CLINICAL
PSYCHOLOGY

CLINICAL·
·PSYCHOLOGY

An Introduction to Research and Practice

NORMAN D. SUNDBERG

LEONA E. TYLER

both of the University of Oregon

APPLETON · CENTURY · CROFTS

NEW YORK   Division of Meredith Publishing Company

ACKNOWLEDGMENTS

AMERICAN PSYCHOLOGICAL ASSOCIATION—quotations from: *Ethical standards of psychologists*, 1953; *Amer. Psychologist:* Annual report of the executive secretary, F. H. Sanford, 1951, 6; A study in human behavior: the clinical psychologist, S. R. Hathaway, 1958, 13; Science and ethical behavior, N. Hobbs, & Ethical standards of psychologists, 1959, 14; The myth of mental illness, T. Szasz, & "Sin," the lesser of two evils, O. H. Mowrer, 1960, 15.

COUNSELING NEWS AND VIEWS—quotation from: Professional status and professional policies, H. Bisno, 1960, 12.

EDUCATIONAL AND PSYCHOLOGICAL MEASUREMENT and the author—quotation from: A program of counseling interview research, R. F. Berdie, 1958, 18.

GRUNE & STRATTON, INC., and the author—quotation from: *The technique of psychotherapy*, L. R. Wolberg, 1954. By permission.

HARPER & ROW, PUBLISHERS, INC.—quotations from: *Clinical studies of personality*, A. Burton & R. E. Harris, 1955; *Essentials of psychological testing*, by Lee J. Cronbach. Copyright 1949 by Harper & Row, Publishers, Incorporated. Copyright © 1960 by Lee J. Cronbach.

HOLT, RINEHART, & WINSTON, INC.—quotation from: *Clinical inference and cognitive theory*, T. R. Sarbin, R. Taft, & D. E. Bailey, 1960.

HOUGHTON MIFFLIN COMPANY—quotation from: *Client-centered therapy*, C. R. Rogers, 1951.

INTERNATIONAL UNIVERSITIES PRESS—quotation from: *The clinical interview*, Vol. I: *Diagnosis*, F. Deutsch & W. F. Murphy, 1955.

THE JOURNAL PRESS—quotation from: Rational psychotherapy, *J. gen. Psychol.*, A. Ellis, 1957, 13.

JOURNAL OF INDIVIDUAL PSYCHOLOGY—quotation from: Rational psychotherapy and individual psychology, A. Ellis, 1957, 13.

ALFRED A. KNOPF, INC.—quotation from: *The doctor and the soul*, V. Frankl, 1955.

McGRAW-HILL BOOK COMPANY, INC.—quotation from: *Psychology: a study of science*, Vol. III, S. Koch (Ed.), 1959.

UNIVERSITY OF MINNESOTA PRESS—quotations from: *Group treatment in psychotherapy*, R. G. Hinckley & Lydia Hermann, copyright 1951 by the University of Minnesota; *Clinical versus statistical prediction*, P. E. Meehl, copyright 1954 by the University of Minnesota.

W. W. NORTON & COMPANY, INC.—quotation from: *The psychiatric interview*, H. S. Sullivan, 1954.

STANFORD UNIVERSITY PRESS—reprinted from: *Psychotherapy by reciprocal inhibition*, by Joseph Wolpe, M.D., with permission of the publishers, Stanford University Press. © Copyright 1958 by the Board of Trustees of the Leland Stanford Junior University.

To Richard M. Elliott

Preface

The title of this book, *Clinical Psychology: An Introduction to Research and Practice,* suggests immediately its central intention—to present in an organized manner both clinical inquiry and clinical service. Psychology is one of those rare disciplines—in some ways the only one of its kind—that attempts to combine the deliberate scholarliness of the laboratory with the arts and responsibilities of the practical world of human affairs. Some related fields, for instance sociology and social work, physiology and medicine, have split into different disciplines and separate training structures. But clinical psychologists are psychologists first, and as such they need to be prepared to contribute both to the betterment of individual lives and to the advance of general knowledge.

Research and practice are not easy bedfellows. From time to time attempts are made to divorce one part of clinical psychology from the other; a completely happy union appears unlikely if not impossible. Nevertheless, we believe that the great strength of clinical psychology lies in its attempt to accomplish this difficult undertaking—to maintain at least a lively conversation between the researcher and the practitioner. Improvements in service depend on the discovery and testing of new knowledge; deep and creative insights into human nature—insights of great value to science—come in the intimacy of clinical work with patients. It is true that one man cannot be all things, and an individual clinician must usually emphasize one activity or the other. But the clinician who decides to become primarily a practitioner remains a *consumer* of research. Through his insights and practical "know-how," he can also serve as a questioner and goad to the research psychologist. On the other hand, the clinician who becomes primarily a researcher is constrained to remember the complexity and rich reality of human behavior. Moreover, research is the way to find out what really works. Ultimately, there is nothing so practical as good research.

In this book we have tried to clarify the identity of the developing profession and to outline ways of thinking that will make it possible for the two kinds of clinicians to remain in touch with one another. For these reasons, we have used research examples at the ends of chapters and written special chapters on research in clinical psychology as a whole, on assessment, and on psychotherapy. We have tried to embody a critical concern with research questions in the discussion of each practical topic. Our view of research has been broad, including descriptive as well as experimental studies, and we have looked at the implications for clinical work in physiological, social, and developmental psychology as well as in traditional areas. Moreover, on the practical side, we have brought cases into almost every chapter and given concrete examples of the kinds of interaction that occur in psychotherapy.

Another of the ways in which we have tried to facilitate the fusion of research and practice is to use a conceptual framework, which, though imprecise in many ways, keeps the length and breadth of human life before our eyes. In the process of selecting concepts and principles as tools to use in understanding clinical work, we arrived at what might be called an organized eclecticism. The whole framework of the book rests on a developmental foundation. We view development as a constantly changing system of relationships—relationships between inner aspects of the individual's personality and relationships of the individual to other persons and to the larger social order. We have placed considerable emphasis on choices and decisions as salient features of developmental processes and have kept constantly in mind the decisions made by both clinicians and patients in the course of clinical work. Both assessment and therapy are considered within this broad developmental framework.

The book is divided into four parts. The three introductory chapters present the problems and principles underlying the rest of the book. The seven chapters on psychological assessment cover the ways in which clinicians arrive at decisions and develop "working images" about patients and their situations. In the nine chapters on psychotherapy we have classified the varieties of psychological treatment on the basis of the kinds of personality change at which they aim rather than on the basis of techniques they use. The final three chapters deal with clinical psychologists as persons and with the profession as it fits into the larger society.

We view this book as a means of introducing the student to a kind of thinking he can apply to the patients and the situations with which he will work rather than as a technical manual from which he can learn skills. Consequently we have omitted detailed descriptions of tests and the interpretations made from them. We assume that a really extensive coverage of intelligence and personality testing will be an important part of a student's graduate program. Similarly we decided to omit any detailed discussion of psychopathology. Like testing, it deserves a much more thorough treatment than we could have given it in this book and will also be covered in other phases of a clinician's training. We have, however, tried to provide many illustrations of individuals with different kinds of pathology and of how tests are used, and in the appendix we have listed 50 important clinical tests.

The book is written primarily for the student beginning his graduate work in psychology. We hope that it may also be useful to advanced undergraduates in psychology and to graduate students in related fields such as psychiatry, social work, and education. We hope also that professional workers in the mental health field may find that the book ties together some ideas and research findings and helps them organize the large unwieldy mass of knowledge that has accumulated so rapidly in the sociopsychological professions.

Some readers may wonder which sections each of the authors has written. The book is truly a cooperative venture. It has grown out of ten years of talking and working together in the development of the clinical and counseling programs at the University of Oregon. Though Miss Tyler was responsible for the first drafts on most of the chapters on psychotherapy and Sundberg for the chapters on assessment, each of us has revised and re-revised the other's work so often that the original author has been lost sight of.

It has been exciting to try to organize our ideas about clinical work and the findings of research in this still new and changing field. We believe that clinical psychology, along with the other behavioral sciences, is standing at the dawn of its influence in human affairs. Just as "wars begin and end in the minds of men," so too can the individual mind, as Milton said, "make a heaven of hell, a hell of heaven." Thinking of the promise and the peril involved in trying to help others, we have a feeling of humility as we commit these efforts to print. We hope students will take up the challenge of making sense and science out of this fascinating interplay of service and search.

N. D. S.
L. E. T.

Acknowledgments

A multitude of people have helped make this book possible. Directly or indirectly we have gathered ideas and inspiration from our teachers and colleagues, our students and friends, our families, and our patients and clients. We wish to thank them all, even though we can list only a few names.

Richard "Mike" Elliott, to whom this book is dedicated, has occupied a very special place in the lives of both of us—a wise counselor, a humane and inspiring teacher, and a critically constructive editor. Gardner Lindzey has also given the manuscript a careful, critical reading. Among the instructors and professional colleagues who have contributed greatly to the development of one or both of us, we want to mention Starke Hathaway, William Schofield, Donald Paterson, Paul Meehl, and Robert Leeper. A number of professional friends have given us examples and made suggestions for research or other material. We are particularly grateful to Herbert Bisno, Robert Boyd, Joel Cantor, Charles Dicken, Raymond Fisher, Fred Fosmire, Vincent Glaudin, Harrison Gough, Theodore Johannis, Paul McReynolds, Gerald Patterson, Phil and Maxine Schoggen, William Singer, David Sterne, and John Watkins.

One of the authors (Sundberg) wrote part of this book while on a Senior Stipend from the National Institute of Mental Health and while working at the Institute of Personality Assessment and Research at the University of California at Berkeley. We are most grateful to NIMH and to the IPAR staff, especially to Donald MacKinnon, for that help. Valuable secretarial and clerical assistance on various parts of the text has been provided by Lou Downey, Jennifer Hanke, Joanne Ward Peyton, and Florence Varner. Donna Sundberg has not only contributed the largest amount of secretarial help, but has also made constructive suggestions and furnished the deep encouragement and support so necessary in writing a book.

N. D. S.
L. E. T.

Contents

PSYCHOLOGICAL ASSESSMENT

Utilization versus change
A conceptual basis for eclecticism

Third possible direction: clinical psychologists as specialists
in human relations
Conflicts and problems in professional development
Conflicting trends and training decisions
Prospects for continued growth

Appendix A. Fifty Tests of Importance in Clinical Psychology   501

Appendix B. Guide for a History-Taking Interview   508

References   511

Index of Research Examples   539

Index of Cases and Illustrations from Cases   541

Index of Names   543

Subject Index   550

One

INTRODUCTION AND CONCEPTUAL FRAMEWORK

1 Patients, Communities, and Psychologists

All of us depend on our fellow men for help in developing and sustaining our own ways of life. Each week, there are many occasions in which we have sought help from others and numerous instances in which help was sought from us. As a general rule men go about the process of living without much trouble. Society has evolved convenient ways for remedying common disturbances. But when these disturbances are highly personal and emotional, and when they affect other people's lives adversely, there may come a point when a person feels he must seek psychological help or when others feel bound to bring him to the attention of professional authorities. The following people had reached that point:

Ricky, a fearful eight-year-old

Ricky had the misfortune to be born into a very disturbed family situation. His young mother was an immature, irresponsible person who would have preferred to be out having a good time to taking care of a baby. She had not really wanted to get married but had become pregnant. Ricky's father had various unskilled jobs which just kept the small family off the welfare rolls. They moved around from place to place. Ricky was colicky as a baby and demanded much of his mother's attention. When he got older but before he learned to walk, the mother got tired of staying with him so much and would leave him in his crib for long periods while she went to the store or visited with neighbors. When he started to climb out of his crib, she would spank him and frighten him. Sometimes his grandmother (his father's mother) who lived nearby during some of this time would find him crying alone in his crib.

When his grandmother objected, his mother would become very angry. When Ricky was a year-and-a-half old, his mother left her husband, who eventually got a divorce. From then on Ricky lived with his grandmother.

By the time Ricky started school, he was noticeably different from other children. His speech was lisping and halting. His movements were odd and rather effeminate. He was afraid to play with other children, and he made very little progress in his reading. At the start of his third year in school, the teacher held a conference with the grandmother and suggested that she consult the child guidance clinic in the next town. The clinic examined the boy thoroughly, finding a normal physique and IQ but considerable educational retardation and psychological maladjustment. Why was Ricky so fearful of others and of trying to learn? The clinical staff could not be completely sure. The early infancy with the rejecting and neglectful mother seemed important. The father's frequent absence and generally inadequate personality seemed important. There might be some hereditary predisposition toward malfunctioning, since there was considerable maladjustment and crime for several generations on both sides of the family. Ricky's grandmother seemed to be a positive influence in his life, but perhaps she was too indulgent and encouraged his feminine interests and activities.

In spite of these unpromising aspects of the case, the clinic staff still felt that it would be fruitful to attempt psychotherapy with Ricky, at least on a trial basis. After several weeks of play therapy, Ricky had made enough progress so that the staff decided to continue for a longer period. Ricky's grandmother participated in counseling, and the school teacher and principal met with the clinic staff to plan a program which would encourage Ricky's participation in school work and group play. After a year and a half, Ricky had improved enough in his social and educational life that his therapy could be terminated. A follow-up interview a year later showed that progress had continued. The clinic felt on the whole that Ricky's treatment had been successful, although early childhood experiences had undoubtedly left "scars" that might predispose Ricky to breakdown in the future.

Harold, a withdrawn, pedantic adolescent

Harold's childhood had been similar to Ricky's. He was the product of a youthful marriage that ended in divorce. He too was brought up by his grandparents. Though early school records showed a tendency toward isolation and strangeness as compared with other children, he did not come to the attention of a clinic until his senior year in high school. Perhaps he would have come earlier if he had not done so well in school. Starting out as an average student in the lower grades, he concentrated more and more on school work, where he found his only pleasure. Tests indicated that he was highly intelligent, and much of his work reflected this ability. In English he was particularly interested in poetry and was given to writing sonnets concerned with death. He made many allusions to Greek mythology and used long, uncommon words like *patrimorphic, scrannel,* and *sacculated.* High school English teachers were at a loss to know whether his poetry expressed disordered thinking or real profundity.

Harold might have continued on his way to become an eccentric poet publishing in off-beat magazines or a philosophy professor, as he stated he wished to be, had it not been for a growing disengagement with social reality. He became tardy in turning in his school assignments and finally did not hand them in at all. He would show his poems to the English teacher but refuse to write an assigned theme. At first some of the teachers respected his independence and originality, but they eventually became irritated with him. His school marks became poorer and poorer in late high school. At the same time, he became more and more isolated from others, although he had never been very social. He grew very tall and became thinner and thinner. He never spoke with his grandfather, a railroad conductor, often away on long trips, who had little in common with Harold's intellectualism. With his grandmother Harold played occasional games of checkers. He spoke little with her and would often not even answer questions she asked.

One morning his grandmother found him in his bed unconscious. She finally was able to rouse him and discovered that he had taken several of her sleeping pills. Quite concerned, she took him to the family physician on the pretext that he needed a physical check-up. To the physician he confided in his characteristic hesitant and quiet voice that he had taken the pills because he could not "distinguish the semblance of life and the semblance of death." The physician discussed with him the seriousness of his act and convinced him that he should voluntarily enter the state hospital for a 30-day observation period. There he was studied by a psychiatrist and tested by a psychologist, and the grandmother was interviewed by a social worker. Harold expressed bizarre beliefs and strange thoughts, such as the notion that he had been born of royal blood. He had ideas that other people were watching him all the time. He was diagnosed as schizophrenic, but as it was felt that he could be treated in an out-patient clinic, he was discharged from the hospital. While he was on the waiting list for the mental hygiene clinic, he made another "suicidal" attempt, this time taking aspirins. The initial attempt at therapy in the clinic involved a strong "here-and-now" orientation to focus Harold's thoughts and actions on immediate environmental problems. Some success was achieved with this approach, for Harold was able to enter a college and take a limited course load. However, after several months he broke off treatment. Later, at the insistence of his college advisor, he established contact with the college counseling center and has continued in college as a part-time student. What his future will be is not at all clear.

Marie, a depressed and desperate woman

Marie had grown up as the oldest child of a large farm family. Her father was a cold, austere German, interested in amassing more farm land and running the family as economically and efficiently as possible. Her mother seemed to be either sick or busy with a new baby most of the time. Consequently, Marie became the hard-working housekeeper for the family. When she married Harry Williams at an early age she continued this role, keeping a neat house, devoting herself to the care of her three children, and finding little time for enjoying the "frivolities" of life. Her husband, whom she had found attractive because he had the warmth and conviviality she lacked, became more and more dissatisfied with her overattention to her family and started to go out more and more on drinking bouts with business friends.

In her early 50's Marie found herself essentially alone. Her children had grown up and left home. Her husband was working or out with his business friends most of the time. She had no friends of her own. In the next few years things became worse and worse. She began to think that her husband was gone so much because he had found someone else. She suspected a certain secretary at the office. When on one occasion she saw the secretary buying a present in a men's clothing department, she thought her suspicions were confirmed. Still she did not want to question her husband because she feared he might become angry. She turned to prayer and for a time went to church every day, but this did not erase her fears. She became more and more depressed and distracted. She did not want to leave the house. All day she lounged around in a bathrobe. She let her grey hair become straggly. She began to have trouble in getting to sleep. She thought that there was something wrong with her stomach, perhaps a nameless disease uglier than cancer, and she would eat very little. Mr. Williams, aware of this gradual change, tried different things—encouraging her to go out, buying a new television set, praising any moves she made toward improving the house. When sometimes he became angry, she would just look away. He got sleeping pills for her when she refused to go to the doctor herself. She, however, became more and more disturbed. She roamed the house at night and in her desperation would sometimes wake him up. She started saying that life was not worth living. When he failed in all his attempts to get her to see a physician or go to a hospital, Mr. Williams finally inquired from the county health department as to how he might force his wife to see someone. They suggested that he sign commitment papers.

When he did so she became extremely angry, since the act confirmed all of her ideas that her husband was trying to get rid of her so that he could marry his secretary. Mr. Williams then called an ambulance. She was overpowered, given a sedative and taken to the county psychiatric ward.

The psychiatric examination resulted in a diagnosis of involutional psychosis, and a course of electroconvulsive therapy was prescribed. After twelve treatments Marie was much more relaxed and less concerned with her worries. While on the ward she became acquainted with some other patients her age and found in their group therapy meetings that some of them were also suffering from the loneliness and despair she had felt. She began to pay more attention to her appearance. After she was dismissed she continued to return to the community hospital for group therapy every week. With the encouragement of her therapist, she became involved in some of the ladies' groups at her church. Gradually Marie began to find a place for herself in life again.

Ricky, Harold, and Marie are only three of millions of persons who have become psychologically disturbed to a serious degree. For a more complete picture we would need to mention many more, like the following: Vera, a middle-aged woman who had become an alcoholic; Mick, a rebellious adolescent who had been arrested and brought before the juvenile authorities several times for stealing cars; Ronnie, a mentally retarded boy who was able to get along fairly well until in his early adolescence he tried to assault a little girl; Margaret, who had such high blood pressure that she had to give up her job and reorient her life; George, an old, "back ward" schizophrenic whom the hospital had assigned to a new rehabilitation program; Jack, a former safe cracker, who had become morose and touchy at his prison job; Tino, an adolescent heroin addict; Sally, a little brain-injured girl who was having a hard time learning to read; and Johnny, who had severe asthma that appeared to be of psychogenic origin. There are many, many more of all ages with disorders of all degrees of severity, coming from all kinds of families and backgrounds, and with all kinds of talents and abilities. These are the people who come seeking help from the psychologist and his colleagues.

FACTORS THAT DETERMINE THE SELECTION OF PATIENTS

The screening that separates out from the general population the small group of people the clinician sees is a process in which an affirmative answer to one of two questions is arrived at: Is a person so worried that he seeks psychological help himself? Are others so concerned that they bring him in for psychological help? The potential client of a clinic is either personally distressed or socially deviant. He is a burden either to himself or to others. The self-initiated approach to the clinic occurs especially among the anxious, neurotic persons who make up a large proportion of the clientele of private practitioners. Many self-referrals also come to public clinics and hospitals. The other-initiated approach is characteristic of seriously disturbed psychotic people, mental defectives, and criminals who turn up at the clinics connected with courts and state institutions. Many of these persons have been legally committed to these institutions, thus being no longer independent citizens. These different paths to clinical settings are also in part determined by such restrictive factors as the fees charged by private practitioners, the availability of public services, hospital admission policies, and the degree and kinds of law enforcement.

Both the intentional and the influenced arrivals at the clinic are in part dependent upon just how severe a condition must be before society or somebody in society views it as a psychological disturbance. A study of different cultures and of attitudes during different historical periods shows wide variation in the way people conceive of mental abnormality and strange behavior (Zilboorg, 1941). During the last hundred years the prevailing attitude has moved toward classifying many of these peculiar or unusual forms of human behavior as illness. Terms such as *mental illness, mental health, psychopathology,* and *psychotherapy* reflect this widespread acceptance of the idea that such kinds of behavior are instances of sickness and therefore need medical attention and treatment. This broadened concept of sickness in the last century has done much to remove the stigma current in earlier times—the notion that persons who are markedly peculiar or different are intentionally malicious or are possessed by an evil demon. The illness viewpoint has been supported by the discovery that some disturbances, such as general paresis, have definite organic causation. It may very well be that more of the psychoses, asocial sociopathy, and much mental deficiency will be found to have specific organic causes.

The approach to mental illness as disease has many strong supporters. On the other hand, the idea that a condition is an illness has certain disadvantages that some psychologists and psychiatrists have begun to notice lately. The disease concept does imply an organic causation, and when this is stretched to cover disorders that are in fact nonorganic, it tends to perpetuate attitudes of dependence upon specific treatments instead of calling attention to disturbances in the ways people live. Even in demonstrated organic disorders, the effects of social and psychological influences are not properly appreciated if one's thinking is limited to the usual concept of an illness. The psychologist Mowrer (1960a, 1960b) emphasizes the problem of *values* in mental illness to such an extent that he would even apply the word *sin* to neurotic behavior. The psychiatrist

Thomas Szasz (1960) also argues that the notion of mental illness camouflages the fact that we are really dealing with problems of value, problems of how to make good choices, and problems of deviation from psychosocial, ethical, and legal norms. He has stated his argument this way: "Our adversaries are not demons, witches, fate, or mental illness. We have no enemy whom we can fight, exorcise, or dispel by 'cure.' What we do have are *problems of living*—whether these be biologic, economic, political, or sociopsychological. . . . Mental illness is a myth, whose function it is to disguise and thus render more palatable the bitter pill of moral conflicts in human relations" (Szasz, 1960, p. 118).

No matter what terms are used,[1] the fact that people come as patients to clinics and hospitals is important both to them and to society. The size and nature of the patient population rests upon how the question: When does a person perceive himself or when do others perceive him as sick? is answered. The definition society gives for the *sick role* may importantly affect the form that a neurosis or mental illness assumes (Stainbrook, 1959).

We do not yet know as much as we should about how people view mental illness and health and what determines when and where they go for help. Seeking light on these questions, Gurin, Veroff, and Feld (1960) used two-hour interviews in a survey of the worries and self-perceptions of a sample of 2460 American adults. They found that feelings of happiness centered around the home and were conditioned strongly by feelings of economic security. The reactions of persons with little education to their problems tended to take the form of physical symptoms, whereas the more educated tended to react to stress with psychological symptoms. Many men reported competition between the demands of home and job, feeling insecure about both. It was shown that the way in which Americans view their mental health is strongly influenced by sex, age, and education. In the part of the study dealing with how people obtained help with their difficulties, it was found that one out of seven had sought help in the past, especially women, younger persons, and those who had the most education. Among those seeking help, 42 per cent reported problems relating to marriage, 18 per cent problems relating to personal adjustment, and 12 per cent problems relating to their children. The largest number (42 per cent) had consulted clergymen; the next largest (29 per cent) had consulted general phy-

[1] In the absence of a more acceptable term, we will continue to use the term *mental illness,* more or less equating it with such terms as *psychological abnormality* or *behavioral deviation.* The term *mental health* is also difficult to define (Jahoda, 1958; Smith, 1959), but again we shall continue to use it even though some other term like *psychological effectiveness* or *personal competence* might be preferable. Perhaps the best solution is to think of mental health as a chapter heading in a book used not to describe a boldly defined entity or pattern, but as a descriptive title for an exposition of certain ways of behaving and of questions that may be raised concerning them.

sicians; only 18 per cent had consulted psychiatrists or psychologists. Of those visiting clergymen or physicians, 65 per cent stated that they had been helped; of those visiting psychiatrists, only 46 per cent said it was worthwhile. These findings reflect in part the fact that the more severely troubled persons tend to see specialists like psychiatrists and psychologists; so it may not be surprising that they are less likely to feel helped by their consultations. The authors concluded that many people feel anxious and insecure, that people have a better chance of dealing with their troubles if they see that they themselves are involved and don't just blame others for their condition, that education has an important influence on mental health, that most people have to rely on themselves for help with their worries, and that the problem of adequate professional help is particularly serious for the lower socioeconomic groups.

LABELS AND CLASSIFICATIONS

Society has labelled distressed and deviant people and their conditions in various ways—delinquents, lunatics, neurotics, criminals, psychosomatic disorders, behavior problems. Every century adopts its own system for describing those who are "different." An adequate system of description and classification which is likely to remain in favor indefinitely has not yet been devised.

One profession which has given particular attention to developing a classification system is medicine. Over the centuries medicine has had the responsibility of deciding whether a person is sick or not and, if he is sick, prescribing how he should be treated. The traditional approach has been to collect observations of as many patients as possible who seem to have similar symptoms or complaints. After a physician has seen a number of people who appear to have a similar disorder—perhaps a high fever followed by skin blotches which disappear in a few days—he reports this set of symptoms and gives it a name. Over the years many disorders have been pigeonholed in this way.

Such collections of *series* of similar cases have been made in which the symptoms are mental and behavioral. Among the mental illness thus labelled, the following are examples: *neurasthenia*, proposed by the American psychiatrist, Beard, in 1869; *paranoia*, by Vogel in 1764; *dementia praecox*, by Kraepelin; and others like *constitutional psychopathic inferiority*, and *psychasthenia*. These are only a few of the terms proposed to describe one or another of the forms of mental illness.[2] Many of them are seldom used today.

[2] For an interesting and brief review of the development of psychiatric nosology from Hippocrates to Kraepelin, see Veith (1957).

Eventually, the hodgepodge of names needed systematization. Many such classificatory systems of psychiatric terms were proposed. The one that has been most influential was drawn up by Kraepelin, a psychiatrist who had been a student of Wundt. His system, originally proposed at the end of the nineteenth century but much revised now, has become the basis for the official nomenclature adopted by the American Psychiatric Association. This system is used by all private and public institutions in reporting the diagnoses of their patients. The latest form of this diagnostic system (American Psychiatric Association, 1952) is summarized in the following outline:

I. Disorders caused by or associated with impairment of brain tissue function.
   A. Acute brain disorders
     Examples: Acute brain syndromes associated with intracranial infection, alcohol intoxication, trauma, circulatory disturbance.
   B. Chronic brain disorders
     Examples: Chronic brain syndromes associated with congenital cranial anomaly, central nervous system syphillis, intoxication, brain trauma, cerebral arteriosclerosis, intracranial neoplasm.
II. Mental Deficiency.
   Classified as mild, moderate, and severe.
III. Disorders of psychogenic origin or without clearly defined physical cause or structural change in the brain.
   A. Psychotic disorders
     1. Involutional psychotic reaction
     2. Affective reactions
       a. Manic-depressive reaction, manic type
       b. Manic-depressive reaction, depressed type
       c. Manic-depressive reaction, other
       d. Psychotic-depressive reaction
     3. Schizophrenic reactions
       a. Schizophrenic reaction, simple type
       b. Schizophrenic reaction, hebephrenic type
       c. Schizophrenic reaction, catatonic type
       d. Schizophrenic reaction, paranoid type
       e. Schizophrenic reaction, acute undifferentiated type
       f. Schizophrenic reaction, chronic undifferentiated type
       g. Schizophrenic reaction, schizo-affective type
       h. Schizophrenic reaction, childhood type
       i. Schizophrenic reaction, residual type
     4. Paranoid reactions
       a. Paranoia
       b. Paranoid state
     5. Psychotic reaction without clearly defined structural change, other than above
   B. Psychophysiologic, autonomic and visceral disorders
     Examples: Psychophysiologic reactions of the skin, respiratory system, cardiovascular system, gastrointestinal system.
   C. Psychoneurotic disorders
     1. Anxiety reaction

   2. Dissociative reaction
   3. Conversion reaction
   4. Probic reaction
   5. Obsessive-compulsive reaction
   6. Depressive reaction
   7. Psychoneurotic reaction, other
D. Personality disorders
   1. Personality pattern disturbance
      a. Inadequate personality
      b. Schizoid personality
      c. Cyclothymic personality
      d. Paranoid personality
   2. Personality trait disturbance
      a. Emotionally unstable personality
      b. Passive-aggressive personality
      c. Compulsive personality
      d. Personality trait disturbance, other
   3. Sociopathic personality disturbance
      a. Antisocial reaction
      b. Dyssocial reaction
      c. Sexual deviation
      d. Addiction
         (1) Alcoholism
         (2) Drug addiction
   4. Special symptom reactions
E. Transient situational personality disorders
   1. Transient situational personality disturbance
   2. Gross stress reaction
   3. Adult situational reaction
   4. Adjustment reaction of infancy
   5. Adjustment reaction of childhood
      a. Habit disturbance
      b. Conduct disturbance
      c. Neurotic traits
   6. Adjustment reaction of adolescence
   7. Adjustment reaction of late life

This outline serves to give the reader an impression of the breadth and variety of disorders that come to psychiatric attention. In this outline is an interesting "sign of the times"—the use of the word *reaction* in labeling disorders. *Reaction* plainly suggests not so much a fixed state or a permanent pigeonhole for a condition as an interactive process, and this is a reflection of current attitudes which stress the possibility of change—that mental illnesses are treatable and the patient's behavior can improve. It is also interesting to note that there is under each main heading a "catchall," or miscellaneous category, to use for a patient who does not fit the given categories easily. This provision indicates how difficult it is to fit all kinds of abnormal behavior into definite classes. The diagnostic manual also provides additional descriptive phrases for modifying and elaborating on the diagnosis. Since the psychologist frequently works in psychiatric settings or is called upon to discuss psychiatric conditions, it is important and even obligatory that he should have a knowledge of psychiatric terminology.[3]

Although the official psychiatric classification system is useful to the psychologist, it has some serious disadvantages and inadequacies. (1) *It does not refer directly to the specific etiology* or causation of the different mental disorders, on the one hand, *or specific treatments,* on the other. It fails to specify relationships to theories of behavior or personality dynamics which the psychologist must always be thinking about. (2) As psychiatrists use the system, diagnosis is *often for other than strictly descriptive purposes.* A diagnosis may be used in a hospital for purposes of ward placement or the administrative handling of a patient. It may determine whether a disturbed soldier is classified as having a service-connected disability or not. For such reasons, administrative or legal considerations may sway the diagnostician in borderline cases. (3) The psychiatric system *has the limitations of any typology.* It identifies certain supposedly correlated clusters of symptoms which very few people actually fit. In real life people vary along many dimensions and from time to time. With almost every case there are certain exceptions which must be taken to the official diagnosis. (4) The psychiatric nomenclature is *poorly developed in a scientific sense.* An attempt is made at the description of disorders, but these are not specified in any concrete operational way. As a result considerable unreliability of diagnosis is to be expected, although one well-designed study (Schmidt & Fonda, 1956) found that there was fair reliability for major categories. (5) But the most serious inadequacy of all from the psychologist's point of view is that it *does not pretend to cover the wide range of problems with which psychologists deal.* There is nothing in it, for example, about learning problems or speech and reading difficulties. It has no categories in which to place the kinds of diagnosis that underlie the decisions clinics must make about children, such as placement of dependents in foster homes and recommendations about probation and parole for delinquents. It leaves out the large area of vocational maladjustments, the difficulties a person may run into in his job. It leaves out marital and sexual problems, except in their extreme sociopathic forms. The increasingly challenging problems relating to aging and retirement find no place in this system. Finally, it does not include any of the positive kinds of personality "deviation" which psychologists need to assess: high intelligence, creativity, and unusual stability and strength.

[3] Clinical students will usually become familiar with the terms in the above outline through courses in abnormal psychology and psychopathology. Those who are not familiar with them should study the complete psychiatric diagnostic manual (American Psychiatric Association, 1952). Dictionaries of psychiatric and psychological terms (e.g., English & English, 1958; Hinsie & Campbell, 1960) are also of value, as are textbooks of abnormal psychology, psychiatry, and psychopathology. Perhaps most valuable of all and certainly among the most complete is the *American Handbook of Psychiatry,* edited by Arieti (1959).

Despite all of these objections and limitations, the psychologist will find that he can organize at least some of his thinking around the psychiatric diagnostic system. There must be a starting point for any discussion of problems in this area, and the psychiatric terminology furnishes an accepted medium for communicating what consensus there is. Furthermore, as Meehl (1959b) argues, there may be good underlying reasons for the persistence of this terminology; perhaps there is, for example, a "disease process" at the base of schizophrenic or sociopathic symptoms. If diagnosis is unreliable, it may be due to our poor tools of measurement and inadequate training methods. The lack of psychodynamics in the system may not be an objection after all, because all of the social and learning dynamics can be superimposed on this basic disorder as the patient's personality structure develops. Meehl believes that the principal psychiatric disorders should be treated as *constructs* for which we are developing sets of indicators through tests and other procedures. Thorne (1955) has ventured to propose a much extended diagnostic system.

Perhaps with time the inadequacies can be overcome. It may well fall to research psychologists to improve and extend the present system or to develop better ones. Certain alternatives and extensions which have been proposed will be discussed in later sections. But as with the weather, there is much talk about behavioral classification, and little gets done about it.

COMMUNITIES AND BEHAVIORAL DISORDERS

The process which brings the patient and psychologist together involves an interaction with the community of which the patient is a part. The patient occupies a place in his family, his work group, and his circle of friends and acquaintances. The evaluation, either by himself or by others, which leads him to psychological help is made in this community. The shift in his behavior in response to clinical actions has a reciprocal influence on the community.

Because there is such variety among behavior disorders, society needs to make a variety of provisions for their treatment and care. In less industrialized and poorer societies, few special measures can be taken in behalf of the mentally ill. These unfortunate people, if not sheltered by their families, where they may be a great burden, are allowed to roam about getting whatever sustenance they can gather. Even in the United States and other industrialized countries, there is a wide range in different communities with respect to how much the mentally ill are tolerated and how much care they receive.

The care and treatment of the most severely disturbed cases can usually be handled best by an *in-patient institution*—that is, a hospital or other institution which can provide round-the-clock observation and care, special control to prevent the patient from harming himself or others, and various special therapies. The first institutions for the mentally ill in the American colonies were established only shortly before the Revolutionary War (Lewis, 1959). In the mid-nineteenth century an impassioned exposé by the humanitarian Dorothea Dix of the brutality, filth, and neglect which characterized the supposed "care" of mental patients led to the establishment of many additional mental hospitals and the improvement of conditions within them. By now all states have public mental hospitals, and there are many private and federal ones as well. The head of a state mental hospital is usually a psychiatrist. Staffs vary greatly in size and quality depending on the size of the patient population in a state, on economic conditions, and on the attitude of people in general. In a properly run hospital there is a department of psychology with a Ph.D. clinical psychologist in charge, though in many instances it is badly understaffed. Besides the mental hospitals there are such other kinds of in-patient institutions where psychologists are on the staff as institutions for the mentally deficient, prisons and juvenile reformatories, and the psychiatric wards in private sanatoria, general hospitals, and medical schools.

Less severe or "ambulatory" cases can be treated in *out-patient services.* These services may be offered by public clinics or by psychiatrists or psychologists in private practice. There are a great variety of out-patient services. In the 1920's and 30's in the United States the child guidance movement fostered the establishment of many clinics for children, a development which is still expanding. Many out-patient services in smaller communities are multipurpose mental hygiene clinics accepting both children and adults and dealing with a wide variety of problems. There are also out-patient services connected with hospitals and institutions. Out-patient clinics are usually organized around a *psychiatric team,* consisting of a psychiatrist, a social worker, and a psychologist. In larger clinics there are several persons from each profession.

Psychologists are not limited to work in public clinics and hospitals. A growing number of psychologists go into private practice (Blau, 1960). Clinicians work in many settings where the persons seen would not be called patients, but perhaps clients or just personnel cases (in industry and offices) or subjects (research institutes). Clinical psychologists can be found in colleges, schools, industries, marriage counseling centers, juvenile court staffs, and so forth.

The variety of places in which clinical psychologists work is indicated by the 27 chapters in the *Survey of Clinical Practice in Psychology,* edited by Rubinstein and Lorr (1954). This book describes the first psychological clinic in the United States, the clinic still in operation at the University of Pennsylvania. There are descriptions of other famous early institutions which clinical psychologists have helped develop—the Institute for Juvenile Research in Chicago, the Vineland (New Jersey) Training School, and the Worcester (Massachusetts) State Hospital. In addition, the book describes the work of psychologists in Veterans Administration installations; military posts; counseling centers; industrial situations; court clinics; rehabilitation centers; school systems; reading, speech, and hearing clinics; an alcoholic clinic; and a psychiatric clinic.

The variety of ways in which clinical service can be provided is undergoing examination and vigorous experimentation. Robert Felix (1961), former director of the National Institute of Mental Health, has summarized the new trends: (1) much greater variety in the treatment of mental patients, (2) more concern for prevention and early detection and treatment of mental illness, and (3) much earlier return to the community and to work. Among the new developments following this expanded conception of the relation of the patient, the community, and clinical facilities are such services as the following: walk-in clinics, where a trained person sees the patient when he first appears at the hospital or clinic and indicates psychological disturbance; emergency services with a psychiatrist on call at all times; visits to patients' homes by the psychiatric team for diagnosis and treatment; night hospitals where patients stay for care and treatment in the evening or night but continue jobs in the community during the day; day hospitals to which patients come for treatment and training during the day but return to their homes at night; sheltered workshops where handicapped patients can do useful work in the community; use of hospitalization for short periods; and provisions for aftercare for patients when they leave the hospital. The gap between the community and the institution is being narrowed, and people are beginning to look at mental illness in a new way. For the first time in history the number of patients in mental hospitals is beginning to decline.

Among these changes there is a strong movement toward developing small community mental hospitals, perhaps as part of general hospitals, instead of the large state hospitals, some of which take care of five or ten thousand inmates. Legislation such as the Short-Doyle Act in California, has provided funds for the establishment of small community units. To these, patients can go for brief periods without the disruption of their lives and relationships caused by going to a large, distant, and impersonal institution. Hospitalization is being seen more as an open situation where help is available for mental patients to come and go as their condition varies without having to undergo difficult formalities. Prominent in introducing these innovations is Maxwell Jones, whose book *The Therapeutic Community* (1953) is based on the proposition that treatment should be obtained not so much at the hands of doctors and specialists but in the normal interactions of healthy community life.

Communities and institutions are increasingly becoming objects of study by social scientists in an effort to discover how to rehabilitate the mentally ill and the socially deviant. These changes are challenges to the creativity of clinical psychologists to develop new methods of assessment and treatment of patients and especially to design new ways of doing research and of checking on the effectiveness of new treatments.

PATIENTS' PATHS THROUGH CLINICAL SERVICES

The willingness to reexamine mental health facilities should extend to the administrative procedures and decision-making activities involved in the course of a patient's contact with an agency or situation. The simplicity, responsiveness, and courtesy with which the relationships between patients and agency personnel are arranged have great significance either for recovery or for increased disturbance of patients. The timing of the response an anxious person encounters is often very important. It can be taken for granted, for example, that everyone approaching a clinic, especially for the first time, is fearful about how he will be received. If patients are required to wait for long periods of time, this may seem to them to confirm their suspicions that they, themselves, are worth little, and this can depress them still further or heighten their anxiety over what may happen to them.

It would seem important to provide an opportunity for talk with the patient when he is most anxious. Some clinics attempt to see everyone when he first applies, even if only for a short while; this is done in the walk-in clinics mentioned in the last section. Recently there has even been some interest in setting up emergency telephone watches so that a qualified professional person can establish contact with people when they become disturbed and open up a channel immediately which will get them appropriate attention. Research evaluation of this idea is needed to check on its actual worth and effectiveness.

The first step in the patient's journey is to gain *admission* to a mental health service. Out-patient services and many hospitals will take self-referrals upon submission of an application form. At some, written recommendation by a physician is required. There can be out-patient referrals from many sources—physicians, schools, courts, welfare agencies. Hospitals frequently get patients by *commitment*. Requirements for commitment depend on state laws. Usually a petition must be signed by a close relative, and there must be an examination of the patient by two physicians, followed by the decision of a judge at a hearing.[4]

The admission procedures of clinics and hospitals involve examination

[4] The reader interested in a general introduction with more details about commitment procedures is referred to Davidson (1959). Locally applicable information may be obtained by calling a county courthouse.

by a psychiatrist, and frequently also by a psychologist, together with interviews of members of the patient's family by the social workers. After a period which may range from a few days to several weeks, a decision is reached regarding *diagnosis* and *disposition*. The period of *treatment* or *management* follows. If this treatment is successful, or perhaps for some other reason, the patient may be *discharged* from the hospital, or contact with the clinic terminated.

The processes of the institution or agency, then, consist of a sequence of decisions about the kinds of experiences that will be therapeutic for the patient. In the making and communicating of these decisions the clinical psychologist plays an important role. Since clinicians and other staff members are fallible and often overworked human beings, there are frequent opportunities for the breakdown of these important processes. Ultimately the mental health of the staff gets itself reflected in the quality of its work with patients. And vice versa, the kinds of conditions that prevail among the patients have their effect on the morale of the staff.

THE DEVELOPMENT OF CLINICAL PSYCHOLOGY

We have looked at the kinds of persons a clinical psychologist attempts to help and the settings in which he works. Now let us consider for a few moments the history of the profession itself. Clinical psychology is largely a twentieth-century phenomenon, but activities similar to those of the clinical psychologist have been carried on for generations. There were wise counselors of human behavior among the Greeks, so wise indeed that any contemporary clinical psychologist will be better able to help people if he has sought to understand what they taught. The Bible describes the assessment devices used by Gideon in selecting his warriors and the test used by the Gileadites to detect Ephramite fugitives—the correct pronunciation of *Shibboleth*. The vitality of Shakespeare's plays, centuries after they were written, testifies to his ability to penetrate to the very depths of human experience. However, it was not until 1896 that Lightner Witmer established the first psychological clinic at the University of Pennsylvania for the psychological study of problem children. At that time there was much excitement about the new laboratory psychology recently imported from Germany. Its methods seemed to give a new direction to the age-old effort to understand man's nature. Witmer saw that these same methods might help in understanding the individual child.

At about the same time a number of other workers became interested in this possibility. The most famous and influential of these was Alfred Binet, in Paris. The publication of his intelligence scale launched the mental testing movement and gave psychologists a remarkably serviceable set of tools to use in their study of the individual person—tools that worked better than the "brass instruments" adapted from the laboratory. As time passed, many tests were devised in attempts to measure other characteristics besides intelligence, and clinical psychologists received their first recognition as experts in the use of tests.

Up to the time of World War II, the majority of the clinics in which psychologists worked were designed to meet the needs of children. Although at first there were many varieties of children's clinics sponsored by many kinds of agencies and organizations, by the middle of the 1930's something like a standard pattern had evolved. A clinic team which usually included a psychiatrist, a clinical psychologist, and a psychiatric social worker had become the accepted thing. The psychiatrist with his medical background acted as clinic director and was in charge of the treatment of each case. The psychologist did the testing that was necessary and often supervised the educational measures that were recommended—contacts with teachers, remedial work in speech or reading, educational and vocational guidance. The psychiatric social worker did much of the interviewing of parents and others from whom information about the child's problem could be obtained. The three members of this team would confer and work out a plan of treatment together. The treatment at this time was more likely to involve changing the environmental influences at work upon the child than psychotherapy. The psychologist probably had a master's degree or even just a bachelor's degree and was considered a specialist in the use of a limited number of tests and techniques. It was very seldom that he had a doctor's degree or would have been considered a scientist with sufficient breadth of training to take all of human behavior for his province.

The unprecedented demand for psychological services that occurred during and after World War II and the large number of academic psychologists who were swept into clinical work in the course of their military service brought drastic changes. Although the number of children's clinics continued to increase, a new emphasis upon adults and their problems developed rapidly. The testing of intelligence and special aptitudes was no less necessary than it had been, but more attention was now directed to the complex and difficult fields of personality and motivation. Psychotherapy became a central concern, and psychologists who had carried great responsibilities for treatment in military programs were no longer content to play a role subsidiary to medicine and psychiatry. They demanded professional recognition from psychiatrists on an equal basis.

It was at this juncture, in 1945, that planning and direction became prominent in the development of the profession, although committees to consider training needs and other aspects of professional growth had exercised marked influence for a number of years previous to this time. The American Psychological Association, whose members include both experimental and applied psychologists, found it necessary to consider carefully the whole problem of how clinical psychologists should be trained. The Veterans Administration decided to underwrite a large-scale training program to provide new staff members which it anticipated its many hospitals and mental hygiene clinics would require. Clinical training programs accredited by the American Psychological Association were set up in the graduate schools of universities. Standards of training were laid down, codes of professional ethics formulated, and procedures were established for certifying professional psychologists.

The graduate training program recommended by the Committee on Training in Clinical Psychology in its report to the APA in 1947 set, or at least crystallized, a pattern of training that provided for the inculcation of both systematic psychological knowledge and specific technical skills. The provisions for both theoretical and applied aspects of the profession stipulated that practical experience must accompany classroom work. Keeping in mind the previously mentioned principle that the clinician was to be a scientist as well as a practitioner, the committee recommended emphasis on three areas: diagnosis, therapy, and research.

In 1949, a two-week conference on training in clinical psychology was held in Boulder, Colorado, just before the Denver meeting of the American Psychological Association (Raimy, 1950). Representatives of training institutions, mental health service agencies and allied professions discussed thoroughly the issues that had arisen and were arising. The general policies embodied in the 1947 committee report were reaffirmed. The clinical psychologist was to be a scholar as well as a practitioner broadly trained to the level of the Ph.D. Research should be considered to constitute at least as important a part of his professional work as diagnosis and therapy.

In the early 1950's another specialized area of applied psychology began to take definite shape. *Counseling psychology* developed out of vocational guidance and was more closely related to education than to medicine. In their concern with positive mental health and with choices and decisions of all kinds, counseling psychologists find that their territory sometimes overlaps that of the broadened clinical psychology that has grown up.

Nonmedical kinds of psychological work received more emphasis than they had previously been given at a conference at Stanford in 1955 (Strother, 1956), at which counseling psychologists were well represented. Attention was given to problems within the normal range of behavior, the sorts of difficulties any person may experience in trying to achieve the best he can with his own special assets, limitations, and circumstances. This conference stressed preventive mental health and the role psychologists might play in community activities.

In December, 1958, a third conference on training in psychology was held in Miami, Florida (Roe, Gustad, Moore, Ross, & Skodak, 1959).

The group who came together at this conference reviewed the entire field of graduate training in psychology, experimental as well as clinical. Again they reaffirmed the intention to maintain the combination of research and practice in the work and training of all varieties of applied psychologists, clinical and counseling included. They recognized that curricula were becoming unwieldy and made a number of recommendations designed to prune course requirements sufficiently to permit students to obtain first-hand experience in research work and to become really prepared to function as researchers. Possibilities were explored for post-doctoral programs designed to develop high-order professional skills and nondoctoral programs to train service workers to meet special kinds of pressing psychological needs.

The continuing emphasis on research by clinical psychologists has been accompanied by a broadened interpretation of the meaning of research. In the summer of 1958 a group of distinguished experimental psychologists met to try to formulate more precisely the factors that are essential in the training of a good research worker (APA, Education and Training Board Ad Hoc Committee, 1959). The upshot of their thinking was a demand that relatively more attention be placed on actual experience in research. One thing especially has been overlooked in our training— experience in developing creative hypotheses. All in all, what seems to be the best kind of training is a sort of apprenticeship under an outstandingly good research man. This recommendation would certainly fit the training of clinical psychologists as well as general psychologists.

Thus it has come about that the central feature of clinical psychology as a profession is its two-sidedness—theory and practice, science and service. Those who made the basic decision to have it so have had their eyes on the continued development of psychology as a whole. Clinical psychology is still a very new field of knowledge. If its practitioners should become satisfied to apply for the rest of their lives the ideas and skills characteristic of our present level of development, they would continue to make great errors in diagnosis and treatment—errors which may perhaps be unavoidable today but we hope will not be a decade hence. The clearing made by psychologists of the past and present in the encircling jungle of ignorance is still painfully small. There must be cooperative work in the task of enlarging it. Furthermore, if research psychologists were to turn aside from clinical activity they would give up what may prove to be their richest source of seminal hypotheses. In fact, if one looks at the work done in recent years in such areas as perception, motivation, and learning, one sees much influence from the ideas generated in clinicians in their close contacts with patients over long periods of time. An outstanding example, is Freud's influence in the development of theories of perception, especially concerning the way perceptions become distorted when persons are defending themselves against anxiety-producing stimuli.

DISTINCTIVE FEATURES OF CLINICAL PSYCHOLOGY

Out of all the discussions and conferences with their thoughtful consideration of the work we are doing and might do, some fairly clear ideas have taken shape about the distinctive characteristics of this profession—how it differs from the other disciplines and professions to which it is related. Perhaps the thing that distinguishes the clinical from the experimental psychologist most sharply is the clinician's emphasis on the *individual* case. For example, every psychologist must take an interest in the problem of learning and be familiar with the large amount of research that has been carried out in attempts to explain how it occurs. But the clinical psychologist concentrates on the learning problems of one patient. Let's call him Henry Landis. The clinician tries to see how Henry Landis is alienated from his wife and his associates. He explores the problem of how Henry came to learn to see the world in his own characteristic way and to behave in his own characteristic manner. Furthermore, he tries to think of present and future learning situations in which Henry's unsatisfactory habits may be changed for the better.

Another example is motivation. All psychologists must know something about motivation, and many of them devote their whole research careers to exploring the general principle of motivated behavior. But the clinical psychologist tries to understand just what is "driving" Henry Landis. What are the sources of *his* anxiety and what goals is *he* striving to attain? Many psychologists are concerned with the effect of stress on human personality. For our hypothetical clinical psychologist, the task is to find out just how Henry Landis is reacting to the loss of his job and the threat of divorce, and how his situation can best be alleviated. To sum up, the general psychologist typically directs his attention to some one area of human experience or some one aspect of human behavior and makes observations on a number of persons in an attempt to find common features upon which to base general statements. The clinical psychologist directs his attention to one person at a time, observing many features of his behavior.

The clinical psychologist's interest in the individual has extended to cover ongoing living groups, which is only a natural outgrowth of his interest in whatever affects persons. More and more the clinician's work includes such social groups as families, the patients in a hospital ward, and even a complete community. But he is concerned with the ongoing behavior and with the living situation of actual people rather than with the framing of general psychological or sociological laws. He carries with him to his study of any group his concern for the maximum development of each individual involved.

This emphasis on the individual, the person, is the most salient feature of clinical psychology as a profession, but there are others. Historically,

as indicated earlier in the chapter, there has been an important connection between clinical psychology and the practice of medicine. This
is why clinicians usually refer to the people they work with as *patients*,
although they may use the word *clients* when they work in nonmedical
settings. Even now, a very large proportion of the members of the profession are working in medical settings in close cooperation with psychiatrists and other physicians and with psychiatric social workers,
nurses, and aides. The term *medical psychologist* is sometimes used, but
the term is too narrow a label for the profession as now practiced. The
concern of the medical profession is with the person whose capacity to
meet the demands of life has been so severely impaired that it is possible
to label his condition a "mental illness." But as we have seen, clinical
psychologists are interested in *many* varieties of deviant behavior, whether
they are properly considered forms of mental illness or not. From one
point of view, clinical psychology looks like *applied abnormal* psychology.

Even this sort of expanded definition does not constitute a really
adequate statement, however. Many clinical psychologists work for
schools, industries, and community agencies and deal almost exclusively
with human problems that fall within the normal range. As newspaper
columnists, magazines, radio, and television make people aware of the
prevalence of psychological difficulties and the means that are available
for coping with them, more persons with minor problems seek help.
Increasingly the demand is for broadly trained psychologists who can
give the kind of help needed by normal persons under unusual stress.
Increasingly, too, today's vigorous mental health movement is leading
to an emphasis on prevention as well as cure, and it has become the task
of some psychologists to identify factors that may lead to difficulty for
some child or adult *before* rather than after such difficulties arise. The
broad activities of clinical psychologists and the variety of situations with
which they must deal is revealed by the definition of *clinical psychologist*
in the newest revision of the *Dictionary of Occupational Titles* (Reported
in APA Division 12 *Newsletter*, Summer, 1960):

CLINICAL PSYCHOLOGIST (profess. & kin.) 0-36.20. A PSYCHOLOGIST. Diagnoses
mental and emotional disorders of individuals in clinics, hospitals, prisons, and
other institutions, and administers program of treatment: Interviews patient,
studies medical and social case history, observes patient in play or other situations, and selects, administers, and interprets projective and other psychological
test findings to diagnose disorder and formulate plan of treatment. Treats psychological disorders to effect improved adjustment through various forms of
treatments, such as milieu therapy, play therapy, psychodrama, etc. Selects
approach to use in individual therapy, such as directive, nondirective, and
supportive therapy and plans frequency, intensity, and duration of therapy.
May collaborate with various professions, including PHYSICIANS and various
specialists in medicine, such as PSYCHIATRISTS, PEDIATRICIANS, NEUROLOGISTS,
INTERNISTS, etc.; SOCIAL WORKER, PSYCHIATRIC; and other specialists in developing treatment programs for patients, based on analysis of clinical data.

May instruct and direct students serving psychological internships in hospitals and clinics. May develop experimental design and conduct research in field of personality development and adjustment in industry, school, clinic, and hospital; and on problems of diagnosis, treatment, and prevention of mental illness. May serve as consultant to social, educational, welfare, and other agencies on individual cases or in evaluation, planning, and development of mental health programs. May utilize teaching, research, and consulting skills involved in the more advanced levels of professional service. May specialize in one of following: behavior problems, crime and delinquency, group therapy, individual diagnosis and therapy, mental deficiency, objective tests, projective techniques, and speech pathology.

Thus, although a firm knowledge of psychopathology is obviously necessary for every clinical psychologist, the province of clinical psychology is considerably broader than medical or abnormal psychology. And attitudes and social demands are changing so rapidly in our modern world that it would be impossible to predict with any certainty where its boundaries will shortly lie.

The extension of clinical psychology into nonmedical areas often leads to difficulty in distinguishing it from counseling psychology. Although there is a good deal of common ground so that many psychologists, for example, belong to both Division 12 (Clinical Psychology) and Division 17 (Counseling Psychology) in the American Psychological Association, there is still enough difference in emphasis and special skills that it seems advisable for the time being, at least, to maintain some differentiation in job specifications and training programs. One way of stating what this difference is is to say that counseling psychologists are basically concerned with the decisions and choices *every* individual must make, whereas clinical psychologists are basically concerned with special problems and difficulties *some* individuals face. For example, a well-trained counseling psychologist knows a great deal more about occupations and their requirements than a well-trained clinical psychologist typically does. Similarly he knows more about aptitude and school achievement tests, less about tests for exploring the so-called "deeper" levels of personality.

Much of what the authors have to say in this book is applicable to both specialties. Because of the variation from place to place in what a psychologist is expected to do and because of the constant shifts and regroupings that occur in the rapidly-changing psychological professions, it seems desirable for both clinical and counseling psychologists to acquire much of the same background of knowledge and many of the same skills.

Perhaps as time passes, we shall see more differentiations within the psychological helping profession. *Rehabilitation psychology,* for example, has recently developed some features that distinguish it from both clinical and counseling psychology. We need not be too jealous of our professional prerogatives in any of these special areas. The important thing is to make our plans and organize our training programs so that all the kinds of work we wish to do can be accomplished.

Partly because of this uncertainty as to just what the clinical psychologist ten years hence will be expected to do, the boards and committees which have given the most serious thought to problems of definition and training have insisted that the clinician should be *first of all a psychologist*. He should be thoroughly familiar with the body of knowledge about human behavior that has been built on the efforts of his fellow scientists, past and present. Furthermore, he should, himself, contribute to the continued growth of this science. He must maintain the skepticism and curiosity out of which come new ways of investigating old problems. Then he can take advantage of whatever opportunities for research he finds in the situation in which he works. And he must know research methods well enough so that he can handle the complex kinds of data his observations give him. The ideal then is that each clinical psychologist should leave this world not only healthier, but wiser than he found it.

HOW SCIENTIFIC IS CLINICAL PSYCHOLOGY?

With all of the brave words that have been said and the ambitious programs that have been formulated, for many people there remains a sincere doubt as to whether clinical psychology can ever really be scientific. Practice, both diagnosis and therapy, comes closer to what we ordinarily term art than science. The clinician proceeds from moment to moment without formulating clearly the reasoning underlying the shifts in his approach, even, it may be, without pausing to check whether his previous hypotheses have been verified or not. An interview cannot be set up and organized like an experiment. It is no wonder that experimental psychologists who prize psychology's scientific heritage and prospects are uneasy about the large numbers of their colleagues in the profession who seem to be proceeding along very different paths from their own. Let's keep the distinctions clear, they say. All of this effort to improve the functioning of individual human beings may be useful, even valuable, but psychological science comes out of the laboratory rather than the consulting room, and until the ideas clinical workers come up with are put to some sort of experimental test, they have no accepted scientific standing.

A number of differences between the two types of approach have been widely discussed. The first has to do with the *generality* of science. A scientific *law* applies to all cases of the type to which it refers. Observations of the movements of raindrops, tides, and shooting stars may have produced a curious assortment of facts about storms, tides, and meteors, but no one thought much of them as science until the general law of gravitation took shape in Newton's mind. Clinicians, too, can certainly generate such laws out of their observations of individual human beings, but it is peculiarly difficult to validate them because the conditions under which observations are made are difficult, if not impossible, to duplicate or repeat. Is the essence of science the developing and stating of general laws and their validation? This is the crux of the matter. Freud considered himself a scientist because he was distilling general principles of broad scope and great significance from his meticulous and penetrating observation of individual patients. The majority of academic psychologists will not be disposed to call Freudian theory scientific until its "laws" have been established through some sort of experimental test. There seems to be a difference between European and American practice in this regard also. We on this side of the Atlantic, for example, are more conservative, more restrictive about what we are willing to call scientific than are most German psychologists.

Another characteristic of work that is clearly scientific is the provision for rigid controls to rule out all sorts of errors that could lead to wrong conclusions. In a scrupulously planned psychological experiment, as many conditions as possible are specified in advance. As each subject is tested, he is given the same instructions, stands in the same position, receives the same amount of encouragement or reward as did his predecessor. Because economic level, intelligence, or academic standing may affect results, subjects are chosen so that these things will be comparable from group to group. Because other experiences during the period an experiment is scheduled to last may also produce changes in the subjects, control groups who have all of these experiences except that of acting as subjects in the experiment are observed for purposes of comparison. In addition, complex statistical methods are resorted to in further analysis of the variables that affect the obtained data. If such elaborate precautions are necessary to enable us to secure data that we can use in the formulation of general scientific laws, how can the haphazard observation the clinician makes in the situation where practically no controls exist possibly have any scientific standing? Here again, however, some definitions of science are broader than others. A considerable proportion of our knowledge in geology and biology has come from field observations without adequate controls, yet such knowledge is generally conceded to be scientific. Perhaps, too, it can be said that all of the sciences in their early stages were based on uncontrolled observations. Controls are a comparatively late development, historically speaking.

Another of the standards science has set up for itself that does not seem to be applicable to much of the work of the clinical psychologist is detachment, or objectivity. The scientist is not supposed to be personally involved in the outcome of his experiments, or at least to let his outlook be biased by what he wishes or believes. The clinical worker, especially when he is acting as a therapist, must really care about the person he is attempting to help. Any appearance of detachment may seem to the client like coldness and lack of interest. Under such conditions he will not feel free to express himself, and the process the scientific clinician hoped to study will not occur. So goes the argument. It is not altogether convincing, however. Scientists in all fields of endeavor do become personally involved in the work they are doing but have managed to work out over the years sufficiently objective procedures and methods of analysis to serve as effective checks on wishful thinking and to make for sound conclusions regardless of what their conscious and unconscious wishes are. It is not inconceivable that analogous methods for clinical psychologists will gradually be evolved. No sharp line between experimental and clinical psychology can really be drawn on the basis of imputed objectivity.

There is one other difference, perhaps less basic than these. Science advances most successfully when variables can be quantified. Many of the most important characteristics with which clinical workers must deal are highly resistant to meaningful quantification, and many excellent clinicians are nonmathematical, if not actually antimathematical in their thinking. Here too, the contrast is not a sharp one. Not all sciences and scientists use mathematical tools in their work. Nor, fortunately, do all clinicians repudiate them. Many ingenious methods have already been worked out for applying quantitative methods to clinical research problems.

Increasingly, the discussion of how scientific it is possible for psychology to become is centered around the concept of prediction. This concept has become a sort of touchstone. If it is said that the basic aim of science is prediction and control, then a psychologist, clinical or otherwise, who can make predictions that "come true" is operating as a scientist. Because this is an assumption all varieties of psychologists seem to be taking for granted, it deserves more scrutiny than any of the other ideas we have been examining. Evidence has been accumulating that the kinds of thinking clinical psychologists normally do about the persons with whom they work does not lead to as accurate predictions about them as can be made by applying purely statistical methods to the test scores and other information that is available about these individuals. The book *Clinical and Statistical Prediction* by Meehl (1954) highlights the problem. We shall be discussing it in detail in Chapter 8. What we should like to stress here is that prediction is not all there is to science. Particularly in biological science, scientists have often endeavored to *explain* rather than to predict. Scriven (1959) and Mayr (1961) have called attention to the fact that evolutionary theory is not based on prediction. It is possible scientifically to explain the past even when prediction of the future is impossible.

Prediction is a useful *tool* to be used in checking explanatory propositions. This is the main function it serves in science. Scientists make predictions about the outcome of experiments in order to determine whether the hypotheses to which their theories give rise are sound. This is a fundamental part of scientific method. It does not necessarily follow, however, that the scientist would feel competent to predict what the same object or kind of material he used in the experiment would do under natural conditions. With all of our knowledge of falling bodies, we still do not even try to predict just how far an irregularly shaped rock on an uneven slope will roll when dislodged in a storm next January. With all our knowledge of growth processes in plants, we do not attempt to say just where the end of a certain tendril of a growing vine will be at the end of the summer. Engineers know a great deal about stresses in the qualities of materials, but they allow a large factor of safety in bridges they build because they cannot predict just what will happen under the complex influences brought to bear on them as they are actually used.

When psychologists set as their *goal* the prediction and control of human behavior, they go far beyond what most other scientists attempt. For scientific work, all that is really necessary is that one be able to make a prediction of what will happen under experimental conditions when as many as possible of the influences that would affect behavior under normal conditions have been controlled. More remote predictions that become necessary when we attempt to apply psychological knowledge to human affairs can be made in probabilities or in broad general terms. When the highway engineer puts up a sign "Watch for rocks on road," he is making such a prediction. He knows that there is an appreciable probability that some rocks are going to be dislodged and roll as far as the highway. The psychologist in an applied area can hope to do his fellow man a similar service if he can say "Under conditions like this, watch out for delinquency, or anxiety, or poor reading habits." It is not required that he predict precisely the behavior of the individual delinquent, neurotic, or nonreader. We can retain prediction as a useful technique of scientific research without committing ourselves to a promise that we will ultimately predict everything.

The great strength of the clinician as compared with the statistician is in his *creative* ability. From his rich experience and intimate and long-term contact with people, the clinician is in an excellent position to *generate hypotheses*. A part of scientific work that we do not as yet understand very well is the process out of which new ideas arise. The clinician who is deeply interested in human beings and observes and thinks about them, trying to arrive at solutions to human problems, may be able to make important contributions to the development of his science through his hunches and hypotheses. Needless to say, he should also participate in the scientific checking of such guesses or hunches. Thus when we clear away some of the exaggerated or unwarranted statements about science, there no longer seems to be so broad a gulf between experimentalists and clinicians—or for that matter, between scientists and artists in general. As we read the history of science, we see how impossible it would be to make any simple statements as to the essence of scientific work. Philosophies and points of view change from period to period. Stress falls at one time on rationality as opposed to irrationality, at another on induction as opposed to deduction. In the work itself, there is a magnificent continuity. Scientists of one period reject the general theory of the previous period but incorporate into their own theory the knowledge that it contained. Scientific method is a much broader concept than experiment or than the currently popular "prediction and control." It is a kind of approach to the world, characterized by values and attitudes more than by specific techniques. Scientists and artists have the same need to observe carefully and to organize what they see, the same respect for skill and craftsmanship. Historically, the two careers have common ancestors. The Renaissance sculptor was both artist and engineer. (It is interesting that the Artist scale on the Strong Vocational Interest Blank has a high positive correlation with most of the scientific scales.) If we broaden our view of what science *is* to make it cover what scientists actually *have done* and *are doing*, we shall not need to be so concerned about whether or not clinical psychology is truly scientific. As F. C. Bartlett (1955) so aptly phrases it, "It may be that all the great scientists are people who work as artists in a field which everybody considers to be scientific."

SUMMARY

Contacts with clinics and hospitals are initiated either because persons have become anxious about themselves or because other people are disturbed about their deviant behavior. The screening process or the decision as to who needs clinical care depends in general on the way a particular society defines abnormality and who is to be considered mentally "sick." The attitudes taken toward mental illness both of the professional and the lay public are proper areas for study by clinicians. Among those who do come to the attention of clinicians, there is a great variety of peculiarities and complaints. The official psychiatric diagnostic system provides a way of classifying some of the disorders which is initially useful but which does not meet the full needs of the clinical psychologist; it should be extended and put on a sounder and more scientifically defensible basis. The clinical settings to which patients come are first, a variety of in-patient institutions (such as mental hospitals, prisons, and institutions for the mentally defective) and second, out-patient clinics (such as child guidance clinics and counseling centers). Clinicians also work in nonmedical settings where the persons who come for help are usually called clients or just personnel cases. The usual ways in which persons are admitted as patients and progress through hospitals and clinics may work toward or against their mental health.

The history of clinical psychology as a separate profession began with the establishment of Witmer's clinic for problem children in 1896. Up to the time of World War II, clinical psychologists worked mainly with children and considered testing to be their primary function. Since World War II, many kinds of clinical services for adults have been set up, and the scope of psychologists' activities has widened. Through a number of conferences held under the auspices of the American Psychological Association, decisions have been made that graduate programs in which clinical psychologists obtain their doctoral degrees should emphasize scientific theory and research along with practice in psychological skills. Combining research and practice presents difficulties, but clinical psychologists are staking their claim to professional recognition and their judgment of the best way to advance human welfare on a synthesis of the two.

Clinical psychology has certain features that distinguish it from other specialties. It differs from general or experimental psychology in its focus on individuals and what they do in the situations into which life has thrown them rather than on general laws of behavior. It differs from abnormal psychology or medical psychology in the breadth of its scope. It differs from counseling psychology in that it is more concerned with difficulties and troubles, less concerned with occupational decisions and other everyday experiences all persons face.

All through its history, there have been many critics who questioned whether clinical psychology could ever really be a part of science. If we avoid overly restrictive definitions of what a science is, we can see the work clinical psychologists do and the kind of contributions they are peculiarly fitted to make as very valuable in the building of an inclusive science of human behavior. A clinician comes to feel that science and art are not as different as they are sometimes thought to be.

SUGGESTED READINGS

NUNNALLY, J. C., Jr. *Popular conceptions of mental health.* New York: Holt, Rinehart, & Winston, 1961.
    This is a report of a five-year research project on the communication of information about mental health. The techniques for measuring attitudes toward mental health in the population at large and the procedures for studying

changes in attitude are of special interest to clinical psychologists working in community mental health.

MOWRER, O. H. What is normal behavior? In L. A. Pennington & I. A. Berg (Eds.), *An Introduction to clinical psychology.* (2nd ed.) New York: Ronald, 1954.

Mowrer presents a lively imaginary discussion among experts from different professions—a physician, educator, philosopher, sociologist, anthropologist, psychologist, and others. Each argues for his point of view on normality. Mowrer's conclusion, with which many might not agree, is that conformity to social ethics is the ultimate criterion.

LINDNER, R. M. *The fifty-minute hour: A collection of true psychoanalytic tales.* New York: Rinehart, 1954.

The very readable stories of five people Lindner saw in therapy. One story, "The Jet-Propelled Couch," has been published in *Harpers* and also made into a television show. All of them are dramatic.

WILSON, D. P. *My six convicts.* New York: Rinehart, 1951.

This bestseller is an account by a clinical psychologist of his work in a prison. Wilson's primary aim was to do research on drug addiction. He describes many interesting and instructive incidents illustrating the problems of testing convicts and training them as research assistants.

BETTELHEIM, B. *Truants from life.* Glencoe, Ill.: Free Press, 1955.

This book includes four long case histories of schizophrenic and seriously disturbed children seen at Dr. Bettelheim's Orthogenic School. The School is a psychoanalytically oriented residential treatment institution connected with the University of Chicago.

BURTON, A., & HARRIS, R. E. (Eds.) *Clinical studies of personality.* New York: Harper, 1955.

Case histories prepared by clinicians with a wide variety of backgrounds. The diversity of theories and approaches both to therapy and assessment techniques are well illustrated.

RUBENSTEIN, E. A., & LORR, M. (Eds.) *Survey of clinical practice in psychology.* New York: International Universities Press, 1954.

The variety and versatility of clinical psychologists are very well documented by this book in which 27 psychologists describe their work.

ARIETI, S. (Ed.) *American handbook of psychiatry.* Vols. I and II. New York: Basic Books, 1959.

This reference book is a comprehensive presentation by 111 authors of the history, concepts, techniques, and problems of American psychiatry. Its two volumes and one hundred chapters contain a great deal that is of interest to clinical psychologists. Of particular pertinence to this discussion are chapters 1, 2, 6, 7, and the several chapters describing the different psychoses, neuroses, organic conditions, psychopathic conditions, and psychosomatic disorders. Relevant to later chapters in this book are the discussions of therapy, an account of the contributions to psychiatry of other fields, and an exposition of the legal and administrative aspects of psychiatry.

WATSON, R. I. A brief history of clinical psychology. *Psychol. Bull.,* 1953, 50, 321-346.

A concise account outlining the development of clinical psychology from its early origins to the mid-century. The author, a well-known clinical psychologist, distinguishes two traditions, the "psychometric" and the "dynamic," and goes on to describe the manner in which clinical psychology came to be applied in a wide variety of institutions.

BECK, S. J., & MOLISH, H. B. (Eds.) *Reflexes to intelligence: a reader in clinical psychology*. Glencoe, Ill.: Free Press, 1959.

This book of readings contains many of the original articles and reports in which ideas in the present book first appeared. As an introduction the reader might look at the first two parts, including brief quotations of "clinical wisdom in former times" and excerpts from Darwin, William James, Dewey, and others relevant to clinical psychology.

ROGERS, C. R. Persons or science? A philosophical question. *Amer. Psychologist*, 1955, 10, 267-278.

In a very personal way, Rogers faces the duality of values in clinical psychology—the clinician's desire both to be of service to people and to advance knowledge. When he engages in therapy the clinician is involved in experiencing and accepting another human being. In scientific research on therapy, he views the person as an object and studies the manipulation of behavior. These aims seem incompatible, but Rogers attempts to integrate them by pointing out that science itself rests in people; its communication depends on intersubjective acceptance. Because of his personal values, a therapist chooses at one time to *live* an experience in therapy, and at another time to *examine* it. Further value comes in the way the psychologist uses knowledge gained from scientific examination. The therapist attempts to be maximally constructive in his use of knowledge.

BRONOWSKI, J. The creative process. *Scient. American*, 1958, 199, 59-65.

In this lead article of a particularly interesting issue devoted to innovation in science, a man who is at home both in literature and mathematics discusses the relations between creativity in art and in science. He finds much that is similar and notes that great periods of both occurred together in ancient Greece and the Renaissance. He argues that innovation in either field happens only when a person perceives beneath apparent disorder a deep new unity. He sees the same imaginative incisiveness in Planck's proposal of the quantum theory and Blake's metaphor: "A dog starv'd at his Master's gate / Predicts the ruin of the State." For a book exploring the relations of art, science and values, see Bronowski (1958).

BRAUN, J. R. (Ed.) *Clinical psychology in transition*. Cleveland: Howard Allen, 1961.

This is a collection of articles from the *American Psychologist* dealing with important issues confronting the profession. Among the 32 articles, the reader will find topics pertinent to almost every subsequent chapter in this book. It would make an excellent supplement to this book, showing how such psychologists as Meehl, Kelly, Hobbs, and others deal with significant problems of clinical psychology. Of particular pertinence to this chapter are the following: Szasz, "The Myth of Mental Illness" and "The Uses of Naming and the Origin of the Myth of Mental Illness"; Ausubel, "Personality Disorder is Disease"; Shoben, "Toward a Concept of the Normal Personality"; and Nunnally and Kittros, "Public Attitudes Toward Mental Health Professions."

2 Mainstreams
of Theory

One reason clinical work is so taxing is the confusion resulting from the multiplicity of events going on in every human life. The development of a conceptual framework for handling them is a problem both for the individual clinician seeking to understand a human being and for the science of clinical psychology. In clinical work one deals with a stream of experiences, the patient's and one's own. Explicitly or implicitly, every clinician faces the necessity of constructing a conceptual framework that will impose some order on this mass of psychological material. Such a conceptual framework involves the clinician's views about the nature of man and society and about himself in relation to the world. However, much of this framework may remain unverbalized, unrecognized, and unsystematized.

THE PROBLEM OF ORGANIZING CLINICAL KNOWLEDGE

During most of its short history reaching back hardly more than a century, psychology has been organized around different general *theories* or *schools* of thought. The need for organization is so widely felt that a commanding figure like Sigmund Freud, whose psychology approaches a *Weltanschauung* in scope, finds a receptive audience among workers in all the psychological professions. Many psychologists find their conceptual framework by identifying with one of the theoretical points of view which happen to be prominent in the subculture in which they are immersed. Markedly original thinkers become leaders in psychoanalysis, client-centered therapy, group dynamics, and other varieties of psychology, gathering schools of followers not only because their views have a clarifying utility, but also because social-political influences are likely to become powerful in a profession and in professional training centers. Even when psychologists do not consciously adopt a particular framework or espouse a certain theory, they may nonetheless behave according to its implicit assumptions and principles.

In the case of the scientist, whether he recognizes it or not, theoretical concepts determine what kind of observations he will make and thus what kind of scientific work he will do. A psychologist whose main job is research is pretty sure to feel satisfaction and security in locating a congenial variety of overall theory and adopting it as his basic orientation. If it is inadequate in some respects, his research will demonstrate this inadequacy, and he may get the credit for a constructive modification. If it does not generate all the kinds of experiments that might be done on various problems, he can safely assume that some other experimenter, viewing his world from the vantage point of a different theory, will do them. The time and energy of any one researcher is limited anyway. He cannot do everything.

For the practicing clinician, however, the existence of conflicting theories poses a real problem. His task is to understand a human being in all his complexity. If he approaches the task using only the conceptual tools provided by one theory, he is almost certain to miss some aspects of the personality he is trying to understand. Orthodox psychoanalysis emphasizes intrapsychic motivation and mechanisms but pays little attention to the influence of social organization. Learning theories of a conditioned-response type focus on what the person is doing but cannot be stretched far enough to throw light on the kind of organizing concepts he uses. Theories about the physiological components of emotion are likely to suggest therapies that relieve tension rather than therapies aimed at discovery of unconscious conflicts. If a clinician disregards some aspects of personality because his preferred theory does not sensitize him to it, he may in an individual case overlook a crucially determining factor.

Furthermore, a clinician finds it very difficult to maintain strict theoretical orthodoxy because he is constantly running up against conflicting interpretations of the same observations or facts. Each client he encounters has his own brand of psychological theory, whether or not it is clear and explicit enough so that it could be given a name. Each colleague with whom he works differs from him to a greater or lesser extent in theoretical orientation. It is almost impossible for a clinician to choose a theoretical system and maintain it in its entirety, a fact that may be fortunate. Freud himself was constantly remodeling and elaborating his ideas to the end of his life.

UNDERSTANDING ONE'S OWN ASSUMPTIONS

The first task of the clinician, in practice as in training, is to discover the conceptual framework under which he is already operating. It is our belief that whether the clinician follows a named theory or not, he would benefit from trying to make his beliefs explicit. Then he can readily examine and test and revise them and he can communicate more effectively with his colleagues.

How does one discover the assumptions on which he operates—his professional life style? The task is not easy. It is as difficult as gaining insight in psychotherapy, for during much of the time our ways of behaving as clinical psychologists are so habitual that we cease to be aware of what we are doing. What is presented to us are three things: our own stream of consciousness, the evaluative feedback by which we feel what others think of us, and our own behavior products. From this mass of data we may inductively draw principles and generalizations and test them. This is the procedure of self-analysis. A clinician can listen to his own recorded interviews and study a series of his reports. He can ask himself: "What kinds of things do I respond to? What sorts of remarks do I make repeatedly? Have I noticed the same things others would see? What have I overlooked?" When one finds repetitive behavior in oneself, it is useful to ask why. For instance, a clinician we may call Dr. Salisbury frequently recommends job changes to his patients. Is this because he assumes that the work situation is more important than other influences— or is he avoiding touchy topics? Dr. Sterns, on the other hand, finds homosexual tendencies in almost all of his patients. Is this because he assumes that sexual role confusion is very common in our culture—or because of his own selective perception? It is possible for a clinician to learn something about himself by careful study of his own work and by seeking supervision and consultation. One of the reasons for the interdisciplinary approach in work in mental health is the value of others' viewpoints in compensating for any single clinician's limited vision.

Along with an awareness of his own predispositions, every clinician should have a thorough understanding of the basic topography of personality. He must have command of conceptual skills which he can use in understanding other human lives. He will find that a grasp of many sorts of concepts need not make for a barren eclecticism in his own thinking. He himself, drawing on his unique pattern of life experience, tends to organize his ideas in a way that is his own. As he considers his own life and the lives of others and as he reads and thinks, the distinctive lines of his own personality theory become increasingly apparent. The previous chapter stressed the fact that each clinical psychologist, whatever his specific tasks, is in some sense a scientist searching for new knowledge. Each is also in a real sense a theorist adding those organizing concepts that stand out from his special vantage point.

Our aim in this chapter is to set forth what seem to us the concepts of personality stressed in present-day theories which are likely to be valuable in this personal theory-building. This poses a real problem—which concepts to include?—since it seems unnecessary to crowd in here many things which can be found in books on psychological theories. What is important is to include the assumptions *which make a difference* in clinical practice. If assuming one thing rather than another leads the clinician to ask this question rather than that, to look for certain things in a case history, to adopt certain attitudes and ignore other possible ones, to make certain interpretations, or in general, to behave in one way rather than another in the clinical setting, these assumptions are important enough to include in the clinician's framework. We have tried to select the concepts that do make such a difference.

At the end we outline a synthesis of these ideas about man, society, and the self which have come to seem to us most meaningful. It constitutes a general frame of reference under which the detailed topics considered in the rest of the book may be subsumed. Our intention is not, however, to gain adherence for this particular theoretical orientation. It is rather the more modest one of pointing the way to the basic ideas themselves, of encouraging reading about those that seem most fruitful, and of helping the clinical student begin his efforts to synthesize his own theory, an effort which if he is wise he will continue to make throughout his life.

CONCEPTS FROM THE LABORATORY

Man is first of all a living creature, and the biological principles that characterize all of life must be understood if we are to understand him. Many of these principles are rather vaguely familiar to all of us, but one upon which psychologists and physiologists in our time have come to place great stress is not so generally known. It is the process to which Cannon gave the name *homeostasis*. It refers to the processes by which the body maintains constant inner conditions in the face of drastic changes in the environment. The thermometer goes up and down as weather changes, sometimes varying as much as 60 degrees Fahrenheit within a single 24-hour period, but the temperature within the body varies very little from the customary 98.4 degrees. A person eats an unusually large meal, including many complex varieties of proteins, fats, and carbohydrates, but the concentration of sugar and other chemicals in his blood remains constant, as it must if life is not to be threatened.

It is only comparatively recently that we have appreciated what a complex thing this maintenance of steady states within the body is. It requires a very large number of adjustive mechanisms, including delicately coordinated reactions of glands and nervous system, which function automatically without any volition on our part. It is only with the advent of automation and our increasing use of equipment like thermostats, electronic controls, and high-speed computers that we have been able to imitate such self-regulating processes. Awareness of the near ubiquity of these "field" processes, at least in our corner of the universe, is coming to permeate all scientific thinking.

Psychologists have used the concept of homeostasis a great deal in their theories of human behavior. For one thing, behavior itself is often a component of the physiological homeostatic processes themselves. The acts of folding one's arms, drawing one's body into a compact ball, or even getting out of bed to find an extra blanket, are part of the process by means of which constant temperature is maintained. The idea of homeostasis has figured largely in theories of *motivation*. Psychologists have noted the cyclical nature of hunger and other drives. A tissue need initiates an active period of restless seeking which leads eventually to eating and cessation of the search. After this reduction of the drive comes a quiescent period which is followed by another cycle of seeking, consummation, and quiescence. Many theorists have proposed that all drives arise out of some sort of disturbance of inner equilibrium and the need to remove such disturbance. It would appear now that this idea cannot account for all of human motivation. Research evidence is accumulating that human beings seek change and new experience as well as steady states. But homeostasis is still an important concept in understanding motivation. It also helps us to make sense of many otherwise puzzling characteristics of perception. Size and shape constancy, for example, can be thought of as homeostatic processes that serve to stabilize the external environment for the person.

Another vitally significant concept related to homeostasis is the idea of *stress* and the person's response to it. Selye (1956) has been investigating a complex phenomenon he calls the *general adaptation syndrome;* a series of reactions involving secretions of the pituitary and adrenal glands. These have widespread effects on many other physiological processes. Stress is a very general concept. It occurs in illness, injury, emotional strain, and to some extent in all of the situations involved in living. Many features of the Selye formulation are useful in theories of personality. The idea of simultaneous processes in opposite directions that serve to maintain a delicate balance can be generalized to many areas of thinking. The idea that there is a temporal pattern to responses to stressful situations has important implications. Temporary stress, being stimulating, calls out constructive reactions; prolonged stress is debilitating and if unchecked leads to a general breakdown of these adaptive mechanisms.

From what has been discovered in the psychological laboratory, clinical workers have constructed their fundamental theoretical conceptions of learning. Since J. B. Watson in 1914 led the American "behaviorists" in rebellion against the "structuralists"—psychologists like Wundt and Titchener who were attempting to analyze conscious experience into its elements—*learning* has been a central topic in experimental psychology. Under what circumstances does change of behavior occur, especially those changes that are in line with the organism's needs? The standard formulation in behavior psychology has been in terms of stimulus and response, and its general plan of research was to search for ways of joining responses to stimuli under controlled conditions. Pavlov's experiments showing how the reflex response of salivation in the dog could be attached to a wide variety of new stimuli seemed to the early behaviorists to represent the essence of the process in which they were interested. The *conditioned response* became the prototype of all learning. *Reinforcement* and *extinction, generalization* and *discrimination* became basic concepts, applied in explanation of all sorts of situations.

Learning theories in the past forty years have become increasingly complex and their fine points need not concern us here. But every clinician in all his work and his thinking makes use of some of the concepts of the stimulus-response learning theorists. In understanding clients, he is often trying to analyze the stimulus conditions through which a person has come and the responses he has learned to make to them. In treating many conditions he will identify useful responses the client now has in his repertory and attempt to get them attached to the sorts of stimuli the person is likely to meet. Clinicians differ in the extent to which they use the stimulus-response way of conceptualizing their work, but they must all make room somewhere in their thinking for theoretical ideas as to how learning takes place.

At about the time the behaviorists rose in revolt against the dominance of structural psychology, another group parted company from it on quite a different issue. The *Gestalt* psychologists objected to the breakdown of experience into elements. *Gestalt,* a German word, means organization, and this group of workers placed the emphasis on the characteristics of the whole rather than the parts. Unlike the behaviorists, who had concentrated their attention on learning, this group saw *perception* as their central problem. What they discovered about perception in their experimental work constitutes a permanent part of the store of psychological concepts indispensable to the clinician.

The unifying thought running through the experimental findings of Gestalt psychologists is that perception is not simply the passive registration of stimulus energies affecting the sense organs. Perception is an active sorting and organizing process with its own laws. Unless experimental conditions are deliberately manipulated to make it impossible, what one sees is a *field* differentiated in part as *figure* and in part as *ground.* Things are seen as *objects* rather than abstract geometrical forms, and these objects appear to be the same objects under all conditions, that is, approximately the same in size, shape, and color even when viewed from different distances, different angles, or in brighter or dimmer lights. A stationary picture followed quickly by another stationary picture of the same figure in a slightly different position will register as perceived *movement* of the figure from one place to the other. We are all familiar with this phenomena in motion pictures. The sudden shifts and reversals in perception such as those we find in the familiar Necker cube and Rubin vase illustrated in most elementary psychology textbooks are important to the perception psychologists as evidence of the organizing principles that underlie all our experience. Though most of their research has had to do with rather simple visual phenomena, there is no reason to limit perception to these. Perceptions can be thought of as unconscious as well as conscious, emotional as well as relatively indifferent, learned as well as innate, and as having motivational characteristics.

People differ widely from one another in the way they perceive things. The influence of wishes, needs, and past experiences on what is observed has been a very active research topic in recent years. It is mandatory that the clinician should be thoroughly familiar with the psychology of perception so that he can over and over again remind himself that the persons with whom he works, both clients and colleagues, may be living in quite different phenomenal worlds than his own. One of his first responsibilities to a patient or client is to become as sensitively aware as he can of his particular ways of perceiving the world.

Out of the intense interests that some experimental psychologists have taken in perception have come learning theories somewhat different from the stimulus-response variety discussed above. These are usually called *cognitive* theories because they are concerned with the thoughts, cognitions, concepts, and other inner processes that change as learning proceeds rather than with the responses or actions, which to the centralists seem secondary. Learning can be seen as basically a matter of changes in *concept formation*. Concepts constitute the categories into which a person sorts the incoming stimulation so that he can deal with it effectively. An important feature of cognitive learning theories is their emphasis on *insight*, the grasping of the relationships between the parts of a situation so that organization is possible.

Concepts like homeostasis, reinforcement, and insight, based on thousands of experiments in laboratories in widely separated places, are the most dependable tools the clinician brings to his tasks. He knows that these processes occur. It is his job to see in what particular ways they operate in the life of the person he is attempting to understand. As the body of accepted knowledge in physiology and psychology increases, the clinician's ability to make correct judgments should become greater.

CONCEPTS FROM THE CONSULTING ROOM

Fully as influential as the concepts arising from experimental research have been those that have arisen from the efforts of gifted psycho-therapists generalizing from and organizing what they have observed in working with patients. Standing out as by far the most influential of all these has been Sigmund Freud. His ideas have become woven into the fabric of all of our thinking about personality so that it is now next to impossible even to discuss personality without using some Freudian concepts. Freud and the psychoanalytic movement which he fathered have stimulated both violent opposition and fanatical adherence. Nowa-days, few psychologists would deny that psychoanalysis constitutes the single most important personality theory, but few would deny that it needs considerable modification. It will be impossible to do full justice to the breadth of Freud's thinking here. The reader must go himself to Freud's original writings (especially 1913, 1914, 1933, 1949) and the many descriptions of his system by his followers, such as Fenichel (1945), and critical evaluations, such as Madison (1961), Hook (1959), and Sears (1943). Here we shall take up only a few of the most important principles which he developed in fifty years of observing and thinking deeply about his patients and himself. He conceived of psychoanalysis as having three areas of contribution: a personality theory, a mode of research into the human mind, and a form of psychotherapy.

The most pervasive of Freud's ideas is the conception of personality as the *interplay of intrapsychic forces.* Psychoanalytic theory places primary emphasis on *motivation* and dynamic interaction. This inter-action often takes the form of two forces opposed to each other. The *id,* containing the chaotic primitive animalistic urges, fights for expression and satisfaction of its needs with the *ego* and its subsystem, the *superego,* or conscience. The basic energy of life, the *libido,* a sexualized con-structive instinct, was seen in Freud's later writings as opposed to the death instinct, a destructive aggressive urge. The *pleasure principle,* by which a person lives early in life as he strives toward immediate gratification of his wishes and needs, is opposed to the *reality principle,* which allows for the realities of the social and physical world. A clinician using psychoanalytic concepts is constantly aware of the wishing, striving, seeking, searching aspect of people and of the inner conflicts which prevent the expression of their needs and wishes. As we have said, laboratory psychologists have also made a place for motivation in their theories, but there it is a less salient concept than in psychoanalysis, and clinical workers tend to use psychoanalytic formulations, which are anthropomorphic and convenient, more than the abstract and technically sounder concepts of the experimentalists.

The second major psychoanalytic idea which has exercised a profound influence on our thinking about personality is the concept of *unconscious processes.* As clinicians we assume when we listen to what a person says about his motives and goals that a large part of his actual motivation is undetected and inaccessible to him. It is only through painstaking attention to the indirect effects and expressions of the unconscious processes that we can get some clues as to what they are. The assumption that much motivation is unconscious is an advantage for the clinician in that it makes apparently irrational behavior at least potentially lawful and understandable.

A third broad Freudian principle that has permeated practically all thinking about personality is the concept of *anxiety* and *defenses against anxiety.* Theorists differ in their ideas about the source of the anxiety that is at the root of all neurotic symptoms, but they would agree fairly well on the proposition that neurotic symptoms and much of normal behavior as well constitute defenses against anxiety, a kind of behavior that serves to keep it within manageable limits. The basic defense mechanism, or as some more behaviorally oriented psychologists call it, adjustment mechanism, is *repression.* Repression is the mechanism by which threatening feelings and impulses are excluded, denied entry to consciousness. Repression occurs because the individual feels threatened, but, it is to be added, the attempted repression is never completely successful. The repressed needs and desires and urges are expressed in roundabout ways, by slips of the tongue, displaced reactions to things, and dream symbols. The expression may take the form of neurotic symptoms. There are, of course, a number of other defense mechanisms which are fairly well known: rationalization, projection, reaction formation.

A fourth contribution psychoanalysis has made to our thinking is emphasis on the critical *importance for personality development of infancy and childhood.* Freud produced convincing evidence that the life of a child is not a time of idyllic bliss and innocence, but rather one when urges are strong and conflicts are many. Freud put particular stress on the notion of *infantile sexuality,* which to him meant a progressive development of children through distinguishable periods of pleasurable erotogenic activities—successively the oral, anal, and genital periods. Furthermore, his emphasis on the Oedipus complex pointed toward the inevitability of a child's intense longing for affection from the parent of the opposite sex. Along with this concept he postulated castration anxiety whereby the parent of the same sex could appear to be a powerful threat to the young child. The discovery of such relationships within the family became ground for developing the idea that besides *intra*personal conflicts, there were also *inter*personal relationships and conflicts. Contemporary thinking about therapy, about methods of child training and education, and about ways of analyzing differences between societies and social classes have all been deeply influenced by these Freudian principles.

We might have selected many more psychoanalytic concepts for special mention. Psychoanalysis is an intricate and involved system well worth all the study that is needed to understand it thoroughly or to dissent from it intelligently. The broad principles we have singled out are some that must be incorporated, or at least dealt with, in almost any personality theory that can be formulated today.

The predominance of orthodox Freudian psychoanalysis has in the judgment of many persons led to an undervaluation of certain useful concepts embodied in modifications of the system. Two major deviations from Freudian conceptualization have been theories centering around cognitive processes and theories emphasizing the social and cultural aspects of personality. The lead in both these lines of deviation was taken by Alfred Adler. Instead of seeing persons as especially to be understood through their intrapsychic conflicts, he asserted that the individual who is an irreducible whole, could be known through his social goals and his relationships to other people, especially with his family. These taken together distinguish his particular "style of life," and this, rather than sexuality, betrays his basic motivation. In analyzing any bit of behavior, neurotic or normal, Adler would ask the question: What is this person's social purpose? The "guiding fictions" or "mistaken notions" of a person seeking to relate to his fellows are at the basis of his neurosis, if he has one. Many present-day psychologists who do not think of themselves as Adlerians are emphasizing the cognitive and social aspects of personality in their theoretical formulations.

From all the complexities of thinking for which Carl Jung is noted comes one idea that has influenced the work of clinicians belonging to many schools. It is the concept of *creative* or *constructive unconscious processes*. Jung in his doctrine of *individuation* holds that psychological health is a matter of learning to express one's self more completely. Jung, because he is frequently very difficult to follow and even outright mystical in the judgment of most critics, has had rather less influence on American psychology, in which the keynote is empiricism, than on European thinking. Nevertheless, his famous concepts of introversion and extroversion and the word-association test he developed have had wide influence.

Otto Rank is another psychoanalyst whose name ranks high with psychologists who find it natural to think of human motivation more in terms of self-actualization and creative self-expression than in terms of biological drives. His emphasis was on the *will* and on the individual's struggle by separating himself and achieving independence to find his own unique personality and place in the world.

Many sorts of syntheses of these and many other concepts from a variety of personality theories are possible. The more a clinician knows about all of them, provided he is alert and does not feel the need to maintain a strict theoretical orthodoxy, the better equipped he is for his work. Although it is simpler to seize upon one theory and stick with it, it is likely that the clinician whose mind is open to conflicting evidence and novel hypotheses will accumulate a more useful set of concepts and serve his clients better. Fortunately, personality theorists are becoming at the present time more and more concerned with attempts to reconcile and unify concepts and to put theories to the test. Thus, as time goes along, somewhat easier channels of communication have opened between various divergent groups.

CONCEPTS FROM THE STUDY OF GROUPS AND SOCIETY

Much of our knowledge in the human sciences has come not from laboratory experiments but from observation and study of persons in real life situations. This has been particularly true with regard to the problem of the relationship between the individual and his society. The cultural anthropologists, the sociologists, and the social psychologists are modifying our thinking about mentally ill people and behavior deviation in general. An early instance of an effective sociological approach of this sort is the work of Durkheim. He formulated the concept of *anomie*, a condition without organization or system, the feeling a person may have of not belonging to society, of not having a "place." Durkheim used *anomie* to explain the development of mental aberrations and suicide.

When it was noted that in some cultures psychosis-like behavior was an accepted thing, a reexamination of our ideas about what is "abnormal" was clearly called for. The finding that there is tremendous variation in behavior and in value systems from people to people, and even between social classes and racial groups in a single country, has made us aware of the overriding effects and importance of social influences. In recent years social psychology has developed rapidly, and now we are on the lookout for sources of stress in communities and in organizations as we study the etiology of mental illness.

If we seek to explain the behavior of individuals, we have to bring in social concepts. Every time we set out to describe a person, we resort to relating him to one or another group. To say, for example, that someone is a man or a woman is already to have placed him in a group which it is assumed one knows a good deal about, and, because this is so, the individual must also be known to some extent. If you tell his age and his occupation, you are assigning him to other groups. Although in general there are greater intragroup differences than intergroup differences, it is still true that the successive identification of the groups to which a person belongs enables one to say a great deal about him. So powerful is the standardizing influence of groups.

"Every man is in certain respects like all other men, like some other men, and like no other man" (Kluckhohn & Murray, 1955, p. 53). As individuals, we share much with other people, some things even with other animals—such as living in a given physical environment with its storms, the features of its terrain, its edible and inedible plants, and we also share such physiological needs and limitations as are imposed by hunger, sexual desire, finite physical strength, and so on. With other peoples we may share a common language or common ways of doing things. *Culture* is "a great storehouse of ready-made solutions to problems which human animals are wont to encounter" (Kluckhohn & Murray, 1955, p. 54).

Of all concepts in social psychology and in cultural anthropology, the one which does most to link the individual with his society is the concept of *role*. Sarbin (1954, p. 225) defines a role as "a patterned sequence of learned actions or deeds performed by a person in an interaction situation." In defining particular roles two different things must be kept in mind. One is the *function* the individual has in a group, what he does, the characteristic contribution he makes. The other is the behavior *expected* of the person who fills a defined position in a group. In both its aspects, the actual and the expected, a role cannot be understood unless the group is specified and understood. Any confusion which may arise between the two meanings is dispelled to some degree if we differentiate between *role expectations* (obligations and responsibilities) and *role behavior* (what the person actually does in a given group). The possibilities for *role conflict* develop when an individual is expected to play one role that interferes with his simultaneously playing another role. For instance, role conflict may occur when the father of a family finds his employer expects him to give up many evening hours to his job while his family expects him to stay at home and do things with them.

One feature of modern life which is surprisingly often ignored is the importance of *large organizations* and institutions in directing and controlling the lives of the people who comprise them. Millions of our citizens work for formally organized entities—such as business corporations, schools, and government. As Max Weber pointed out, it is the ideal of every bureaucracy to have each individual performing assigned duties in an efficient, machine-like manner as set forth in a table of organization. Perhaps there may be an *informal organization* which modifies and runs counter to the *formal organization,* but still when a person joins a given organization, much of his behavior is defined and prescribed. Unless he conforms, at least within limits, he will not be able to retain his position. A nation's way of governing its people is translated down into distinct influences on individual human behavior.

Prohibition was associated with large-scale gangsterism in the United States. There were many suicides at the start of the depression. Changes in tax laws, marriage laws, labor laws, adoption laws, traffic laws, criminal codes, laws governing military service, rationing, and social security affect people directly as well as the provisions the state makes for the aged and mentally ill. The kind of sanctions which prevent Negroes from living in certain districts of town and segregate them in slum areas seem to be related to the rates of occurrence of delinquency and schizophrenia. Increasingly, as we move from the "fire-fighting" of social ills to "fire prevention," the clinical psychologist must be concerned with these community correlates of mental illness and maladjustment.

Social concepts are important to our understanding of an individual in still another way. George Herbert Mead pointed out that a child's self-concept develops from the "reflected appraisals of others." Even when a person is by himself, he has within him effective traces of many of the people he has known. Although he is not interacting with them at the time, he may behave as if he were. It is not uncommon for a person to feel guilt upon doing certain things which would have been punished by his parents in the past, or to feel a surge of anger at the mere idea of an insult which there is no chance he will ever encounter. His solitary plans are related to his social purposes.

Another line of thinking comes from the direct observation of people in living situations. Barker and Wright and their associates (1955) have done studies in the *ecology of behavior*. Ecology is the study of organisms in relation to the environment to which they are more or less successfully adapted. This concept has to do with the on-going natural interaction of human beings. Barker's methodology was to observe his subjects wherever they naturally go rather than to bring them into a laboratory or to interview them in the usual clinical manner. His work sharpens our awareness of how much goes on in the life of a person even during a single day and how difficult it would be to categorize all that he does in an adequate manner.

Undoubtedly the theorist who has had most success in showing the relations between personality and social phenomena is Kurt Lewin. We have no space here for going into much detail about Lewin's system, accounts of which have been presented by Leeper (1943) and Deutsch (1954). Lewin's most enlightening concept was the *life space*. By this he meant the perceived *psychological* environment, rather than the physical environment. What is always required as we attempt to understand a person is that we find out how *he* sees his world, whether or not this view corresponds to that of others who know him or to our own. Whether or not we follow Lewin in calling such personal views of the environment "life space," we use the concept constantly.

It is the great variety of these different approaches to understanding individuals through social concepts which impresses us most and leaves us asking for some way to integrate them. The likelihood that such an integration can be effected in the near future is not great, though many interesting formulations have been proposed. Meanwhile, the clinician will find his observations and reflections on the nature of interpersonal relationships and on the influence of situations on behavior a rich source of ideas and hypotheses.

CONCEPTS FROM INDIVIDUAL DIFFERENCES AND THEIR MEASUREMENT

The other large body of knowledge that has come mainly from research in the field rather than laboratory investigation is made up of what we have learned about individual differences in psychological characteristics. Once it became apparent, at about the turn of the century, that differences in intelligence could be expressed in quantitative terms, the way was open for work on all sorts of "mental measurements." Tests as devices for measuring psychological characteristics or traits have been given to many millions of people—school children, soldiers, job applicants, and all sorts of other groups.

If we look at the basic concepts, rather than at the tools of measurement, that have arisen in this line of research, the first that comes to mind is the *trait* concept itself. Like other major ideas we have been discussing, its origins go back much farther than scientific psychology. But our methods of measuring in numerical terms have forced us to ask what it is we are measuring. We speak of a trait when we single out one aspect of an individual personality, some quality, some ability which he shares with many, perhaps with all, human beings and then measure some performance ("output") believed to be indicative of this quality, or ability, so that we can state in quantitative terms how his performance compares with those of a large population of other people. For example, an intelligence test, by showing us how much below or above average an individual is in the performance of a specified set of tasks under standardized conditions, is supposed to indicate how *much* of the trait intelligence, or problem-solving ability, the individual possesses. Such a device is particularly helpful in situations where the need is to be able to sort out individuals and place or assign each of them to a group or a situation where he will best fit in. Clinicians find trait concepts both a help and a hindrance. On the one hand, they must keep in mind this normative evaluative way of looking at persons, for society itself uses it constantly, but on the other they must be sensitive to their client's essential nature in an overall nonevaluative way, to his absolute worth as a person.

Even if there were only ten human traits, each of which could be measured on a seven-point scale, the combinations would add up to more than 56,000 kinds of individuals. So it is understandable that the trait concept has of late been combined to an increasing degree with the more significant concept of *patterns* of traits. This is a move in the direction of expressing individuality in quantitative terms. In many different areas of practice and research, the trait-pattern method of describing a person has come into use. Counselors at employment offices look for combinations of scores on the separate tests of the General Aptitude Test Battery for the occupations that require such combinations. Physiologists like Roger Williams measure separate metabolic activities with regard to different kinds of food and describe the person in terms of this pattern of metabolic reaction rather than in terms of one overall metabolic rate. This is an approach which the clinician often finds enlightening, and its use will surely be expanded as fast as methods can be devised.

The third contribution that work in individual differences has made to our theoretical thinking is not exactly parallel to the others. It is a sort of basic prescription that we apply the logic of *probabilities* to all thinking in this field. The concepts underlying the whole technology of mental testing are statistical concepts based on probability theory. When a psychologist finds, for example, that a mentally retarded child obtains an IQ of 58 on the Stanford-Binet test, he automatically interprets this as a range of scores within which the child's IQ *probably* falls, rather than as an exact score. It is such thinking that technical knowledge of individual differences fosters.

CONCEPTS FROM RELIGION AND PHILOSOPHY

It is well for psychologists to remember that they are far from being either the first or the only group of professional people who have thought long and deeply about human nature. Philosophers and religious leaders have been concerned for centuries with man—his nature and his needs. Many of their insights are doubtless direct ancestors of what we take to be basic premises.

Much religious thinking has centered around the concept of the *soul*, and the word *psychology* itself is derived from the Greek word for their idea of a soul. In the personality theories of our day, the *self-concept*, or as some writers prefer, the concept of *ego identity*, carries some of the same sort of meaning, though stripped of mystical or supernatural connotations.

Then there is the vast effort philosophers have given to the problems of *choice, responsibility*, and *freedom*. Psychologists, particularly those dealing directly with human beings who might be aided to live fuller and more meaningful lives, must come to terms with the issues for which these terms stand. In doing so a sort of basic dilemma confronts them. On the one hand, it has been feared that to recognize the reality of freedom and individual responsibility would undermine the determinism that must be postulated if psychology is to be considered a science. On the other hand, to assume that the actions of a human being are completely determined by causal factors in his past history and present situation leads to pessimism concerning the outlook for a person whose background has been extremely unfavorable, and what the practicing clinician needs is optimism and faith in therapy. What psychologists have tended to do is to alternate between the two frames of reference. Boring (1957), in a thoughtful analysis of the problem, justifies this alternation on the grounds that each view of the world is only a sort of model into which we fit events as we observe them, and it is quite legitimate to use different models at different times. Another way to look at the problem is adopted by Feigl (1959). He explains how we often confuse determinism with compulsion. He points out that as we move up the phylogenetic scale, there is more and more *self-determination*. A man, though he too may be the product of antecedent conditions, can control much of his own behavior through cerebral dispositions equitable with his own personality. Feigl arrives at a resolution of the free-will problem in terms of both determinism and individual responsibility. His clarification of the problem will repay study by the clinician who feels doubt, in principle, of the efficacy of a man's trying to behave differently.

In other ways the issue is less troublesome than it once was. More complex and subtle ideas concerning the nature of causation growing out of new conceptions of the physical world have made some notions of determinism obsolete. These include the ideas of systems dynamically interacting and of feedback, instead of simple mechanical causation, and Heisenberg's principle of indeterminacy, in which observation itself interferes with the thing observed. Predicting what individuals will do in probabalistic terms and for a limited time only, as discussed in the previous chapter, will make it unnecessary for the psychologist to rule choice and responsibility out of his thinking about a person's life. Even more important than these trends is the development in our time of powerful new logical and mathematical tools that made it possible to apply scientific methods of study to the decision process itself. It is such changes in the general climate and in specific tools of our thinking that now warrant the use of *decision* as a focal concept in clinical psychology.

A DEVELOPMENTAL FRAMEWORK FOR CLINICAL USE

What sort of conceptual framework is broad enough to encompass so many ideas from different sources—ideas that a clinician uses in his work? As we indicated at the start of this chapter, if he commands such a conceptual framework, it will enable him to keep in order the unwieldy body of detailed knowledge he needs to draw upon in understanding individual cases. It will aid him in organizing his observations and inferences into clear patterns that can be communicated—sometimes to the client himself, as when an interpretation is given as part of therapy, sometimes to other persons who may be able to help the client.

There is no perfect way to put together a satisfactory conceptual framework. Even the best of existing theories are loose and imprecise on many points, and many of them are too limited in scope to be usable in clinical work. For instance, a rote-learning theory or a neuropsychological model are of little value in explaining patients' interaction with complex environments. In doing clinical work we must confront the wide expanse of a person's life. We must include in our thoughts about cases such matters as a boy's power struggles with his domineering mother, an adolescent's progressive withdrawal and development of bizarre delusions, a man's neurotic reaction to an industrial accident, a woman's suicidal attempt following the birth of a child, and an old man's mental deterioration. The clinical view is a long and wide view of human life, sweeping from birth to death and from physiological to cultural influences. In reviewing our clinical experiences and the way this book is written, the authors have found themselves thinking in terms of *development in interactive systems*. Even though such a view does not constitute a precise theory or a perfect synthesis, we find the orientation very useful.

Development can be defined as a process of *patterned change*. In its broad meaning, it includes a vast range of phenomena. As English and English (1958, p. 148) put it, "Its application ranges from molecular changes in crystals or bones to changes in purposes, ideals, or the structure of society." Thus physiologists, neurologists, biochemists, anatomists, anthropologists, sociologists, and many other kinds of professional workers besides psychologists are concerned with patterned change in one form or another. But the clinical or counseling psychologist must mark off some aspects of it as his own particular province, if he is to use it to guide his day-to-day work with patients and clients. The particular changing pattern, or development, with which he is concerned is embodied in an individual's *experience* and in his *behavior*. "Experience" includes many things—ways of perceiving self and the world, conceptual structures by means of which his perceptions are screened and organized, and the motivational components of his experience, such as needs and interests. "Behavior" includes his habits, skills, general styles of talking and acting, and many other specific things. Needless to say, behavior and experience are not unrelated and the ultimate concern of a clinician is with the person, the unity that underlies them both.

The individuality a psychologist tries to seize in his attempt to understand a person takes the form of a unique pattern, changing continuously from conception to death. In order to cast this formidable idea in a more workable form, the concept of developmental *stages* has been formulated. The total process is broken down into a limited number of periods, each of which can be studied separately or in succession. There is no one best set of dividing incidents to mark where each stage begins and ends. Biological events can be chosen as landmarks—birth, puberty, the menopause—but they are few in number. It can probably be done better using the social transitions deemed most important in a particular culture as the basis for separating stages. Sometimes a combination of biological and social stages is used. Early in life there appear to be *critical periods* during each of which certain social skills should be learned in order to build a base for further normal development. The evidence from studies of imprinting and sensory deprivation in animals suggests early experience may have powerful effects. The evidence on deprivation of maternal care with human infants is less clear, but profound effects are also found there (Yarrow, 1961).

Perhaps the most useful way for a psychologist to think about life stages is embodied in the concept of *developmental tasks.* The periods that comprise a human life can be distinguished from one another on the basis of what the developing individual is expected to accomplish during each period. Thus we consider infancy to be over and early childhood to have begun when the person has learned to walk, talk, feed himself, and control bladder and bowels. We think of adolescence as the period when he must learn to become independent of his family, establish heterosexual relationships, and make dependable plans for adult life. Old age or senescence is the period after retirement when the person must come to terms with the fact that he is no longer needed in his occupation and must learn to organize his life around the leisure activities that are open to him and that will make life seem worthwhile.

For the clinician, this focus on developmental tasks serves well as an organizing conceptual framework. It stimulates questions such as: How did Mrs. Y as a little girl get along with her family? Which developmental tasks of adolescence was she unable to accomplish? How can she learn now what she failed to learn at that time? How are certain habits she adopted then affecting her life adversely now? To change an undesirable pattern that has been established over a long period of time is never easy. Its features most open to change are those over which the individual himself has some control. Thus to think in terms of developmental tasks, past and present, is to place emphasis where it belongs—on things the patient or client may *do* or be able to *learn* to modify an existing pattern in such a way that the changes inevitably occurring as life goes on will improve its effectiveness in later stages.

Somewhere within this general framework of development as patterned change, each of the diverse concepts outlined in the early sections of this chapter can be placed. Some of them have to do with the *pattern* aspect, other with the *change* aspect. Study of the patterns of human life, seen as cross sections of processes with a time dimension, includes whatever seems significant in the way of basic physiological patterns and thus makes a place for concepts like heredity, homeostasis, and the mechanisms for adapting to stress. The study of perception in the individual is also a study of the patterns into which his world is organized. The trait and factor approach to the study of a personality is a way of identifying a pattern of measured characteristics. The analysis of a person's basic needs and characteristic defense mechanisms is another way of looking at the unique pattern of his personality. From the broader social viewpoint, the pattern includes the person in his social situation with lines representing his relationships to other persons—their special forms and colors—all salient features of the total design. And perhaps most clearly of all, the person's organized choices, his *plans* for his own activity, to use the term Miller, Galanter, and Pribram (1960) have elaborated in their approach to theory, constitute a pattern we need to understand. The psychologist who uses development as a conceptual framework can make use of any or all of these theoretical ideas as he seeks to construct as detailed and comprehensive a view as possible of the pattern of one person's life.

In thinking about patterns of development, the central concept is that of *systems,* a concept that occurs in all sciences. Development occurs within a system and in relation to other systems. A system is made up of objects or parts related to each other and interacting within certain limits or boundaries. Galaxies, cells, persons, families, and factories are systems. As we look at human beings, we can distinguish several levels of analysis: (*a*) the *organismic system,* the homeostatically controlled physiological interaction within the body; (*b*) the *personality system,* the organized interaction of abilities, interests, motives, defenses against anxiety, and so on, within an individual; (*c*) the *group system,* the interaction of a primary group such as a family or friends; and (*d*) the *institutional system,* any one of many large organizations with their economic and political interactions. In his daily work the clinical psychologist will focus most frequently on the middle two systems—on personality and primary groups—but he needs to have other kinds of analysis in mind. With some patients it may be very helpful to understand the physician's analysis of the organismic system, such as the breakdown of normal brain functioning due to the bursting of a cerebral blood vessel.

Systems have a number of important characteristics which help us in understanding the persons with whom we deal. For one thing, there is a *relative openness or closedness* to "inputs" and "outputs" across the system's boundaries. Human beings are relatively open systems, ingesting food and excreting wastes, engaging in social behaviors, and so forth.

Within the system there are *communication* patterns; there are intra-personal as well as interpersonal channels of communication through which some messages easily pass and others get delayed or confused. A system must have a method of *self-regulation*. In order to regulate itself there must be *feedback* and controlling reactions when homeostatic balance is upset. This applies in the family as well as the cell; when father gets terribly angry at mother there must be some reestablishing of a new working relationship in order for the family to stay together. This controlling function also includes the rewards and punishments influencing learning. Within the system there is a dynamic interplay of the subsystems so that a cooperative *reciprocity of functions* is established. For example, in order to maintain a family there must be some system for obtaining, preparing, and distributing food to the children and adults; if the mother hates to cook, often, at least in this culture, the father will take over much of that responsibility. Another important characteristic of systems is their *purposive adaptability:* that is, the system can work in many different situations to arrive at the same ends. A husband can support his wife and family in many different ways. A hostile person can find a great variety of ways to injure others—by cutting humor, vicious gossip, withholding of assistance, and physical violence. This purposive adaptability is an integral part of the last characteristic we will mention. Systems have *developmental directions and stages*. The human organism has a life cycle from birth to death. It is impossible to reverse that direction. In the development of a family there are also directions and stages: courtship, marriage, young children at home, older children away from home, dissolution of the relationships by death or separation. Even in large organizations developmental patterns can be discerned, such as the early reforming spirit of a new fundamentalist sect turning into the formal dignified organization of an established church.[1]

Many of the concepts we cited earlier in this chapter can be incorporated in the *change* aspect of development in systems. Here too there are physiological principles derived from observation of the especially rapid processes of prenatal change and the slower postnatal processes of maturation, growth, and senescence, in both animals and man. The idea that psychological growth tendencies persist throughout life can be given a place in this overall framework. Such an assumption has been important to many therapists, especially Jung and Rogers. The core of personality containing both self-concepts and generalized role behavior —the experience and behavior reflecting a sense of personal continuity even in different situations—is what we mean by *identity*. Aspects of a person's identity are continually evolving as he meets new life situations

[1] This review of the concept of system is a very brief one. The interested reader is referred especially to the discussions by Hearn (1958) and Miller (1955).

that cause him to question "Who am I really?" Concepts concerning learning of all kinds belong here also, whether they have to do with the acquisition of specific motor habits or the modification of cognitive patterns. The part social and cultural influences play in the socialization of the child can be considered as part of the change aspect of development. Decisions made by or about a client can be seen as signposts pointing to the direction of change in the period they initiate.

This in bare outline is a sketch of a kind of conceptual framework broad enough to accommodate a wide range of concepts about human personality, but definite enough to suggest ways for a clinician to begin his task of understanding an individual. In such a system, pathology is conceptualized as a special kind of changing pattern. Schizophrenia, for example, is to be thought of not as a disease entity of a precise character, but as a line of development taken by certain persons in certain situations. What one discovers studying a given patient, however, is the total pattern of his unique individuality, not just its schizophrenic aspects. As the schizophrenic individual has gone through his life cycle until the present time, he has developed in a series of interacting systems. His typical role behaviors in close groups, his deficiencies in physiological function, and his inadequacies in problem-solving have determined a pattern of development that ultimately incapacitates him for normal living.

Such a developmental viewpoint affects one's approach to both diagnosis and therapy. Diagnosis in the individual case is always an attempt to grasp as adequately as possible the total pattern the person presents, not just the assigning of a typological or psychiatric label. In the analysis of the changing pattern of a person's life one must look at the role he plays in significant interpersonal systems, his skills as they function in life, his emotional adaptations to stress, and his general directions of development. These concepts will be further elaborated in the chapters on assessment.

Psychotherapy constitutes an attempt to change the pattern enough so that subsequent development will turn in the direction of its strong healthy features rather than its conflicted, self-defeating, nonproductive idiosyncracies that are unadaptive and perhaps pathological. In the chapters on therapy we will see how different kinds of therapists try to do this through influencing roles and interpersonal interaction, through promoting greater utilization of present skills and changes in habits, through stimulating emotional insight and reorganization, and through encouraging the patients to reexamine their values and their perceptions of self. These approaches (paralleling the assessment analysis in the preceding paragraph) can be thought of as varying emphases on different aspects of personality. They are all concerned with development. It is because developmental change is always in process in a human being that psychological treatment is possible. The therapist is like a gardener who can have some influence in shaping and conditioning plants whose general characteristics are largely determined by inherent processes beyond his control.

SUMMARY

Faced with the double need to describe and treat the complexity of human living, how shall the clinician organize his thinking? A theory of human behavior in its present state is far from unified and only small parts here and there have been tested. Though he will not lay claim to having a tightly systematized theory, the clinician knows at least that he needs a conceptual framework. One way for him to develop his own conceptual framework is to examine closely his implicit working rules and then try to systematize them, along with whatever assumptions underlie them. Another way is to apply to clinical problems the concepts that have proved effective in various areas of research and practice. Some of these come from the laboratory, such as homeostasis, motivation, stress, learning, and perception. Some of them are products of clinical work itself—especially some of Freud's pioneering ideas, such as unconscious processes, intrapsychic conflict, defense mechanisms, and the psychosexuality of early childhood. Derivative offshoots from orthodox psychoanalysis have emphasized sociocultural and cognitive aspects of personality. From research on the nature of the social field, we have learned to think in terms of such concepts as role, institution, culture, and the natural ecology of human behavior. From the psychology of individual differences and psychometrics, we get the concept of traits, of patterns, and of the probabilistic nature of behavior. The philosophers and religionists have taught us to think of self, identity, choice, and responsibility. The philosophy of science has furnished a logical and critical framework. In attempting to synthesize these many ideas, we have used a developmental framework—seeing individual and group living as a process of patterned change with critical periods and developmental tasks throughout the whole life span. Each person who proposes to work in clinical psychology should be challenged to set about developing his own synthesis, recognizing as he does so that he faces a task he can never expect to complete.

SUGGESTED READINGS

FEIGL, H. Philosophical embarrassments of psychology. *Amer. Psychologist*, 1959, 14, 115-128.
    Feigl, a philosopher who has written widely on the philosophy of science and who is closely acquainted with psychology, compares philosophical analysis with psychotherapy—philosophical analysis trying to make fully ex-

plicit the conceptual conflicts that are responsible for our intellectual disorder and psychotherapy trying to reduce or eliminate our emotional conflicts. Feigl analyzes the "free will versus determinism" argument, "explanation versus understanding," and problems of defining subject matter and constructing theories. In this very readable article he advocates adoption of a "liberal" operationalism.

HEBB, D. O. The American revolution. *Amer. Psychologist,* 1960, 12, 735-745.
This address by the first foreign president of the APA is an analysis of the American psychological revolution, which is called Behaviorism, and a call for extension of this revolution to include the thought processes and particularly the self-concept. According to Hebb, mediating processes interact between stimulus and response, perhaps in a way similar to the "plans" described by Miller, Galanter, and Pribram (1960) in their analogy with the computer. Some of Hebb's discussion of the self-concept and the body image comes close to problems of clinical conceptualization.

ERIKSON, E. H. *Childhood and society.* New York: Norton, 1950.
Erikson combines a psychoanalytic and anthropological view of man. Man's long dependence during childhood has the advantage of permitting extensive learning, but it has the disadvantage of leaving a residue of emotional immaturity. In the life span of development Erikson discerns eight stages characterized by a nuclear conflict or choice at each stage: (1) trust versus mistrust in others during infancy (replacing the traditional oral stage), (2) autonomy versus shame and doubt somewhat later on (replacing the anal stage), (3) initiative versus guilt as the child begins to move out and explore relations with others, (4) industry versus inferiority as he meets the requirements of school or the culture (replacing the latency period), (5) identity versus role diffusion as he moves into adolescence, (6) intimacy versus isolation as he chooses whether to love a person of the opposite sex and work with others, (7) generativity versus stagnation as he assumes parental responsibilities, and (8) ego integrity versus despair as he moves into old age. For an excellent presentation of Erikson's concept of identity see his later monograph (1959).

Several attempts to develop theory relevant to clinical problems

Students of psychology will be familiar with the usual systems and theories in personality, learning, and social psychology. Among broad interdisciplinary attempts to develop a theory taking into account psychopathology and clinical problems, there is Abt's (1956) whose transactional approach to clinical psychology describes what he conceives as the basic unit of interpersonal transaction embedded in a larger social process. Grinker (1956) and several other psychiatrists and behavioral scientists meeting in conferences for several years attempted to arrive at a unified theory of human behavior. They agreed on three basic principles: homeostasis, the transactional principle ("meaning a reciprocal relationship among all parts of the field and not simply an interaction which is an effect of one system or focus on another," Grinker, 1956, p. 372), and communication processes. (For a critique of this book see Cartwright's review in the May, 1959, *Contemporary Psychology.*) Leighton, Clausen, and Wilson (1957), in connection with planning a mental health study for a large community, adopted the following orienting concepts: the mutually interdependent functioning of systems, the personality concepts (self, ego-ideal, and superego), socialization, identification, sentiments (emotional action tendencies directed toward some object), values, roles, and social organization. The Mental Health Research Institute at the University of Michigan has been working on broad behavioral theory, reports of which frequently appear in issues of their journal, *Behavioral Science.*

An excellent introduction to theory building with an application of general systems theory to social work is provided by Hearn (1958). James Miller (1955) presents another good overview of general systems theory.

3 Clinical Research

In the varieties of people who come to the clinic there is much that puzzles the clinician. Research is the systematic seeking of answers to puzzling questions. In this chapter we shall look at the clinical psychologist's great interest in research and his responsibility for conducting it and also explore the advantages and disadvantages of doing research in a clinical setting.

THE SPIRIT OF INQUIRY

Why? This question comes naturally to human beings. Shortly after a child learns to talk, he starts asking questions in various forms. Children, like cats, are notoriously curious. Without fears induced by adults, they will eagerly examine bugs and plants, climb on high places, and manipulate things in strange ways. Scientific research is simply a more or less elaborate expression of this basic spirit of inquiry into the processes of nature going on around and within us. It is true that complex tools of observation and intricate experimental and statistical procedures must often be employed to avoid reaching erroneous conclusions. But the basic motivation and attitude is curiosity, search, fascination with knowing. It is the precious resolve to inquire and to find out that psychologists wish to encourage and preserve. Some psychologists who become immersed in the daily pressures for service lose this ambition, some fail to see how they can combine research with clinical practice, and some, perhaps, lack the requisite skills.

The research process has two aspects—the generation of ideas and the development of methods for checking them, or as Reichenbach (1938) has called them, the context of *discovery* and the context of *justification.* The significance of any piece of research depends on the significance of the idea behind it. In clinical work, there are frequent opportunities to make contact with some really significant aspect of human living. The clinician cannot retreat to an ivory tower when a despairing patient tells him he is contemplating suicide or when patients engaged in group therapy start aggressively attacking each other. Human emotions and lives are there to be observed and studied, demanding that we make some sense of them. It is this "making sense" of the human game that is basic to research. The clinician gets his hypotheses and hunches from many sources: previous research findings, doubts of what others have claimed to be true, personality theory, learning theory, "accidental" happenings, dreams, almost anywhere.

The second aspect of inquiry is important too—moving in to check-up on an idea. The generation of good ideas and sudden insights, creative ones, is important and makes a good story—Archimedes' "Eureka" in the bathtub, the falling apple that supposedly jolted Newton into giving birth to the principle of gravitation, Fleming's discovery of penicillin in a mold that had accidentally formed in a laboratory dish, the idea for the bubble chamber that the young Nobel laureate, Glasser, got while opening a can of beer. Many clinicians, too, get such insights into the whys of human behavior—the great Freud was one. But the dramatic event sometimes turns our attention away from the fact that these scientists have spent years of preparation before the insight and that they usually have labored to solve the problem many, many times unsuccessfully. Only a mind which is prepared can appreciate the importance of the sudden insight or the lucky accident. There is even a name for the ability to extract value from an accidental happening and to utilize it creatively, *serendipity.* But we must remember that the final proof that the insight has value comes from its subsequent checking through the use of techniques which the scientist must be able to devise. The checking of hypotheses requires much persistence and ingenuity. Every step of these procedures must eventually be communicated to one's fellow scientists in the report of the research so that they can repeat the observations if they wish. Unfortunately many ideas seem great when they come but cannot stand up when tested. The chances are very much against any random hypothesis being true. Still, the more new ideas that are tested, the more likely it is that some of them will prove true.

As tentative hunches about human behavior are confirmed or rejected, the body of knowledge is increased. A good piece of research suggests further research. New ideas are generated. Old methods are improved. Gradually the spirit of inquiry, together with hard work, produces a science of human behavior.

FORMULATING QUESTIONS AND PLANNING RESEARCH PROJECTS

In developing the plan of his research, a scientist usually proceeds by *successively refining his original question*. His first problem is to find out and state very clearly what he means by the terms and processes involved in the question. When this has been done the rest of the research can often be carried out in a straightforward way. In the beginning, however, the clinician may have a question or an impression that is very vague, like the following: "I have an idea that schizophrenia is caused by conflicting communications from parents in childhood" or "I've noticed that one town in our state sends our state hospital year after year more paranoid patients than another town of about the same size; what are the differences between these two?" or "I wonder what would happen if we should change the administration of the Thematic Apperception Test so that patients were asked to tell us the most *unlikely* story to go with the picture" or "My ideas of role theory suggest to me that psychopaths are deficient in their ability to take the other person's point of view; how could I check on this notion?" In such a vague state, though the idea for a research project is there, it would be impossible to carry out a useful piece of research to test it. The next steps consist in the clinician asking himself repeatedly what is meant by each of the various terms and propositions it involves and checking the relevant scientific literature until it is clear that some kind of procedure can be tried out to study the point at issue. Usually it is necessary to try out several different procedures with different subjects to see which works best. In the process, the original ideas and questions may be altered somewhat. The development of a piece of research is a process of constant interaction between the thinker and actual operational research procedures.

For a more extensive example, let us take a question that might be asked in a mental hospital: "Does X, a new drug, really improve the condition of schizophrenics, as it is reputed to?" Immediately we wonder what exactly is meant by "improve." Suppose we decide to observe the patients that are given X in a particular ward and record our judgments as to whether they seem better afterwards. Such an approach may go wrong in many places. One important source of error would be the influence both on the patient (actually, of course, a number of patients) and on the observers of the knowledge that that particular patient is being given a drug supposed to lessen his symptoms of schizophrenia. We know from many studies that both suggestion and anything in the way of special attention are potent influences for change in human beings. As a result, the best drug research programs now use *placebos*, or harmless neutral substances which are identical with the experimental drug in appearance and taste.[1] Furthermore the placebo and the experimental drug are used in a *double-blind* design; that is, it is arranged so that neither the patients nor the staff members who work with the patients and are to judge their improvement know which pill each patient is receiving. For our elaboration of the question, then, we would choose to use a double-blind design. But there are further questions about improvement and what it means. What are going to be the *criteria* of improvement—the indicators of change? There are several possibilities— ratings by the psychiatrists or other clinical staff, changes in the results of tests administered to the patients, observations by aides and others recorded in the form of ratings or checklists, and objective indices like discharge from the hospital or successful placements in hospital jobs. For this project we might decide on one or several of these criteria. Another decision to make would be the kind and size of *sample* of patients. In making this decision we would need to remember to include a *control group* of patients who would receive the placebo instead of the drug and whose treatment otherwise would be identical with that of the experimental group. Perhaps it would be possible for the patients to serve as their own controls by giving them the placebo for a time, then the experimental drug X, and then again the placebo. Decisions would need to be made by the medical member of the research program as to what amounts of the drug to give and what would be a reasonable experimental period to administer the drug at a given strength. The researchers would need to plan the general atmosphere in which the experiment would be conducted and to secure the cooperation of both patients and staff in the project. The researchers would be looking ahead to the kind of procedures which they would use for determining whether any differences between the groups that turned up were actually statistically significant or whether they were such as might well be obtained by tossing a coin. Several different statistical procedures would have to be reviewed to determine which was best for the kind of data collected. The researchers would also be thinking ahead about the interpretation of data, whichever way things turned out, and looking for indications of ways to improve the research if they or someone else should wish to repeat it.

RESEARCH DESIGN AND STATISTICS

There are many different strategies for attacking the research problems in which clinical psychology is vitally interested. Since human behavior is not the exclusive province of any one branch of psychology, clinicians have to keep an eye on the research done in perception, learning, and

[1] For an interesting discussion of the historical development of the recognition of placebo effects, see Shapiro (1960).

personality. Important clinical research is found in the allied disciplines of physiology and sociology. If a technique of measuring anxiety is used in a learning study, this has clinical implications. Biochemical methods of studying adaptation to psychological stress are something the clinician must know about. Whoever follows any of the journals in which clinical psychologists commonly publish, such as the *Journal of Abnormal and Social psychology, Journal of Clinical Psychology, Journal of Consulting Psychology, Journal of Counseling Psychology, American Journal of Orthopsychiatry, Journal of Personality*, will find that many different research methods and designs are employed, such as experimental variation of stimulating conditions, factor analyses of test results, surveys, matching studies, group comparisons, designs involving analysis of variance. All of these varied approaches, however, can be classified under three main headings:

1. *Descriptive research.* Sometimes the basic data and variables of an area of interest are so unclear that we must first identify and describe whatever we can find. We would need to use interviews, observations, or questionnaires to *survey* a sample of the population we are interested in. Surveys provide a scrutiny of an area of interest and may assist in the selection of variables for further research. Descriptive research is often very important in clinical and social psychology because behavior, especially when it is observed outside the laboratory and without controls, is so complex that we are still at a very early stage in understanding most of its patterns. Simple descriptive statistics usually suffice for such research such as frequency counts, means, and standard deviations. Sometimes tests of the significance of differences between group means are also employed.

One example of descriptive research is the survey of Americans' views on the problems of mental health (Gurin, Veroff, & Feld, 1960) mentioned in Chapter 1. Another example is the "behavioral census" of a state hospital population by Fjeld and his colleagues (1957). This study was really the first attempt to survey in a systematic way the entire population of a large hospital. For every one of nearly two thousand patients, nine case-history items and eleven behavior ratings were collected. The main result was a broad description of the hospital population. One finding, among several interesting ones, was the fact that men behaved relatively better than women in a variety of personal and work tasks. A third example is the work of Roger Barker and his associates (1951, 1955) in studying the activities of children in a Midwestern community. Though perhaps not strictly a clinical one, this work is important for revealing a serious deficiency in the work of most psychologists, clinicians included. Barker rightly points out that both clinicians and experimentalists will continue to receive only somewhat distorted views of human behavior if they go on studying people too exclusively in highly artificial situations. Observing phenomena as they occur in natural settings is a respected part of sciences such as astronomy, geology, and biology. Barker has advocated the study of *behavioral ecology,* a term which, as mentioned in the last chapter, covers the intricate and adaptive relations between the natural psychological habitats of people and the structure, dynamics, and content of their on-going behavior. In carrying out such studies, Barker and his colleagues made extensive recordings of children's behavior throughout the day and surveyed the "ecology" of the community to learn which kinds of behavior occurred in different settings. We shall have more to say about this kind of research in Chapter 7.

2. *Relational research.* Many descriptive studies go beyond the simple descriptive survey of events or persons to study relationships. In such work, people are still taken as they are, that is, they are not exposed to conditions set up for the purpose of changing their behavior, although the observations may not be made in their natural habitats. After measuring the variables in which he is interested, the researcher correlates them and often follows with a factor analysis of the table of correlations. Sometimes different groups are compared using appropriate tests of statistical significance. Studies in social and developmental, as well as clinical, psychology frequently take this form.

A few examples may serve to make clear what this kind of research is like. Suppose that a clinical psychologist is interested in the relationship between "authoritarian" attitudes and maladjustment. As his measure of authoritarianism he uses one of the versions of the F scale, as presented in the well-known book by Adorno and others, *The Authoritarian Personality* (1950). As his measure of maladjustment, he uses the Minnesota Multiphasic Personality Inventory (MMPI). He decides to use three different kinds of population samples—college students, hospitalized psychotic patients, and convalescent hospital patients who are not psychotic. After each subject in each of his three groups has completed the F scale and the MMPI, the investigator correlates the F-scale scores with each MMPI scale in turn. He examines the correlations to discover whether an overall relationship seems to exist and then to see whether some kinds of maladjustment, as expressed in particular MMPI scores, are more closely related to authoritarianism than other kinds are and whether the relationship is closer in some kinds of population sample than in others. Special statistical procedures are available for him to use as he makes each of these judgments so that he will not base conclusions on "chance" differences.

There are many variations on this simple design. Factor analysis is a way of locating a limited number of basic variables that can account for the intercorrelations between large numbers of variables. Eysenck, R. B. Cattell, and Guilford have made extensive use of this technique in their studies of personality. Another kind of variation is to hypothesize at the beginning, on the basis of some personality theory, what the expected correlations between variables are and then run a correlational study to check these hypotheses. One might, for example, explore the relationship between the frequency of aggressive acts committed by children and extent of aggressiveness in fantasy, as measured by the Thematic Apperception Test, taking into account two intervening variables: inhibitory control, measured by a questionnaire, and situational provocation, measured by reports of the amount of time spent in interpersonal activities. Any issue of one of the journals referred to earlier will furnish other examples of relational research.

3. *Experimental research*. Experiments involve the actual manipulation of variables. Modern statistical procedures permit us to discover relationships between the several independent variables and the dependent variable and to determine which particular effects upon the latter are associated with which particular changes in the former. The same sorts of statistics employed in descriptive and relational research including factor analyses are used in experimental research, but most commonly contemporary research prefers to avail itself of various forms of experimental design based on the analysis of variance.

The advantages of the experimental approach over the others is that in the controlled situation the experimenter is in a position to observe what happens; he can vary the conditions as he wishes, and he can exactly repeat the experiment when he or someone else wishes. The experimental method is frequently used for testing hypotheses and establishing general laws in science. In the field of clinical psychology more and more experimental work is being done, although it seems unlikely that it will ever be possible to subject people living under natural conditions to many of the controls needed in experiments. However, this is not to deny that many laboratory experiments on learning, concept-formation, motivation, and so forth may profitably be duplicated using the mentally ill as subjects as well as normal persons.

Some examples of research in which experimental methods are being used in clinical psychology or studies of personality are experiments varying the rewards given to patients working on concept-formation in a Skinner box kind of situation; research like that of Krasner and others (1958a, 1958b) in verbally conditioning patients where the frequency of using certain kinds of words is increased by the experimenters' differential reinforcement of them; or the studies of Lazarus and Speisman (Lazarus, 1962) on varieties of "defense techniques" such as denial and intellectualization, thought to reduce the effect of anxiety in subjects viewing a film on the gory subcision rites of a primitive tribe. Despite the limiting factors we referred to, it is likely that there will be more and more use of experimental methods in clinical research as the body of sound systematic theory grows. Cronbach in his APA presidential address (1957) compared what he called the correlational and the experimental method. He pointed out that both kinds of research are needed. Frequently the experimental approach in its attempt to develop general laws disregards interesting data on individual differences. The correlational approach in its emphasis on individual and group characteristics overlooks the study of processes. Certainly in clinical psychology there is plenty of room for the further exploitation of all methods.

The clinical psychologist has to have an understanding of basic statistics in planning and carrying out his research and in evaluating that which others do. In addition to providing a medium for reporting or summarizing research findings, statistics are a valuable tool for checking the significance of findings and for showing that they cannot readily be dismissed as due to chance. Kogan writes of clinical work, "Perhaps the chief function of statistical research in this area is to inhibit the human tendency to indulge in self-satisfying explanations which are unwarranted by reality" (1952, p. 532). Clinical psychologists will have had an introduction to statistics in their graduate work. Even if a practicing clinician feels inadequate in handling statistics, there is usually enough statistical consultation available in any area to keep him from feeling reluctant to do research for that reason.

The challenge is not so much to one's command of statistical finesse as to one's ability to plan sound research procedures directed at significant problems. Kogan, after reviewing clinical research publications, wrote, "In the writer's opinion the greatest need in clinical research is not so much a wider knowledge of the technical aspects of statistics but rather a more serious consideration of experimental design, of population specification, sampling control and relevance to systematic theory" (1956, p. 326).

SPECIAL CONSIDERATIONS IN CLINICAL RESEARCH

Before leaving the matter of research design, it might be useful to mention some of the special problems that beset clinical research. One of these difficulties arises from the fact of *multiple interaction* in human events. The clinician in interpreting and designing research must keep in mind the possibility that results may be influenced by many different things. When using human beings as subjects, especially in complex clinical situations, it is difficult to control all the variables. However, there are statistical procedures that permit one to handle the interaction of several variables.

Another, yet related, problem is *patterning*. In studying an individual many test scores are accumulated, perhaps by the use of tests like the Rorschach or MMPI, each with its many scales. The score on any given variable is not to be interpreted by itself but in relation to other scores. For example, on the "neurotic triad" of the MMPI, if the D (Depression) score is lower than the Hs (Hypochondriasis) and Hy (Hysteria) scores, we have the so-called "hysteriod V" pattern, the interpretation of which is quite different from the interpretation to be given if D is higher than the other two scores. Configural scoring (Meehl, 1950) is needed to take account of possible patterning of items within a test. The problem of depicting patterns is not yet well solved statistically, although there have been several useful proposals (Cronbach & Gleser, 1953; Osgood & Suci, 1952; McQuitty, 1959). On the other hand, some studies have shown that configural methods do not provide any improvement over conventional procedures (e.g., Michael, 1959; Yandell, 1955). Until these patterning and interactional problems receive more sophisticated statistical solutions, many interpretative procedures must continue to be qualitative instead of quantitative.

There can be no more fundamental task confronting the clinical psychologist than *how to study individuals.* Traditionally science studies masses of data and groups of similar phenomena and strives for general laws. However, in clinical work and practice we are most of the time confronted by one person, and our undertaking is to understand him. How are we to set about describing his uniqueness? The answers to this problem are partly conceptual and partly methodological. In working with an individual, the clinician should ultimately be able to relate much of his behavior to general laws. The clinician will also gain understanding of the individual by comparing him with other persons. Beyond these approaches looms the problem of the complexly patterned personality and the long life history of episodes that have helped to make the individual unique and which the clinician must examine for consistencies and repetitive "themes." There must also be a place in psychological science for the study of single events. Allport (1937, 1961) has been among American psychologists the most insistent that personality involves idiographic as well as nomothetic knowledge. *Nomothetic* is an adjective we use for general laws that apply to human nature in general or the characteristics which groups of persons share. In contrast, *idiographic* refers to knowledge of a particular event or a unique individual.[2] Methods for carrying out idiographic research are slowly being developed. One way of doing this, for example, is to treat a set of repeated measurements upon a single individual in much the same way as we ordinarily treat a set of measurements from different individuals. Thus the standards of so-called *ipsative* measurement (Cattell, 1946) are obtained from a population of measures of the individual rather than from measures of a group

[2] For detailed arguments on the idiographic-nomethetic controversy, see Allport (1937) and Rosenzweig (1951), who favor the idiographic side, and Meehl (1954) and Phillips (1956), who raise objections. For recent discussion of statistical inference and the single case, see Chasson (1960).

of individuals. Growing out of such an idea is *P* technique, a way of factor-analyzing many measurements from one individual to study the effect of time or changed conditions (Luborsky, 1953). The semantic differential (Osgood et al, 1957) is another technique. The methodologies for studying individuals are much in need of further development, but clinicians see in what they already have some powerful tools for coming to grips with the individual as an object of study.

The possibility of *extra-experimental influences* in human situations also affects clinical research. We have already mentioned the problem of the disturbing effects introduced by knowledge of procedures on an experiment, effects the double-blind design is intended to avoid. In any study involving human judges, extraordinary care must be taken to see that the judges are not contaminated by any knowledge they possess of the subjects that would influence their judgments. All of their information must come from observation within the intended confines of the experimental situation. For instance, in one study a handwriting expert was asked to judge the degree of maladjustment of several subjects from their handwritten TAT stories. He was able to do a very good job, but the question remains whether his judgments were based on the handwritings itself or on the content of the stories, which in some cases seemed to indicate considerable disturbance. In this case it would have been better if the subjects had *copied* identical paragraphs.

Another consideration in clinical work is the problem of the *criterion*. In most studies with a practical bearing, it must be decided what is to be taken as the critical variable, or variables, given the purpose of the study. There must be some index of success or failure on a job, of the presence or absence of mental illness, or of improvement or no change in psychotherapy. Underneath the choice of a criterion is a value question: What *should* psychotherapy accomplish? What do I *want* this test to measure? After deciding what sort of evidence may be accepted as relevant to one's goals, then methodological problems arise. Many large assessment programs have had great trouble with the criterion (Office of Strategic Services Staff, 1948; Kelly & Fiske, 1951), because the subjects were not exposed to environmental situations sufficiently similar that judgments of ultimate outcome could be validly compared. The judgments themselves used for criteria may be unreliable. The criterion itself may have dubious significance as "evidence" for answering the question that has been raised. In any clinical study much attention must be paid to clarifying the criterion and developing reliable and valid measures for criterion scores. In clinical work the criterion is particularly difficult because we are often interested in predicting how successful patients will be in meeting the complex demands of daily life.

Another vastly important topic is the *ethics* of research with human beings. For example, how much stress may one properly use in an experiment? Will the conduct of research interfere with improving the condition of patients? Is it ethical to *mislead* subjects in an experiment? Some of these problems are discussed in the APA's publications on ethical standards (APA, 1953*a*, 1953*b*, 1959). In all research work, the psychologist must keep in mind that the welfare of the patient or subject is primary. If it is necessary to mislead a subject, say as to the purpose of an experiment, or to put him under stress, the researcher's responsibility is to hold a session with the subject following the experiment in order to make perfectly clear the nature of the study and to alleviate any worries he may have about himself or his performance.

Also there are the *administrative considerations* in obtaining the cooperation of colleagues in clinical settings. Psychiatrists, social workers, and nurses are busy people. In their zeal for serving patients, some may be uninterested in research, or even opposed to it. Some colleagues may view a research project as a threat to the continuance of established procedures in which they have invested their egos. There are the practical problems of finding time for research in the turmoil of crowded hospitals and clinics. Fortunately, it still remains true that most mental health specialists have been trained to appreciate the need for research and will do their best to accede to reasonable requests for cooperation.

These are only a few of the special problems in carrying on clinical research. There are others, like sampling problems in the choice of subjects, the selection of stimuli, and the needs for cross-validation and for repeating studies when the results are not beyond question. A study repeated with a fresh sample of subjects serves to test the adequacy of its methods and the soundness of the original interpretations. Replication guards against *ad hoc* explanations. Frank has warned us: "It seems to be literally impossible to present a person with a set of data that are so random that he will not be able to read a relationship into them" (1959, p. 23).

Despite all these cautions, however, it should be borne in mind that research must not be stultified by overemphasis on statistical niceties or compulsive exactness. Someone has pointed out that the most carefully designed research is often about trivial problems, whereas really important questions tend to find their answers in experiments that are sloppy in design and poor in statistical checks. This, of course, is not always true. It is to be hoped that there will be more good research design applied to the really significant problems of clinical work and mental health as clinicians become more and more sophisticated and competent to undertake research.

THE LANGUAGES OF CLINICAL PSYCHOLOGY

At the core of what research in clinical psychology is trying to accomplish is its need for a language adequate to express its thought and findings. The language clinical psychology employs must be such that it can be translated into action—the everyday operations of the clinic as well as the conduct of research. Such a language is important because it influences the selection of variables for research as well as the interpretation of results. Just as there are African tribes who have no concept of money and as Eskimoes have a highly elaborated vocabulary for describing different forms of frozen water, so whatever language we employ will inevitably limit our accomplishments in some areas, or cause us to overlook them entirely, and lay great emphasis upon and minutely differentiate what is to be found in others.

It is not easy to develop an adequate language for describing human living in all its rich complexity. And it is difficult in another way to translate or to reduce this complexity to a medium that lends itself to research operations and the proper statistical designs. Many of our terms for human behavior are emotional and highly pictorial rather than exact. How can one experimentally define terms like Jung's *racial unconscious,* Freud's *repression* or *superego* or a Rogerian therapist's *unconditional positive regard* for his client? Many such terms have double meanings and fuzzy edges. Often yawning gaps are detectable in the system of relationships among terms. Yet the terms and the formal relationships in a clinical language are supposed to be reliable, economical, broad in coverage, and heuristic.[3] Obviously we, in our contemporary Tower of Babel, must be content with the best approximations—there are several— that we can get to an adequate language. We need to remind ourselves, too, that dealing with the phenomena of clinical work is more important than splitting hairs. The Medieval scholastics never found the answer to the question of how many teeth are in a horse's mouth. Their overconcern with theories and the opinions of authorities prevented them from finding a horse and actually taking a look. Decrying the ritual of overemphasis on the precision of definition, Cattell has written, "If anything can be fully defined, it is pointless to investigate it" (1956, p. 15). So, while aiming to evolve more precise and flexible language, our task should be to study and describe better what we actually find as we work with people.

One of the problems of describing the phenomena encountered in clinical psychology is that there are at least three domains of communication, each with its different language. First, there is the *domain of everyday practice.* The clinician interviews patients; he must grasp what they are saying and ask them questions about what they seem to be telling him; he must tell them what he finds by his diagnostic procedures; he must conduct therapy in a language patients understand. Clinicians have tended to ignore these necessities, perhaps assuming that anyone who

[3] For a discussion of the language of psychology, see Mandler and Kessen (1959). Rotter (1954, Chapter 3) has paid particular attention to the language required by clinical psychology. Allport (1958) provides a useful introduction to considerations about the units of analysis to be used in personality research.

grows up in our culture and has a college education can communicate
well. This conclusion is very much open to question. The specialized nature of clinical training may even raise barriers that increase the difficulty
of communicating with ordinary people. Gough (1952, 1956, 1960*a*,
1960*b*) is one of the few clinicians who has emphasized the importance
of building tests for measuring "folk concepts" and for doing research
to discover the best common adjectives (trait vocabulary) to be used in
describing behavior.

A second area in which the clinician must employ a special language
is the *domain of professional-administrative communication*. The psychologist writes reports, attends staff conferences, and participates in
interdisciplinary programs. Many of the concepts used here and the
variables needed for research in this domain are different from those encountered in everyday life. This is a language partly supplied by the psychiatric nomeclature which we discussed in the first chapter. We can
talk to our colleagues of schizophrenia and hysteria pretty confident
they will understand us. Some psychoanalytic terminology has been so
widely diseminated and accepted that it also serves usefully to communicate what we mean. The language of hospital organization and administration is straightforward and serviceable.

One possible research technique for studying professional communication is the *Q* sort. For this purpose a large set of statements is prepared.
The subject sorts these into a series of piles graded from highly appropriate to highly inappropriate with respect to the facts of a designated subject or situation. A variety of statistical techniques are available for
analysis of the results of the sorting (Stephenson, 1953). The statements
in the *Q*-sort decks may use everyday language suitable for sorting by
patients themselves. Or they can employ more technical language, such
as the following from a *Q* deck developed by Block (1957): "Takes an
ascendant role in his relations with others"; "Overcontrols his impulses;
is inhibited; needlessly delays or denies gratification." *Q*-sort statements
may be *phenotypic*, that is, descriptive of directly observable phenomena,
or *genotypic*, that is, descriptive of inferred relations or psychological
states in the subject to which, or whom, the statements are supposed to
apply. A mixture of phenotypic and genotypic description was used in a
large project on the language of clinical psychology in progress under
the direction of Meehl (1960) and his associates at the University of
Minnesota.

The third kind of language that clinicians need is in the *domain of
personality and behavior theory*. The clinician requires a conceptual
framework that will embrace the development of personality, the etiology
of psychopathology and the physiological and social influences that mold
behavior. Such a theoretical language will differ at some points from
both the everyday and the professional languages. It should make for

better communication between clinical psychologists and their less specialized research colleagues. As yet we have no completely satisfactory theoretical language, despite some grand attempts. Psychoanalysis towers above all as the greatest effort so far. Freud intended that it should constitute a personality theory and not be just a system of clinical treatment. In recent years, with the development of ego psychology, there has been more of a *rapprochement* with such laboratory concepts as intelligence and perception. Psychoanalysis also has provided a strong stimulus to personality research. Other attempts of less far-reaching social significance, but nevertheless valiant and important endeavors to systematize personality theory and to provide a synthesis of the practical and research languages, are the following: Rotter's theory of social learning (1954), Leary's system of interpersonal diagnosis (1957), Kelly's theory of personal constructs (1955), and Rogers' self-theory (1959*b*). As yet there has been no systematization of a special language for the developmental viewpoint the authors would like to see grow in influence.

Several of these systems will be discussed in more detail later in the book. Factor analysts believe their method will provide a clinical language. Cattell (1957) has proposed a Universal Index for factors he has identified in a large number of research studies. Eysenck (1960) has recently proposed a "rational" diagnostic system and a "behavior therapy" based on two dimensions of personality, neuroticism and extraversion-introversion, both with significant implications for behavioral learning theory. These examples are enough to indicate that there are indeed many languages in which the clinician may converse.

THE SOCIAL PSYCHOLOGY OF KNOWLEDGE

Like all fields of knowledge, clinical psychology will develop in interaction with its sociocultural field. If we knew more about how knowledge has developed in the past, we might be better able to direct the course of clinical research in the future. Though as yet little studied by psychologists, it would appear from the work on the sociology of knowledge originating with Mannheim (1936) and more recently elaborated by Stark (1958) that there is considerable substance to the hypothesis that the development of any field of science is related to the values and the socioeconomic status of those who work in it. What this might mean for the future of clinical psychology is a fascinating topic to speculate upon, but nothing more solid than speculation seems feasible at the moment.

Even in the short history of psychology one can see evidences of *fads, swings in interest,* and *social movements.* Certainly Wundt's laboratory where introspectionists were trained was quite different in outward appearance from the laboratory of Olds, who investigates motivation in animals by planting electrodes in their brains. Now that the tirades of the early behaviorists against introspection have outlived their sociological and political timeliness, we have lived to see introspection return to a respected place in the laboratory as psychologists have become interested in perception and phenomenology again. Dallenbach (1955) has compared the popularity of psychoanalytic theory at the present time with the popularity of phrenology a century ago. Though they differ widely in content, there are striking similarities between them when viewed as sociopolitical movements.

Trends, if not faddism, are also evident in the rise and fall of certain areas of psychological publication (Louttit, 1957). In the field of clinical testing one obvious trend was the rise during the 40's and 50's of projective techniques and the relative decline of intelligence tests (Sundberg, 1954, 1961a). The reasons for such changes, including the swings in clinical practice and research, have not always been clear. Often popular theories and procedures "just fade away" not because anyone has come forward to disprove them or supplant them with something demonstrably better, but just, apparently, because other things became more popular.

Sociopsychological factors enter into the *choice of research topics.* Beyond the effects of "booms" or swings in popularity of theories and methods, a number of extraneous influences are powerfully operative. In academic circles, where advancement in rank is determined by the mandate to "publish or perish," research workers often scramble into areas where a quick pay-off may be expected rather than settle down to attack long range or complex problems. In colleges of arts and sciences where clinical subjects are lacking and there are hordes of "captive" students it is not surprising that short-range studies and problems requiring normal and verbally competent subjects predominate. When a new laboratory is set up or new sources of financial support become available, changes occur in the kinds of problems that are attacked. Frequently scientists decry the overemphasis on applied research, believing that this leads to neglect of basic research, but the direction from which important additions to knowledge will come is not always determined along such a simple dichotomy as applied versus pure. For instance, Lewin's study during World War II of the influence of group discussion in shifting the meat-using patterns of housewives (1943) had definite consequences in the future development of social psychology. The kind of situation in which the clinical psychologist works naturally has an influence on the selection of research topics and even on the outcome of the research. In one of a very few studies of the social psychology of clinical research, Levy and Orr (1959) analyzed the provenance and the findings of 168 studies of validity in the Rorschach test over a five-year period. They found that studies emanating from academic settings, as contrasted with clinical settings, were oriented toward the testing of theories or constructs more than toward relating results to practical criteria and that higher validities turned up in the construct than in the criterion studies. Levy and Orr concluded that it might be very profitable to launch a general investigation not only into processes of research as it is conducted in various settings, but into the biases and personalities of the researchers, and into the pressures and ideologies to which they may be subject.

Another aspect of this general problem is an understanding of the *conditions affecting research*. We have already mentioned the opposition of some mental health workers to research and the difficulties the psychologist encounters in finding time for it in a busy clinical schedule. Staff relationships in hospitals have important effects which are encouraging or discouraging to research. Financial encouragement of research is very important also, although Clark (1957) has found that really eminent psychologists do not complain about lack of support. Sometimes it has been alleged that better research comes from individual rather than group research work, but Clark's survey of psychologists failed to confirm this claim. Another question, undoubtedly belonging under any list of conditions favoring or hindering research, is the question how best to train students for their careers as researchers. As we said elsewhere, a number of leading research psychologists (Education and Training Board, APA, 1959) have recommended that students should be given opportunities to learn the spirit of research as well as its techniques while apprenticed to qualified research workers.

What, then, is the best strategy to insure the rapid development of clinical knowledge? It would certainly seem important to provide the kinds of training and the financial support mentioned above and to break down any social-psychological obstacles that hinder participation in research by clinical staffs. In addition, it would seem very important not to let the development of clinical knowledge become confined to any narrow research sector. In fact, Dittmann (1960) has gone so far as to claim, in reviewing the work of an eminent psychiatrist, that it is questionable whether much progress in ideas in personality and clinical psychology has come from formal research itself. Freud, Piaget, and others who have contributed a great deal to psychological knowledge have concentrated on observing a few individuals closely and in great detail. While it is true that their conclusions have to be treated as hypotheses to be tried out, tested, and varied in many ways on a wider array of human beings, we can not, *ab initio*, exclude their methods from psychological science. There is a place for *clinical exploration*, the empirically oriented investigation of phenomena. As has been stressed in the previous chapter, science is not limited to the laboratory or the computing room. The kind of scientist we are talking about does, however, constantly check himself and concedes that his conclusions are open to revision. Darwin, another astute observer and searcher for scientific laws, even kept a notebook in which he entered *negative instances* because he suspected he was more likely to forget these than the instances which, agreeably to him, confirmed his theory. This kind of clinical exploration requires a long period of observation leading to a preliminary statement of principles, then more observation followed by refinement and revision of the principles. It includes the public communication of these ideas and sincere openness to change in the light of new findings, which, perhaps, is rarest of all. This, though not a formal research design, accords with the spirit of science and falls well within the confines of respected inquiry. It is something all clinicians may engage in. Rogers has defended it in these words:

> It is my opinion that the type of understanding which we call science can begin anywhere, at any level of sophistication. To observe acutely, to think carefully and creatively—these activities, not the accumulation of laboratory instruments, are the beginnings of science. To observe that a given crop grows better on the rocky hill than in the lush bottom land, and to think about this observation, is the start of science. To notice that most sailors get scurvy but not those who have stopped at islands to pick up fresh fruit is a similar start. To recognize that, when a person's views of himself change, his behavior changes accordingly, and to puzzle over this, is again the beginning of both theory and science. I voice this conviction in protest against the attitude, which seems too common in American psychology, that science starts in the laboratory or at the calculating machine (1959 *b*, p. 189).

SUMMARY

Research begins with a spirit of inquiry. It has two main aspects: asking as pertinent and precise questions as possible and systematic probing for answers to them. The developmental stages of research planning seem to involve successive refinements of the question until a stage is reached at which clearly designed operations can be carried out. The completion of one piece of research often leads to another, and so the spiral of refinement continues on and on until the well of ideas is temporarily played out. There are three basic kinds of research in psychology; descriptive or survey research, relational research for interrelating different observed events or characteristics, and experimental research, in which variables are purposely manipulated in order to observe resulting changes. Clinical research presents a number of special problems: multiple interaction of variables, patterning, study of the individual, extra-experimental influences, the criterion problem, ethical considerations and principles, and administrative strategies. One obstacle to the rapid development of clinical research is the absence of a clear medium for communicating ideas in this field. A serviceable language is needed in three separate domains of clinical psychology—everyday practice, professional and administrative relations, and theory. The choice of areas for research investigation and the creativity of clinicians are influenced by what goes on in a given culture. It is important not so to limit our ideas of what is appropriate in research that we hamper genuine creativity and exploration of clinical problems beyond the boundaries of the orthodox.

SUGGESTED READINGS

CRONBACH, L. J. The two disciplines of scientific psychology. *Amer. Psychologist*, 1957, 12, 671-684.

Cronbach, in his APA presidential address, identifies two streams in the history of psychology—experimental and correlational psychology. Experimentalists deliberately and systematically manipulate the conditions under which observations are made in order to record the effects of each change. Correlational psychologists scatter into many areas and set about studying relationships as they are found under so-called "natural" conditions; most of the workers in individual differences, social and developmental psychology, personality, and so on are of this kind. Cronbach contrasts these two aproaches and points out that each can contribute to the other. He discusses the need to study processes experimentally and at the same time to observe individual variety. Research designs can cover the interaction of treatment and individuals. To secure a complete psychology we must have the contribution of both approaches.

SCHWAB, J. J. What do scientists do? *Behav. Sci.*, 1960, 5, 1-27.

This article is a sophisticated analysis of certain points where decisions must be made and alternatives in planning scientific research weighed. The author bases his analysis of research strategies on an examination of thousands of scientific papers written over the last five centuries.

ROTTER, J. B. *Social learning and clinical psychology*. New York: Prentice-Hall, 1954. Chapter II. Some major problems of clinical psychology; Chapter III. Criteria for a language of description for clinical psychology.

Rotter points to problems in clinical psychology as he seeks to develop constructs which describe and explain its subject matter. He points out the dangers of overgeneralization, of labelling and categorizing. He reviews the language employed by psychologists in discussing faculties, types, traits, psychoanalysis, and learning theory. Later on in the book he presents the postulates of his own social learning theory.

Reviews of clinical research

The interested reader will find the following reviews an excellent way of locating the significant research in clinical psychology: *Annual Review of Psychology*; the several volumes of *Progress in Clinical Psychology*; and the reviews appearing in the *Journal of Clinical Psychology* for a number of years since 1950. For an overview of statistical techniques and research principles as applied to clinical research, a number of reviews and symposia are valuable (Cronbach, 1954; Kogan, 1953, 1954, 1956; Symposium, 1950; Symposium, 1952).

Two

PSYCHOLOGICAL ASSESSMENT

4 The Nature
of Clinical Assessment

The working clinician is a student of human behavior, but he is a student with certain purposes. He is studying the actions of real people and his aim is to help them toward more satisfying and effective living. Because human behavior is very complex, the clinician must concentrate his efforts upon delimited problems and test his methods for their soundness as well as their utility. If he attempted to report all the behavior of an individual even in a brief span of time, he would be overwhelmed by data. What aspects of human behavior does the clinician pay attention to? What are his goals in trying to understand another person? What are the processes by means of which a trained person forms his impressions of another person, infers the underlying causes of his behavior, identifies and evaluates his difficulties, formulates alternative courses of action aimed at their alleviation, and finally decides what he should attempt to do? In this chapter we will describe the nature of assessment from several points of view.

AN EXAMPLE OF CLINICAL ASSESSMENT

First, and before getting involved in theoretical abstractions, let us take a brief sample of what a clinician may think and do as he proceeds with a clinical assessment. The case of Dolores which follows is not really "typical," if any case can be called that, but it does serve to bring out many of the problems and processes of assessment:

The juvenile court of a distant county has requested the mental hygiene clinic to evaluate a 14-year-old girl, Dolores Aiken, who frequently plays

truant from school and tells other children fantastic stories about her relations with boys. The court is considering removing her from her home.
Her alcoholic mother is often away from home, leaving the younger children
to shift for themselves; her father is in jail off and on, and two of her older
brothers have been sent to reform school. The family is what is known as
a "hard-core" family with which welfare and other agencies have been working for many years.

At the staff conference it is decided that the psychologist should look into
this case along with the psychiatrist and social worker. The staff reasons
that Dolores' case is likely to involve a problem of differential diagnosis,
perhaps a decision between a character disorder or early schizophrenia. They
also recognize that it is a family problem and a challenge to the community.
This family feels alienated from society and oppressed. Before proceeding
further, the clinician calls the juvenile court in order to clarify the referral.
He indicates that the clinic should be able to reach a diagnosis of the girl
and form an impression of the family situation, but will probably not risk
making any recommendation about whether or not to remove her from her
home, since this is a more complex matter than can be dealt with at a distance
and within limited time. He makes appointments with Dolores and her
mother. Mr. Aiken refuses to come to the clinic. The psychologist's job is to
study Dolores' personality and see how she views the family situation. The
psychiatrist also interviews Mrs. Aiken.

The first impression the psychologist forms of Dolores is that of a small,
plainly dressed girl who seems to be putting up a front of casualness and of
being ready and willing to talk. After chatting with her for a time and then
interviewing her in more detail, he starts to administer the Rorschach test.
When the test is about half over, Dolores bursts into tears. The clinician
immediately shows sympathy. He stops the test to talk with her about her
fear of being sent to a psychiatrist and of being taken away from her family.
He grasps how frightened she was about coming to the clinic. While feeling
and registering sympathy for her, he is also wondering why she cried at this
particular time. Is crying her typical reaction to strain? Is she especially
anxious in unstructured situations? Is something in the content of her responses
on the Rorschach related to her breaking down? Might her crying mean an
attempt to influence the clinician? As Dolores' composure returns, the psychologist goes on with the Rorschach test and then administers an abbreviated
form of the Wechsler Intelligence Scale for Children. Dolores also answers
the California Psychological Inventory (CPI) while she is waiting for her
mother to return. The psychologist becomes more familiar with her attitudes,
thoughts, and feelings about herself and her family as the testing session continues.

After three hours of interviewing and testing are over, he is confronted with
the task of selecting and organizing the most pertinent findings to form an
accurate and enlightening picture of her for staff discussions. In preparing
his report, he brings in the statistics on cases like this to show what the statistical prediction of delinquency is likely to be for a girl of Dolores' age,
general history and family background. There are also statistical predictions
of delinquency based on some of the CPI scales. In preparing the report, however, most of the psychologist's time goes into an attempt to integrate all the
qualitative impressions he has gathered about Dolores. He checks his test
findings and his hypotheses against the case history and the report from the
school.

At the case conference, the psychologist, psychiatrist, and social worker present their findings, and a composite picture of Dolores and her family begins to emerge. The staff decides that the findings do not support a psychiatric diagnosis for Dolores at this time, other than the vague and essentially meaningless one of "adjustment reaction of adolescence." The staff is agreed, however, that the outlook for her is unpromising. The habits she has formed by age 14 are not at all appropriate for coping with her present environment or the tasks she faces ahead of her—such as adjusting to her developing sexuality, learning to judge people correctly and form secure relationships with them, and becoming a responsible homemaker. It seems likely that she will become more delinquent unless she can make progress in establishing helpful relationships, emotional and social, with some one or more persons. An alcoholic and promiscuous mother makes a very poor model for a developing adolescent girl. Dolores lives too far from the clinic to make counseling there possible. She does seem to be rather close to one of her teachers, and she gives evidence of average ability in school when she tries. Perhaps the possibility of securing special attention from this teacher might be explored. Also a counseling relationship might be established with one of the women on the staff of the juvenile department. The other members of the family are a problem. Ideally the whole family should be given firm but sympathetic guidance in an effort to bring about some affiliation with the community. However, there is no denying that the prospects are discouraging. The staff decides to report these findings and impressions to the juvenile court. After two hours devoted to the case, the staff meeting breaks up with a feeling that the problem of hard-core families is a very large one requiring much more in the way of community facilities and of research on understanding and treatment.

There are several things to note about this illustration. For one thing, what happened in the case—both before and after the clinic came into the picture—was very much tied in with the community. It could not be considered independently. The manner in which the referral was made has an effect on the structure of the assessment process. The fact that the family lived at a distance from the clinic limited the contacts with its members to nearly minimum. The psychologist was able to see Dolores for only one session, though for a rather long time—three hours. It should also be noted that the clinic did not accept some of the role which the juvenile court wished to thrust upon it. Perhaps the clinic had reason to suspect that behind the request lay some bickering between the court and the welfare agencies in the community. Having accepted the referral the clinic limited itself to reporting a description of Dolores and her family and did not feel it should take the responsibility of recommending separation from the home without a much more thorough understanding of the situation than was possible under the circumstances. The juvenile court recognized the reasons for this limitation of clinic responsibility and would use the clinic's report in the light of its more intimate understanding of what might possibly be done in the community.

We note that in assessing Dolores the psychologist did much more than administer a few tests and report the scores. He was trying, even in this instance when time was limited, to conceptualize a person. He observed her behavior and turned over in his mind several hypotheses about what was going on. As he got a firmer impression of her and studied the test results, he ventured to formulate a picture of the salient features of her personality. He used not only "clinical" approaches to develop his understanding of her but also "statistical" ("actuarial") approaches to compare her with others. The other members of the clinical team were doing much the same thing in their contacts with Dolores and her mother. At the staff conference, there was an amalgamation of several points of view. Together they came to a final impression through a process of group interaction, in which, hopefully, any clear misperceptions were put aside and they arrived at a realistic and useful conclusion. In this case, where there was a real consensus, the staff was pessimistic about the girl's future.

As we review this sample of clinical work, it is important to raise the crucial question of the utility of the assessment process. Some people may be disposed to argue that such a process is a waste of time. The mental hygiene clinic that accepted the case of Dolores spent about 20 man-hours of costly professional time in interviewing, testing, reading records, writing reports, and holding staff conferences. Did the clinic's work help Dolores? Did it help the referring agency come to a practical decision? Are there better ways of making an assessment? Would the same amount of effort have been better employed in other activities, such as therapy, community consultation, or research? These are important questions which cannot be easily answered. Perhaps as we are able to analyze and understand clinical assessment through research, we can more convincingly answer some of these questions. In the meantime, the decisions and actions of clinicians, which have profound effects upon the lives of people, carry so much weight that we psychologists must use all the means we can command to keep them under critical scrutiny and to improve them.

THE MEANING OF PSYCHOLOGICAL ASSESSMENT

The case of Dolores is only one example of assessment procedures. There are other clinical settings—state hospitals, medical schools, institutions for the mentally defective, speech and hearing clinics, prisons, private clinics, and many others. Each setting has its own kind of referral system and its special community with which the patient interacts. Each setting has some way for evaluating the clients or patients who come to it and assigning them to some form of treatment or management. As we shall argue in the next section, assessment is an inevitable aspect of clinical work. But just what is assessment?

There are several ways to answer the question. Very simply psycho-

logical assessment consists of *the ways we go about understanding others.* — *Λ B.*
Thus we are concerned with how we form impressions of others and
make judgments about them. These processes occur in daily life as well
as in clinical work. Another definition characterizes assessment as the
systematic| collection, organization, and interpretation of information *n/3*
about a person and his situations. This definition points to the organized
and intentional communication that is involved—a repeated emphasis
in this book. Another way to say it, this time with a stress on the relation between clinical assessment and its research and experimental
parallels, is the following: Assessment is the *description, explanation, and*
prediction of behavior of individuals in their natural living situations.
This definition points toward the attempt to develop exact ways of measuring behavior and of testing hypotheses. Always, as was pointed out in
the first chapter, the working clinical psychologist is interested in real
persons and their daily lives rather than in general laws derived from
artificial situations. Perhaps the most satisfactory way to define assessment is in terms of the functions and purposes it serves in the clinic.
This approach would define clinical assessment as *the processes used*
for| decision-making \and for developing [a working image| or model of
the person-situation. These twin functional goals of assessment will be
discussed at considerable length in later sections.

The word *assessment* itself also has a history which contributes to the
meaning of the term. The dictionary meaning of the word *assess* is to
set or fix the value of property for the purpose of taxation. Probably the
first use of the word in the psychological sense was in the book *Assess-*
ment of Men (OSS Staff, 1947), which was a report of the selection of
men for special assignments in World War II. The staff of the Office of
Strategic Services wanted a different word from *psychodiagnosis.* Diagnosis has been traditionally associated with medical evaluation of disease.
But in this work, the goal was not the discovery of pathology but the discovery of the *worth* of an individual. The OSS staff needed to establish
the strengths of the person—his ingenuity, leadership, and courage in
carrying out a difficult and dangerous mission. The word *assessment* with
its emphasis on the evaluation of the worth of something seemed like the
most appropriate term.

Now the evaluative work of the clinical psychologist needs to turn
more and more to the positive and constructive forces in the person.
Psychological treatment requires the enhancement of the developmental
processes as well as the removal of sources of disorder and disturbance.
As in the analogy with a plant mentioned in Chapter 2, the therapist not
only identifies plant diseases and parasites so as to exterminate them, but
also to enrich the conditions which promote growth and blossoming. So
assessment is becoming a more appropriate word than *psychodiagnosis*
for what the clinical psychologist does. When it is necessary to distinguish

between the two major uses of the world, we will use *clinical assessment* to refer to the assessment carried on in clinical settings and *programmatic assessment* to refer to large research projects for studying personality. The latter kind of assessment will be discussed in Chapter 10.

THE INEVITABILITY OF ASSESSMENT

In the upsurge of "dynamic" psychotherapy and counseling after World War II and the disillusionment with the earlier promises of some testing techniques, there was a reaction against psychodiagnosis and testing. Criticisms of the psychiatric classifications also led to doubts about the value of diagnosis. Some psychologists (and many social workers and psychiatrists) began to argue against all psychodiagnostic activity. There was a heated debate for and against diagnosis (especially by Rogers and Thorne). The debate still continues, but the broadening of the meaning of psychodiagnosis and the introduction of the assessment concept has put the issue in a different light.

No matter what we do for patients, some assessment is always involved. To take a common academic example, a student comes to the university mental hygiene clinic the weekend before final examinations. He sees the psychologist (or social worker or psychiatrist,) for an interview. The student reports sleep difficulties, anxiety about his part-time job, and a feeling of being inadequate for his school work. The psychologist, familiar with many cases like this, is alert for signs of serious disturbance or for evidence of strength enough to carry the person through this stressful period. By the end of the hour, the student becomes less anxious and indicates in what he says about previous accomplishments that he has usable personality resources. The clinician decides that this is probably a transitory problem which the student can handle with some support. He arranges an hour on his appointment book two days hence for the student to use if he wants to come in again. No tests are given, no extensive history taken. Was assessment involved? It certainly was. The psychologist "looked for signs" and "evidence," classified the problem as a transitory one, and made a decision about a future plan of action. All of these behaviors are part of the assessing process. Assessment also occurs during long-range therapy contacts, both at the beginning and at any time at which decisions are made about shifts in the course of treatment. Furthermore, the process of forming a "working image" of a person is not limited to the initial stages of contact with a person, but continues to some extent throughout.

The question then is not one of *whether* to do assessment but *how* it should be done. It is here that disagreement is greatest and research evidence scarce. The differences center around such questions as these: Should there be a *formal* assessment with administrative provision for specialized services? What should the *timing* of assessment procedures be? Should *standardized procedures* such as tests be used? Such questions are researchable, but as yet there is very little evidence about them. Does the early assignment of tests have the detrimental effects on therapy that some people believe it has? To what extent do the various assessment procedures increase the value of therapy? What research there is on these questions will be discussed in Chapter 10, but it can be said now that the questions are still much bigger than the answers. In the meantime, it seems to the authors that the strategies for assessment must be flexible and adapted to particular clinical settings. Furthermore, assessment procedures should never be used for their own sake. One uses tests and interviews for the welfare of the patient, not for research or administrative routine alone. Each clinical psychologist should know his competencies and his role so that he can apply whatever assessment procedures will help most in each individual situation.

THE FUNCTION OF ASSESSMENT IN THE MAKING OF DECISIONS

Earlier we pointed out that clinical assessment might be defined in terms of its functions and that its two primary functions are decision-making and the development of a working image. Decisions and descriptions are, in a sense, the "products" of the assessment process. In studying individuals and their living situations, the clinical psychologist and his colleagues try to facilitate and improve these two products. A third result, an important "by-product" of assessment practice, is a contribution to knowledge in general. We will take up this purpose in Chapter 10.

Decision-making is a basic aspect of clinical work, as it is indeed in all of life itself. In the case of Dolores Aiken, someone had to make a decision about whether or not she should continue living in the damaging atmosphere of her home with a criminal father and an alcoholic mother. In psychotherapy, patients come to decisions about marriage, divorce, job changes, and ways of rearing children. Each of these decisions requires a choice between alternatives, each alternative having certain values. The values are often conflicting.

Two different orientations characterize clinical work. There are *decisions about the patient* and *decisions with the patient.* Decisions about the assignment of patients to wards or to different kinds of treatment are similar to decisions about personnel selection in industrial or educational institutions. A mental hopsital is interested in operating efficiently so as to produce maximum gains in mental health at a minumum cost to taxpayers. When psychotherapists are limited in number, the patients who may be expected to profit most from treatment have to be selected. Decisions of this first kind are made in the interest of *institutional values.*

Decisions of the second kind bring in *individual values.* When a person decides to take up an occupation, to undergo training, or to marry, he is, generally speaking, concerned about maximizing his own satisfactions and his own effectiveness. A psychologist can help the individual to assess his special tendencies, interests, abilities, and purposes. Assessment procedures can help the person to identify possibilities for action, to evaluate the appropriateness of various alternatives, and to clarify his own values.

In most clinical assessment, decisions involve both individual values and institutional values. In a mental hospital, a patient cannot be turned away as one would a job applicant, because there is nowhere else for him to go. The hospital must usually accept its patients as they come and then try to fit each into a program that will benefit him most. Furthermore, assessment procedures are also used to help the institution adapt to individuals. Selection and training of psychiatric aides and nurses can be oriented to the particular needs and characteristics of patients. The effort to maximize both individual and institution values is a major task for psychological assessment.

The study of the decision-making process promises to contribute much to future developments in applied psychology. In its rigorous form, decision theory has been applied to economics and related areas. The application closest to clinical psychology is Cronbach and Gleser's (1957). As yet it is most useful in personnel selection where institutional values predominate, but there are implications for individual orientations. Some general aspects of decision theory are: (1) Emphasis should be on *payoff* or outcomes, not on specific techniques. (2) Questions of the validity of tests or other assessment activities should be considered as problems of *improving on existing procedures,* rather than improving on chance. (3) *Strategies of assessment* or whole sequences should be the object of concern; one asks about the contribution of both test and nontest procedures to the ultimate outcome. (4) *Examination of values* is fundamental to assessment; decisions are made that will maximize movement toward goals. All of these principles will be stressed in later sections of this book.

THE DEVELOPMENT OF THE WORKING IMAGE OR MODEL

The making of decisions is not all there is to clinical assessment. To some degree the clinician always builds up a *picture* of the person with whom he is dealing. In some cases of short contact and immediate decision, this picture-building is minimal. In extensive contact, especially for therapy, a detailed picture is often needed. This function of assessment is what we have called the development of a working image or model. By the working image or model we mean the *clinician's set of hypotheses*

about the person and the situations in which he presently or potentially ⁿᵇ
operates. Such hypotheses develop inevitably from contact with a patient.
They are exemplified in such statements as these: "Fred is the sort of
person you can depend on when you tell him to do something on the
ward." "Alice is not sure of herself now; maybe after she's worked at her
new job for a while she'll feel more wanted." "You never can tell how
George will be; some mornings he's as clear as a bell, other times he's
hallucinating wildly—it almost seems as if there's some kind of off and
on switch in his head." Aides, psychiatrists, and others develop more or
less accurate and helpful models of the patients with whom they work.
Psychological case reports and case conferences go beyond decisions
about the assignment of patients. They disseminate information and establish attitudes which are carried out into the wards and consulting rooms.
A striking illustration is given by Stanton and Schwartz (1954), who describe the improvement of a withdrawn schizophrenic woman on a hospital ward as a result of deliberately changing her reputation with the
ward personnel.

The use of the words *image* or *model* remind us that always the impression we have of another person is partial, limited. As we develop the
image of the patient or client with whom we are working clinically, we
need to be forever conscious of the possibility that we may be overlooking information, overweighing or enlarging the importance of some data,
and misinterpreting the significance of others.[1]

The use of the word *working* in the term is intended to suggest a
parallel with the *working hypothesis* in psychological experiments. The
clinician can view his situation somewhat as the experimental psychologist views his. When he starts investigating an area he first gets hunches
or directional leads about the state of affairs. Often he can explicitly state

[1] We will use the terms *working model* and *working image* interchangeably, though
they do carry somewhat different connotations. *Model* points to the constructed
quality of this concept but implies more structure and precision than the concept
often possesses. *Image* emphasizes the *perceptual* character of the notion. We
recognize the risk of ambivalence we run in using the word *image*. On one
hand, this word calls up connotations of the kind of duplicity, manipulation,
and Madison Avenue huckstering portrayed in *The Image Makers* (Dryer, 1958).
On the other hand, the word has been used constructively and scientifically in *The
Image*, by Boulding (1956), and in *Plans and the Structure of Behavior* by Miller,
Galanter, and Pribram (1960). *Image* to these men means an internal representation
of people and situations. Other terms such as "cognitive map" (Tolman) or "schema"
(Bartlett) are related expressions. Sarbin, Taft, and Bailey (1960, p. 107) have
proposed the term "module" as the "cognitive counterpart of the organization of
objects in the ecology." Oldfield (1947) has used the term "homunculus" to refer
to the image the interviewer has of the interviewee. Pepinsky and Pepinsky (1954)
have used the term "hypothetical person"; McArthur (1954) refers to a "clinical
construct" and a "dynamic model of a person"; Super (1957) mentions a "picture
of a client"; Goldman (1961) uses the term "model" of a person; Meehl (1954,
1959) covers this assessment function in discussing the "concept of the person" and
the clinician's aim to provide a "personality description." All of these refer to a
hypothetical and only approximate representation of the person.

these in the form of working hypotheses. He develops definitions for his basic terms and procedures that will permit him to test his hypotheses. Then he revises his hypotheses in the light of any evidence he has gathered while testing them. In a similar manner the clinical psychologist can begin by informally attempting to specify his hypotheses and hunches about a person and his situation and then proceed to check them and revise them as new evidence comes in. The working image is a kind of "hypothetical construct" with an admitted surplus meaning over and beyond the available data. It includes more than the recorded report concerning the patient, in that it is shaped by both verbal and nonverbal interactions that have never been caught in the record. The working image is the best approximation a clinician can achieve of a *representation* of the other human being.

This image is revised as acquaintance continues. In many ways it can be seen as a creative product like an artist's painting. Major outlines and structures first appear, but further nuances and details are added as the painting progresses. Eventually perhaps research on interpersonal perception and the formation of impressions of others will clarify the concept of working image. As we shall see in Chapter 10, Q sorts and other assessment devices may be used to analyze the ways people see one another.

AN OUTLINE OF THE COURSE OF ASSESSMENT

After seeing the "end-products" of assessment, decisions and the working image, let us take a look at the whole course of assessment from beginning to end. Figure 1 is a diagram of the way assessment proceeds. They are four major stages: (1) the *preparation stage* during which the clinical psychologist and his colleagues are apprised of the patient's problem and lay plans for the study of the case; (2) the *input stage*, during which they collect information about the patient and his living situation (and potential plans); (3) the *processing stage*, during which they organize and "assign meaning" to all the information collected; and (4) the *output stage*, during which they communicate findings and interpretations to others and make decisions about clinical actions. Figure 1 gives examples of clinical activities for each of these stages and shows the general course of development in assessment. In some clinical settings and with certain cases, of course, some of the parts of the stages will be omitted. For instance, there may be no mechanical processing of data or statistical procedures. Some places will not hold intake conferences or case conferences. But in general this is a fairly typical picture of assessment from the clinical psychologist's point of view.

Much of the remainder of the assessment part of the book will be devoted to a clarification of the activities outlined in Figure 1; so there is

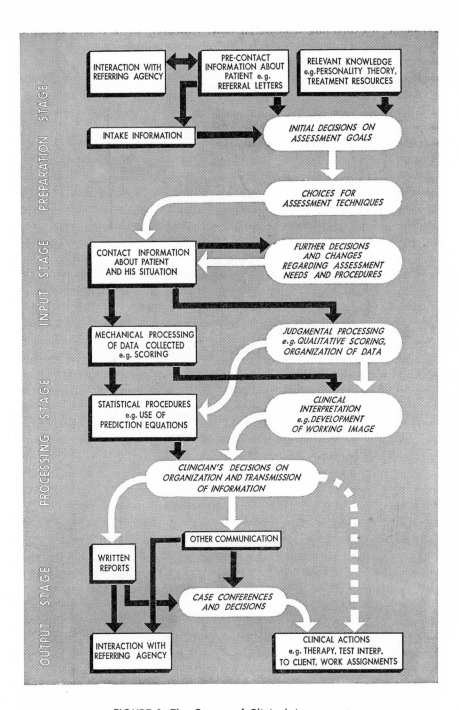

FIGURE 1. The Course of Clinical Assessment

no point in explaining it in detail now. However, there is one very important thing to note now in preparation for the more extended treatment of the issue in Chapter 8. It is the *clinical versus statistical prediction* issue, a burning problem to psychologists since Paul Meehl's book appeared in 1954. The diagram shows some parts in rectangles and some in circular outlines. The activities described within circular outlines are the clinician's cognitive processes—his decisions, judgments, hypotheses, interpretations, selections, and so forth. The clinical assessment process depends all along the way on the wisdom and skill of the clinician. Mechanical and statistical procedures are only a small part. Clinical assessment is not a routine personnel procedure, such as one finds in busy college admissions offices or employment services. Holt (1958) has pointed out that the assessment problem is one of statistical *and* clinical prediction with many places for clinical judgment to enter. Although the point of view of the present authors is that clinical judgment is involved throughout the assessment process, we also believe in the value of research to improve the mechanical and statistical tools which can be put in the hands of the clinician. The future expansion of standardized procedures for behavioral prediction is inevitable and commendable—if at the same time clinical judgment for their use also be enhanced.

REFERRAL QUESTIONS

The practicing clinician must set his sights differently for each individual patient whose assessment is undertaken. Every patient requires a somewhat different approach. It may happen that the clinician does not even have the proper tools to use in a puzzling case and must invent them. The special problems of the case are primary, and the clinician will adapt his techniques to whatever he considers the appropriate formulation of the goals in each individual case. In defining the specific goals for a case he must always consider the nature of the referral.

The process of referral in clinical work is important because it sets the *framework* in which assessment goes on. It does not define the psychologist's goals. This is his responsibility as master of his own craft. But the circumstances of referral and the information from referral letters and telephone calls do tell the psychologist something about the role and purposes of the referring persons as well as about the patient. The circumstances of the referral constitute the social setting in which assessment must be planned and treatment recommended. Patients, of course, do not always come to the attention of the clinician through a referral. Sometimes the clinician himself may see someone on the ward or the playground who is obviously in need of special help and will go out of his way to get in touch with him. Sometimes the psychologist's purpose is to select persons for research. However, most commonly patients come to the clinician through referral. Voluntary or self-initiated referrals apparently have a better prognosis for successful response to psychotherapy or counseling than compulsory referrals (Habbe, 1939; Kirk & Headley, 1950; Williamson & Bordin, 1941). The kind of referral no doubt reflects the patient's motivation.

As part of a survey of assessment practices in public clinical services in the United States (Sundberg, 1961a), there were a number of findings, hitherto unpublished, relevant to referral. Data came from 185 respondents to a questionnaire, including psychologists working in the following five kinds of agencies: VA hospitals and clinics, state hospitals and institutions, out-patient clinics, counseling centers, and university training clinics. One of the questionnaire items was "What are your principal referral sources for psychological testing?" For the total group, the following were most often named as referral sources, in order from most to least frequent: physicians and psychiatrists, other departments and personnel in the institution, social agencies, schools, routine administrative practices (e.g. routine admission testing), self-referral, and courts. This list comprised almost all of the referral sources mentioned. Notably infrequent were referrals from nonmedical professional people, such as lawyers and ministers, and referrals from business and industry.

When referrals were classified by their sources into two groups—intramural, such as referrals from staff psychiatrists and through routine hospital procedures, and extramural, such as community physicians, schools, and social agencies—there were striking differences. The VA proved to have very little connection with referral sources in the community; 97 per cent were intramural. Psychologists in state hospitals and institutions received two-thirds of their referrals from intramural sources. In the other cases, one-fourth or less of the referrals were intramural. The out-patient clinics were most closely related to the community, with 90 per cent of the referrals originating from outside.

In private practice the patterns of referral may be quite different from those in public agencies and institutions. Blau (1959, p. 34) reported on 1200 referrals to three clinical psychologists in private practice. Of these 58 per cent were self-referrals, 8.5 per cent came from schools and agencies, 7 per cent from psychiatrists, and 15 per cent from other physicians. Seventy per cent of the cases referred were children. Among the self-referrals, over half were the result of recommendations by former patients to their relatives or friends. Very few referrals came as a result of the psychologists' listings in the telephone book. It can not be assumed that Blau's data, however, are representative of private work in general. In the APA survey of private practice in Los Angeles reported by Clark (1957, p. 201), the kind of referral most frequently mentioned was by physicians, including psychiatrists. Undoubtedly there are great variations in referral sources for both private and public psychological services, depending on the nature of the agency and the reputations and specialties of the persons involved. (Statistical findings such as these, also depend on the manner in which the survey questions are phrased, and the data we have cited were collected by methods which were not equivalent.)

More directly related to the purposes of assessment is the nature of the referral questions. In the nationwide survey of public psychological services mentioned above, the following item was used: "List the most common referral questions; what help are you asked to give?" Such an "open-end" question produced a variety of responses which could be classified in several ways. Among the functions of assessment which require the reaching of decisions, diagnosis was mentioned by 47 per cent of the respondents and recommendations for treatment and the planning of therapy by 36 per cent. The description of personality as a function of assessment was frequently noted, with psychodynamics being mentioned by 39 per cent of the total, intelligence evaluation by 38 per cent, intellectual impairment by 24 per cent, educational evaluation by 25 per cent, and appraisal of vocational fitness by 19 per cent. A variety of other purposes were cited, such as determination of criminal responsibility, personnel selection, and evaluation of readiness for discharge.

When referrals are broken down by age levels, the *developmental aspects of assessment problems* become very apparent. As we have mentioned in the chapter on clinical theories, every society sets certain developmental requirements or tasks which must be met by each person as he moves from infancy to old age. Various kinds of penalties or deprivations will be the consequence of failing to meet society's pressures in these matters. In the light of such pressures it is interesting to speculate on the fact that certain psychiatric disorders tend to occur more frequently at one age than another. Social expectations and legal responsibilities are often tied to particular ages. For instance, one place in life at which certain disorders occur is in the first few years of school. Usually by the second or third grade a child is expected to know how to read, and if he does not, it will not be long before he has serious difficulty in keeping up in school.

In this report Blau (1959, p. 26-27) cites the percentages of different sorts of problems presented by children, adolescents, and adults coming to private psychologists. The classifying of problems at intake was done by the psychologists, not by the referral source, which might have had different notions. Among referrals of children aged twelve or less, social maladjustment was found in 60 per cent of the cases, educational difficulties in 50 per cent, and developmental disabilities (such as bed-wetting and poor eating habits) in 50 per cent. Among adolescents aged 13 to 16, 75 per cent showed social maladjustment and 20 per cent came in with educational and vocational problems. Of the adult referrals, 90 per cent were rated as having emotional difficulties and 40 per cent marital problems. Other surveys also have shown the frequency of developmental difficulties. Even one extensive study of normal children (MacFarlane, Allen, & Honzik, 1954), revealed that certain behavioral difficulties and emotional crises are associated with partciular periods of development.

Before leaving the matter of referrals, we might take a closer look at their meaning to the assessing psychologist. The function of the agency or hospital, the reputation of the agency in the community, and the definition of his own role by the psychologist enter into referrals. The psychologist can increase or decrease the number of referrals of a given sort either intentionally or by adopting some habitual course of action which he does not recognize. Long delay in taking up a case, a poor report, or superficial examination may serve to warn the referring party that he had better look elsewhere when he wants psychological help next time. The psychologist should attempt to keep communication lines open, letting his referring sources know by examples just what his abilities are and also what are the limitations of the services he can render.

Generally it is a good idea for the psychologist, unless he knows a referring person so well that he can assume it is unnecessary, to talk to him and explore thoroughly what he wants. Almost always additional information can be had about the patient which will assist in the psychologist's assessment. Sometimes, however, both parties may prefer, for valid reasons, that a "blind" evaluation of the patient be made. In such a case the psychologist may see the patient or his test results without knowing his history and other facts. The object of such a procedure is to obtain independent impressions of the patient, and it will be assumed that if the psychologist agrees with the referring person, the diagnostic conclusion is more likely to be correct. Ordinarily, however, the psychologist will want to have fairly complete knowledge about the patient at the outset. If a medical chart is available or a social history has been taken by a social worker, he will want to go over these before making a decision about what tests to administer or what other procedures are indicated. In carrying out his plan of assessment, he will also want to keep in mind the kinds of decisions that will have to be made and what therapeutic program is likely to be possible considering the condition of the patient and the resources of the agency.

DETERMINING GOALS FOR INDIVIDUAL CASES

A key decision early in the assessment of a case is the choice of a plan for the study of the person. Stemming from the chosen goals of the study will come the specific techniques, such as tests, to be used. Frequently the strategy is modified as the assessment proceeds, but having an initial plan prevents one from using a miscellaneous mixture of procedures and a time-consuming shotgun approach. The goals may be rather specific:

What is the psychiatric diagnosis? What is the patient's functioning intelligence? With more involved cases they may be quite complex: What recommendations are there for psychotherapy? What is the nature of this patient's relationship to his father?

There are four factors in the determination of assessment goals: (1) the referral source, which we have already discussed, (2) the institutional or agency needs and limitations, (3) the patient himself, and (4) the assessing psychologist, who is the final judge. The psychologist keeps all the others in mind as he works toward a statement of his specific goals.

The institutional or agency needs will orient the assessor to such problems as these: "Is this mental hygiene clinic equipped to handle a case like this, or would it be better to refer to a state hospital?" "Since it is only three months before this service closes for summer vacation, would it be helpful or harmful to start psychotherapy?" "Because of legal requirements, we must have a good evaluation of intelligence." "What should the official psychiatric diagnosis of this patient be?" "No one on the staff has handled a case like this before; let us work it up with extra thoroughness for a better understanding of the general problem." "Since our social worker is on vacation, the psychologist will also have to cover the social history and interview the patient's wife." At an intake conference, or through general knowledge of the agency and his role, the psychologist includes considerations like this in his assessment plan.

Particular goals also depend on the interaction with the person most concerned with the outcome—the patient himself. It goes without saying that his understanding of his problems and his wishes should help to determine assessment goals. As he interviews the patient, the psychologist should be alert to his reasons for coming to the clinic. In the case of self-referrals, the patient will nearly always have questions that he wants answered: Why am I so nervous? Can you help me stop worrying? My wife says she wants to leave me; why doesn't she love me any more? My children fight all the time; how can I stop them? Even in the case of involuntary referrals, such as court cases, delinquents, young children, and committed psychotics, the patient nearly always has some question on his mind: Why am I here? Has someone got it in for me? There's nothing wrong with me; why is everyone raising such a fuss? As we shall see in the next chapter, the understanding of the patient's purpose is a fundamental part of the assessment itself. It should also enter into the early decisions about what else is to be assessed.

It is generally agreed that if psychotherapy is to be successful, the patient's cooperation is essential. Some clinicians will agree with Hubbard, who writes: "Probably no test should ever be given unless the client (or his parent if the client is a child) has requested it; this means a consideration of the client's real wishes and following them rather than following some casework goal the agency may have in mind" (1949, p. 338). However, it is not to be supposed that most clients or patients will have the necessary knowledge to choose specific tests. In psychiatric hospitals some psychotic patients will be largely unaware of what is happening and incapable of judging what is best for them. Despite the limitation that such cases impose on Hubbard's prescription, the patient's willingness to be tested and to engage in a cooperative effort to solve his problem is very important. The psychologist should not use tests or other procedures unless he is convinced that they will be of value to the patient. There are times when he senses that testing procedures are likely to interfere with his relations with the patient. Sometimes patients are actively resistant. A paranoid psychotic may refuse to answer questions; an aggressive or brain-damaged child may not do as he is asked. In such cases the clinician can obtain some information by observation alone, but it is more desirable if a cooperative effort can be directed toward goals meaningful to both the patient and clinic.

The final arbiter on the goals of the assessment is the psychologist himself. Only he knows the instruments he is to use. Furthermore, the process of assessment involves problem-*finding* as well as problem-*solving*. The initial problem presented to the clinic is only a small part of the definittion of assessment goals. Even highly experienced psychiatrists have been known to overlook important diagnostic details. Patients cannot be expected to have complete insight into problems or knowledge of clinical tools. Family informants may be pressuring the psychologist to come to a certain conclusion. (Some even have been known to try to encourage a diagnosis of psychosis so that the patient can be locked up and declared legally incompetent.) They also may have their own ideas of what treatment should be given. Through ignorance, intention, or oversight, persons he interviews may lead the psychologist astray.

In the national survey of services already mentioned, some responding psychologists complained that referral letters were very meager, consisting of nothing more than "Psychologicals, please." A content analysis of the psychologist's responses to the question about referrals suggested that they perceived persons referring patients to be more interested in the patient's liabilities (the negative side of his behavior) than in his assets (the positive side), more oriented to report on his supposed individual characteristics than on his interpersonal adjustments, and not very knowledgeable about psychological concepts. Whether these biases can be said to indicate something about the referral sources or about the perceiving psychologists is not clear, but in any case it would appear that part of the task of the psychologist is to restructure the goals of assessment to fit each case as best he can.

Blau gives a good illustration of the value to psychological assessment of flexibility no matter how strong might be previous impressions of the case the psychologist has gained from the referral source:

A five- and one-half-year-old girl was referred by a local pediatrician. He stated, "The school says the child is retarded but I would like this checked." Indeed, the youngster walked in an ataxic manner, exhibited chorea-form movements of the hands, and verbal response was minimal. The school psychologist reported a mental age of two years, four months as measured by the Stanford-Binet. Shortly thereafter the child was tested at the local Child Guidance Center, with a resulting Wechsler Intelligence Scale for Children Full-Scale IQ of 48. The two evaluations were in close agreement, and a diagnosis of "Mental Deficiency, Imbecile Type, Exogenous (brain-injured)" was made. The detailed clinical history revealed no specific circumstances to indicate encephalopathy. The family situation, however, was very stressful during the child's developmental years. During the clinical examination, while a Critical Flicker-Frequency Test was being administered, with little apparent attention from the child, she suddenly remarked, "The light is flickering." Routinely noted as a remark during testing, we were suddenly aware that this supposedly defective, brain-injured child had exhibited appropriate verbal behavior compatible with a mental age of eight years. Careful evaluation during several examination periods indicated many of these unusually appropriate behaviors. Neurological and electroencephalogic examination was requested and revealed no evidence of organic pathology. A tentative diagnosis of childhood schizophrenia was followed by intensive psychotherapy for the child, as well as for the parents. At the end of six months, a Full-Range Picture Vocabulary Test revealed an IQ of 115. After two years of the family program, the youngster, still under intensive treatment, had started school, and was beginning to read. The original plan to place her in the state institution for mental defectives was, of course, abandoned (Blau, 1959, p. 47).

The seriousness of an incorrect assessment is illustrated by Blau's case and by others that almost any clinician can recall. If Helen Keller had not had the good fortune to attract the interest of a great teacher, she would very likely have become either an inmate of an institution or a tragic burden to her family as long as she lived. The assessor's task is to detect in each individual those special characteristics which can be built upon by proper training and treatment.

As Figure 1 has suggested, the clinician's initial decisions of assessment goals also stem from his background knowledge and experience—his theoretical orientation about personality, his knowledge of similar persons and situations, and his understanding of treatment resources. The experienced college counselor seeing a case of "examinationitis" is automatically alerted to certain signs; his goals are to rule in or out a more serious condition and to make plans if necessary to support the student through the stressful time. Likewise the hospital psychologist considering assignment of patients to work programs ("industrial therapy") is familiar with the requirements of various jobs and knows what to look for in a patient. The more complicated question of understanding the "criterion" situations of daily living will be examined in a later chapter. However, it should be mentioned here that goals of assessment need to be related to the demands and rewards of the situations being considered for patients. The clinician needs to "study the criterion" to determine whether the patient will fit a given situation or not. Assessment goals are partly chosen by the theoretical orientation of the clinician himself. As Chapter 2 stated, every clinical psychologist has at least an implicit theory. He has hypotheses about the nature of schizophrenia, the conditions likely to reduce anxiety, and the importance of early traumatic experiences. These preferences will orient him in his assessment goals. He will look for an Oedipus Complex or not even think of it; he will treat diagnostic classification lightly or give it careful attention. Finally out of all of these sources of influence, the referral question, the patient's wishes, the institutional needs, and his own understanding of the case so far, the psychologist will come to a set of specific purposes.

GENERAL OUTLINE FOR FORMULATING A CASE

Each individual patient will require unique assessment purposes, but there are general guides that can be kept in mind, at least for fairly complete case studies. After an extensive case study the psychologist or psychiatrist is usually expected to present his "formulation of the case"—his organized statement of the patient's personality, including his interpretation of the present personality "dynamics" and psychopathology, the etiology or antecedent conditions, the prognosis for the patient's future, and his recommendations for therapy and disposition. Such a formulation is often presented at case conferences and included in written reports.

The outline that is given below presents a set of questions that exemplify what might be used for such a case formulation. It has been developed from many sources and fits in with the authors' orientation toward interactive development. (For similar outlines, see Huber, 1961, p. 34; Berg, 1954, pp. 114-120; Menninger, 1952, pp. 101-106; Wells & Ruesch, 1945, pp. 5-11). We will elaborate on the major features of this outline in the subsequent assessment chapters and return specifically to it in the chapter on report writing (Chapter 9). The guide, with its sample questions, follows:

A. Present functioning
 1. Functioning in groups and living situations
  What are the important situations in the patient's life? What are the primary groups with which he affiliates?
  How does the patient interact in these groups? What role does he assume? How consistent is he from group to group?
 2. Functioning skills and abilities
  What is the level of the patient's intelligence as he functions now? Is there evidence of changes from earlier periods in his life, of intellectual impairment from brain damage or emotional disorder?
  What strengths and weaknesses does he show in his work or academic performance? What potentialities have not been developed?
  Does he show disorders of thought and distortions of reality? What are his problem-solving skills?

3. Physiological limitations and effects
   What physical restrictions are placed on his functioning?
   How well does his "body image" correspond with reality?

B. Motives and emotions
   1. Interpersonal purposes
      What is the patient attempting to accomplish by his typical interaction
         patterns? How does he "teach" others to respond to him?
      What are the interpersonal effects ("gains") from his symptoms?
   2. Emotional characteristics
      What is the patient's characteristic mood? How anxious is he? What are
         his fluctuations in emotions?
      How does he express his emotions? How controlled or how impulsive is
         he? Is there a disparity between his self-report and his objective dis-
         play of emotions? How appropriate are his emotional expressions to
         his age and situation?
   3. Intrapsychic conflicts and adjustive reactions
      How does the patient react to anxiety? What are his typical defense
         mechanisms and "self-protections" against threat?
      What is the intraphysic function of his symptoms? How do they relate
         to his adjustment to stress?

C. Self-concept and core belief system
   1. Identity
      Who does the patient believe he is? What are the central assumptions
         or unquestioned beliefs about his own nature?
      Is there evidence of delusions and other distortions about his beliefs
         about himself?
   2. Values and authorities
      What are the basic values, interests, and goals implied by his present
         behavior and his choices throughout his life?
      Whom does he accept as an authority? Whose word would be un-
         questioned?

D. Development and change
   1. Choice patterns
      What were the "turning points" in the patient's life? What are the
         kinds of alternatives the patient has chosen at these significant points
         in his history? How has he gone about making these choices?
      What alternatives does he face now?
   2. Situational developments
      In what kinds of situations has the patient functioned poorly or well?
      What changes are going on in his present situation? What shifts in
         role are expected of him? What are the sources of support or stress
         from significant others? What developmental tasks is he facing?
   3. Capacity for learning and change
      How capable is the patient of shifting roles, learning new ways of re-
         acting to stress, reorganizing his self-conceptions?

E. Diagnostic impressions
   1. Psychiatric classification (if appropriate)
      What category in the official psychiatric diagnostic system (American

Psychiatric Association, 1952) does this patient match most closely, and why? What are the second or third alternatives, if any?
2. Disorders of ability and performance (if appropriate)
What are the patient's disorders of speech, reading, academic performance, etc.?
What classes of jobs is he qualified for presently and with training?

F. Recommendations and prognosis
   1. Developmental needs
      What changes need to occur in the patient in order to meet the demands of present or potential situations?
   2. Situational changes
      What kind of home, work, or ward situation would be conducive to the patient's development?
      What kind of counseling or psychotherapy should be done with the family or other people who are important in his life?
   3. Special assignments or training
      Are there any special kinds of treatment, such as occupational therapy, industrial therapy, or training courses which would be of help in rehabilitating the patient?
   4. Psychological effects of somatic treatments
      What benefits or difficulties might accrue from drugs, electroconvulsive therapy, etc.?
   5. Psychotherapy
      Is psychotherapy likely to be of value? If so, what kind and by whom?
      Is group therapy or counseling indicated?

ASSESSMENT AS AN INSTRUMENT OF SOCIAL ACTION

As we read the case of Dolores Aiken and examine the purposes of psychological assessment, it becomes apparent that assessment does not arise in a social vacuum. Psychologists have become interested in clinical work in response to the interests of society and the spirit of the times. The very fact that we have developed techniques for assessing *individuals* reflects a social and political philosophy which emphasizes the worth of the individual. The growth of humanitarianism as an ethical attitude has reached the point where society ideally seeks to find the "best place" for each person to promote his maximum development. Psychological assessment is part of this enterprise.

A second social reason for assessment, and perhaps one that is more cogent and down to earth, is the recognition by large social organizations that any organization can run most efficiently and smoothly if there is a planned coordination between the individual and the institution. The personnel programs of industries, the pupil placement and special educational programs of schools, and the assignment of hospital patients to wards, to therapeutic duties and forms of work, and to positions in the community are direct expressions of the need to align institutional and individual needs and abilities. These gigantic personnel programs have greatly stimulated the development of psychological tests.

The social value of smoothly functioning organizations and institutions is obviously a justification for occupational placement. It is not so obvious that social needs are being served when a patient goes voluntarily to a private psychotherapist. However, it has long been considered desirable that somewhere within society a place should be provided for people who are seriously maladjusted or deviant. Today, although, of course, less compulsion is involved than formerly, there are, nevertheless, strong social pressures to find ways of handling people with problems so that they may get along more easily and be less of a burden to those around them.

Ultimately, an examination of the purposes of assessment leads back to the basic relation between the individual and society. In the United States, millions of people take psychological tests every year. This means that schools, colleges, businesses, and governmental agencies are letting test results enter into decisions about human lives. Psychological assessment is both a response to and an influence on sociopolitical values. Many questions can be raised about the wisdom of this course. Intelligence tests, the content of which often have a middle-class bias, may discriminate against lower-class children. Whyte, in *The Organization Man* (1956), has shown how psychological tests may be used to produce conformity and stifle any form of individuality that might interfere with the organization's smooth-running machinery. To what ends shall we turn our science? Assessment techniques, like most tools, can be used for a diversity of purposes, some destructive and some constructive. The ultimate question is put to the assessor himself, and the answer resides in the competence and ethical responsibility of the psychologist.

SUMMARY

The nature of psychological assessment has been the subject of this chapter. Assessment can be seen as the way we go about understanding others; as the systematic development and communication of information about a person and his situation; as the description, prediction, and explanation of individual behavior in natural living situations; and as the processes used for making decisions and for developing a working image or model. It is inevitable that there be some procedures for assessing patients in clinics and hospitals, although these may not be formal and obvious. In decision-making both institutional and individual values enter into the evaluation of alternatives. The working image or model is a set of hypotheses about the person who is to be studied and about the situations that surround and affect him. The course of assessment can be broken down into a *preparation* stage, in which early information and the clinician's background of knowledge are used to make plans and decisions about how a case is to be investigated; an *input* stage, in which information is gathered by interviews, tests, and other procedures; an *information-processing* stage; and an *output* stage, in which decisions and conclusions are translated into reports and clinical actions. Referrals for assessment help determine its goals. Many referrals to clinical psychologists come from physicians or psychiatrists, through schools, and through social agencies. Clients themselves also often initiate contact. The sorts of cases that are referred exhibit general trends according to the age and sex of the patient and the developmental tasks which may be facing him at the time. The individual goals of assessment must not be uncritically accepted from the referring agency but must be formulated by the psychologist himself. The process of assessment is a reflection of an influence on the society in which it takes place; the psychologist needs to examine the ethics and social effects of his practice.

SUGGESTED READINGS

MEEHL, P. E. Some ruminations on the validation of clinical procedures. *Canad. J. Psychol.*, 1959, 13, 102-128.

In this invited address before the Canadian Psychological Association, Meehl presents his views on the purposes of assessment and raises important questions about validation. He argues in favor of retaining psychiatric diagnoses. He urges that psychologists should emphasize practical prediction as well as the development of theories and construct validity. (Sections of this article can also be appropriately read in connection with later chapters on validity and research.)

CRONBACH, L. J., & GLESER, GOLDINE C. *Psychological tests and personnel decisions.* Urbana: Univer. of Illinois Press, 1957.

This slim volume presents ideas which, if followed through, would create extensive changes in methods and research in assessment. Instead of concerning themselves with single tests as present test theories do, these authors focus on ultimate outcomes—on the making of decisions. They apply decision theory ("rational behavior in the fact of unknown states of nature," p. 2) to the testing enterprise. The psychologist must consider combinations and sequences contributing to decisions among alternatives having certain values. The middle sections of the book present complex statistical details, but the first two and last two chapters furnish an easy-to-read overview of decision theory as applied to psychological problems.

RESEARCH EXAMPLES

NOTE: At the end of most of the following chapters, there are brief reports of research studies selected because of their originality, sound methodology, or general significance. They are but a few of many worthy to be chosen. All are good studies, though they may have limitations, and their findings often may need to be checked. Each should be seen as a steppingstone to further research. The reader is urged to examine the original articles and to consider how he might extend and improve the study.

DAILEY, C. A. The practical utility of the clinical report. *J. consult. Psychol.*, 1953, 17, 297-302.

This study is interesting because it is one of a very few attempts to identify the decisions made about patients in the course of their hospital stay and to study how clinical procedures contribute to these decisions. Dailey's first step was to collect a long list of decisions from the clinical staff members of the VA hospital where the study was made. By eliminating overlap he reduced this list to 32 kinds of decisions. Examples on the first list are: Should this patient be admitted to the psychiatric ward? Should he be allowed visitors? Should he have a special diet? If he is to have psychotherapy, should the therapist be male?

In developing the measure of contribution to decision-making, Dailey took an important next step. He asked ten clinical psychologists employed on the hospital staff to answer 32 decision questions for the average patient in his hospital. This step furnished a baseline against which to measure the amount of *new* information contributed by the psychological report. Then two clinicians read nine psychological reports, without having any other knowledge of the patient, and checked the decision list. Their answers were compared with the baseline answers. The score given each report was the difference between the judges' answers and the baseline answers.

This score was then compared with certain characteristics of the psychological report. It was found that 26 per cent of the decisions based on the report were different from the baseline. The number of new contributions was correlated .27 with report length, .43 with number of technical terms, and .32 with personal terms, all of these being significantly different from chance.

This study has some limitations. One wonders what the validity of these decisions was. For instance, would there be a correlation between these decisions and the judged success of the actual decisions? There is no report of the correlation of the report-based decisions with actual decisions about the patient. It is not known whether the clinician's baseline answers are actually the base rates on decisions in the hospital. Also it is likely that one could not readily generalize to other hospitals because of the different possibilities for decisions in different settings. Despite all of these shortcomings, the study is interesting and original. It treats of problems calling for much more research.

SCHMIDT, H. O., & FONDA, C. P. The reliability of psychiatric diagnosis: a new look. *J. abnorm. soc. Psychol.*, 1956, 52, 262-267.

The assumption that psychiatric diagnosis is unreliable is widely held but has actually been subjected to very little careful study. Schmidt and Fonda concluded after surveying the literature that a good research design for such a study should include the following: a patient sample, representative of the population to whom the diagnoses applied; a sample of diagnosticians, representative of the population of psychiatrists; a representative sample of clinics and hospitals; widely used diagnostic nomenclature; and independent assessment by several diagnosticians.

Following their own recommendations, the authors arranged for independent diagnoses by pairs of psychiatrists on 426 admissions to a state hospital. The first (tentative) diagnosis was made by one of a group of eight psychiatric residents during the patient's first week in the hospital on the basis of the information available at admission and on an interview. The second (official) diagnosis was made by one of three chief psychiatrists during the patient's third week in the hospital, this time on the basis of a full staff conference utilizing social history, psychological case reports, and so forth.

The results showed 84 per cent agreement for major diagnostic categories between the tentative and the official diagnosis, roughly equivalent to a Pearson *r* of .90. The hospital diagnostic base rates in the major groupings were 45 per cent organic, 38 per cent psychotic, and 17 per cent character disorders. About four-fifths of the classifications into these three major groupings were in agreement. The reliability of the schizophrenic diagnosis ranged between .73 and .95. Otherwise agreement *within subtypes* occurred in only half of the cases and was almost nil in cases involving neuroses and disorders of personality.

The study failed to provide complete independence of judgment by two psychiatrists. The official diagnosis was made with the resident psychiatrist present at the staff conference, although his tentative diagnosis was not announced. Also the official diagnostician had a great deal more information at hand than the tentative diagnostician. Finally such a study of the reliability of diagnosis can reveal nothing about generalizability to other clinical settings or the long-term stability of personality. It does provide support for a finding of other research, namely that reliability for major classifications of mental disorder is likely to be much higher than for subdivisions within major classifications.

WITTENBORN, J. R., & HOLZBERG, J. D. The generality of psychiatric syndromes. *J. consult. Psychol.*, 1951, 15, 372-380.

This study is part of a larger research program in the development of a quantified method for psychiatric diagnosis. It employed rating scales usable by a psychiatrist, nurse, or other competent observer to record discernible symptoms in a standard manner. From these ratings a profile can be prepared which can be compared with various known patterns. In this particular study the preliminary form was applied to the 250 patients admitted to a state hospital over a six-month period. The ratings were made as part of the psychiatrists' case examinations. The rating scales included items like: "Ideas change with spontaneous rapidity," "Refuses to eat," and "Has made attempts at suicide."

The 51 rating scales were correlated with each other. The matrix of inter-correlations is presented in the article. This matrix was submitted to a centroid factor analysis and a series of rotations. There was a conspicuous tendency for symptoms to cluster. The clusters agreed excellently with those obtained in an earlier study of a VA population. The eight clear-cut symptom clusters were labelled as follows: Paranoia, Schizophrenia, Excitement, Manic state—Depressed state, Anxiety, Hysteria, Paranoid Condition, and Phobic-Compulsive reaction.

The consistency of the two studies with established diagnostic groupings and with clinical impressions is notable. Wittenborn continued the development and application of these scales in an extensive research program. A monograph (Wittenborn, Holzberg, & Simon, 1953) describes the rating scales and further applications in detail. Some excellent critiques of the rating scale have since been published in Buros (1959). For a general review of scales for rating psychopathology, see Lorr (1954).

5 Interviewing

In trying to learn about the behavior of other persons, the two principal ways are through interrogation or observation. We either "ask 'em" or "watch 'em." Interviewing is the prime instrument of assessment, partly because it offers an opportunity for seeing the person's behavior first hand while both the patient and clinician are bringing up important topics. With hardly an exception, all clinicians use interviewing as the first and foremost method of assessment in their daily work. In this chapter we will try to see how the participants meet and act in the interview, what the assessor gets from the interview, and the different ways in which interviews can be used.

THE INTERVIEWING SITUATION

As with a television camera, let us now move in closer for a look at the actual situation in which clinical assessment takes place. Then from a near though somewhat detached position, let us ask some questions about the assessment situation and the factors influencing it. We shall concentrate on the prototype of all assessment situations—the clinician and his patient in an interview or testing period. Many of the same questions and the ideas back of them are relevant to other assessment situations, such as those involving groups of persons or where there are several observers instead of one.

The first thing we notice about the clinical psychologist and his patient is that they are talking to each other. If we watch the scene a little while, we can see that they are not just chatting or gossiping, as friends might. It is true that when Mrs. Olson, the patient, comes in, she and the clinician greet each other and chat conventionally for a minute about the

102

weather and the difficulty she had in finding the clinician's office, but it is not long before the discussion takes a more serious form, and the patient is talking about things that trouble her. We notice that the clinician does very little talking. His full attention is on the patient; he seems to be listening intently, as if he wished to understand completely everything Mrs. Olson is saying. From time to time he breaks in with a question or two, and later on in the interview, after a brief explanation of what he is going to do, he takes out some testing materials and asks the patient to respond to them. At the beginning of the interview the patient appears to be tense and uncertain, and the clinician also seems a little tense, but as the interview proceeds, both become more relaxed. It is clear that the clinician has helped Mrs. Olson feel at ease and at the same time to speak directly about the problems she seems to be facing. We notice that though the room in which they meet is an office, there are evidences in it of some concern for comfort and quiet attractiveness. It does not look sterile like a hospital room or cluttered and hectic like a business office. There are two good reproductions of paintings on the wall, curtains at the window, a pleasing rug. Such objects, though secondary to the relationship between the clinician and patient, help to set the tone of the situation. As the interview moves on, we notice that the clinician looks at his watch. Time is running short. Mrs. Olson is still talking actively. The clinician tactfully mentions that their time is almost over and that he has one more thing he would like to ask her. After discussing this point, he tells her the clinic will telephone her in a few days to outline future plans with her. He stands up and shows her to the door.

Observing such a scene, we wonder about many things. What is the clinician trying to do? What brings the patient to his office, and what does she want? How is this interview related to what may be going on elsewhere in the clinic? How typical of clinical work in general is this kind of scene?

The first interview is only a small part of the total assessment situation. Both the talk and the testing have gone on within a larger context. The clinician already knows a good deal about Mrs. Olson from the manner in which she was referred. Perhaps he has seen a referral letter or a summary of an intake meeting at which her case was discussed. Probably he has spent some time preparing for the meeting. He has read the case folder on Mrs. Olson. Since testing seemed indicated, he has picked out certain tests he will probably use and has placed them close at hand. He may have talked the case over informally with a colleague. He may have read reports of other professional workers who have seen her. A social worker's report, for example, may have supplied a considerable amount of information. The patient's medical record may be available. Furthermore, the clinician himself may have seen Mrs. Olson in other situations before the interview. Even if he only got a glimpse or two of her behavior in the informal situation of the waiting room, he will have impressions of her—how she related to the receptionist, whether she talked with other people, whether or not she read any of the available magazines, whether she seemed anxious or impatient while waiting. If she had been on a hospital ward, he would have had opportunities to learn what impressions the aides, nurses, and other persons had of her. All of these many sources of information are absorbed into the total activity we call assessment. The clinician's purpose, the way he decides to focus the interview and his choice of tests, all are conditioned by such data as these.

The interview with Mrs. Olson is but one sample of an assessment interview, every one of which differs, sometimes a great deal, from every other. Three principal groups of factors (each of which will require a lengthy description after they have been listed) make for variation among assessment situations: (1) *The characteristics of each of the two participants*, including their attiudes toward the interview, their motives or purposes, their emotional reactions, and their thought processes and adaptive behavior in this special situation. (2) *The interactive process*, including the kinds of communication that take place and the development of a relationship between the participants. The term *interactive process* refers only to what goes on while the clinician and patient are in each other's presence. (3) *Special procedural features of the situation*, including the amount and kind of focusing that occurs during the interview, the degree of structure or ambiguity in the interview or testing, and the context within which certain features of the interview develop or are brought out.

HOW THE PATIENT APPROACHES THE INTERVIEW

When a person such as Mrs. Olson comes to an assessment interview, one of the first things we want to know is *why* she has come. It can be assumed that the patient has many and often varied feelings about coming to a psychologist. Reaching a firm decision to seek the help of a psychologist or being forced to seek it is likely to be a rare and significant event in any person's life. Perhaps before a patient comes he recalls such colorful phrases as "headshrinker," "mind reader," and "bug doctor." He may wonder if the psychologist will try to hypnotize him and make him do things he does not want to do. He may imagine that the psychologist is someone who can "fix everything up." As students of psychology, we recognize how false such stereotypes are, but we can sympathize with some of the patient's ideas and feelings when we think how we have felt when we have gone to a physician for some vague and disconcerting symptoms or when in trouble we sought the advice of a lawyer or banker. Over and above our anxiety we are curious about what the "expert" will do and what he will expect us to do. We may even resent his prying and pushing, as he tries to size up our situation and what we should do about it.

The clinician can understand things much better if he knows what the patient expects and wants from the interview. How is he to discover what the patient thinks and feels about coming to him? In most cases it is possible to infer his attitudes from observing his initial behavior. The patient may be eager and interested, distrustful and quiet, or angry and irritable. He may take the intitiative in a vigorous handshake or sit in the chair without being invited to and start talking immediately. On the other hand, he may hold back his hand, move slowly, and respond only when questioned. Each individual person has his own revealing way of entering the situation. One reason the opening remarks and initial actions are important is that they are indicative of the way in which the patient approaches this kind of a human relationship. In a sense, he is "teaching" the psychologist how to respond to him. In order to make sure of the impression he is forming, it may be appropriate for the clinician, after the initial greetings and small talk, to refer to the patient's feelings about coming for an interview, to remark that he must be unsure about what it is all about, or if he is talking to a child, to ask him why his mother brought him to the clinic. Such an opening may lead quite naturally into questions and answers which will help the clinician and patient work out a mutual purpose for the meeting.

Understanding the patient's approach to the interview situation not only tells something about his general approach to similar interpersonal situations and helps work out common purposes, but also supplies clues as to the degree of validity there may be in much of what he asserts in the interview and in his responses to those tests where evasion is possible. Both in tests and in interviews patients will have a test-taking or interview-taking *attitude*, or *set*. This is the patient's preparatory adjustment or readiness for perceiving or acting in the situation. The self-pitying neurotic comes in all set to parade every one of his misfortunes, but the hardened delinquent "ain't gonna tell nobody nuttin." Whether the patient's set coincides with the clinician's wishes or not, it is valuable in helping him understand the patient and in appraising the information he gets from him. This inital set may very well change during the interview. Sometimes the clinician can quite clearly direct it as may be necessary to do when giving instructions about taking the tests. Often it is helpful to discuss the patient's attitudes toward the procedures and to "work through," or reduce, any resistances encountered.

The patient's *purpose* or *motive* in coming to the interview has a decided influence. Is he coming because he himself anxiously wants to get help, or is he coming because others have frightened or threatened him or because he has hopes of manipulating someone? Did he come in acquiescence to part of a routine hospital procedure? Did he come under court order? Is this his first visit to a psychologist or is it one of many? The question is not whether the patient is motivated or not, for there is no such thing as an "unmotivated client." The clinician's problem is to find out *what* are the patients motives with respect to the interview, what he hopes to get from it. The patient is very likely to be troubled or have a complaint or symptom which he wishes to be rid of. However, he may not see himself as required to do anything at all to produce such a change, and he may enter the interview hoping that his telling about himself will help the doctor cure him. During the course of the interview it may be that his motivation will change if he finds the experience gratifying. He may then be motivated to respond in the interview because he finds he likes the new relationship with the interviewer. The kind of content the patient chooses in his conversation and his resistance to changing the subject, as well as his direct statement of why he is here, all tell the clinician something about his purposes.

Another influence on the interview is the patient's *emotional involvements.* Many patients come to the psychologist with considerable fear and anxiety. This anxiety may be advantageous if it leads the patient to cooperate as best he can with the psychologist so that he can get help, or it may be a handicap if he fears, for example, that the psychologist will find out something which could be used to make him do something he is unwilling to do. It is well known also that anxiety can affect test performances. The patient is unlikely to be able to exhibit his maximum ability when he is upset.

Other influences on the course of the interview are what we call the patient's *adaptive techniques.* An interview puts some pressure on the patient to respond to a new situation. The patient perceives that he is expected to respond in a certain way, or perhaps to reveal his thoughts and feelings. How does he adapt to this pressure? The chances are that his behavior in the interview will be like his behavior in similar situations. It may be his habit to withdraw when he encounters stress in his relations with another person. He may become very evasive or he may became agitated and uncontrolled. He may be very sensitive and respond in the way he thinks the interviewer wants him to just to oblige him. Many patients who are new to such interviews are mystified about how they should act. They may be completely at sea about how to play the "patient's role." On the other hand, old-timers around hospitals know so well how to play it that it is difficult to "get to" them. Often, too, it is useful to see the patient's adaptive techniques as attempts to "teach" the interviewer how to behave toward him, for instance, to treat him as a dependent little child or as a mistreated but courageous martyr. Most of the foregoing characteristics of the patient—his attitudes, purposes, emotional state, and adaptive techniques—can be summarized under the terms *role expectation* and *role behavior.*

It has now become clear that understanding the patient's approach to the interview is part-and-parcel of the whole assessment process. In trying to understand these things, one will not only be adding to the interview, but also to one's ability to communicate a useful working image and recommend appropriate clinical actions. The patient comes to the interview with certain predispositions. These may change in order that some commonality of purposes between the patient and clinician be established. If the patient perceives the clinician as having goals too foreign to his own, or as being insensitive and incapable of understanding him, he may be very reluctant to participate not only in the interview but in other contacts with the clinician. Polansky and Kounin (1956) have studied the development of first impressions in different "helping" contexts. They have shown how actively the client evaluates the professional person, especially trying to estimate the expert's competence, personal motives, and friendliness.

HOW THE CLINICIAN APPROACHES THE INTERVIEW

Just as the patient comes to the interview with his own predispositions and biases, so does the clinician. Every clinician will become a more skillful interviewer in proportion as he sees clearly how he is conducting himself and what his personal idiosyncracies in interview situations are. Such self-insight can be a valuable corrective, but it is still more important that the clinician keep his interest focused primarily on the patient. In other words, it would never do for him to concentrate more on watching his own style as an interviewer than on understanding the patient. The clinician who is overly concerned with asking his questions just right or with keeping the testing equipment *exactly* in order is bound to betray this self-consciousness to the client. In the interview, understanding the client, not oneself, is the main thing. However, this need not entirely prevent the clinician from noting what he is doing, and, of course, he can study his own methods of approaching the interview situation in retrospect after the session is over. Listening to taped recordings of interviews is helpful.

What should be the clinician's attitude or *set* toward the interview? If a primary function of the clinician is to facilitate the communication of almost anything and everything which is disturbing the patient, the clinician must be ready to respond in ways which will encourage the patient and keep him relaxed and trustful in the clinician's presence. Rogers (1942, pp. 87-89), in writing of the counseling interview, lists several characteristics which a clinician should exhibit: Warmth and responsiveness, permissiveness in expression of feeling, absence of any suggestion of moralistic or judgmental attitudes, and complete freedom from pressure or coercion of any kind. The clinician centers his attention on the client and is responsive and encouraging. Rogers' list is a help in describing the ideal "posture" for a clinician. On the other hand, it must also be recognized that there is some conflict of goals in an assessment interview. The patient is to be encouraged to express himself freely, but if he completely dominates and monopolizes the interview, the clinician may be unable to elicit material important for diagnostic purposes. At times it may even be worth the risk to introduce stress or deliberately confront the patient with a problem or an inquiry with a hint of challenge in it in order to assess his ability to handle it. The clinician also will have to impose his own time limits on the interview, and these are inconsistent with letting the patient meander aimlessly and lose himself in trifling details. The typical clinician makes a compromise here. His attitude is basically warm, interested, and nonjudgmental, but he maintains control over the interview in that he sets some limits, making sure that discussion covers important topics. Very frequently he is permissive early in an interview, letting the client choose whatever topics he wishes to talk about, but before the assessment period is up, he may try to gather loose ends together and seek to have the gaps filled in. If, along with the interview, the clinician makes use of standardized tests, he must of course adhere to the standard administration procedures. If he hints or coaxes the patient to greater effort than the test instructions suggest, he cannot use the test's norms in the usual way. (However, this does not prevent him from doing exploratory work or "testing the limits" after the standard method of administering the test is finished.)

The clinician's *purposes* will have an influence on the course of the interview. At one level there are the more obvious "official" purposes of the clinician. These may include his desire to understand the patient's complaints and symptoms, to predict how he is likely to respond to therapy, or to obtain for the clinic a general picture of the patient's personality. With each particular patient there are likely to be specific goals, for example, a differential diagnosis between sociopathic personality and schizophrenia, or the identification of deep-down conflicts to be worked through in individual therapy. It is a great help to the interviewer when he can have his chief goals clearly in mind before he sees the patient, providing he remains sufficiently flexible to recognize that he may need to revise them in the course of the interview itself.

We need to face the possibility that considerably less rational and more personal and emotional motives may also play a part in the clinician's conduct of an interview and in determining his relationships with a client. The very things which are the hallmarks of a clinician's special field— observing and analyzing abnormalities of behavior—may suggest less desirable aspects of his personal motivation. The clinician finds himself exploring certain problems about which the patient is sensitive, and his motive in doing so may take on a neurotic character if he probes and pries beyond what is necessary for his avowed clinical purpose. In an insightful and provocative chapter on the interpersonal dynamics of the assessment situation, Roy Schafer (1954) has analyzed the primitive, unconscious aspects of the clinician's activities. The psychologist is officially supposed to examine patients. Schafer points out that such an examination may take on the *voyeuristic* connotations of a "peeping Tom" looking into the intimate and juicy details of others' lives without any responsible relationship to them. The psychologist is sometimes expected to put questions and make decisions in a way which is unmistakably *autocratic,* or at another time he may be appealed to to render judgment as if he were an *oracle,* with special personal powers for seeing hidden meanings. Finally, if he is asked to help others his assistance may take on *saintly* connotations. All of these roles may appeal to the unconscious needs of psychologists, but with self-insight and a sense of personal security, the clinician is not likely to go far wrong. He should have enough humility and humor to recognize these dangers and check with the reality of records and the judgments of others.

Closely related to the clinician's motives, and like them affecting the character of the interview, are his *emotional involvements*. In general, he needs to maintain an attitude that is interested, but calm. He may respond to the patient with empathy and understanding, but not with pity and maudlin sympathy. Though in some kinds of therapy there may be a place for excited responsiveness, the clinician must not lose himself, as a sympathetic friend would, in the terrors and delights of the patient's world. The clinician may allow one foot to rest in the patient's world, but he will always keep the other in reality. An attitude of "deeply interested detachment" is an ideal. Every now and then, however, a patient may be able to strike the emotional Achilles heel of the clinician. If the client shouts in angry, abusive terms, the clinician may give vent to a natural tendency to get angry in return. This is not always a mistake, for there may well be a therapeutic effect in showing the patient that he is human too. In assessment interviews such extremes of emotional participation seldom arise, largely because assessment usually comes early in the series of contacts with the patient. With an attitude of professional interest, the clinician notes anger as an important datum in the information he is collecting. He realizes that the anger is not really directed at him alone, but reflects more general feelings and frustrations. A patient may unconsciously need to arouse hostility in everyone around him and so justify his paranoid tendencies. Or the patient's hostility may echo an old feeling he had toward his father. In such a situation the interviewer is helped by the intellectual activity of trying to understand what precipitated the emotional outburst. He may want to check whether there was something about his own manner or something he said that could have awakened these deep feelings in the patient. In this way even the observation of his own behavior and feelings may contribute data to his understanding of the patient.

Finally, the clinician will be influenced the interview by his *adaptive techniques* and his problem-solving ability. Since every patient and every interview is in some ways unique, there are frequently occasions when things do not run true to form. The clinician must be able to adapt quickly to any special situations his patient may bring up. The psychologist whose ability to untangle human problems is limited will find himself having trouble as he interviews many kinds of clients.

The inexperienced clinician tends to run to extremes in evaluating an interview. He tends to blame either himself or the client for a bad interview. The truth of the matter is that both are involved in what occurs and neither one should be "blamed." The ever-present aim should be to study what occurs during an interview so as to understand it better. The patient may be unresponsive for some completely extraneous reasons. No clinician can get along well with all patients. However, every clinician is usually able to develop a working relationship with many kinds of patients. (This might suggest a research project on the hypothesis of a relation between effectiveness in clinical work and ability to establish relationships with a wide range of people.)

One wide difference between clinician and patient in the way they adapt to the special situation which the interview presents is the amount of *training and experience* the clinician has had. Good training should have provided the clinician with an understanding of himself as an assessment instrument and a knowledge of how to combine such skill as he has with the tools and techniques his professional training has equipped him with, such as tests and the strategies of structured interviews. These include techniques of interviewing he has learned. For instance, a lot has been known from the time of the pioneer study by Muscio (1916) up to the latest studies of public opinion polls about how the form of a question can bias the interviewee's answers. Though there are many things of this kind to be learned about interviewing techniques, all the techniques are overshadowed in importance by the interactive processes and particularly by the personal relationships that develop in interviews.

THE INTERACTIVE PROCESS IN INTERVIEWING

In the interview two persons come together with a *mutuality of purpose*, at least to some degree. To the extent that they are *en rapport*, there is a comfortable and unstrained relationship between them. Rapport is not the whole aim of the interview unless it marks the beginning of therapy, but at least minimal rapport is a necessity if the clinician is to be successful in gathering much information about the subject and to make progress toward his ultimate aim of getting a view of the client's way of perceiving his world.

The interaction that takes place in the interview can be seen in several ways. First it is a kind of *transaction,* an exchange of valued actions or experiences, a process of giving and receiving. According to their individual motives, each of the two participants will endeavor to get certain things from the interview and be willing to give something in exchange. Adolf Meyer, as Muncie (1959) points out, saw the interview as a kind of *negotiation* between two people to enable them to arrive at common goals. A client, for instance, may be very willing to give out information about himself if he can receive at the same time reassurances, advice, or just a listening ear. The kinds of things exchanged are limited by the structure of the interview, each person's perception of his role, and the like. A patient may desperately want sympathy, reassurance, and love, but the interviewer, having in mind the larger goal of the patient's development and maturity, finds himself in good conscience barred from gratifying him in the way the client longs for.

Another aspect of the interview is the *relationship* that is established between the participants. This involves their interpersonal feelings—the emotional closeness or distance between them, their liking or disliking for each other. Each new interview undoubtedly to some degree echoes earlier relationships with similar persons who have at some time entered the participants' lives. When one of us meets a person for the first time it commonly happens that we start comparing the person with someone already familiar: "She looks exactly like Aunt Myrtle when she was young;" or we rack our memories in vain to discover whom the new acquaintance resembles but are disconcertingly sure that there is a likeness—a haunting one. When this relationship goes farther and the patient starts acting toward the interviewer "as if" the latter were his father or mother, we have what the psychoanalysts call *transference.* If, on the other hand, the interviewer gets overly involved with the client, we have *countertransference.* When this happens the participant's own emotional needs have entered so strongly into the relationship that there may be interference with the process of helping the patient. Transference and countertransference occur, of course, in the interviews of more sustained and intensive therapy rather than in diagnostic interviews, although elements of them may enter early into the relationship. Even during a first interview a psychologist will do well to take note of his feelings of liking or disliking as these intrude upon the "interested but calm detachment" of the ideal attitude.

The interview may be seen as *communication.* Communication is a process of sending and receiving messages, or meaningful information, from one person to another. Communication theory must include the following: a source of the message (one person) and a destination for it (the other person). In between is a medium or channel of communication (such as spoken or written words or nonverbal movements), perhaps with some *"noise"* attached. The person who is the source of the communication must *encode* the message by putting it into signs that are comprehensible to the other, and the person receiving the message must *decode* it in order to understand it. Errors and disturbances can happen at any point along the way. This analysis of the process of communication as it applies to interviewing is of some help in understanding what may go wrong when we try to understand other persons. For instance, a patient may decode a statement in a very different manner from that in which the interviewer encoded it because he does not share the same signs or "language." An interviewer hearing a delinquent say he "made out" with a girl must take into account differences in language in different regions. In one part of the country it may mean he has had intercourse with the girl; in another part it means simply that he arranged a date or kissed her. Another useful term in discussing communication is *feedback,* a term derived from the ability of servomechanisms to govern and control their own activities. In social psychology feedback refers to one's perception of the effect one's own activities have upon others, for example, observing how many smiles or how much laughter the joke one has just told produces. In interviewing, the clinician is constantly receiving feedback from the client, and he in turn is reacting to the client's communications in ways the client may be quick to detect and be influenced by; in this way feedback enables each of the persons to govern or modify his behavior during the interview. When there is some disturbance in this feedback system, communication is impaired or altered.

Our modern emphasis on words, which extends to the typical subculture of clinics and colleges, may make us forget that communication is *nonverbal as well as verbal.* The root meaning of the word *interview* is a view between people—two people seeing each other face-to-face. One reason that the interview is usually much preferred as a medium of communication to correspondence by mail or telephone, or to test results alone, is that it provides an opportunity for nonverbal forms of communication and observation. Nonverbal communication is likely to be less under our control because we are less aware of it. Research has barely started on the communication value of gestures, actions, marks, signs, objects, sounds, smells, touch, and so on (Ruesch, 1959; Ruesch & Kees, 1956; Dittmann & Wynne, 1961). Almost certainly some of the causes of mental illness lie in disturbances of communication that goes on in families (Bateson, Jackson, Haley, & Weakland, 1956).

Interviewing may be seen as *interactive learning.* Inevitably during the interview, some modification (which may be fleeting) of each participant's behavior will occur through his interaction with the other.

It is not the aim of the assessment interview to modify the patient's behavior, but research on verbal reinforcement indicates that definite modifications of verbal behavior do, in fact, occur. It is important that the assessment interviewer be aware of the way in which he is affecting the client. In some cases it is very clear how an interviewer can increase or decrease certain classes of responses. If the patient says, "Every now and then I have a dream about going into a deep, dark cave," and the clinician says, "Yes, tell me more" and leans forward eagerly, the patient is likely to respond by telling more dreams. If the clinician perks up whenever sex is mentioned, he is likely to get more sexual content in the interviews. Intentionally or not, the interviewer is bound to be engaged all the time in encouraging or discouraging certain kinds of responses, and the patient is similarly learning to behave a certain way in the presence of the interviewer and to reinforce some of the interviewer's behavior. This phenomenon makes it very difficult to standardize an interview or even, to some extent, the administration of a test.

The research on effects of reinforcement on verbal behavior out of which this concept of the interview as an interactive learning situation has developed grew out of Skinner's work on learning. Krasner (1958a) has reviewed the literature on this subject. In such studies the subject is asked to produce words in the presence of the experimenter and the experimenter alters his behavior when the subject says certain words— then it is observed whether or not the subject has increased his production of these particular words or of the class of words to which they belong. It has been found that signs of interest and approval such as saying "mmm-hmm" or "good" or nodding the head when the subject happens to say the kind of word the experimenter is interested in will serve as reinforcers and increase the production of such verbal responses as the pronouns *I* and *we*, names of animals, and others. So far there has been little interest in research on the other side of the interaction—namely the effect of the client on the interviewer—but undoubtedly this exists to some extent too (Masling, 1957, 1960), although it is implicitly assumed that the interviewer is more in control of the situation and will adhere more steadily to the pattern he intended. Controlled variation of interviewer responsiveness has been studied in a long series of experiments by Saslow and Matarazzo (1959). They have found a surprising amount of lawfulness in the interview and are able to study the effect of such things as interviewer silence and interruption of the client's talk. (See the research example at the end of this chapter.)

Another way of thinking about interviewing is to take it as a *developmental sequence.* We study the sequential nature of the interview interaction, noting what happens at its beginning, toward the middle, and at the end. As Hathaway has pointed out in reviewing nondirective therapy (1948), there is a "hello-goodbye phenomenon" in interviewing. Cultural expectations have an effect on how one starts an interview or a series of interviews and how one ends them. Patients often bring in a "ticket"—a complaint that will admit them to therapy or diagnostic attention. They tend to have self-centered problems at the beginning of the interview series; at the end when they are breaking off an interview they tend to say goodbye by showing gratitude and saying they are better. This goodbye phenomenon confuses the objective evaluation of the effectiveness of therapy. Individuals differ a great deal in their way of starting to terminate an interview session. Some of them seem to save up particularly important details to the end, when they quickly blurt them out either in an attempt to prolong the interview unsuitably or to prevent deep discussion of them at the time. The initial ways in which patients act in individual interviews seems to be especially significant, revealing in capsule form what the patient has been thinking about and his attitude toward the interview. Another effect of time on interaction is the question of how short, frequent interviews differ from longer, more infrequent interviews. Perhaps there is some relation here to massed versus spaced practice in learning. In any case, a rich field for research on the interview lies open before us.

THE PHYSICAL STIMULUS CONDITIONS OF THE INTERVIEW

One of the conditions affecting the interview is the *physical setting.* This should be a quiet, pleasant room. How the chairs are arranged and whether there is a desk between the participants are things that surely have an effect. Perhaps the reader knows the feeling of having to sit in a very low chair while being interviewed by someone who towers over him. *Freedom from distraction* is very important. Interruptions from the telephone or from noises of traffic or children playing outside, may very much affect the way the patient feels about talking and prevent the interview from becoming the intense and intimate conversation it often should be. *Privacy* is ordinarily of the utmost importance. It can be assumed that the client will feel much freer to talk about himself if he knows that no one but the interviewer will hear even a word or two of what he has to say. (Parenthetically it may be remarked that along with physical privacy goes the clinician's ethical responsibility to respect the social privacy, or confidential nature, of the patient's revelations. For instance, if he wants to record the interview, he should get the patient's permission to do so.) The physical situation in which the interview itself occurs, the closeness of the chairs, the softness or harshness of the lighting, the warmth or coldness of the room's style are very likely to be felt by the client as a communication of how the clinician feels about him and about the interviewing relationship. Conditions such as these are often so subtle that people may be unaware of why they feel comfortable or uncomfortable, and even that they do feel as they do, but they, nevertheless, have marked effects on the course of the interview.

Ideal physical conditions sometimes are not possible. When this is the case it is a good time to remember—as really we always should—that the personal relations established between clinician and client are always more important than the physical setting. The physical setting assumes importance only in relation to its influence upon the client-clinician relationship. Someone has even gone so far as to say, with truthfulness, "A good therapist can do therapy in a barn." Buildings are not as important as people. Office decor—the modern Danish furniture, the reproduction of the Impressionist painting on the wall—can also become stereotyped and damaging, as columnists lampooning the psychiatrists' "Libido Lane" in Beverly Hills have shown. Frequently, too, informal interviews in the hall or on the street are valuable just because of their apparent casualness.

STRUCTURING THE INTERVIEW

The purposes of an interview will determine the way it is structured. It is its purpose, whether history-taking, differential diagnosis, or therapy, that distinguishes an interview from ordinary conversation. When the purpose of the interview is assessment, the purpose might be stated in such ways as these: "to explore Mr. DeSilva's relations with his family, especially his wife and son, and to get a picture of his ability to plan realistically for a job" ; "to review briefly the somatic symptoms Mrs. Grant complains about and then to explore intensively the possibility that tensions over relations with her husband may lie behind them"; or more generally, "to understand the patient's reason for coming to the clinic, to examine his complaints in detail, and to obtain a social, medical, and educational history."

Interviews vary a great deal in the degree to which they are structured. Bordin's research (1955) has made it clear that the degree to which the interview is ambiguous or structured is largely controlled by the interviewer. Structuring may occur in one or more of three areas: *content,* the topics that are discussed; *goals,* the ends toward which the interview works; and *closeness* of relationship, that is the degree to which the interview is emotional rather than rational-factual.

Structuring may vary all the way from very general (such broad questions as "Tell me something about why you came here") to very specific (the specific questions of a survey interview or a police interrogation into minute details of a crime). Very similar to the distinction between general and specific structure is the difference between *scanning* and *focusing.* It is often a good plan to start an interview by scanning, sweeping broadly over, important areas of living: "What led up to your coming to the clinic?" "Tell me about your family," and "How have things been going with your work?" Then from time to time when the clinician believes he sees an opening that may lead to closer understanding (and if the relationship is good), he may focus on a question in some detail: "Tell me exactly what happened the morning you first noticed the pain" or "Why is it that Mr. Meyers seems to be watching you?" Bugental (1954) in an outline to be used in analysis of typescripts of interviews has coined the phrase *topical concurrence*. He describes five levels of "concurrence" with the previous topic of conversation. The response may be passive, responsive, developing, diverging, or changing. The range is from "mmm" or "I see," at the passive end, to "Now, suppose you tell me about something else, your education," changing the topic. To this list might be added some of the structuring done in research with the interaction chronograph described at the end of the chapter (Saslow & Matarazzo, 1959); at planned times the interviewer makes no response whatsoever and at other times he contradicts whatever the subject says.

Above everything the effect of the structure of the interview on the patient needs to be kept in mind. In general one is interested in getting the patient to tell his own story and so the direction taken by the conversation is left open to permit him to select what is most important to him. This is especially true at the beginning of an interview. Some patients, however, find an extremely unstructured situation unsettling. In such cases the greater the ambiguity of the situation, while the social pressure to respond is great, the greater will be the anxiety of the patient. For this reason, it may be desirable that the clinician at the beginning of the interview give an anxious client some clear feeling of what is wanted.

KINDS OF INTERVIEWS

Among assessment interviews, there are several kinds of purposes and structures. We will mention some common ones.

Intake interview

As the name suggests, the purpose of an intake interview is to establish a relationship with a client and to obtain and impart some preliminary information needed by one or the other participant. This information usually includes identification of the client, in some detail, listening to his complaints, explaining any fees to be charged, and clarification of the patient's expectations about the service he is likely to obtain from the agency or hospital or clinic. Often during this initial contact the interviewer raises the question whether the agency can appropriately handle the patient's problems or whether he should be referred elsewhere. In this sense, the intake interview results in a "contract" between the patient and the agency. Because considerable knowledge of community facilities is often necessary, and because of special training in intake work, the social worker usually does the intake interviewing. Frequently the intake interview may develop into a case history interview, to be described next. The first contact with the agency is a very important one; it may set the tone for all future contacts.

Case-history interview

Nearly all clinical work requires close study of the background and history of the patient. When this information comes from an interview with the patient himself and includes his recall of those events which seemed important prior to the onset of the disorder, it is called an *anamnesis*. *Case history* is a broader term and is applicable when information is also obtained from other persons. A case history would cover such topics as: history of the complaint, childhood development, description of the patient's parental family and, if he is married, his present family, educational and occupational history, sexual adjustment, interests, and medical history. Though in larger institutions and agencies social workers usually take histories, the psychologist will often find it desirable to be prepared to do so. Appendix B presents an outline guide for taking a case history and refers to other sources.

Mental status examination

This kind of interview is traditionally the responsibility of the psychiatrist, but clinical psychologists also should be able to conduct it. The possible usefulness of this kind of examination should always be kept in mind, especially when there are hints that a psychosis might be present. In some institutions it is the psychologist who teaches medical students and psychological interns to give this kind of interview. A mental status examination usually covers six areas: *mental content,* which includes evidence of such symptoms as delusions, hallucinations, preoccupations, or phobias; *sensorium and intellect,* the person's orientation to "time, place, and person," evidence of intellectual level, and memory; *emotional tone,* a term used to cover both overt signs of emotion and the patient's subjective report of his emotional life; *insight,* answers to questions of whether the patient knows he is ill and what he thinks caused his mental illness; *stream of speech,* the rapidity, organization, and peculiarities of speech; and *attitude, appearance, and behavior,* which includes a resumé of the patient's behavior and his social life during the most recent period. For a more extensive account of this kind of interviewing, see Wells and Ruesch (1945), Menninger (1952), or a textbook of psychiatry.

There are many other kinds of structured interviews which meet special needs. For instance, *brief screening* interviews as used in military induction centers in order to spot recruits unfit for service. Then there are the interviews *associated with testing*, which serve to explain purposes and procedures, develop rapport with the patient, or, after testing, report and explain findings. Another kind of interview is the *discharge or exit interview*, used for finding out why an employee is quitting his job or for discussing the termination of his treatment with a patient just before he leaves a hospital. There are also many different kinds of structured *research interviews* (See Maccoby & Maccoby, 1954).

EXAMPLES OF INTERVIEWING

In this chapter we will present two examples of early history-taking. Both of them are intended to assist the interviewer in planning therapy, but they are two very different approaches. The first one will particularly emphasize the structuring activities of the interviewer as he scans the areas of living that are usually important to know about in all cases and as he responsively probes to follow-up important leads. The second one will emphasize the patient's associations and be far less structured. Part of these differences spring from the clinical settlings involved and part from the theoretical leanings of the interviewers.

The first case, Bob Simon, is the client of a psychologist in private practice. (The psychologist has an eclectic theoretical background with a strong influence from Adolph Meyer's thinking.) Bob is a 23-year-old unmarried college senior. He came to the psychologist for help in overcoming a lack of self-confidence and fear of meeting others which he feels will be crippling to him in his chosen occupation—high school teaching. The following interview is the second meeting of the psychologist and Bob, the first one being a ten-minute discussion when Bob came to the office. That first meeting was mainly a matter of making decisions about acceptance (the psychologist deciding it was an appropriate case for his services) and "contractual" expectations (the client agreeing to pay the fees involved and to take the recommended test and the psychologist getting some idea of the motivation of the client for therapy). The following is a series of excerpts from the next hour's interview. The psychologist is following a semistructured interview guide, writing down notes on the client's responses as the interview progresses. (The *Ir* indicates the interviewer's remarks and the *Cl* the client's.)

Ir. (After a brief introductory exchange about the MMPI which the client had taken.) All right. Today I'm going to do something that I will probably not do in the future. As I indicated before, I would like to be more active in asking questions today than later on—to direct your attention to a number of areas that you might not get around to otherwise. It would save some time. Let's clear some historical material out of the way first. Do you know anything about the conditions of your birth?

Cl. Well, I was two months premature and in an incubator for several weeks, I guess. By Caeserian section. It was a question of saving my mother I guess. That's about the only thing.

Ir. You know quite a bit about the terms—the conditions of your birth. Many people do not. How did you get to know this?

Cl. I was told in the course of history. I don't remember exactly when it came up. I think my parents or relatives talked. I don't know how much I weighed at birth. I could find out.

Ir. Were you expected to live?

Cl. I guess it was a question of touch-and-go for a while. I'm no major miracle, but I guess there was some question involved.

Ir. Do you know whether this shaped your parents' attitudes toward you when you were a child?

Cl. I suppose it did. I don't know how it could have been otherwise. (Pause.)

Ir. Moving on up some months or years, were you told anything about when you began talking, walking, things of this sort?

Cl. I've been told, but I forgot. I'll find out.

Ir. If it's not a lot of trouble, I'd like to check into it. What about the difficulties which many children have? Were you a problem eater, have feeding problems and so on?

Cl. Yes. I've been told that several times. I'd drink water. Yeah, they had trouble feeding me, I guess. I don't know for how long. My mama says that if she knew then what she knows now she'd never have worried; she'd have made up for it, you know.

Ir. What about other problem behavior, like nail-biting, or night terrors, or things like that?

Cl. Well, just stuttering. I was a very acute and chronic and uncomfortable case of that. Only a little nail-biting. I remember some.

Ir. Could you tell me more about the stuttering?

(The client describes how stuttering seemed to come and go and be very bad at times. The psychologist notes that he has no trouble now in the interview and asks if he had speech therapy. The client says he did not and tells how his mother was sympathetic about it.)

Ir. What happened with your stuttering?

Cl. I don't know. It was something that I was bound and determined to get over one way or the other. I remember how I used to practice words beginning with *s*. I remember being acutely aware of the problem, speaking very much slower, making conscious efforts to speak clearly, and it seemed to drop dead more or less. I didn't understand it. It wasn't explained to me.

(After some more exploration of the stuttering which reveals little more detail, the interviewer moves on to questions about health. The patient reports some decrement in hearing in one ear due to several middle-ear infections as a child. He describes his health as generally good and reports that he has an annual checkup with a physician, whom he says the psychologist may consult if he wishes. The interviewer brings up his school history, and the client reports a good academic record but a feeling of not being liked by the other children.)

Cl. I remember one time I came home from school crying most of the way, telling my mom that nobody seemed to like me. I don't remember why.

Ir. From what you say, I have the impression it wasn't that they disliked you, but that no one bothered to like you. You were a nonentity, as if you didn't exist. Is that right?

Cl. Yeah, that's it. I just don't know why. (Pause.)

Ir. When did you graduate from high school?

(Going on, the interviewer inquires into the client's college interests and takes up his work record and attitudes toward earning money. The client spent a year and a half in the army and is now in the reserves. Leaving that topic, the interviewer brings up the subject of sex.)

Ir. What about your sex development? When did you first learn about sex and from whom?

Cl. Not from my parents. I think in junior high school they showed us a movie on the conception of a baby. I remember not understanding that. Still I'd learned a lot of language and terms from kids in the neighborhood. Some of them had spent time in a reform school. I didn't have any experience— either homosexual or heterosexual—until last year in the army really. From these other guys, when I was a kid, I learned the reported techniques of attacking a girl or defending yourself from them. When I was in the fifth grade I started taking some boxing lessons. I met some very tough kids, and they were about the only ones that taught me about sex. I'm amazed I didn't get more involved.

Ir. When you first learned about sex, what kind of reaction did it arouse in you?

Cl. I don't remember any surprise, any shock. My reaction was close to equal to learning about astronomy or something objective. I pursued it somewhat academically like anything else, I guess. I wasn't raised in a prudish family.

Ir. You mentioned experience last year in the service. How did that come about?

Cl. Well, this might seem like old stuff to you. I went out with a friend to the town near the camp where I was in training. It was suggested that we go to this place and that there would be booze and tail available. It turned out to be that both was the case. I don't remember any particularly traumatic experience being involved. My reactions were what I'd expected them to be. Nothing out of the ordinary.

(The interviewer leads briefly into other areas of sex experience including masturbation and fantasies and then moves into another topic, self-description.)

Ir. Now I want to ask you about something a little more complicated than what we have been talking about before, Bob. Imagine that I don't know a thing about you. Imagine that it is important that I get an accurate picture of you in just a very brief time. How would you describe yourself?

Cl. As I am right now, or as a function of the past?

Ir. Anyway you wish, describe yourself. You want to give somebody a capsule sketch of what you're like.

Cl. Well, I would say that I'm an overly defensive person, more easily hurt than I would like to be, having much more discomfort in meeting people than I would like to have, more difficulty in getting along well with the people that I have met, some ability to carry on fairly well with a few people. (Pause.) Well, that's not as efficient as it could be. Is that okay?

Ir. Uh-huh. What would you regard, speaking very candidly and without excessive modesty, as your outstanding assets?

Cl. (Pause.) Well, the ability to arrive at a well-founded decision given certain facts. Something I picked up from chess playing, I think. Academic work. An interest in a wide variety of subjects. A mastery of very few.

Ir. So you're an analytical type person.

Cl. But how much that is a product of what I want to be I don't know.

(The interviewer goes on to question the client about his greatest handicaps, the concrete difficulties to which he would like to adjust in the next years, what attempts he has made with these difficulties, and some concrete examples of successes and disappointments.)

Ir. One last area and then we can call it quits today. We haven't talked much about your family. What comprises your family?

Cl. Father, mother, and one brother and a sister.

Ir. Where is your brother relative to you?

Cl. Two years younger.

Ir. How would you describe each of these persons in your family? Let's begin with your father. What kind of a person is he?

Cl. Well, that's hard for me to answer because he has changed so much within the last four years. Before that he was very harsh. Domineering at certain times. Sometimes cruel. Not interested in things academic, they were physical things. I remember he thought that wrestling matches were great stuff. He took my brother and me to them when we were quite small, and I remember reacting to them with something in the way of shock at the bloody spectacle. I don't know why. Since then he's made a lot of improvement.

Ir. How is he now?

Cl. More gentle. More interested in academic things, more interested in political things, less interested in sports. Maybe I just notice this more now.

(The description of other members of the family is continued. The client tells about the delinquent behavior of his brother and his parents' reactions.)

Cl. My brother has a very sadistic sense of humor. Somebody on television gets trampled underfoot by a horse and he'll laugh his head off. I thought the situation was tragic. I think if he were my kid I'd get some professional help for him. But these things flow like water off my parents' backs. That's bad, I think. They've rebuked him but never sought help. He's like me. Average intelligence but he started the university and dropped out after a few weeks. Just wasn't interested in it. He seems to react only to very exciting and spectacular things. He doesn't go out for a beer or two, he goes out for 15 or 20, plus a fifth of vodka, plus three or four girls a night.

Ir. The family that you describe then, Bob, is one that seems to be rather devoid of ties. Is that right?

Cl. In a way, it is. But superficially, we're pretty good. I don't remember going on an enjoyable picnic with my parents. I don't remember ever in my life talking to either one of them for more than five minutes about any one subject. I can't remember them even talking to each other except maybe in an argument.

(After a little more description of the family, the interviewer begins to close the discussion toward the end of the hour.)

Ir. It's getting to be about the end of our time. Is there something that we've overlooked here that you think we should add in at this time?

Cl. Why, I thought of something while we were talking about something else. It's mainly sleep. When I get up in the morning, I feel very much tired, usually nauseated. And I have some trouble getting to sleep. I don't usually take sleeping pills but I have sometimes. When I was a sophomore I took No-Doz pills to keep awake and then sleeping pills to go to sleep when I wanted to.

Ir. Okay. Well, now next Wednesday, let's shift over to a conventional psychotherapy procedure. I've been trying to get background material this time. Next Wednesday we will start in with you exploring the topics which seem most important to you at that time. See you then, Bob.

Such an interview as this provides a broad survey of the person's present outlook on life and the beginnings of many aspects of his history. No doubt the reader of this abbreviated interview has already gained many impressions—a sketchy picture of what Bob Simon is like. If you see him as a serious, rather literal young man, frightened by the manifestation of almost any emotion but seeking desperately to enrich his affective experiences, a person with confidence in the power of psychotherapy whose desire to be a "good" client suggests that he tends characteristically to seek support from others, you see him as the interviewer did.[1]

The second example is an excerpt from a book on clinical interviewing by Deutsch and Murphy (1955). It illustrates an early diagnostic interview with a depressive patient. The interview follows a modified psychoanalytic technique emphasizing the patient's associations. Some of the interpretative thoughts of the interviewer are indicated in the parentheses between the comments of the interviewer (again abbreviated *Ir*) and patient (abbreviated *Pt*). The patient is a white, widowed WAC veteran aged 31. Her presenting complaint on admission to the hospital was that she was weak and exhausted. Her symptoms had started two years ago when she gave an illegitimate child up for adoption. Physical examination had disclosed very little disorder except some malnutrition. She was admitted to the psychiatric ward in a wheel chair, nervous and perturbed. On the ward she has shown marked emotional lability, throwing objects in anger at times and being very depressed at others. On one occasion she threatened suicide. The interview and the authors' comments are as follows (Deutsch & Murphy, 1955, p. 36-38):

Ir. How are you feeling today? Your doctor has told me a little about your condition and your troubles.

Pt. You want me to tell you about it, huh?

Ir. Yes, if you wish to do that.

Pt. Well what do you want to know; I mean, I don't know.

(The usual opening and usual reticence of a patient who knows so much and does not want to know. We are always primarily interested in feelings, as these are the complex, primitive, substratum roots from which grow many diffuse fantasies, ideas, rationalizations, and verbalizations.)

[1] For those readers acquainted with the MMPI, Bob Simon's code was '28 367 4 − (78) 2, 8, 16. See Chapter 8 for a partial explanation of MMPI codes.

Ir. How do you feel?

Pt. How do I feel? Well, I still have the *weakness* I had when I came. I am *tired.*

Ir. *Weak* and *tired?*

Pt. Yes.

Ir. That was the reason why you came?

(Here she appeared doubtful, so we could press forward.)

Pt. Well, yes.

Ir. There were other reasons, too?

Pt. Well, I couldn't find any other reasons to come to the hospital except that. That was all I could find. I was just exhausted. I went to the hospital, so they admitted me for exhaustion.

Ir. You had other troubles?

("Troubles" is ambiguous and was deliberately chosen to get further association to "weak," "tired.")

Pt. Oh, I had problems.

Ir. What problems do you mean?

(Problems must lead to the past and to the child.)

Pt. Well, I have financial problems, and housing problems, and *everything.*

Ir. What do you mean?

Pt. Well, if I could find a place to live and—it's hard to get along with a *child,* you know, all alone.

Ir. What do you mean, hard to get along with a *child?*

(The interviewer proceeds cautiously.)

Pt. Well, it is hard to go out and work and come home and work and pay all the expenses and everything. Of course, I don't think that's all my *troubles,* just that alone.

(Here she takes up our word, *troubles*—a good sign, so we use her word, "problems," which makes her feel understood and she feels better—laughs.)

Ir. That is only one of the problems, you mean?

Pt. That's only one, yes. (Laughs)

Ir. What are the other problems?

Pt. Well, I guess being alone is one of them too, all *alone* in the world, feeling insecure.

Ir. Alone?

(She pleads for sympathy. The interviewer cannot take sides. Why *must* she be alone?)

Pt. Oh, yes, all alone—no relatives, no family.

Ir. *Always,* you mean?

(Instead of sympathy, she is guided toward the past.)

Pt. Well, not always, no, since I was sixteen or seventeen.

Ir. Then you were on your own?

Pt. Yes.

Ir. What happened?

Pt. Well, my *family died* and *left me.*

(She talks somewhat like a child for whom the loved or hated person who left is like dead.)

Ir. Left you?
Pt. Yuh. They died.
Ir. Your parents died, you mean?
Pt. Yes, my family.
Ir. What do you mean, family?

(As soon as possible in an interview, we try to get the patient's setting in a family constellation in the past as well as the present.)

Pt. Well, mother, father, grandmother. That was all the family I had except my *sister*. She's still in the South. She's seventeen years old.
Ir. Your sister?

(She excluded the sister from the family. Did she want her to be dead? Or are there two families: one before her sister was born, and one afterwards?)

Pt. Yes.
Ir. And she can't help you?
Pt. Not much, no. I always had to help her.
Ir. You helped?
Pt. Oh, yes. Up until about two years ago.
Ir. Until fifteen you had to help her?

(Now she is also talking of helping the little girl as if she were a mother who must die. This misunderstanding of the question hints that she has returned to the past in more than memory, i.e., it indicates a regressive state.)

Pt. Yes, since fifteen, since I was fifteen.
Ir. Since you were fifteen?
Pt. Yes.
Ir. What do you mean, in which way?
Pt. Well, I had to look after her when my mother died so my father could work, and watch her, take care of her, and see that she was fed and everything.
Ir. You had to do that?

(She asked for sympathy at the level of childhood and she betrays her bad conscience in relation to her sister.)

Pt. Oh yes, sure. And then when my father died, well, she was placed in an orphanage for six years. She is now with my aunt.

(She too is an orphan and all alone.)

Ir. With your aunt?
Pt. Yes.
Ir. So you didn't have to take care of her any more?
Pt. No, I couldn't do it any more.
Ir. And now she does not need you?
Pt. No, I don't think so. She is getting old enough now; she can look after herself a little.

("A little" means she should be able to take care of herself.)

Ir. Do you miss her?
Pt. Well, yes, I do, I miss her.

Ir. Since she was almost a child to you?
Pt. That's right. Almost. Almost the same.
Ir. Since you had to take care of her?
Pt. Yes, she was with me most of the time when my father died until she was placed in an orphanage. She *always* kind of looked up to me like a *mother*.

(This important statement expresses clearly that she felt "always" like a "mother" who later lost the child. This foreshadows the future.)

The interviewer continued to explore the patient's associations in this way. This interview led to the characterization of the patient (Deutsch & Murphy, 1955, p. 61) as having had "a defective mother-child relationship" during which an "infantile hysterical neurosis" developed. The difficulties of having an illegitimate child "plus her guilt feelings over her unconscious, hostile and aggressive fantasies . . . led her to give up (lose—send away—kill) her baby and this in turn led to her giving up and acting out upon herself her sadomasochistic fantasies expressed in the form of a depression." These conclusions came, of course, from a much more extensive exploration of the case than is presented here. However, this excerpt has served to illustrate some of the features of the case. This excerpt compared with the earlier one also illustrates the differences in structuring according to the different purposes of the interviewer.

CRITICAL EVALUATION OF THE INTERVIEW AS A METHOD OF MEASUREMENT

As we must have made clear, much of the interviewing that goes on during assessment is not oriented toward measurement. It may be designed to develop rapport, to provide an opportunity for the expression of feelings, to introduce testing procedures, or to aid the patient who is in transition to another agency or treatment. However, since the interview is almost always also a method of gaining certain kinds of information or data, we are under obligation to ask questions about its reliability, validity, and any other evidences of its dependability.[2]

Such questions are complex, because the interview is not restricted to the use of any single method. Interviews are of all sorts and vary along every dimension imaginable. The characteristics of interview *processes* themselves are open to investigation. We have already mentioned some process studies, and many more will be found in the chapters on therapy. At the moment we shall look only at the *outcomes* of the interview, its contribution to the total assessment.

The question of the *reliability* of the interview method has usually been answered by comparing the judgments of different interviewers of

[2] The concepts of reliability and validity will be defined and discussed in detail in the next chapter.

the same person (technically *inter-rater reliability*). Psychiatric diagnosis is one area where reliability of this kind has been rather extensively studied. As mentioned in an earlier chapter, the problem is complicated by the need to get a system of psychiatric description that is clear and unambiguous and has been thoroughly taught to the clinicians who make the diagnoses. The heterogeneity of the patients and the coarseness of the system of classification also affect the results. Agreement between interviewers could easily be obtained if they were required to diagnose a series of patients, each one of whom was either a Mongoloid imbecile, a case of anxiety neurosis, or a chronic schizophrenic. However, a number of the studies of psychiatric diagnosis when the cases are unselected show considerable unreliability, with disagreement on as many as 50 per cent of the cases (Ash, 1949). The study by Schmidt and Fonda (1956), reviewed at the end of the last chapter, obtained higher reliability, and in cases where the training has been good and there is also good agreement on the classification scheme, reliabilities can run over .80 (Newman, Bobbitt, & Cameron, 1946). Vernon (1953), after surveying the literature on a variety of interviews, concluded that reliability coefficients of around .50 and .60 are most common.

In addition to the reasons for unreliability mentioned above, there is also interviewer bias. In the classical study of bias in interviewing, Rice (1929) arranged to have social workers interview a large number of destitute men in New York for twenty to thirty minutes, using a set of questions to guide the collecting of their economic and social histories. Each man interviewed and his interviewers were required to record their judgments of the reason for his destitution. One interviewer, a fervent prohibitionist, reported that 62 per cent of the men were poverty-stricken because they drank too much and only 7 per cent because of adverse economic conditions. Another interviewer, who was a Socialist, judged that only 22 per cent were destitute because of drink, whereas 39 per cent were reduced to poverty because of economic conditions. Rice also found that the men's own judgments tended to agree with those given by their interviewers and he called this effect "contagious bias." However, a later repetition of the study (Wyatt & Campbell, 1950) has failed to support Rice on this latter point.

We must admit that the *validity* of the interview as an assessment method is much less than could be wished. In reviewing the issue of clinical versus statistical prediction in Chapter 8 we will be pointing out that the validity of the interview is no higher than that of statistical methods, and in some studies it has proved to be lower. When the interviewing is not compared with the results of tests, its predictive validity and that of observational methods are very suspect. For instance, Vernon (1953) cited two British studies: In one (McClelland, 1942) primary school teachers' judgments of pupils did not predict secondary school performance, and in another (Himmelweit & Summerfield, 1951) the predictions of a board of university teachers interviewing entering students correlated zero with the marks these students obtained a year or two later.

The validity of the interview varies greatly with the purposes for which it is done and with the way the data and judgments of the interviewers are recorded. Some studies of estimates of intelligence by skilled interviewers have shown high correlations with test results (Hanna, 1950; Snedden, 1930). Some of the brief psychiatric screening interviews were effective in predicting gross maladjustments (Wittson & Hunt, 1951). In general, though, clinical interview methods are susceptible to distortion and the influence of personal bias. The less clearly they are structured the less reliability and validity they are likely to have. It is also very difficult to put one's finger on the parts of the interview that are invalid because objective methods of analyzing the data are almost impossible to devise. A number of interesting questions arise in relation to the problem of validity: What kinds of information can an interviewer obtain that will be most useful for the different clinical purposes? In what ways can interviews add to the validity of the assessment process when other procedures are used? How can we account for individual differences in degree of validity which different interviewers can obtain? These questions will be raised again in the chapter on assessment research.

What can we conclude about the use of the interview in clinical assessment? First, there seems to be no doubt at all that the interview is here to stay. Nearly every clinician, if allowed only one procedure for assessing a patient, would choose to use an interview. Its nonmeasurement uses alone seem to be enough to justify its usage in the opinion of clinicians. Wherever a test is available to do a certain job it will usually be better to restrict interviewing to purposes other than those competing with the test. Future answers to the problem of the proper place of the interview will depend on intensive research into interviewing processes. These may lead to the development of training programs to exploit the special advantages that interviewing undoubtedly has. In the meantime, as clinical psychologists we need to be aware of the dangers of bias and distortion and to do everything we can both to form our impressions and report them with care and skill. It is also a pretty fair conclusion that the interview is most valid when the influences and predictions attempted in the course of it are confined to what may happen in similar situations and in the *immediate* future. Interviewing gives us no license to indulge in grandiose predictions of a patient's long-time future.

SUMMARY

Clinical assessment can be analyzed according to the characteristics of its participants, the nature of the interactive process, and the sorts of tests and other procedures used. We have tried to describe what the clinician and the patient bring to the interview in the way of attitudes, purposes, emotional states, and adaptive techniques. In analyzing the interview, we have looked upon it as a transaction, a relationship, and a communication process, one that involves both verbal and nonverbal communication and that can be analyzed sequentially. It is the clinician's responsibility to keep firmly in mind the purposes of the interview and to develop its structure along lines that accord with these purposes. Important aspects of structuring are content, goals, and closeness of relationship. Among the major kinds of clinical interviews are the intake interview, the case history interview, and the mental status examination. Interviewing is mainly used for nonmeasurement purposes and with problems for which tests are not readily available. As a measuring instrument, the interview has been shown to possess questionable reliability and validity. However, the more it is structured and the better trained the interviewers are, the more it can be depended on for valid measurement. Because many of its purposes avowedly do not require measurements and because of its great flexibility, the interview is likely to continue to be the most widely used assessment procedure.

SUGGESTED READINGS

BINGHAM, W. V. D., MOORE, B. V., and GUSTAD, J. W. *How to interview.* (4th ed.) New York: Harper, 1959.

This is the fourth edition of a classic introduction to the interview. Different parts of the book differ a great deal in quality, and much of it is more pertinent to personnel practices than to clinical psychology. The first two chapters, however, contain a good review of the literature.

KAHN, R. L., and CANNELL, C. F. *The dynamics of interviewing: Theory, technique, and cases.* New York: Wiley, 1957.

This book, though primarily based on the experience of the University of Michigan Survey Research Center with the interview as it is used in surveys, goes far beyond this. The authors, who have been influenced by the theories of Lewin and Rogers, are interested in the clinical aspects and psychodynamics of the two-person interpersonal situation. The transcripts of interviews from a variety of professional settings are valuable for study and discussion.

MASLING, J. The influence of situational and interpersonal variables in projective testing. *Psychol. Bull.,* 1960, 57, 65-85.

This review is applicable to all assessment procedures, not just projective techniques. Masling reports research findings on the effects of different instructions in taking projective tests; effects of special influences upon the situation, such as stress, drugs or hypnosis; examiner influence; and influence of the subject on the examiner. The bulk of the studies do indeed indicate that changes occur as a result of such influences, but the extent of these influences and the interrelationships among them are still to be discovered.

KRASNER, L. Studies of the conditioning of verbal behavior. *Psychol. Bull.,* 1958, 55, 148-170.

Krasner reviews and compares 31 studies of verbal conditioning. The original stimulus for this very active line of research came from Skinner's ideas on operant conditioning. In the most typical situation a subject utters disconnected words continuously with the experimenter selectively reinforcing certain ones by nodding or saying something. The majority of the studies report positive results (an increase in the kind of verbal response being used as a criterion) from the use of generalized conditioned reinforcers such as "good" and "mmm-hmm."

RESEARCH EXAMPLES

Saslow, G., Matarazzo, J. D., and Guze, S. B. The stability of interaction chronograph patterns in psychiatric interviews. *J. consult. Psychol.*, 1955, 19, 417-430.

This particular study, part of a research program covering several years, furnishes important evidence on the reliability of the major research technique, the Interaction Chronograph. The authors are concerned with the development of a standardized structure in the interview which can be used for many investigations into personality. The Interaction Chronograph, originally developed by the anthropologist Chapple, is a device which allows an observer to record in time-units the behavioral interaction of two individuals in terms of some ten or more variables. The ten variables, such as tempo, dominance, and initiative, are defined in detail.

The standardized interview, which the Interaction Chronograph measures, requires the experimenter-interviewer to follow a definite sequence. In the present research there were three stages: (1) 10 minutes of nondirective interviewing (the free period); (2) then a period of silence on the part of the interviewer, either to the extent of 12 remarks by the subject or for 15 minutes (the silent stress period); (3) 5 minutes of free nondirective interviewing; (4) a period in which the interviewer interrupts 12 remarks of the patient, or waits 15 minutes (the interrupting stress period); and (5) a 5-minute free interview. In total there are 20 minutes of free interviewing plus a maximum of 30 minutes of stress.

In this study 20 patients from an outpatient clinic were interviewed independently by two different psychiatrists. The order of interviewing the patients was randomized between the two interviewers. The interviewer always started out as follows: "My name is Dr. ——. Can you tell me how you happened to come to the clinic at this time?" An observer using the Interaction Chronograph apparatus in the next room counted interactions and recorded the interviews. The resulting scores for each patient with the two different interviewers were correlated and similarities and differences in parts of the interview were studied.

In general, there were highly significant correlations indicating high reliability and marked stability in patient-interaction patterns under the same conditions. However, when the interviewer introduced stress in his approach according to the predetermined plan, there were marked changes in the patient's reactions.

This study furnished an important foundation for later work that investigated many other characteristics of persons in such a situation. For a more recent review of the research program see Saslow and Matarazzo (1959). Among still later reports in this extensive series, Phillips et al (1961) have shown some interesting relationships between Interaction Chronograph variables and content variables from the same interview. Although correlation coefficients are modest, the data do suggest that persons who speak faster and less often have interview content that is more oriented toward others and play more dominant social roles. Patients who tend to submit to interruptions and are more hesitant show more noninterpersonal concerns in their speech content and are more submissively hostile with others.

If the reader consults the original article reported here, he may find it interesting to compare this kind of research on interviewing with an entirely different one by Giedt (1955) in the preceding article in the journal. Giedt recorded ordinary interviews with four patients and presented them in various forms to clinicians to study the influence of different cues upon prediction of patients' responses. Surprisingly there is a suggestion that visual cues may impair predictions.

STARKWEATHER, J. A. Content-free speech as a source of information about the speaker. *J. abnorm. soc. Psychol.*, 1956, 52, 394-402.

A distinction can be made between the verbal and vocal aspects of speech. The verbal aspect has to do with words and linguistic units, and the vocal with tonal variation and voice quality. Some theorists hypothesize that there are two kinds of communication going on, with the verbal channel carrying semantic information and the vocal channel carrying affective communication. Verbal-vocal incongruence may be characteristic of persons in conflict. In this particular study (the author's Ph.D. thesis), these different characteristics of speech were related to the theory that persons with essential hypertension are in a constant struggle over the control of hostile impulses.

Subjects were drawn from military officers participating in an assessment study. Three groups of 10 each were selected on the basis of two measures: blood pressure and scores on a scale by Harris for measuring the hypertensive personality syndrome (HPS). Of those with high blood pressure, 10 had high HPS scores and 10 low HPS scores; the third group had low scores on both measures.

Each subject's voice was recorded in a role-playing situation and three 20-second samples were selected for this study. The resulting 90 speech samples were presented to college student judges in three forms: a normal recording, a typewritten transcript, and a mechanically filtered content-free recording. The judges were asked to rate the speech samples on scales of aggressiveness and pleasantness.

The results were studied by analysis of variance applied to these ratings. The reliability of the judgments was acceptable. The high blood pressure groups showed a significant lack of verbal-vocal congruence. With combined judgments, significant differences were found between groups for "aggressive" judgments of both content-free and normal information. Starkweather interpreted the finding of greater relative usefulness of content-free speech as evidence for the importance of the vocal aspect in assessing personality.

For another approach to the analysis of emotionality in interviews, see Dittmann and Wynne (1961). These researchers coded interview excerpts for linguistic characteristics (junctures, stress, and pitch) and paralinguistic features (vocalizations, voice quality, and physiological set). While they established reliability for the linguistic coding, they were not able to demonstrate any relationship to emotionality. They concluded that their detailed breakdown into vocal elements seemed less promising and practical than Starkweather's more global approach.

6 Clinical Use of Tests

Ask any intelligent person to free associate to the word *psychologist* and the chances are that before many words are out he will mention *tests*. The use of psychological tests in the United States has exceeded the expectations of even wild dreamers a half century ago. A few years ago *Newsweek* stated that the annual sale of test booklets and answer sheets to schools was 122 million and the figure had increased 50 per cent over sales five years earlier (reported in Goldman, 1961, p. 1). Surveys of test usage in business, industry, and government would be equally impressive. Testing in the large organizations is used mainly for the institutional decision-making we have discussed in Chapter 4. Even in clinical settings where testing is much more on an individual basis, there is a great amount of testing going on. In public clinical services it has been estimated that there are at least 700,000 individuals tested every year (Sundberg, 1961*a*).

This wave of testing in America, now extending to other countries, is not without its drawbacks and opponents. Columnists decry the inaccuracies and the kinds of values perpetrated by tests. (For example, see Banesh Hoffman's article, "The Tyranny of Multiple Choice Tests" in *Harpers*, 1961.) There is no doubt that there can be much injustice from naïve and misguided use of tests. Psychologists themselves are concerned about the ethical and scientific problems involved.

The solution is not the prohibition of all tests. *Not* using a test when a good one is available is as unethical as misusing one. The truth of the matter is that *tests are tools*. In the hands of a capable and creative person they can be used with remarkable outcomes. In the hands of a fool or an unscrupulous person they become a pseudoscientific perversion. The student of clinical psychology needs to learn all he can about these

131

tools so as to use them wisely. He will need to know which tests to use with which kinds of patients in which kinds of situations. He will need to master the research studies on tests and learn how to contribute to greater understanding of them by his own research.

The purpose of this chapter is to cover the general principles of the clinical use of tests. Specific tests will be used as examples. Appendix A lists 50 important assessment techniques to which the reader should refer for a brief description and for further reading. The details of specific tests are too numerous to cover here. The student of clinical psychology will need special courses on tests and supervised experience with some of the most important tests during the course of his training.

SOME EXAMPLES OF WHAT TESTS CONTRIBUTE IN CLINICAL CASES

Why are tests used? There comes a time when the less systematic procedures are not enough. In planning a building an architect not only looks at the site and talks with the client about what he wants, he must measure exactly and order the correct amount of materials. Likewise a physician giving a physical examination is not content with a patient's report of his symptoms, he measures the patient's blood pressure, looks at the optic disk for signs of intracranial pressure, and taps the patellar tendon to check the knee jerk. These are standardized procedures which the architect or the physician can use to compare with past experiences they have had and to indicate problems that need to be solved. They are tests and forms of measurement.

Likewise it is true that a highly experienced clinician can do much assessment by interviewing and observation alone. But in order to do a thorough and accurate job he would need to have many of the qualities of a test itself—breadth of coverage of the given area, subjective norms so as to compare a patient with others, and accurate knowledge of the relationships of present and future behavior. There are few clinicians who are as accurate as well-prepared tests. As we shall see elsewhere when clinical methods are pitted against statistical methods, it is the clinician who comes out second best. The implication of these findings is that tests and other statistical devices should be used whenever they are available and appropriate, and the clinician's time saved for other purposes. The following are some examples of how tests might usefully be brought into assessment:

On a neurology ward of a hospital, a psychologist is asked to determine whether Mrs. Tyson's symptoms, loss of memory and vague thinking, indicate a hysterical reaction or brain damage. He reads the medical chart and talks with the referring neurologist. The neurological findings are minimal. The psychologist decides to administer tests that have often been used in such a differential diagnosis. One test, the Bender-Gestalt, frequently shows rotations and distortions when a brain-damaged person copies the figures. But Mrs. Tyson does not show such changes. Furthermore on the MMPI she shows a pattern that is common for hysterical patients. The psychologist's report to the neurologist helps him to make a diagnosis and suggests that a program of psychotherapy be instituted.

Alfred Norton, nine years old, was referred to the child guidance clinic. He had grown up on a farm and at the age of six started school in a small town nearby. He was obviously slow in school work. He could read only a few simple words. He usually played with younger children or by himself. On the recommendation of the teacher and because the school had no psychologist to test him, the family brought Alfred to the clinic. After an intake interview with the mother, the clinic staff immediately decided that Alfred's level of intellectual functioning should be carefully evaluated. Interviewing Alfred or generally observing him would be helpful and interesting, but would not settle the important question of his potential for going on with the regular school routine. Another equally important purpose the psychologist and the rest of the staff had in mind was the need to ascertain whether there were additional reasons for his school difficulties and whether they could be corrected. Were there eye troubles that could be corrected with glasses? Did Alfred have perceptual distortions suggestive of brain damage? Was he insufficiently motivated to do well in school because of fears, anxieties or other emotional problems? Among the various aspects of intellectual functioning, did he do better on some than others? If so, how could these be used to help the teacher in her program for teaching Alfred to read? All these questions, and doubtless others, occurred to the psychologist as he was planning his appointment with Alfred. He chose to give the boy the Stanford-Binet because this well-standardized and developed test provides for testing lower mental age levels than another major test he considered. He chose also to administer the Gray Oral Reading Test in order to get a quick indication of Alfred's reading ability. He decided to keep in reserve other possibilities, such as the Bender Visual-Motor Gestalt Test or a storytelling test, until he could see how well Alfred did with the other tests and how much his attention wandered.

Another psychologist works in the state penitentiary. He is developing selection methods for therapy groups. In a professional journal he has read about a behavior rating scale which has given some promising results in assessing the potentiality for effective interaction in a VA group. The psychologist decides to use this test and some other procedures in a project with the combined purposes of research and therapy for the prisoners.

These are just a few examples to remind us of how tests make special contributions in assessment. The variety of patterns in which assessment techniques might be conducted is infinite. Tests may or may not be given. Among tests, there are literally thousands that might be chosen. The order and timing of the testing may vary. Each case needs to be planned to carry out the best strategy for answering the important question—to arrive at the special goals of assessment in the case, as discussed in Chapter 4.

One assessment consideration of special significance is the planning for psychotherapy. This question is of such importance that we will discuss it with each chapter in the section on psychotherapy. A book that is of particular interest in this connection is *Case Studies in Counseling and Psychotherapy* by Burton (1959). The purpose of the book was to examine a wide variety of theoretical approaches and kinds of clients or patients. Each therapist answered a set of questions about his case. For our present purposes there were two questions of special interest: "Optimally, what criteria do you use for accepting or rejecting patients for psychotherapy?" and "Do you make a diagnosis before psychotherapy begins?" Though this is not a formal study, in reading over the cases and the answers to these questions, one can obtain indirectly an impression of the value placed on tests in therapy planning. In the fifteen exemplary cases formal testing was mentioned in only three instances. The therapists made their decisions and determined the course of therapy on the basis of interviews primarily. In the child therapy cases there was also use of informal procedures such as drawing, storytelling, and doll play. The collection of cases in this book was not specifically intended to sample the use of tests with therapy, but it does serve to point out a serious question about the use of tests. They seem to fail to meet the needs of many practicing therapists for deep understanding of the patient, or perhaps they introject something into the relationship which therapists do not want.

If we look at books on diagnosis and research, we find a very different picture. An example is *Clinical Studies of Personality,* also edited by Burton (1955) in cooperation with Harris. In this book nearly every case demonstrates the use of several psychological tests. There are a wide variety of not only traditional tests, but also specially designed measures and informal assessment procedures. In any research project in the clinical area, including research on psychotherapy, there is, of course, an extensive use of tests.

We might formulate a tentative answer to the question posed at the start of this section: Why are tests used? They are not used much when the purpose is the establishment of a close intensive working relationship with an individual. They are used extensively when the purpose is the objective study of the person. The contribution of tests seems to be greatest whenever careful and standardized ways of comparing people are needed. In fact a test has been defined as "a systematic procedure for comparing the behavior of two or more persons" (Cronbach, 1960, p. 21). *Systematic comparison* is the strength of tests. Human experience and human memory are limited and fallible as compared with normative tables and correlation coefficients. To what extent these systematic comparisons might help in psychotherapy itself is still an open question. There are certain other questions and limitations about tests which we will discuss at the end of the chapter.

TESTS FREQUENTLY USED IN CLINICAL SERVICES

What tests are most frequently used in clinical work? In the national survey (Sundberg, 1961) we mentioned earlier, 185 hospitals, counseling centers, and clinics answered a questionnaire inquiring into psychological assessment practices and checked the frequency with which they used specified tests. There were thirteen tests that were used by at least half of the respondents. Starting with the most frequently used tests, they were the following: Rorschach, Draw-a-Person, Thematic Apperception Test, Bender Visual-Motor Gestalt Test, Stanford-Binet, Wechsler Adult Intelligence Scale, Minnesota Multiphasic Personality Inventory, Wechsler-Bellevue Intelligence Test, Goodenough Draw-A-Man Test, Wechsler Intelligence Scale for Children, Kuder Preference Record, House-Tree-Person test, and the Goldstein-Scheerer Tests of Abstract and Concrete Thinking.

This survey also investigated the major changes in clinical usage of tests in the last quarter century using the results of earlier surveys (Louttit & Browne, 1947). Between 1935 and 1959, there was a 76 per cent turnover among the top 20 tests. Only a quarter of those that ranked in the top bracket a quarter century ago still remain there. The top 20 tests probably account for the majority of all clinical test administrations. The staying power of the Stanford-Binet in its various revisions and the Goodenough Draw-a-Man are outstanding. The most striking changes have been the increase in the use of projective techniques and the decreased emphasis on intelligence testing.

The survey revealed differences, of course, among the different kinds of clinical services sampled. Particularly notable are the differences between counseling centers, on the one hand, and state hospitals or similar institutions and out-patient clinics, on the other. Counseling centers, confronted with problems of vocational and educational decisions, naturally make more use of tests, and they emphasize vocational interest tests, like the Kuder Preference Record and the Strong Vocational Interest Blank, and ability and aptitude tests. The more psychiatrically oriented hospitals and clinics emphasize more the tests of psychopathology and personality such as the Rorschach and MMPI. The overlap among other kinds of services is fairly great.

It may be well to mention that a test's popularity should not of itself be taken as a mark of validity or effectiveness nor of what test experts might recommend. There are many possible influences on test popularity, such as ease of administration and scoring, current trends in the training of psychologists, and test promotion by publishers. The correlation between rate of publication on a particular test and the extent to which the test is used was only .46. This suggests that many of the most popular tests are not generating much research. Examples of large discrepancies between popularity and publication, with the former running ahead, are the Draw-A-Person test and the Vineland Social Maturity Scale. Though a clinician will not ordinarily prefer tests because they are popular, he should be well acquainted with them since he is likely to run into them often in his practice and in clinical publications. The list mentioned earlier in this section does not exhaust the tests he should know, since many good tests, either new or not widely known, are not on this list. The reader can refer to Appendix A for a list of tests the authors consider important to know.

HOW TESTS ARE DEVELOPED

"Case histories" of our leading tests would make interesting stories. Each is the product of an interaction between a social need, professional traditions and standards, individual creative insights, and careful scientific research. The famous Binet intelligence test, as most students know, grew out of a problem first faced by school officials in Paris who wanted to do something about the children who seemed not to profit from regular classes. Binet was shrewd enough to realize that the problem could only be met *by measuring, not a limited form of behavior like reaction time, but complex activities like following directions, solving problems, and employing words correctly.* Then followed decades of research during which Binet and those who became interested in the same problem developed the potentialities of this idea. Binet contributed the concept of mental age; Stern, the intelligence quotient; Terman and his co-workers, the well-constructed Stanford-Binet Scale which has recently been revised by Merrill. This test alone has been involved in countless decisions about children, the breadth and variety of its applications adding much to the understanding of intelligence in general.

The Rorschach technique[1] grew out of the insights of a Swiss psy-

---

[1] The word *technique* is frequently used to designate the less standardized assessment procedures such as projective techniques, and the words *inventory* and *questionnaire* are applied to paper-and-pencil procedures for evaluation of personality and attitudes. The APA Committee on Psychological Tests (1954) advises that the word *test* be restricted to well-standardized procedures, such as most intelligence and

chiatrist who noted the differences in what patients reported seeing in inkblots. He surmised that these differences significantly related to their psychopathology. An important underlying notion stated later by others as the "projective hypothesis" is that *people confronted with an ambiguous or unstructured stimulus situation tend to respond to it in terms of their own inner needs, attitudes, and more generalized ways of perceiving the world.* Binet and others had discovered the potentialities in the common inkblot for evoking imagination, but Rorschach went farther. He developed a standard set of inkblots and systematic methods for scoring and interpretating the results. He got ideas for his interpretations partly empirically from giving the test to a large number of patients and partly also from Jung's theory of personality. Whether the patient chose, for example, to respond to the whole blot or to some detailed part of it was taken to be symptomatic of a basis and characteristic interest in large ideas or in small details of the world. In a similar way, reactions involving color, movement, and form were found to be significant indicators of underlying character. After Rorschach's death in 1922, others began to see great potentialities in his system. In the decades of the 30's the Rorschach began to spread rapidly both in Europe and America. It reached a peak of popularity along with other projective techniques in the decade following World War II. Present-day use of the Rorschach is based upon an accumulation of experience and research in which a great many people have shared. There are several major scoring and interpretive systems. All told there are more publications on the Rorschach than on any other psychological test.

The Minnesota Multiphasic Personality Inventory (the MMPI) is an altogether different sort of test, also with a story of its own. Midway in the 1930's, Hathaway, a clinical psychologist, and McKinley, a neuropsychiatrist, saw great potential usefulness in supplementing the psychiatric interview with an inventory of statements which could be subjected to statistical analysis. For example, the patient could be asked to respond "true" or "false" to such statements as "I frequently have headaches," "Someone is plotting against me," and "My family does not like the kind of friends I have." There had been much discouragement over inventories which had preceded the MMPI. Those earlier tests had mostly consisted of items scored according to the author's notions of what the item indicated. This "rational" approach assumed first that the designer of the test knew the meaning of the item to the subject and second, that the subject was giving an honest self-report. Hathaway and McKinley's most important idea was that sets of items, or scales, of the inventory could be developed empirically (instead of rationally) by *selecting items which statistically differentiated between normal and*

---

ability tests. However, in this book we will follow common usage and frequently use the word *test* as a generic title for all kinds of systematic assessment procedures.

abnormal groups. For instance, only items which depressed patients answered significantly more often than normal people were included in the Depression scale. Thus all sorts of items were useful, even ones that the authors themselves might not have anticipated—subtle as well as obvious. There were other important ideas growing out of this basic notion. For instance, the MMPI makes use of scales of test-taking attitude, providing some indication when a patient is distorting or faking his responses. Research starting in 1937 with a WPA project had produced by 1945 the major part of the MMPI. Since that time many people have used the test and added to "MMPI lore." There are at least one-hundred additional scales, sets of test items, which purport to measure personality characteristics such as anxiety, ego strength, and hostility. The MMPI had been responsible for more publications than any other personality inventory to date.

Similar accounts could be told about many other psychological tests. The Strong Vocational Interest Blank, for instance, made use of empirical methods of selecting items even before the MMPI. This test, the life work of E. K. Strong, measures the degree of similarity between an individual's interests and those of samples of persons who have been highly successful in certain occupations and professions. The test is a tool of great importance in the hands of vocational counselors all over the country. The Thematic Apperception Test, developed as part of Murray's assessment program at Harvard, provided a way of inferring characteristic needs and perceptions of environmental "presses" of a person through stories elicited from him "projectively." The Goldstein-Scheerer Tests of Abstract and Concrete Thinking were developed over the years from close observation of brain-injured people and from theories about the way their thinking is limited and obstructed. The Wechsler tests, so widely used in clinical testing of intelligence, consist of a battery of different subtests. The Wechsler IQ is based on deviation from the average for the subject's own age group rather than on Binet-type mental age. A great many other tests have contributed much to clinical assessment, many as tools with which to explore individual differences in personality and some of them as evidence for particular theories of personality or psychopathology. Despite their range and accomplishments, the need for good new procedures is far from satisfied, and the future for research in these areas is indeed bright.

The fact must be faced, however, that the development of a good test is a long and arduous process. It may begin when a psychologist with an original twist in his thinking fastens upon some trait he is determined to assess—his domain of interest—and has a hunch about a new method of testing it. He defines this domain of interest usually in terms of some ultimate goal—a dimension or scale that he would like to have available. Behind the construction of the test, no matter how empirical the process, there is some theoretical notion of what should go into it and what it should do. Three theoretical sources of dimensions can be discerned: (1) personality theory, such as the Jungian typologies or Freudian stages of fixation; (2) theories of internal consistency, such as the proposals of factor analysis that dimensions should be derived out of the intercorrelation of items; and (3) concepts found to be in use in the culture. The latter might be occupations, which Strong used in constructing his test. They might be differentiations made in handling social problems—psychiatric diagnoses (such as used by the MMPI), levels of mental retardation, delinquency, and so forth.

No matter what the source of the scale or dimension the test-maker is ultimately trying to achieve, there are various procedures for selecting the items or stimuli. The principal division which we have already mentioned in telling about the MMPI, here is between a *rational* versus an *empirical* way of choosing items. Using a rational, or *a priori* approach, the test-maker reasons logically from his theory about what content should go into a scale and writes out items to fit his theory. Using an empirical approach, the test-maker starts out the same way but collects a great many items into an item pool. At the same time he selects criterion groups who will be answering the items. In the final form of the test he uses only the items which statistically differentiate between these groups.

Following the initial development of content and dimensions there are four *principal* aspects for the test-maker to perfect. The test must provide for systematic use by others, providing a *standardized method of administration and scoring.* There must be comparison groups or norms against which to judge an individual's results. When the test is nearing its final form, the test-maker must study its *reliability* and *validity*. These concepts will be explored in detail later in this chapter. Even after the test is published in its completed form, there will be much to learn about it—applications to different problems, new studies of validity, new norms from different samples. As a guide to the person who is developing a test and to the user evaluating it, the American Psychological Association (APA Committee on Psychological Tests, 1954) has provided a manual of recommendations.

A CONCEPTUAL FRAMEWORK FOR THE TEST-TAKING PROCESS

In evaluating and interpreting tests, it is important to become aware of everything that may affect the results we obtain from their use. The test response, which is a sample of behavior, is a function of both the person and the stimulus configuration. The stimulus configuration in turn may be analyzed into test stimuli and their context. The test stimulus is usually the main focus of the patient's attention, but many other features of the physical and social environment may affect the way he responds.

We can control the test stimulus itself sufficiently by duplicating the test materials so that they are the same for everyone. The context in which the test is taken is more difficult to control. A number of external factors like lighting, timing, and test instructions can be standardized, but how an individual is going to interpret the testing context is another matter. In administering personality tests, one of the first things we learn is that every person is different in his understanding of the test situation. It may be as important to know *how* a person takes a test as what test he took.

In recent years considerable interest has been awakened in what we may call *response style*. This phenomenon, sometimes also called "response set," or more broadly, "test-taking attitude," is illustrated when a subject manifests a more or less consistent tendency to make a particular kind of response to a test. Some response styles are related to the form of the test stimulus. The familiar "error of central tendency" in rating is one example; that is, when in doubt about how to check a particular trait, some raters tend to check the middle position. Research has shown that the psychologist can deliberately alter the average ratings of a group by moving the range of choices for answers up or down. Response styles vary from individual to individual, however, not just in dependence on the form of the test. Some individuals, for instance, manifest more of a tendency to guess in taking a test, and so answer many questions which others would leave blank. Other response styles which have been studied extensively are *social desirability,* the tendency to endorse items supposedly esteemed by one's peers (Edwards, 1957, 1959); *defensiveness,* the tendency to deny weaknesses (Smith, 1959) and its opposite, *self-disclosure* (Jourard, 1959); *acquiescence,* the tendency to agree or answer "true" to test items (Couch & Keniston, 1960); and *deviation,* the tendency to be different or take an extreme position on various kinds of items (Berg, 1958, 1959). Confronted with such response styles, there is a difference between the psychometrically inclined psychologists who seem to see them as sources of error in testing that need to be eliminated or corrected, and the clinically inclined psychologists who pounce on them as valuable indicators of personality. There have been some attempts to introduce controls for response style, notably the Edwards Personal Preference Schedule, which forces the subject to choose between alternatives matched on social desirability. However, the effectiveness of this procedure is questionable. Other tests, like the MMPI (Meehl, 1945), attempt to take advantage of test-taking attitudes as aids that can help in interpretation. In any case, all of us can agree that it is important to try to understand the expectations of the subject in the testing situation. A suspicious patient, afraid that his responses are going to be used against him, will naturally approach a test differently than a relaxed, sociable person. The free-wheeling and careless psychopath may not even read many of the items on a questionnaire. If we can clearly identify a person's way of going about taking a test and see it through his special purposes, we are already well along in our interpretation of him as a person. An advantage in individually administered tests, like the Wechsler tests or most projective techniques, is that one has an opportunity to observe the patient closely and to get clues about his attitudes toward the test. When using paper-and-pencil tests, the clinician must be especially alert to detect these attitudes: usually he will want to chat enough with the patient in administering the test to understand what is going on.

A number of research studies have also demonstrated the influence of *situational and interpersonal variables* upon test results. Masling (1960), in a review of these studies, distinguishes (*a*) influences due to the methods of administration, such as instructing experimental subjects to make a good or bad impression or emphasizing particular features of the test stimuli; (*b*) influences due to the testing situation, such as stress induced by lack of sleep or by social isolation or the influence of drugs or hypnosis or special training and experience; (*c*) influences traceable to the examiner, intentional or otherwise, such as his physical characteristics, the "warmth" he displays toward the subject, or the sorts of verbal behavior he happens to reinforce; and (*d*) influences originating in the subject, himself, such as his friendliness or hostility. The subject's past experience is certain to play some part in the way he faces the sociocultural implications of the testing situation, also his previous personal experiences with tests or similar challenging situations. Although much more research needs to be done in this area, there seems to be ample evidence that most of the factors mentioned can influence the outcome of a test. The subject faced with the testing situation, which is always more or less unstructured, will utilize all available cues as to how he should see his task. The more clearly he knows what he is supposed to do and the less he is disturbed by his own anxieties and by outside distractions, the more sure we can be that the test is doing what it is supposed to do.

In summary, then, we can list a great many things which affect a test response, which need to be considered both in constructing a test and in interpreting the data obtained from it:

Stimulus characteristics
    The test stimulus content per se.
    The form of the test as it affects response set.
    Sequential or patterning effects of previous parts of the test on following ones.
    Method of administration.

The physical context and outside distractions.
The interpersonal context, including examiner influences.

Characteristics of the person
   Response style and test-taking attitude, including interpersonal motivations
      in the situation, such as defensiveness or acquiescence.
   Physiological-psychological conditions, such as fatigue, emotional strain, and
      fluctuations in attention and memory.
   Ability to comprehend test instructions and items.
   Sociocultural interpretations of the items.
   Personal experience with the stimuli.
   "Inner" variables, e.g. more enduring to attributes of personality, such as
      motives, conflicts, defenses.

From such a list we can see that test interpretation is not simple. The "projective hypothesis" which states that a person projects into an ambiguous stimulus situation his own personal needs and wishes now begins to be seen as constituting only one way of interpreting his responses. Further problems arise when we start raising questions about how safely these responses may be used as a basis for generalizing to his actions in everyday life. A later chapter will go on to a more detailed examination of test interpretations.

EVALUATION OF TESTS

Before one can judge the worth of a test, he must know a good deal about it—*become acquainted with the test*. There are several sources of information about any test. The one most quickly thought of is its manual. A general reference of great value is the Buros *Mental Measurements Yearbook* in its various editions (Buros, 1941, 1949, 1953, 1959), which lists tests, authors, and publishers and includes thorough and critical reviews. A third good source of information are the textbooks on psychological testing (e.g., Anastasi, 1961; Cronbach, 1960; Nunnally, 1959) Specimen copies of tests can be usually obtained from the publishers or copies can be obtained through universities or testing centers. It is often a good idea to take the test oneself while one is as naïve as possible about it. This may furnish one with a "patient's eye view" and point out problems of administration and interpretation. Or the test may be tried out on friends and, if possible, on a sample of the kind of subjects with whom it will eventually be used. If some subjects are interviewed afterward, this will throw further light on test-taking attitudes and reactions, and also evoke questions and doubts from them.

It may be wise—in fact it usually is—to go beyond the test manuals, Buros' *Yearbooks*, and texts to the important journal articles on a test, and if necessary, additional material can usually be had by writing the author or by consulting testing experts in the community. Because new tests are always coming out and old ones become outdated or prove inadequate, the testing situation is continually changing.

Actually the process of becoming acquainted with a good test never ceases. As we become increasingly familiar with a test, we usually see more and more in it. Thus in many ways, older tests may be more valuable than new ones—because the clinician has built up his own dependable internalized methods of using them. The clinical utility of a test improves with age if it is being continually studied. Experienced Rorschachers, "MMPI'ers," or Wechsler specialists can somehow extract much more from a protocol or profile than even the literature on it claims. At the same time, we must remember that this kind of experience and clinical know-how has its dangers. A clinician can become so "overly sold" on a test that he loses his objectivity and willingness to be critical of it. He can no longer see its limitations. The antidote for such hardening of the testing arteries is continuing research on how the test is actually working out in one's own situation. Checking one test against other tests, checking with other clinicians, seeking for confirming or disconfirming impressions independently derived, and following a tested patient's history and subsequent behavior may keep the cutting edge of a test fresh and sharp.

Another part of the process is *evaluating the practical aspects of the test*. One such practical question is: What does a given testing procedure cost in materials, training, time, and effort? Is its contribution to decision-making about the persons who compose our clientele worth the cost? Every test requires certain amounts of time from the patient, the examiner, the scorer, and the interpreter. Some tests like the MMPI, CPI, and various paper-and-pencil intelligence tests require very little administrative supervision. They do require that the patient be free to spend perhaps an hour answering a test, but time may not be much of a problem on a hospital ward or in an out-patient clinic where the patient has to do a good deal of waiting anyway. Another consideration is whether it is likely to hold the interest of the individual tested. This is especially important with children. The items in tests like the Stanford-Binet have been selected especially with this in mind. Other practical matters are the amount of training needed to administer and score a test, the availability of equivalent forms if it is necessary to repeat it, and, of course, its cost.

A psychologist in any particular clinic or hospital also needs to check about *fitting a test into the general framework of local clinical procedures*. He must be satisfied that a test will "pay-off" in supplying answers and generating hypotheses that meet both his own particular needs and those of the institution for which he works. If such a test does not at first appear acceptable to the clinician's colleagues, he must either drop it or be able to convince them that it is worthwhile in terms of eliciting the kind of behavior in which he and his colleagues should be interested. Technical validity studies furnish partial answers, perhaps, but even more important ones spring from the way the clinician conceives his task and the opportunities it gives him to help his institution fulfill its purpose. A highly reliable test valid for predicting school grades or recidivism might not seem at all interesting to a particular clinician because it does not provide the heuristic, hypothesis-generating characteristics which he deeply desires either for research or clinical purposes.

Lastly and very importantly, there is the process of *evaluating the technical adequacy of a test*. Unfortunately, there is not always as much technical information about a test as one could wish. Also, since each clinical situation is somewhat unique, a clinician cannot assume exact correspondence between the situation from which studies have been reported and his own situation. In evaluating the technical adequacy of tests, the research attitude is extremely important—a concern for evidence both negative and positive, a detached willingness to "test the test." Convincing sales talks are no substitute for statistical evidence.

The question of technical adequacy involves the matters of validity, reliability, objectivity of scoring, norms, and interpretation aids. Validity ranks first in significance; here is the "meaning" of the test. We shall devote the next sections to validity and reliability. *Scoring objectivity* is a problem only when judgment enters where numbers must be assigned or the responses be classified by categories. Evidence for scoring objectivity or lack of it is often discussed under the term *inter-rater reliability*, the degree of similarity between the quantitative judgments made by several persons. Test *norms* permit us to know how a patient's performance compares with that of other persons with whom he may be appropriately compared. Test publishers often furnish norms for a number of different classes of subjects so that the appropriate one may be chosen. Some research workers are beginning to realize the desirability of additional *aids to test interpretation*. For instance, test-users can be supplied with a list of adjectives or descriptive statements which have been proved to characterize high and low scorers on a test (See Gough, 1957; Meehl, 1956a). It is a safe prediction that future test research will result in further developments along this line.

VALIDITY

Put in simplest terms, knowledge of a test's validity answers such questions as: What does the test result mean? What is the test good for? What can be accomplished with it? Does it work? Does use of the test enable any psychologist to perform his task better? The concept of validity, then, is basic to the whole idea of a test. Its ramifications tie in the nature of scientific experiments and even the philosophy of science, since it involves the concept of evidence. Validity, unlike reliability, reaches out to something other than the test itself. One cannot simply ask: How valid is Test X? The question should be: How valid is Test X *for* predicting school achievement, or *for* differentiating between depression and schizophrenia? Research on a test's validity tells the kinds of decisions for which it can be used profitably. Validity is not just the degree with which a test measures what it purports to measure, as many textbooks say. What a test may be used for may not be apparent at the time of publication. To study a test's validity is to study its value for many purposes. With increasing knowledge of a test's performance, its validity in a variety of applications becomes better known.

How does one make the connection between the test and any given variable we would like to be describing or predicting? There are two general ways—by thinking about the test and by trying it out in the field of human action—by logical or speculative ways and by empirical ways. The ultimate proof of the pudding is always empirical demonstration—does it work? No matter how much the protagonist of a test may theorize, one finally must ask him what are his correlations and significance figures. However, with psychological testing now in its growing phase, there are very many areas of human assessment for which we just do not have sufficient empirical evidence. Until the research results are in, we must test our impressions against logic and theory. We study test items to see if they adequately sample the domain or area we are interested in. We must critically examine not only content but also the instructions and the item form itself. By logical analysis and psychological understanding we attempt to discern what goes into the responses to the test. This understanding requires that we become intimately acquainted with the test—take it ourselves, give it to others, peruse the items, interrogate subjects who have taken it.

Sometimes we run across the term *face validity*. This term refers to the logical or apparent validity of a test. For instance, the Meier Art Judgment Test involves having the subject choose the better picture in a set of two pictures, one a painting done by a master and another picture a good deal like it but deliberately altered in such a way as to violate some principle of good composition. There are many sets like this on the test. It is assumed that a preponderance of choices of the original painting indicates good artistic judgment. The test is then said to have face validity. The question arises: validity for what? In sober logic and without further evidence all we are entitled to claim is that people who score high on this test apparently have good artistic judgment, since they agree with the people who developed the test. If we use the score for choosing persons who possess artistic creativity, or for selecting applicants who are likely to do well in art school, we are making claims which go far beyond the test and which need to be checked empirically.

Similar reasoning applies to rating scales used with psychiatric patients. A behavioral checklist such as may be used by attendants in an attempt to get at the personal and social adequacy of patients may have face validity. An aide checks whether a patient dresses himself or not, whether he gets in fights with others or not, and so forth. The scale would consist of a series of items like this, with the total score being the number of positive or constructive activities checked for a patient. Such a scale provides a good way of getting a record of a patient's behavior. But when we generalize from this behavior-rating scale and assume it reveals how constructively the patient will behave at other times in other places, we are drawing unwarranted conclusions. When the scale is put to some special use—for instance, for selecting patients who are permitted to leave the hospital on trial visits or for predicting who will respond to therapy—we must ask the empirical question: What is the validity for this purpose? We must subject it to an empirical test.

The research designs most often used in studies of empirical validity are of two sorts: comparisons of groups and correlations between different measures within the same group. In both designs the basic question is whether the test can discriminate between persons who have the trait we are interested in and those who do not. A matter of crucial significance in studying a test's validity is the selection of a *criterion*— the index or measure of outcome or some other characteristic to which we want the test to relate. It must be a reliable and quantified measure. Often several criteria may be used. For instance, in predicting success on a job, we may use supervisor's ratings, amount of work produced, employee's ratings of satisfaction, or amount of turnover in a job. The criterion must be "external" to the test, that is, something must be known about it wholly independently of any knowledge provided by the test. If a test is devised for the purpose of differentiating between neurotics and normals, the criterion group could be a group of patients diagnosed as neurotic by psychiatrists who did not have the aid of the test in making the diagnosis. The crucial question of whether the test is any good or not would hinge on whether test scores of neurotics were statistically different from normals. The problem becomes more complex when a variable like "anxiety" or "an unresolved Oedipus Complex" becomes the "criterion," for they have not been clearly defined behaviorally. As we shall see later in discussing construct validity, such intrapsychic states or conditions may more properly be spoken of as having behavioral indicators instead of being called criteria. Criteria must be exact, operationally defined, measures of what we wish to predict or describe. Several cautions must be kept in mind when one is evaluating validity. If the groups are large, for instance, made-up of one or two hundred individuals, significant group differences seem to be obtained rather readily. However, these differences may be of little value for psychological purposes because the overlap between the groups is large. One should always look for some measure of overlap when validity figures for large groups are reported. Another common but misleading matter is a report on validity of a test based entirely on the sample used in deriving the original scales. If items are selected because they are statistically significant in the original group, then naturally any validity coefficients are likely to be high for that group. This problem can be solved by applying the test to another group—by *cross-validating* the test. Other cautions can be found in the *Technical Recommendations* of the American Psychological Association (1954).

Another problem that enters here is the need to compare validity measures with *base rates*. As Meehl and Rosen have shown, in an excellent discussion (1955), the practical value of a test should be measured by how much it improves upon an already achieved level of experience. If in the past, 80 per cent of the patients admitted to a given psychiatric hospital have been diagnosed as schizophrenic, the chances are eight in ten that a new patient will receive that diagnosis. A test purporting to differentiate schizophrenics from others must improve on this rate to be of practical value for the neuropsychiatric hospital. Otherwise it would be just as well or better to use the experience-table data. We will discuss and exemplify this matter further in Chapter 10.

The size of validity coefficients is seldom very high, and we must be satisfied with different levels in different areas of testing. Ability tests, including intelligence (or general ability) tests, usually furnish higher coefficients than personality tests. In well-designed studies, the correlation between intelligence test scores and indexes of success in school or college generally fall between .40 and .60. Ghiselli (1955) has summarized hundreds of validity coefficients in research published between 1919 and 1955 on personnel selection and placement. The highest validity coefficient for intelligence tests was .61, and one test of mechanical comprehension gave a coefficient of .66. The average for all intelligence tests was .38 against criteria of successful outcomes of training programs and .19 against criteria of success on the job. What correlated most highly with criteria of job success were indexes from biographical data blanks —providing an average coefficient of .41. The importance of such life-history data will show up in several places in our discussion of assessment.

In order to judge whether a validity coefficient is high enough to warrant using a test, we can only judge in relation to its intended context. The basic question is whether or not the test provides an improvement over whatever alternative methods there are. We used to think that validity coefficients below .50 were of little value and noted that it took a correlation of .86 to account for half of the variance in prediction —or to be 50 per cent better than chance. As Cronbach and Gleser

(1957) have shown, this conclusion was based on inappropriate assumptions. In Cronbach's opinion (1960, p. 349) "Coefficients as low as .30 are of definite practical value" (1960, p. 349), and occasionally tests of even lower validity are useful if they measure something not covered by other tests. Cronbach refers to Strong's comments (Strong, 1943, p. 55) to the effect that the test critic who is contemptuous of low positive correlations may be willing to accept information of no greater dependability when he plays golf or goes to see a physician. The correlation between golf scores on the first and second holes of an eighteen-hole course in championship play is about .30, and the reliability of medical diagnosis is near .40.

There is another aspect of the need to evaluate validity coefficients in reference to the context in which the test is to be used. This is the consideration of the needed breadth and exactness of the information one wishes to obtain. Cronbach and Gleser (1957) apply to testing the principles of information theory, which Shannon developed for the study of electronic communication systems. The two main concepts are *bandwidth*, the amount of complexity of information one tries to obtain in a given space and time, and *fidelity*, the exactness and sharpness with which a specific message is reproduced and communicated. (The latter concept is familiar to those owning home Hi-Fi phonographs.) The classical psychometric ideal, as Cronbach (1960, p. 602) explains, is a test with high fidelity and low bandwidth, that is, a measure of a specific ability with high reliability and validity coefficients. At the opposite extreme, interviews and projective techniques are extremely wide-ranging; they sample behavior and attitudes from many situations in a person's life but only with very limited reliability and validity. An aptitude test may devote an hour to obtaining one score; an interview may cover dozens of topics in an hour. Between the extremes there are intermediate bandwidth tests, and different parts of a test may have different bandwidths and fidelities. The Verbal IQ on the Wechsler is highly valid for many purposes, but the patterns of subtests have quite limited value, and interpretations from single items are quite untrustworthy. A few tests like the Strong Vocational Interest Blank and the General Aptitude Test Battery cover a wide selection of topics and have relatively high fidelity for each subtest.

In general, when evaluating tests, one has to decide what the assessment task requires—high fidelity or broad bandwidth or some combination of the two. Cronbach states "All the validity studies we have reviewed substantiate Shannon's principle: increases in complexity of information are obtained only by sacrificing fidelity" (1960, p. 602). In planning a test battery for a patient, the sequence of assessment procedures must be considered. Often in clinical work, one might want wide band techniques for early stages, permitting exploration of many areas, stimulating hypotheses, and allowing for later shifts of attention. Wide bandwidth is especially important when there are many alternatives for treatment planning. However, if a decision must be made concerning only a few treatments available in a hospital, such as electro-convulsive therapy or discharge, then it would be useful to develop more specific tests for predicting outcomes from these procedures. In general, instruments having narrow bandwidths are desired for final irreversible decisions.

DIFFERENT KINDS OF VALIDITY

In evaluating a test, the potential user should not be content with a single kind of validity study. Not only should the test be tried out with different kinds of subjects in different situations, but also different kinds of validity should be studied. The APA *Technical Recommendations* (1954) lists four kinds of empirical validity which enjoy general acceptance: content, concurrent, predictive, and construct validity.

Content validity answers the test-user's question: How well does this test sample the topic, or content, that I am interested in? Any test can only encompass a rather small sample of a wide population of possible items. This sort of validity is important for any test; it is especially important for achievement and proficiency tests. When seeking to measure a student's knowledge of American history, the user of a test wants to know that the test items are of proper pertinence and scope. In evaluating tests, one should look at the manner in which the sample of items was developed and judge how typical it is of the universe of possible items. Quantitative evidence on this point is often lacking or difficult to obtain. In the case of personality tests, it is not always clear what their content should be. Thus Berg (1959) has argued for the unimportance of item content in personality testing, and Wiener (1948) has shown there are subtle as well as obvious items. However, on personality inventories, original selection must come from some pool of items and this should be defined and adequately sampled.

Predictive validity answers the test-user's question: How well does this test predict *future* performance? *Concurrent validity* answers the question: How well does this test check with other evidence available *now*? Both predictive and concurrent validity require the use of an external criterion and therefore may be considered instances of *criterion validity*. They differ only in the *time* at which the critical evidence is to be obtained. A new intelligence test may be straightway tried out to see how it correlates with other well-known intelligence tests such as the Stanford-Binet, or it may be used to predict school grades for which is would be necessary to wait for evidence. The difference in time is of considerable importance, since usually in clinical psychology what we really want to do is to predict a patient's future behavior. For this reason we want to look particularly for evidence of a test's predictive validity.

Construct validity answers the test-user's question: How well does this test reflect (or show the possession of) some trait, quality, or construct presumed to underlie performance on the test? This kind of validity requires some kind of hypothesis or theory about the nature of what is being tested. Interest is not in sampling behavior directly related to the criterion, but in using the test to measure a hypothesized state or quality, as anxiety, intelligence, or ego-strength. In a study of this sort one must specify operationally what is to be called a measure of anxiety, but one does not claim that the criterion *is* anxiety. Anxiety cannot be measured directly, though the inference that one is "getting at" anxiety is justified if test performance can be shown to be related to such indicators as the tension reported by the patient, psychiatrists' ratings of anxiety, amount of palmer sweat, or other physiological indications. The term *indicator* is more appropriate in speaking of construct validity than criterion (Meehl, 1959). A set of interconnected indicators, the relevant conceptual framework, or model, is called a *nomological net* by Cronbach and Meehl (1955). Both a logical and an empirical attack are required to develop a nomological net, and the procedure may be deductive or inductive. Deductively, the psychologist armed with his theory predicts that such and such a variation from person to person or from occasion to occasion will occur if he uses this test, and then he gathers data to discover how well his predictions are confirmed. Inductively, he might arrive at the same hypothesis by noticing that on scale X, persons of various kinds score high; his hunch then is, this is because they possess a hypothetical something he calls, let us say, "independence of judgment." From this inference he must make some predictions deductively and then proceed to check them. It is ordinarily necessary to have many measures to establish the construct validity of a test.

There has been a lively debate over construct validity. Loevinger (1957) has advocated sweeping aside all other notions of validity. She believes that the task is to develop measurements of traits which have "real existence" and are widely applicable and basic, rather than to develop tests for use in making practical decisions and predictions. On the negative side, construct validity has come in for criticism on several counts. Bechtoldt (1959) objects to its lack of logical precision and charges that it is an attempt to bring in vaguely defined variables instead of operationally defined concepts. It is too easy to deceive oneself about what one is proving, he believes, and too difficult to define constructs and the nomological net empirically. Supposedly unitary concepts that seem to be desirable like "anxiety" or "suicidal tendencies" or "homosexuality" shatter, on inquiry, into many different meanings (Jackson & Bloomberg, 1958; Farberow, 1959). A final argument against construct validity is that overemphasis on it may lead us to forget the practical side of psychological testing. Little (1959) has pointed out that construct validity is all right for theoretical psychology, but clinics and hospitals need answers to questions like: Is this patient likely to attempt suicide? Will psychotherapy help enough to be worth diverting our limited staff? He emphasizes the importance of "effective validity"— the making of predictive statements for practical use. Undoubtedly during the next decade contention over construct validity will continue to be lively.

RELIABILITY

Reliability refers to the consistency, reproducibility, or accuracy of test results. To measure the consistency of a measuring device such as a test, it is necessary to take more than one measurement of the same variable, using the same subjects, in order to allow forces to play which induce variability. If these scores vary widely, then the test cannot be relied upon, for its results are inconsistent. Clearly a test must have reliability if it is to have validity. The larger the variability due to chance (by which we mean any factors irrelevant to test purposes), the less faith we can put in any score obtained from it. In interpreting test results we should think of a test score such as a child's IQ of 115 not as a point, but as a sample with a range of scores. The child's "true" IQ probably falls somewhere between 110 and 120 assuming the test is highly reliable. The less reliable the test, the wider the range within which the true score might fall.

There are two major ways of measuring reliability. After an interval, the test can be given again to the same subjects in order to discover how much scores or two forms of the test composed of similar sets of items can be given for the purpose of comparison. Thus reliability breaks down into two concepts: *stability*, as measured by the retest method, and *equivalence*, as measured by testing with equivalent forms of a test or by observing internal consistency, that is, by splitting the test in two and studying how closely scores on the two halves agree, the so-called *split-half reliability*. The differences between these two approaches make it desirable with most tests to obtain measures of both kinds of reliability. With some kinds of tests one or the other kind is inappropriate. For instance, in a timed ability test in which scores can improve with practice, test-retest reliability would be misleading. In personality tests there are also problems in retesting after a long time interval, since personality may change over time.

Peak (1953) has elaborated on the equivalence or homogeneity of observations under the term *functional unity*, pointing out that it is basic to measurement that we find "something that holds together" in the ongoing stream of behavior and interaction. To measure this unity operationally such methods may be used as item analysis, intertest correlations, and factor analysis. Thus factor analysis contributes to the development of unity or homogeneity in a test, and the so-called *factorial validity* is not true empirical validity.

These basic concepts we have been discussing apply very broadly in assessment work. The relation between the concepts of reliability and validity can be seen if one thinks in terms of internal and external relations of the test—or for that matter not only tests but test batteries or a clinical team—any assessment system. Reliability deals with internal relations—the consistency within the system and its parts. Validity is concerned with external relations of a system with higher and lower systems—the relation of a test to other tests or to future outcomes. One can stop at any level of organization in the hierarchy of assessment and speak of these two concepts—the reliability and validity of items, of tests, of batteries of tests, of the clinician-battery system, of the psychiatric team.

COMBINING, VARYING, AND SUPPLEMENTING TEST PROCEDURES

It is rare that one test is given in isolation. In planning for the psychological assessment of a case, many problems usually present themselves. Some of these can be clarified by the interview and the case history. The initial scanning of the case by broad bandwidth procedures will often uncover areas that need more specialized and exact testing by instruments with higher fidelity. This procedure of scanning and focusing is carried beyond the interview. A group of tests given together are called a *test battery*. Most commonly in clinical work, such a combination of tests is especially chosen for a particular patient with his unique problems. Most psychologists who have worked for some time in one clinical setting, however, find themselves giving certain combinations of tests much more frequently than others. In some situations it is possible to develop routine screening batteries, made-up, for instance, of a brief intelligence test, the MMPI, and a sentence completion test, to be given to every new admission to a hospital or clinic. Such brief batteries take little staff time, provide a lot of information, and help select those patients who are in need of more intensive study. They also are useful for research purposes. The danger of routine dependence on such a battery is that patients may also get *only* routine evaluation. It would be catastrophic if such a battery should become the sole and habitual method of assessment. Every case must be given as close individual attention as possible.[2]

[2] For an extensive discussion of selection and interpretation of test batteries, see Brower and Abt (1958).

Faced with an unusually difficult assessment problem the psychologist may risk devising an original kind of investigation or introduce variations in the usual tests. His new procedure and the variations will, of course, have the disadvantage of not being standardized and norms will not be available, but still it is possible that they will prove enlightening. With young children or with cases of special defects, a psychologist often has to depend on his ingenuity. With a four-year-old who does not talk, the psychologist can get some idea of his passive vocabulary by playing a game in which he is asked to bring objects which the psychologist names. In one case of suspected hysterical deafness, a psychologist was able to demonstrate to himself and to the patient that she actually could hear. With a psychogalvanometer recording fluctuations in response to emotional stimuli, the psychologist, standing where the patient could not see him pronounced a list of emotion-loaded words. Often, in administering an intelligence test, the psychologist may get the impression that the patient actually knows more than he is able to express. The psychologist can complete the regular administration of the test, but later on go back to selected parts, repeating questions and perhaps proferring hints to see how easily the person "catches on." Klopfer's Rorschach administration specifically suggests such a procedure, called *testing the limits,* to see if the person can perceive popular responses or give other kinds of responses in which he seemed deficient. McReynolds has developed a promising standardized method for this Rorschach procedure (1951, 1954).

Observation constitutes a most important supplement to test information. *Observations during testing* include noting verbal comments and any unusual nonverbal activity. A patient may make excuses for what he thinks is a poor performance; he may not treat a test seriously or he may be unduly worried over whether he is doing well or not; he may attempt to sidetrack the testing altogether by bringing in extraneous topics of conversation. Oftentimes the patient's actions will speak louder than his words. He may express willingness to take tests, but then prove refractory by giving laconic, scanty responses on the Rorschach and TAT. The psychologist observes the appearance and behavior of the patient during testing for clues to his test-taking attitude and his personality in general. There may be significance in his restlessness or the retardation in his rate of speech, in movements toward and away from the examiner, in interruptions of normal breathing, amount of smiling, and many other forms of behavior. It is, of course, impossible to keep a running record of all such behavior. The clinician has to depend on his experienced observational habits to keep track of what should be recorded. Sometimes he can make jottings about revealing actions on the margins of test blanks. Immediately after the test session a fuller record can be completed. A standard rating scale or checklist, such as the Maryland Behavior Checklist (Berenson et al, 1960) can be very useful.

In training students it is desirable to have them make phonographic recordings of testing sessions and to use one-way screens for observation.

Observation outside of test situations is also important. In child guidance clinics, play sessions are recognized as valuable opportunities to observe how a child reacts in a free and generally pleasant situation. The toys and equipment of a playroom permit the psychologist to set up special situations which duplicate some of the problems that arise between parent and child and in school, to see how the child handles them. Sometimes it is useful to bring several members of a family into the playroom to observe the ensuing family interaction. Home visits may clarify many points in assessing the family situation. Observation on hospital wards contributes much to understanding interpersonal behavior. It allows the observer to comprehend how patients react to the authority of attendants, what sorts of spontaneous activities occur. There are standardized techniques for recording observations: the Haggerty-Olson-Wickman Behavior Rating Schedule for use with children and a number for use with psychiatric patients, such as the Wittenborn Psychiatric Rating Scales, the Hospital Adjustment Scale, and the Multidimensional Rating Scale for Psychiatric Patients. Some studies with these scales have demonstrated the value of using observations of actual behavior of patients on a hospital ward instead of records of "mental" symptoms. The hospital treatment and training program for psychotics may improve their social behavior so that many are able to do limited work outside or be placed in foster homes; however, the patients' delusions and mental aberrations may not change. A behavior rating scale thus may be indicative of this potential for improvement even when measures of psychiatric symptomatology are not useful. A general conceptual framework for assessing situations and additional techniques and research on observation will be discussed in the next chapter.

Having tested, interviewed, and observed the patient, the psychologist has on his hands a great deal of information, both objective and impressionistic or inferred. From the beginning this material will have started to develop into a kind of meaningful picture. As he studies the data further, a pattern with sharper outlines will begin to emerge and this the psychologist, when he feels he can put trust in it, will communicate to others.

A CRITIQUE OF THE PLACE OF TESTS
IN CLINICAL ASSESSMENT

As mentioned at the start of this chapter, tests are tools that can be used wisely or foolishly, constructively or destructively. The psychologist deciding to use a test in making an ethical and philosophical choice as well as a technical one. Human values are involved in the choice. The kind of procedures selected for assessment have implications for treatment and attitudes far beyond the procedure itself. The technical aspects of evaluating tests are covered in earlier sections of this chapter and in other chapters. Here, at the end of this chapter we want to survey the assets and liabilities of tests in their clinical context. First, let us review the reservations and outright dangers of which clinicians need to be aware.

a. Test results depend on the attitudes of the person taking the test. As indicated earlier in this chapter, there are many aspects of the testing situation and of the patient's test-taking approach which must be considered in interpretation. Before interpreting a result we must be certain whether the testing occasion has approximated a standard one, and if not we must take this into account in the interpretation.

b. The value of tests depends on the competence of the interpreter. Test interpretation cannot be automatic. Poorly trained or inexperienced examiners operating under the guise of clinicians will not be able to extract much value from the tests they give. It is true that there are many uses for less trained clerical help in administering, scoring, and preparing tests for clinical interpretation, but the final decisions in application to individual cases must be made by a skilled clinician. As yet very few tests provide ways of interpreting the results for individual cases. Test norms and validity coefficients do not tell what words to use in a report. Test manuals need to present illustrative cases on applications in different clinical settings, and research is needed on useful ways of reporting results.

c. There is a danger that the psychologist may become overly dependent on tests. A psychologist sometimes uses tests as "an easy way out" or to cover up his lack of interviewing skill. Tests may blind him to clues and evidence right before his eyes if he is too completely engrossed in test scores. Skillful observation and interviewing are still the basic features of assessment, not testing.

d. The use of tests may structure the relationship in undesired ways. The total effect that testing will probably have on the client should be weighed before testing is started. Do we want to set up in the client's mind the expectations of authoritative and detached handling of his problems which tests often imply? Rogers (1942) has pointed out that the use of tests and diagnostic procedures may prejudice the situation in an antitherapeutic way. When the experienced clinician gives tests, he is careful not to give an impression that tests in themselves solve problems. He may engage the patient in testing as a cooperative effort for this patient's benefit. Too often in psychiatric hospitals and clinics, patients are not informed about the reasons for diagnostic tests nor the results of them.

e. There are large gaps and questionable areas in the use of tests in clinical work. One such area is psychotherapy—whether tests can be of value in shortening or improving treatment of patients. There is considerable information on selection for various kinds of treatment in institutions, but the value of tests for individual psychotherapy is still an open question.

f. Selection techniques being developed from criteria of past performance tend to perpetuate past standards and conformity. This danger is the crux of Whyte's argument against tests in *The Organization Man.* Bureaucracies, both public and private, pick new employees using tests developed on past evidence of job success. Whyte argues that these tests can be used to keep out men who are creative or would encourage change. Some of the recent work on creativity in school and college students suggest that selection on the basis of current intelligence tests and past school records weeds out the original or highly specialized person. Psychologists must be alert to the kind of personalities and abilities inadvertently chosen by his selection procedures. It is possible to devise tests which specifically seek out the creative and nonconforming person.

g. Tests are not appropriate for many people with special defects or difficulties. There is a limitation, to the generalizability of the norms and validity data on tests. The psychologist must know when the conventional interpretations of a test score must be departed from.

h. Tests may make us put too much emphasis on the individual tested and so overlook the importance of his life situation. Tests have a built-in individualistic bias. Test norms, for instance, are based on samples of a population—not on interacting groups. There is no provision, in most existing tests, for conditional applications depending on the context of the person. Since typical tests have nothing to say about the situation that a person is in, this may be forgotten. The psychologist must incorporate his client's situation in the interpretation of any test. We will have much more to say about this point in Chapter 7.

i. All test interpretation is probabilistic. As we have seen, validity coefficients are seldom as high as we would like them to be. The psychologist must often keep his fingers crossed if he is to avoid claiming too much for his tests.

Almost all of these reservations about tests boil down to the statement that tests are tools dependent for their success on the skill and wisdom of the user. There are many situations in which a skilled clinician knows enough to avoid testing altogether. The important thing is to know tests and the clinical situation well enough to put them together advantageously. Now let us look at some of the special advantages of tests when they are appropriately employed:

a. Tests are often better than the alternatives to them. Tests can only be judged in relation to the other possible procedures that might be used for assessment. As we have seen interviewing is time-consuming and open to very serious questions of reliability and validity as a measuring instrument. In Chapter 8 we will review the research on clinical versus statistical prediction, which suggests that tests in combination with properly developed interpretive techniques are effective. The question of effectiveness and "incremental validity" will also be covered in Chapter 10.

b. Tests have a high degree of communicability. It is possible to print directions and test materials so that other people can do the same thing as the originator of the test. Tests are more precisely reproducible than less formal and less standardized methods.

c. Tests are relatively free from personal bias. Tests may differ a great deal in their objectivity, but as compared with informal methods of evaluation, they are likely to be less affected by personal prejudices and psychological blind spots, because of the need to check against norm groups and research results.

d. Many tests are amenable to exact statistical analysis. Many tests can be checked to discover whether they are working well or not. If a certain item is of no value, or if an entire test contributes nothing, it can be dropped. Unless something can be proved to be right or wrong, it is impossible to evaluate it clearly. When methods are informal, it may be difficult to distinguish what is useful in them from what is useless.

e. Tests often are more economical than their alternatives. In many instances having the client record his answers on paper saves the expensive time of a trained interviewer. Even when a clinician administers a test individually, as he does with a Wechsler test or Thematic Apperception Test, time may be saved if the standardized situation elicits more information in less time than does an interview. Still more professional time is saved when tests can be given to groups.

The stage we have reached in test development at the present time leaves much to be desired. We may hope and believe that great achievements lie just ahead in this field.

SUMMARY

Knowledge and skill in the use of tests are indispensable to the clinical psychologist. This chapter has been devoted to an evaluation and some description of test usage. (An acquaintance with specific tests will have to be obtained from special courses and study. Appendix A lists some tests which are most important for clinical work.) A test is a systematic procedure for comparing behavior. The history of test development is an account of how certain instruments were created as products of an interactive process in which the originator's insights, society's needs, and meticulous research all played their part. Any potential user of a test seeking to ascertain how useful it will be to him needs to study the test manual, to look up what is said about it in Buros' *Yearbooks* and in text-books; he will want to try it out, perhaps first taking it himself, then giving it to others and studying the results and how the subjects react to it. Also, he will want to know how much it costs to use a particular test and how appropriate it is in relation to local clinical needs. Evaluation of the technical excellence of a test involves a study of its reliability, validity, scoring objectivity, norms, and aids to interpretation. Validity is an index of what a test means—the degree to which a test measures, predicts, or describes whatever it may be used for. There are four common kinds of validity—content, concurrent, predictive, and construct validity. While all kinds are important, for practical clinical purposes, the indexes of the worth of a test for predicting future behavior is particularly valuable. Reliability is an index of the consistency of the test—its stability over time or the equivalence of different forms or parts of the test. In clinical usage, tests are combined in batteries, and adjustments and changes are made to fit the test to the special needs of the case being studied. The dangers and advantages of tests were listed.

SUGGESTED READINGS

BIBER, Barbara, MURPHY, Lois B., WOODCOCK, Louise P. & BLACK, Irma S. *Life and ways of the seven-to-eight year old.* New York: Basic Books, 1952. See "Stenographic record of psychological examination." Pp. 631-639.
  This book describes in detail the authors' observations and research with ten children in an experimental school in New York. The record of a testing session provides a good illustration of the richness of interaction that makes individual test administration far from routine or mechanical. In the process of taking the Porteus Mazes and other performance tests, Douglas asks about a dent on the table, sings tunes, talks about fear and lying, inquires about the examiner's stop watch and writing, and comments on how well or poorly he is doing on the tests. The reader may be interested also in other sample records, such as those of the painting period and of the problem-solving situations.

GOLDMAN, L. *Using tests in counseling.* New York: Appleton-Century-Crofts, 1961.
  This book covers in detail considerations about selection, administration, and interpretation of tests. Of particular pertinence to this and later chapters are the discussions of clinical and statistical approaches to test interpretation and the case illustrations. Though the examples from counseling settings and vocational problems are often prominent, there would be much carry-over of Goldman's points to clinical applications.

General introductions to tests

A large number of books present general introductions to testing. Cronbach (1960), Anastasi (1961), and Nunnally (1959) are particularly good. In the areas of clinical psychology and personality there are many examples of which the following are a few. Watson (1951), Weider (1953), and Garfield (1957) demonstrate the use of tests in clinical settings. Louttit (1957) describes the

clinical approach to children and methods used with them. Allen (1958) and
Anderson and Anderson (1951) contain brief introductions to a wide variety of
personality assessment devices. There are, of course, innumerable books and
manuals on specific tests. The best single source for references on any test is
the series of *Mental Measurements Yearbooks* (Buros, 1941, 1949, 1953, 1959).

RESEARCH EXAMPLES

FISHER, G. M. Differences in WAIS Verbal and Performance IQ's in various
diagnostic groups of mental retardates. *Amer. J. ment. Defic.*, 1960, 65, 256-
260.

Fisher notes Wechsler's assertion that mentally defective individuals usually
obtained higher Performance IQ's than Verbal IQ's on the Wechsler-Bellevue
scale, the predecessor of the Wechsler Adult Intelligence Scale (WAIS), and
reviews a number of research studies that support Wechsler's statement. In
his review of the studies with the Wechsler Intelligence Scale for Children
(WISC), however, Fisher finds considerable inconsistency on this score.
Wechsler also states that individuals suffering from organic brain disorders
often obtain Verbal IQ's which are higher than Performance IQ's. In this study,
Fisher's purpose is to study this Verbal-Performance discrepancy in mentally
retarded persons, some of whom have evidence of brain damage as compared
with others who do not.

The sample was gathered from the files of two large institutions for the mentally defective in California. Fisher collected information on all persons who
had been given the full WAIS and met certain diagnostic criteria. The total
number of subjects was 508. The WAIS Verbal IQ's averaged from 61 to 76
in the various diagnostic groups, and the Performance IQ means ranged from
59 to 77.

The main finding was that the 271 subjects who were diagnosed as undifferentiated and familial (or "garden-variety") mental defectives showed no
significant difference between Verbal and Performance IQ's, in contrast to
Wechsler's findings with the earlier scale. In the brain-injured groups, only
subjects with the diagnosis of central nervous system infection and other organic nervous disease showed a Verbal IQ significantly higher than the Performance IQ. The subjects whose deficiency was due to epilepsy or birth
trauma did not show a significant difference. One further finding refers to the
variation, or dispersion, of the Verbal-Performance IQ differences. Wechsler
had found that samples of persons with IQ's below 80 showed smaller standard
deviations than normal samples. This finding held up for the familial group in
this study, but not for the other diagnostic categories, who showed no significant
difference in dispersion from the normal WAIS group.

It would seem then that the Verbal-Performance discrepancy is not a clear-
cut diagnostic indication and more work is needed to ferret out connections
with different etiologies. There is the suggestion in this research, however, that
diffuse organic pathology may have different effects than more localized lesions,
and the attempt to distinguish familial from organic mental deficiency is given
some encouragement by the results.

REITAN, R. M. Validity of the Trail Making Test as an indicator of organic
brain damage. *Percept. mot. Skills*, 1958, 8, 271-276.

The Trail Making Test is a simple procedure that has been found, over a
number of years, to be of use in detecting intellectual deficit from organic

brain damage. This study is based on larger groups than were used previously and provides preliminary norms for evaluating performances of adult subjects. The Trail Making Test consists of two parts, each with 25 circles distributed over a white sheet of paper. On one sheet, the circles are numbered from 1 to 25, and the subject's task is to draw lines connecting the numbers in sequence as quickly as possible. On the other sheet, the circles include numbers from 1 to 13 and letters from A to L, and the subject is asked to draw lines connecting numbers and letters alternately in an ascending sequence. The score is the number of seconds required to finish each part.

In this study the test was administered to 200 patients with clear evidence of brain damage, for example, diffuse cerebrovascular disease, intrinsic brain tumor, traumatic head injury, and to a control group of 84 patients hospitalized mostly for neurological disorders, such as paraplegia, but not having any history or clinical evidence of brain damage. The groups were comparable with regard to sex distribution, age, and education.

The results showed striking and highly significant differences in the performances of the two groups on the Trail Making Test. The original article presents frequency distributions of scores which may serve as preliminary norms. Cutoff points for maximum differentiation between the brain-damaged and normal groups are discussed.

Reitan reports on some of his clinical observations of patients taking the test. He notes that the test does require an alertness and concentrated attention, measures of which have often been found to be sensitive to effects of brain damage. He relates the findings to other work in this general area. This publication is only one of a large number of studies of psychological aspects of brain dysfunction by Reitan and his associates. For a study using the Wechsler-Bellevue and the Halstead Neuropsychological indicators, see Fitzhugh, Fitzhugh, and Reitan (1961).

DEMMING, J. A., and PRESSEY, S. L. Tests "indigenous" to the adult and older years. *J. counsel Psychol.*, 1957, 4, 144-148.

The authors argue that most intelligence tests are constructed to fit the interests and problems of children or young adults. The decline in the curve of intellectual ability beyond middle age may appear greater than it is owing to lack of items appropriate for the older persons. In order to develop a test with suitable content, the authors attempted to select items related to the everyday life of older adults. They developed three objective tests covering (1) use of the yellow pages of a telephone directory, (2) common legal terms, and (3) information on people who perform services needed in everyday life.

The authors administered these three new tests to a sample of inmates of a state penitentiary aged 20 to 50 years, most of whom were in their 30's, and to elderly persons in evening school classes and Golden Age Clubs. In addition to the new tests they also gave these subjects the Army Beta, the Otis Self-Scoring test, the Minnesota Paper Formboard, and the Bennett Mechanical Comprehension test.

The results, shown in tables, indicate a progressive decline on the four "traditional" tests with age and increases on the three new tests. The authors conclude that the tests they developed might have value in assessing the practical information of older people who are to be returned from institutions to the community.

This study, though limited in many ways and certainly in need of repetition, does suggest a very interesting and important point for the study of elderly persons. Just as it would be inappropriate to expect a young child to be interested in purchasing real estate or qualified for driving a car, so it seems inappropriate to expect elderly people to be proficient in childish activities. With a rapidly increasing number of elderly people in our population, psychologists are going to be faced more and more with the problem of discovering what older people can successfully do and at the same time are really motivated to do in daily living. For further information on the problem of geriatrics and aging, see the review by Inglis (1958) of methods of assessing cognitive deficit in elderly psychiatric patients. Also the appropriate chapters in Birren (1959).

BAUGHMAN, E. E. An experimental analysis of the relationship between stimulus structure and behavior on the Rorschach. *J. proj. Tech.*, 1959, 23, 134-183.

In an excellent review made by Baughman earlier (1958*b*), he had reported that he found a remarkably small number of studies out of the thousands on the Rorschach in which stimulus properties had been systematically varied. The purpose of this study was to study how Rorschach responses changed in a normal population as a function of several stimulus properties of the inkblots.

The subjects were 648 employees of an insurance company. The subjects were divided into eight groups equated for age, sex, IQ, and education. Two of the eight groups were given the standard Rorschach; the rest were given specially modified forms of the test in which the modifications were made in the color, shading, and figure-ground contrast of the blots while their basic form was kept the same.

The resulting data are presented in detail so that students and users of the Rorschach can make use of the tables as basic references in their work. The major point, supported by his statistical analysis is that the properties of ink-blots other than form do affect the responses of subjects in contrast to what had been found in some earlier more limited studies. In discussing the results, Baughman states, however, that the effect of structure upon content is fundamental. It can be seen that some scores (such as for Movement, Animal per cent, and Populars) are related directly to content, but other scores not directly related to content (such as scores for Detail and Space) are also linked to form. Baughman concludes that it is difficult to generalize regarding color and shading effects and the context of each individual card must be considered. This study is interesting for its experimental variation of Rorschach stimuli, and its norms are valuable because the number of subjects is large. The study does not contribute anything directly to the question of the validity of the test. Baughman does have something to say about examiner reliability.

In other articles (1958*a*, 1959*a*) he has presented a standardized method of inqury for the Rorschach. (In administering the Rorschach the subject is first asked to free associate to the inkblots; subsequently he is asked to explain where and why he saw what he reported; this latter part of the administration is called the inquiry.) Baughman argues that the usual approach in inquiry leaves too much room for variation among examiners and is one of the reasons for the disagreements among different Rorschach studies.

SEIDEL, Claudene. The relationship between Klopfer's Rorschach Prognostic Rating Scale and Phillips' case-history prognostic rating scale. *J. consult. Psychol.*, 1960, 24, 46-53.

Seidel has applied two prognostic scales to a clinical sample to determine their interrelationship and their ability to predict outcome. The Rorschach scale (presented in Klopfer, Kirkner, Wisham, & Baker, 1951, and discussed further in Klopfer, Ainsworth, Klopfer, & Holt, 1954) is a quantitative measure of "ego-strength" derived from Rorschach scoring categories. The Phillips' scale (1953) is derived from ratings of items pertaining to recent sexual adjustment

and past and recent personal relations. The main work of this study was carried out on 63 white, male schizophrenic patients selected from the files of a
large mental hospital. Only patients who had been given Rorschachs within four
months of admission were used. The follow-up data on these patients showed
that 31 of the 63 had been hospitalized continuously for three years or longer
and 32 had been discharged in less than three years with a psychiatric evaluation of "recovery" or "social recovery."

The findings of the study included a correlation of .30 between the Rorschach
and case history scales using total scores. There was a correlation of .46 between the case history scale and the Rorschach form level score alone (a rating
of the appropriateness of patient's perception to the form of the inkblot, usually
interpreted as a reflection of good contact with reality). The criterion of recovery in less than three years after admission also correlated significantly with
the prognostic scales: .40 with the Klopfer scale total, .44 with the Rorschach
form level alone, and .46 with the Phillips' case-history scale. These scales were
thus demonstrated as having predictive validity, which would encourage further
use of them.

MURSTEIN, B. I., and WHEELER, J. I. The projection of hostility on the Rorschach
and Thematic Stories Test. *J. clin. Psychol.*, 1959, 15, 316-319.

This is a report of research on the differential effects of the Rorschach and
thematic stimuli. The authors hypothesized a negative correlation between the
projection of hostility as it is revealed by the Rorschach and by thematic tests.
They reasoned as follows: The TAT being more structured and closer to reality
(with pictures of people, *etc.*) would elicit expressions of hostility if the person
is sufficiently secure, but a really hostile person who is anxious about his expression of hostility will deny it on the TAT. However such a hostile, insecure
person would reveal his hostility on the less structured and less realistic
Rorschach.

The subjects were 36 female patients aged 33 to 60 years. The authors used
ten pictures, six from the TAT and four from another series. The stories these
pictures and the Rorschach inkblots elicited were scored for hostility according
to scoring techniques worked out in other studies. The correlation between
thematic hostility and Rorschach hostility was not significant. However, productivity is known to be a very important variable in projective techniques.
Some subjects give many answers and some very few. When productivity was
controlled by partial correlation techniques, there was a significant negative
coefficient ($-.41$) between thematic and Rorschach hostility scores. The
authors concluded that their general hypothesis was supported, namely that
hostile persons project in a relatively unstructured situation but repress hostility
in a more structured and obvious situation.

This study is interesting because of its attempt to relate two tests by a
systematic theory. Unfortunately the number and nature of the subjects employed do not warrant any broad generalization from the findings with this
group. The study should be repeated by others. Elsewhere, Murstein (1959)
has presented an extensive review (which the reader will find valuable) of
stimulus variations on thematic techniques and a conceptual framework related
to Helson's adaptation theory. See also Murstein's and Pryer's review (1959)
of the concept of projection.

GOUGH, H. G. Theory and measurement of socialization. *J. consult. Psychol.*,
1960, 24, 23-30.

This article presents the theory and development of the Socialization scale of the CPI (Gough, 1957). The author points out the similarity of his theoretical position with that of G. H. Mead: socialized behavior is behavior based on a proper viewing of oneself as a social object. Gough's major point is that a scale measuring such a theoretical dimension should not just separate delinquents from nondelinquents but should differentiate along the whole range of the socialization continuum.

In the main body of the article means and standard deviations for the So (Socialization scale) are reported on 41 research samples, totalling 1294 male delinquents and criminals and 9,001 male nondelinquents, 784 female delinquents and 9,776 female nondelinquents. A rank ordering of the various samples on the So scale, which is a psychological measure, agrees closely with the way they would be ranked sociologically, according to their actual adjustment to the standards of society. Those nominated as "best citizens" in high school are at the top of the list, followed by applicants for medical school and banking executives. At the bottom of the list are inmates of federal reformatories. Several studies by other investigators demonstrate the validity of the scale over the whole socialization continuum.

This article is a demonstration of the theoretical foundation of an empirically developed scale. The CPI was mainly developed by selecting from an item pool those items which statistically differentiated between normal and deviant groups. In the development of the So scale, items were selected to differentiate also between gradations of behavioral deviation. The CPI aims to measure "folk concepts" of interpersonal dimensions. Those dimensions, such as socialization, responsibility, and dominance, are presumed to be transcultural (not peculiar to the culture in the U.S.A.). Gough (1960) has recently reported tentative evidence that the validity of the So scale holds in several other countries.

7 Assessing Development in Life Situations

Behavior is a function of person and situation. This is a basic formula to which most, if not all, psychologists would subscribe. Yet psychological assessment has been almost exclusively concerned with measuring personal or individual variables. Clinicians have failed to incorporate situational variables systematically in their practice. Tests provide, as we have seen in the preceding chapter, comparisons with populations—not comparisons with interacting groups in which individuals might actually function. Much psychological research makes the tacit assumption that human behavior is a function of personal characteristics alone.

Yet we know that the expression of personal tendencies is dependent on the conditions surrounding the person. We require environmental supports for any action we contemplate. Our behavior is stimulated by changes in the environment. We catch the excitement of football crowds. We are reminded of a happy event when we hear a certain tune. At a party with friends we may be playful and humorous, but at straight-laced Aunt Minnie's house we will never crack a joke. In our modern society, the demands large business and military organizations make on those who join their ranks are strong and insistent. All of these considerations are requiring psychologists now to begin to develop ways of studying situations so as to place situational variables in the equation of behavior. The aim is what might be called *conditional prediction*. We should be able to say: *If* this kind of person goes into this kind of situation, *then* such and such will probably happen; if he goes to this other situation, then something else is likely. Assessment of situations may help psychologists solve the criterion problem which has plagued them so long.

In clinical cases, it is not difficult to find examples illustrating how important situational variables are: the man who goes through most of his life without difficulty until forced into retirement; the child whose symptoms begin at the time of the birth of a sibling; the disintegration of a family when the father is sent to prison; the "transient situational disorders" of soldiers under the extreme stress of prolonged combat; the change in behavior of even a chronic schizophrenic when he is placed on a new and lively ward. In looking at these examples, we do not say the situation caused the breakdown or recovery. The same situation may have a positive effect on one patient, a negative effect on another, and little influence on a third. It is the *interaction* between person and situation that is important.

In this chapter we will take up the problems and methods of assessing situational variables and life histories for clinical purposes. In doing this we will try to make more explicit the implications of the orientation toward interactive development described in Chapter 2. The goal of this kind of assessment is to see the person in relation to the stream of interaction as his life unfolds. It requires a horizontal (ecological) and a vertical (historical) view of the person. There is a heavy emphasis on the *systems* of which each person forms a part. Such an orientation is complex and unfortunately vague here and there, but it is the kind of orientation that seems necessary for clinical work. People's lives *are* complex, and our concepts and methods are still at too early a stage of development to express this complexity with complete clarity.

METHODS FOR OBTAINING INFORMATION ABOUT SITUATIONS

In a rough way, a situation can be defined as the perceivable environment with which the individual interacts. Situational variables are the dimensions on which situations differ from one another. The contents of the environment are not only physical objects but also social organizations and cultural heritages, all of them "outside" the individual. In order to be influenced by the situation, the person must be able to sense them in some way, of course. However, many things happen which the person does not perceive until his "attention" is called to them. These problems of what attention means and how the meaning of environmental objects is "incorporated" in a person's experience are only a few of the many theoretical and experimental problems with which psychologists must wrestle. The intent of this chapter, however, is not to review theories (of which there are important ones by Lewin, Murray, Brunswik, Osgood, and others) but to deal in a rather common-sense way with the practical problem of assessment of situations as they face clinicians every day.

Although there are few standardized techniques for assessing situa-

tional variables, there are a host of "looser" approaches based upon interviewing and observation. The traditional method is, of course, *interviewing*. The interviewer asks the patient to describe his family and to tell of
incidents in his life that are important to him. In assembling a case history a clinic interviews relatives and other informants as well as the
patient. It may be that supplemental written reports from the patient and
his family are collected, letters of application and autobiographies. In
any case, from these reports of the participants in the important situations
of the person's life, the clinical psychologist can build a picture of what
those situations are like. These kinds of reports are very useful. They are
often the only kind of situational assessment which can be done under
the time-pressures of clinical work. However, they do need to be recognized for what they are—reports by highly ego-involved participants removed in time and space from the original scene. One is reminded of
some of the anthropological studies of Japanese "national character"
carried out during World War II. Using informants' reports, newspapers,
art, myths, history, these anthropologists made "studies of culture at a
distance." In many cases these studies too were very useful, but no anthropologist would be content to let his science rest on such evidence
alone.

Another approach is direct *observation of natural living situations*. With
the resurgence of interest in family interaction, mental health workers
are discovering again the value of home visits (see Ackerman, 1958, for
instance). By visiting the actual place where a family lives, the clinician
can form an impression of the way in which the neighborhood influences
the family members, the way in which the size and shape of the house
and yard affect their interaction, the kind of care and interest parents
show toward the children, and the patterns the family interaction itself
takes. Other loci of interaction might also be observed—the work setting,
the classroom, and the playground. Sometimes the clinician can find
records of observations that will be of value in understanding a case,
anecdotal records kept by some schools. In many cases, however, these
will be inadequate because of the unsystematic way in which observation
and records were made. The advantage of direct observation in the home
or place of work is that it enables the clinician to see much more clearly
just what is going on than the patient's reports do. There are several
difficulties. The principal one is that such observation is time-consuming
and expensive. Another is that the presence of the observer in the situation may distort it somewhat. Furthermore, if measurements of any kind
are to be used, observations must be systematically recorded and coded.
Satisfactory recording and coding procedures are not easy to set up. Most
of the hospital behavior rating scales mentioned elsewhere are oriented
toward recording the behavior of individuals, not describing situations
or even changes in the interaction of individuals in different situations.

The methods of studying behavior settings developed by Barker and Wright probably come closest to filling the need; they will be discussed soon. Although it is difficult to observe situations directly, it seems probable that excursions into this largely unexplored area would pay off handsomely in our understanding of mental illness and health.[1]

A related approach is the *observation of controlled situations*. The research psychologist may modify natural situations so as to observe the effects of the changes. The clinical psychologist may introduce variations in ongoing therapy groups for the same reason. One can observe situations, such as therapist-patient interaction, through a one-way screen using special recording devices such as the Interaction Chronograph or motion picture film. There is no sharp difference between natural and controlled situations, of course. The important question about artificial situations is how well conclusions based on them will generalize to behavior in "real life." One advantage of controlled situations is that one can study special problems, like stress, frustration, or creative ingenuity, which occur very rarely under normal conditions.

The principles discussed in Chapter 6 apply to the techniques of interviewing and observation as well as to tests—principles about reliability, validity, and norms. In a sense any test is a miniature situation. There are some tests expressly designated *situational tests,* which we will mention later on in this chapter. The difference between most psychological tests and the procedures for assessment of situations with which we are now concerned is a difference in focus of observation, or frame of reference. With tests the focus is on attributes of a single person; with situational assessment the focus is on the interacting system or the context in which an individual's behavior develops.

STEPS IN ASSESSMENT OF SITUATIONS

In assessing situations, as in assessing individuals, the exact content and extent of the program to be carried out varies with the needs of the case, the functions of the agency, and the role of the psychologist. In many clinical settings, unfortunately, there is very little time for doing much more than a quick study of the person, but even here the psycholo-

[1] Some very dramatic differences can be shown in the behavior of animals in different situations. The seriousness of overlooking situational effects and the need for natural life observation is demonstrated by the contrast between the earlier reports on the behavior of baboons based on observation in zoos, and the recent work of Washburn and DeVore (1961; also see Sahlins, 1960). Earlier reports described the animals as incredibly savage and aggressive in their relationships, characteristics now believed to be a result of the constriction of the zoo and consequent frustrations. Washburn and DeVore observed baboon troops extensively in their natural habitat in Africa and describe how troops establish a remarkably stable and peaceful society. A social hierarchy exists in which older and stronger animals are very protective of the others.

gist needs to keep in mind the situations in which the patient operates. In many clinics and institutions it is the job of the social worker to assess the life situations of the patient, and there is no point in having the psychologist duplicate what the social worker has already done. However the information about the patient's life situation is obtained, the psychologist always needs to consider it as he interprets test results, plans treatment through individual or group therapy or ward activities, and carries on research.

Here are some examples of questions about situations which clinical psychologists may face: What can be done to alter the home situation of a five-year-old boy so that he will be less persistently hostile and aggressive? What can be done to reduce the opportunities for suicide in an acutely depressed woman? What work possibilities are there for a man with a crippling fear of crowds? How can a patient's family be helped to accept a patient when he returns from the hospital? Why is this therapy group unable to move forward? How can the activities of this hospital ward be reorganized to promote therapy? In planning for an expansion of a hospital, what kind of architectural design would be best? What kind of mental health facility does this community need? Any clinician could give many other examples.

In our discussion in this chapter we shall place a major emphasis on the *people* in a patient's immediate situation and his own *interpersonal* behavior. This does not mean that we can ignore other aspects of situations, such as the effects of larger organizations and communities. But the clinician will most often find himself looking directly at the interpersonal drama and will be dealing with it directly.

The process of assessing the situation in a clinical case consists of four steps: (1) First one must *identify the significant interactive systems*— especially the primary groups that are of most importance in the patient's life. The present family and work setting are usually of great significance. Potential systems of interaction—different wards, alternatives for jobs, various foster homes—must also be identified and analyzed. (2) The next step is to *study the characteristics of each of these systems*. The characteristics to be studied will be discussed more extensively later on, but they include such aspects as the roles of the major participants, the rules for interaction, and the kind of communication that goes on within the system. (3) A third step is to *compare the characteristics of the patient and the system*. It is important to know what role he typically plays, how his perception of the situation corresponds to that of others, and whether his skills and resources are adequate for the tasks he is expected to carry out. (4) The fourth and last step in this assessment procedure is to *plan for utilization of situational resources or for change in the system, the patient, or both*. This final step requires that the assessor consider the kind of intervention that the clinic or hospital staff will attempt to make in the on-going behavior of the individual and his environment. He may need to think about the effects different forms of psychotherapy might have, or the way in which the personality of some particular therapist might interact with that of the patient. The possible effects somatic treatments and drugs might have on the patient's behavior must be taken into account. So must changes in place of residence, attitudes of other people, and general "social climate." In every case there are likely to be several alternative ways to handle a problem. Assessment involves evaluating these alternatives, assigning probabilities of success to each.

IDENTIFYING THE SIGNIFICANT SYSTEMS

The human organism is a system in a continuous flow of energy transactions with the environment—taking in oxygen, food, sensory stimulation and giving out carbon dioxide, refuse, motor actions. The physiological system and the personal-psychological system can be differentiated for purposes of analysis, as we have shown in earlier discussions. We have in the last few chapters been speaking largely about the *intrapsychic* system of personality—the abilities, attitudes, conflicts, adaptive techniques of the individual. Now we come to the individual's interaction in the larger systems of his physical and social environment.

The nature of a person's commerce with his environment has been demonstrated by Barker and Wright (1955), whose observational research on the behavior of children in their natural surroundings was introduced in Chapters 2 and 3. One of the reports from this large research program describes a normal eight-year-old girl, called Mary Ennis, as she lives a day in her small rural town called Midwest (Barker, Schoggen, & Barker, 1955). In the 14 and a half hours between rising in the morning and going to bed at night, the investigators found Mary engaged in 969 episodes (behavior-habitat interaction units) such as "telling mother she wanted yellow socks," "listening to class discussion about a story read aloud by the teacher," and "kicking a tin can." About half of the episodes were spontaneously initiated by Mary. Nearly all of the episodes were psychologically completed. Only 6 per cent were classified as incomplete. Rather surprisingly, there were no instances of frustration, and only one episode ended in failure. (Though Mary's record is somewhat sparser than others in this regard, there is a suggestion here that so-called "traumatic" incidents may be exceedingly rare in natural life. However, there certainly may be large differences between a small-town setting like this and a crowded city slum.) During this day Mary used 571 different objects as essential supports for her behavior and transacted behavior with those objects 1882 times. The authors describe these objects as flowing through her psychological habitat at the rate of a different object every 1.6 minutes. The most common objects were other persons, who figured in 33 per cent of Mary's transactions. Additional objects included school supplies, furniture, plants, clothing, play things, parts of her body, foods, animals. The object capturing the largest amount of Mary's attention was her mother with whom 6.5 per cent of her transactions occurred. But even at eight years of age, Mary's social contacts outside the home were four times as frequent as with members of her family. The investigators classified 30 per cent of her interactions under the heading of "domination of others." Mary used this mode of interaction more than did the other children they studied. The next most frequent classifications for Mary were nurturance (26 per cent), resistance (16 per cent), appeal (16 per cent), submission (14 per cent), aggression (8 per cent), and avoidance (2 per cent). Altogether, the amount of "authoritative" action on Mary's part almost exactly equalled the amount of "subordinate" behavior.

Although there is this enormous amount of interaction between an individual and his environment, there is also a great deal of *selection*. There were over 200 behavior settings in Midwest, some of them not available at this time of the year or forbidden to children, but still many more than Mary used. Also the total number of objects available in Midwest was approximately 1,200,000, of which about half might be available on a given weekday. Mary's use of 571 objects, therefore, must have involved a great deal of choice. There would probably have been a large amount of consistency from day to day had it been possible to follow Mary for some period. Despite the selection involved and the consistency over time, the recording of the great flow of behavior presents a massive task. As yet, there has been relatively little application of Barker's approach to clinical settings even for research purposes. One exception is the thesis of Rose (1959), who recorded the behavior of patients on a continued treatment ward of a VA hospital. Such a gigantic effort is impossible to expect in the course of ordinary clinical assessment. However, it may be possible to apply ecological concepts in a less ambitious way.

Barker and his co-workers have given us one concept which is particularly important in the assessment of situations—the concept of *behavior setting*. By this they mean an independent area of a community where characteristic patterns of behavior occur, areas which are generally recognized by the citizens. Using interviews, observation, and records (such as newspapers), Barker and Wright (1955) developed reliable ways of identifying behavior settings. They are things like the Cub Scout Den meeting, the Fourth of July celebration on the Courthouse Lawn, the delivery route of the Grand Union Tea Company man, the school playground, streets, and sidewalks of the town, and meal and bathroom situations in the home. Examples of behavior settings from Rose's work (1959) on a hospital ward are the dayroom, noon medications, doctor's rounds, haircuts, showers, preparing for bed, the visit of the Gospel singers, occupational therapy, and group therapy. In each of these behavior settings there are certain expected behaviors, certain demands, and appropriate objects in the environment to suggest and support the behaviors. Often there are quite dramatic changes in behavior when a person moves from one setting to another. In Midwest, for example, little Margaret Reid's hyperactivity and verbosity gave way like magic to passivity, submissiveness, and silence when she passed from the behavior setting of her own backyard to the neighbor's birthday party. On any given day in Midwest, a person might be presented with about 200 behavior settings. Because of the selective process to which we have referred, however, the average eight-year-old participates in only about 16 settings.

If we are to apply ideas from research on behavior settings to clinical situations, we must do two things—develop an overall picture of settings that are available in the patient's daily life and choose which of the many settings presently or potentially available should be studied in detail.

The psychologist can obtain the overall picture or *situational survey* by interview. He might start like this: "Tell me about a typical day for you. When do you get up in the morning and what do you do?" Then in imagination he follows the patient through his day, attempting to see what the patient notices and what he may be overlooking and identifying the principal settings in which he behaves. He might think of a person's life as though it were a play and ask himself: What are the stage settings, the props, and the characters present in each scene?

Each person is allotted only 24 hours a day and 7 days a week. His *distribution of time and energy* reveals his way of perceiving and interacting with his environmental opportunities. He is not a passive organism, but a seeking, motivated, deciding one. His interactions are limited, of course, by what is available externally as well as internally. Keeping his opportunities in mind, we can see that his report of his use of time and energy represents his *choice patterns* for daily living. In this daily living a high degree of ritualizing and scheduling will ordinarily be apparent over any period of time. If we are able to view a person's life over a long time span, it may be possible to see large shifts in daily patterns of behavior. These may represent points of decision and may possibly reflect crises in the patient's life.

In addition to collecting information from the patient, one can also obtain it from informants[2] or from observations made on the scene—the home, for instance. Clinical applications might be made of procedures like Gough's Home Index (1949) which has a report filled out by the subject on the number of books in the home, the presence of a radio, and so forth. Items could be summed to give a measure of socioeconomic level;

[2] Hoffman (1957) has developed a "behavior-day interview" for research on parent-child interaction.

it is easily imaginable how such a procedure might be developed to measure the values emphasized in the home. These different sources of information can provide material for later comparisons between the way the patient perceives his environment and the way others perceive it.

The choice of what situations to explore in detail depends on several factors. When the assessor encounters discrepancies between different observers or finds places where conflict and emotional involvement are high, he knows that more detailed analysis is required. To some extent his theoretical predispositions and the clinical role he plays in the case will guide him in his selection. A clinician convinced of the importance of family interaction usually investigates his home situations. If vocational counseling seems indicated, the clinician concerns himself with work settings. A psychologist in a hospital is likely to emphasize interactional systems on the ward. In any case, the clinician selects a few situations he considers important enough to assess in detail.

ASSESSING INTERPERSONAL SYSTEMS

Often the most significant situations are the primary groups with which the patient is affiliated. Face-to-face relations with close friends and relatives are likely to provide the most highly charged emotional experiences of life. Thus one's perceptions of these relations are likely to be distorted. The number and kind of close groups a person belongs to will vary as he develops throughout his life. Of special importance are his two families: the *family of orientation,* in which he learns his initial modes of interaction from his contacts with mother, father and siblings, and his *family of procreation,* in which he develops his adult ways of relating to his marriage partner and children. Other influential primary groups are friendship pairs, teenage gangs, teacher and classmates, boss and co-workers. In clinical settings there are special groups to be considered— ward associates, doctor and staff, therapy groups.

Because the interview is a two-person group we have already discussed some important aspects of group interaction in our chapter on interviewing. We considered the role expectations, purposes, emotional involvements and adaptive techniques of the participants, and the interaction itself as viewed from several standpoints. These concepts are applicable in larger groups and in natural living situations. There are, however, some aspects of natural groups that make them different from arranged groups meeting by appointment. In the home, for example, the field of interaction is larger—the coming and going is much less regular and controlled. The members of natural groups are more concerned than the members of arranged groups about who is included and excluded. In groups larger than two, characteristics arise that are not found in the simpler combinations. A hierarchy of dominance arises so that there are leaders and followers. Role differentiation becomes more specialized.

When we analyze groups as interpersonal systems, we must ask four kinds of questions. The first has to do with the *structure* of the group: Who are the actors? What roles are available for them to play? What are the power relations among them? What are the rules for interaction? These questions lead to insight about the positions people in the group occupy. The language we have been using suggests a drama; we can also view the group as a game. Once people are brought into a game of baseball or bridge, they must fill various positions and abide by certain rules. In baseball the pitcher is the person who makes most of the decisions and yields most of the power. He stands in the center of the field. He decides when and how to throw the ball. Most of the action is organized around him. The batter, catcher, umpire and others occupy clear positions and have certain powers. A family is organized in a somewhat similar way. Mother, for instance, may have the position of power with regard to activities around the house. Each child has certain tasks he is expected to do. It is possible for a family to be organized in a way that repeatedly produces conflict and frustration. For instance, if several young children are expected to go to bed at an early hour and are told to get into the bathroom and do the chores by themselves, a piling up in this area of the house will occur and squabbles about who gets to use bathroom facilities first will be frequent. Gump, Schoggen, and Redl (1957) have shown the coercive effect of the structure of different camp activities on the behavior of campers. For instance, there is quite a contrast between the activities of swimming and fire-tending. During swimming, an activity which allows great freedom for all to participate in some way, the campers engaged in relatively little conflict. In taking care of the camp-fire, one boy had to be in charge and arguments frequently developed.[3]

The second kind of question has to do with the *processes* of the group: How are decisions made and conflicts of interest resolved? How well do the members of the group communicate with others? In what ways are emotions such as anxiety and affection transmitted through the group? How do the energies of the members become mobilized for action? Each of these questions is a large and important one. Decision-making, communication, transmission of emotion, and mobilization for action—each of these is a topic worthy of a book in itself. We must content ourselves now with just mentioning them. As yet there are no precise assessment techniques for these processes. The interviewer who is attuned to them, however, will be led to ask questions such as: "How did you and your family come to decide on your going to college?" "When your husband comes home tired and irritable as you say he frequently does, what happens? Tell

---

[3] Gump and Sutton-Smith (1955) and Sutton-Smith (1959) has published very interesting analyses of the radically different kinds of interaction patterns produced by the rules of different children's games.

me about the last time this occurred." "Most families find it easy to talk about some things and difficult to talk about others. How is it in your family?"

The third kind of question has to do with the *developmental tasks* of the group: What are the directions of change in the group over time? What problems are of concern now? What behaviors are rewarded or punished? What skills and knowledge are emphasized and needed for meeting present tasks? Is the group attentive to the developmental needs of its members? The sorts of problems of a new family or a new therapy group are quite different from those of groups that have been together for a long time.[4]

The fourth kind of question has to do with the *physical environment* of the group as it influences behavior: Are there sufficient resources for carrying out the activities the group needs to do? What effects on behavior are there from the architectural arrangements and the surrounding "neighborhood"? What sort of interests and activities are stimulated by the physical objects available? Psychologists in their concern for subjective feelings and inner conflicts sometimes fail to pay enough attention to the influences of environmental objects. Such influences are amply demonstrated by noticing the differences in group behavior when a small child and his mother are visiting a house with lots of breakable and attractive knickknacks. If such objects are within the child's reach, the hostess and the mother may be in a state of constant agitation. If they are locked away in a cabinet, the scene will be much more peaceful. As another example, the arrangement of the chairs in a classroom—whether in rows facing the instructor's podium or in a circle—has an influence on the amount of group discussion which takes place. (Also see the report on Sommer's study at the end of this chapter.)

One of the few precise techniques which has been developed to study groups is *sociometry*. (The word could be used in a broad sense to cover all kinds of measurement of groups, as is its present meaning in the journal *Sociometry*; however, we will use the more traditional and narrow meaning here.) Stemming from the work of Moreno, sociometry provides a means of assessing the attractions and repulsions within a defined face-to-face group. This approach, therefore, would be mainly useful in studying what we have called the structure of the group. If used repeatedly it can be helpful in charting changes and developments of this structure. The procedure starts out in a simple fashion. Each person in the group is asked to nominate or rate other members in terms of some dimension or contemplated action—persons preferred as work partners, personal liking for other members. The lines of attraction between mem-

---

[4] Duvall (1957) has described the "family life cycle" showing how families expand and move through certain tasks and problems as the children grow up, and how they contract as the parents age and finally die.

bers can then be plotted graphically to make a sociogram. Figure 2 shows a hypothetical sociogram of ten boys in a camping group. Greg, who receives many choices, is called a *star*. Ivan who neither chooses nor is chosen by anyone is an *isolate,* a term that is sometimes used to cover others like Dave and Dick who were chosen by no one. Also the sociogram reveals cliques of mutual choices, such as the trio, Greg, Rick, and Jim, and the isolated pair, Chuck and George. Quantitative indexes for individuals can be developed by summing the numbers of choices and

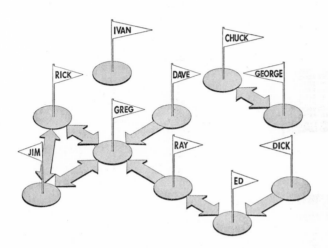

FIGURE 2. Hypothetical Sociogram of choices for companions on an overnight hiking trip. The boys were told they could pick one or two other boys or else go alone.

rejects for each person. More complex statistics can be used for measures of group cohesiveness and compatibility. (For more detailed accounts of procedures and statistical treatments, see Lindzey & Borgatta, 1954, and Glanzer & Glazer, 1959).

The reliabilities and validities of sociometry compare well with those of psychological tests. Despite fluctuations in social relations, there is considerable constancy in an individual's level of popularity. Gronlund (1959) points out that sociometric choices are as stable as intelligence and achievement measures in elementary pupils over a one-year interval. The possibility of high validities is shown by Byrd's report (1951) of a correlation coefficient of .80 between sociometric choices by school children and later actual choices for fellow actors in doing an impromptu play. Gardner and Thompson (1959) have standardized an adaptation of sociometry for school children. They include questions about whom the subject would seek out for discussing a personal problem and whom he admires.

The bulk of the research using sociometry has been in educational, industrial, and military settings, though some version of the technique has frequently been used with therapy groups. The full value of this technique for clinical assessment is yet to be realized. It seems logical that sociometry would be of great value for it makes use of some of the most fundamental qualities in human relations. As Lindzey and Borgatta (1954, p. 406) point out, in showing that sociometry requires little training of the judges, "the rater is asked to apply exactly those particular, unique, and sometimes irrational criteria he has spent a lifetime developing. . . . Liking and disliking, accepting and rejecting are part of the process of daily living."

COMPARING THE PATIENT WITH HIS PRESENT AND POTENTIAL SYSTEMS

While identifying and analyzing the significant systems in the patient's life, the clinician has naturally been thinking about how the patient fits into these systems. In the third step of the process, he proceeds to do this more explicitly. There seem to be three interrelated areas in which comparisons of patient with systems need to be made—role behaviors, perceptions, and functioning skills.

One task in this comparison is to *identify the roles the patient plays (or would play) in each system.* Knowing something about the structure of the family or other group, the question is how the patient fits into it. As we mentioned in Chapter 2, roles are the behaviors that go with a certain position in a social structure. A *position* is a set of expectations about the obligations and the rights of a person who occupies a particular place in a social structure. Positions are something like a set of places at a dining table. The father of the family sits at the head of the table; the mother at the other end. The children rush in and go automatically to their accustomed places. Once the positions at the table are filled, certain role behaviors begin. Someone starts the dishes around the table. Members of the group pass the food to each other, expect to share in it themselves, and engage in customary family conversation. Positions and the role behaviors that go with them are not immutable. Because they are learned ways of interacting, new learning may modify them. On occasions when guests are visiting, for example, there is a reshuffling of positions. The development that occurs over the years also changes the ways in which children enact their roles. In the typical middle-class family the

parents expect more of their children as they grow older—more politeness, more care in handling food. Thus roles are developed in fairly well-
defined social structures. Any given person, of course, occupies many roles
in the different systems in which he participates—father of the family,
salesman, grocery shopper, fisherman.

Information about the obvious roles played by a patient are easy to
come by from hospital records—occupation, marital status, religion. Related to these are the demographic data or background information about
the patient—his father's occupation, the location of his home, his income.
These "ecological attributes" apparently have a very high relationship
with behavior. Several studies mentioned in detail elsewhere show that
a great deal of the accuracy of clinical judgment arises from the judge's
knowledge of the social positions occupied by the person whose behavior
is being predicted. The so-called "stereotype accuracy,'" accurate predictions based only on the knowledge of basic background material and not
on details about individual behavior, is a powerful component in many
of these studies. It can be interpreted as deriving from knowledge of
major life roles. Thus in all assessment it is important to keep in mind
these obvious role attributes of a person.

Some positions and roles are apparent to all, but others that show up
in family interactions are more subtle. In arguments between mother and
father a child may serve as a go-between when communication breaks
down. Or he may serve as an object on which the father displaces his
anger against the mother. A son may be a substitute love object for a
frustrated mother. A careful case history will sometimes show that a
daughter's attacks of asthma always occur soon after fights between
parents; by serving as the suffering one the child distracts the parents
from their own hostilities and brings them together again. The purpose
behavior serves is not always easy to identify, but we can often furnish
the key to the understanding of complex interactions.

The second important task is to *compare the patient's perceptions of
the system with the perceptions of others.* Many aspects of the system
mentioned in the last section can be used for comparison—the way
decisions are made, the values of the significant participants, the exchange
of affection, the satisfaction with physical arrangements. On each of these
different areas of the system the questions now are: How does the patient
see it, and how do other persons see it?" Comparisons of the patient's
analysis of the situation with that of the clinician is also helpful.

It is probably better not to say that the purpose of comparisons like
these is to evaluate the patient's perception of "reality." Since the situation can only be understood ultimately in terms of the perceptions different persons have of it, there are many different "realities." This fact
is beautifully illustrated in the Japanese film *Rashamon* (developed
from the story "In a Grove" by Akutagowa, 1952). It depicts the murder

of a man in the forest from the viewpoint of three different observers. The notorious robber depicts a combat to the death. The wife of the murdered man says he begged her to kill him after he witnessed her disgraceful rape by the robber. The murdered man, speaking through a medium, declares that he killed himself because of his wife's disloyalty. The gross distortions of a psychotic patient, such as failure to know what city he is in or his delusions about Hitler or the Virgin Mary, are so different from what most people hold to be "facts" that we consider them "breaks with reality." But we must always remember that there is always some disagreement between participants in a system about what its "facts" are. When these disagreements are very disturbing, it is important to locate them and to resolve them in therapy.

/ The third task in "patient-system comparisons" is to *ascertain the skills and knowledge needed for the patient to function effectively in the system.* This area is of special importance because of the possibility of training patients to function in a particular system—present or future. Besides sizing up his fitness for a job in a vocational sense, we must also consider the "job" of living in a family or a community group. The homemaker and mother is required to have an incredibly large number of abilities—keeping family expenses within the limits of family income, preparing interesting meals day after day, settling quarrels between children. Clinical psychologists and psychiatrists, in contrast with counseling psychologists and social workers, are prone to overlook such realistic details of everyday life and forget that they play very important parts in the breakdown or rehabilitation of a patient. The clinician cannot afford to be ignorant of these areas. In large agencies and hospitals he may be able to turn over the assessment and treatment planning to a specialist such as a rehabilitation counselor or a social worker but in many situations he must do the work himself. In all cases the conceptual framework he uses in assessment should have a place for these ideas.

Sometimes this third step—the general comparison between the individual and the systems of which he forms a part—can be made quite precise. If job specifications exist, it may be possible to compare the measured abilities of the individual with the job requirements and thus make fairly exact predictions, using actuarial tables that specify success and failure rates for persons of different levels of ability. Less exactly, some psychologists (Stern, Stein, & Bloom, 1956) recommend the development of a "hypothetical model" of the effectively functioning person in a given system. This model takes shape after intensive interviewing and observation of the standards of the people in the system who will be judging the prospective participant. The assessor must set aside his own value judgments and construct a model based on what these judges value in the person, such as the criteria for promotion actually used by a school administrator in promoting a teacher, or the grading system the instructor in a course actually applies. The assessor can then compare the candidate for a position with this hypothetical model and make a clinical judgment as to his suitability for the job. In clinical studies comparing persons with situations, we may consider the developmental needs of a patient relative to the systems in which he will interact. Such an analysis may point to discrepancies which can be lessened by training, therapy, or other procedures.

ASSESSING INTERPERSONAL TRAITS OF INDIVIDUALS

Before going on to the fourth step—planning for change—we will pause first to take a look at a special kind of assessment which is related to the step we have just been discussing—the assessment of interpersonal attributes of individuals. It is important to recognize that we have shifted our frame of reference when we move from interpersonal systems to the interpersonal characteristics of a single person. It is the difference between watching a team in a football game and watching one of the players. In the first case, we note the various formations the team takes in offense and defense; in the other case, we see the style and skill with which the person plays his position. The object of the study of interpersonal characteristics of an individual is usually to identify the traits he shows in many different interpersonal situations. Trait assessment focuses on the individual; role assessment, on the group within which he interacts.

Research and theory in social psychology since World War II has increasingly pointed to two basic interpersonal dimensions. In the many studies of leadership (e.g., Petrullo & Bass, 1961), these two aspects have been identified in various ways: leadership by "initiating structure" or by "consideration of others," the "task-orientation" versus the "social-emotional orientation" of people in problem-solving groups, interest in "production" versus interest in "socialization." In rational or factor-analytic studies of procedures for assessing interpersonal characteristics of individuals, these two dimensions have also appeared. Reviewing many of these studies, Foa (1961) designates them as Dominance-Submission and Love-Hostility. The two dimensions show little or no correlation. Individuals can be described as dominant and loving or dominant and hostile, submissive and loving or submissive and hostile.

These two dimensions form the primary axes of Leary's diagnostic system—the most extensive approach to describing interpersonal characteristics and relating them to clinical purposes. On Leary's circular psychogram (1957, p. 65) shown in Figure 3, the top is the interpersonal direction of dominance and the bottom, submission; the right side is friendliness and the left side, hostility. This psychogram depicts how Leary has elaborated greatly on these two dimensions, breaking them

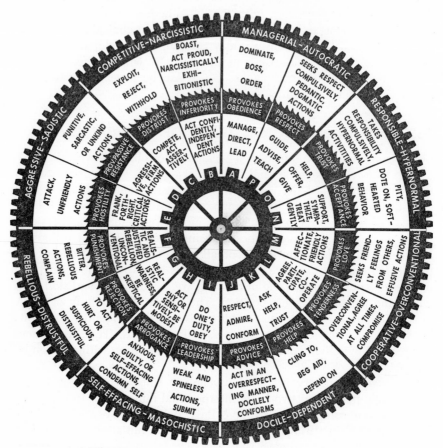

FIGURE 3. Classification of Interpersonal Behavior into Sixteen Mechanisms or Reflexes

Each of the sixteen interpersonal variables is illustrated by sample behaviors. The inner circle presents illustrations of adaptive reflexes, e.g., for the variable A, manage. The center ring indicates the type of behavior that this interpersonal reflex tends to "pull" from the other one. Thus we see that the person who uses the reflex A tends to provoke others to obedience, etc. These findings involve two-way interpersonal phenomena (what the subject does and what the "other" does back) and are therefore less reliable than the other interpersonal codes presented in this figure. The next circle illustrates extreme or rigid reflexes, e.g., dominates. The perimeter of the circle is divided into eight general categories employed in interpersonal diagnosis. Each category has a moderate (adaptive) and an extreme (pathological) intensity, e.g., Managerial-Autocratic. (After a figure from Interpersonal diagnosis of personality, by Timothy Leary. Copyright 1957 The Ronald Press Company.)

down into 16 sectors, each illustrated by brief descriptions. Specified tests and formulas make it possible to describe a person in terms of these 16 characteristics, which are often paired into 8 octants. Leary's system includes another innovation—a way of recognizing the principal levels of information to be obtained about a person, levels ranging from conscious public information to unconscious private information.

There are several other major systems for assessing interpersonal characteristics. Schutz (1958) has developed tests for three kinds of interpersonal needs—inclusion, control, and affection. Gough's CPI (1957) measures such variables as socialization, responsibility, achievement, and capacity for status. Kelly's Role Construct Reportory Test (1955) represents quite a different approach. After identifying persons who occupy significant roles in the subject's life, his mother, a favorite teacher, an interesting person, he asks the person to describe their similarities and differences. From the subject's own choice of words in these comparisons, the clinician can ascertain the way the person thinks about others—his personal constructs. Kelly argues that leaving the patient free to choose his own ways of characterizing others allows the clinician to grasp more readily what the person's own view of his world is like. Somewhat similar to Kelly's test is the Semantic Differential of Osgood—a way of rating objects or persons to determine their connotative meaning to the subject. Many other tests, especially the story-telling tests like the TAT and Sargent's Insight Test, are oriented toward revealing a person's attitudes toward others.

/ Mention should also be made at this point of the so-called *situational test*—a test of performance in a complex, lifelike setting./ Situational tests gained prominence in programmatic assessment work carried on by the Office of Strategic Services during World War II. The candidate for a position of leadership is placed in a standard situation. For example, he may be given certain materials and a crew of men to work with and assigned the task of building a bridge across a stream. Assessors then observe him while he carries out the task, making ratings and recordings of his behavior. Other situational tests involve role-playing. For instance, the subject is told to play the role of a boss who must fire an old employee. An assessment staff member plays the role of the employee in a standard way. Another form of situational test is the leaderless group discussion (Bass, 1954). Still another form is the *work-sample test* used in industry. For example, an applicant for a job as machine operator is provided with the machine for a specified time and the quality and efficiency of his work is recorded. The goal of the work-sample test is to provide a measurement of individual characteristics under conditions which duplicate those of the criterion situation as closely as possible. Other situational tests may select for study certain rare but exceedingly significant aspects of the ultimate criterion situation, such as behavior under extreme stress. In any case the purpose of situational tests, just as with other tests mentioned in this section, is to provide information on the individual—not to study the situation itself as we have described it in previous sections of this chapter.

ASSESSING AND PLANNING FOR CHANGE IN SITUATIONS

The final step in situational assessment takes into account the processes of change and development in the systems with which we are concerned. This is not the place to go into detail on change in systems, since, on one hand, this would involve a review of social psychology and group dynamics and, on the other hand, it would overlap with the material to be discussed under the chapters on psychotherapy. We will content ourselves with mentioning some general matters which may help to orient our thinking on this topic.

The clinical psychologist needs to become aware of the ongoing processes of change in a system before attempting to intervene by setting up rehabilitation plans. There are two principal kinds of ongoing processes to keep in mind: development and reactions to stress. The *"natural" development of a system* has already been discussed. Identifying the course of this process and the special problems of development in a particular case are essential parts of assessment.

Another process is the *system's reactions to stress*. In clinical work we are very often dealing with crises. A family finally can no longer tolerate the alcoholic rages of a father. An adolescent attempts suicide. A psychosomatic ulcer becomes unbearable. These symptoms are alarming reactions to stress. Sometimes, however, extreme reactions subside quickly. Older clinicians are able to distinguish between a momentary turbulence and the more long-range and perhaps more serious stresses and reactions. The experienced person has seen the course of change in similar families or persons many times. He knows when to overlook the violent threats and wild emotions of the moment and how to give emergency treatment.

There seems to be a general pattern characterizing reaction to continued stress in social groups as well as in single organisms. Stemming from the work of Selye to which reference was made in Chapter 2, studies have been made of stress reactions in a variety of systems. (See Miller, 1955, Torrance, 1961). The first reaction seems to be a brief period of shock in which efficiency is lowered. The second reaction is overcompensation an intensive effort to deal with the stress. If the stress continues there is either a catastrophic collapse or an oscillation in effectiveness until adaptation is achieved. Keeping this general model in mind during assessment helps the clinician to understand the overelaborate reactions of a patient to acute stress and the oscillations he shows as he frantically tries to reach an equilibrium. It also helps him to recognize when he is dealing with a patient who has collapsed—given up. The clinician's appraisal will lead him either to accept the lower level of functioning or to try to find ways to expose the person once more to stressful problems. This amounts to a decision between what is sometimes referred to as "covering" versus "uncovering" therapy.

A central problem in planning for change in systems is that of *assessing and working with whatever motivation there is for change*. Nonclinical studies of small groups suggest that change is more effective and lasting if the members themselves participate in planning for it. In clinical work, the members of a family or of a therapy group can often be helped to identify and clarify problems, to search for possible alternatives, to make decisions together, and to follow-through into action. In many clinical situations, however, problem-solving may not follow this pattern. The emotional involvement of the group members may make it hard for them to keep their attention on the tasks. In such cases, the clinician's intervention may be designed to resolve emotional problems rather than to facilitate the carrying out of group tasks. Another problem in the clinical situation is that not all members may be motivated for change. Parents, for example, can see what is "wrong" with their child, but not what is "wrong" with themselves. Still, in most cases the family or other system will have some recognition that something is wrong and that something needs to be changed. This is the motivation with which one must work at the beginning.

In groups where there is strong motivation for change, the clinician's job is *to help search for and clarify alternatives*. The variety of possibilities for change is infinite. It is often surprising, however, how blind patients can be to these alternatives. The clinician attempts to "unfreeze" their rigid views of their situations so that other possibilities can be explored. The possibilities the clinician sees for change will often have been suggested by earlier steps in the assessment of situations. They may include such tactics as redistributions of time and energy, shifts in the groups with which the patient affiliates, changes in the rules or physical arrangements of a ward, changes in the reputation of a patient in a school or ward, training for new kinds of social interaction, and so forth. There are usually resources in the present situation which can be used if we only can see them. In the chapters on therapy we will consider in more detail the utilization of resources and the process of planning for change.

ASSESSING LIFE HISTORY

In both persons and situations there is a life-long process of change and adjustment. As we pointed out in Chapter 2, the clinical psychologist must see the person as a complex system with a time dimension. Whether he is seeing a person briefly for a decision about placement on a hospital ward or working for years with a patient in intensive psychotherapy, he needs to see the contact as an excerpt from a larger, longer pattern—the life history of the person. This life history will combine both personal and situational variables. It will include a picture of a person's choices and developmental tasks as they relate to present assessment goals.

The caution needs to be inserted that the specific assessment goals in an individual case will determine the extent to which the life history is studied. The object of clinical work is not to write a biography nor to conduct a personality research project. The extent of a particular study will be limited by the nature of the task—deciding whether Fred Pearson should be committed to an institution or not, or developing a working image of Mrs. Antonio, whose psychological conflicts underlie her painful migraine headaches. But knowing something of a patient's life history throws light on present problems and suggests future plans.

A central feature of the assessment of life history is the study of the person's choice patterns. Information will usually be obtained by interviewing the patient and other informants.[5] First one identifies the major periods of shift in a person's life: perhaps marriage, leaving to go to college, shifts in occupation, onset of symptoms. Then one inquires into the circumstances of the person at these periods of change (and most probably stress) looking for evidence about the way decisions were consciously or unconsciously made. Did the individual take an active stand, or did he let things happen to him? Did he consider long-range effects of possible courses of action, or was he influenced mainly by considerations of benefits in the present and immediate future? Various other aspects of these "times of change" can also be considered.

In examining choice patterns one needs to keep in mind the developmental tasks characteristic of various periods of life. If the patient does not mention his adjustment to his developing sexuality in adolescence, the clinician wonders why. If the occasion seems appropriate, he inquires in some subtle way about this area of life. In order to make use of the developmental-task notion, the clinician must have some knowledge of normal development and "subjective norms" about expected averages and deviations. An illustration of the possibility of constructing such

_____

[5] One of the authors of this book (Tyler, 1961) has been developing an assessment technique for studying choice patterns of individuals. The stimulus materials consist of one large set of cards, on each of which the title of an occupation appears, and another set, each of which has on it a common leisure-time activity. Working with one set at a time, the subject first separates these into liked and disliked groups. Then he sorts the items into whatever categories he wishes, being instructed to group things which seem to him to go together. This freedom of procedure allows the subject himself to tell how he conceptualizes an area of life. The assessor interviews him extensively to uncover his modes of thinking. Norms for the quantitative aspects of performance—number of positive and negative items, number of positive and negative categories, and the like—can be developed. The actual content of the categories the person uses, however, is idiosyncratic.

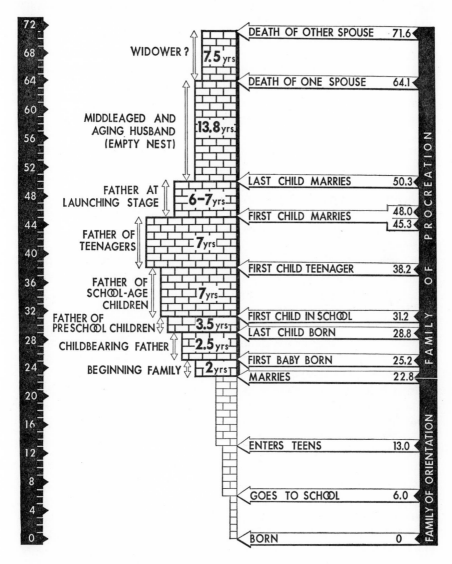

FIGURE 4. Profile of the Life of the Midcentury Husband and Father

(After a figure from Duvall, 1957, p. 18. Used with permission of J. B. Lippincott Co. Data from U.S. Census for 1950 from Paul C. Glick, The life cycle of the family, Marriage and family living, 1955, 17 (1), 3-9; and from National Office of Vital Statistics, Births by age of mother, race and birth order, United States, 1953, U. S. Department of Health, Education, and Welfare Report, 1955, 42 (13), 294.)

norms is provided in Figure 4, which is a reproduction of Duvall's profile of a man based on census data (1957, p. 18).

A picture of the role development of the person begins to emerge. The clinician sees what kind of role the person has tended to assume in family and other groups. As he explores the life history of a patient, he should pay particular attention to the role implications of the patient's memories of early events. These earliest recollections (Mosak, 1958) seem to relect the patient's perception of the place he occupied in relation to the significant persons in his life. If there is a consistent thread running through these recollections, one may hypothesize (along with the Adlerian theorist) that they serve as "guiding fictions" in his present activities.

There are many other aspects of life history—physical functioning, births and deaths in the family, economic problems. To help him organize and interrelate all of the information, the clinician may wish to prepare a chronological chart. Adolph Meyer early advocated such longitudinal outlines, and many others have also used them. (For illustrations, the reader is referred to Richards, 1946; Cobb, 1953; and Burton, 1959, pp. 164-165 & 195). Figure 5 shows one possible life-history chart. This chart can be used in taking notes on major events, choice points, and disturbances of a person's life, as one reads over a case history. In preparing to write a case study or psychological report, such a chart can be very useful as a source of hypotheses about conditions that have influenced the development of the person and stresses that may have led to his symptoms. It helps organize the confusing details of a case history. One may see, for example, how a child's psychosomatic disorders started when a younger sibling was born or how a man's income and productivity improved when he was working under supervision rather than independently. Gaps and holes in the history also become apparent as we study such a chart.

For several reasons it has been difficult to work out exact ways of studying life history. In the first place, what is a life history? What the person tells you himself may be a gross distortion of the facts, whether through lapse of memory, unconscious distortion, or intentional omission. The histories we obtain from other informants, such as wives or parents, are also subject to distortion. Furthermore, to delimit the area to be studied as life history is difficult, because the broad scope of life makes it impossible really to know what is important and what is not. Finally, the history of each individual is so different from that of another that it is difficult to develop comparable procedures. While there is no real solution to these problems of distortion, delimitation, and individual differences, we can set up specific definitions for specific research purposes. Some beginnings of research on life history have been made.

One practical research question is whether the inferences clinicians typically make from case-history data are warranted. We usually assume

FIGURE 5. Life-History Chart

*Patient's name*_____ *Age*_____ *Sex*_____

Family constellation: (Names of brothers and sisters and number of years
older or younger than patient)

Father: (Occupation, education, and age at time of patient's birth)

Mother: (Occupation, education, and age at time of patient's birth)

Major childhood community: (Kind of neighborhood, friends, activities)

Patient's earliest recollections:

Marital family (Family of procreation): (Names of wife and children)

Year	Age	Major Events in Life Situation	Physical & Medical Events	Psychological Functioning
19____	Birth	(For each year describe major events, e.g. who cared for patient at birth, births of siblings, deaths, school problems)	(Describe onset, cessation, and changes in severity of symptoms, illnesses, injuries, etc.)	(Onset, cessation and changes in any psychopathological symptoms—also periods of greatest effectiveness, productivity and satisfaction)
19____	1			
19____	2			
	etc.			

that certain events in a person's life are particularly meaningful, but we have not really checked these assumptions in a systematic way. Some discrepancy between the beliefs clinicians hold and the facts is demonstrated in a research project by Hovey (1959). He asked six psychiatrists and psychologists working daily with neuropsychiatric patients to check a long list of history items indicating whether they are significantly associated with neuropsychiatric conditions. He then compared these answers with a list derived from actual case histories of psychiatric patients and veterans. Hovey found that the clinicians were right about the predictive value of 73 per cent of the items. But there were many errors. Among the items erroneously predicted to be indicative of mental illness were the following: "From time to time I had nightmares as a boy; I used to stammer or stutter; My home was broken by separation or divorce of my parents by the time I was 12 years old." In a study of an entirely different sort, Barron (1954) reports that many successful and mentally healthy graduate students have had incidents in their backgrounds which would be considered traumatic or pathological. Schofield and Balian (1959) in a study of schizophrenics and normals, which is presented in an expanded form at the end of this chapter, found "traumatic histories" in a fourth of the normal subjects. The authors caution against oversimplified ideas that any single event or deprivation necessarily leads toward schizophrenia, and they urge that more intensive studies of case histories be made in order to detect "suppressor" of "immunizing" factors in the lives of those normal people who do not succumb to mental illnesses.

One systematic assessment device is the standardized questionnaire or record blank. Many personality inventories and job application blanks include items about the history of the person. It is very seldom, however, that an attempt is made to cover the life history in any broad and systematic fashion. Hovey has developed a Self-Interview Inventory for psychiatric patients themselves (1958), and Briggs has developed the M-B History Record for use by informants in describing the patient. The latter has been applied in a few research studies with some promising results (Briggs, 1959; Wirt & Briggs, 1959). At the present time, however, there are rather few attempts to study life history intensively by quantitative methods. If we accept the dictum that the best predictor of the future is past performance in similar situations, then it would seem that life-history research would be very profitable. Perhaps we shall have more of it in the future.

CRITICAL COMMENT

The development of exact procedures for assessing situations and life histories is an enormous task. Most people agree about the ultimate worth of such research. Research efforts are hampered, however, by something the reader has probably noticed—the vagueness and lack of precision of concepts in this area. Some psychologists would consider it wiser to put research energies into more tangible projects which promise quicker pay-off. But, vague or not, these problems must be considered by practicing clinicians. Rather than to discourage research on them, it would be wiser for us to praise and encourage any adventurous psychologists who attempt to attack them.

We have not yet made up our minds about the relative amounts of emphasis to be given personal and situational variables. Some psychologists take an individualistic point of view and insist that persons are highly consistent in their behavior, if we have a deep enough insight into them and can see beneath situational variation. Some are extreme situationalists. For example, Coutu (1949) argues that it is useless to assess personality at all since situations determine behavior to such an extent that we can speak only of "tendencies-in-a-situation." Only research will settle the question. We need research that will separate the temporary from the enduring traits. But we must also remember that if assessment studies teach us one basic fact, it is that there must be a careful analysis of the criterion situation. For clinical work we must realize that the ultimate criterion is adequacy of interaction in living.

What would seem to be needed for clinical usage is an analysis of the major situations in the daily life of the patient—especially covering the patient's family, his work or school setting, and his recreational or peer-group relations. Within the daily circle of intercourse with the environment, the major roles would need to be identified along with the accompanying expectancies and boundaries of behavior and the flexibility with which others will respond to role changes in the patient. These interacting systems would need to be classified in such a way that similarities of interactional patterns could be detected and used in the making of clinical decisions. For instance, one should be able to say that this delinquent boy would probably do well in the highly structured environment of a certain family, where communication is clear, but poorly in the permissive environment of another family, where communication is poor.

In addition to these mentioned earlier, there are a number of possibilities for research related to the assessment of situations. One suggestion is that local applications of existing techniques be encouraged and expanded. Too often clinicians assume that a validity study done somewhere else will apply to their own hospital or clinic. This may not be true. Clinical populations vary greatly, and the expectations of one community are not like those of another. Therefore, we need to develop local norms and to do local validity studies. Allport, in this discussion of situationalism (1958), has suggested that assessment should increase the use of devices for self-report on behavior in different situations. Cattell (1957, pp. 426 ff), in considering the development of a taxonomy of situations for conditional prediction, suggests that we could classify situations according to common elements found by factor analyzing descriptive statements about them. The assessment of development in life situations is an area awaiting some future clinician's insight as to what variables and values to insert in the formula: Behavior is a function of person and situation.

SUMMARY

Although most psychologists recognize the importance of the interaction of persons with their environments, there are almost no practical procedures for assessing situations. While precise and quantified methods are lacking, we can make use of interviewing and of observation in both natural and controlled situations. The four steps in assessment of situations and the following: (1) identifying the significant interactive systems; (2) studying the characteristics of each of these systems in which a patient participates; (3) comparing the patient with the system; and (4) planning for the utilization of situational resources or for change in the person and situation. Several writers recommend using the interpersonal traits of individuals as the focus of assessment. If we accept such procedures as Leary's or Kelly's, we must remember that their concern is still with individuals, not with group interaction. Emphasis on the development of persons and situations over time leads to a consideration of ways of assessing the life history of persons. Assessment of both situations and life history is still in an early stage of development; too little research has been done.

SUGGESTED READINGS

ROTTER, J. B. Some implications of a social learning theory for the prediction of goal-directed behavior from testing procedures. *Psychol. Rev.,* 1960, 67, 301-316.
   Rotter pleads that the problem of psychological assessment is very inadequately conceptualized. Rotter's framework of social learning theory rests on the general formula that the potential for certain behavior to occur in a situation is a function of the subject's expectancies about the magnitude and value of reinforcement for that behavior. Thus situational assessment would be based on the categorization of situations according to the predominant reinforcements as determined for any culture group.

DUVALL, EVELYN M. *Family development.* Chicago: Lippincott, 1957.
   This an introductory text to the sociology and social psychology of the family. The orientation is toward the developmental nature of families including an identification of the problems and tasks of the following "stages": establishment, expectant phase, childbearing, preschool children, school children, teenagers, families as launching centers for independent children, the middle years, and the aging years. The clinical psychologist will find a wealth of background information from studies of families.

LIPPITT, R., WATSON, Jeanne, and WESTLEY, B. *The dynamics of planned change*. New York: Harcourt, Brace, 1958.

This book covers the wide spectrum of purposeful attempts to change systems including personalities, groups, organizations, and communities. The authors diagnose each of these systems in terms of internal characteristics (distribution of power, mobilization of energy, and communication) and external characteristics (correspondence between internal and external reality, goals and values for action, and skills and strategies for action). They identify five general phases in the changing of a system: the development of a need for change, the establishment of a relationship between the system and the change agent, working toward change by clarifying the problem and exploring alternative routes and goals, generalizing and stabilizing changes that have been achieved, and terminating the relationship.

THOMAS, H. Problems of character change. In H. P. David and H. von Bracken (Eds.), *Perspectives in personality theory*. New York: Basic Books, 1961.

In this paper Thomas emphasizes the importance of research on personality trends that can be seen only if we observe a long period of an individual's life. He summarizes briefly a study of 4000 German school children now in progress and a number of miscellaneous studies of life histories of individuals, such as reports by people who spend long periods of time in war prisons. He reviews the work of Charlotte Buhler on life stages and some more recent studies of the same problem.

RESEARCH EXAMPLES

PHILLIPS, L., and RABINOVITCH, M. S. Social role and patterns of symptomatic behaviors. *J. abnorm. soc. Psychol.*, 1958, 57, 181-186.

The purpose of this research was to develop a classification system through a study of relationships between symptomatic reactions. It was based on an examination of the case-history data of 604 patients having at least two symptoms on admission. The sample covered a broad range of diagnostic categories. It was drawn largely from a state hospital although there were some subjects from an outpatient clinic and a jail. The total was randomly divided into two halves—one half serving as the pilot group for the initial analysis and the other half serving as a cross-validation group on which to test the stability of the devised categories.

Examination of the records turned up 39 discrete presenting symptoms which occurred frequently enough to be included. All possible pairings of these 39 symptoms would result in 741 different pair combinations. Each symptom was examined statistically for tendencies to pair or not to pair with every other symptom. It was found, for instance, that the symptom of "drinking" often combined with "irresponsible behavior" but seldom with "self-deprecatory ideas." Also "suspiciousness" occurred frequently with "hallucinations," "sexual preoccupations" with "feelings of perversion," but infrequently with "drinking," "rape," "headaches," or "suicidal ideas." On the basis of the analysis of the pilot group, the authors hypothesized that symptoms tend to occur in three major groupings they labeled (1) "avoidance of others" (2) "self-indulgence and turning against others" and (3) "self-deprivation and turning against the self." The validity of this classification system has support in the analysis of the second half of the sample.

The authors relate their findings to the theories of Horney and Fromm. They prefer to interpret them in terms of a theory of development of interpersonal roles. Patterns of role-taking represent the individual's implicit assumptions as to the nature of his relations with others. Psychopathology represents a dominance of genetically early levels of functioning. The category of "avoidance of others" is considered most primitive and might be related to early social and emotional isolation from others preventing normal development of self and reality testing. The "self-indulgence" category represents a genetically high level. This category shows no disturbance of thought but does include tendencies to aggress against others if one's needs are not met. The third category "self-deprivation" represents a still higher level of development, one where social standards have been introjected. Under stress a person of this kind turns against himself and shows symptoms such as "not eating," "headaches," or "suicidal attempts."

One of the limitations of this study or any other study of ordinary psychiatric case histories is the possibility that some of the organization that is discovered is really based on the concepts held by the original interviewers who may tend to omit items that do not fit the case well. A systematic history-taking system would be better for research purposes. It is interesting to compare this study with two research examples mentioned elsewhere—the factor analysis of observed behaviors by Wittenborn and Holzberg (1951) and the comparison of case histories of schizophrenic and nonpsychiatric patients by Schofield and Balian (1959), both reviewed elsewhere in this book. They handle rather similar problems but differ in methodology and interpretation of results. This study goes much further from the data in its theorizing than the others do. For later extensions of this work see Zigler and Phillips (1960, 1961).

WIRT, R. D., and BRIGGS, P. F. Personality and environmental factors in the development of delinquency. *Psychol. Monogr.*, 1959, 73, No. 15, 1-47 (Whole No. 485).

This study relates personality characteristics and case-history factors in a long follow-up study of delinquents. In 1948 all ninth-graders in the Minneapolis schools had been administered the MMPI, a total sample of about 4000. Hathaway and Monachesi (1953) reported the results of an extensive analysis of these data and identified certain codes as being related to subsequent delinquency. In particular a 489 code (the Psychopathic Deviancy scale highest followed by the Schizophrenic scale and Hypomania scale) was frequently associated with delinquency in boys and a 025 code (the Social Introversion scale highest followed by Depression and Femininity) was seldom associated with delinquency in boys. Wirt and Briggs conducted a follow-up in 1956. The authors were interested in comparing nondelinquents and delinquents representing each of the code types. They located 71 to 73 boys from each of the four possible combinations—*delinquency-prone* personality with and without a history of delinquency and *delinquency suppressor* personality with and without a history of delinquency. The environmental data were gathered from records of social agencies; also there were interviews with the subjects, a Q sort by the interviewer, and a standard history questionnaire from the mother. Data from the four different groups are compared.

Some of the numerous results are as follows: Certain profiles on the MMPI and the fact of the family having had contact with a social agency taken together successfully differentiated boys with delinquency records. Forty-two per cent of the boys with 489 codes whose families had agency contact had become delinquent, whereas only 11 per cent of boys with 025 codes who had become delinquent were extremely deviant. Among boys with delinquency-prone personalities (489 codes), the greatest differences between those who became delinquent and those who did not centered around family sufficiency and occupational-educational level. The delinquent group came from worse homes with poor family ties; there were records of disease, poverty, dissocial behavior in the family, absent mothers, and disparity of views between mothers and sons.

This study is of value not only for what it contributes to our knowledge about delinquency and the information it gives us about MMPI patterns, but also as a demonstration of a method for combining personological and sociological data. An additional study, using the same ninth-grade MMPI pool, exemplified another kind of design and a sophisticated statistical technique. Rempel (1958) applied a multivariate statistical analysis to MMPI's and school records of a large number of delinquents and nondelinquents. By a combination of the two kinds of data he was able to correctly identify 74 per cent of the nondelinquents and 67 per cent of the delinquent boys.

Both of these studies as well as the book by Hathaway and Monachesi (1953) exemplify the research possibilities in a well-planned collection of data from a large population in a community or region. This approach makes it possible to do true prediction studies. Measurements are made *before* delinquency or mental illness occurs. Later follow-up in social agency files locates the deviant or disturbed groups. Then the research worker can go back to the data and check which measures actually relate to later events.

HERBST, P. G. The measurement of family relationships. *Hum. Relat.*, 1952, 5, 3-36.

This article is one of the significant steps in the development of the conceptual and methodological framework of family assessment. Herbst derives his basic concepts and hypotheses from Lewinian theory and applies them by means of a Family Questionnaire, which is presented in an appendix to the article. Starting from the assumption that the behavioral field of a person or group is a dynamic whole with interdependent parts, Herbst identifies three concepts: (1) the *family field*, defined in terms of activity regions; (2) the *family structure*, as defined by the power relationship between husband and wife; and (3) the *tension balance* arising out of opposition to changes and decisions.

The Family Questionnaire consists of 33 items, designed to be answered in this case by 10- to 12-year-old school children in Melbourne, Australia. The questions sample four activity regions of the family: household duties, child care and control, economic activities, and social activities. The temporal sequence of "a day at home" is also sampled. For each item the subject is to check who does the activity and the amount of disagreement between the parents regarding what might be done. An example is the first item: "Who decides at what time you have to get out of bed? How often do your parents disagree as to what time you ought to be up?" In answer to the first part the subject checks *mother, father, other adults, myself* (the subject), *brother(s)* or *sister(s)*. For the second part of the item the subject checks whether disagreement is *often, sometimes,* or *never.* The article provides instructions on how to score the questionnaire and how to derive indexes of tension and power.

Herbst identifies four patterns of husband-wife interaction: Husband Dominance, Wife Dominance, Syncratic (or mutually cooperative), and Autonomic (or a high degree of separation or autonomy in activities). These four patterns are derived by using certain cutting points on the scores coming from the Family Questionnaire. (For an extension of this notion and a different way of measuring the four basic patterns, see the Wolfe study mentioned below.)

Using the responses of the 96 children in his sample, Herbst found that the general degree of tension in Syncratic families was lower than the others. However, in looking at separate regions of activities, he found that this kind of interaction did not necessarily result in reduced tension. A decrease of tension in one aspect of family relationships might be associated with an increase of tension in the family as a whole.

Herbst's Family Questionnaire is far from being a well-developed assessment technique. Studies of its reliability, validity, and the influence of response set would be needed. It would need to be changed for applications in other geographical areas and with clinical groups. Though this study is rather weak methodologically, it is very stimulating conceptually and has led to other work. Herbst himself (1954, 1957) has added considerable conceptual and empirical elaboration of situational assessment.

An example of subsequent research is the report of Wolfe (1959) on power and authority in the family. Using a survey sample from the Detroit area, he determined from a small set of items about decision-making in the family the following two indexes: the relative authority of the husband and wife and the degree of shared authority. With these two indexes he determined demographic characteristics. Some of Wolfe's conclusions were as follows: Husband Dominant families are generally high on mean annual income and general social status, whereas Wife Dominant families are generally low. A strong need for love and affection on the part of the wife is a source of power and authority for the husband. Wives in Syncratic families are likely to be well satisfied with their marriage, while wives from Autonomic and especially Wife Dominant families are likely to be low in marital satisfaction. The authority of the wife increases over the years of marriage so that Husband Dominant wives are apt to be younger, and Wife Dominant wives are older.

SOMMER, R. Studies in personal space. *Sociometry,* 1959, 22, 247-260.

Surprisingly little is known about the way people use space. There are two ways in which *space* is defined for research purposes: (1) in the geographical sense, as in the studies of the territories of animals or adolescent gangs, and (2) in the personal sense as the organism moves about, illustrated best by studies of the proximity animals allow other creatures before taking flight and by the cross-cultural studies of "nose-to-nose" distance in conversations between two people. Sommer was interested in personal space rather than territoriality.

The study took place in the staff dining hall of a 1500-bed mental hospital in Saskatchewan, Canada. Data were gathered by two observers who were eating with other staff members. There were 13 rectangular tables each with eight chairs around them. When the observers agreed they could both observe a given table, they started checking who conversed with whom in terms of their positions around the table. Interobserver reliability was high (.91). The first part of the study showed that the greatest amount of interaction occurred at the corners of the table. Side-by-side and face-to-face interaction occurred less frequently, and more distant interactions were much more rare.

The second part of the study involved active experimentation. As they came to the door of the cafeteria, subjects were handed a card with a proverb on it which they were told to discuss with people at their table. Observations were made as before. The study was carried out in a staff dining hall, at a meeting room for the community mental health association, and in dining halls for patients. The interactions of the nonschizophrenic patients were similar to the normal groups. However, the schizophrenics were significantly deviant, choosing distant interactions or opposite interactions more commonly than corner-to-corner interactions which were most common in the other groups.

The third part of the study employed a "decoy"—a confederate of the experimenter who was already seated in a particular chair. The subject was asked to go to the table to discuss a particular topic with the decoy. Decoys and subjects of both sexes were used in various combinations. The typical results showed that females sit "closer" to female decoys than to males and also closer than males would sit to decoys of either sex. Schizophrenic patients, however, did not show this typical pattern.

The author interprets the results as indicating that schizophrenics have an impaired concept of social distance. The methods of this study could be applied to other kinds of interaction. The cafeteria seemed to provide a re-laxed and natural situation in which to study interaction. Clinicians familiar with the behavior of hospital patients often have noted differences in pref-erences for beds, placement of chairs in the day room, etc. It seems very likely that there is much to learn from studies of territoriality and personal space that would suggest how to increase constructive interpersonal relations and how to design hospitals better.

SCHOFIELD, W., & BALIAN, LUCY. A comparative study of the personal histories of schizophrenic and nonpsychiatric patients. *J. abnorm. soc. Psychol.*, 1959, 59, 216-225.

The authors point out in the currently popular view that the seeds of mental illness are to be found in life experiences, especially in critical periods of childhood. In a survey of over 300 studies of life histories of psychiatric pa-tients, they found fewer than 10 which included data from a reasonably com-parable control group. The purposes of this study were to examine the life histories of "normal" persons for evidence of psychiatric problems and to compare the histories of these people with histories of schizophrenics.

The schizophrenic sample consisted of 178 hospitalized patients on which there were comprehensive personal history statistics. The "normal" sample was mainly composed of medical patients coming to the same hospital who showed no evidence of present or previous psychiatric disorder. The selection of the nonpsychiatric sample was dictated by an attempt to match on age, sex, and marital status. The life histories of the 150 normals were collected by a comprehensive clinical interview. After the interview the interviewer im-mediately recorded data on a standard schedule for recording developmental, personal, social, and medical history, the same schedule which had been used with the schizophrenic sample. MMPI's were also available on the normal sample.

The single most impressive feature of the statistical comparison was the sizable overlap of the normal and schizophrenic samples on distributions for personal history variables. Of 35 major aspects of early history and adjustment, 37 per cent failed to show a significant difference, and on an additional 14 per cent it was the normals who showed a significantly greater frequency of undesirable or "pathogenic" characteristics. Specific items that were higher for normals than for schizophrenics were: frequency of poverty and invalidism in their childhood homes, poorer heterosexual adjustment and adequacy of sexual outlet, and a greater incidence of an intellectualized or ritualized orientation toward religion. Divorce in the childhood home approached significance.

The schizophrenics showed a significantly high incidence of unfavorable history items having to do with withdrawal and poor relationships with others:

poor relations with parents, unfavorable attitudes toward school, less occupational success, more social withdrawal, lack of poise, narrow interests, limited aspirations, vague life plans, and lack of initiative. However, the extent to which these same characteristics were found in normals argues strongly for caution in interpreting any single event as traumatic or pathognomonic. Schofield and Balian judged that nearly a fourth of the normal subjects had "traumatic" histories but their MMPI's did not indicate that they were very different from the rest.

The authors concluded that many theories about the etiology of mental disease in early experience need to be carefully checked. Patterns of life events rather than single events should be studied. They suggest that research might identify "suppressor" experiences or psychological processes that immunize normals with deleterious early experiences against psychological breakdowns. (For a brief discussion of a hypothetical X factor, an ability to resist psychological stress, see Pascal, 1951).

8 Interpretation

How does the psychologist "make sense" out of the myriad impressions and diverse bits of information which come to him during assessment? On the outline of the course of assessment given in Figure 1, we are now in the processing stage. The observations, interviews, and tests that have provided the "input" are being processed, analysed, and organized preparatory to the "output" stage in which resulting impressions and judgments are to be communicated to others. Among the various activities at the processing stage, we will focus on the most important, the clinician's interpretative activities—the way he extracts meaning from the information available. There is some ambiguity about the word *interpretation*. Besides using it to refer to the clinician's diagnostic work, psychologists use the term to describe certain aspects of therapy. There it refers to statements the therapist makes to the patient explaining his behavior or pointing out relations the patient has not suspected. In this chapter we are considering mainly assessment or pretherapy interpretation. We will take some examples from therapy situations, however. Though there are many differences between diagnosis and therapy in the interpretative process, there are also many commonalities. Assessment actually goes on during periods labelled therapy as well as during periods labelled diagnosis or assessment.

GENERAL CONSIDERATIONS

A basic assumption, common to all science, is that there is some order to the events of the world. In psychological interpretation the task is to *find* the basic order underlying the complexity of information about a patient. Freud expressed this assumption as the principle of *psychic determinism*.

197

Even dreams, slips of the tongue, and seemingly senseless acts of violence can be explained if one understands the needs of the person and the context in which he behaves. It is this order we seek as we interpret the facts we have assembled.

The actual way in which skilled clinical psychologists go about the business of interpretation cannot be explained as one simple technique at the present time. The very diversity of personality theories and the existence of such issues as "clinical versus statistical prediction," "individualism versus situationalism," and "interpersonal versus intrapsychic explanations" indicate that there are different ways of looking at the process. If we ask clinicians to tell how they make judgments about the case, we get a great variety of answers. Furthermore, many clinicians cannot explain very clearly how they do go about the job. Some say that they relax and let their unconscious "resonate" to the patient's statements. Others decry intuitive interpretation and insist that they follow a rigorous and mechanical method.

As we consider this problem, let us keep in mind some background facts stressed in preceding chapters. First of all, the clinician's perception of *his role* has an important influence on what he does with the available information. It helps to determine the question he tries to answer, the alternatives for disposition of the case he considers, and the amount of time he spends on analyzing the case and writing the report.

Another important factor in interpretation, as in the previous stages of assessment, is the clinician's *conceptual framework*, the assumptions he makes about the nature of personality, psychopathology, and person-situational interaction—his own "philosophy of life." This framework furnishes the basic ideas which will be combined with the specific data. Sarbin, Taft, and Bailey (1960) have called this the "postulate-system" of the clinician. The postulate system originates from inductive generalizations on his experiences, from the theories he accepts, from analogies with similar situations, and from authoritative statements made by teachers and others. Much of the conceptual framework of the clinician is untested. It would seem likely the better clinician would be one who is more open to new and more subtle ways of construing his world and more able to perceive both positive and negative evidence.[1]

Each bit of information that has been collected about a person can be viewed in three ways. There are three kinds of questions we can ask ourselves as we attempt to fit it in to the total picture. First, what does this mean as a *sample*? Second, with what does it *correlate*? Third, is it a *sign* of some underlying condition?

A psychologist's observation, the score on a test, or whatever is

---

[1] The clinician, like any other person, may have a relatively "open or closed mind." Rokeach's work (1960) on dogmatism and rigidity of belief systems could very well be applied to professional people as well as to patients.

available is a *sample* of a population of events. All that the psychologist has is his limited record of the patient's history and the notes from the diagnostic study. How generally do these pieces of information characterize the person, or how specific are they to this time and place? The patient's expression of hostility toward his mother does not necessarily mean that he hates all female authority figures, but we might hypothesize this.

The datum can also be viewed as a *correlate* of something else. What would this observation be related to? On the basis of research or clinical experience, what should one expect? As a clinician considers a patient's feelings that others are persecuting him, he looks for feelings of special worth or special powers, since it is common for paranoid people to develop grandiose reasons for the attention others seem to give them.

A datum can also be seen as a *sign* of underlying feelings or causes. Agitation, a flushed face, and changes of the topic of conversation suggest anxiety stemming from internal conflict. What motives, traits, or social pressures account for the agitation? What would psychoanalytic theory, learning theory, or role theory suggest? In combining information from various sources one checks inferences from one kind of data against other kinds of evidence. If a test shows a poor attention span, for example, one looks for evidence of attention difficulties in school work, associated characteristics like hyperactivity, and background characteristics like anxiety in the home.[2]

LEVELS OF INFERENCE

As we think about the "in-between" process linking "input" to "output"— the process we call *inference*—it will be helpful to distinguish three levels at which it occurs. Figure 6 illustrates this idea. Let us look carefully at what the clinician does at each of these levels.

Inference Level I: At this level there is a minimum amount of inference. The information about the patient or client is as directly related to resultant action as it can ever be. In nonclinical work this kind of inference frequently occurs. For example, a prospective student applies for entrance to college. He sends in his grade record and takes an entrance examination. The admissions officer accepts him if he is above a certain cutting score, rejects him if he is below it. Similarly, in screening for emotional disturbance in the armed services psychologists used a routine test and a checklist, followed perhaps by a five-minute interview. If they detected no gross deviation from normal they passed the inductee. If they

---

[2] The observant reader may have noticed that the sample, correlate, and sign approaches are parallel to the different kinds of validity (content, criterion, or construct) discussed in Chapter 6. It is interesting to note the similarity of the interpretive processes used by the clinician and the validation procedures used by the statistical measurement specialist.

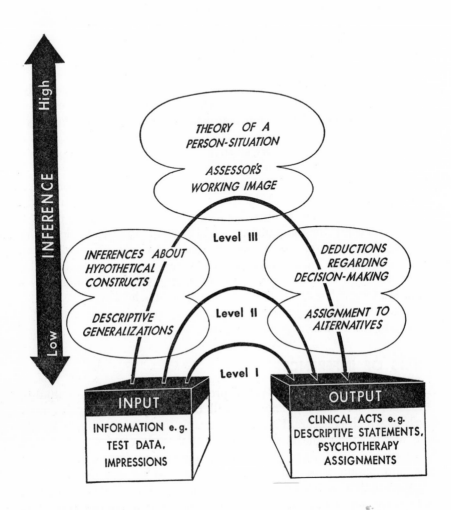

FIGURE 6. Levels of Inference in the Assessment Process

noted some disturbance, they sent him to another interviewer for more intensive evaluation. A well-trained clerk or even a machine, can make such inferences. We do not generally think of Level I as being very "clinical"; yet, as Meehl has pointed out (1956a), it is potentially an important level for clinicians. It produces standardization and efficiency in the operation of a program. Its main disadvantage is that it provides no way of dealing with exceptions to general trends and unique or idiosyncratic events.

If we were content with this level of inference, we could dispense with theory altogether. We would need only to check outputs against inputs, never bothering to guess what goes in between. Skinner has advocated an experimental psychology of this type, in which the organism is treated as a "little black box." Much might, perhaps, be learned by experimental work of this kind, with clinicians as subjects. It certainly is true that many gifted clinicians function extremely well without being able to explain what it is they are doing. They are like Feigl's "diagnostic dog," who belonged to a physician. He would bark in a peculiar way whenever a patient with incipient cancer entered the office. The dog's bark was a useful aid to diagnosis though no one knew why. Feigl says, "I suggest that the clinical psychologist, and the empathizer generally, is his own diagnostic dog. If, and only if, a high 'batting average' can be established, on the basis of subsequent objective evidence, is he entitled to some confidence in this diagnoses" (1959, p. 121). However true this may be, most clinicians want to know more about assessment than this. They are eager to go beyond the level of bare correlation to discover something about their own internal processes, even though they admit that such speculations are hazardous.

Inference Level II: At the next level above simple correlation between input and output, there are at least two kinds of inference. The first is *descriptive generalization.* Here one attempts to state what is generally true about some observed characteristics. For instance, during an interview with a patient a clinician may observe several instances of slow body movements and long delays in answering questions. The descriptive generalization he uses in interpreting these facts is that at the time of observation the patient was "retarded motorically." If he discovers later that the patient eats and sleeps poorly and says that he is sad and discouraged, the clinician may then use the term *depressed.* This term can be thought of as a broader descriptive generalization, or an example of a second kind of inference, a *hypothetical construct*—an inner state which is more than a pure description of behavior (MacCorquodale & Meehl, 1948). A construct often implies an etiology or causal condition, perhaps physiological. Level II inferences, whether they are descriptive generalizations or hypothetical constructs, permit us to make deductions with regard to the patient's needs and treatment.

Inference Level III: This level differs from Level II only in its inclusiveness and integration. Here one attempts to form a consistent overall *theory of the person-situation.* Such an attempt involves the kind of thorough-going exploration of the person's life situation we have discussed in the last chapter, and explanatory speculations about the developmental, social, and physiological underpinnings of his behavior. To be completely successful it requires a coherent integrated theoretical system of hypotheses and deductions. Most clinical work is not pitched at such a

high level, in part because most of our theories of personality are themselves very difficult to apply consistently to an individual.

At a less pretentious Level III position, we do seem to be using something like a simple "theory of a person" in all assessment work involving
contact with patients. It is the loosely organized set of hypotheses and
hunches about a person and his situation which we have called the
working image. This image of a person undoubtedly starts to form as
soon as we get one or two bits of information about him. It grows very
rapidly in the first few minutes after we meet him. It is in terms of these
partly verbalized, partly unverbalized images of people that we make
our decisions and use our clinical techniques.

The different levels of inference and the use of statistical and clinical
processes in practical work is well stated in Goldman's metaphor comparing the interpretative process to a bridge:

We stand on one side of a river with our client, trying to help him to explore
some of the territories on the other side, so that we may better decide where
among the various communities on that side he would like to live. The question
at hand is: Which bridge would suit our needs best? To complicate the situation none of the bridges leads to the places being considered but only to points
from which those places can be viewed, sometimes not very clearly. Furthermore, on the opposite bank one cannot travel very well between bridges, so
that each time one has seen the view from the far end of a clinical or a statistical
bridge, he must return to this side of the river. To get another view of the
countryside, a different bridge must be crossed. Counselors can help their
clients to locate the bridges, to make the trips across, and to try to make out
the different views from the other side—of the job, the college, or whatever.
Later, the client must make the trip to his destination alone, without the
counselor as guide; only at that time will he, or we, truly know how he will
fit into that community (Goldman, 1961, pp. 188-189).

STATISTICAL AIDS TO INTERPRETATION

As Goldman points out, both statistical and clinical bridges are available.
In this section we will examine these statistical bridges before we consider the more "clinical" processes of interpretation. As the word *aid*
suggests, the use of statistical procedures never gives us the complete
interpretation, even at Level I. Clinicians must always decide what kind
of statistical aids are appropriate for an individual case. Statistical
processes are tools used by clincians rather than substitutes for clinical
judgment.

The clinical psychologist often uses quantitative procedures to compare
persons with others and to make predictions. To do this he must be able
to make an *exact classification of the individual*. The basis for classification can be a test score produced by the operations of either a clerical
worker or an IBM machine on an answer sheet the individual has filled
in. This may be a nonmechanical judgment the clinician makes on the

basis of an observation or a Rorschach protocol. Classification can also
be based on history categories, such as age, sex, occupation, presence or
absence of syphilis. It would also be possible to use categories and codes
derived from interviews, reports on home atmosphere, or job requirements. The first essential requirement for the use of this method is that
the clinician have available some kind of clear and unequivocal slot in
which to place the person. (To simplify the terminology, we will usually
refer to this quantity as either a score or a category.)

The second requirement is that some previous research has provided
an *exact procedure for relating the score or category to other events or
outcomes*. It must be possible to place the score in a table to see how it
compares with others or to insert it in a prediction equation. Before going
on to discuss these mechanical procedures for comparison and prediction,
it might be useful to point out that though this procedure is mechanical
and apparently nonpsychological it resembles in many ways what a psychologist does without the benefit of these exact procedures. Lacking research evidence the psychologist is likely to assume relationships and
to act as if they exist. On the basis of previous experience with aggressive
children, a psychologist predicts that a new boy will not respond well to
play therapy. Every psychologist has a set of subjective norms on which
he compares people even if he does not have objective tables. He may
think, "the new patient, Henry Peterson, is one of the most severely disturbed schizophrenics we've had at the hospital; he has certain features
that remind me of George Gerlich and others that remind me of Calvin
Achipeligo." The clinician is acting like a mechanical comparison-maker
even when he lacks exact evidence. We shall have more to say about this
resemblance in later sections.

The simplest kind of statistical aid to interpretation is a *table of base
rates* (what insurance men call *experience tables*). To construct such a
tool, one tabulates instances of the kinds of cases that interest him. A
psychologist working on a hospital admissions ward may check the files
for the past year and tabulate the number of cases diagnosed as anxiety
neurotics, sociopaths, schizophrenics, manic-depressives, and others. He
can also tabulate the kinds of decisions about treatment that were made
for different diagnoses, for males and females, for different age groups
and occupational groups, or for "first admissions" and "readmissions."
In using base-rate information to make predictions about a new case,
he will first locate the subgroup to which the new patient belongs. He
can then read off from his table what decisions have been made in the
past about the treatment of such patients and how the treatments turned
out. How he will use this information in dealing with this particular
patient depends upon many things such as his observations of unusual
features in this patient's case or his knowledge of changing trends in
the treatment of this condition. But knowing this base-rate information

helps him prevent possible errors. As Meehl and Rosen (1955) have pointed out very well, it is often true that additional statistical and clinical procedures do not actually improve on base-rate predictions. Unfortunately, the clinicians too seldom take the time to tabulate base rates, even though they are almost always available in the clinic's files.

A special kind of base-rate table is the *expectancy table,* which relates test scores to criteria of later success. An excellent example is the graph developed by Carlson and Fullmer (1959) shown in Figure 7, relating the scores received by tenth-graders on the Iowa Tests of Educational Development to grades received in the freshman year of college. A particularly valuable feature of this chart is the indication that the score a student obtains is related to a range or spread of college grades. Statistical prediction gives us probabilities, not certainties.

A simple and related kind of statistical aid to interpretation is merely the *table of norms* for test scores. One locates the individual's raw score on the distribution of scores for a normative sample. The table will tell you whether the person is in the high, low, or middle range of the comparison group. A single derived score such as a standard score or percentile rank gives us this sort of information if we know the norm group on which it is based. We have mentioned in Chapter 6 the cautions that must be observed in using these scores. We must be sure that the norm group is appropriate for the individual being considered. For example, the usual test is standardized on the general population with normal faculties. With a blind or crippled child, some norms may not be appropriate. The psychologist can develop local or specialized norms for tests in the same manner as he ascertains local base rates. We must always remember also that norm tables tell us nothing about the reliability and validity of tests. In order to take unreliability into account, we should think of a score as a range rather than a point. What a score means about a person must be decided on the basis of studies of the empirical validity of the test.

Normative data may be utilized in a more complex way by making *profile comparisons.* Many texts are made up of several subtests or scales. When these are all studied against the common standardization group, it is possible to plot the scores and to examine the resulting configuration. The greatest elaboration of methods for comparison of profiles has occurred in work with the Minnesota Multiphasic Personality Inventory. An example is the MMPI profile shown in Figure 8.

It is possible to summarize the information in the graphic profile by a number called the *profile code.* This system developed by Hathaway, requires that one rank in descending order the numbers of the scales on which the person scores 55 or above. There are a number of other rules too complicated to discuss here. Having this profile code, the psychologist can turn to the information provided in the MMPI Atlas (Hathaway &

ITED Composite Score	Chances in 100 of Earning College GPA of			Expected Range of College Grades				
	2.0	2.5	3.0	F	D	C	B	A
29-30	97	86	62					
27-28	95	80	50					
25-26	91	70	40					
23-24	86	60	29					
21-22	78	49	19					
19-20	60	38	13					
17-18	59	28	8					
15-16	48	19	4					
13-14	38	12	2					
11-12	27	7	1					
9-10	18	4						
7-8	12	2						
5-6	7	1						
3-4	4							
1-2	2							

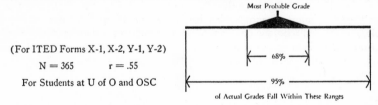

Most Probable Grade

68%

95%

of Actual Grades Fall Within These Ranges

(For ITED Forms X-1, X-2, Y-1, Y-2)

N = 365   r = .55

For Students at U of O and OSC

FIGURE 7. Expected College Achievement as Predicted by Performance on Iowa Tests of Educational Development Taken in Tenth Grade

(From Carlson & Fullmer, 1959, p. 11. Used with permission of the University of Oregon.)

Meehl, 1951). It tells him what diagnostic groups are likely to include people with such codes and provides brief case histories of persons who have scored this way. This information may help with prognoses and suggest areas to be investigated. A brief glimpse of how profile comparison

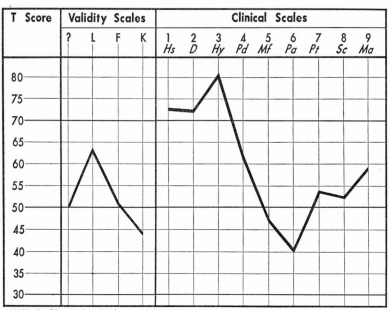

MMPI Profile Code: 3<u>12</u>′ 49– 6(47) 8; 3; 9.

FIGURE 8. An MMPI Profile and a Profile Code

The 3<u>12</u>′ indicates that 3 (the Hysteria scale) has the highest score and 1 (Hypo-chondriasis) and 2 (Depression) are next highest. The line underneath the 1 and 2 indicates that they are within one point of each other. The accent mark (′) indicates that 3, 1, and 2 are all above a T score of 70. Next in rank below these three scales is 4 (Psychopathic Deviate) and 9 (Hypomania). The dash indicates that the other clinical scales fall between 45 and 55 except for 6 (Paranoia), which falls below 45. The 47 in parentheses indicates the T score on Mf (Masculinity-Femininity) which is not included in the clinical scales. The 8, 3, and 9 indicate raw scores on L (Lie), F (Infrequent answers), and K (Defensiveness) respectively.

might be used in clinical interpretation is provided by Hathaway's report (1955) on the MMPI code from which the profile shown in Figure 8 has been reconstructed. Hathaway is presenting a case of "low back pain" in a 35-year-old woman. Part of his discussion of MMPI results is as follows (Hathaway, 1955, pp. 71-72):

This profile did not indicate a severe neurosis but was certainly clearly of the type observed in hypochondriacal and conversion-type hysterical cases. The

Atlas gives diagnoses of psychoneurosis; hypochondriasis, mixed; and hysteria, in that order of frequency. Reactive depression and suicide are often mentioned. . . . These data strongly indicate a functional rather than an organic problem.

Coding systems for other tests, such as the Strong Vocational Interest Blank (Crites, 1959), the Kuder Preference Record (Callis, Engram, & McGowan, 1954) and the Rorschach (Hales, 1952) have been suggested. In his review of studies using complex profile-analysis methods, Michael (1959) concluded that the results have been disappointing. One difficulty is that profiles tend to be unreliable, since differences between pairs of scores are less reliable than the individual scores themselves. However, Meehl and Dahlstrom (1960), in the study mentioned at the end of this chapter, were able to derive rules for the use of MMPI profiles that enabled them to make successful predictions.

The *regression equation* is another statistical aid to interpretation. Out of the correlations of test scores with a criterion, an equation can be developed for predicting individuals' achievement on the criterion. When several tests are used, a *multiple* regression equation is required. An illustration is provided by Garrett (1958, pp. 406-409) and mentioned in Goldman (1961, p. 176). A study of the relationship between college grades and two predictor variables, general intelligence and number of hours per week devoted to study, produced the following prediction equation:

$$X = .57Y + 1.12Z - 66$$

Here X represents the honor-point record being predicted; Y stands for the intelligence test score, and Z stands for the number of hours of study per week. With a given student named Smith, the predicted number of honor points for the year can be easily computed from his intelligence test scores and his report on hours of study. For instance, if Smith's intelligence score is 120 and he reports that he studies 20 hours per week, our best estimate of the number of honor points he is likely to make is 25.

$$(.57 \times 120) + (1.12 \times 20) - 66 = 24.8$$

Another simpler way of bringing data from several tests to bear on a decision is what is usually called the *multiple cutoff* procedure. For   many kinds of decisions we do not need to consider the whole possible range of scores on the variables from which predictions are being made. If in the preceding example, we are interested only in helping Smith decide whether he has a good enough chance of college success so that he should apply for admission, all we need are cutting scores for the two predictive measures. If on the basis of evidence that 50 per cent of students with intelligence test scores below 110 are disqualified before the end of the first college year, we have set a cutting score of 110. We first check Smith's record to make sure that his score is higher than this. If previous evidence has enabled us to set a cutting score of 12 hours a week for the variable "study time," we can see at a glance that Smith's study time is also above the minimum. Thus we can give him the "Go ahead" signal without making any computations.

Another kind of statistical aid consists of *differential group comparisons*. These methods can be used when prior research has identified significant differences between groups on the given measures and a formula has been derived which yields a number showing how similar any given person's scores are to those of the reference groups. As a hypothetical example, if clerical workers are high on a test of perceptual detail and low on a test of mechanical comprehension, but certain factory workers are the reverse, then such a formula weights scores accordingly. If a new applicant for a job scores low on perceptual detail but high on mechanical comprehension, the formula would indicate that he is more similar to factory workers than to clerical workers.[3]

One reason that clinicians do not use the more complex statistical aids very much is that as yet very few have been developed for clinical situations. Their largest application has been in schools and industries where large populations must be screened and assigned to different activities. Such situations involve what in a previous chapter we have called institutional decisions. Some of the clinical psychologists' work may be very similar to this. For instance, he may work on personnel selection of psychiatric aides. Clinical assessment aimed at classification for treatment purposes is less similar. One cannot just tell a patient to go away, as one can a job applicant. Furthermore, the values that enter into these decisions are values about sickness and health, even life and death. An example is the suicide problem. Suicide is very rare in the general population, or even in the psychiatric population. Even a good test administered in a patient group would provide only low probabilities of suicide for a given patient. Perhaps even the highest score on the test might predict for patient X only one chance in four of his committing suicide. Going by base rates or by the test predictions alone, one would predict that the patient will not commit suicide even if no special precautions are taken. But a patient's life is an important matter; so if the probability of suicide

[3] One such method is the discriminant function. (See Tiedeman, 1954). Whether discriminant methods or regression methods are more useful and meaningful is an argument as yet unresolved. (For a discussion of the issue, see Goldman's chapter on "statistical bridges.") If a person looks at the life history of the individual as a series of choices, then some procedure which allows for placement in one category or another is necessary and the continuous dimensions of trait psychology and regression equations are not appropriate. (See Tyler, 1959.) One decides either to be married or not; one is born male or female. For research on choice patterns, nonparametric statistics applied to categories leading to statements of probabilities would seem to be more appropriate than correlation methods.

for this patient is even a little greater than average, the psychiatrist in charge is likely to order removal of sharp objects from his room, special round-the-clock care, and the like.

THE STATISTICAL VERSUS CLINICAL PREDICTION ISSUE

Psychologists are agreed about the usefulness of all these statistical tools as aids to the interpretative process. They agree that it is desirable for clinicians to apply their research skills to the problems of developing such aids and to take the responsibility for decisions about which should be utilized in each case. There has been a long-drawn-out argument, how-ever, over the question as to whether what a good clinician does in organizing information about a case goes beyond this and accomplishes purposes that regression equations and other statistical techniques cannot accomplish. In order to compare the effectiveness of statistical and clinical methods in combining data, investigators have asked a clear, practical question: Which produces a more accurate prediction of be-havior in some life situations?

The controversy over this issue was brought to a focus with the publication in 1954 of Meehl's book, *Clinical Versus Statistical Prediction.* Since then many articles and symposia on the subject have been published. Time after time, research studies contrasting the two ways of combining the same data arrive at the same conclusion—that the clinical method does not result in greater accuracy of prediction than the statistical method does. In many instances the clinical predictions are clearly less accurate.

A good example of such a study, the first one in Meehl's series, is Sarbin's 1943 attempt to predict college grades. For the statistical ap-proach, a clerk simply inserted each student's college aptitude test score and his rank on high school grades into a regression equation developed from an earlier sample. For clinical predictions, psychologists were given the same scores plus a variety of additional data including other test results and a biographical form. They were also allowed to interview each student before making their predictions of the grades he would receive at the end of the first quarter in college. The predictions by the clerk using the regression equation correlated with actual grades .45 for men and .70 for women. For the psychologists, the respective cor-relations were .35 and .69. The two sets of correlations do not differ significantly. The equation did fully as well as the psychologists. Meehl and others have reported many other kinds of studies involving a variety of predictions—flying skill, parole violation, outcomes of psychotherapy.

In 1956 Meehl presented a study in which the attempt was made to produce a description of personality (a working image, in our terms) by mechanical methods. Halbower (1955) in a doctoral dissertation under Meehl's direction derived a set of Q-sort statements associated with certain MMPI profile codes of VA mental hygiene patients. Then a fresh batch of MMPI profiles was submitted to several trained clinicians and to a clerk who worked automatically according to rules derived from the previous statistical research. Both the clerk's and the clinicians' results were compared with the criterion, the Q sorts of therapists who were well acquainted with the patients. Once again the clinicians were not able to improve on the mechanical "cookbook" approach. The research of Marks (1961) and others to be mentioned in Chapter 10 have confirmed this general finding.

When one looks for evidence from carefully controlled studies on the other side of the question, evidence that would demonstrate the superiority of clinical prediction, he finds very little, and there are serious questions about what he does find. Holt (1958) presented a persuasive argument about the necessity for considering a wide range of judgmental activity in the clinician. (Meehl's book had intentionally limited its survey to studies of the two different methods of combination of the same information.) Holt argued that it is important for the clinician to study the criterion and test his judgments—to become a sophisticated rather than a naïve judge. Holt's data on the prediction of success of psychiatric trainees in the Menninger school included both the statistical predictions from a variety of tests and the predictions of two "sophisticated" psychologists. The statistical formula gave what appeared to be good predictions for the initial group, but did not work for the next group of psychiatrists. One of the clinicians made assessments that correlated fairly highly (.57) with the criterion. Holt does not tell us, however, whether these judgments were equally accurate in the second group. In another study, Trankell (1959) found that psychologists' assessments of candidates for flight training in Sweden were more highly correlated with success than the test results were. Both Holt and Trankell emphasize the importance of trained judges, sophisticated judges, sophisticated about the situation for which they are predicting. Though both of these studies served to keep the controversy open, they did not do away with the necessity for the clinician to stay on the defensive in his battle with the actuary. The bulk of the research still indicates that actuarial prediction is more accurate than clinical prediction.

It is obvious, of course, that we cannot immediately replace clinical prediction by statistical prediction, since, as mentioned before, there are as yet very few statistical procedures available for use in clinical situations. Also, as Holt has pointed out, much of the furor over clinical *versus* statistical prediction has involved a narrowed attention on what the clinician actually does. The methods of combining data are a small part of the total role of the clinician in assessment, as our diagram of the assessment process (Figure 1) illustrates. There are many points at which clinical judgment must enter—decisions as to the goals of assessment,

what information to collect, how to organize and report information. As
Meehl (1956*b*) points out, we cannot make a statistical prediction for
the individual case unless the conditions match reasonably well the
particular conditions under which the statistical formula was derived.
It is very seldom that we have situational variables in our formulae.
Then, too, when special events, such as accidents, occur, the statistical
approach will not be applicable, and we clinicians must necessarily, as
Meehl says, "use our heads instead of a formula." Also, as we have
noticed before in discussing individual decision-making, individual
values play a large part in counseling and therapy so that general
formulae are not applicable except as information for the patient and
therapist when a client is being helped to make choices. Holtzman (1960)
has pointed out that clinicians have to be on hand in order to collect,
interpret, and apply data. What we can say on the basis of present
evidence is that wherever available, statistical methods are to be recommended for data processing. Some day when clinical psychology has
advanced further than it now has much of the processing of data that
now requires clinical judgment may be done by machine. Perhaps the
most important thing about the clinical versus statistical controversy is
that it demonstrates the desirability of devoting much more attention to
research so that assessment work can be simplified and redirected as
well as improved. Meehl makes this point well in his main conclusion:

> There is no convincing reason to assume that explicitly formalized mathe-
> matical rules and the clinician's creativity are equally suited for any given kind
> of task, or that their comparative effectiveness is the same for different tasks.
> Current clinical practice should be much more critically examined with this in
> mind than it has been. It is my personal hunch . . . that a very considerable
> fraction of clinical time is being irrationally expended in the attempt to do, by
> dynamic formulations and staff conferences, selective and prognostic jobs that
> could be done more effectively, in a small fraction of the clinical time, and by
> less skilled and lower paid personnel through the systematic and persistent
> cultivation of complex (but still clerical) statistical methods. This would free
> the skilled clinician for therapy and research, for both of which skilled time is
> sorely needed. (P. E. Meehl, *Clinical versus statistical prediction*, Minneapolis:
> University of Minnesota Press, 1954, pp. vi-vii.)

CLINICAL INFERENCE AS TAXONOMIC SORTING

One of the outgrowths of the thinking stimulated by the controversy
over clinical and statistical prediction has been the development of some
theoretical formulations about the logic of the clinical inference process.
Sarbin, Taft, and Bailey (1960) have presented a theoretical analysis
in terms of what they call *taxonomic sorting.* They see the thinking
process of the clinician as fundamentally a process of syllogistic reasoning of the sort familiar to any student of philosophy. From a postulate
system based on his whole background of experience and from his

awareness of his role in this assessment, the clinician formulates a *major premise:* "Improvement in psychotherapy is frequently associated with an intact ego, mild anxiety, and high motivation." From his assessment of a patient called Mr. Jones, by means of tests and observation, the psychologist arrives at his *minor premise:* "Jones is a member of the class of persons characterized by an intact ego, mild anxiety, and high motivation." This act of placing the person or occurence in a class— the act that produced the minor premise—is called *instantiation.* From these two premises a conclusion follows: "Jones will probably improve with psychotherapy." In summary, it can be said that "The clinical inference is a conclusion which follows from the collocation of a major premise, derived from the clinician's postulate system, and a singular minor premise achieved through observation" (Sarbin et al, 1960, p. 83),

Sarbin and his associates hold that this process differs from ordinary syllogistic reasoning mainly in the fact that it is probabilistic. Presuming that research has shown that 60 per cent of similar cases improve with therapy, we have no logical way of knowing whether Jones fits in the group of the 60 per cent who improve or the 40 per cent who do not. However, because decisions must be made, we treat information from previous experience "as if" it were pertinent to Jones. More exactly we should say, "The probability that Jones will improve in therapy is six in ten" or "The statement 'Jones will improve in therapy' has a credibility of 0.6." If we accept this analysis of interpretative activity, we would require that a clinician identify his major and minor premises, check their validity, and avoid the logical fallacies in coming to his conclusions. The clinician must work toward a scientific estimate of the probabilities involved and formulate them as exactly as possible.

The clinician's task is more complicated than this simple formulation would suggest, however, because he must usually make a sequence of inferences in order to come to a final decision about a patient. The probability values attached to the premises at each stage depend upon the preceding events. (This is what is called a *stochastic* process.) Because of previous experience (in some cases based on tabulations of base rates), a diagnostician has a certain probability to work with as soon as he decides that a person is a mental patient. For instance, he may know that six patients out of ten are schizophrenic. The tests the clinician gives and the questions he asks at this stage serve to shift the probability value for this particular patient up or down, and the clinician decides either to adopt the minor premise, "This patient is schizophrenic," or to adopt another one, such as "This patient is neurotic." If he chooses the "schizophrenic" premise, he then starts the next stage of the inference process as he attempts to decide whether this is *reactive* schizophrenia" or *process* schizophrenia." Again he uses any means available to him (tests, interviews with the patient's family, for example) to enable him to "instantiate" the patient in the "reactive" category or the "process" category. The next step in the inference process involves probabilities of favorable or unfavorable outcomes in whichever category he chooses. The conclusion of the complex logical process is either "The prognosis for this patient is favorable," or "The prognosis for this patient is unfavorable." He can attach an exact probability value to each of these conclusions if he knows the probability values of the successive branches of this "tree." Usually, of course, the clinician does not know these exactly, but he may in his thinking use estimates of them even when he is not aware that this is what he is doing.

It is this kind of thinking that Sarbin, Taft, and Bailey have in mind when they characterize the whole process of clinical inference as taxonomic sorting. It is a sequential process of assigning the assessee to categories—of deciding which premises patients fit, these premises being statements of probabilities rather than certainties.

CLINICAL INTERPRETATION AS EMERGING SYNTHESIS

There are many clinicians who would be reluctant to say that interpretation is never anything but this categorizing process. Part of assessment work is the assignment to classifications carrying certain probabilities. But is this all? To the working clinician it certainly "feels" as if he is doing something more significant and fundamental when he discovers the deep fear of disapproval that keeps Mr. Tucker from using his talents, or the ambivalence toward women that arose from Harry Simpson's frightening experiences with his parent's sexual sadism and is now reflected in his dreams. Taxonomic sorting seems like a logical analysis after the main work is done. It is logical, not psychological. It is limited to producing conclusions about the person rather than an understanding of what we might call the "shape of his life." To hardheaded thinkers like Sarbin, Taft, and Bailey, such a phrase has an unwelcome, mystical ring. They can point to the outcomes of the clinical and statistical prediction studies as evidence that "understanding" does not lead to a greater number of correct predictions than does manipulation of probabilities.

But does failure to predict accurately necessarily invalidate nonstatistical varieties of clinical inference? In discussing psychological theories in Chapter 2, the authors of this book take the position that prediction is not the whole aim of science. It is a convenient tool in scientific work, but it is not the only tool that can be used in the accumulation of knowledge and the testing of theories. One could even argue that a clinician often hopes to stimulate unpredictable behavior in patients with whom he works. Rogers has called our attention to the loss in predictability that typically occurs when a neurotic patient moves toward a healthy sort of personality integration. Evaluation of how successful one's predictions are is certainly one way to check the adequacy of his concepts, but it is not necessarily the only way. In Reichenbach's terms, mentioned in Chapter 2, taxonomic sorting more nearly fits the kind of thinking called "justification" rather than the kind of thinking called "discovery." Their view restricts itself to only part of the work of the assessor. Meehl in his review of the Sarbin, Taft, and Bailey book points out several other shortcomings and concludes: "Whatever plausibility the resulting conceptualization has is achieved by ignoring the really interesting cases of personological inference" (1961, p. 391).

We have asserted in previous chapters that a psychologist, during the course of his assessment work with a patient, develops a working image of the person. There seems to be a process by which a more-or-less unified perceptual picture occurs—a complex of hypotheses or beliefs about the patient and his situation. He is then able to make statements about the patient beginning with "This is the sort of person who would. . . ." He communicates these statements to others, presumably affecting the others' own working images of the patient. Admittedly such a concept as the working image is vague and much in need of conceptual clarification and empirical test of its implications. If we assume the possibility of some such cognitive process and we set aside for the time being the question as to whether it is worthwhile to have such a working image and make such statements, we still face the question: How are such "models" formed? Something beyond the taxonomic sorting process we have been considering seems to be involved.

Taking a cue from some clinical research workers who have been interested in this problem (McArthur, 1954, and Shneidman, 1951, p. 206), we might use the term *emerging synthesis* to describe the search for an image of the person. Research workers of this sort look for life themes. They point to the occurrence of sudden insights that sometimes clarify the whole character of the person and promote a deeper understanding. They speak of a clinician's sympathy and ability to "understand" a case. McArthur (1954) speaks strongly for the need to be inductive, rather than deductive, about a case, saying that the very categories in which the facts are to be cast must arise from the case. He quotes Tomkins' discussion of TAT analysis: "The logic of the individual's fantasy itself must be our ultimate criterion" (1947).

Unfortunately, there are very few systematic reports of the thoughts of clinicians which might illustrate this rather vague process of emerging synthesis. The problems and possibilities for research on the formation of impressions of the others and on "thinking aloud'" will be discussed in Chapter 10. Here, let us look at some illustrations that have been published, all of them highly condensed retrospective accounts of the interpreter's cognitive activity. For an example in which one can see taxonomic sorting but that is hard to see as nothing but that process, let us turn to the one Meehl gives in describing how clinical, as contrasted with statistical, predictions are made.

A patient has been developing insight into her ambivalent attitude toward her husband. She begins to show some gross manifestations of hostility against him; for example, she tears up a series of short stories he wrote some years ago, telling him he knows perfectly well that they were no good anyway. Do we deal here with a relatively unmixed expression of hostility previously repressed by the patient, or are there other components in her need structure contributing to this behavior? She reports that one evening, feeling very nervous, she went out alone to a movie and as she was walking home, wondered if he would be "peacefully sleeping" upon her arrival. Entering the bedroom, she was terrified to see, for a fraction of a second, a large black bird ("a raven, I guess") perched on her pillow next to her husband's head. Asked to give her thoughts in connection with a raven, she says that she shouldn't have called it a raven, it was probably just a crow; in fact she doubts that she said raven in the first place. Insistence that she did say raven elicits irritation. She recalls, "vaguely, some poem we read in high school, I guess I don't know anything else about it."

What prediction enters the listener's mind with this reference? The prediction is mediated by a miniature dynamic hypothesis. The reference is almost certainly to Poe's poem; one guesses that the thematically important content determining her hallucination is connected with the preceding thought about her husband peacefully sleeping. The hypothesis forms itself: Nervous and upset, she goes out alone to a movie while her husband, unmindful of her, is able to "sleep peacefully." The fantasy is that, like Poe's Lenore, she will die or at least go away and leave him alone, with the bird croaking "Nevermore." Then he'll be sorry, not able to sleep peacefully, etc. We formulate the further hypothesis, which included our hypothesis about the determination of the particular hallucination, that she is concerned about her husband's need for her and would like to know how important she is to him. This leads to a prediction as to the leading themes we expect in the rest of the session. The prediction has a wide latitude, i.e., a *class* character is specified for the behavior, as always. But we anticipate that her (unguided) associations will touch upon the theme of punishing her husband, by going away somehow, that he would be sorry if she did, and the like. We also permit ourselves some leeway as to time, in that the development of the theme may not begin strongly until the next session, *etc.* But we do not make a vacuous prediction, since some manifestations of the Lenore fantasy are to be expected, and fairly soon. Her subsequent remarks in the same interview return repeatedly to the general topic of her husband's lack of concern for her condition, and his "sublime confidence" that she will "never do anything rash," which turns out in further talk to cover both suicide and unexpectedly leaving him. Fortified by these confirmations, we begin to attach considerable weight to the hypothesis that her hostile reactions are overdetermined, being in part attempts at testing the limits of his love and acceptance. Systematic attention to this hypotheses is well rewarded in the succeeding sessions.

The interesting question here is this: What are the general statistical uniformities which are allegedly able to generate the initial hypothesis? I presume the situation of a woman hallucinating a raven next to her husband's head is unique, and hence cannot define a reference class for any relative frequency, either known or unknown. To what larger class can the event be ordered? It would be a nonsensical classification, and would completely cut across the categories and dimensions which are really involved here, to consider the

obvious larger classes, *e.g.*, having halucinations of birds. I do not suppose anyone would seriously maintain that hallucinating birds is statistically associated
with the desire to test a husband's love, or the unconscious fantasy of leaving
him. The general principles involved here are not difficult to state; but what
impresses me is their relatively vacuous character *insofar as generating the particular hypothesis is concerned.* (P. E. Meehl, *Clinical versus statistical prediction,* Minneapolis: University of Minnesota Press, 1954, pp. 48-50.)

Colby, in *The Skeptical Psychoanalyst* (1958), also discusses the interpretive activity of the analyst. He points out how the analyst organizes
the information from the patient into sets of similar objects, such as
bills, money, and clippings, and how he associates to these and reaches
hypotheses about the patient. The basis for this thinking partly lies in
the theoretical background of the analyst, for the psychoanalyst has been
trained to see a correlation between anal functions and overconcern
with money and clippings. Colby presents the illustration as follows:

A patient reports:
   I let all the bills pile up on my deck—it's full of bills, magazines, articles
I've cut out of newspapers to read, stock market reports, little notes I've made
to remind me to do something. Just a whole mess of stuff. Each month it gets
bigger and bigger and I keep telling myself that someday I should get in there
and clean it all out. I can understand the bills because I don't like to part with
money but to save all that other junk makes no sense at all.

   Let us assume that this is the first time an analyst has heard these statements
from this particular patient. As he listens to them, what enters his conscious
awareness? It would go something like this:

Bills mean money again. Yesterday he mentioned being stingy with tips.
Magazines, newspaper clippings, reports, notes—they all concern paper. He
collects paper in various forms. Anality, since money, paper, and accumulation
are involved. "To clean it all out" would go with that, too. Watch for further
indications of retentiveness. How about punctuality, stubbornness, orderliness?
He's usually late. Don't see any stubbornness yet. Very neat and clean in appearance. But remember X who was so neat but changed his underwear only
once a week. Should I ask him here about cleanliness? (Kenneth Mark Colby,
A skeptical psychoanalyst, New York: The Ronald Press Company, 1958, pp.
28-29.)

   As another example of clinical thinking, here is Goldman's report on a
vocational counselor's test interpretation:

Ted says he's unsure about engineering as a career but he seems vague in his
reasons. As we were discussing it, interests seemed to be his main concern,
but perhaps more important, though he is reluctant to admit it, is some concern
about abilities. After discussing this for a while, we decided to use tests in
both areas, since he seemed to block on any further discussion of his feelings
and those of his family about this decision. College aptitude test scores are low
average for freshmen at the college he's considering, which means they're even
lower as compared with engineering freshman there. This suggests (*inference*)
that he would have a hard time in that program; incidentally, this is the same

prediction I'd make from his high school record (*confirmation* or *verification*). Since he's well aware of the requirements for engineering college, why has he chosen this goal and why is he reluctant to discuss the ability area? Let's leave this for a moment and look at the interest profile. On the Strong, he has a much more pronounced cluster on Group IV (Technician) than on II (Physical Sciences), and his Occupational Level score is also more appropriate for the technician or even skilled-worker level. All this would imply that his expressed goal is at too theoretical a level and requires too much academic preparation. Why, then, did he choose it? Or did he? (Apparent *contradiction,* with just the suggestion of an hypothesis to explain it.)

What's the family constellation . . . father a draftsman . . . Ted said he was sorry he never finished college . . . mother was an elementary teacher before marriage . . . college graduate. I wonder if all these pieces fit together to form a picture of a boy whose own ambition and interests would lead him to a skilled mechanical or maybe a technician level—perhaps not unlike his father (*hypothesis*). Sounds like a socially aspiring family whose upward mobility requires college level goals for their children (*hypothesis*). Could it be that Ted's evasiveness when I asked him about his family's feelings about careers means that they're pressing him pretty hard to be an engineer? Might be even more specific than that—maybe father is projecting his own unfulfilled ambitions on Ted.

If this is true—and I'm not at all sure it is, but we can try to explore it when I see Ted again—Ted would receive considerable pressure at home not to give up his engineering goal; maybe I'd have to talk with his parents and try to help them to see the situation. Might even be worse than that: Ted's whole self-concept—the way he wants to live, kinds of friends, girl he'll marry—is based on a high professional occupational level. Is all this pressure so great that he'll just have to make a try at engineering? Maybe this would give him enough drive to study so that, especially at the less competitive college, he would make it.

This gives me some hypotheses to work on when I see Ted again. As we go over his test results—or maybe I can get him to talk about self-concept and family without bringing in the tests—I'll try to get him to explore some of these areas to see how accurate my "model" of him is. What would be his best choice? Well, we'll have to see first whether we've included all relevant factors; for one thing, I don't know how he really feels about all this—he has been pretty evasive about it last time we talked. Then maybe I'll try to help him see the alternatives and the likely implications of each. After that, he'll have to decide which course of action is most likely to meet his (and his family's) needs. It might help to have his parents in for a talk (Goldman, 1961, pp. 68-69).

The differences between the *taxonomic-sorting* and *emerging-synthesis* approaches to clinical interpretation are partly a matter of levels of inference, as explained above. Those who espouse taxonomic sorting prefer to remain at low inference levels and avoid "global" concepts of the person. Partly the differences have to do with the source of the concepts or hypotheses. Sarbin will not admit to anything more than the syllogistic process in the origin of hypotheses, whereas the others assert that hypotheses may include something close to "creative hunches," "sudden insights." Both approaches would admit the possibility of theories about individuals but they differ in the emphasis placed on the individual's unique life history. The emergent synthesizer would assert that not only the hypotheses but the concepts or classifications themselves should arise from the study of the case itself. The clinician gets his concepts about the case not by using a predetermined taxonomy, but perhaps by inventing new categories and descriptions suited to the individual patient.

The most important difference may have to do with attitudes toward interpretation. The emergent interpreters are predisposed to be very open to broad ideas and hunches. They encourage their unconscious minds to "resonate" to the unconscious of the patient. The sorters prefer exact probabilities and logical relations. It is a difference between a preference for rigorous detail and analytic modes of thought and a concern for underlying "truth'" even if it must be vaguely formulated. This dichotomy is not confined to approaches to clinical interpretation but permeates the thinking of many scientists, as William James long ago pointed out in his dichotomy of the tough-minded and the tender-minded. Perhaps research will eventually give us the basis for more definite conclusions about what clinicians actually do and what they should do.

IMPROVING CLINICAL INTERPRETATION

Even though some of the basic questions about interpretation have not yet been answered, research has already given us evidence about many practical matters. Since there seems to be no way in which we can dispense with clinical judgment in the forseeable future, we should do what we can to improve it. It was somewhat disconcerting to find, in a series of studies to be reviewed in Chapter 10, that psychologically untrained persons, such as student nurses, physicists, and typists have often equalled or excelled clinical psychologists in making accurate predictions. Thorne (1961) has suggested that the achievements of educated common sense might be regarded as establishing a base rate against which professional clinicians' predictions should be judged. We should be able to do better than this. Reflection of past experience and research suggest several recommendations along with some pitfalls to be avoided.

1. *Develop local base-rate and expectancy tables for use whenever they are appropriate.* Experience tables are fairly simple to develop and they are likely to pay off well. For suggestions on simple punched-card systems for keeping records, see Keller, Rosenblum, and Ebling (1956) and Stubblefield and Camp (1959).

2. *In collecting new information, give attention to an optimal and limited amount of information.* Strange as it at first seems, it may not be helpful to have a lot of information. The fact that the successful statistical procedures make use of only a few variables (usually no more

than three) suggests that the clinician may be trying to take in too many things at once. Hoffman (1960) has been producing evidence that when a person is asked to judge any trait in others, he uses only a few items of information, even though many more are available. The masses of information on their cases which clinics typically collect may actually increase confusion rather than accuracy of diagnosis and prognostication.

3. *Select information carefully and weight it correctly.* The heart of the undertaking consists not in increasing the amount of data, but in getting the right kind. The exact kinds of data for which the psychologist should look depend on the particular case and the purpose for which he is making his assessment. Commonly, his general strategy should be first to scan the life of the person and his situation broadly and then to focus on the particular aspects of both which seem most prominent.

4. *Be especially careful about making predictions concerning "low probability" events.* The lesson from a knowledge of base rates is that the probabilities are increasingly against the clinician as he makes predictions of events very different from those that usually occur. It is very tempting to show original and dramatic clinical insights, but these need to be checked very carefully against the probabilities.

5. *Do not jump to an overly high inference level.* It is possible to get too far away from one's data. A clinician faces two dangers: (*a*) being overly simple and thus missing the latent and unconscious meanings of things, or (*b*) being overly abstract and subtle and thus missing the obvious meanings of things. At the present time the second type of error appears to be more common (Soskin, 1954, 1959). This warning against high-level theorizing applies to practical problems only. For new research and theorizing, let us leave the doors open to any kind of speculation.

6. In interpretation *be very skeptical of principles and premises that are not tested empirically.* The largest difficulty for the clinician according to Sarbin, Taft, and Bailey (1960) is the failure to use major premises that are empirically supported. The clinician in his search for certainty and desire to see patients helped is lured to consider theoretical and authoritative assertions which have not been tested, such as: "Psychotherapy can succeed only in cases where the patient's ego-strength is adequate." Whether the clinician should or should not use such additional considerations in any given case is open to debate, but it is clear that he should not let them lead him to disregard empirical evidence that is available.

7. *Become thoroughly acquainted with the facts of the situation you are trying to predict.* This may be the most important counsel of all. The outcome you are trying to predict determines what information you need to collect as relevant to the situation. In clinical work we often have too vague a notion of the possible alternative courses of action, such as various treatments which might prove beneficial to a given patient. If

we are going to predict whether or not he will have to return to the hospital, we need to know what his home and job are like. If we are predicting his response to group therapy, we need to know the kinds of groups in which he might be placed.

(8.) *Whenever possible, make use of other judges—especially those similar in background to the person being studied.* Studies (e.g., Chowdry & Newcomb, 1952) have shown that one predicts best for people similar to oneself. Lower-class people can predict most accurately what other lower-class people are likely to do. Religious people can predict best the responses of other religious people. Part of one's ability to predict comes from the mere fact of similarity. Being unlike the person you are trying to understand constitutes a difficult handicap and the clinician needs to recognize his limitations.

9. *Keep a record of your own "batting average."* Every clinician has his special strengths and weaknesses, but many do not recognize what these are. It would be possible for any clinician to develop a form for recording predictions in some exact fashion at the time he writes his assessment report. Then he could follow-up on these predictions regularly and see with what kinds of patients and problems he does well with and where his difficulties occur.

SUMMARY

This chapter is concerned with the way a clinician interprets the information he has collected about a patient—the intermediate process that links "input" to "output" in the system. A psychologist's conceptual framework and the way he sees his role in the agency and in the particular case under consideration serve to direct his thinking into some channels rather than others. Inferences can occur at a low level, with little or no theory entering into them, or at an intermediate or high theoretical level. Many kinds of statistical aids to interpretation are available. Research in which inference processes were evaluated according to the outcomes of predictions based on them has indicated that low-level inferences remaining close to known statistical relationships produce more accurate predictions than inferences based on higher and more abstract levels. Sarbin, Taft, and Bailey have constructed a theory of clinical inference as a kind of probabilistic logic following standard principles of syllogistic reasoning except that the premises and conclusions are stated as probabilities rather than certainties. In this theoretical formulation, clinical inference is essentially *taxonomic sorting*. Many clinicians are not convinced that this theory is adequate to cover all kinds of clinical interpretation and prefer to think of the process as an *emerging synthesis*. Whatever its contribution to a comprehensive theory of clinical interpretion turns out to be, research done so far gives us a basis for a number of practical procedures and cautions: (1) Develop local experience tables and other statistical aids. (2) Concentrate on a limited amount of information. (3) Select and weight information carefully. (4) Be especially careful about "low-probability" events. (5) Avoid high inference levels. (6) Be skeptical about untested major premises. (7) Become thoroughly acquainted with the criterion situation. (8) Make use of appropriate judges. (9) Study your own diagnostic record.

SUGGESTED READINGS

MEEHL, P. E. *Clinical versus statistical prediction.* Minneapolis: Univer. of Minnesota Press, 1954.
This is one of the most influential books in clinical psychology. The central problem is how to predict a person's behavior. Meehl analyzes methods of inference from class membership. He considers the special powers of the clinician. The main section of the book is Meehl's review of a large number of studies which have contrasted the predictions of clinicians with predictions based on statistical procedures. In none of the studies was the clinician able to improve on the statistical prediction. Meehl himself attempts to straddle the fence, saying that statistics are indispensable, but also showing that clinicians do make special contributions, such as creative insights. This book touched off a controversy that has been argued in many a symposium and journal article. As a sample of another point of view, see Holt (1958).

SARBIN, T. R., TAFT, R., & BAILEY, D. E. *Clinical inference and cognitive theory.* New York: Holt, Rinehart, & Winston, 1960.
The authors state their central problem: "How does the behavior analyst proceed from raw data to refined inference?" (p. 4) They propose a general model for inference based on the logician's syllogism. They deny that there is any special kind of clinical intuition or insight and assert that clinical inference is only a special form of statistical inference. In the course of a thorough analysis of the clinician's conceptual activity, a cognitive theory is developed. The authors relate their proposals to a wide range of research. The whole book is highly recommended. The first and last three chapters are particularly pertinent to this chapter. Also see Meehl's critical review (1961).

MEEHL, P. E., and ROSEN, A. Antecedent probability and the efficiency of psychometric signs, patterns, or cutting scores. *Psychol. Bull.,* 1955, 194-216.
This is an important article describing base rates and their relationship to psychological assessment. The authors point out many of the errors which are likely to be made in clinical research. They show that the practical value of any psychometric score depends jointly on its intrinsic validity and the distribution of the criterion variable in the clinical population. Information on base rates of patients' characteristics can be readily obtained by file research. They show how test development should ordinarily be concentrated on characteristics having base rates near a 50-50 split.

HOFFMAN, P. J. The paramorphic representation of clinical judgment. *Psychol. Bull.,* 1960, 57, 116-131.
Hoffman presents a statistical procedure for studying the clinician as a processer of information. He asks judges to make decisions about a large number of individuals, giving them a standard set of data on each person. For instance,

the judges may be given high school rating, per cent of self-support, parents' education and be asked to rate each individual on intelligence. By studying the judge's choices statistically, it is possible to determine the weights the judge attributed to high school ratings, etc., in his ratings. In further work it would be possible to study the effects of amount and kind of information, of training, for the judge and other procedures.

Cases illustrating clinical interpretation

The student and practicing clinician can gain considerable understanding of how tests and other psychological data are interpreted from reading case reports. It is particularly helpful to start with the data themselves—the test protocols, interview summaries, profiles, and the case history—trying to interpret the material first by oneself, before looking at the expert's interpretation. A systematic way of doing this is to use an adjective checklist (such as that of Gough, 1960a) or to perform a Q sort (using a Q-deck like that of Block, 1961). When two or more people use these techniques it is possible to make general comparisons and to locate sources of differences in opinion. This kind of study of cases, whether employing systematic procedures or not, enlarges the clinician's subjective repertory. Burton and Harris (1955) present a large number of cases that would be useful for this purpose. Over a number of years the *Journal of Projective Techniques* has presented extensive information on cases—first the original protocols and data and later the interpretations of experts on each of the tests. See the Case of Gregor (*J. proj. tech.*, 1949, 13, 155-205 and 433-468; also reprinted in Weider, 1953), the case of Jay (*J. proj. Tech.*, 1952, 16, 297-345 and 444-475), and the Case of El (*J. proj. Tech.*, 1961, 25, 131-154, 252-267, and 371-411).

RESEARCH EXAMPLES

MEEHL, P. E. A comparison of clinicians with five statistical methods of identifying psychotic MMPI profiles, *J. counsel. Psychol.*, 1959, 6, 102-109.

In Meehl's book (1954) no study showed clinicians able to do better than statistical predictions. In this study, Meehl attempted to see if the same conclusion still held five years later for his favorite test, the MMPI. He collected a total of 861 MMPI's from seven different places. Forty-seven per cent were profiles of psychotics and 53 per cent of neurotics. These profiles, unmarked, were turned over to 21 clinicians who were expert in interpreting the MMPI, with instructions to sort them into two groups, psychotic and neurotic.

Against the clinicians he pitted five statistical methods. Four of these were the linear discrimination function, Lykken's technique, the Hathaway codes for neurotics and psychotics, and the Taulbee-Sisson signs. (For details see the original article.) The fifth method was the Meehl-Dahlstrom rules (described in detail by Meehl & Dahlstrom, 1960), a rather complex set of signs and countersigns derived by an interplay of clinical impressions and statistical checking.

The result of this contest was another defeat for the clinicians, except in the case of the discriminant function which was least successful of all. The other four actuarial and configural methods were all superior to the clinicians. The best method proved to be the Meehl-Dahlstrom rules. It achieved a hit rate of 74 per cent, the pooled clinicians 69 per cent, and the median individual clinician 66 per cent. There was considerable variability among individual clinicians in their accuracy.

Perhaps the most interesting aspect of the study is that the best method has been derived from a combination of clinical and statistical considerations. This suggests that many clinical ideas if tested and systematized might provide very useful actuarial methods. The trouble is that clinicians, who are full of hypotheses about patients, seldom have a sample of cases on hand adequate for a thorough tryout. Clinicians should make a more strenuous effort to record their unverbalized assessment approaches in ways that can be checked. The range of performance among clinicians also suggests that the differences between good and poor clinicians should be explored and explained in further research.

KOSTLAN, A. A method for the empirical study of psychodiagnosis. *J. consult. Psychol.*, 1954, 18, 83-88.

Kostlan (as part of a doctoral dissertation) addressed himself to the following problem: "Which of several sources of cues permits the clinician to make the most valid inferences when he uses them in certain combinations?" (p. 83) In this research, four sources of information often used in a clinic were employed: the social case history, the MMPI, the Stein Sentence Completion Test, and the Rorschach examination. Test scores and social histories were obtained from five VA outpatients. These materials were presented to the judges under five different conditions: four of them with one source of information missing (an example would be the MMPI, SSCT, and social history minus the Rorschach) and a fifth with identifying (face sheet) information only.

The judges were 20 clinical psychologists with at least two years of diagnostic experience. Each judge was systematically assigned records of five patients, one set from each of the five conditions. Judges were told to study the information available as in a typical diagnostic study. Their task was to fill out a specially devised 283-item true-false checklist of psychological inferences about the patient systematically derived from sentences in psychological reports. The criteria were two: an "internal" criterion consisting of checklist items agreed on by six of eight criterion judges using all four sources of information, and an "external" criterion was based on the progress reports of the patient's therapists.

The results of this latin-square analysis of variance design led to the following conclusion (p. 86): (*a*) Minimal data (the identifying data alone) permitted inferences which were better than chance. (*b*) Without social case histories, the clinicians were no more accurate in their inferences than they were on the basis of minimal data. (*c*) The batteries that included both the MMPI and the social case history were superior to the others. (*d*) There are large differences in the accuracy with which particular patients can be diagnosed. (*e*) Clinicians differ in diagnostic skill.

For additional confirmation of many of these findings, the reader would do well to consult the study by Soskin (1959). The criterion was different. Soskin required clinicians to predict the subject's characteristic behavior in defined situations. The kinds of data given the clinicians were different (observation of role-playing, the Rorschach protocol, or a battery of tests) and the particular kind of data given each clinician was in addition to the basic biographical data which they all received. However, the major results of Soskin's study were similar to Kostlan's. None of the sources of information produced improvement over predictions from basic data alone. In addition, Soskin found that giving the Rorschach to the clinicians changed their judgments toward inaccurate estimates of maladjustment. He also found that student nurses could predict as well as clinicians using basic biographical data. These two studies and others similar to them in some respects constitute a serious challenge to researchers to discover just what kinds of information are most useful in clinical assessment.

9 Communicating Assessment Information

The course of assessment depicted in Figure 1 in Chapter 4 funnels down to the clinician's judgment about what to tell others about the patient, how to communicate his impressions and findings. In what ways shall he combine and draw out the most important things from the mass of data? How might he present his conclusions in an effective way? The clinician sitting down to prepare a report is not very different from the artist facing a blank canvas. Whatever strokes and colors he first places on the canvas organize the space and set a pattern that leads to other things. It is possible to change the composition or even to start over again, but if the finished painting is successful it communicates an idea, an organization, a feeling. The report of the psychologist, like a work of art, communicates the pattern of the patient's life. It should facilitate constructive and practical decisions and aid the development of the patient in his interactions with the clinic or hospital.

DIFFERENT KINDS OF COMMUNICATION IN CLINICAL SETTINGS

Keeping formal records and preparing reports are important parts of every clinic's operation. Medical charts are kept in hospitals, cumulative records in schools, case files in clinics and agencies in order to preserve the information about clients and patients which is most useful. Years later it may be necessary to go back to these records when a case is reactivated. Records also serve as reminders in handling ongoing cases. They are indispensable in every large institution where reports must be routed from one specialist to another. Well-kept records constitute gold mines of data for the clinical researcher in search of evidence in support or refutation of some hypothesis. Conscientious report-writing and record-keeping are a major part of the responsibility of every clinical psychologist.

Not all communication about a patient need be formal. In most situations much of the on-going hour-to-hour communication is informal; it is necessarily so and not less effective for this reason. Talk and discussion, at both scheduled and unscheduled times, and accidental interactions between staff members and between staff people and patients make up a large part of the communication that is carried on in a clinic. Staff members are trained to occupy given roles, and professional ethical codes help structure relationships, but there is no doubt that informal communication is a powerful factor in the running of an institution and the development of a therapeutic or antitherapeutic climate for patients. Much of what is very important is not recorded on the charts. Also, since clinical settings are places where human beings work with and for other human beings, all the possibilities for covert influence, prejudice, symbolic interaction, informal power structures, occur just as they do in ordinary life.

CLINICAL RECORDS

During the course of a person's progress through a clinic or hospital, there are several points at which records are compiled. A very common pattern of records on a patient runs about as follows:

1. *Records of initial contact.* The patient first contacts the institution through a telephone call, a personal visit, or an application blank. At this point a record is started, if the contact appears to have been made seriously and the case is appropriate for the clinic or hospital to accept. The person is registered by obtaining such necessary information as name, age, sex, names of relatives, income. These items of information are often recorded on a *face sheet* which is attached to the front of the patient's chart or record.

2. *Intake information.* Usually the next step is the scheduling of an interview by a professional person, most often a social worker, but sometimes a psychiatrist or psychologist. The interviewer records his findings as a *case history* for the patient's chart. There may be interviews with relatives of the patient or other informants. The patient's own report, or anamnesis, should be distinguished from informants' reports. Typically

other materials, *letters from referral sources, schools, and physicians,* will be added to the chart at this time.

3. *Special case-study information.* At this point it may often be decided in the clinic that the patient will need special evaluations by the psychologist, psychiatrist, and others. The psychologist will see the patient, introducing whatever procedures seem desirable, and add his written *report of the psychological examination.* (The actual test protocols and notes will be filed separately for future reference, especially for use in connection with research.) The *psychiatrist's report* may also be added to the chart, although a complete report by the psychiatrist is often delayed until all the information is in.

4. *A running account of the case conference and case progress.* After the case conference involving all the professional personnel concerned is held and also after any other decision or action has been taken regarding the management of the case, *case notes* are entered on the chart. In the section for case notes, anyone who has a share in handling the case can see at a glance the skeleton outline of actions and decisions. On a psychiatric ward, the nurses enter their reports of observations of patients.

5. *Record of treatment.* The *psychotherapy notes* may be kept in a separate confidential file if the main chart or file is to be widely available; otherwise they would be kept in the main folder. Such records will vary in fullness according to the customs of the institution. They should be of sufficient length to cover the main content and impressions of the session or sessions but not so long that going through them may become an undue burden on the therapist or other reader.

6. *Closing records.* A *final case summary* is prepared by the psychiatrist, psychologist, or other person who is mainly concerned with the case. It is intended to be a record of the case for future reference and is often placed just behind the face sheet when the case records are finally stapled together and put away in the inactive file. Closing a case also usually requires *further correspondence with the interested agencies and referring persons.* All in all a complete case file or chart may become a document ranging anywhere from 10 to 100 pages in length. In cases where the patient returns many times to the agency and where the contact is intensive, the chart is indeed a weighty volume.

STUDYING THE WHOLE CASE

Let us turn now to the preparation for the report. The clinical psychologist is sitting at his desk with the information spread before him. There are the test records, the patient's chart, and statistical comparisons and predictions. He has already started making inferences and interpretations of the case, and is now beginning to organize and select from among these many impressions. In the experience of most clinicians, the organization of a report does not spring out at once. Sometimes it is necessary to read through case material many times before themes begin to emerge and conclusions become clear. The pattern may be slow to emerge, just as in perceptual experiments it takes a while to find a hidden figure or to see reversible figures change. The psychologist must actually *study* the case thoroughly.

There seems to be no single best point of entry into a case. It often is wise to scan the whole case rapidly to look for outstanding characteristics before getting bogged down in details. Having a notepad available and perhaps an outline like the one suggested in the next section, the psychologist jots down points as he reads the material. Though he may have strong attitudes based on early observations and theoretical biases, he needs to reserve judgment and objectively look at the facts. As groupings of notable data grow from the case itself, he begins to get ideas and hypotheses and speculations about basic themes in this person's life. He checks these hypotheses against other data and develops subjective impressions of the probabilities attached to each of these hypotheses. Thus, over a period of time he begins to feel very sure about certain conclusions and less sure about others.

As he organizes the material into a report, the foremost guide the clinician has in mind is: What are the questions this report is to answer —the purposes of this assessment work? These questions and purposes were given initial formulation at the onset, as mentioned in Chapter 4, but often the psychologist in the process of assessment may uncover significant features of the case which had not been suspected before. If the clinician's purpose is differential diagnosis, he will be seeking evidence both for and against each of various possible diagnoses as he reads over his material and thinks about it. When his purpose is to prepare a description of the person as a first step in planning therapy, he will be sensitized to detect evidences of interest in therapy, anxiety over certain life problems, underlying conflicts, and so on. When decisions involving court action or school placement need to be made, he looks for evidence in the record that would point toward good or poor adjustment in any contemplated moves. The clinician's task is to fix firmly on the most important features of the patient's case, and his situation, and to communicate just what he understands them to be.

Certain things will prove helpful in shaping the report. Congruencies between several tests or repetitions of a test are good clues. When evidence for schizophrenic behavior and ways of thinking is found in the MMPI, the Rorschach, and from his own observation, the clinician will be sure of his diagnosis. *Discrepancies* between various tests or observations may be equally significant, though they raise more difficulties. What if the MMPI suggests psychotic personality trends, but the Rorschach points toward neurotic characteristics? Perhaps such differences need to be interpreted in the light of differences in the tests or in the way the patient took the tests. In any case, inconsistencies of this sort must be run down just as far as any clues can be unearthed.

For the clinician *deviant behavior* of any sort is of unusual interest. After considerable experience in a given working situation, he develops more or less explicit expectations of what his patients are going to do when confronted with certain tests, certain turns in interviews, and the like. If a patient behaves quite differently than normal persons or than other patients who seem to have something in common with him, or maybe in comparison with himself on other occasions, then the clinician takes special notice. This deviation may be some particular act, like suddenly stopping in the middle of a test and bringing up an entirely unrelated topic, or it may be an odd omission, like failing to notice the gun on a TAT card. It may be an isolated response which seems to have special emotional significance for the patient. One important point to remember is that the normal curve has both a high and a low end. Deviation may be constructive as well as destructive. Some positive and desirable characteristics turn undesirable when present in an extreme degree—as when adjustment becomes scrupulous overconformity. Of course, the clinician does not concern himself solely with deviations— far from it; it is exceedingly important for him to size up the patient's *typical behavior,* for it is the usual, the typical, conduct of a person with which unusual acts are compared and which will figure heavily in any decisions and planning that are done for him. Every psychologist needs to bear in mind the dangers of "overpathologizing" near-normal people, or anybody, for that matter. One of the greatest advantages of standardized procedures is that they provide norms against which to check clinical judgments that run to extremes, or that illustrate the opposite error of failing to note how far some individuals do depart from the average in respect to some trait.

Another organizing idea is the search for *diagnostic signs.* This idea is borrowed from the medical concept of *pathognomonic cues,* or indicators of a specific underlying disease. Thorne in his book on clinical judgments calls such cues "the key to all diagnostic processes" (1961, p. 42). When the task is differential diagnosis, the clinician will be looking for a sign, or more commonly the pattern of signs, associated with a given condition. In the cases of some physical or neurological disorders the pathognomonic cues are quite clear. An Argyll-Robertson pupil (a pupil responding to accomodation but not to light) and a paretic colloidal gold reaction from a sample of cerebrospinal fluid are almost certain to mean a neurosyphilitic infection and a diagnosis of general paresis. On a somewhat different level, a person's inability to pronounce familiar words, except for a few short or highly emotional ones, though he can react appropriately when he encounters the same words in speech or writing, identifies the condition of motor aphasia. This is a behavioral syndrome, a rather circumscribed one, and it commonly means there is a lesion in the speech area of the frontal lobe (Broca's area). With functional disorders, it is much more difficult to specify clear pathognomonic cues. Some of them are fairly clear, for example, a "glove anaesthesia," where the numbness does not follow the anatomical distribution of nerves, suggests hysteria. Hallucinations and disorientation, in the absence of organic pathology and with a history of increasing social withdrawal, suggests schizophrenia. When we come to the neuroses and near-normal cases of maladjustment, we find fewer clear diagnostic signs. A very large number of cases, probably the majority among those referred to psychologists, will have a mixture of indications for different disorders. It is a question whether the assumption underlying the pathognomonic sign approach, namely that there must be an underlying disease entity, is appropriate to many of the kinds of cases with which a clinical psychologist will usually deal. In any case, the research-oriented clinical psychologist will be interested in testing any potential cues that might help him in his job.

A METHOD FOR ORGANIZING INTERPRETATIONS

In making order of the complexity of a case, psychologists develop working habits which fit their own clinical settings and theoretical leanings. In this section we will return to the general outline for the formulation of a case presented in Chapter 4. We will not repeat the details and the illustrative questions of that guide, and the reader may find it useful to review them. The outline is intended for the instances in which a thorough case study is required. There are, of course, more limited assessment goals—for instance, the interpretation of a routine battery on a clear-cut case or the report on a short intelligence test for a psychiatrist who merely wants to check his impressions. This outline is intended as a suggestion. The reader is urged to develop his own system, perhaps using this as a model.

Figure 9 presents the recording chart for organizing observations and hypotheses which we have called the Assessment Analysis Chart. For actual use it should be placed on a large sheet of paper. This chart is a modification and extension of an outline proposed by Walter Klopfer in his useful book on the *Psychological Report* (1960, p. 36). It is to be used in organizing one's thinking about a case before actually writing the report. This method is particularly recommended to students and their supervisors, but experienced clinicians might also profit from using it. After the student has administered the test battery (previously planned in consultation with the supervisor), he sets up this outline. On this outline, he is encouraged to jot down his hypotheses and inferences

IDENTIFYING INFORMATION

Name _____ Address _____

Age _____ Sex _____ Marital Status _____ Occupation _____

Education _____ Reasons for Referral _____

ASPECTS OF PERSONALITY AND SITUATION	Identifying Data	SOURCES OF INFORMATION					
		Testing				Other	
		Obser- vations	WAIS	MMPI	TAT etc.	Case history & physical examination	Home or work observation
Roles in primary groups							
Functioning skills and abilities							
Emotional characteristics and control							
Intrapsychic conflicts and defense techniques							
Self-concept, values, and authorities							
Diagnostic impressions							
Indications for treatment and rehabilitation							

FIGURE. 9. Assessment Analysis Chart

as freely and daringly as he wishes as he reviews the assessment material. Later he has a full discussion with his supervisor.

At the column heads of the Assessment Analysis Chart, various sources of information are listed, one column being for impressions gleaned from the identifying information alone. This column should be filled out *before* the clinician sees the patient or reads his record. The reasons for giving this preliminary attention to impressions are two: First, it emphasizes these basic data, which have been found in a number of research studies to contain a great deal of predictive power. Second, it explicitly alerts the clinician to whatever personal impressions or biases he may have in approaching the case. Next come any observations made by the psychologist during testing followed by columns for each of the tests administered. In a hospital or clinic in which the psychologist's assessment functions are confined to testing, his entries would stop at this point. In a situation where he is expected to function more broadly and to prepare a full case report, he would list other sources, such as the case-history information, the physician's report and observations in the home, school, or ward. In any given column under the particular source of information, the clinician or student-clinician will jot down whatever interpretations and hypotheses he finds significant and related to the various areas listed at the left of the chart.

The rows across the page provide opportunities to record hypotheses in each of the major areas outlined for a thorough case study. The suggested topics (somewhat modified from the outline in Chapter 4) are as follows: (1) roles and interpersonal purposes in primary groups; (2) functioning skills and abilities; (3) emotional characteristics and controls; (4) intra-psychic conflicts and defense techniques; (5) self-concept, values, and authorities for beliefs; (6) diagnostic impressions; and (7) indications for treatment and rehabilitation.

This chart provides a way of looking over in condensed form all of the information that has been gathered in the course of assessment. From such a chart, adapted to the needs of a particular setting, the clinician can get a picture of how particular sources of information contribute to conclusions. Going down the columns he notes the various ways in which individual tests and other materials add to the whole. Going across the rows he sees how different sources of information concur or disagree. This either strengthens a conclusion or suggests that he look closer into the nature of the disparity. Is the difference in intellectual picture on the Rorschach and WAIS due to differences in the patient's ability to tolerate ambiguity? Are there other structured situations in which he does well? As a result of this comparison, an overall picture of the patient and his situation develops which can be used in the next and final step, which is to write the report.

EFFECTIVE COMMUNICATION IN REPORTS: SOME QUESTIONS TO CONSIDER

The most important thing to keep asking oneself as one writes a report is: What are the main points that emerge from this particular psychological work-up and how am I to make sure the reader will understand them? Unfortunately there is no one clear, simple outline for every report. As Tallent, after years of research on writing reports, has stated, "The conclusion is overpowering that there is no best way or correct way to carry out this duty" (1960, p. 5). Good reports are like fine portraits, providing special insights into the characteristics of the individual patient.

Who will be reading the report? It makes a big difference if the report is to be read by a teacher in a class for retarded children, a counselor in a high school, a social worker in a welfare agency, a pediatrician in a remote town, or a psychiatrist working in the next office. The level of language used, the length of the report, and even the kinds of things reported will be determined by the interests and responsibilities of the reader vis-a-vis the patient and by the readers' sophistication in psychological matters. The report-writer, drawing on his general knowledge and his recollections of specific interactions that occurred in past cases, needs to tune his report to the expected reader's abilities and needs.

The clinician has to have in mind both what Hammond and Allen (1953) call the *primary reader,* the person to whom the report originally goes, and the *secondary reader,* usually a research worker or administrator. These two kinds of readers are pretty certain to have conflicting needs. The busy psychiatrist or educator will want main facts and conclusions. He will not have time for detail nor be interested in it. On the other hand, the research worker will want careful recording of details, especially any quantitative ones. The psychologist's report cannot easily serve both purposes at the same time. In a clinic and hospital the psychologist must be mainly concerned to communicate effectively with the primary reader, since the patient's welfare is his uppermost concern. Research needs are also important, especially in the long run. However, they can be served best by preservation and careful labeling of original test materials, recorded interviews, and other documents, so that research workers can easily identify and use them, although sometimes a separate research-oriented report will need to be written.

In what kind of language should the report be written? Since most of us are prone to assume that other people understand what we say and write better than they usually do, the misjudging of the reader's ability to understand our language is a serious and frequent cause of poor report-writing. Psychologists themselves adhere to such different theoretical positions and approach assessment from such different backgrounds that it is difficult even for them to communicate with each other.

The situation becomes worse when we must communicate with non-psychologists. Even when we are writing to very capable people in mental health professions we cannot expect them to understand special jargon like "color shock," "confabulation," "regression equation," or "an MMPI code of 27." Klopfer has asserted, "If the clinical psychologist really comprehends what he is attempting to communicate, a technical language level is really unnecessary" (1960, p. 58). He urges clinicians to write in a basic English that any reasonably intelligent layman can understand. He illustrates his recommendation with several "translations" from psychological and psychoanalytic jargon. For instance, a patient's "great desire for affiliation" becomes the patient "would very much like to have friends"; "personality dynamics" becomes "interesting character-istics of this person"; and a patient who was "extremely narcissistic" is described as "so intensely preoccupied with himself that he finds it very difficult to become interested in other people" (1960, p. 59-61). So the terms used in the report and the degree of abstraction permitted must be carefully adjusted to the reader's level. It is allowable to use a term like "obsessive-compulsive" when writing for a psychiatrist, but a school teacher encountering it might be lost. A report that does not carry the intended meaning can be worse than none at all. As a check on the communication value of a report not intended for fellow-professionals, it is often a good idea to have a secretary or other nonprofessional person read it over and tell you where it seems vague, obscure, or meaningless. A telephone call or a conference with the recipient may help to clear up difficulties and also tell you something about writing better reports in the future.

How detailed should the report be? Aside from the ever-threatening problems of jargon and vagueness there are questions of detail. Should the psychologist report the IQ? Should he quote patients' remarks verbatim? Should he only report general conclusions? Again the role and interests of the reader should be kept in mind. A vocational counselor might wish to have exact details on a person's intellectual level and tested vocational interests which a psychiatrist would want to know about only in a general way. To readers such as physicians, judges, and teachers who have had no special training in interpreting psychological tests, it might be misleading and against the best interests of the patient to report exact findings. The writers recall instances when physicians and teachers have handed psychological reports directly over to the patient's relatives to read. If there can be the slightest question of this happening, a report should be boldly marked "confidential," and the fact that it is so should be explained in a letter. If such breaches of profes-sional confidence should continue, the psychologist would have no alter-native but to stop working with the referring person.

On the other hand, a report with no detail, along with a barrage of abstract generalities, is hopelessly vague and not likely to be convincing or persuasive. Some evidence and a concrete example or two, at least, have a place in every psychological report. In fact, one study of criticisms of psychological reports by psychiatrists revealed a good number of complaints over their lack of raw data and their wordiness (Tallent and Reiss, 1959). Parenthetically, it may be pointed out that there is a distinction between *psychometric detail* and *behavioral illustration*. Statements such as "F plus is 69 per cent" or "Block Design is the highest of the Performance subtests" communicate very little. However, illustrative statements made by the patient or samples of his behavior may clarify a more formal description a great deal. For instance, when speaking of a patient's strong dependence on mother figures, it might be well to add, "On several stories made up about TAT pictures, the patient described the older female figures as 'strong and supporting' and told how younger people are 'lost without her.'" Or even more specifically, a patient's bizarre definitions on the Wechsler might be brought in to illustrate schizoid tendencies, or a patient's particular way of completing a sentence might be cited to throw light on his attitudes toward his family. Such direct quotations and reports of behavior illustrating salient and yet typical features of the client's behavior may be as important as anything that comes up in an early interview or in therapy. They do a good deal to make the record convincing.

How long should a report be? Probably most psychological reports tend to be too long. Foster (1951) states that it is a rare report that needs to be longer than one page, but few psychologists would agree to such a rigid rule. The needs of readers and the complexities of cases vary too widely to make a definite limitation. The most important thing is that the report communicate clearly just what it is intended to say. Occasionally an involved case intensively studied will require several pages, but such a report should always contain a summary planned to save reading time when the reader is in a hurry, and often, in addition to this, a covering letter should call attention to salient points.

THE PROBLEM OF INDIVIDUALIZING THE PSYCHOLOGICAL REPORT

In a number of publications over the last few years, psychologists have denounced "pseudo-reporting," a kind of writing which substitutes generalities, trivialities, and ambiguities for specific, clear, and practical communication. Meehl (1956) has coined the term *Barnum effect* to stigmatize spurious descriptions composed of a mixture of stereotypes and evasion. Tallent (1958) has labelled another kind of report an *Aunt Fanny report* because it contains mostly information that would be true of anybody's "Aunt Fanny." Klopfer (1960) has condemned reports that seem subtly designed to play up to a psychiatrist or to sell some point as if it were merchandise as *Madison Avenue reports*. Other kinds of reports that have come in for criticism are (Thorne, 1961): Pollyanna reports, prosecuting attorney briefs, cookbook reports, safe-hedge reports, and abstract, theoretical, head-in-the-clouds reports.

Many of these miscarriages of communication are illustrated by a report written by one of the present writers. The report was a completely blind analysis of the case of a schizophrenic veteran; it was written before the writer knew anything about the patient except that he was a new admission to a Veterans Administration hospital and his case was to be worked up for "A Case Study of Schizophrenia," a discussion by several psychologists at a state psychological association meeting, January, 1956. Nevertheless, it rang surprisingly true to the actual presentation of the case.

This veteran approached the testing situation with some reluctance. He was cooperative with the clinician, but mildly evasive on some of the material. Both the tests and the past history suggest considerable inadequacy in interpersonal relations, particularly with members of his family. It is doubtful whether he has ever had very many close relationships with anyone. Those few that he has had were tinged with a great deal of ambivalence. He has never been able to sink his roots deeply. He is immature, egocentric, and irritable, and often he misperceives the good intentions of the people around him. Projection is one of his prominent defense mechanisms. He tends to be basically passive and dependent, though there are occasional periods of resistance and rebellion against others. Although he shows some seclusiveness and autistic trends, he is in fair contact with reality. Vocationally, his adjustment has been very poor. Mostly he has drifted from one job to another. His interests are shallow and he tends to have poor motivation for his work. Also he has had a hard time keeping his jobs because of difficulty in getting along with fellow employees. Though he has had some relations with women, his sex life has been unsatisfactory to him. At present he is mildly depressed, although a great deal of affect is not shown. What physical complaints he has appear mainly to have a functional origin. His intelligence is close to average, but he is functioning below his potential. In summary, this is a long-time inadequate or borderline adjustment pattern. Test results and case history, though they do not give a strong clear-cut diagnostic picture, suggest the diagnosis of schizophrenic reaction, chronic undifferentiated type. Prognosis for response to treatment appears to be poor.

This completely blind analysis is based on the following assumptions:
1. The usual veteran referred for psychological testing is not likely to be an obvious or clear-cut diagnostic case. There is no need for testing unless there is indecision about what steps might be taken in his behalf. Consequently, hedging is to be expected in a report anyway.
2. There are some modal characteristics of patients coming to VA hospitals. In placing bets on what the patient is likely to be like, the best guess would be a description of the modal personality. For instance, most of the veterans coming to this hospital are chronic cases who have not succeeded in jobs or in family life. Also, the best guess on intelligence would obviously be average intelligence, but since the person is a psychiatric patient it is likely that he is not functioning at his best.

3. This is a schizophrenic case (according to the plan for the program). Given the general classification schizophrenia, one can work back to some of the characteristics which belong to such persons and have a fair chance of being right.

4. Certain modal behaviors of the clinical staff provide clues. They use certain words, resort to jargon. They have a preference for certain diagnoses. A large percentage of the cases wind up with the diagnosis of schizophrenic reaction, chronic undifferentiated type.

5. There are some "universally valid" adjectives which are appropriate for almost any psychiatric patient, such as *dependent, immature, irritable,* and *egocentric.*

6. In the less clear areas where modal characteristics do not stand out, it is safe to write a vague statement or one which can be interpreted in various ways. Readers can be counted on to overlook a few vague misses and to select the descriptions which jibe with their own preconceptions.

7. All of this is intended to say that we have much in common with the old fortune teller, and that what we need are better ways of dealing with individuality. Knowing modal personalities is very useful; it certainly adds to ease of social communication; however, we are sometimes fooled into thinking that we know persons when actually all we know are our own stereotypes.

The problem of individualizing a psychological report is not an easy one. As Forer (1949) and Sundberg (1955) have shown in research studies with college students attempting to identify their own personality descriptions, it is extremely difficult to differentiate fake "universally valid" statements from bona fide attempts at interpretation. Indeed, both the students and their friends were unable to do so. Tallent (1958) has made several suggestions for individualizing the psychological reports. Modifying and adding to his suggestions, the following can be made: (1) Do not mention a general finding which is true of almost everyone unless it is one that is unmistakably important to keep in mind. (2) Indicate the individual's special characteristics as exactly as possible by illustrating how a trait is manifested, by quantifying the strength of a trait or by indicating the degree of probability of such behavior, by describing the situations in which such behavior becomes overt or important, and by stating the level of overtness of subtlety at which the trait is detected. (3) Describe the interrelationships of characteristics rather than mention them separately. (4) Avoid "shotgun" listing of all possible findings, "wastebasket" classifications, and vague generalities. Report only what is pertinent and relevant. Focus on the important problems and decisions in the case as you have analyzed it. (5) Make an honest statement of the circumstances of your testing and observation, and state the limitations of your procedures and of your understanding of the case. Never fear to say, "I don't know."

THE FORM OF THE REPORT

The psychological report must be in the correct form to fit in with the remainder of the patient's clinical record. If his social history is already on the chart it need not be repeated. However, if the psychologist's interview and testing should unearth new, significant aspects of the history or throw a new light on it, such items should be included. In a small clinic or private office where there may be no one else to take the history, the psychological report may contain it as an integral part. The psychological reports we are about to reproduce as illustrations were taken from regular "team" settings and so are restricted to the more typical functions of the clinical psychologist.

Some student psychologists tend to find report-writing easiest if they organize the report around the tests administered. The fault in such a procedure is that it ignores the fact that the main interest of the reader is not in the tests but in how the report answers certain crucial questions about the patient. For this reason it is generally much better to organize the report around such topics as the patient's intelligence, personality, and clinical diagnosis. The Assessment Analysis Chart helps to organize just such a report. Some psychologists seem to prefer to write in narrative form without section titles, but generally it is easier for the reader and makes the content clearer if section titles or underlinings are used.

We know that a large number of possible topics may be covered in a psychological report.[1] No one format is recommended, since different cases demand different treatment. However, the report will typically cover such things as: (1) *Basic identifying data,* such as the patient's age, sex, marital status, occupation, and education. (2) *The reasons for referral,* to serve as a kind of orienting framework for both writer and reader. (3) *Behavioral observations* of the patient made by the psychologist during the interview and testing session, with intent to show anything significant about his personality, test-taking attitude, or disabilities (if any) that might affect test interpretation. (4) *Tests administered* or special observational procedures employed. (5) *Intellectual functioning* of the patient and any signs of impairment. (6) *Personality description and dynamics.* These occupy a prominent place in the report, touching upon such matters as conflicts, attitudes, behavioral peculiarities, control and adjustment mechanisms, deviant mentation, whether the information is derived from tests or observations. Although less often described, *problems that arise from the patient's situation* should also find a place in the report. (7) *Diagnostic impressions.* Though psychologists are not legally responsible for making psychiatric diagnoses in most states, in practice their impressions are usually expected and may make a major contribution. *Prognosis* is often indicated. (8) *Recommendations for treatment or disposition.* These are often made and

---

[1] The reader might profit from looking over the outlines recommended in such sources as Berg (1954), Blau (1959), Taylor and Teicher (1946), and Wells and Ruesch (1945).

should be supported by psychological evidence. (9) A brief *summary* of the report, to be placed either at the end or the beginning.

SOME ILLUSTRATIVE PSYCHOLOGICAL REPORTS

The six illustrative examples of actual psychological reports which follow are taken from the files of a variety of different clinical settings. (Details have, of course, been altered so as to preserve the anonymity of the patient and the institution.) These reports are to be thought of not as models of report-writing but as samples of psychologists' work to be criticized and evaluated. As the reader studies them, he might try to put himself in the place of the recipient of the report. What main impressions of the person are you going to get from this report? What further questions do you feel you would like to ask of the psychologist? At what points is the communication unclear, pretentious, or unnecessary? What picture do you get of the psychologist who wrote the report? Finally, you might try to put yourself in the place of the psychologist to see if you could improve on his report in certain places.

Report on Sally Rhodes, a mental hospital inmate, to the referring ward physician

This report was written by an experienced psychologist, the only psychologist in a very understaffed state hospital. With limited time available and forced to set himself a limited task, he administered just one test.

Psychological Evaluation

Name Rhodes, Sally
Date _____
Age 29
Case number _____
Requested by Dr. _____ (physician)
Purpose Evaluation of intellectual functioning

Mrs. Rhodes is a short, heavy, squarely built blonde person whose speech is like a rapid machinegun flow of words in which she repeats herself again and again. She is very defensive about her low intellect, saying she isn't bright in things like school, but maintaining that she is bright in other ways. She was very suspicious about the purpose of the test, is afraid it will cause her to be kept here in the hospital, and in general presents a very excited appearance. However, she denies her excitement, claims to be very calm and does so in an excited argumentative voice. She feels she has been unfairly treated, is resentful of having her children taken from her, and cannot give a clear coherent logical account of the events leading up to her hospitalization. Her behavior appears definitely manic.

Tests administered   Wechsler-Bellevue (I)
                              Verbal scale IQ 73
                              Performance IQ 62
                              Full-scale IQ 65

The subject is functioning at a defective intellectual level, and her present level of functioning is slightly below her potential, due to the impairing effects of her excitement and the anxiety produced by the threat of the test situation. She relies heavily upon defenses of denial and is full of excuses for her errors. For example, when she misses a question she might say, "I could do it if I had more time," or "I have that question written down at home, and I could have learned it if I'd been told I was going to be tested," or "I could do it if I had a pencil; it's not being dumb if you have to use a pencil." She has a very low fund of general information, her thinking is quite concrete, and she is so excited that it was necessary to repeat almost every question. She doesn't interpret reality accurately, is very insecure with regard to her intellect. One feature was consistent throughout, and that was that she would never admit that she was as dull as she really is; she clings desperately to anything that will permit her to preserve her sense of being worthwhile and in so doing has to rely upon uneconomical, almost pathological, and very unstable defenses.

Diagnostic Impression from his limited observation: Mental deficiency with hypomanic defense by denial, accompanied by some paranoid features which probably have a fairly realistic basis. Her social adjustment has always been about in line with the above mentioned intellectual level. She will probably always be a ward of the state either in or out of the hospital.

                                              (Name)
                                              Psychologist

Report on Chuck F., a child guidance clinic case, to the clinic staff

Report of Psychological Study

                                   F., Charles N. ("Chuck")
                                   Male, age 10, born _____
                                   Clinic No. __
                                   Interviewed and tested
                                   (date) by (Name)

Reason for referral

Chuck was referred to the clinic by the school with a history of disobedience at home, running away from school, poor school work, and taking or destroying other children's property. The family physician's report is essentially negative.

Previous tests

The school reports a Stanford-Binet IQ last year (date) of 91. He averages at the 3.1 grade level of achievement tests though he is now near the end of the fourth grade.

Tests administered

        Wechsler Intelligence Scale for Children—6 subtests
        Rorschach
        Michigan Picture Test—8 cards

Observation

Chuck is a robust, healthy appearing boy. This healthy appearance is at odds with his lethargic, "tired" manner. Although he appears to have no motor or speech defects, the lack of energy was evidenced in his soft, colorless, and somewhat monotonous speech. He is left-handed, and though he does not wear glasses, his behavior on the coding subtest in the WISC (eyes within 2 inches of the page) leaves some doubt as to his visual acuity.

When asked what the two activities he liked best and least were, Chuck said that he liked "going to the woods" and baseball best and "hated" school and cleaning his room. He claimed that no one had said anything about why he was coming here. When asked if his father had come with them he said, "No, he stays home and watches the ball game." This was the only reference to his stepfather.

Chuck gave up easily on items in the WISC and responded quickly but briefly on the projective tests. The general picture of low vitality was the central impresison received from his behavior. It is difficult to assess the quality of the testing relationship. It was my feeling that Chuck was "going along" with anything suggested, patiently, but not enthusiastically.

Test results

Intellectually Chuck has normal ability (WISC Full Scale IQ, 99), despite his poor school record. He was particularly poor on items having to do with practical reasoning about human problems (the Comprehension subtest). He shrugged his shoulders and said that he "didn't know." When I persisted with questions beyond the standard requirements, he was able to answer some of the items.

In regard to personality characteristics, aside from the indications of immaturity and unsettled sexual role which might be expected in boys of his age, the most notable feature is an interpersonal orientation of passive submission. The general impression he gives is one of apathy, perhaps as a result of feelings of inadequacy and ineffectiveness. His stories reflected three themes: (1) sadness, (2) control by authority figures, and (3) being the recipient of action rather than the actor. These findings are consistent with the relationship with the examiner and the test-taking behavior. It also seems to fit in with the teacher's statement that he "seems afraid to let others like him." His quick response to the projective tests suggests, along with compliance, an adequate perception of reality and the possibility of a richer fantasy life than he ordinarily reveals.

Summary

Chuck gives the impression of a boy who feels uncertain of his own ability. He seems to have given up overt attempts to "control the situation" himself. His intellectual ability is such that he should not have too much difficulty in meeting the school's academic requirements. It is my opinion that Chuck is capable of entering into a warm relationship with others, if it is in an area in which he feels somewhat competent. In the light of his interests in outdoor life and in baseball, any organization, such as Boy Scouts or Little League, where he could have a successful experience in a social situation, would be advisable. The conflict between his parents reported in the social history is undoubtedly being reflected in his attempts to run away and in distracting fantasies. His behavior and the test results are not indicative of a typical predelinquent pattern. If psychotherapy is available, he would probably respond well. Perhaps a woman therapist might be able to relate with him more quickly in the light of his passive resistance with me and his very active problems with his father. It is also strongly recommended that his vision be carefully examined.

(Name)
Clinical Psychologist

Report on Mrs. C., a new patient at a psychiatric out-patient clinic, to the clinic staff

Mrs. C. is a 44-year-old divorced woman. She is a practical nurse but is currently unemployed. She is living with her 60-year-old mother who helps take care of her two children. Her manner is noticeably reticent and somewhat depressive and there is some degree of emotional withdrawal. She volunteers virtually no information, and even when she is directly questioned, her responses are guarded and cryptic, and she is generally uncommunicative. In the testing situation she was very cooperative, but her participation is more on the basis of submissiveness than of intrinsic interest in the proceedings. She was administered the Rorschach, Sentence Completion, Thematic Apperception Test, and the Minnesota Multiphasic Personality Inventory.

The Rorschach shows a basically hysterical type of personality structure, the presence of substantial obsessive trends and significant indications of paranoid pathology. Sexual maladjustment is clearly evident and the indications of weakened reality contact seem to be related to the sexual problems. The patient is very resistant to attacking or even facing her basic problems, and this corroborates the impression one gets in attempting to interview her. There is a virtual absence of any insight. The MMPI shows significant peaks on the Hysteria, Paranoia, and Depression scales. This kind of pattern has been found to be common with neurotic patients, although a significant degree of paranoid involvement is suggested. The TAT is, for the most part, rather bland except for the presence of a considerable number of themes involving highly aggressive acts. The most salient and pervasive feeling that emerges is the paranoid one of a defenseless person in a hostile and brutal world in which violent aggressive forces are always lurking and may strike one or one's loved one when they least expect it.

The Sentence Completion Test brings out most clearly the paranoid ideation which is suggested in the MMPI and Rorschach. She feels that she is extremely ill and that her condition is almost hopeless: I am very—"sick," and My greatest hope—"is almost gone." To further inquiries about these she says, "I feel that if my eyes, my ears, and my throat were thoroughly studied, they would find something wrong," and, "I don't think I'll ever be healthy and strong again." Although a nurse, she is unable to explain how a local eye, ear, and throat condition could cause her to be so severely and hopelessly sick, and she shows no interest in attempting to explain it. She is confused and baffled by many inexplicable experiences she has had and projects motives and interpretations into many common daily occurrences; for example, from sentence completions, I want to know—"Why some people behave so strangely"; I secretly—"Feel that something must have happened in 19— that I don't know about"; If only—"People would tell me the truth." In the inquiry on these items she replies, "None of these things are too important, but so many of them happened to me. For example, when my brother-in-law's leg was broken, and I was present in the doctor's office, my brother-in-law remarked to the doctor, 'She's an excellent diagnostician,' referring to me. All the doctor said was, 'Well, I got you.' What did he mean by that? That's bothered and puzzled me ever since. The same kind of thing that's been happening that I can't explain is why the seriously sick diabetic patient I was nursing was suddenly taken off all medication. And also the last patient that I had that none of the doctors or nurses did anything for. I can't understand these things." In the same vein, What puzzles me—"why one of the doctors talks about married men and men in high salaried positions." In the inquiry she responds, "The way he'd lower his voice or look at me when he'd get around to talking about those things. I don't know what his motive was, but I felt there was some reason behind it."

Along the same lines, and by dint of much probing, since the patient is very guarded and cryptic in all her responses, additional evidence of paranoid ideation was elicited. She has visited fortunetellers twice. In both cases the fortunetellers told her about a particular man who would come into her life significantly. She relates many strange events which have happened around her house which she feels are all related to the return of this man into her life. She relates a recent experience in which she felt extremely good and symptom-free for a day or so, and she feels that this happened because she was given a massive dose of "dope" which was put in some coffee which was returned to her by a girl in a neighboring apartment who had borrowed some coffee from her. These experiences, all of which are baffling and troubling to her seem to have increased in frequency since 19—, and she feels that the attitudes and feelings of her friends and associates toward her have changed. She is unable to account for these unusual experiences, but she feels that she is being used as a psychological experiment by someone who is causing these things to happen to her so that he can study her reactions to them.

Impression. On first impression derived from an initial interview, Mrs. C.'s superficial manner and guarded communicativeness conveys the picture of a person in good contact who is suffering from a reactive depressive state as a result of protracted and severe stress in a realistically difficult marital situation. The termination of the marriage in divorce and her stringent economic prospect of having to support her two children enhances this impression. On the basis of psychological testing and a searching and probing type of interview, however, evidence of substantial paranoid pathology, moving toward systematization, is elicited. It is felt that this patient is quite seriously ill, and the outlook is poor, inasmuch as her present uncommunicativeness makes her unavailable for a psychotherapeutic approach.

Psychological consultation report on Mr. Deeter, a patient in a general medical hospital, to the referring physican

Psychological Consultation Report

This 35-year-old man, Mr. Deeter, was referred to this service because of signs of mental deterioration associated with a 15-year history of *grand mal* seizures. Until this year he has averaged 4 to 5 seizures a year. He has had 3 seizures during October 19—. In this evaluation the Rorschach, Wechsler Verbal Scale, and Memory-for-Design test were administered.

Though there is no previous IQ score for comparison it would appear that this patient shows little intellectual deficit. The earned score of 108 is in the normal range, and the ability he displays is generally good. There is a certain compulsiveness and occasional bizarreness to his responses, however, that can readily interfere with his ability to demonstrate his intellectual capacities. Similarly, there is little evidence that cerebral pathology is interfering with his skills or his ability to perceive accurately. In fact, he demonstrated surprisingly good visual-motor ability. However, Mr. Deeter does show some clear psychopathological signs. Beneath his rather controlled and benign exterior there is strong hostility. He does not show any overt psychotic indications but he is capable of perceptual distortion and of bizarre thought. Psychologically he protects against overt manifestations by withdrawal and avoidance. In particular he shows little capacity for rewarding relationships with others. It is judged that at this time the patient does not present a very stable personality. Psychiatrically, the prognosis would appear to be poor. Diagnostically, this is not a clear picture inasmuch as the outstanding feature of the present evaluation is the personality instability. It may be that his seizures have a secondary effect in preventing any overt psychiatric symptoms from appearing. It is recommended that if possible this man be referred again in the near future for re-evaluation by this service.

Diagnostic Impression
Chronic brain syndrome associated with convulsive disorder. 009-550
a. Manifested by impaired reality testing and some bizarre thought and by social withdrawal and avoidance signs.
b. Precipitating stress undetermined.
c. Predisposition undetermined.
d. Impairment moderate to severe.

Report to the rehabilitation team on Mr. Engel, referred for vocational rehabilitation by a physician

Mr. Engel, a 41-year-old patient, was referred by Dr. _____ for vocational rehabilitation. During the initial interview he appeared somewhat tense, holding his body rigid and not allowing himself to relax. At the same time, he appeared emotionally flat, describing an incident where he quite impulsively hit a man on the head with a paint gun. He stated that he felt "good" after hitting the man, giving the impression that he derives little guilt from hostile and impulsive actions. His previous records contain a prediction that he would continue to behave in rather psychopathic ways, and from the patient's description of his own behavior, this prediction seems to hold up.

He has held a number of jobs the past few years, most of which were related to driving or servicing trucks and automobiles. He states that his longest single employment lasted seven years, when he hauled cars and moved Army equipment prior to and during World War II. Since his marriage (he now has four children), his work record has been unstable. He appears to have used alcohol excessively and has been in jail a number of times, necessitating his wife to request state aid.

This man's impulsive actions appear to be of an erratic nature so that he may seem fairly stable for some length of time before any impulsivity breaks out. Although his control over his behavior at times appears quite poor, he seems to be able to give rational explanations for his behavior after it has happened. This suggests that he tries to give the impression that he has good control over his behavior when he really has little.

He was administered a Wechsler Adult Intelligence Scale, a Kuder Preference Record, a Cornell Index, a Minnesota Multiphasic Personality Inventory, and a Purdue Peg-Board. He appeared to be motivated to do well on these tests and showed no flippancy or careless attitudes toward testing. On the Intelligence Scale he received a Full Scale IQ of 85, a Verbal IQ of 91, and a Performance IQ of 78, suggesting that he is of dull normal intelligence. The Purdue Peg-Board was given to test the coordination of his hands and suggests that he is probably a little below the average in this ability.

On the Kuder Preference Record he scored highest on the Social Service (98 per cent) and Musical (78 per cent) areas of interest and lowest on Mechanical (12 per cent) and Outdoors (26 per cent). This suggests that there might be some conflict between this man's interests and his vocational pursuits. There is a little higher accordance between these interest areas and his stated desire to work as a hospital aide or practical nurse. The difficulty here is that he might express some of his impulsivity toward patients or fellow employees.

The testing results also indicate that this man may handle anxiety by developing a variety of psychosomatic symptoms or by acting aggressively toward his surroundings and deriving little guilt from any antisocial actions he may commit. Any long-range plans for this man should take into account his occasional impulsiveness, his tendency to develop physical complaints when put under stress, and his admitted excessive use of alcohol at previous times.

Report on Mr. Farrel, to the mental hygiene staff

Problem

This 35-year-old married, accounting clerk, with a history of a loss of skull bone and residuals of the removal of a benign brain tumor, was referred to the Mental Hygiene Clinic by his private physician for a psychological evaluation. This evaluation is directed toward demonstrating alleged psychological deficits, for example, "poor memory," stemming from brain trauma. The problem, further, is to rule out a psychogenic emotional disturbance. The following tests were used as an aid in reaching the clinical opinion:

    Wechsler Adult Intelligence Scale
    Bender-Gestalt
    Rorschach
    Routine Research Battery (including Draw-A-Person, a special inventory, and selected TAT cards)

Observation

The veteran is a balding man of medium height and build whose neat grooming and pale color mark him as a white-collar worker. He related socially in a deferent manner with an obedient, overpolite, almost apologetic attitude. Throughout the evaluation he gave evidence of high manifest anxiety: nervous laughter, flushing, perspiring, hurried speech, self-derogation. As his tension mounted, he exhibited a striking tic-like mannerism wherein he simultaneously blinked, wrinkled his nose, and raised his upper lip. This was done rapidly and resembled the facial movement of a rabbit sniffing.

Intelligence

The patient's functional intellectual ability is best characterized as "average" for men of his age (Full Scale IQ, 107). This overall intellectual status reflects the veteran's ability to recall old learning, acquire new associations, and solve problems of both abstract and concrete nature. There are no specific deficits in his pattern of performance which might suggest a selective decrement in skills. It is noted, however, that the veteran tended to be "bright" when responding to verbal material and "low average" when doing performance tasks. To some extent this discrepancy is a matter of being unable to hurry effectively. It is not a matter of depressed intellectual "power" since the most difficult performance tasks can be solved by this man slowly but surely. As long as a problem situation is clear-cut, making for objectivity, the patient functions with little or no hint of psychological impairment. For example, visual-motor organization, immediate and remote memory, and manipulation of number symbols—often the most sensitive dimensions reflecting the deficits of brain damage—were sound. None of the confusion, concreteness, and perceptual distortion typical of organic deficit was demonstrated. Overall alertness, concentration, and clarity of thought were shown as the patient responded to intellectual demands that had a "right" or "wrong" answer. In contrast, the patient functioned pathologically when he was forced to cope with novel, ambiguous situations. There was a striking regression in the level of adequacy when the patient was forced to rely on his own cues and trust his own feelings. Rather than conventional perception and rational inferences previously demonstrated at a superior level, the veteran sharply deteriorated to autistic explanations. These results show that he is capable of crude conceptualization and distorted reasoning under conditions where his deepest feelings become involved. Without doubt this is the most significant observation made concerning the man: It is possible for him to look like two different people in his ability and reasoning, depending on the nature of the situation. Severe psychopathology is present in a latent form of deteriorating thought processes rather than manifest in terms of specific deficits in intellectual skills.

Personality

This man is capable of giving the appearance of social and vocational adequacy while defending himself desperately against panic which now strains his ability to maintain contact with external reality. He is the sort of person who has emphasized rigid control of behavior and intolerance for his emotional impulses. There are few behavioral outlets for any but the most conventional needs and his dogmatic, authoritarian beliefs make the thought of unsocial feelings unacceptable. The inflexibility of the control system dealing with feelings is paying the price of a high level of subjective discomfort and manifest anxiety. Nevertheless, an appearance of good adjustment is maintained in familiar environments where there are reality props to help repress the wild ideas generated by fear. This intense anxiety destroys any experience of well-being and narrows the veteran's inner thoughts to frightened preoccupation with bodily function. Stimuli that normally would elicit interpretation within a wide framework are constricted to this panicky concern with self-function even when it is necessary to use autistic logic to achieve it. Energy which might be invested in human relationships, cultural interests, and spontaneous emotional expression has been turned inward to be consumed in depressive rumination. While he reassures himself in a Pollyannish fashion that there is nothing the matter that can't be fixed, he is desperately concerned about his very existence. This threat makes him emphasize rigid controls more than ever, renders him more subservient to dogmatic authority and less capable of expressing rebellious feelings. The increased sensitivity due to the shaky state of defenses is apparent in cautious, suspicious attitudes which have a paranoid ring. He fears revealing not only his unusual ideas but also his natural sexuality. Embarrassment results when sexual stimuli enter consciousness and he reacts with angry disgust to the sexual behavior of others. All in all, it can be said that there has been a process of disintegration in a rigidly controlled personality so that further decompensation would produce a paranoid psychosis.

Conclusions

On the basis of psychological evaluation, it is adjudged that this patient is suffering from a psychogenic emotional disturbance of severe proportions rather than psychological defects directly traceable to brain damage. It is entirely possible that the emotional trauma of brain surgery was a significant etiological factor in the psychopathology now observed. The symptoms and complaints which have been described in this case—including "poor memory" —may be accounted for by panic which this patient is fighting off. Diagnostic impression: Anxiety reaction with incipient paranoid psychosis.

Treatment

It is recommended that this veteran be treated as an incipient paranoid psychotic with emphasis upon chemotherapy and a supportive medical relationship. The support can best be given by an understanding manner which does not attempt to uncover inner feelings but accepts those that are volunteered. Straightforward medical reassurance concerning organic disease coupled with sympathy for the burden of such worry should be of value. Above all, it should be kept in mind that this man is functioning to the limits of his capacity because of emotional stress, and his responsibilities should be lightened when this can be done without loss of self-esteem. It is not unlikely that this patient will be treated eventually in a neuropsychiatric hospital.

Summary

This patient was psychologically evaluated to demonstrate alleged psychological deficits stemming from known brain trauma. No objective evidence of such specific intellectual deficits was demonstrated. Severe psychopathology was judged to be present, however, in the form of personality disintegration, best described as an anxiety reaction with incipient paranoid psychosis.

FOLLOW-UP REPORTS

In order to judge the effectiveness of his psychological reports, the clinician needs to have some feedback from those who use them. Sometimes it is possible to get an articulate and sympathetic colleague or supervisor to express his straightforward judgments of their effectiveness. In addition to this kind of follow-up, it is most helpful for the psychologist to find out whether a report he has sent in has led to any action or not. Perhaps he may even discern that it has not ever been read. This clearly suggests that something in the local situation is amiss. Perhaps the significance of the report was not properly appreciated. Maybe the person who should have read it merely decided it was too long. On the other hand, perhaps the local situation needs to be improved by educating the potential readers. In any case, the clinician whose reports run into difficulties should be alert to possible ways to improve his future communications.

A special form of feedback on interpretation of assessment information occurs when the clinician gives *interpretations of test results to clients*. This is commonly done in counseling centers and educational situations. Although there is less interpretation of tests directly to psychiatric patients, it may happen that they are curious about test results, and when they are it is often possible as well as kind to explain them. In his report on the disposition of 1200 cases seen by three clinical psychologists in private practice, Blau (1959, p. 35) reports that 40 per cent of the cases were seen for test interpretation, recommendations, and follow-up only. The subject of test interpretation in counseling and psychotherapy will be covered in later chapters. We mention it here to call attention to the fact that it gives the psychologist an opportunity to improve his understanding of assessment. Perhaps a session may be begun with some inquiry into what the patient recalls of a test and what questions he would like to ask about it. From there one moves into a simple explanation of the test results and what they may mean to the patient. Because the patient may ruminate about their meanings for some time, it is often wise to schedule a second interview at a later time. The patient's view of the tests, his emotional reaction to various aspects of them, and the modifications the clinician has to make to apply recommendations to the patient's circumstances give the clinician further opportunities to see where his interpretations could be improved.

CRITICAL EVALUATION OF PSYCHOLOGICAL REPORTS AND COMMUNICATION

Since the psychological report may involve crucial decisions about the patient's life, it is very important both for him and for the psychologist. It is the primary documentary product of the practicing psychologist. Though in recent years the importance of the report is reflected in the findings of several research studies, the larger problem of clinical communication can scarcely be said to have been seriously approached as yet by systematic research.

Where the psychological report stands or falls is in its *general clinical utility*. In a study partially summarized at the end of Chapter 4, Dailey (1953) started out by developing a list of decisions ordinarily made in clinical work. He then had judges read reports and check the list of decisions that could be made on the basis of the content of the reports. The correlations between various characteristics of the report and the number of new, clear, and useful decisions was then computed. Contrary to some of the conclusions reported in this chapter, Dailey found significant, though moderate, correlations between the utility of the report and both the length of the report and the number of technical terms in the report. Doubts and questions may be raised because of the limited scope of the study, but its conclusions certainly suggest that many of the assumptions psychologists are prone to make about report-writing should be tested. Two other studies are of interest in connection with the same topic. Klopfer (1960) reports an unpublished study he carried out with Suczek in which staff members were asked to check a list of terms to indicate their impressions of a patient after attending a conference devoted to his case. They found agreement was restricted to those characteristics about which there had been specific pronouncements by the psychological consultant. This finding suggests the importance of clarifying exactly what one means in a report and not leaving much to the reader or the listener to infer. The desirability of a *certain kind of specificity* in a report is emphasized as the outcome of a study by Ullman, Berkman, and Hamister (1958) on the prediction of benefit from placing a VA patient in a nursing home. They discovered in general that psychological reports on these patients added nothing to prediction above the prediction obtained from length of hospitalization. However, they did find that reports specifically appraising likelihood of conformity to the requirements of a group situation predicted nursing-home adjustment significantly, whereas routine reports did not.

There have been several studies of the *sources of difficulty in communication* in reports. Robinson and Cohen (1954) analyzed the content of 30 reports prepared by three graduate students who held internships. They found evidences of significant *systematic bias* in them. The tendency of one student was to emphasize aggressiveness in his reports, of another to emphasize dependency. Grayson and Tolman (1950) compared the *differences in the definitions* given by psychologists, on the one hand, and by psychiatrists, on the other, to 50 crucial terms frequently used in psychological reports. They found a number of significant differences, such as that the psychologists proved to be wordier and more intellectual in the definitions they gave. Naturally there were wide individual differences, and both groups also gave a good many vague and loose definitions. Garfield, Heine, and Leventhal (1954) compared *ratings of the value of reports* made by several judges representing different mental health professions. Social workers rated the value of the reports higher than did members of the other professions, and they were less critical. Cuadra and Albaugh (1956) studied the *communication of intended meanings* by report writers. They constructed multiple-choice items incorporating the material included in four representative psychological reports. These items, together with the reports, were then distributed to 56 judges, representing six professional groups in a VA Hospital. The judges were asked to select from each multiple-choice item the alternative which the author had either clearly stated or strongly implied. The particular meaning that the writer of the report stated he had intended to convey was used as a criterion for correctness. Analysis of the data showed that: (1) Correspondence between the author's intentions and the judges' interpretations, for all professional groups combined, was only 53 per cent. (2) There was statistically significant variation among the professional groups in the accuracy of their interpretation, the psychologist judges being most accurate and the nurses least accurate. (3) There was considerable variation within all of the groups in their interpretations of the reports. (4) The greatest breakdown in communication occurred when the judges did not agree with the report writer's emphasis or with the presence or strength of some personality characteristic the writer believed they had detected. Datel and Gengerelli (1956) studied the ability to match individuals with Rorschach interpretations. Though psychologists could do this with better than chance accuracy, their success depended greatly on the heterogeneity of the samples.

In conclusion, it can be said that the scientific study of clinical interpretation and communication is a wide open area for research. Current practices in clinical work have "grown like Topsy," with far too little evaluation of their underlying assumptions. The next chapter will explore further some of the research issues and problems in psychological assessment.

SUMMARY

The value of psychological assessment ultimately depends on how well the psychologist gets his communication over to the person who uses or acts upon his report. Communication may be informal and oral as well as written. The psychological report is one of several kinds of case records; its nature and scope will be affected in part by what is covered in other records on the same case. In organizing the assessment information into a report, the psychologist keeps the purpose of the report uppermost in mind. He looks for congruencies and discrepancies, for deviant and typical behavior, and for diagnostic signs. The Assessment Analysis Chart should help in organizing data for the report. In order to have effective communication one must be particularly concerned with the interests and needs of the primary reader. The danger of lapsing into psychological jargon is ever-present. Though the report should not be overburdened with test detail, concrete illustrations may be strikingly valuable in communicating a point. The report should be pointed and brief enough to make it likely that it will be read. The psychologist must seek to individualize his report and beware of writing what have been dubbed pseudo-reports displaying the "Barnum effect." The chapter included for purposes of discussion a number of actual psychological reports from different psychological services. The psychologist must manage to follow-up on his reports to see how well he is communicating. There has been but little research on the general clinical utility of reports, though some problems of communication have been identified, such as the fact that a psychologist may betray a systematic bias in his reports. It has also been shown that there are characteristic differences in the way different professional groups on the clinical team define terms.

SUGGESTED READINGS

KLOPFER, W. G. *The psychological report: Use and communication of psychological findings.* New York: Grune & Stratton, 1960.
    This is an excellent book on report-writing from a man who has had a great deal of practical experience in varied settings. It discusses the purpose, focus, style, language, and organization of the psychological report. It describes for students an excellent method for organizing the multiplicity of assessment materials in preparation for writing a report. It contains numerous extracts from reports and one complete case. For another reference on report-writing which pays particular attention to the language and construction of reports, see Hammond and Allen (1953). The book by Huber (1961) also provides some very helpful suggestions and illustrations concerning report-writing.

RESEARCH EXAMPLES

DATEL, W. E., & GENGERELLI, J. A. Reliability of Rorschach interpretations. *J. proj. Tech.*, 1956, 19, 372-381.
    This is an investigation of the similarity of psychologists' interpretations of Rorschachs. The authors collected blind interpretations of Rorschachs on 18 neuropsychiatric patients from 27 clinical psychologists. These psychologists were then asked to match for a set of patients the several Rorschach interpretations made by other psychologists. The psychologists were presented with the reports in a systematic way (a two-way factorial design).
    The overall results for the group attained a high level of significance; that is, psychologists were successful in matching to a particular patient the interpretations made by different psychologists. However, when details are examined, some strikingly negative findings appear. Forty-eight per cent of the judging psychologists did not perform at a level significantly better than chance. Also much of the successful matching occurred with very heterogeneous groups of patients. To cite an example, if a schizophrenic, a mental defective, a neurotic, and a sociopathic personality were in the group, it was easy to differentiate reports about them correctly. If, however, the whole group was made up of neurotics, it was difficult to do better than chance. Such a finding detracts from the overall significance of the matchings. Psychologists might legitimately be expected to do better than they actually did with the less heterogeneous samples. The authors concluded that a substantial majority of these Rorschach reports had very little communication value. Individual differences among psychologists in respect to their reports ought to be studied more than it is.

LITTLE, K. B., and SHNEIDMAN, E. S. Congruencies among interpretations of psychological test and anamnestic data. *Psychol. Monogr.*, 1959, No. 6, 1-42 (Whole No. 476).

The primary purpose of this study was to investigate the agreements, or congruencies, among personality descriptions when such descriptions are based on different sources of information. Congruencies were examined for different subjects, different assessment instruments, and different interpretive tasks. The 48 clinical psychologists who served as test judges were experts in the tests used; 12 each interpreted the Rorschach, TAT, MAPS, and MMPI. The tests were obtained from 12 male subjects of normal intelligence; 3 from each of the following categories: normal neurotic, psychophysiological, and psychotic. In addition to the test data a comprehensive psychiatric case history was submitted. The typed case histories (the anamnestic materials) were judged by 23 psychiatrists and one psychologist, half of them psychoanalytically oriented.

Each judge, using the test or anamnestic materials assigned him, made five kinds of interpretive judgments: diagnostic label, rating of degree of maladjustment, a 76 item Q sort of social behavior and adjustment items, a 117 item true-false questionnaire with items like those on psychological reports, and a 100 item true-false questionnaire of a factual nature about the subjects' past and present life. (The procedures and cases are described in such detail in the monograph that the study could be repeated by other researchers.)

The bulky data were analyzed by correlation analysis of the various methods. The monograph presents the findings in detail. In general the results are disheartening to anyone hoping to find that these common assessment procedures have high validity. Even though the judges were experts in their particular tests, the best they could do amounted to only a small increase over chance variation. This small increase might be considered useful for screening purposes by anyone who overlooks the fact that the tests, especially the projective techniques, are as time-consuming as they are. The MMPI fared slightly better in the outcome, and it also has the practical advantage of requiring less time. There were certain limitations in the procedure, such as the fact that only blind interpretations were used. This study certainly raises questions about the value of having merely the results of a test, without additional information. No attempt was made to go into the validity of a test if there is added material. The use of psychiatrists' consensus of judgment based upon the anamnestic material as a criterion of validity of the tests can also be questioned; the psychiatrists were not given the full facts about each subject and did not interview him.

Little and Shneidman's study makes an interesting comparison with the somewhat similar study by Silverman (1959) in the monograph that follows it in the series. Silverman studied the validity of projective-technique interpretations by 30 clinical psychologists with varying amounts of experience. The interpreters' Q sorts were correlated with the Q sorts by psychiatrists after 35 or more therapy sessions. The patients taking the tests (Rorschach, TAT, HTP, and Most Unpleasant Concept) were 10 young adult males beginning treatment in a clinic. The results indicated significant agreement of interpretations with the criteria. There was no significant difference connected with less or greater experience among the psychologists. Psychologists who had undergone analysis did significantly better. However, it needs to be remembered that the criterion was the judgment of psychiatrists who were analytically oriented. Interpsychologist agreement on the cases was significant, though the correlation was only .34. Whether the projective techniques really added significantly to evaluation is not clear from this study, but the author is more optimistic than Little and Shneidman.

10 Research in Assessment

In this chapter we will summarize the directions that research in assessment has taken. Since the preceding chapters have included many references to research, with examples, we will select only certain areas for more extensive reporting: the general effectiveness of assessment, the problem of "incremental validity," the process by which our impressions of other persons develop, an introduction to "programmatic assessment," and the implications of the current development of computers for assessment.

THE DIRECTIONS OF RESEARCH IN ASSESSMENT

Looking for the broad field of research in assessment, it is possible to discern five paths that pass through most of the terrain, so to speak. The interests of research workers have led them to investigate clinical procedures, clinical problems, the personnel who carry on clinical work, and the processes and outcomes of assessment. We will discuss each in turn.

1. *Research oriented toward assessment procedures*. This is the largest of the five areas of investigation. It includes the construction and elaboration of tests and techniques. The clinical psychologist interested in this kind of research finds he can accomplish much with already existing tests. They may be applied to new populations, to securing local norms, to studies of the influence of response sets, to discovering how scores change with age and socioeconomic status, to prediction studies. In addition to the use of old tests, many new ones are being constructed. Whether

it is desirable that there should be so many new tests is an open question. Many psychologists decry the plethora of "little" tests, each of which has had only a very limited amount of work done on it. They maintain it would be wiser to concentrate research energies on already existing procedures. Still there are large gaps in the testing armamentarium that need filling—tests of situational variables, of life-history variables, of problem-solving. Also a good many of what we have called the old tests are so poorly developed psychometrically that there is more promise in starting from scratch than in trying to refine them.

In procedure-oriented research, there needs to be a sensible balance between psychometric finesse and practical clinical needs. Clinical assessment requires a sequential and flexible testing strategy. In many instances, procedures of very dubious psychometric refinement, such as interviews and some projective techniques, are of great value in providing the initial orientation to a case and in suggesting areas for more intensive investigation. When it comes to clinical work, many psychometrically sophisticated tests such as forced-choice scales or tests developed by factor analysis have not yet proven very useful. In any attempt to improve assessment procedures, the whole assessment process should be considered. The ultimate arbiter is the pay-off or outcome—Does this test actually select those who will profit from therapy, or does that technique detect a true picture of a patient's important conflicts and problems?

2. *Research oriented toward clinical problems.* Instead of being concerned with *how* to assess, some research focuses on *what* is being assessed. This involves concentration upon the particular disorders and deviations of the persons who come to the clinic—the problems of psychopathology, psychosomatics, delinquency and crime, speech disorders, mental retardation, and so forth. The psychological assessor's concern here is with differential diagnosis, predicting the course of the pathology or deviation, its etiology, and group and community differences in such deviant behavior. He uses assessment procedures to investigate these questions.

Often, since his interest is not for the time being in test development, he uses existing tests, accepting whatever validity they have as measures of anxiety, authoritarian attitude, or whatever. Of course, he must be wary of assuming more validity for a particular test than has been demonstrated. Actually, procedural and problem research have many implications for each other. The feedback of information from problem-oriented research is important for understanding the tests used. Thus an experimental study of the effects of frontal lobe lesions on planning ability as measured by the Porteus Mazes has implications for the interpretation of the Porteus in other types of cases.

3. *Research oriented toward clinical personnel.* Psychologists working in a mental hospital or state institution often become involved not only

with assessment of the patients, but also with assessment of the personnel who deal with patients. Common problems are the selection of psychiatric aides and the screening of volunteer workers. Another is how to select patients who are qualified to hold hospital jobs. The influence of aides and other personnel on the therapeutic climate of a hospital is exceedingly great. Institutions with incompetent personnel, where the turnover is high, or where there is feuding between the administration and the clinical staff present especially challenging problems. The development of procedures for assessing and rating personnel for advancement is also very important. The effectiveness of training programs for aides and other personnel need to be studied.

The fitness of the professional staff itself should be appraised. The great expense involved in training psychiatrists, psychologists, social workers, nurses, and occupational therapists makes their proper selection very important. Later on, in discussing programmatic assessment we will refer to studies of trainees in clinical psychology and psychiatry. In medical schools the psychologist is likely to be called in to help in the development of selection procedures for medical students. In the community the selection and evaluation of mental health counselors of different kinds may call for psychological assessment. Psychologists have for many years been involved in school guidance and counseling programs. They may be called on to help in the selection and training of pastoral counselors. All these personnel research programs involve not only the selection and development of procedures, but also the analysis of community mental health programs and methods of evaluating training.

4. *Research oriented toward assessment processes.* In Chapter 19 on research in psychotherapy, studies are classified as either *process* or *outcome* research. A similar distinction can be made in the case of assessment. In Chapter 4 we listed the steps in the assessment process. At each step there are special processes on which research can focus: the initial decision as to why assessment is to be undertaken, the particular tests and techniques chosen for gathering data, the thoughts and actions of the clinician during his direct interaction with the patient, the judgmental processing of what information is obtained, the clinical interpretation process, decisions about the transmission of information to others. Also the group processes in assessment come in for research—the decision-making in intake conference, the problem-solving aspects of conferences where therapy is planned, the way a working image of a patient is developed and transmitted through the staff who are to deal with him. Research on this process aspect of assessment is increasing. In earlier sections we have mentioned a number of relevant projects. In a later section of this chapter we will turn our attention to the process through which a working image or model of the patient is formed.

5. *Research oriented toward assessment pay-off.* This is an outcome

side of assessment. From a practical point of view it is the most important: How well does all of this effort pay off? In order to get our answer, criteria of the accuracy of our predictions, of probable outcomes of clinical acts, and other criteria, must be set up. We will begin our consideration of this kind of research by focusing on two concepts: *effectiveness of assessment* and *incremental validity.*

Before leaving this overview of research in assessment, the problem of keeping up with the research literature might be mentioned. Already publications related to just one assessment technique, the Rorschach, number on the average about three per week. If a clinician or a student conscientiously tries to keep informed about this test and the hundreds of other tests and techniques, as well as with the other kinds of research going on, his problem is likely to become overwhelming. As is true among all the sciences these days, the breakdown of technical communication has become desperately apparent. Some industries have found it is more expensive to search through the literature using present outmoded library procedures than it is to repeat the research itself. (For discussions of this problem, see Kent, 1959, and the report of the APA board of Scientific Affairs, 1959). It will be some help to the student or practicing clinician to develop his own system of abstracting and filing research in the areas of his special interests. (For a description of punch-card systems for doing this, see Casey et al, 1958, and the suggestion of Kirk, 1958, for classifying literature.)

THE EFFECTIVENESS OF ASSESSMENT

The hard-headed administrator has the right to ask, "Just what do we gain by having a psychologist do assessment work in our clinic?" The tender-minded humanitarian is justified in asking, "Is assessment contributing to the welfare of each individual patient?" Psychologists themselves should occasionally stop and ponder: "Is what I am doing right now really worthwhile? Am I wasting time interviewing, giving tests, and writing reports?" Some psychotherapists have even charged that assessment—or at least what they call diagnosis—is in general injurious. Just going through these procedures may lead the patient to be overly dependent and to form a false impression of the authority and omniscience of the clinician. In a survey of clinical psychologists' opinions and practices, E. L. Kelly (1961) found only half of them considering a diagnostic work-up always, or even usually, essential for therapy.

The position we have taken is that assessment is inevitably part of the whole clinical process, once we come face to face with a patient. In some manner we must make a decision whether or not to accept this patient as suited to the kinds of service we can render, and, if he is, which procedures should be undertaken. Unless we flip a coin, decision-making involves some sort of assessment procedure. Furthermore, assessment is bound to lead to communication of a picture of the patient to other persons, giving them impressions which affect their behavior toward him. The question, then, is not whether to have assessment or not, but how to carry it out. Should the receptionist make decisions? If so, which ones? Should only the social worker or the psychiatrist be the assessor? Should we use simply a little interview and immediately launch into therapy, or should we use more involved techniques?

The validity of assessment is not limited to the validity obtained by using any single technique. Too often we study only the validity of an individual test. In actual practice, tests may be combined in various patterns, and additional procedures employed. The understanding we seek can be best obtained from the findings of this whole assessment process and the differential effects of its parts.

If we are serious about studying the effectiveness of assessment, we are led immediately to the problem of criteria. As we have mentioned several times in this book, criteria are ultimately questions of value. The purpose and "philosophy" of an agency or person or program determine what results are wanted. Given clarification and definition of what is important or of what the outcome of clinical work should be, then the criteria of these need to be specified and measured. There is undoubtedly a wide agreement on general statements of value; for example, assessment procedures should lead to decisions that maximize the development of the patient's satisfactions and his effectiveness and that minimize the distress he may cause to society and the cost of his treatment. However, the further definition of these values in detail, the identification of them, and the assignment of proper weights to use in combining them are not simply achieved. We have only just begun to specify values for research on clinical work.[1] In clinical attempts to recommend forms and treatment, we have never done a "job analysis" of what treatment is or what sorts of life situations patients must face. We have too often been satisfied with our impression of what goes on in the clinic and with our "global" knowledge of life.

Before going on, perhaps we should again mention the important distinction between institutional and individual decision-making. As Cronbach and Gleser (1957) have pointed out, the typical institutional decision, such as one determining how aides are selected or how assignments to a work program are made, requires a large number of decisions about people. The institutional decision-maker tends to use a fairly con-

---

[1] As mentioned earlier, the book by Cronbach and Gleser (1957) is a very important source for understanding attempts to analyze these problems. The distribution of criterion variables (base rates) in the population of reference is an important consideration in studying decision-making, as Meehl and Rosen (1955) have pointed out. Goodman (1953) has presented an analysis of social values in the prediction of prisoners' responses to parole.

stant philosophy or value system. On the other hand, individual decision-making, such as choice of one's job or whether to seek a divorce, is something that may occur only rarely in an individual's life. The individual decision-maker chooses between alternatives according to his personal values, which may differ decidedly from those of other persons. In clinical and counseling work our task is often one of helping the person to clarify his values so that he may make his decisions in the light of these. When we use standardized tests, we can inform the person how he compares with others and what his probabilities of success may be if he makes a given choice, but the ultimate decision has to be his own.

Despite the fundamental importance of individual decision-making in clinical work, there are, of course, many occasions when the psychologist is involved in institutional decision-making. There are *selection problems*[2]: With limited time available for therapy, which patients should be offered this service? Is this prisoner sufficiently "rehabilitated" so that he can be put on parole? Very often there are *classification problems:* Is this patient schizophrenic? Should this patient be assigned to individual or group therapy? Which patients should be assigned to which kinds of industrial therapy? These decisions involve institutional policies and the availability of personnel and equipment, as well as considerations of what will be of most value to the patient. As yet there has been very little application of decision theory in clinical settings. It will be easier to work on common institutional decisions first, though gradually better means will be developed for understanding individual values (Morris et al, 1960) and contributing to individual decision-making.

In doing research on the effectiveness of assessment in clinical decision-making, there are a variety of directions research can take. For one thing, there is *the identification of clinical decisions and the alternatives involved.* Dailey's study (1953), reviewed in an earlier chapter, is one of the few explorations of this question. His study of a VA hospital identified 32 questions which might be raised from the time a patient is admitted until he is discharged—from "Should this person be admitted to the psychiatric ward?" to "Should he seek membership in a community AA group?" Dailey obtained these by asking staff members to list the kinds of decisions they had to make frequently. They might also have

---

[2] Cronbach (1960, p. 359) implies that all clinical decisions are essentially classification decisions, e.g., choices between treatments. Even discharge from a hospital is not done to fill a quota but to give the person the most beneficial treatment. However, when there is pressure for hospital space or the time available for treatment in an out-patient clinic is limited, there must be selection. Also the clinical psychologist at work on such hospital personnel problems as screening aides or volunteers, is required to make selection decisions. The distinction between selection and classification, which is important for choosing and interpreting tests, depends essentially on how much responsibility the institution assumes for those who are rejected; in classification it puts *every* person in some class or subjects him to some kind of procedure for which the institution is responsible.

been obtained by observation or from analyses of case and staff conferences.

Looking into the probability of success in connection with each alternative course of action leads to larger problems. A full study would require a kind of job analysis specifying the abilities and personality characteristics required for success in each of the alternatives that are open. If it is a question of instituting treatment, it would involve an *analysis of the "work" of the patient in each of the various kinds of treatment situations.* How much verbal ability does this kind of psychotherapy require? What sorts of interpersonal characteristics are found in those who comprise an effective group? When a patient is brought up for a case-conference decision, his characteristics would be matched with the requirements of the clinical procedure. At a more remote level, there would be *an analysis of the "work" of the patient in the contacts of daily life.* What sorts of problems do former patients commonly run into in various sectors of the community? What kinds of personal characteristics are required to handle these problems? How much complaining and bizarre behavior can the patient's family tolerate?

One resource that might be used in this "job analysis" part of the decision-making problem is Flanagan's *critical incident technique* (1954). In a research program in a VA hospital, Flanagan and Schmid (1959) asked staff members to give them exact descriptions of incidents "in which the patient did or said something which suggested improvement in his condition" and of incidents "in which the patient did or said something which indicated the need for further hospital help." The experimenters then classified the 854 incidents they obtained into categories representing different types of critical behavior, such as aggressive versus considerate behavior, irrational versus rational behavior. On the basis of these categories a Patient Observational Record Form was constructed which had good reliability. It is still too early in this research program to see the outcome of the procedure, but the approach suggests interesting possibilities.

The next step after a "job analysis" is the development of *assessment procedures.* We have already discussed many possibilities, although certainly a genuine attempt to develop a decision-making program for clinical use would have to develop new tests and procedures. Another step in the process is *the strategy for combining information to make a final decision.* In two previous chapters we have discussed ways of doing this. The discussion of clinical versus statistical prediction falls under this heading. As indicated earlier, statistical combination, by means of multiple correlation, multiple cutoff scores, and so on, has generally been shown to work better than the clinical methods. These statistical methods are usually available only when there are large numbers of similar decisions to be made, namely in the case of institutional decisions. Thus, for making decisions *about* individuals, such as predicting success in a job or in therapy, statistical procedures, if available, should usually be relied on. There are, of course, exceptions to this rule. However, when we engage in decision-making *with* the person, as we do in psychotherapy, we can only give the results of pertinent information to the individual for his own use. Regression equations are seldom useful.

INCREMENTAL VALIDITY

When a clinical decision is to be reached, the contribution each bit of information can make to the total picture has to be considered. How much, we wish to discover, does any given assessment procedure add to the prediction obtainable from other sources of information? This is the question of *incremental validity*, as Meehl has termed it (1959b). This question can be raised in connection with various parts of the assessment task.

We may ask, for example: *Does an individual test or other assessment technique add anything to prediction over what we already know from the base rates for the appropriate population?* Meehl and Rosen (1955) mention a study (Hanvik, 1949) in which a scale was developed for differentiating between psychogenic and organic low back pain. It was found that 70 per cent of the psychogenic cases scored above a certain cutting score and 70 per cent of the organic cases below. If this test is used in a neurology service where 90 per cent of the patients are in fact organic, testing everyone to detect the psychogenic cases would yield a great many "false positives," people who were labeled psychogenic but were actually organic. However, such a situation would not be typical. More commonly the neurologist refers only questionable cases to the psychologist for testing. Thus the base rates in which we are interested are those of the select group referred. Perhaps records of such past referrals or of patients with minimal signs show that 90 per cent are ultimately diagnosed as psychogenic. In this case a person achieving a high score on the test can be diagnosed as psychogenic, but low scores are difficult to interpret. In either case, the test is of little value because knowledge of the base rates alone provides such high accuracy of classification. It is in situations where the base rates are closer to a 50-50 split that the tests are more likely to improve prediction. However, if a certain kind of decision is very important, such as in the detection of brain tumor or suicidal tendencies, the hospital may be willing to consider many "false positives" in order to catch the few "true positive" cases. In such a situation, even a test of low validity with adverse base rates may be useful.

Another problem of incremental validity arises when we ask *whether a given assessment procedure adds information beyond that available from necessary or routine techniques.* The most common question is whether a test contributes useful information beyond what is obtainable from an interview or case history. Winch and More (1956) have compared ratings given by judges using respectively only interview information, only the case history, or only the TAT. These ratings were compared with criterion ratings derived from a panel of five experts using all three kinds of information. Winch and More found that the interview and case-history data provided increases in correlation with the criterion, but that the TAT made no statistically discernable contribution beyond the other sources. The question can also be asked in reverse—whether the interview contributes anything beyond what a test can give. As we know, several studies have shown that clinicians using interviews could not improve on the prediction of academic success made on the basis of ability tests alone (Sarbin, 1943; McClelland, 1942; Kelly & Fiske, 1951). On the other hand, Sines (1959) found that the interview coming early in an assessment series did contribute to the prediction of the personality picture that psychotherapists developed later on.

When we come to life-history information the incremental validity question becomes: *Does this information add anything beyond the judgment obtained from the basic identifying data?* Kostlan (1954), whose study was reviewed at the end of Chapter 8, systematically varied the information available to clinicians by eliminating sources of information one at a time. The four sources of information were the Rorschach, MMPI, a sentence completion test, and the social history. The criterion he used was number of agreements with the statements in the filed psychological reports. He also collected so-called stereotype judgments based simply on knowledge of age, education, occupation, marital status, and source of referral. His striking finding was that the only one of the sources of information that could not be subtracted without loss of predictive power was the social history. Only this contributed above and beyond the stereotype judgment. Sines (1959) also found that the picture based on biographical data held its own in comparison with tests and other information. These studies and similar findings from others (Gage, 1953; Crow, 1957) suggest the predictive power that resides in knowledge of primary role affiliations. Evidently judges can go a long way in predicting behavior if they can classify people as to age, sex, occupation, and so on. These findings lend credence to Sarbin's concept of clinical judgment as taxonomic sorting (discussed in Chapter 8). However, awareness of the dangers of stereotyped thinking and of the great overlap between groups on almost any dimension keeps clinicians from feeling comfortable about relying entirely on this kind of prediction.

Research on incremental validity in another area makes for modesty on the part of clinicians. This is when the blunt question is asked: *How much better are predictions by trained clinicians than those of untrained persons?* Soskin (1959), in a study similar to Kostlan's, asked clinicians to answer questions derived from knowledge of the actual behavior of a subject. He provided them with different kinds of information such as scores on psychological tests or the opportunity to observe a subject in a role-playing situation. All judges received basic biographical data. None of the types of critical data he provided them with improved their accuracy over the level achieved by study of biographical facts alone. Furthermore, student nurses were as accurate as the clinicians in their inferences from the biographical data. Even when using a psychological test, the clinicians' predictions may not be inherently superior. Goldberg (1959) gave Bender-Gestalt designs from brain-damaged patients along with some from psychiatric patients to two groups, clinicians and secretaries. The latter did as well as the former except for those clinicians who had had an exceptional amount of training. Sarbin, Taft, and Bailey (1960, pp. 262-263) in a count of fourteen relevant studies found only five in which the psychologists were superior to nonpsychologists, and in a similar count, only two of ten studies in which psychologists were superior to beginning psychology students. Kremers (1960) found no improvement in prediction when students in a Dutch university had taken courses in psychology compared with when they had not. The reason for this lack of superiority of trained persons is not yet clear. Training may lead clinicians to err in overemphasizing signs of maladjustment (Soskin, 1954, 1959). There is also some suggestion that clinicians may be prepared to take a greater risk and play more long shots than others (Sarbin, Taft, & Bailey, 1960, p. 263). Much more work is needed on the training of what may surely be considered the major assessment instrument—the clinician himself.

Some of the studies just mentioned have been less concerned with decision-making than the development of an accurate description of a personality—a working image, as we call it. A common design for such research is to see what procedures best approximate the criterion—the description reported by the therapist after considerable contact with the patient. One such study is Meehl's "cookbook" study mentioned in Chapter 8. Another example is a research project reported by Marks (1961) on the validity of the diagnostic process in a child guidance clinic. In this extensive study on 48 cases of mothers and children in treatment, criterion Q sorts were obtained from the therapists after ten hours of therapy. A variety of predictions were collected from different clinic workers at different stages. In addition to regular assessment procedures the MMPI was given to both parents. Child stereotype Q sorts were also obtained from judges on the basis of their conception of the average clinic child. The most striking finding was that the MMPI interpreted blindly by clinicians did as well in predicting the criterion as did the full assessment study by psychologists, and better than the evaluations made by caseworkers after three hours of interviewing. These MMPI interpretations and the general clinical descriptions correlated more highly with the criterion than the stereotype judgments did. The overall agreement between the psychologists and the therapists was "discouragingly low." Considering discrepancies between assessors and therapists and the value of the blind interpretation of the MMPI, Marks concluded that present diagnostic practices may be "an extravagant waste of time" (p. 35).

Marks' discouragement over the value of present assessment practices for actual work in the clinic raises other questions such as whether group decisions are an improvement over those arrived at by individuals. In a study in a VA clinic, Wiener and Raths (1959) concluded they are not. The whole process of evaluating patients needs thorough investigation. Among the questions Meehl (1959b) brings up in his discussion of incremental validity are how much time may be saved by assessment procedures and how good is the quality of the help they provide in treating the patient. Hathaway (1959) has raised other questions about the efficiency of clinical assessment. He estimated that at least 40 per cent of the time spent by clinicians in testing is completely wasted. For instance, the Rorschach takes four hours of clinical time, according to Odum's study (1950). In the light of the findings about its validity, it is questionable whether this most widely used test in clinical work deserves the amount of time it requires. Research should ferret out what is valuable in this or any other procedure from what is not. It may be that some of the work of the clinician might be taken over by subdoctoral psychometricians who have been properly trained for special testing work. This would free the clinician for important work on therapy and research. And in order to know what is the best way to conduct assessment, we must have research.

PROCESS STUDIES: FORMING WORKING MODELS OF OTHERS

Clinical practice is carried out in interpersonal situations. Much of the effectiveness of assessment and treatment will depend on an understanding of interpersonal psychology. Parenthetically, it might be stated we should not be misled into thinking that clinical work deals with nothing but interpersonal relations; constitutional deficiencies and various forms of physiological functioning are examples of other influences on human behavior that may be profoundly important in clinical work; no amount of interpersonal understanding would make an imbecile normal or rid a paretic of his syphilitic infection. Nevertheless, all assessment and therapy is carried out between persons. "If there is to be a science of interpersonal behavior, it will rest upon a cornerstone of social perception," Bruner and Tagiuri (1954, p. 650) write in their review of research on the perception of people.

There are two research approaches to the perception of others: research oriented toward _accuracy of perception_ and research oriented toward the _process of perception_ itself, whether it is accurate or not. For the first kind of study a criterion of accuracy is selected such as consensus of others, expert opinion, or self-report. The experimenter seeks to determine how accuracy is related to differences in judges (such as age, intelligence, experience, similarity to the patient) or to differences in the characteristics of the persons being judged (age, intelligence, characteristics of voice), or to differences in procedures for collecting judgments (ratings, different order of presentation of information). Accuracy studies in clinical work have been covered briefly in the previous section. For a review of such studies see Bruner and Tagiuri (1954) and Taft's review of ability to judge others (1955).

Process studies do not concern themselves with the troublesome problem of whether judgments are accurate or not. Instead they focus on the manner in which impressions are formed. Thus a phenomenon like the "halo effect" in rating becomes an object of interest and study rather than an obstacle to be avoided or controlled. Process studies go into the kinds of impressions that result from experimental variation of prior information, the context in which information is given, and the psychological set or role of the judge. Bruner and Tagiuri (1954) and Tagiuri and Petrullo (1958) have provided us with extensive reviews of process studies. The prototype for much of this work goes back to Asch's experiment (1946). Asch gave groups of students two lists of words describing a hypothetical person. The adjectives on both lists were the same except that one list included the word _warm_ where the other had the word _cold_. The students wrote sketches of the person from the list they received. The sketches of students who had been given the _warm_ list differed markedly from those receiving the _cold_ list. Asch concluded that a change in a single important interpersonal quality made for a broad change in the basic perception of others. His results were confirmed and extended by several later investigators. For instance, Luchins (in Hovland, 1957) has shown that when two conflicting descriptions of a person are presented (e.g., a person is called introverted and then extroverted at different times in the study), the subjects were most influenced by the descriptive material they encounter first. He explained these findings in terms of the difficulty of overcoming the initial perceptive set, or _Einstellung_.

The way the clinical psychologist and his colleagues form impressions of patients is open to similar kinds of research. Some of the studies of incremental validity mentioned in the previous section exemplify possible methods. The effects can be measured by Q-sort descriptions or adjective checklists used to characterize the patients being studied. Influences upon the clinician-judge can be variations in the information given about the patient, variations in the experience itself, variation in the theoretical orientation of the judge himself, etc. The reports of Rubin and Shontz (1960), Marks (1961), and others mentioned earlier are pertinent.

An entirely different way of approaching the study of the clinical process is the naturalistic one. In origin it goes back to Duncker's methods of studying problem-solving (1945). The experimenter attempts to capture the reactive "thoughts" of the clinician as he is forming his impressions of a case. One way to do this is to interview the clinician afterwards regarding how he went about conceptualizing the person, but recall is notoriously distorted. "Stimulated recall" seems likely to serve better: a tape recording of an original interview is played back to the clinician and he stops from time to time to dictate the recollections it stimulates in another tape recorder. Another method is called "thinking aloud." The clinician, having been furnished new case material, dictates his reactions to it immediately. Though it is impossible to get all his ideas down, with practice this method seems to produce a fair approximation to the thinking processes of assessment.

When this "thinking aloud" procedure is adopted, an important ingredient is the development of a system for coding the clinician's thoughts. One scheme of classification has been developed by Koester (1954) in a university counseling center. He may have been the first person to apply this procedure to assessment. The transcribed record is first broken down into response units in each of which the counselor had expressed a single idea. These response units were sorted into one of six categories derived from the literature: (1) indeterminate or uncertain responses, (2) interpretation without reference to any other data in the case, (3) comparisons and evaluation of the data without interpretation, (4) hypotheses based on a synthesis of data, (5) evaluation of a hypothesis or interpretation, and (6) expressed need for additional data. Koester found that his ten counselors used all six categories of response, the most frequently used being category 4. The results generally showed that individual counselors were consistent in the use of these categories when working with different cases. Parker (1958) extended Koester's approach to a series of three interviews with a client.

Drawing on clinical research in both the person-perception tradition and the problem-solving tradition, let us examine several questions and issues. One important question on which we have considerable evidence is: *How quickly does the clinician form a stable image of the patient?* A clear answer from these studies is "very quickly." Parker (1958) found no increase from the first to the third interviews in the richness anf diversity of the clinician's hypotheses. Meehl (1960), reports that therapists' Q-sort descriptions of patients have stabilized to the level of the terminal reliabilities (in a long series of interviews) by the second to fourth therapeutic hour. Rubin and Shontz (1960), using a Q-sort description of cases of paranoid schizophrenics, also found that psychologists form a fairly complete clinical picture early in the diagnostic process. This basic conception changed only in details as more information was added. Of additional interest is the fact that Q-sort descriptions of the paranoid patients correlated very highly with composite prototypes of patients done before seeing any data. The clinicians had been able to differentiate clearly in their prototypic descriptions between paranoid, catetonic, and hebephrenic patients. It was almost as if the clinician, on the basis of a small amount of initial information, said, "Well, he's a paranoid," and once he had classified the patient the clinician stuck close to that basic image.

The result brings us to another basic issue in the assessment process: Is the process one of *taxonomic sorting* or *emerging synthesis?* The discussion of these two approaches has already been expanded in our chapter on interpretation. As yet research is too scanty to give a conclusive answer. There seems to be evidence on both sides. Parker did not confirm Koester's conclusions that the diagnostic process is a hierarchical one progressing from interpretation and synthesis to the forming and evaluating of hypotheses. On the contrary, Parker concluded that counselors used these processes in a global interrelated pattern. The issue is related to the still larger one of the frame of reference or theoretical orientation of the clinician. Only a start has been made in research into this topic. Parker found that clinicians with a "more richly developed" concept of the client did not make more accurate predictions than others.

Another broad question is this: What kinds of information produce changes in the working image? As Asch demonstrated, adding the words *warm* or *cold* to two otherwise identical lists of characterizing adjectives caused subjects to produce different descriptions of the person. However, other experimenters have shown there is less differential effect from words like *polite* and *blunt.* In a more clinical study, mentioned earlier, Soskin (1959) showed that Rorschach data tended to elicit more pathological descriptions of the person than did role-playing observations. Undoubtedly some kinds of information presented early in the assessment process keep the clinician more open to new observations about the client than other kinds. The effect of basic identifying data and stereotyped information seems to have this effect of early freezing of the working image.

Studies of both incremental validity and impression formation have implications for training. Many clinicians now assert as McArthur does in commenting on Parker's paper (1958, p. 262) that students beginning their specialized study should start with global material like dream series and autobiographies and be kept away from item-like data as long as possible. This puts emphasis on developing an understanding of themes in personality and the use of theories about individual persons.

Others, looking in the opposite direction, point to the importance of training in the use of basic biographical data. They cite studies showing how accuracy of judgment is enhanced by case-history and stereotyped information. Such clinicians would train people to take base rates into account. They insist that we have overemphasized clinical subtleties and individual variation in our clinical training. Crow and Hammond (1957) found that stereotypes were markedly stable, whereas differential accuracy in diagnosis was not. Crow (1957) also found that training in responding to individual differences and the abandoning of stereotypes resulted in a decrease in accuracy of prediction. However, the kind of stereotypes which people are to be trained to use needs clarification. Knowledge of one kind of person does not necessarily generalize to other kinds (Chowdry & Newcomb, 1952).

Another question, too, is how well accuracy in assessment correlates with therapeutic ability. There is some suggestion that the correlation is low (Horrocks & Nagy, 1948; Sundberg, 1952), in which case the question arises as to whether we want to train for assessment accuracy or for something else. The problem of how best to train clinicians is clearly no simple one.

PROGRAMMATIC ASSESSMENT

So far we have been speaking mostly about clinical applications of assessment. There is another kind of assessment involving large programs organized for the intensive study of individuals. Their purposes are to investigate individual differences in personality and often to develop ways of predicting such qualities as professional success, military leadership, creative productiveness. In Chapter 4 we mentioned that these research studies might be said to use *programmatic assessment*. Another name for this, the one Taft uses in his review (1959), is "multiple assessment," since this approach uses many techniques and many assessors observing and judging the subjects. These programs, though they are usually not directly concerned with clinical patients or clinical problems, have contributed so much to our present understanding of clinical assessment that an introduction to them, though it can be only brief, seems appropriate.

The history of programmatic assessment of personality starts with Henry Murray and his group at the Harvard Psychological Clinic, although the Hartshorne and May studies of character and the work of Simoneit in Germany were influential predecessors. In *Explorations in Personality* (1938) Murray and his colleagues reported an intensive study of young college men by a great variety of techniques. In the course of this program Murray developed a pluralistic personality theory and also his well-known Thematic Apperception Test. When World War II came both the German and British armed forces were using large-scale assessment programs for selecting officers. In the United States the Office of

Strategic Services (OSS Staff, 1948) was given the task of choosing men for dangerous and specialized assignments such as dropping behind enemy lines to organize underground resistance groups. Since World War II a number of ambitiously conceived assessment programs have been carried on, notably the Michigan VA study of clinical psychologists (Kelly & Fiske, 1951); the Menninger study of psychiatric residents (Holt & Luborsky, 1958); the Chicago study predicting success of ministers, teachers, and college students (Stern, Stein, & Bloom, 1956); and the studies of the Institute of Personality Assessment and Research at the University of California at Berkeley. The latter institute, abbreviated IPAR, has been studying various aspects of effectiveness in personality— military effectiveness (MacKinnon et al, 1958); personal soundness in graduate students (Barron, 1954); conformity (Crutchfield, 1955); and the personal characteristics of creative writers, architects, research scientists, and mathematicians.

All these assessment programs have involved the intensive study of individuals by a wide variety of techniques. Usually the sample of subjects has been selected because there is interest in some important role or occupation. Since any thorough-going study of a group of individuals is very costly, its subjects have generally been persons whose training is expensive and who are considered in some way especially important to society. The assessment has usually involved observation of subjects in "living in" or "house party" situations, where the subjects' behavior may be observed or studied experimentally by a large number of judges. The research strategies of the more recent assessment programs basically involve a correlation of many predictors with several criteria of success. The studies vary in the extent to which they rely on clinical or statistical procedures and the kind of conceptual systems that have dictated the design of the research (Taft, 1959).

Paralleling a division we have found in much of our consideration of assessment, some programs have emphasized theoretical model-building more explicitly than others. All these programs have relied on theory, for it is hard to imagine a planned program that would not derive in some measure from a conceptual scheme. In that sense there are really no "naive" empirical studies, although most studies may "throw in" certain tests and techniques on vague hunches that they might work. One approach, which might be called the *model-building approach,* involves first an intensive study of the criteria with a view toward developing a "model" of the successful person in the criterion situation, and making inferences about his traits and their dynamic interplay. The next step is to select the measures which will supply indicators of these constructs or dynamics. The *work-sampling approach* also involves an intensive study of the criterion, but the attempt is not to infer a model of the successful person, but to duplicate the conditions of the criterion as completely as possible in the assessment program. Inferences and hypothetical dynamics are kept to a minimum. The latter approach means that similar judges are used, not psychologists, in judging the character of the assessee; attempts are made to duplicate conditions of stress on the job, and the like, to make them as similar as possible to the ultimate criterion situations. Holmen, Katter, Jones, and Richardson (1956), in their more than usually successful assessment of army officer candidates, employed observers who were themselves recent officer candidate school graduates. Peer ratings were also used. Average ratings by assessors correlated .55 with pass-fail records of OCS. Peer ratings correlated .58 with the criterion. These ratings correlated higher with the criterion than test results.

The predictive weight of interpersonal evaluation is also demonstrated indirectly by an unexpected finding in the Menninger study (Holt, 1958). Following their original design, the psychologists had collected judges' ratings of "liking" for the subjects, intending to use the ratings to correct for the judges' biases. However, they found that those ratings correlated higher with the criterion of success in psychiatric training than any other measure. Perhaps the reason this correlation was so high was that "liking" reflected a really important factor underlying much of what constitutes the work of the psychiatrist—his interpersonal attractiveness.

When placed beside the effort they cost and the high expectations they arouse, the findings of these assessment programs may be considered somewhat disappointing (See reviews by McNemar, 1952; Thorndike, 1960; Clark, 1960). However, in stressing the low correlations between predictors and criteria, many reviewers have overlooked their less tangible contributions to the development of personality theory—the new methods of assessment that have been devised and the weeding out of fruitless procedures which had survived long use simply on the strength of "faith validity." In the history of assessment, these large-scale programs must be credited with having had enormous impact. For instance, the Kelly and Fiske report on the VA study of clinical students (summarized at the end of this chapter) would be chosen by many as an important turning point in assessment research. Their work spelled out the weaknesses of clinical predictions and instigated all of us to become more critical. The postwar wave of enthusiasm over projective techniques has subsided after a more realistic look at their achievements. Undoubtedly psychologists were too confident in the first place. Cronbach (1960, p. 600) quotes William James as warning that "psychology can establish general expectations but cannot hope to give biographies in advance." Too much opportunity resides in the operation of a host of factors for us to believe that easily made predictions will not be upset. We have only to remember, for instance, how a depression or a war can alter the course of individual lives. Still, the hopes and needs which gave rise to assessment programs in the first place continue to spur us on, and the values of programmatic assessment must continue to be exploited. The important thing is to gain enough understanding of what has been achieved in past attempts that future success can be maximized.

Several lessons may be learned from the results of these massive assessment programs:

1. First in importance, probably, is *the necessity of placing more emphasis on precise specification of the criteria.* When criteria are ratings, school grades, or the successful completion of a line of work, subjects going to different schools or military posts may be exposed to extremely different circumstances both in the way of opportunities and handicaps. Criteria of this sort are not standard or consistent from place to place. Judges' ratings may be extremely unreliable. Or the criteria may be overly simple, or just trivial. Careful analysis of the accomplishments of a group of men may indicate that many of them are good in certain things and poor in others. An overall rating obscures these differences, but it might be that predictors would be able to help differentiate them.

2. Along the same line, it is necessary that *the assessors should be thoroughly familiar with the criterion situation.* Cronbach states: "The most important requirement for valid assessment is that the assessors have a clear understanding of the psychological requirements of the criterion task" (1960, p. 589). In some cases it would be possible, as in the study of officer candidates just cited, to use assessors who have themselves been exposed to the procedure being studied. Programs should include provisions for selecting individuals who would make good assessors. The pooling of judgments from a large number of assessors also raises reliability and validity.

3. *Situational influences on behavior need to be brought into the predictive system.* It may be that future developments will succeed in making predictive statements like the following possible: "Person X in a situation where ability A is called for and amount of stress B is present and where his closest interpersonal relations are with people sharing characteristic C will perform at peak efficiency. In various other specified situations, on the other hand, he will do so and so." Particularly important, there has been little assessment of the behavior of the subjects in their natural field of operations; "living in" the research center for the weekend of the assessment is a very unusual situation. As yet we have very few tools for assessing situations in general, as has been pointed out in Chapter 7.

4. *Several points about the predictive value of tests and techniques* have come out of these studies. Just as Binet found years ago, there is considerable usefulness in structured tests and complex work samples. Unstructured tests requiring much use of theory and subjective judgment have not shown up well. Of the multitude of tests used in the VA study, only the Miller Analogies Test, a high-level intelligence measure ap-

propriate to the sample, and the Strong Vocational Interest Blank, an empirically constructed test, had high correlations. But even many structured tests have been tried and found wanting. Often these tests were devised for purposes quite removed from that of the assessment program, however. In developing tests, it seems we cannot overlook the need to study the criterion situation. Cronbach summarized his advice on assessment as follows: "For today's applied psychologist minimum interference is clearly best. The test which duplicates the general factor underlying the day-to-day demands of the criterion situation is a good predictor" (1956, p. 186). After reviewing the methods of all the personality assessment programs, Taft (1959) advised that objective techniques be used whenever possible.

5. *Statistical procedures* that are much more sophisticated than the usual correlational methods are probably needed. With hundreds of measures on individuals, methods need to be devised of getting at complex patterns of personality.

6. *Human errors and organizational problems* beset any research study of this magnitude. Many of the measures depend on judgments; in some cases the judges are poorly trained and no attempt is made to screen judges for their judging abilities. Inevitably errors in communication enter; also in the recording and analysis of data.

Cronbach (1960, p. 591) has summarized much of the process and problem of assessment in the diagram reproduced in Figure 10. The goal of the study is to predict success on a job. The criterion (6d in the diagram) is the merit rating by a supervisor. Three types of prediction are depicted, all stemming from the subject's behavior during the assessment period: The predicted merit rating (6a), derived from a theoretical model of the subject's person, the observer's impressions (6b), which can be used directly as a prediction, and the predicted merit rating (6c) from a test-score "cookbook." This diagram shows how there are possibilities for many weaknesses in the links of assessment. Simply because of the greater number of links (and more opportunity for "slippage" between related activities), the use of intervening theoretical models and clinical predictions is more hazardous than when straightforward psychometric and statistical methods are employed.

Another major problem is the linkage between the subject's personality at the time of assessment and the final criterion—the supervisor's rating. The job requirements, the changes in a subject with time, the limitations of the supervisor's knowledge of the subject, and the supervisor's values are all factors which influence the final rating. Even with perfect knowledge of the subject's personality at the time of assessment, the assessor's prediction could not be perfect. In fact, it is possible that assessment studies may be doing an excellent job of revealing a person at the time he is assessed. The problem is that the other links in the predictive chain,

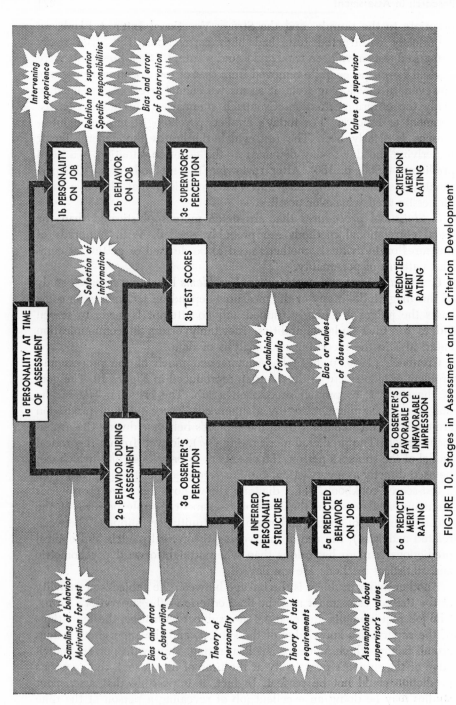

FIGURE 10. Stages in Assessment and in Criterion Development
(After a figure from Cronbach, 1960, p. 591. Used with permission of Harper & Brothers.)

such as the values of supervisors are not estimated sufficiently. Once more we are brought squarely up against the problem of how we are to study life situations in all of their complexity.

5 IMPLICATIONS OF COMPUTERS AND ELECTRONIC DEVICES FOR THE FUTURE OF ASSESSMENT

In a large assessment program it becomes impracticable to undertake the analysis of enormous quantities of data without the aid of computers. Probably this will also become true in the field of medicine as more complex programs of individual diagnosis and prediction are embarked upon. The tremendous potentialities of modern computers and new electronic devices are still only barely glimpsed. It may be that their development will go as far in revolutionizing psychology as automation has in transforming industry. Psychological assessment would seem to be in line to be profoundly affected. The majority of procedures now in use may be completely outdated, and the role of the clinical psychologist radically changed.

How is this possible? The computer is basically a "stupid" mechanism—really just a set of switches. What it accomplishes is dependent on the data which are fed into it and on simple step-by-step instructions given to it. We must not become unrealistic in dreaming about what computers may do nor forget that they can only perform the operations that are programmed into them. All the same, their potentialities are impressive. The modern computer has the ability to handle huge quantities of data with great speed. It can store an enormous mass of information in its "memory" and retrieve it instantly. Furthermore, the data-processing activity is only the beginning. What is more exciting for psychological research is the ability of the computer to use "logical" procedures—to manipulate symbols in systematic ways—and thus perform humanlike feats of problem-solving, learning, and playing games. Computer programs have been developed that enable the machine to "learn" rather quickly how to beat its inventor at checkers or chess. The computer's program can instruct the machine to "check for differences between this new symbol (a set of impulses) and an old one, and if they are the same, apply one rule, but if they are different, apply another." By building up a sequence of instructions the scientist can set a machine on such a complex course that even he cannot anticipate the results.

From this process of developing programs for computers arises a valuable byproduct. Because the machine can use only the most simple "language," the scientist himself is forced to specify exactly what he means. There can be no vague talk with a computer. The psychologist studying concept-formation must analyze the way things are similar or different and then state step-by-step how to compare one thing with another (Hovland, 1960). Then as he tries out a program on a computer, he finds out where he must learn more about the process. This byproduct —the reciprocal influence of the machine upon the scientist—even apart from the final action of the computer, is of great service in developing a science.

Before going on to the uses of computers, we should note that many other electronic procedures besides computers are being developed. They will contribute to clinical assessment by aiding in the collection of information. For one thing, it is likely that the present enthusiastic development of teaching machines will encourage experimentation with "testing machines." One of the great problems with much of our testing is the lack of uniformity of the stimulus context. It would be possible to develop complex testing environments, like booths, in which the stimuli surrounding the person being evaluated are precisely controlled. Even interpersonal stimuli might be approximated through the use of closed-circuit television with taped programs. Complex programming for stimulation and recording of the subject's responses could be developed. These data could then be turned over for computer analysis as outlined later. Another possibility for the collection of data is the use of telemetering and telecommunications devices for "observation at a distance." The value of the "telemike" which permits observers to hear distant conversation is demonstrated by the work of Alpert (1961) in recording the interaction of teachers with pupils. After the teachers got used to wearing the microphone, it was found that the number of instances classified as "punishing" (teachers' negative comments to the children) jumped 40 per cent over the number detected by visual observation alone.

New electronic techniques may also be of much assistance in the use of data already collected. A great problem is the lack of adequate ways of communicating knowledge (APA Board of Scientific Affairs, 1959). One new development might be "automatic libraries." If it becomes possible to organize large numbers of hospitals and clinics and to develop standard procedures, the consultation researches of a clinician could be enormously increased. When he goes to plan assessment procedures, or finds some unusual results with a test, or comes to interpreting a test pattern, he could punch the characteristics of the case into a machine. It would search its enormous memory and supply him with pertinent and recent data on similar cases. It would furnish base rates and outcomes. It could assist in diagnosis, as outlined below. It might not only supply statistical data but also might be able to furnish microfilmed copies of case histories and other information.[4]

---

[4] The ethical and legal implications of such a procedure may prove serious. The possibility that privacy will be violated or that information will be misused, not to mention machine errors, will be problems to be solved if such a system develops. Vandenberg (1960) mentions that one woman was kept imprisoned for a considerable time because of an error in the functioning of a punch-card machine. Of course, such problems will not be entirely new, for we know human errors can occur now in clinical work.

Now let us look at the direct uses of the computer itself. In the energetic developments in computer processing of information we see great prospects for research in assessment. *Statistical analysis,* or data (1) processing, which is the commonest of the three general ways in which computers can be used (Vandenberg, 1960), is already fairly well known. In assessment research it is now possible, for instance, to intercorrelate a vast amount of data and to perform factor analyses and other statistical procedures which would have been impossible a few years ago because of the labor involved. (For a simple punch-card system for recording and analyzing data, usable by graduate students with small incomes, see Campbell & Caron, 1961).

A second usage of computers is the beginning work on *logical diagnosis* (2) (which is related to the more general usage called "artificial intelligence"). If enough knowledge exists in a particular area of medical diagnosis (Ledley & Lusted, 1959), a table of the incidence of symptoms with different diseases can be established. The base rates of various diseases can be listed using age, sex, previous history, etc. When a particular case comes up for diagnosis, it can be compared with tables in the computer's memory and probabilities assigned to different parts to give a differential diagnosis. Treatment can also be handled as a problem of optimum strategy in the contest between the physician and aberrant nature or adverse conditions. Unfortunately, diagnosis is not as clear in psychiatry and clinicial psychology, as in some other areas, but with more specification of descriptive schemes and greatly expanded knowledge of the course of symptom development and alleviation such a system will achieve a greater level of usefulness.

A third usage of computers is for *simulation of human processes.* Here, (3) in contrast with the second group of uses, the scientist is not simply interested in accurate outcomes, but also in having the computer parallel the process all along the way whether the human being is right or wrong. Illustrations noted by Hovland (1960) include research on computer simulation of concept information, learning, pattern recognition, and problem-solving. In assessment work, there is the intriguing possibility of simulating the clinical assessment process itself. The research worker could use the "thinking aloud" technique discussed earlier to provide a record of the steps a clinician goes through in organizing and interpreting assessment data. Then the researcher would set up a computer program to duplicate these steps and come to the same conclusions. By studying and varying this computer program it might be possible to understand and improve on present assessment procedures. Other possibilities are the duplication of the group assessment processes. Bales (1959) has pointed to this possibility. In the study of life history, the psychologist might start out with conditions at age 10 and then give the machine life events along the way in order to see if it could predict a breakdown at age 30. In research on psychopathology, the clinician might try the challenging possibility of simulating schizophrenic thinking. In research on treatment, he might attempt to duplicate the course of interpersonal interaction.

As we sketch these tremendous possibilities for computers and electronic devices, we may begin to wonder if there will still be a place for the clinician in that remote future if and when these problems are solved. But Holtzman (1960) reassuringly points out that the machine cannot interact with the patient as the clinician does. Though potentially it can process data better than the clinician and free him from many chores, it cannot use its results in subtle interaction with a person. A limited interaction is indeed conceivable. But if values are given to it and the machine figures out the best strategies for treatment it is still true that values were first supplied to it by human beings. No danger, then, that we shall lose our clinical jobs to these machines—at least in the near future!

SOME CONCLUDING COMMENTS

A few additional points need to be made. It should be clear by now that the authors see assessment as a broad attack on the problems of understanding human behavior. Developments in many other fields have implications for assessment. In a sense, almost all psychological research is relevant to assessment, since at any point a contribution may be made to our knowledge of the characteristics of individual persons. Though most of these studies will not prove immediately relevant to clinical purposes, every now and then there will be the valuable exception. An example is the application of an experimentalist's "oddity," the spinning Archimedes spiral, in a number of studies on the detection of brain damage. The clinical psychologist needs to be especially well rounded in his knowledge of human beings. It is not enough merely to have psychological literature at his fingertips. Unquestionably the clinician is at present the most important clinical instrument and, as a decision-maker, a purveyor of human values. As such, he needs to have been steeped at firsthand in human experience and the ways of human beings from intimate work with people as well as from studying great and insightful literature and art and from a broad appreciation of the historical movement of human society. In a later chapter on the personal development of clinicians we shall revert to this theme.

It should also be clear that in discussing research in assessment we have found it necessary to pick and choose what should be covered. Many pertinent areas of research could not be covered in detail. Among these partially neglected areas the most important is research oriented toward clinical problems such as mental deficiency, schizophrenia, crime and delinquency, speech disorders, and psychoneurosis. Knowledge of psychopathology and behavioral deviation is indispensable for clinical workers. For instance, differential diagnosis, a common task in clinical work, requires the clinician to be able to discriminate clearly between schizophrenia and sociopathic personality, between hysteria and organic disorder, and the like. Though we have given frequent references and examples in this area of knowledge, our coverage has been limited, since we assume that our readers will need to become thoroughly acquainted with it in other places—books, courses, and practica.

Another field we have touched upon but slightly is the use of physical and physiological measures for assessment purposes: the electroencephalo-gram, the galvanic skin response, measures of body type, and so on. These measures are particularly important for psychologists working in a medical setting. Some psychologists, for instance, are specialists in reading EEG records for evidence of brain damage. Other psychologists are specialists in using the polygraph ("lie detector") in assessing individuals suspected of crimes. This area of knowledge, like that of psychopathology, is too large and important to be covered superficially. (For an excellent review of psychophysiological research especially as it applies to therapy, see Lacey, 1959.)

What is the future of the practice of assessment in clinical work? From time to time we have mentioned the opposition of some clinical workers to testing and formal diagnosis. Though a survey (Sundberg, 1961) showed no drop in testing and formal diagnostic work in recent years, still it is the impression of the authors and others that there has been a marked decrease in interest in diagnosis in many of the leading clinical centers. Meehl (1960) reports that a survey of the opinions of 168 psychotherapists of various theoretical persuasions showed only 17 per cent felt that prior knowledge of the patient's personality greatly speeds therapy. Support for this impression also comes in part from the fact that the work of testing is often shifted to trainees, while experienced staff members spend their time in therapy, supervision, or research. Some psychologists advocate the use of psychometricians trained at the master's degree level just to do the assessing. Others advocate resorting to statistical clerks and "cookbooks" for this function. The practical uses to which assessment procedures are put in the future should ultimately depend on their utility for case planning and treatment.

As we have stated at the outset, it is not a question of whether one should use assessment, but how best to do it. Assessment is the process of getting to know the patient in some fashion. Whenever any patient is handled clinically, sound decisions have to be made. They should be made on as scientific and practicable a basis as possible. The question is how to make the most effective use of our clinical resources, including time, in serving these ends. No matter which direction assessment takes in the future, there is bound to be plenty of room for research and creative development.

SUMMARY

It has been the aim of this chapter to survey research in assessment, pointing out its orientations toward developing procedures, studying clinical problems, selecting and training clinical personnel, understanding the assessment process, and evaluating outcomes of assessment. A basic question is how effective assessment is or could be made. Questions raised concerning validity cannot be answered by referring to a single test or technique, but require examination of the whole assessment process —the adequacy of decision-making and how the working image of the person is to be developed. There has been very little attention to the study of clinical decision-making and no "job analysis" of the requirements of situations to which patients are assigned. Incremental validity raises the question of the contribution of each part of the assessment process to the ultimate products. Some of the questions are these: Does a test add anything to prediction over the base rates? Does a procedure contribute information that goes beyond what can be obtained from such an indispensable technique as interviewing? Does it add anything beyond that obtained from the bald identifying data? Can clinicians using certain information improve on the predictions made by untrained people using the same data? The answers furnished by research so far should make clinicians very modest about both their instruments and their own achievements. One finding that comes up again and again is the importance of case-history data.

Some research focuses on the process of assessment instead of its outcome, or the uses to which it is put. This is where the study of interpersonal perception, or how impressions are formed of others, and also studies of clinicians' "thinking aloud" come in. The question whether the assessment process is more one of taxonomic sorting or of synthetic emergence will be answered at least in part by such inquiries.

Programmatic assessment employs many techniques for the study of many subjects by many assessors. Some of the results and problems of these programs were discussed, with particular emphasis on the need for analysis of the criterion situation. The application of computers and electronic devices to assessment work has enormous implications for future development.

SUGGESTIONS FOR FURTHER READING

BASS, B. M., & BERG, I. A. (Eds.) *Objective approaches to personality assessment.* Princeton, N. J.: Van Nostrand, 1959.
This conference report provides a good overview of the procedures and

problems of research using objective personality techniques. The definition of objectivity is broad. The twelve chapters include a historical review, underlying theory, discussions of multivariate and pattern analytic methods, exposition of the "deviation hypothesis," discussion of social desirability, objectivication of projective techniques, the study of leadership, and clinical judgment and efficiency. Contributors were Watson, Super, Cattell, McQuitty, Berg, A. L. Edwards, Holtzman, Bass, W. A. Hunt, Hathaway, J. Miller, and Pepinsky.

LINDZEY, G. (Ed.) *Assessment of human motives.* New York: Rinehardt, 1958. This book is a report on a conference which brought together a wide variety of psychologists in an attempt to define as clearly as possible what is meant by motivation from various theoretical viewpoints. Lindzey provides an introductory framework. Chapter subjects include constructive alternativism (G. Kelly), cognitive dissonance (Festinger), cognitive control (Klein), regression in service of the ego (Schafer), the dynamic calculus (Cattell), Murray's personality system, psychoanalytic observation (Janis), and Allport's analysis of the units of personality assessment.

BURDOCK, E. I., SUTTON, S., & ZUBIN, J. Personality and psychopathology. *J. abnorm. soc. Psychol.,* 1958, 56, 18-30.
This article presents a comprehensive conceptual framework for assessment. It was developed in connection with a research program on schizophrenia and gives examples of techniques that are used in research on schizophrenia. This biometric model conceptualizes the behavior of individuals as a set of overlapping domains of ascending psychological complexity: physiological, sensory, perceptual, psychomotor, and conceptual. The authors assert that there has been too much preoccupation in the past with conceptual thinking and they urge a more balanced approach to research. The methods they describe range from naturalistic observation through controlled experiments to attempts to modify personality.

Reviews of assessment research

Reviews of assessment theory and research appear frequently in the *Annual Review of Psychology* and in *Progress in Neurology and Psychiatry.* The reviews of general clinical research mentioned in Chapter 3 also cover assessment. Buros' *Mental Measurement Yearbooks* include reviews and appraisals of both tests and books on assessment. From time to time reviews of special forms of assessment appear, often in the *Psychological Bulletin.* Examples are Yates (1954) on the validity of some psychological tests of brain damage, Swenson (1957) on research on human figure drawings, Taft (1959) on programmatic assessment, Murstein and Pryer (1959) on concepts and tests of projection, and Rotter (1960) on the development of assessment procedures based on social-learning theory.

Potential uses for computers in psychological research

For a short introduction to the possible uses of computers in psychology, the following readings are suggested: Hovland (1960) has supplied a very readable overview of many possible uses of computers in psychological research, with particular attention to computer simulation of thinking. Two symposia, one in the April, 1960, issue of *Behavioral Science* and another in the Spring,

1961, issue of *Educational and Psychological Measurement* cover the impact of computers on research in psychology and the social sciences. A detailed consideration of the logic underlying medical diagnosis is presented by Ledley and Lusted (1959). The Mayo Clinic (Symposium, 1962) has taken promising steps toward the automatic processing and interpretation of the MMPI.

RESEARCH EXAMPLES

LYKKEN, D. T. A study of anxiety in the sociopathic personality. *J. abnorm. soc. Psychol.*, 1957, 55, 6-10.

Cleckley has identified a condition he calls "primary sociopathy" in which the chief clinical characteristic is lack of normal emotional accompaniments of experience. Such persons are different from sociopathic personalities having neurotic or dissocial characteristics. One hypothesis of Lykken's study (a Ph.D. dissertation) is that among persons diagnosed as sociopathic personalities, those who appear to show Cleckley's syndrome would be defective in ability to develop anxiety (in a conditioning situation where they must anticipate a warning signal associated with an electric shock) and would be less capable of avoidance learning. Lykken hypothesized also that they would show little manifest anxiety in life situations normally conducive to this response (as indicated by responses to anxiety scales).

The subjects, obtained from a variety of institutions, were diagnosed as sociopaths and divided into two groups: 19 subjects who met criteria for primary sociopathy and 20 subjects who were classified as neurotic sociopaths. In addition, there were 15 college and high school subjects, matched with the sociopaths for age, intelligence, and socioeconomic background, who served as controls. All subjects were given the same tests and exposed to the same experimental situation, which is described in detail.

Results: The primary sociopaths showed significantly less anxiety on the questionnaire, less galvanic skin reactivity to a conditioned stimulus associated with shock and less avoidance of punished responses on a test of avoidance learning. The neurotic sociopaths scored significantly higher on the questionnaires (the Taylor Anxiety Scale and the Welsh Anxiety Index of the MMPI).

This kind of study is significant because of its implications for the theory of sociopathic personality. It demonstrates, within the limits inherent in any one study, the defective emotional reactivity of the so-called primary sociopath. These significant findings should be checked and extended by follow-up studies. Of particular interest would be developmental studies of the etiology of defective reactivity.

McREYNOLDS, P., & COLLINS, Beverly. Concept-forming behavior in schizophrenic and non-schizophrenic subjects. *J. Psychol.*, 1961, 52, 369-378.

Schizophrenia, usually referred to as a thinking disturbance, is a condition *par excellence* for the study of concept-formation. McReynolds and Collins wanted to study the characteristic patterns of conceptual behavior of schizophrenics, seeing whether they could mobilize their resources for solving a task even though they often used loose standards in classifying or conceptualizing.

Four groups (one experimental and three control groups) were used in this study, carried out in a VA hospital: 18 schizophrenics judged as having thinking disturbances, 20 schizophrenics not manifesting thinking disorders, 20 nonpsychotic hospitalized psychiatric cases, and 25 college students. The principal measuring technique was a concept-formation task. Each subject was given a tray on which were 80 small cards each with a different word on it—the name of a common object, such as chair, leaf, cloth, shoe, cow, tobacco. The instructions were simply to arrange the cards in groups that go together with as many or as few in each group as he wished. From this task these four kinds of data were obtained: number of cards put in groups, number of groups or categories, total time for the task, and judges' ratings of the quality of the concepts. The instructions for these ratings, based on reading a subject's groupings and his rationale for the groupings, were described and illustrated in detail, running from adequate, well-rationalized categories, through vague and awkward groupings, to bizarre categories (such as grouping *napkin, diamond, saddle, ink,* and *picture* together because "these are particles").

Some of the results came out in the expected manner. Schizophrenics of both kinds had more difficulty in grouping the cards, leaving more of them uncategorized. The schizophrenics with thinking disturbances were remarkably slower in their categorizing behavior. The two schizophrenic samples differed significantly from the two nonschizophrenic samples on the concept quality ratings. Perhaps the most surprising result was that *all* groups used the best kind of reasoning most frequently—the quality rating described as "an adequate rationale with an appropriate grouping of cards." Even the schizophrenics with considerable thinking disturbance used the adequate groupings most often, thus showing that much of the thinking of these people is still reasonable—at least about the common objects used in the card-sorting task.

McReynolds and Collins believe that the concept-forming procedure would be useful for further research though it is not yet a clinical diagnostic tool. In extending the work different kinds of words might be used on the cards. There also needs to be a further study of the relationship of categorizing behavior to functioning intelligence. With part of the sample a correlation of .46 between this task and the WAIS vocabulary score was obtained.

BECKER, J. Achievement related characteristics of manic-depressives. *J. abnorm. soc. Psychol.,* 1960, 60, 334-339.

Becker's research is a clever combination of several lines of endeavor: the hypotheses of socially oriented psychoanalysts, the work of McClelland and his associates on achievement, and the assessment techniques produced by psychologists interested in measuring authoritarianism. Becker posits that the manic-depressive condition is a reaction to a strong emphasis on achievement and conformity in early experiences in the family. The person places a great conscious value on achievement (he has high Value Achievement) but he has not internalized this value (he does not have a high Need Achievement). Becker's principal hypotheses were as follows: (1) Manic-depressives will describe themselves as more ambitious and achievement-oriented than controls. (2) Manic-depressives will subscribe more strongly to authoritarian ideology than the controls. (3) Manic-depressives will profess a more traditional ideology with regard to family roles and statuses than the controls.

Among the procedures used for measuring the variables involved were the following: four TAT-like cards, stories of which were scored by McClelland's method for evidence of Need Achievement, a Value Achievement attitude scale developed by DeCharms, the California *F* (Fascism) scale, and the Traditional Family Ideology scale. Each of these measures were administered to 24 remitted manic-depressives and 30 nonpsychiatric controls matched on important variables.

The manic-depressives, as predicted, scored significantly higher than the controls on Value Achievement, the F scale and the TFI scale. There were no significant differences on the Need Achievement measure. An interesting side-light was that the conscious valuing of achievement increased with age in the manic-depressive group but not in the controls, and contrary to reactions of normals, increasing amounts of education were not associated with decreasing authoritarianism in the manic-depressives. The author interprets the results as being in line with environmental influences in the development of the manic-depressive condition.

CROW, W. J. The effect of training upon accuracy and variability in inter-personal perception. *J. abnorm. soc. Psychol.*, 1957, 55, 355-359.

The purpose of this study, so arresting in its outcome, was to test the effect of training in interpersonal relations on ability to predict the responses of others. The subjects were 72 senior medical students randomly assigned either to an experimental or to a control group. The experimental group was in-structed in physician-patient relationships and given training in more pro-longed contact with patients than the control group was able to have. It was expected that the students in the experimental group would become more accurate in interpersonal perceptions of other persons.

At the beginning, during, and at the end of the year, students were asked to estimate the real status and self-ratings of patients presented in sound-film recorded interviews. Actual self-ratings and relevant MMPI scores were used as criteria for scoring the medical students' predictions.

Contrary to expectation, the experimental group became significantly less accurate than the control group. The variability of their estimates increased. The author suggests that training programs devoted to increasing interpersonal sensitivity run the risk of actually decreasing accuracy of perception. Increasing the trainee's responsiveness to individual differences apparently leads him to lose sight of stereotype or basic role data. A piece of research like this presents a sharp challenge to those engaged in the training of clinicians. We need to know much more about what goes into the various kinds of tasks clinicians perform. Also questions arise about the sorts of tasks for which accuracy of interpersonal perception would be useful and the kinds of tasks for which special sensitivity to individuals is needed.

KELLY, E. L., & FISKE, D. W. *The prediction of performance in clinical psy-chology.* Ann Arbor: Univer. of Michigan Press, 1951.

This massive assessment program has had a profound effect on clinical psychology. It might be seen as the turning point in the optimism about clinical psychologists' abilities that prevailed following World War II. Along with the later book by Meehl (1954), it has forced psychologists to become more realistic, and therefore more modest, about their skills of clinical prediction. Though most of the effects were sobering, it also provided encouragement to those who have all along maintained that well-developed objective measures are of value.

This monograph reports on this five-year research program. Its primary purpose was the evaluation of a variety of procedures as predictors of later success in graduate training and professional function in clinical psychology. In 1947 and 1948 several hundred college graduates who were seeking ad-mission to or actually entering the VA training program in clinical psychology in some 40 universities were evaluated by a wide variety of techniques. During the first year 137 subjects were brought to Ann Arbor in groups of 24 for a five-day stay at the assessment center. During the second year they were tested in other centers. The predictive measures were derived from a battery of objective tests, a battery of projective techniques, two interviews, and a series of situational tests. This large mass of data including many judgments made by assessors possessing different kinds of information formed the predictor variables. The criterion variables were the students' academic records and various ratings of success in clinical work.

Only a small portion of the very numerous findings of the study will be mentioned here. The subjects proved to be remarkably like other graduate students in psychology, differing mainly in possessing greater interest in people and persuasive activities. There were significant differences between various institutions in the interest and abilities of the graduate students. With respect to the criteria of success in clinical psychology, there was wide variation in the conceptions of the university professors and training supervisors. Ratings of clinical competence appeared to be as much a function of the role of the rater as of the person rated. When it came to predicting success in clinical psychology, intellectual aspects could be predicted surprisingly well, validities ranging from .35 to .60. The more clinical aspects of training were much less predictable. Social skills were predictable beyond chance but less so than the intellectual aspects. The validities of the 1947 group did not hold up well for the 1948 group. The criteria themselves were seen as very fallible.

Only a small proportion of the objective tests correlated with the criterion measures. The most generally useful of the objective tests were the Miller Analogies Test and the Strong Vocational Interest Blank. Predictions based on the credential file and the objective test profile were almost as accurate as those based on intensive study of the person with projective techniques and observation. Predictions of success based on single projective techniques tended to produce very low correlations with criteria. On follow-up none of the rated criterion measures differentiated students with less training from those who had more, and the authors concluded that it is an open question whether additional years of experience and present training procedures lead to any measurable improvement in clinical skill.

A summary of the study and additional information from a later follow-up study can be found in Kelly and Goldberg (1959).

Three

PSYCHOLOGICAL
APPROACHES TO TREATMENT

11 Ideas of Psychotherapy

It may be that a slightly frivolous historian in a time to come will look back on our twentieth century and label it *The Age of Psychotherapy*. Hundreds of thousands of men, women, and children are seeking help from thousands of "therapists" of one kind or another: psychiatrists, psychologists, marriage counselors, school counselors, social workers, and clergymen—ministers, rabbis, and priests. Dozens of books are written each year presenting the theory and practice of psychotherapy to technical specialists, students, and the general public. Psychotherapy figures prominently in novels, plays, movies, and television programs. What is it that all these participants are attempting to accomplish? In this chapter we will analyze their purposes and some of the ideas about how they are to be achieved, as they have been set forth by the psychotherapists who have written about their profession.

WAYS IN WHICH GOALS OF THERAPY HAVE BEEN FORMULATED

In this field even more than elsewhere in clinical psychology, complex and elaborate theories have arisen. Undoubtedly Freudian psychoanalysis is the most influential, but the impact of the views of Adler and Jung, Horney and Sullivan, Rogers, Mowrer, and many others has been strongly felt. Instead of discussing these theories one at a time, however, we shall attempt a different kind of classification.

In the theories as they stand there is considerable confusion, arising

287

from various sources. One source of confusion is that the ideas of every theorist undergo continual modification as he lives and works. The concepts Freud stressed in 1910 are not identical with those upon which he rested his theoretical structure in 1935. Rogers' second book on psychotherapy differs markedly from his first. Thus, it is difficult to write for the beginning student of clinical psychology an account of one of these comprehensive theories that includes *all* the concepts, early and late, actually incorporated in the thinking of some of its adherents.

Another reason for confusion in the theories therapists have produced about therapy is that they overlap. If such theories are taken up one by one, the student is confronted with the task of judging for himself how great this overlapping is. This is especially difficult for an inexperienced person because much of the common ground is found in practice rather than in conceptualization. Psychologists and psychiatrists, when *writing* about their work, are most likely to stress the aspects they consider to be unique or original, while they slight the aspects that fit in with many other theoretical orientations. Thus the student trying to find a way of approaching his own professional tasks is likely to assume that the differences between theories are sharper than they actually are, and he may conclude that he is required to identify himself with one and only one of the theorists and to repudiate the others. The richness of his own theoretical formulation and the range of his helpfulness to others may be diminished by such a decision.

Therefore, instead of outlining the different complex approaches to therapy connected with the names of Freud, Rogers, Sullivan, and the other founders of systems or schools, we shall discuss first the principal purposes therapy has been thought to accomplish by some influential thinker at some stage of his development. We shall then look for common threads and basic issues and attempt to put the separate pieces together in a new way.

The first of these major purposes basic to some kinds of therapy might be labeled *strengthening the patient's motivation to do the right things.* It is the oldest of the aims we shall discuss. Suggestion in all its forms, ranging from gentle advice to the use of hypnosis to produce tendencies to act in specified ways, is one kind of procedure through which this purpose is carried out. Encouragement and inspiration, whether administered through informal praise and appreciation or through books and sermons, are intended to serve this purpose. Long before there were any professional specialties like psychology, this kind of treatment was constantly attempted. In our own time, therapeutic organizations like Alcoholics Anonymous attribute most of their success to this kind of influence.

A second purpose of therapy that has often been stated is *to reduce emotional pressure by facilitating the expression of feeling,* the process called *catharsis.* When the average layman thinks about therapy, it is probably this meaning he is most likely to connect with it. Dozens of motion pictures have given dramatic portrayals of a sudden relief from neurotic symptoms and anxiety following a flood of emotional expression touched off when contact is made with some repressed memory. Like suggestion and inspiration, the use of this process of emotional expression covers a wide range of depth and intensity, from the common "blowing off steam" at work or at home to the use of drugs or hypnosis to enable a patient to relive a traumatic experience.

A third way of formulating the purpose of therapy makes use of concepts from the psychology of development. Therapy aims to *release the potential for growth.* A basic growth tendency in every person is postulated, a tendency toward maturity and integration. Unfortunate circumstances or adverse influences can block or temporarily reverse this process, but cannot destroy it completely. What therapy aims to do is to remove these obstacles, whatever they are, and allow the person to start growing again along the lines of his own unique pattern. The psychotherapist should not be thought of as a mechanic, locating and repairing defects in a piece of equipment, but rather as more like a gardener, removing weeds, providing light, nutrients, and moisture to stimulate a plant intrinsically disposed to grow. Two aspects of developmental theory may be distinguished. One calls for *the analysis of each life stage* in childhood to ascertain what kinds of neurotic symptoms and faulty character structures may have arisen from failure to negotiate it successfully. The discussions by psychoanalysts of symptoms arising through arrested development at the oral, anal, phallic, or latency period have this focus. The emphasis psychoanalysts place on the necessity for *transference*, a term signifying the process of projecting childish attitudes onto the therapist, comes from the conviction that early periods must in some sense be relived emotionally if personality reorganization is to occur. The other aspect of developmental theory, expressed more clearly by Jung and by Rogers than by Freud, places the emphasis on *development as a process that continues throughout life*, whatever the early handicaps have been. A person is so complex that many avenues of growth and creativity are open to him if they can only be recognized and encouraged. Whether the emphasis is on unraveling the tangled strands of childhood or on opening up new vistas for the future, developmental theories have in common the assumption that therapy means discovering ways of facilitating a natural process rather than undertaking the construction of something new.

A fourth way of stating the purpose of therapy is *habit change.* Neurosis or maladjustment are viewed as the end result of a learning process in which undesirable or ineffective habits have been formed. For many reasons these may be difficult to get rid of, once the person is saddled with them. The task of the therapist, then, is to arrange learning situations in which the patient can modify such undesirable habits or replace them by others. There was real excitement among psychologists when J. B. Watson reported in 1920 that an irrational fear for furry animals had been experimentally produced in a child using conditioned response methods, and when M. C. Jones reported a few years later that conditioning could also be used to remove such fears from children's experience. These experiments seemed to point the way to a rational, scientific kind of therapy free from mystery and uncertainty. The years since the 1920's have sobered hopes for simple methods of "emotional re-education," as many irrational fears have proved to be impervious to such treatment. But straightforward conditioned response methods are still used quite widely in the treatment of behavior patterns such as enuresis and alcoholism, and the modification of social habits such as shyness and tactlessness is often attempted through planned learning situations. Probably more important, however, than these specific applications of the psychology of learning to particular kinds of cases is the task some theorists have undertaken of reformulating *all* the principles of psychotherapy in terms of learning. A thriving partnership between psychoanalysis and learning theory has resulted in an attack on some interesting research problems. Most psychologists engaged in therapy would agree in principle that therapy *is* learning. They would agree much less well about just what the faulty habits are that need to be changed, and what sort of learning process it is that therapy sets in motion.

A fifth purpose of therapy, in some ways related to the two preceding ones, is *the modification of the cognitive structure of the person,* by which is meant the interrelated set of concepts and fixed ideas that determine his perceptions of the world around him, of other persons, and of himself. Theorists who approach the problems of therapy from this direction have surmised that the roots of a person's difficulties lie in his basic misconceptions about the nature of things, mistaken ideas he acquired at some former period of his life. He is likely to be quite unaware of these cognitive structures. The conclusions to which they lead him are axioms, taken for granted. A generation ago Alfred Adler discussed the effects of this phenomenon under the graphic term, *life style.* More recently, George Kelly in his *Psychology of Personal Constructs* (1955) has presented not only a coherent theoretical statement of this point of view, but also a number of ingenious methods for identifying the basic cognitive structures in an individual and for helping him to modify them if they need changing. The theoretical formulations of Carl Rogers have emphasized the importance of clear, finely differentiated perceptions of self and the world as a basis for effective living. As many clinical psychologists see their task today, the aim of therapeutic activity is to make a client aware of his basic cognitive structures and enable him to produce some change in the pattern. Change will often come automatically once the person becomes aware that one of his "personal constructs" is inconsistent with other aspects of his personality. Lecky's oft-quoted little book, *Self-Consistency* (1945), stimulated much thinking along these lines.

A sixth stated purpose of therapy is *self-knowledge,* broadly defined. This, like habit change, can be an extremely inclusive concept. It is basic to most counseling and rehabilitation activities. The client is given aptitude and interest tests and helped to examine his own capacities, attitudes, needs, background, and opportunities. Self-knowledge is also prominent among the goals of psychoanalysis. The attempt to bring unconscious material into consciousness where the ego of the person can cope with it is so basic in therapeutic procedure that for many theorists this growth in self-knowledge *is* therapy. The word that has been much used as a label for the process of attaining self-knowledge is *insight.* As a theoretical concept, insight is not being stressed as much at present as it was in previous periods. There has come the recognition that an intellectual awareness of all the recesses of one's personality does not necessarily make for psychological health. There must be some emotional quality to such insight if it is to be effective, and it has proved to be very difficult to state how the word is to be defined in these emotional terms. Furthermore, striking improvements occurring in the absence of any manifestation of insight whatever have seriously challenged those who would use self-knowledge as a central therapeutic concept. In short, it seems that insight is neither a necessary nor a sufficient factor in therapy. Nevertheless, it still has its place as an important organizing concept, and the procedures most commonly used in therapy perhaps serve this purpose better than any other.

The last type of theory to be considered here emphasizes *interpersonal relationships.* According to such a theory, we must look for the sources of all psychological ills in the person's relationships to the "significant others" in his life. Here too some therapists place the emphasis on the very earliest periods of life as the time when the patterns for future relationships are laid down. They hope, by understanding what occurred then, to find ways of modifying these patterns so that they will no longer exert unhealthy influences on present relationships. Other workers pay more attention to their client's current relationships to spouse, children, friends, and colleagues. They hope to find relationships which may be changed for better rather than, to identify the remote childhood origins of the difficulties. One major resource inherent in all types of therapy for producing change in interpersonal relationships is the fact that the client is at the time experiencing a new relationship, without the defects of those previously formed—his relationship to the therapist. A strong emphasis on *communication* distinguishes the interpersonal theories of therapy. Isolation and estrangement are involved in much psychological disturbance. One way to combat them is to improve communication.

Furthermore, the possibilities for therapeutic intervention are not limited to the things that can happen between just two individuals. The unique advantage of *group therapy* is that it allows the participants to establish new relationships, observe and study them, and modify them in constructive ways. Patients can make emotional contact with others as individuals; they can also practice the different *roles* they must play in dealing with other people—whether children, bosses, co-workers, or strangers. Clinical psychologists join sociologists in the interest they take in the mental health effects of *social systems*. As a natural extension from the interpersonal approach, some psychotherapists have been asking: Should we be attempting to treat this individual at all? Would it not be a sounder procedure to try to improve some particular social system of which he is a part, and thus increase the level of health and soundness of all the persons who are caught in it? Thinking of this sort has stimulated careful scrutiny of the social situation to be found in a mental hospital— the whole institution and the individual ward—in a search for ways to change the relationships of physicians, nurses, aides, and patients to one another. The work that marriage and family counselors do often rests on a consideration of the kind of a complex system the wife, husband, and children together constitute rather than on the psychological character- istics of one member of the family. The therapist sees the importance of understanding, and perhaps changing, the dynamics of the small groups encountered in the course of living—work groups, recreation groups, and classroom, for example. The implications of this therapeutic approach are very far-ranging. It has even been said that our whole modern society is a kind of neurotic organism needing therapeutic re- organization.

In many situations, psychologists join in collaborative efforts with physicians providing *somatic treatment*, such as the use of drugs, shock therapy, physiotherapy, or other forms of medical treatment. Physiological changes can have direct effects on behavior, or they may make a person more amenable to ordinary psychotherapy. Even nonpsychiatric patients, such as persons who must undergo surgery and are anxious and dis- traught, can be helped by brief psychotherapy or counseling. In all somatic cases, psychological treatment must be coordinated with medical treatment. The psychological goal in such cases will fall under one or more of the purposes of therapy we have discussed.

COMMON FEATURES

It is not possible to distinguish very sharply between the leading schools of psychotherapy on the basis of such aims as we have been outlining. Most writers put stress on more than one of these purposes, selecting dif- ferent combinations, weighting them differently, and finding different kinds of links between them. Rogers, for instance, stresses the ideas of catharsis, self-knowledge, perceptual shifts, and creative growth. His publications over the years show that he has emphasized catharsis less and creative growth more as time has passed. Freud's early formulations centered on catharsis and self-knowledge, but he later shifted the focal point to development and interpersonal relationships in infancy and childhood. Adlerian therapists devote a good deal of attention to perceptual and cognitive structures and social relationships, but use suggestion and advice to promote self-knowledge and habit change. One of the reasons for the many controversies in the field of psychotherapy may be that there are so many ways in which complex theories can be contrasted with one another!

The procedures actually used show much common ground. In the first place, all methods of personal therapy must concentrate on bringing about *a sufficient lowering of the patient's level of anxiety so that he will be able to permit himself to explore the painful areas of his experience.* An interview where the person is guaranteed privacy, freedom from interruptions, and complete confidentiality has the effect of making him feel at least a little safer than he does at other times in other places. Special group situations may also produce this relaxed attitude. More important is the whole attitude of the therapist and the feeling he communicates to the patient in many subtle ways that he is no longer *alone* with his troubles. The strength of another person has been added to his own.

Dealing with anxiety is one of the basic skills that a psychotherapist must acquire, and it can never be learned from books or lectures. It is not accomplished by simple kinds of verbal reassurance, no matter how earnest. Furthermore, the goal can never be to eliminate anxiety completely, because anxiety constitutes the principal motivation for undertaking therapy as well as the chief reason for resisting it. Some therapists approach the problem of reducing anxiety by combining tranquilizing drugs with psychotherapy in the treatment of severely disturbed cases. To calm a person enough so that he can face all kinds of potentially threatening inner feelings and outer situations and cope with them may be a valuable treatment maneuver. But to carry this so far that he no longer cares what happens to him or no longer sees the sharp outlines of unyielding facts is not therapy. One of the reasons alcoholics have responded less well to psychotherapy than many other types of neurotic patient is that drinking has become a habitual way of reducing their anxieties—too much.

The second thing that all varieties of therapy attempt to do is to create *a strong personal relationship that can be used as a vehicle for constructive change.* In individual therapy this is a relationship between patient and therapist; in group methods the ties between group members may be the important ones. Research by Fiedler (1950*a*, 1950*b*) has suggested that the nature of this relationship may be very similar for kinds of therapy that are differently labeled. It is a significant fact that many theoretical writers, as their experience increases, come to place much more emphasis on this variable. At first, Freud insisted most on the necessity of achieving *insight*; as time passed, *transference* took its place as his central concept, and he turned his attention to the way in which the patient relates himself to his doctor during the different stages of treatment. More recently in psychoanalytic writings there has been a strong emphasis on *countertransference*, or the way in which the doctor relates himself to the patient. Other theorists also talk about the therapeutic *interaction*—what the situation means to the therapist as well as to the client.

The important idea arising from all of this discussion is one that beginning students sometimes miss—that it is necessary for the therapist himself to participate on a deep emotional level in the psychological process that constitutes therapy. Verbal techniques and skills are no substitute for this emotional participation. There are hazards for the doctor as well as for the patient in launching out upon the deep waters the two of them must traverse together. Learning to deal with such hazards is a far more difficult thing than learning to say something appropriate in response to a client's remark. We shall have more to say of this later.

Another common feature in many diverse systems of thinking about psychotherapy is an emphasis on *communication as a way of enabling the patient to establish connections with his own inner and outer worlds.* Obviously, any talking involves communication to some degree. It might be maintained with some plausibility that all psychological disorders *are* essentially communication problems and that treatment consists in repairing or installing lines of communication so that they will connect the patient with the complex human world in which he must function and assist him in articulating his own thoughts and feelings, thus making them more accessible. At any rate, some of the most essential of the therapist's skills are the ways he has of facilitating free expression in the client with whom he is working. This, like the emotional participation discussed above, is not just a matter of knowing what to say. It consists rather in a sensitive awareness of the way the other person feels, a general perceptiveness that makes it possible for him to pick up faint clues and to grasp meanings in confused and halting attempts to say something—or even in silence, for that matter. A sense of being understood acts as a powerful motivating force for a troubled client, encouraging him to try to communicate more of his experience. To provide this understanding requires great effort as well as extreme sensitivity. One must listen to the other person with a kind of concentrated yet relaxed attention that one seldom brings to the other situations of life. It may even be that it is this *interested attention* rather than the understanding itself that promotes further effort on the part of the client, since occasional failure to grasp some particular meaning seems not to impede therapeutic progress. However, needless to say, if the therapist, well-meaning though he may be, never quite understands what the client is trying to say, the therapeutic process is hardly likely to continue for long.

One of the limitations of psychotherapy as commonly practiced today is that it is almost impossible to make it available to troubled persons whose verbal skills are limited. Most of the patients who receive this form of treatment from private practitioners or public clinics are middle-or upper-class persons of above-average intelligence and with better-than-average education. Even in these privileged parts of the population (Hollingshead and Redlich, 1958) many individuals are unable to express themselves very well verbally. It has occurred to many psychologists who are impressed with the enormous need for therapy that greater use must be made of *nonverbal forms of communication.* In clinics for children the use of toys, finger paints, clay, and many other kinds of equipment and materials as media in which they can express themselves has become standard procedure. Even very young children are able to express in such ways thoughts and feelings which they are quite incapable of putting into words. Child therapists must learn to receive communications coming to them in these forms. Some attention has been given in recent years to ways of encouraging nonverbal kinds of expression in adults also. One method, Moreno's psychodrama, has been in use for a considerable period of time and a fairly large body of literature concerning it has accumulated. Therapy using music, painting, or the dance has been tried. Group therapy using activities is not uncommon. There have been nonverbal attempts to condition regressed patients in hospitals. All these new ways of dealing with patients remind us that when we say that communication is essential to therapy we must be sure that we do not define communication too narrowly.

One additional feature characterizes all forms of psychotherapy: *some degree of commitment on the part of the patient, his decision to participate, to try.* This, like the other aspects we have been discussing, is not a simple matter and cannot be brought about by the therapist's use of some particular technique. It is often said, for example, that therapy can occur only if the client takes the initiative by seeking out the therapist, if only by calling the clinic for an appointment. Most professional workers try to arrange things so that this will be the way in which therapy begins. If a college teacher is concerned about the state of mind of a student in his class, the counseling psychologist who is consulted will suggest that the student—not the instructor—call the Counseling Center for an appointment. But the principle involved here is far broader and more fundamental than policies with regard to appointment procedures. Even a person who makes his own arrangements for interviews may feel passive and ambivalent about the whole procedure. On the other hand, rebellious clients forced into therapy by relatives, employers, courts, or school administrative officers may shift their attitudes and make the sort of commitment we are talking about. Especially in early interviews, the therapist's skill can contribute to this end. It requires that one carefully avoid any contest of wills, any obvious or subtle attempt to control the client. But one must also avoid what looks like indifference, an attitude that what the client decides to do is immaterial to the therapist. What the therapist's whole attitude (it cannot be communicated by words alone) must say is: "I really want to help you. I hope you'll give this a trial. But I'm not going to force you or trick you into compliance. The decision really does rest with you." The therapist must be able to communicate hope to the client but without promising anything except sincere effort. What he is asking the person to do is to invest something of himself—a great deal, really—in an enterprise for which a successful outcome cannot be assured.

Once this commitment has occurred, therapy becomes a sort of *partnership*. Menninger (1958) has called the arrangement a *contract* in which each participant agrees to do something in exchange for something from the other person, and both agree to follow certain implicit rules. This, too, is something that characterizes all forms, all schools. There are differences in the way the work to be done is distributed—differences from case to case as well as from one theoretical school to another. But therapy is work, and hard work, for both participants. Both will go through periods of elation as well as periods of extreme discouragement. Progress will often be followed by relapses. Therapy is one of the most fascinating and rewarding of human undertakings, but it is never simple, never easy.

It is generally agreed that patients and clients, even children (Allen, 1942), must be willing to accept changes in themselves if therapy is eventually to succeed. However, this does not mean that psychologists should refuse to work with poorly motivated clients such as chronic schizophrenics, resentful juvenile delinquents, and patients with character disorders. Even though the attitudes of such persons make formal psychotherapy impossible, desirable changes can sometimes be produced by means of direct suggestion, environmental influences, or group activities. There is always room for innovation and research in understanding and modifying behavior.

UTILIZATION VERSUS CHANGE

There is one kind of difference between the ways in which therapists of different schools look at their systems and techniques that is perhaps sharp enough to serve us as a basis for distinguishing between them. This difference can best be expressed in the form of a question: How much and what kind of personality *change* does the therapist hope to bring about in the patients with whom he works?

Let us recognize at the outset that the change that actually occurs in a patient may bear little relationship to what the therapist intended. As explained in Chapter 2, the inexorable process of developmental change is one of the "givens" of human life. Imposing any sort of therapeutic process upon this natural process may produce something unlooked for. Furthermore, what any therapist actually does may be different from what he supposes he is doing. But with all these ambiguities and complications it is still possible to distinguish varieties of therapy from one another by asking, "Just what is this therapist trying to accomplish?"

At one extreme, there are kinds of psychological treatment in which the major goal is not to change the individual's personality at all, but rather to enable him to *make use of the resources he already has.* Much of the work done in college counseling centers is of this nature. It is assumed that in spite of minor handicaps the student client will be able to lead a satisfying, productive life if, by means of a limited number of interviews and perhaps some well-selected tests, he can get a clear view of what his assets are and make up his mind how he wishes to use them. Much marriage counseling also falls in this category. A woman who comes to a marriage counselor with the hope of improving her relationship with her husband and thus avoiding a divorce is usually not going to be treated for a deep neurotic pattern of overdependency even if the therapist suspects that this is her condition. Instead, she and her husband are given an opportunity to work out new ways of handling the kinds of situations that regularly lead to conflict between them. The aim of the treatment is to use the strengths of both personalities to control any weaknesses they may have and develop a relationship that can itself be a source of strength for both of them.

The purpose of intensive psychoanalytic therapy requiring daily sessions over a period of several years is quite different. The client hopes to come out of the treatment rather profoundly changed, with even his most basic personality needs and emotional processes reorganized. Even here, however, *unlimited* change is not expected. There can be no attempt to make a person over in the image of someone else. The pattern of each patient's unique individuality must be preserved.

Between these extremes there are many other positions which can be taken toward psychotherapy and personality change. In each of the succeeding chapters we have grouped together those systems that appear to take similar positions with regard to the amount and kind of change they attempt to produce. Theories of therapy have proliferated and the number of ways they could be compared with one another is infinitely large. Each psychologist tends to create his own theory of therapy out of concepts he finds congenial, useful, and compatible with one another. The student can begin now to build for himself such a structure.

It is important as he selects those concepts and methods of psychotherapy he finds congenial, that he keep in mind their limitations. In order to help him do this, we have attempted a critical evaluation at the end of each chapter. For these we have drawn on research findings wherever they are available. It can safely be said now that no one of these approaches to therapy is as universally effective as its most enthusiastic adherents believe it to be. Eysenck's 1952 summary of all the available published evidence in the psychiatric and psychological journals indicated that substantial improvement occurred in only about two thirds of the cases regardless of the length or intensiveness of the treatment. This study is presented in more detail at the end of this chapter. Other outcome studies are discussed in Chapter 10. The important point to be noted here is that psychotherapy as currently practiced is definitely no sure panacea. Both the immediate effectiveness and the lasting effects of psychotherapy constitute research problems upon which much work must be done. Whatever his predictions, every clinical psychologist must preserve an attitude of healthy skepticism.

A CONCEPTUAL BASIS FOR ECLECTICISM

Rather than to commit ourselves to one theoretical position and one set of concepts about therapy, the authors have chosen to pay some attention to all of them. This is possible within the framework based on developmental psychology, the outlines of which we sketched in Chapter 2. Life is a process in *time*, a complex process of patterned change. In the passage from one stage to another, all of the factors we have discussed in talking about therapy play some part—growth, habit formation, emotional attitudes, awareness of self and others, conscious choices, roles and relationships, and many others. With or without psychotherapy, elements of a personality pattern that are barely visible at one stage become dominant features at a later stage. Consciously or unconsciously, each person selects the aspects of his ongoing life that are to be emphasized in his continuing development.

Psychotherapists of all kinds have in common this concern with their patients' development. All that they can possibly do is to *modify* patterns of personality they find already existing in the individuals with whom they work. In one case it may seem advisable to do this by showing the patient how to replace a faulty habit with a more efficient one. In another case, it may seem advisable simply to assist a client to mobilize his own energies behind a course of action leading in the direction he wishes to go. In still another case, it may seem advisable to try to increase an individual's awareness of many aspects of his own developmental pattern so that he can replace unconscious selection by conscious choice.

We realize that we have neither the knowledge nor the skills to put this eclectic approach to therapy fully into effect. But the thinking we do about such complex psychological issues is a program for the future as well as a guide to the present, a blueprint for research as well as practice. Much has been learned about the complexities of personality by therapists of many different schools. We have tried to make use of all this knowledge, searching for ways to combine and organize as many different concepts as possible rather than arguing their respective merits. It is our belief that some sort of synthesis of a number of these ideas constitutes the best foundation for the student's own practice and research in psychotherapy.

SUMMARY

Psychotherapy occupies a prominent place in current Western culture. There are many systems of therapy. Their overlapping relationships and the changes in any one system over time constitute a serious intellectual challenge to the person who tries to understand them objectively. Several basic intentions underlie the various therapeutic endeavors, some of which are as follows: to strengthen a patient's motivation to do the right things, to reduce his emotional pressure through expression, to change his faulty habits, to increase his insight or self-knowledge, to modify his thought processes, to release his potential for growth, and to improve his interpersonal relationships. Any single theory of therapy might employ one or several of these aims. In addition, there are approaches which seek to change the social system rather than the individual or to modify the physiological functioning of his body in order to improve his behavior. These various psychotherapeutic approaches hold several aims in common: they all aim to lower the patient's level of anxiety sufficiently so that he may explore the painful areas of his experience, to establish a strong personal relationship between patient and therapist as a means for constructive change, to facilitate communication between the patient and his world, and to secure the commitment of the patient to participation in a joint endeavor with the therapist. These systems of therapy differ in the amount of emphasis they place on utilization by the patient of his present resources as opposed to attempt to change or reorganize the patient's personality. As yet, the broad question of the degree to which therapy is effective remains unanswered. Studies show that about two-thirds to three-fourths of neurotics improve whether they have undergone psychotherapy or not. If one adopts a broad developmental view, concepts from many different schools of psychotherapy can be combined.

SUGGESTED READINGS

WATKINS, J. G. *General psychotherapy, an outline and study guide.* Springfield, Ill.: Thomas, 1960.

This book, a very useful reference, is an organized annotated list of the vast literature on psychotherapy and related approaches. Topics covered include the foundations of psychotherapy in psychopathology and psychodynamics, the theories and techniques of psychotherapy, preparation for psychotherapy through diagnosis and the establishment of rapport, specific therapeutic problems, evaluation of therapy, and research methods. For a brief introductory survey of a wide variety of therapeutic approaches organized into supportive methods (e.g., suggestion, rest, environmental manipulation) and reconstructive methods (e.g., psychoanalysis, psychodrama, client-centered therapy), see the author's earlier publication (Watkins, 1954).

BIJOU, S. W. Therapeutic techniques with children. In L. A. Pennington and I. A. Berg (Eds.), *An introduction to clinical psychology.* (2nd ed.) New York: Ronald, 1954. Pp. 608-631.

Bijou reviews the history and diverse approaches to therapy with children. He discusses child diagnosis and its continuity with treatment. He points out that the child differs from the adult in his motivation for working with the problem (the parent initially being the person who "wants something done"), the capacity to verbalize, the degree of dependency on the surrounding situation, and differences in the therapeutic relationship. Many of the therapy systems involve play and activities, especially with younger children. Of the five child-therapy systems Bijou discerns, three (child analysis, briefer analytic therapy, and expressive therapy) derived from psychoanalysis; the others are Rankian relationship therapy and Rogerian play therapy.

COLBY, K. M. *A primer for psychotherapists.* New York: Ronald, 1951.

This book is a clear and practical introduction psychoanalytically oriented. For Colby's more advanced theoretical statement, see his *Energy and structure in psychoanalysis* (1955).

RESEARCH EXAMPLES

EYSENCK, H. J. The effects of psychotherapy: an evaluation. *J. consult. Psychol.,* 1952, 16, 319-324.

This is Eysenck's famous exposé of the dubious value of psychotherapy. His basic question is this: Does psychotherapy increase the rate of recovery from neurosis over what might be expected without psychotherapy? His study was important because there had been very few earlier systematic attempts to find an adequate control group or to determine base rates for outcome studies.

For his baseline of recovery from psychoneurosis, Eysenck depended upon two sources of information. Landis had collected recovery rates of state hospital patients diagnosed as neurotic. (We should note that it is likely that only severe neurotics were sent to a state hospital. At that time such patients received very little if any treatment other than custodial care.) Another study by Denker had established the rates of recovery of five hundred disability claimants of the Equitable Life Assurance Society, persons who were under a physician's care but received no special psychotherapy. These claimants were investigated in a two-year follow-up. Both the Landis and the Denker data yielded a baseline of 72 per cent recovered or considerably improved.

For the figures on outcomes of psychotherapy, Eysenck located 19 studies in the literature covering over 7,000 cases in which a wide variety of psychotherapeutic approaches had been followed. The diverse reports of outcome were converted to four categories: cured or much improved; improved; slightly improved; and, lastly, not improved, died, or left treatment. The studies were divided according to whether treated by psychoanalysis or by less intensive therapy. The percentage of cured or much improved by psychoanalysis was 44 percent. If only completed cases were used, the rate was 66 per cent. The same percentage for shorter therapy was 64 per cent. These figures show, of course, highly significant differences from the baseline of 72 per cent improvement with patients having custodial or regular medical treatment.

Eysenck concludes that the hypothesis that psychotherapy or psychoanalysis facilitates recovery from neurosis is not supported. He states that the stable two-thirds recovery rate, while encouraging to the neurotic, can hardly be called very favorable for the psychotherapists' claims.

Eysenck's article aroused a storm of objections (Charms, Levy, & Wertheimer, 1954; Luborsky, 1954; Rosenzweig, 1954) and replies from Eysenck (1954, 1955). In general, the objections centered around questions of the comparability of the control and therapy groups on the nature and severity of disorder, the meaning of psychotherapy in the eclectic group, and the judgments of improvement. In regard to the latter, it was averred that psychoanalysts hold higher standards for their ratings of improvement. We consider that Eysenck's conclusions have not been effectively refuted by any published research results. In fact, they have been supported by Levitt's more recent study (1957) of outcomes of child therapy and reasserted by Eysenck (1961). Among psychiatrists, a statement by Appel and others (1951) anticipated Eysenck's findings, and Frank (1959) and others recognize the gravity of the problem.

One of the important related questions is the effects of patients' expectancies regarding whatever treatment they receive. It is difficult to separate effects of therapy from placebo effects (Shapiro, 1960). Frank and his colleagues (1959) found in a well-designed study of out-patients that discomfort had decreased markedly by the end of six months, whether intensive or minimum therapy was used. They point to the importance of a nonspecific expectancy of relief. They did find that therapy was more effective in certain ways. The nature of patient's expectations, individual differences in life situations, and specific effects of different case management must receive much careful research. In the meantime, Eysenck's study has provided a challenge which no psychologist or research worker can ignore.

FIEDLER, F. E. A comparison of therapeutic relations in psychoanalysis, nondirective and Adlerian therapy. *J. consult. Psychol.*, 1950, 14, 436-445.

Fiedler's purpose was to investigate differences between three major schools of psychotherapy and between beginning and expert practitioners. He collected ten recorded therapy interviews from ten psychotherapists. The therapists included from each school at least one expert who enjoyed a national reputation and one therapist who was a novice. There were some specifications as to the choice of the patient in therapy, and the recorded session came sometime between the sixth and seventeenth interview.

Four judges listened to the recordings. They made their judgments by sorting a Q sort deck made up of 75 statements about the nature of the therapist's communication, emotional distance, and status relative to the patient. Each Q sort was then intercorrelated with each of the others and with an Ideal Therapeutic Relationship sort obtained in a previous study by the author.

The results led to the following conclusions: (1) Expert psychotherapists create a relationship closer to the ideal relationship than novices. (2) The therapeutic relationships created by experts resemble those of other experts more closely than they resemble those of nonexperts in the same school. (3) Differences between experts and nonexperts were greatest with respect to communication. (4) Differences between schools were most apparent on status items, with Adlerian and some psychoanalytically oriented therapists adopting a more tutorial role.

This important study does not say anything about the effectiveness of the three schools, of course. It does provide a method of describing the nature of the relationship, the Q sort, which is very usable in research. In another study (1950*b*) reported earlier in the same journal, Fiedler found that therapists of different schools do not differ in their concept of the ideal therapeutic relationship and that nontherapists describe it in about the same way. He concluded that the ideal therapeutic relationship is but a variation of good interpersonal relationships in general.

12 Psychotherapy as Exploration of Resources

In this chapter and the chapters following it, we will look into several different views of psychotherapy. Here we inspect the therapeutic process as the exploration and utilization of the client's or patient's resources—his abilities, motives, interests, relationships—the natural tendencies for behavior which he possesses now or has readily available. Psychotherapy of this kind merges with counseling.

HISTORY AND PHILOSOPHY

The first decade of the twentieth century was a period of unusual importance in the history of American psychology. At about the same time that Freud's ideas were being introduced to a skeptical but fascinated public and Binet's tests were opening up the whole vast field of mental measurement, Frank Parsons published a little book called *Choosing a Vocation* (1906). His ideas caught on immediately and within just a few years a flourishing vocational guidance movement was under way. To start with, it had little to do with psychology, but psychologists soon saw the significance of the movement and began to make contributions to it, devising tests for the assessment of vocational aptitudes, working out occupational classification systems that made psychological sense, and refining interview techniques.

Until fairly recently, however, vocational guidance and clinical psychology had little in common. The aim of guidance is to help a person arrive at sound decisions and thus to set his course in the direction he wishes to go. It has nothing to do with neurosis or psychosis, and concepts of illness and cure are foreign to it. Thus its principal beneficiaries have been high school and college students, although there have always been some agencies designed to serve adults at times when they face vocational decisions.

As time passed, psychologists began to realize that the two areas were not so unrelated as they had at first appeared to be. Uncertainties about occupational choices and other important life decisions contribute to the anxiety underlying various psychiatric symptoms. Personality problems are common causes of vocational maladjustment and must be considered when vocational plans are being made. On the positive side, it has become more and more apparent that work is one of the great stabilizing forces in human life. Many psychotherapists, realizing this fact, have turned their attention to this aspect of their patients' problems and in doing so contributed to the development of a kind of therapy resting primarily on the exploration of resources.

During the 1950's we have witnessed a tremendous upsurge of interest in the rehabilitation of the handicapped. A movement which in the 1920's appeared to be a minor offshoot of the general vocational guidance movement joined forces with those branches of medicine that are especially concerned with the restoration of function to the handicapped. At first only physical handicaps arising from illness and accident were considered, but gradually rehabilitative work was extended to patients in mental hospitals and to the mentally retarded. All of these efforts have contributed to the ideas about therapy we shall review in this chapter. It has become apparent that because of the rich resources the process of development has built into a human personality, it is often possible to disregard a person's weaknesses and handicaps almost completely and instead help him build his future on his strengths or assets.

Fortunately, this is not an all-or-none distinction. Typically, therapist and client weigh and consider both assets and liabilities and work out appropriate ways of dealing with them. What distinguishes *resource therapists* from other varieties we shall consider later is that, instead of attempting to bring about as *much* change as possible in a client's personality, they try to help him utilize as much as possible of the structure that already exists. They attempt to discover some unblocked path along which the person can move forward, develop his unique individuality, and thus transcend, rather than penetrate into, the anxieties and conflicts in which he is enmeshed.

In the previous chapter we stated that therapies differ in the view they take of personality change. Therapy of the sort considered here thinks of change in terms of its *direction* rather than its magnitude or amount. That a person is encountering difficulties may be a sign that he is headed in a direction that is wrong for him or that at some former time he has made a turn leading into a blind alley. The therapist's first aim is to create a situation in which the client can see what shifts in direction are possible for him, and second, to give him confidence that someone will see him through the initial uncertainties that arise because he does change his course.

Although this approach to therapy owes much to the vocational guidance movement, its applicability extends far beyond vocational adjustment. In any kind of situation where a person's forward movement is blocked for one reason or another, these concepts may be useful. Examples could be multiplied. Perhaps it is a husband and wife who have come to realize that their marriage has become intensely frustrating to both of them, and they cannot seem to surmount or get around the obstacles that are preventing the continued development of their relationship. Or a bright young high school girl wishes to get married immediately to the classmate with whom she is deeply in love, but hesitates to cut herself off from the possibility of the career in science she had looked forward to. A young man brought up in a devout Catholic family finds that his beliefs are being undermined by his associations with faculty and fellow students in college.

In all these situations and in countless others, the common feature is that some choice or decision faces the client. He may not see it this way. The situation may be so confused at the outset that it is not at all clear what decisions are possible. And he himself may be so anxious and upset that he is in no condition to make important decisions. The therapist's responsibility is to create a special kind of environment in which difficulties can be faced and overcome. The client must be protected at least partially and for a time from outside pressures. He must be helped to obtain the information he needs and to attack doubt and confusion at their source. He must have his confidence in himself strengthened so that he can take the action necessary to establish the new direction and can accept the consequences of the action he takes. A therapist in this case resembles not so much a physician who cures psychological ills as he does the proprietor of a service station who furnishes road information, supplies fuel, and helps get stalled vehicles moving in the direction their drivers wish to go.

Because of its origins in vocational counseling rather than in psychotherapy, we shall call this kind of technique *counseling* as we proceed with the chapter. The word *counseling*, to be sure, is even more ambiguous than most of the other terms we use in psychological practice. But for want of a better word we shall use it to refer to the kind of therapy we have been describing where the emphasis is put on assets rather than liabilities, on small modifications of direction rather than large changes, either quantitative or qualitative, and on decisions made by the client rather than influences brought to bear by the therapist. Similarly, for the purposes of this chapter, we shall refer to the recipient of the service as a *client* rather than a "patient." It is fundamental to this approach that even though he may be a chronic schizophrenic with 20 years of hospitalization behind him, rehabilitative efforts must start with the assumption that he is a client making use of a service offered him rather than a patient hoping to be cured.

THE COUNSELING RELATIONSHIP

The foundation of the whole counseling enterprise is the relationship between counselor and client. In some ways it is misleading to speak of *the* counseling relationship, because it varies from case to case. A counselor's relationship with Mr. Christie, a mature graduate student in his own field, is of necessity quite different from his relationship with Jane Julian, an 18-year-old first-term freshman. But in his attempt to create a solid, fruitful relationship with each person, a counselor proceeds according to certain principles or guidelines, and these can be specified. First, he must have a genuine, sincere interest in each client, *as he now is.* As Rogers has put it, the client must feel that he is *received.* Such an interest is communicated to the client in many ways— by promptness in meeting appointments, by sensitiveness to doubts and misgivings the client may express at the beginning, by posture and facial expression, as well as by verbal responses to what the client says. Such an interest cannot be faked or simulated. If a counselor finds a client boring or distasteful to him, it is far better that he try to put the person in touch with some other service than that he continue a relationship almost certain to be unproductive.

The second essential is that the client have confidence in the counselor, feel safe with him. It is this requirement that makes what is called *confidentiality* so important. If a person is going to relax his defenses and think out loud about weaknesses as well as strengths, he needs to be sure that these weaknesses will never under any circumstances be held against him because he has revealed them here. But there is more to a feeling of confidence than this. It includes respect for the counselor's competence, liking for him as an individual, probably a favorable disposition toward the field he represents, such as psychology, social work, or the ministry. There is no simple technique by means of which such confidence can be won. It is rather an ongoing process of becoming the kind of person in whom confidence can reasonably be placed and demonstrating this constantly by what one says, what one does, and what one refrains from doing.

The third defining characteristic of counseling relationships is that they are *limited* in many ways and that these limits themselves are used to promote development. Interviews are held at definite times, by appointment, and unless there are unusual reasons, a client is not permitted to overstay his allotted time. There are limits to the services the counselor is willing to give. He does not ordinarily intercede for a client with outside agencies or authorities, although on occasion he may make some recommendation about minor matters like permitting a student to drop a course or move out of the dormitory. There are limits to the intimacy or closeness of the relationship. The counselor does not express his own views in interviews as he would in conversations with friends. He may encounter his clients socially, but he avoids close friendships with them. He also avoids being cast in the roles of other significant persons in the client's life—father, brother, lover—he avoids what the psychoanalysts call transference. Some of this inevitably occurs, because the client, like people generally, may try out any new person he meets in the roles he knows best. But a counselor discourages the continuation of such transference ties by the sorts of response he gives—consistent, realistic, matter-of-fact. The purpose of these limits is to make it clear at all times that responsibility remains in the hands of the client. What is to be done he must do. He cannot depend upon someone else to decide things for him or to protect him from the consequences of his actions.

It is in such relationships that the real power of counseling lies—relationships that are friendly, sincere, dependable, but not close in the ordinary sense of the word. It is the setting up of such a relationship with each unique individual person that mainly constitutes counseling skill. It is this relationship that furnishes the psychological environment in which a person is able to make the choices and decisions through which his own distinctive personality takes shape. Research like that of Snyder (1959, 1961) and his fellow workers at Pennsylvania State University has shown that the effects of different techniques on counseling outcomes are far less striking than the effects of different kinds of relationship. The focus of their research program has shifted from techniques to relationships because of this finding. In practice, training programs for psychologists have not paid enough attention to it, and the efforts psychologists have made to assist in the training of other kinds of workers for counseling activity have not emphasized it enough. Teachers still tend to think that it is counseling *techniques* they need to acquire. Employment service counselors and juvenile court counselors are likely to be technique-oriented. If we are really to make use of the potential counseling resources in our society, we must find ways of making prospective counselors aware of the subtleties of these relationships between people instead of simply trying to tell them what to *do* or *not do*.

THE USE OF INFORMATION

Resource therapy can be distinguished from many other varieties of psychological treatment by the way in which information of many varieties is used. Under the broad term *information* we include background facts about the person's school and work experiences, results of psychological tests, and facts about occupations and social organizations, as well as a multitude of other specific things that may come up in connection with specific cases. It is evident that such facts can have a bearing on any kind of psychological treatment. What gives this method its specific emphasis is that information is treated as a *resource to be used by the client* rather than as background to be used by the therapist for the benefit of the client.

If clinical psychologists are to use this method effectively, they will need to have at their disposal various tests that are different from those they customarily use as a basis for personality diagnosis. For example, an individual intelligence test is often less useful than a well-chosen group test that enables the client to see where he stands in a particular group of persons with whom he may be competing. A projective test designed to probe unconscious levels of personality functioning is often of less value than an interest test that shows him the directions in which he finds it natural to move. Achievement tests and specially constructed vocational aptitude tests also contribute to a client's knowledge of himself.

This *client-centered* approach to information has a number of other implications. For one thing, the emphasis must always be on things the client wants to know. Therefore the relevance of any series of questions he is expected to answer or any set of tests he is asked to take should always be explained to him. This does not always mean that the assessment process must be confined to questions the client raises when he comes in. Part of the counselor's skill consists in reformulating questions in more answerable terms. Furthermore, it is quite possible to add some questions of his own to those the client brings. If, for example, he has doubts about the general soundness of the client's personality that would lead him to question whether counseling is the preferred form of treatment, it is quite possible for him to say without alarming the client, "It might be a good idea if you took a few general tests to start with to give us a preliminary idea of what sort of person you are. That would make it easier for me to help you decide the best way of going at this problem." In other instances where the counselor is carrying out some research project that necessitates obtaining certain kinds of test information from all clients, he can state frankly at the outset that tests are being given for this purpose and explain how the results are to be handled.

Aside from such exceptions that are explained to him ahead of time, a client in a counseling situation is a "partner in the firm." He himself analyzes the significance of his past experience for his present attitudes. If he takes tests, the meaning of the scores he obtains is explained to him as clearly as possible. (This does not mean, however, that the scores themselves with all the involved complications related to inadequate reliability or validity and diverse norm groups, will necessarily be placed before him.) If friends, relatives, or teachers are interviewed, he should know that such contacts have occurred and accept their purpose. He is encouraged to seek out for himself the facts he needs about occupations, hobbies, clubs, or religious beliefs, though the counselor may help put him in touch with the sources of such information.

The reason for stressing this point is that it is important for the success of the whole counseling enterprise that the client keep the responsibility for his own life firmly in his own hands. Decisions must be *his* decisions, and he must know on what basis he made them, else he will not have taken the step toward maturity which it is the chief aim of the counseling process to promote.

We have said in an earlier chapter that the purpose of all therapeutic work is to facilitate development, defined as patterned change. Moment by moment, year by year, the process continues. A person is continually being transformed, but there is order and a measure of predictability in the transformations themselves. The more a person becomes aware of the personality structures he has built up through previous development—his abilities and talents, social assets and liabilities, emotional strengths and weaknesses, wishes, values, and aspirations—the more he is able to influence his own subsequent development by the choices he makes. The main purposes of counseling are to promote this kind of awareness, to facilitate this kind of choice.

STAGES IN COUNSELING

There is a basic pattern to the counseling process, although as in all kinds of psychological treatment, individual cases call for variations on the central theme. During the initial stage in the counseling, the psychologist has three specific purposes. First and most important of all, *he attempts to lay the foundation for a relationship of mutual participation,* such as we have discussed earlier. He does and says whatever is necessary to give the client confidence—to make him feel that he has come to the right place. He encourages him to tell his own story in his own words and does not interrupt while this is being done. But if the client is not able to begin spontaneously, he helps him out with general questions that indicate the areas it may be helpful to consider: "What sort of educational background do you have?" "You might tell me something about your family." "What kinds of work have you done?"

Another purpose the counselor has in mind as he participates in the initial counseling is to *help the client talk of motives as well as memories and to express emotional attitudes toward work, other people, and life in general.* If he is to make choices that facilitate his development in his own unique direction, it is extremely important that he take these things into consideration. The facts that must be considered in such choices are often not difficult to see—the person's abilities and limitations, the possibilities and limitations of the situation in which he must act. It is these less tangible matters that complicate the decision process—such things as judgments about the relative prestige of different occupations, expectations of mother or wife that must be met, fears of being trapped, misgivings about growing up, refusal to accept a physical disability, doubts about masculinity or femininity. The counselor's task is not so much to interpret these things to the client and try to get him to accept them as it is to free the client to face them himself. In the counseling interview he is protected by the counselor's presence from some of the anxiety that ordinarily arises when one confronts such attitudes. He can, as it were, try out alternatives that will not have consequences until he actually puts them into operation in the world outside the interview room. In the counseling situation he is able to express and recognize impulses and attitudes of which he is not ordinarily fully aware.

Still another and probably less important purpose of the initial counseling stage is to *obtain some information about the present and past circumstances and actions of the client.* Just what information seems essential depends upon the nature of the agency and its clientele. Most agencies use an information form of some sort for recording and classifying such facts. A college counseling center will collect data about the counselee's family, educational and occupational experience, hobbies and recreations, and previous and present major and career choices. A social agency dealing primarily with adults will place more emphasis on occupational experience, less on the details of the person's school years. A marriage counselor will seek more information about the various family members and their relationship to one another, as well as about the client's childhood years. A rehabilitation agency collects detailed information about the client's physical condition. To an inexperienced counselor this obtaining of information often seems more important than any other purpose of the interview; he knows that he must fill in all the blanks on the printed information form. Actually, any one bit of information is seldom crucial, many facts are obtainable from records and official sources, and it is quite possible to ask the client to fill in some of the blanks in information forms himself. Thus this purpose should never be allowed to dominate the interview. It is the other less tangible purposes of the interview which make it so important.

The second main stage in the total counseling process consists in *helping the client obtain and organize into a meaningful pattern the informa-*

tion he needs in his choice-making activity. In the vocational counseling setting where these procedures originated, this usually means that the client will take some tests to identify his own interests and aptitudes and will be put in touch with other sources of reliable knowledge about occupations he is considering. A file of all kinds of psychological tests that have been shown to be related to occupational criteria, and a library of up-to-date occupational information are standard resources in college counseling centers. But the scope of the information-gathering aspect of counseling is much broader than this. In a marriage counseling case, sound sexual knowledge or correct legal information may be essential. In cases where values are in question, books on theology or ethics, courses in philosophy, or interviews with clergymen may be sources of enlightenment. Generally speaking, the counselor does not dispense such knowledge. Rather, he puts the client in touch with it, and later helps him to organize and assimilate what he finds.

The third stage in counseling is *the actual making of choices and decisions.* Through helping the client to become aware of his complex and subtle motives and to assimilate the facts that must be taken into consideration, the counselor has contributed to his decision-making in two ways. He has enabled him to avoid premature crystallization and pseudo-decisions that are not really satisfactory. But he has also enabled him to narrow down the field of possibilities so that instead of complete confusion he now has perhaps only two or three clear alternatives between which to choose. At this point the interviewer serves as a catalyst. By communicating his thoughts about these alternatives to a person whose goodwill and understanding he trusts completely, the client is able to clarify his own wishes and goals. Thus he "makes up his mind" and takes some necessary action. When this has happened, he no longer needs counseling (at least for the present). His case can be closed.

To outline the counseling process in this way makes it appear less complex than it is in practice. A psychologist must always be ready to make decisions of his own about shifting to some other kind of treatment in an individual case. It may become apparent before the first interview ends that the person has not reached the general level of maturity where responsible decisions are possible. In such cases, planning for the experience needed in his personal growth may be undertaken. A college boy from an overprotecting home may need to work away from home for a summer to feel at first hand some of the hard realities of life. Another student may have to pursue a professional course of study far beyond his intellectual capacities until he has actually come up against failure before he can think realistically about choosing an occupation. In such cases counseling can simply be deferred until the person is able to make use of it.

In other cases, the possibility of severe emotional problems becomes apparent during the first phase of counseling. What the psychologist does in such cases is to refer the client to another therapist for a different kind of therapy or to shift to another treatment strategy himself, at least for the time being. A thorough personality assessment may precede either of these changes in the direction of treatment.

Any stage of the counseling process as initially outlined may be prolonged in an individual case. Particularly the last or choice-making step may turn out to be much more difficult than the counselor initially anticipated. Many interviews, essentially therapy sessions, may occur before the client arrives at a satisfactory plan. Failure at this point is not uncommon even when all previous stages appeared to progress successfully.

Therapy of the kind we have been considering is brought to a close whenever is is apparent that a clear direction has been established in the client's life, even though many emotional complexes remain still unexplored, many interpersonal problems still unsolved. Evidence from outside the interview room can be combined with what comes up during therapy sessions as a basis for judging whether a change of direction has been established. It may be desirable, however, for the therapist to see the client from time to time to encourage him and help him deal with minor problems that arise.

CRITICAL EVALUATION

Since vocational guidance began, more than a half century ago, a considerable amount of research has been carried on to evaluate its effectiveness. (See Tyler, 1961b, Ch. 13.) In such studies, the subjects have not been patients, but students, veterans, or adults consulting vocational counseling agencies. Generally speaking, the results of such studies indicate that counseling is thought by clients to be helpful and that it contributes to favorable educational and vocational outcomes.

In the area of most interest to clinicians, however, that of personality development, the results are more ambiguous. Generally speaking, counseled clients show no more change in measured or rated personality characteristics than do noncounseled. Berdie (1958) includes in his summary of the results of fifteen years of research on the counseling interview at the University of Minnesota the results of one carefully planned investigation in which 80 experimental subjects were compared with 20 controls who had applied for counseling but did not receive it until a month after the matched experimentals had completed their counseling experience. There was no significant difference between them on a test battery chosen to measure anxiety, defensiveness, and personal problem-solving. Various kinds of experimental controls were more adequate in this study than they have been in many others, the outcomes of which were similar. Berdie's comment (1958, pp. 272-273) on these findings is worthy of special attention since it suggests what therapeutic efforts of this sort may and may not be expected to accomplish:

Some evidence suggests that changes that result from counseling are related to specific problems rather than to broader personality variables. For instance, a student may feel that his development is blocked because of a special problem, he may not be able to study effectively, he may not know how to react to his brother's teasing, or he may not know which student groups would be most receptive to him. A counselor who provides student assistance in solving these problems may hope that once the barrier is removed, the student may be able to develop and grow in the desired direction. This development, though not a direct outcome of counseling, is often made possible through the results of counseling and this may be all that most counselors can expect or hope to achieve.

Of special interest to clinical psychologists is some evidence as to the value of this general approach to hospitalized patients. Stotsky (1956) showed in one study that psychotherapy, defined as talking to a doctor about oneself, ranked lower in the estimation of 60 hospitalized veterans than all but one of the 12 hospital activities they were asked to evaluate. Only bookkeeping ranked lower. But in another study at the same hospital (Stotsky, Daston, & Vardack, 1955), significant differences between 14 experimental subjects and 14 controls on criteria measuring ability to function effectively (work characteristics, grounds privileges, trial visits) were obtained when the eight-week experimental procedure included group meetings on vocational adjustment, individual counseling sessions, and the planning of hospital work activities. This study, like those of students, gave no evidence that a significant change in general personality traits, as indicated by the group Rorschach or psychiatric symptom ratings, was produced.

Another study of some interest in this connection is that of Kir-Stimon (1956) in which 54 subjects classified as suffering from anxiety neurosis were evaluated for job adjustment and personal adjustment about six years after they had experienced Veterans' Administration counseling. The general finding of most interest is that these veterans compared favorably with the general population. Seventy per cent of them were considered to have made a good adjustment.

In summary, it can be said that even rather disturbed persons, many of whom are unable to make use of psychotherapy oriented toward insight and personality change, are able to profit from a kind of treatment in which their resources are brought to bear on the solution of specific problems and the formulation of concrete plans. With the interest in rehabilitation that is characteristic of our times, the advantages in this method of treatment should be increasingly evident.

SUMMARY

One point of view toward psychotherapy is to see it as a process of attempting to help the patient or client utilize his existing resources as much as possible. A *resource therapist,* as he may be called, tries to explore not a person's deep emotional disturbances and unconscious wishes, but the directions in which it is possible for him to move at the present time. He tries to locate and develop assets and unblocked paths. While this viewpoint has mainly grown out of vocational guidance work, clinical psychologists have found the approach more and more useful with many kinds of clients. Efforts at rehabilitation have been extended to mental patients as well as to the physically handicapped. In personal counseling the work of the counseling psychologist and the clinical psychologist overlap. The counseling relationship is the foundation for this kind of therapy and other therapy as well. The relationship involves genuine interest on the part of the counselor in the client as he is, a feeling of trust and confidence in the counselor on the part of the client, and the acceptance by both participants of certain limits upon counseling with respect to time, place, and services. The relationship is much more important than any specific techniques the counselor may choose to use. All information, such as knowledge of test results, is regarded as a resource to be used by the client to help him understand himself and his situation better. If tests are also to be used for research purposes, these purposes and the unavailability of their results should be simply explained to the client. In the initial interviews it is most important for the counselor to establish a relationship of mutual participation, to enable the client to talk about his psychological world, including his attitudes and feelings toward life, and to obtain pertinent information for future sessions. In later interviews he helps the client obtain and organize whatever information he needs into a meaningful pattern, one that may lead to his own actual making of choices and decisions. A critical evaluation of this kind of therapy can marshal a good deal of evidence that it has value to clients with vocational and educational problems; its value in cases where personality problems predominate is less clear. In general, it can be said that many persons unable to benefit from psychotherapy oriented toward insight and change are still able to profit from therapy oriented toward the freeing and development of such assets as they possess.

SUGGESTED READINGS

TYLER, Leona E. *The work of the counselor.* (2nd. ed.) New York: Appleton-Century-Crofts, 1961.
    This book introduces professional people and students with various backgrounds to counseling. In addition to a greater elaboration of counseling prin-

ciples, use of tests, etc., than this chapter affords, it reviews research in the field more extensively.

SUPER, D. E. *The psychology of careers.* New York: Harper, 1957.

Super presents his theory of life patterns incorporating findings from developmental psychology, differential psychology, occupational sociology, and his own extensive research in the Career Pattern Study, in which an entire class of high school boys is being followed through the successive stages of career development.

MUDD, Emily H., and KRICH, A. (Eds.) *Man and wife: a sourcebook of family attitudes, sexual behavior, and marriage counseling.* New York: Norton, 1957.

This book is a collection of material from a wide variety of sources, covering marital problems, sexual relations, parent-child problems, religious attitudes toward divorce and other matters, and general principles of marriage counseling. The basic theme of the book is the effect of an individual's developmental experiences on his or her relationships with the opposite sex. Another useful introduction is Vincent (1957). For a more psychoanalytically oriented approach, see *Neurotic Interaction in Marriage,* edited by Eisenstein (1956). The person interested in these matters can also profit greatly by looking over the issues of *Marriage and Family Living.*

LOFQUIST, L. H. *Vocational counseling with the physically handicapped.* New York: Appleton-Century-Crofts, 1957.

Medical treatment of an illness or injury is only the beginning of rehabilitation. The more complete task includes helping a disabled person to make an effective return to the community. Lofquist shows how vocational counseling starts in the hospital and is coordinated with professional and administrative decisions. The book presents case illustrations of the rehabilitation of diabetics, amputees, heart patients, hypertensives, paraplegics, cancer patients, and skin patients. The book is, however, weak in its presentation of rehabilitation work outside of the hospital in the community.

RESEARCH EXAMPLES

WILLIAMSON, E. G., and BORDIN, E. S. Evaluating counseling by means of a control group experiment. *Sch. Soc.,* 1940, 52, 434-440.

This is one of the earliest studies evaluating counseling. It demonstrates the usefulness of college counseling in a large and well-designed study. The counseled or experimental group consisted of 405 arts college freshmen men and women having complete data in the Testing Bureau. The follow-up evaluation was made one year after counseling. The noncounseled, or control group, consisted of students individually paired with the experimental group on the basis of college class, age, sex, size and type of high school, high school grades, and college entrance examination scores. Each student in the experimental and control groups was personally interviewed by a staff member not involved in the original counseling. All subjects were rated on their adjustment and the nature and certainty of their vocational choices. Their college grades were also recorded.

The comparisons of the two groups showed the following: (1) Students who had been counseled were likely to be better adjusted than the control group. Four-fifths of the counseled group were classified as having a satisfactory adjustment to problems at the time of the follow-up, compared with two-thirds of the noncounseled group. (2) The large majority of students in both groups tended to follow-through on plans they had stated during their freshman year in college or ones closely allied to these. However, among the small number who did not follow-through consistently, there were more individuals from the counseled group. Students tended to be more faithful to plans dating from previous and noncounseling influences than to plans arrived at on the advice of the counselor. (3) The authors interpreted some evidence as indicating that the counselors' assistance yielded benefits to the students even though it was not followed consistently. (4) Counseled students made markedly better grades than noncounseled students.

This thorough study might have been improved upon by the use of more objective criteria of adjustment and of the soundness of vocational decisions. It is possible that the academic grades may not be directly associated with the counseling experience. Both the higher grades and the seeking of counseling may be related to stronger motivation and more anxiety lest they not succeed. Despite these limitations, the results of this study are impressive in contrast with results from studies of psychotherapy.

STOTSKY, B. A., DASTON, D. G., and VARDACK, C. N. An evaluation of the counseling of chronic schizophrenics. *J. counsel. Psychol.*, 1955, 2, 248-255.

This is a report on a program of the Vocational Counseling Service with long-term regressed patients in the "continued treatment service" of a VA hospital. The counseling program was part of a very intensive attempt to activate these "back ward" schizophrenics. Experimental and control groups of 14 patients each were selected randomly. The experimental group received the following services from the counselor: weekly group meetings, individual counseling sessions twice a week, and informal visits to the ward. Before and after the eight weeks' period these data were collected: *Q* sorts, group Rorschachs, Hospital Adjustment Scale ratings, and some other ratings of work behavior and symptoms.

The results indicated that though the two groups remained homogeneous with respect to psychiatric symptoms, ward adjustment, and Rorschach measures, they showed significant differences on four of the five work variables, on *Q*-sort self-descriptions, and on number of trial visits outside the hospital. The authors concluded that such a counseling program was of definite value.

Another counseling psychologist, C. H. Patterson, in his comments at the end of the article calls this a very significant report because it shows the importance of the counseling approach with even very disturbed patients long before they are being considered for discharge. It also demonstrates and evaluates new counseling techniques such as group counseling. The mixture of techniques in the whole program makes interpretation of the effects of any single method difficult. Also, it is likely that it was not this counseling approach per se that proved efficacious. Any kind of attention and personal interest shown these unfortunate back ward cases is likely to have effects. Results from such approaches over a longer term need to be studied. Does the patient soon regress to his former state? What length should a special program be (this one was only eight weeks) to produce the maximum recovery rate?

Another more recent study of chronic patients by Meyer (1960) is of interest. This is a follow-up study of 57 VA neuropsychiatric patients who had been hospitalized for eight or more years and who were referred to the counseling psychologist with a view to planning for discharge. Counseling with such persons involving fairly concrete vocational planning and counseling was continued after the patients were returned to the community, along with the development of work skills and the resolution of family problems. The author concluded that the rehabilitation potential of these patients was surprisingly high. A significant number of the patients in this study were able to rise from unskilled to skilled work.

13 Psychotherapy as Growth of the Self: Client-centered Approach

As was explained in an earlier chapter, it is possible to impose some order upon the confusing, shifting, partially overlapping systems of psychotherapy if we describe them in terms of the amount and nature of the change they attempt to bring about in the patients they serve. The system for which Carl Rogers and his many students and co-workers are responsible has as its aim the release of the natural potentiality for growth assumed to be present in every human being, even though it may be arrested and stifled by personal and situational difficulties. Basically, what they hope to bring to the fore in the life of each client (it is characteristic of this point of view not to use the term *patient* with its connotation of illness and helplessness) is the ability and willingness to be *himself,* in the fullest and most complete sense. Relief of symptoms, improvements in social adjustment, and the resolution of personal problems and conflicts may result from this process as it unfolds, but they are byproducts rather than primary effects. The real goal is that the client should perceive and accept his unique self so that it becomes free to grow and change in its own natural way. At the center of the theory lies the conviction that every individual is capable of constructive, self-directed change, and that the core of every personality is basically good.

318

HISTORY AND PHILOSOPHY

One of the reasons why it is difficult to say outright and in one way exactly what this method of therapy involves, is that the ideas themselves have undergone a process of developmental change. It was in 1942 that Carl Rogers published his first full exposition of the system as it then was, in the book *Counseling and Psychotherapy.* This book was destined to have a profound influence on the thinking of psychologists and many other kinds of related workers—teachers, school counselors, personnel men. It outlined the *technique* of what was at first called "nondirective" counseling, and included an almost complete transcript of a case in which the technique had been used.

It is difficult for students entering the psychological profession at the present time to realize just how revolutionary this book seemed in 1942. Previous counseling texts had been concerned mainly with information about clients rather than with what went on in counseling interviews themselves. Previous books on the techniques of psychotherapy were practically nonexistent, if we except the works of Freud and his followers on psychoanalysis. The demonstration that an interview could be recorded in its entirety opened up exciting new possibilities for research. Up to this time, case reports had always been based on notes taken during or after interviews—notes in which the possibility of errors and biases of many sorts was always present. In many ways this book made a major contribution.

One of the immediate effects was a strong influence on training programs for counselors in a variety of settings: schools, industries, military installations, and veterans' centers. The steps outlined and explained so clearly seemed simple enough that any reasonably intelligent person of goodwill ought to be able to follow them. Many persons who tried it, however, found that the point of view was profoundly uncongenial to them. Thus what was taken as a prescription for good counseling became the focus of much discussion and controversy. "Nondirectiveness" became a touchstone for classifying counselors. Some lined up as disciples, some as critics and disparagers of Rogers and his ideas. Remnants of this doctrinal controversy persist, especially among workers somewhat remote from the main streams of psychological research.

Because of the strong emphasis on research that has always been an intrinsic part of Rogerian theory and practice, the system itself has continually left its more dogmatic adherents behind. Rogers' *Client-Centered Therapy,* published in 1951, differed markedly from the earlier book. No longer is emphasis placed on technique. Nowhere in this volume can one find a series of simple steps to be carried out. The center of attention has shifted inward. It was the *experience* of both client and therapist in the therapy situation, the *meanings* it had for both of them, which had emerged as something far more important than the words spoken or withheld. The outlook for the treatment of clients and building of a science of psychotherapy had become less optimistic and promising than it had appeared at the beginning. There was evidence that therapy was taking longer than it had in the beginning, perhaps because clients with more deep-seated difficulties were now seeking it. Would-be therapists were discovering that it was far more difficult to acquire the attitudes and feelings toward other people that now seemed to be the crucial factors in the therapy than it was to learn to make the right verbal responses.

Since 1951, Rogers has increasingly put the emphasis on a philosophy, a general view of human nature. It is this that a student who wishes to practice client-centered therapy must grasp. It has become far more fundamental to the system than nondirective techniques. We can summarize here only the barest essentials of the theory. For a fuller treatment the student must turn to the writings of Rogers and his associates in more recent years (*e.g.*, Rogers, 1961).

First of all, client-centered therapy calls for a *phenomenological* approach to human experience. This means that it deals with the world as a person sees it rather than with objective realities. Within this personal phenomenological world, it is the individual's concept of *himself* that is most significant. During the course of therapy both therapist and client become aware of what the client's concept of himself is and of how favorably or unfavorably he feels toward this perceived self. When therapy is successful, it is this self-concept that changes. It tends to become more finely differentiated and to be accepted and valued more highly.

The process of becoming increasingly differentiated, thus producing richer, more complex patterns, is one of the most fundamental principles of development. A basic dynamic premise upon which Rogers' system rests is that this growth principle does truly apply to psychological reality, and that there is in each person a strong tendency toward *self-actualization*. The therapist's whole task is to work with this, to free it from shackles of various kinds. He does this by creating a completely nonthreatening situation, and by devoting such intense concentrated attention to whatever the client can express about his self-concept that its outlines gradually become clear and the direction taken in this person's life by the forces of growth can be identified.

To many psychologists, this emphasis on growth forces has seemed mystical and unscientific. Of course Rogers' formulation, like so many ways of talking about personality, is essentially a metaphor rather than a literal statement of fact. But this certainly does not make it unscientific. One of the best documented facts in all of the life sciences is that organisms do grow and undergo a continuous process of developmental change extending from conception to death. The concepts of increasing differentiation and individual uniqueness are basic to developmental physiology and psychology. To think of the differentiation and enhancement of the phenomenal self as a part of this overall process does not involve a great leap of the imagination. Thus, it cannot be considered unscientific to conceptualize the process of therapy in this way. The large amount of research stimulated and supported by Rogerian ideas would suggest that science has been well served by this theory.

While growing in theory and research, the client-centered approach has also had its effect in other fields. Group-centered therapy, play therapy, student-centered teaching, and client-centered counseling in industry are examples. In a recent theoretical statement, Rogers (1959b) has extended many of his concepts to interpersonal relationships, delineating the conditions and processes involved when relations are deteriorating or improving.

THE THERAPIST'S TASK

Because of its initial emphasis on *non*directiveness, it has been customary to differentiate this from other styles of therapy more on the basis of what the therapist does *not* do than on the basis of what he does. In the first place, he does not *diagnose.* The process of diagnosis calls for an objective, evaluative attitude, a weighing of the meaning of whatever symptoms and other characteristics the client shows. This attitude is not compatible with client-centered therapy, which requires empathy rather than evaluation. Furthermore, since the process of treatment is to be the same whatever the client's personality structure, diagnostic procedures are at best a waste of time. Rogers rejected from the beginning the analogy between psychological and medical treatment and the resulting principle that in psychotherapy, as in medical practice, careful diagnosis should always precede treatment. This does not mean, however, that testing and other kinds of evaluation are never carried on. They are often used for research purposes, but in such cases the client is told that they have nothing to do with his therapy, and they are administered by someone other than his therapist.

The second thing the client-centered therapist does *not* do is to make *interpretations.* This is the point of sharpest conflict with the systems of therapy derived from psychoanalysis that we shall discuss in Chapter 16. The client himself may see relationships between his present problems and his past experience, or between an emotional need and a characteristic way of handling an interpersonal situation. The development of this kind of insight is a frequent (though not universal) occurrence during client-centered therapy. But it must be spontaneous. The therapist makes no attempt to suggest such relationships.

The third thing he does *not* do is to dispense *advice or information*. This is the characteristic that makes this system different from much of the so-called supportive therapy used by workers of many theoretical orientations. The therapist does not suggest even tentatively what he himself would do were he in the client's place.

Similarly, he does *not reassure* or attempt in any way to make the client more optimistic or comfortable than he is. Anxieties, hostilities, feelings of isolation and strangeness are faced and explored rather than subdued or diminished.

What, then, does the therapist do in the interview situation? *First of all, he establishes an atmosphere and a relationship that will free the client as much as is possible from any sort of threat,* internal or external. He provides an interview situation that is completely confidential and sets the client's mind at rest on this score if he has any misgivings about it. Within this situation he gives the person his full concentrated attention. He manages to get over to him by one means or another that he is genuinely interested in him—that he really likes him. What is required is the indefinable quality of *warmth,* or "unconditional positive regard" (Rogers, 1957). As mentioned before, the client must feel that he is *received*.

Most of the things the therapist says during the interview take the form of what is usually called *reflection of feeling*. A better term would probably be *communication of understanding*. Through his close empathic listening, the therapist senses a meaning the client is trying to express, perhaps in a very halting fashion. He puts this meaning into words as clearly as he can, perhaps in the form or with the inflection of a question to indicate that he is trying to follow the client rather than to lead him. The client may then object to the therapist's way of putting it, but is likely to go on to try to clarify his meaning still further. The important thing is not that the therapist should be precisely correct in his reflection of what has been expressed, but rather that the flow of significant communication be maintained. At its best, this therapeutic process consists of a progressive clarification of the emotional meanings that the client's experience has for him.

Unfortunately, this kind of therapeutic activity appears deceptively simple, so that would-be practitioners (and critics of the system) often see the husk without the kernel, as it were. Some enthusiastic extremists may decide, for example, that since nondirectiveness is good, they will be as nondirective as humanly possible and say nothing but "M-hm" now and then, regardless of what the client says or does not say. Others quickly learn to parrot back the content of each remark the client makes, prefacing each statement with the words, "You feel . . ." A sequence of responses such as: "You feel that your mother disliked your father," or "You feel that you may get cut in salary" does not serve to clarify emotional meanings of any sort. Others wrongly equate client-centeredness with passivity. Actually, the attitude required is one of intense effort to grasp complex feeling patterns, and a passive, nonparticipating attitude stands in the way of successful outcomes.

Limits of various sorts constitute an integral part of client-centered therapy, since they are one of the principal ways of clearly placing responsibility in the hands of the client. The client must make the best use he can of interview periods of fixed length coming only at scheduled times. He must accept limits on the degree of intimacy he can expect from the therapist, and he is not allowed to depend upon him for decisions about the conduct of his life. The goal is to set up a special kind of clearly defined relationship. A client discovers what it is like to have complete confidence in someone, to like a person very much without developing overdependence and without manipulating him for his own ends. He experiences acceptance without intimacy, friendship without demandingness.

An excerpt from one of the interviews Rogers has published (1951, pp. 152-154) may serve to give the reader a sense of what the process of client-centered therapy is like. It is a portion of a second interview with a young woman. (The S indicates the client's remarks and the C the therapist's.)

S102. It seems—I don't know—It probably goes all the way back into my childhood. I've—for some reason I've— my mother told me that I was the pet of my father. Although I never realized it—I mean, they never treated me as a pet at all. And other people always seemed to think I was sort of a privileged one in my family. But I never had any reason to think so. And as far as I can see looking back on it now, it's just that the family let the other kids get away with more than they usually did me. And it seems for some reason to have held me to a more rigid standard than they did the other children.

C103. You're not so sure you were a pet in any sense, but more that the family situation seemed to hold you to pretty high standards.

S103. M-hm. That's just what has occurred to me; and that the other people could sorta make mistakes, or do things as children that were naughty, or "that was just a boyish prank," or "that was just what you might expect," but Alice wasn't supposed to do those things.

C104. M-hm. With somebody else it would just be just—oh, be a little naughtiness; but as far as you were concerned, it shouldn't be done.

S104. That's really the idea I've had. I think the whole business of my standards, or my values, is one that I need to think about rather carefully, since I've been doubting for a long time whether I even have any sincere ones.

C105. M-hm. Not sure whether you really have any deep values which you are sure of.

S105. M-hm. M-hm.

C106. You've been doubting that for some time.

S106. Well, I've experienced that before. Though one thing, when I make decisions I don't have—I don't think—It seems that some people have

—have quite steady values that they can weigh things against when they want to make a decision. Well, I don't, and I haven't had, and I guess I'm an opportunist (laughing). I do what seems to be the best thing to do at the moment, and let it go at that.

C107. You have no certain measuring rods that you can use.

S107. Yes. M-hm. That's what I feel. (Pause.) Is our time about up, Mr. L.?

C108. Well, I think there are several minutes more.

S108. I was thinking about this business of standards. I somehow developed a sort of a knack, I guess, of—well—habit—of trying to make people feel at ease around me, or to make things go along smoothly. I don't know whether that goes back to early childhood, or—I mean, to our family situation where there was a large family, and so many differences of opinion and all that there always had to be some appeaser around (laughing) and seeing into the reasons for disagreeing and being sorta the oil that smoothed the waters. Well, that is a role that I have taken for a long time. And—I—it's gotten so it really—I mean, before this sort of thing came up I realized that as a person in a social situation or group of people like at—oh, at a small meeting, or a little party, or something—I could help things to go along nicely and appear to be having a good time. And I'd see where someone else needed more punch, or where someone didn't have a partner, or where somebody was bored with that person, and something—somebody was standing in a corner, and I could go out and meet them. And sometimes I'd surprise myself by arguing against what I really thought when I saw that the person in charge would be quite unhappy about it if I didn't. In other words, I just wasn't ever—I mean, I didn't find myself ever being set and definite about things. I could see what I thought might be interjected to make people feel happy, and I'd do that.

C109. In other words, what you did was always in the direction of trying to keep things smooth and to make other people feel better and to smooth the situation.

S109. Yes. I think that's what it was. Now the reason why I did it probably was—I mean, not that I was a good little Samaritan going around making other people happy, but that was probably the role that felt easiest for me to play. I'd been doing it around home so much. I just didn't stand up for my own convictions, until I don't know whether I have any convictions to stand up for.

C110. You feel that for a long time you've been playing the role of kind of smoothing out the frictions or differences or whatnot. . . .

S110. M-hm.

C111. Rather than having any opinion or reaction of your own in the situation. Is that it?

S111. That's it. Or that I haven't been really honestly being myself, or actually knowing what my real self is, and that I've been just playing a sort of false role. Whatever role no one else was playing, and that needed to be played at the time, I'd try to fill it in.

C112. Whatever kind of person that was needed to kinda help out that situation you'd be that kind of person rather than being anything original or deeply your own.

S112. I think so. I remember one summer. We used to go to the YWCA camp in the summers. And our family lived way out near the edge of town. We went with the school groups that went at a certain time during the summer. Well, we didn't know those children very well, because we didn't see them except on Sundays when we went to church. So going to camp wasn't an awfully satisfying experience because I felt quite strange among the children. Well, this summer—I'd been to camp once before—and I think I'd decided that I was going to be one of the popular girls at camp. So I went to camp with these children that I didn't know too well. And I don't remember what I did that summer; but anyway, I came home voted the most popular camper. What I do remember, though, is when I got ready to go to camp—I and I don't know how old I was then—I was not thirteen, I don't suppose; maybe twelve or thirteen, I don't know quite how old; I just decided I was going to be the most popular girl at camp. So I went to camp with that decision, and I did the things that needed to be done. Whatever they were, I'm sure I don't—I mean, it was probably a lot of drudgery too; like making other people's beds and doing other things like that— I'm sure. But anyway I went through a set campaign and came home and was actually chosen the most popular girl at camp (laughing). And it seems that what I've done is do things like that instead of developing a real self.

C113. In other words it's been kind of a planful campaign in each case rather than because you really felt that way or really wanted to be that kind of person. Is that it?

S113. Well, yes. I think so. It seems that it's more—that it's not realistic, or it's not honest, or not—it's not sincere, maybe.

CLIENT-CENTERED THERAPY IN THE TREATMENT OF CHILDREN

While the techniques we have been discussing were designed originally for adults, it has been possible to extend them, with very little modification, to work with children. The idea of growth in the direction of self-actualization is applicable to human beings of any age. The client-centered child therapist respects his small client in the same way that he would respect older ones, and assumes that he too has within himself the capacity for self-help.

His first task, as with adults, is to create a warm, nonthreatening situation in which the child can feel free enough from anxiety so that he can express his real self. But since to put subtle or complicated feelings into words may be beyond his powers, the child is encouraged to express himself in other ways. A well-equipped playroom makes this possible. Pounding and smashing things may express aggression. Painting with somber colors may express hopelessness. Arranging small dolls of both sexes and different ages in the rooms of a playhouse may give a picture of the child's family relationships, as he experiences them. These are only a few examples of the kinds of communication that occur. Axline (1947) and Moustakas (1953) have written books describing client-centered therapy as it has been used with children.

As with adults, the client-centered therapist does not attempt to interpret this behavior, but concentrates instead on making clear to the child that he understands and accepts the feeling he is showing. He stays very close to the child's actual expression. As in adult therapy, limits are very important. In addition to the ever-present time limitations, there are special limits in child therapy on the kind of behavior that will be tolerated. Playrooms are usually built so that one need not worry about messiness or destructiveness, but a child is not allowed to break windows or other permanent fixtures or to attack the therapist physically. Since there are many ways in which aggressive impulses may be expressed symbolically in the therapeutic situation, such limits help rather than hamper therapy.

THE USE OF ASSESSMENT METHODS IN CLIENT-CENTERED THERAPY

Client-centered therapists differ from those who adhere to most other theoretical systems in their attitude toward psychological assessment. As has been indicated in the previous section, they have definitely repudiated the idea that diagnosis should always precede therapy. They do not accept the analogy with medical practice upon which this idea rests, and they insist they have found no evidence in their research that the kinds of classifications commonly resulting from diagnostic assessments are related to therapeutic success. But over and beyond these grounds for skepticism as to the value of assessment, they see more important reasons for coming out strongly against routine diagnosis. The principal one is that the evaluative, judgmental attitude actually interferes with the empathic, accepting attitude on which, as they see it, the success of therapy will depend. Any effort a therapist makes to accomplish a thorough-going objective assessment of his client makes it just that much more difficult for him to adopt the client's frame of reference.

This does not mean, however, that assessment procedures are never used in centers where client-centered therapy is given. Because of the strong research orientation of the movement, there has been from the beginning a concerted effort to ascertain relationships between progress in therapy and various sorts of personality change. Personality measurement is used, then, for research purposes, but not for the selection of clients or the planning of therapy.

One of the results of this special sort of orientation to assessment is that a psychologist almost never administers any tests to his own therapy clients. A client who consents to serve as a research subject will be signed up for pretherapy tests with an examiner who has nothing whatever to do with his treatment. It is made perfectly clear to him that his therapist will not see the test results during the period therapy continues.

Another result of this research orientation is that assessment involves a considerably wider variety of special techniques than are customarily used at clinics where other sorts of therapy are practiced. The Rorschach, TAT, and personality inventories have been used by Rogerian researchers as by others. But along with them a test of the 1930's, like the Willoughby scale, may be resurrected, or new devices, such as Q sorts or situational tests, may be introduced. Early research efforts to record and study interviews led to ways of classifying the therapist's remarks and of studying the shifts in content and affect of the client's words over a series of counseling sessions. The search has always been to find measuring instruments that are suitable for tapping some of the aspects of personality in which theory would predict changes.

Something that might be called assessment occurs, of course, in deciding whether to accept a case. The question arises as to when client-centered therapy is appropriate and when not appropriate. Rogers has not concerned himself much with this question, implicitly allowing self-selection to take place. As the client-centered approach developed at the University of Chicago Counseling Center, many clients were college students. However, it has been applied to adults who are not college graduates, to children in child guidance clinics, and to workers in industry. Snyder (1954) states that the client-centered approach has had its greatest usefulness in dealing with the emotional problems of normal persons, and with mildly psychoneurotic persons. He points out that it seems ineffective or counterindicated in cases characterized by any of the following: psychosis, advanced age, low intelligence, poor ability to verbalize, and excessive dependence. These limitations, however, would apply pretty generally to any kind of psychotherapy. In a publication reviewing recent client-centered work, Rogers (1960) reports an ever-widening range of application extending to psychotics and alcoholics.

CRITICAL EVALUATION

Active organized research programs at the University of Chicago, at Pennsylvania State, and at various other places have investigated both *outcomes* (What kinds of results does therapy produce?) and the *processes* of therapy (What psychological processes occur during the course of therapy?).[1] Scores of Ph.D. dissertations have been devoted to studies in these areas; the bibliography of published studies runs to hundreds of items (See Seeman & Raskin, 1953; Cartwright, 1957).

Still, after nearly twenty years of almost continuous research, it is not possible to answer simple questions with regard to how "good" this method of therapy is, or just what kinds of effects it has on those who undergo it. More and more sophisticated attempts to answer such questions have made us increasingly aware of their complexities.

[1] A more detailed consideration of the aims and methods of outcome and process research is included in Chapter 19.

The simplest of all the possible evaluative questions that can be asked about this or any other form of therapy is: Does it accomplish *anything* that the process of time would not accomplish by itself? Since publication of the Eysenck report (1952) mentioned in the previous chapter, it has been commonly charged that figures showing percentages of cases judged to be improved through therapy do not prove that there is any advantage in intensive psychotherapy over the minimal sort of advice and support a neurotic patient obtains from a nonpsychiatric general medical practitioner. About two-thirds of any group of neurotic patients seem to improve with or without special treatment. How does the success rate for client-centered therapy compare with this "base rate"?

In evaluating Rogerian therapy, it is difficult to make direct comparisons with Eysenck's figures. In most of the studies that have been done, the proportion of cases the therapist would judge "unimproved" has been reported only incidentally, if at all. It would appear, however, that the outcomes reported in these studies fall within about the range that Eysenck claims for the cases he studied. In many of the studies reported in Rogers and Dymond (1954) a counselor rating of the success of the therapy on a nine-point scale was used. Subgroups based on this success rating were differently constituted for different comparisons, but about one-third of the experimental cases were quite consistently classified as unsuccessful.

In addition to the kind of clients whom therapists judge not to have made significant progress, there is another kind of therapeutic failure in which practitioners are taking increasing interests. A considerable number of clients *break off* therapeutic contact after a small number of interviews and thus automatically remove themselves from any further influence the experience might have had on them. The Rogers and Dymond report gives us some evidence on the prevalence of this phenomenon in client-centered practice. Of those who entered the study as experimental clients, 25 terminated after less than six interviews, as compared with 29 who persisted in the treatment.

It should be emphasized once more that neither the failure nor the attrition rate is higher in client-centered therapy than in other varieties. We shall return to the general problem raised by these findings in a later chapter. The only statement that can be made with regard to this particular line of evaluation is that client-centered therapy has not solved the problems of keeping patients in treatment and enabling all of them to benefit by it.

"Outcome" research in client-centered therapy has been most concerned with the nature of the personality changes the experience produces. There have been a large number of such studies, some reporting favorable changes, others not. The most thorough attempt to assess them is the series of studies reported in the Rogers and Dymond volume

(1954). Their importance derives partly from the way the research design handled some of the complexities to which we have referred. The subjects were clients who applied for treatment at the University of Chicago Counseling Center. A standardized program of pretherapy and posttherapy testing was arranged. The control group, similar in age, sex, and socioeconomic status to the experimental group, consisted of subjects who volunteered for a personality research study, and who took the same tests without an intervening period of therapy. The other kind of control used in the experiment, an especially interesting one, was an attempt to find out whether such changes as occur may reflect a certain kind of *motivation* rather than therapy experience. Half of the experimental clients were asked to wait sixty days before being given an appointment with a counselor. They took the assessment tests at the beginning and end of the "Wait" period, as well as at the conclusion of therapy. Changes occurring during the "Wait" period could thus be compared with the changes in the same individuals supposedly growing out of therapy itself. All experimental subjects were also given follow-up tests from six months to a year after the termination of therapy.

Results of the study were in general positive, though rather complex. The more closely the assessment techniques were related to Rogerian theory, the more clearly the effects of therapy showed up. In the Q-sort procedure, for example, in which subjects who had therapy were asked to sort items of personality description into various categories to describe their real selves and then to sort them again to describe their ideal selves, the change was in the direction of closer agreement between the two after therapy. Corresponding changes were not found in the control group or in the "Wait" period. The TAT protocols showed changes in the direction of improved adjustment when they were rated for general adjustment, but not when they were rated by a special system based on psychoanalytic theory. The Emotional Maturity scale was filled out by each subject himself and also by two of his friends. The self-ratings improved with therapy but not the friends' ratings. (Cases their counselors judged to be successful did tend to be rated higher by others, whereas those judged not to be successful were rated *lower*. Thus the "no change" conclusion is in a way an artifact.)

Some of the more important results of this epoch-making study can be summarized if we say that client-centered therapy has been shown to produce a more positive self-evaluation and a feeling of better all-round adjustment. In some clients, the more successful, behavior and relationships with others also improve. In others, the less successful, these behavioral indices of competence in the business of living indicate a decline, accompanied by a defensive verbal insistence that all is well.

Throughout the years since client-centered therapy was initiated, much attention has centered on *process* research, as distinguished from the *outcome* research we have been considering. Interview recordings and typescripts have been broken down into units and analyzed in great detail for increases and decreases in various kinds of verbalization. Clients have been asked to describe their feelings at different stages. Physiological indicators of anxiety, such as PGR responses, have been monitored as therapy proceeded. The description of process has been modified again and again as new evidence came in. Without going into the details of separate studies, let us look at Rogers' formulation of the process.

He sees it as composed of seven stages (Rogers, 1959a, p. 98). At the one end is a condition in which the person is rigid, unaware of his own feelings, unable to tolerate change or to hazard entering into close relationships with people. At the other end is the condition of being open to experience, at harmony with one's own feelings, emotionally close to others. Progress in client-centered therapy seems to involve movement on this continuum which Rogers has chosen to divide into seven stages. Few clients start at Stage 1, and if they do, they are likely to break off the relationship after an interview or two because they cannot tolerate the anxiety it arouses. Few ever reach Stage 7, an ideal state toward which "self-actualizing" personalities move. Therapy works at the intermediate stages, helping each client progress toward fullness of life. In a preliminary tryout of the system, Rogers (1959) had two judges rate excerpts from six of his completed cases on this seven-point scale. Change was measured by comparing the ratings for excerpts from early stages of therapy with those from later ones. There was a rank correlation of .89 between progress measured on this process scale and progress as judged from external criteria. The three cases the therapist had considered most successful showed shifts of 2.3, 2.0, and 1.5 on the process scale. Those the therapist had judged to be least successful showed shifts of 1.15, .62, and .30.

As research and theory-making have continued, less emphasis has been placed on one particular technique and more consideration given to personality processes underlying all kinds of therapeutic change. As stated in Chapter 11, Fiedler (1958b) showed that experienced therapists of three different theoretical orientations agree very closely in what they consider to be a good therapeutic relationship. Strupp (1958) has also investigated this question, and while he has found differences of some kinds between client-centered and analytically oriented therapists, the similarities remain very great. One of the aims of the coordinated research program Snyder has been carrying on at Pennsylvania State was to vary therapists and techniques separately in order to discover whether it was the qualities of the therapist's personality or the technique he was using (leading versus reflective) that produced favorable results. (See Ashby et al., 1957.) The styles of therapy showed only a very slight relationship to measures of change in clients. The therapist's personality traits and the pretherapy traits of the clients showed more. In addition, however, there was a significant *interaction* effect. Some therapists obtained better results with the leading or interpretive treatment, others with the reflective variety. Furthermore, therapists found it very hard to maintain one kind of treatment consistently throughout their contacts with a certain individual, even though they were interested in the experiment and willing to participate in it.

In keeping with this shift of attention from technique to general personality processes, and in an attempt to move toward research-derived definitions of his basic position, Rogers formulated what he considers to be the necessary and sufficient conditions for therapeutic change (1957). The six conditions are as follows:

1. Two persons are in psychological contact. There must be a genuine relationship between them.
2. The client must be in a state of incongruence, to some degree vulnerable or anxious.
3. The therapist is congruent and integrated in the relationship. He is able to be deeply and genuinely himself.
4. The therapist experiences unconditional positive regard for the client.
5. The therapist experiences an empathic understanding of the client's internal frame of reference and endeavors to communicate this experience to the client.
6. The communication to the client of the therapist's empathic understanding and unconditional positive regard is at least to a minimal degree achieved.

One of the noteworthy things about this list is that it is so short. Many of the points of practice and theory upon which psychologists have argued, and around which their loyalties have been organized, do not appear in it. True, the six conditions as they are stated above are too vague for research purposes. Rogers believes that it is most important in these early stages of personality theory to deal with really significant problems, even if statements can only be vague. He has chosen to concern himself with human experience, a most difficult topic. In the article and in later publications (1959*a*, 1959*b*), Rogers has attempted to make clearer what he means by his terms. For instance, he recommends using a client *Q* sort of self-referent items for defining what is meant by the self, for comparison with the therapist's sort and with later sorts by the client. Rogers and his students have made some beginning attempts to relate their work to experimentation in perception (Chodorkoff, 1954).

There have been many criticisms of client-centered therapy. It has been called naive and superficial, useful only for mild disturbances and articulate clients, and lacking in recognition of social influences. Thorne has called the approach too narrow and unitary and fears it fosters stereotyped thinking and treatment. Many psychoanalysts have been particularly opposed to the Rogerian approach, although the evidence that their methods are superior to this one is lacking. The use of self-report in measuring effects of therapy in a number of studies is open to serious question, as Hathaway (1948) and Loevinger and Ossorio (1959) have pointed out. However, no one can deny the tremendous stimulus this movement has given to the development of responsible research in psychotherapy, nor the deep sincerity of Rogers' effort to develop order and system out of his many years of personal experience with clients. The problems of what kind of approach to use with what kind of clients in the hands of what kind of therapists are for future research to illuminate. In the meantime, whether one adopts a client-centered view or rejects it depends partly on the kind of training he has received and partly on how congenial it is to his own personality.

SUMMARY

Client-centered therapy has undergone continual development. In his 1942 book Carl Rogers placed considerable emphasis on nondirective technique. In his 1951 book, Rogers shifted the emphasis to the experiences of the client and therapist. In more recent years the emphasis on the therapist's warmth and unconditional positive regard for the client has been continued along with an attempt to develop a phenomenological theory explicating the self and personal experience. Nondirective technique avoids diagnosis, interpretation, advice-giving, and reassurance. The method mainly used is reflection of feeling. Applications of client-centered therapy have spread to play therapy with children, group therapy, and student-centered teaching. Throughout the history of client-centered therapy there has been a heavy emphasis on research. If tests have been used, it has not been for diagnostic purposes, but for research. The analysis of recorded interviews was undertaken early, and shifts were revealed in the kinds of statements made by the client. The kinds of remarks made by the therapist were classified and related to these shifts. Later research emphasized the use of Q sorts to record self-concepts of the clients and judgments of the therapists. Many other assessment techniques were also used in research. Study of the outcomes of client-centered therapy have generally shown an increase in positive self-evaluation and a feeling of better all-around adjustment. In more successful clients, external behavior and relationships also improve. Some clients do not improve, and in some, behavior and relationships are rated lower after therapy. The findings are complex. Despite the disagreements of many critics, the client-centered approach is a notable exhibit in the development of research in psychotherapy.

SUGGESTED READINGS

ROGERS, C. R. *Client-centered therapy*. Boston: Houghton, 1951.

This book presents the major tenets and applications of client-centered therapy. Rogers discusses his goals and theories in several chapters, and there are a number of chapters on special uses of the client-centered approach, e.g., therapy with children and with groups.

ROGERS, C. R. A theory of therapy, personality, and interpersonal relationships, as developed in the client-centered framework. In S. Koch (Ed.), *Psychology: a study of a science*. Study I. *Conceptual and systematic*. Vol. 3 *Formulations of the person and the social context*. New York: McGraw, 1959, pp. 184-256.

This chapter is the most extensive statement of Rogers' recent point of view. He starts with an interesting and brief presentation of his own theory of therapy and personality change. With the therapeutic experience as the keystone, he expands the theory to cover personality, his concept of the "fully functioning person," a theory of interpersonal relationships, and applications to family life, education, and groups. He relates in quick review various kinds of research which are pertinent to the theory. This chapter is neither clear nor simple in spots unless one has a background in client-centered psychology such as might be obtained from Rogers' earlier books (1942, 1951).

ROGERS, C. R. *On becoming a person*. Boston: Houghton, 1961.

This book is a collection of papers Rogers has written over a period of a decade or more. In them, his thoughts about human nature and the values that underlie his therapeutic and research efforts are expressed with ever-increasing clarity. The book is not directed primarily to psychologists, but rather to workers in all the service professions and to people in general. Thus the beginning student will find it an interesting introduction to Rogers' thinking about personality and therapy.

SNYDER, W. U. *The psychotherapy relationship*. New York: Macmillan, 1961.

This book is an excellent illustration of "organized eclecticism." It developed out of Snyder's earlier association with the client-centered approach and still emphasizes the relationship which is at the core of Rogers' therapy. However, the relationship is now described with the psychanalytic concepts "transference" and "countertransference," and concepts from learning theory are employed. In addition to clarification of feelings, the therapist makes liberal use of interpretations and frequently asks the question: Why? Three principal kinds of content in the book are (1) conclusions from a four-year research project, (2) analysis of a mass of relevant psychological literature, and (3) extensive case material demonstrating an eclectic type of psychotherapy focused on interpersonal relationships. The Affect Scales developed for clients and therapists to record their feelings about interviews would be useful in other research endeavors. As a piece of research, this project has the limitations of being applied to a small, highly selected sample (20 cases, 19 of whom were graduate students in psychology).

BUTLER, J. M. Client-centered counseling and psychotherapy. In D. Brower and L. E. Abt (Eds.), *Progress in clinical psychology*. Vol. III. New York: Grune & Stratton, 1958. Pp. 93-106.

This is a very interesting review of developments in theory and research at the University of Chicago Counseling Center by the man who headed the Center after Rogers moved to the University of Wisconsin. Of particular interest is some new research based on the analogy between psychotherapy and some of the aspects of human engineering. Client-centered therapy is shown to be broadening and becoming less of a "school."

RESEARCH EXAMPLES

RAIMY, V. C. Self-reference in counseling interviews. *J. consult. Psychol.*, 1948, 12, 153-163.

Raimy's research (his Ph.D. thesis work) was one of the earliest in a long series of studies related to the theories of Rogers. It was postulated that a person's self-concept is a significant factor in his personality organization—"the map which each person consults in order to understand himself." The approval, disapproval, or ambivalence a person feels toward himself is related to his adjustment. It was hypothesized that there would be significant shifts toward more favorable self-attitudes in those cases where counseling was judged to be successful.

Raimy's method of measuring attitudes toward the self was as follows: Judges were instructed to read transcripts of interviews and to identify all word groups in which the client made a reference to himself. Each of these self-references was to be classified as positive, negative, ambivalent, or ambiguous. References to others and questions were also identified. Preliminary tryout gave satisfactory reliability. The method was then applied to 111 interviews that occurred during therapeutic sessions at the college clinic. Seven of the 14 cases were considered clearly successful.

Although only the simplest statistics were used, the results seemed to support the original hypothesis very clearly. For instance, one successful case started counseling with self-references that were 10 per cent positive and 40 per cent negative, and ended counseling with self-references that were 57 per cent positive and 0 per cent negative. An unsuccessful case showed 5 per cent positive references at the start and about the same at the close; negative references remained high throughout. The author interprets the results as indicating that successful counseling involves essentially a change in the client's self-concept.

The reader who examines the original study will be able to discern many of its limitations. However, this research was done at the beginning of an important line of research and theory. It is suggested that the reader go on to look up some of the studies described briefly by Cartwright's annotated list of 120 papers about research and theory on client-centered therapy (1957). In more recent years there have been several studies dealing with the relationship between attitudes toward the self and attitudes toward others.

BUTLER, J. M., & HAIGH, G. V. Changes in the relation between self-concepts and ideal concepts consequent upon client-centered counseling. In C. R. Rogers & Rosalind F. Dymond (Eds.), *Psychotherapy and personality change*. Chicago: Univer. of Chicago Press, 1954. Pp. 55-75.

This is a report of one of the studies in the large research program on psychotherapy of the University of Chicago Counseling Center. The program introduced a number of important innovations into research on this subject. Most important of these was the use of control groups and control phenomena in studying the effects of psychotherapy. There were two kinds of control groups: the own-control group and the equivalent-control group. The own-control was formed in the following manner: During the period of the selection of subjects, every applicant at the Counseling Center was invited by a preliminary interviewer to participate in a research project. About 50 per cent accepted and were started on the battery of tests and other research procedures. Among those participating, one-half were assigned to immediate therapy and one-half to a 60-day waiting period. Those clients who waited formed the own-control group. The equivalent-control group was selected from volunteers for a project on "personality research" and were matched with the therapy group on age, sex, socioeconomic status, and student-nonstudent status. The own-control plan includes controls for motivation for therapy and passage of time without therapy. The equivalent-control group makes it possible to compare the subject with persons who were not motivated for therapy, but spent the time in normal living.

For the Butler and Haigh part of the research program, there were two hypotheses: (1) Client-centered therapy results in an increase in congruence between the self-concept and the ideal-and-self-concept in the client. (2) This increasing congruence would be especially marked in those cases judged independently as exhibiting improvement. The self and ideal-self concepts were defined operationally by client Q sorts which took place before and after therapy and at a six- to twelve-month follow-up time. Examples of items in the 100 item Q-sort were: "I am a hard worker," "I really am disturbed," and I am afraid of a full-fledged disagreement with a person." The two control groups were appropriately tested during the waiting period and equivalent time periods. Twenty-five persons received psychotherapy, of which 15 were in the own-control group.

The findings were as follows: In the total client group, the original correlation between self and ideal-self Q sorts averaged .01 (with a range from −.47 to .59). By the end of the therapy, the self-ideal correlation had significantly increased, averaging, .34. On follow-up testing, this correlation remained essentially the same (.32), suggesting the congruence was not due to a temporary "hello-goodbye" effect.

The equivalent-control group started out with a high relationship between self-and ideal concepts (.58), as is common with a sample of the normal population, and made little change over the period of the study (correlation at the end, .59). The own-control group also showed no change in self-ideal correlation during the waiting period, starting and ending with a zero correlation. This group, however, did make a significant change by the end of the therapy. In summary, the several comparisons between the therapy and control groups led the authors to conclude that the first hypothesis was confirmed at a high level of significance.

In order to test the second hypothesis, a group of 17 "improved" clients was selected on the basis of two criteria: ratings of improvement by the therapist at the end of the treatment, and independent ratings based on blind analyses of TAT's before and after treatment. This improved group showed a zero relationship between self and ideal sorts before therapy, but a .44 relationship on follow-up. The gain in self-ideal congruence was significantly greater than for the controls or the "not definitely improved" group of clients, thus confirming the second hypothesis.

This study is only one of several reported in the Rogers and Dymond book. There are other interesting studies on an "attrition group" that did not complete therapy, on ethnocentrism (using the F scale) as a limiting factor in psychotherapy, and on many other aspects of personality change. Rogers summarizes the research program and points out additional problems in a final chapter. It is not possible, of course, to generalize too widely from this one project, for it is likely that a very special kind of client participated in it. But as a demonstration that methods can be devised to solve the difficult problems of controls and that one kind of personality change takes place as a result of one kind of therapy, the study is highly significant.

14 Psychotherapy as Habit Change

Psychotherapists of most schools have held that their work is grounded in the psychology of the personality as a whole. Generally speaking, they do not aim to treat particular symptoms or habits, but look on them as symbolic expressions of motives and conflicts involving the total personality. Thus if a young woman complains of a persistent phobia of railroad trains, they do not attempt to free her of this one special fear, but rather to help her understand and get rid of the general anxiety of which this phobia is presumably one crystallization, or otherwise to modify her personality sufficiently so that she can cope with her anxiety in some constructive way.

But there is another current of thinking about therapeutic intervention. Its course is nearly as long but not nearly as visible as the main stream. It derives from Pavlov rather than from Freud. Its central thought is that neurotic manifestations of all kinds are essentially bad habits. They are *responses*, learned under special circumstances, and later generalized to many other situations. Regardless of how or when such habits were first acquired, the therapist's whole responsibility is to plan a learning situation in which the behavior can be modified, either by extinguishing the undesirable response through nonreinforcement, or by training the patient to make another response incompatible with the neurotic one.

HISTORY AND PHILOSOPHY

Such abnormal symptom-habits as facial tics, hand-washing compulsions, enuresis, or impotence have impressed observers of human behavior for a long while. Since they are habits, they are learned responses to stimuli of some sort. Fifty years of research on learning in psychological laboratories throughout the Western World have taught us a good deal about methods for changing the connections between stimuli and responses. It seems sensible and worthwhile to try to apply some of this knowledge in the consulting room.

But the concept of therapy as attempted habit change goes much deeper than the alleviation of particular symptoms. The fundamental motivational state that seems to underlie all neuroses is *anxiety*. Anxiety can be thought of as generalized fear, and fear is itself a response. It is far more complicated than the responses like salivation and eye-blinking, so extensively studied in conditioned-response experiments, for it may involve widespread activities of the viscera, the endocrine glands, and the skeletal muscles. The important point, however, is that fear responses differ from eyeblinks in degree rather than in kind of activity, so that learning principles applicable to the one should help us understand the other.

Every student in a course in general psychology knows of J. B. Watson's experiments with little Albert. He was a healthy child in his first year who showed no initial fear of a white rat. After a series of learning experiences in which an iron bar behind him was struck loudly just as he began to reach for the animal, the boy began to show the same reaction to the rat that he had naturally made to the noise—starting violently, drawing back, and screaming. Watson was also able to show that these fear responses had *generalized* to a number of stimuli similar in one way or another to the white rat. Albert had learned to fear all kinds of furry or fuzzy objects—cotton wool, a fur coat, a Santa Claus mask.

Perhaps even more important for therapy than Watson's early experiments were some attempts to eliminate such experimentally induced fears by conditioned-response methods. Mary Cover Jones (1925) succeeded in overcoming a child's fear of a furry animal (in this case a rabbit) by presenting the animal to him at a time when he was reacting positively to food. If the experimenter was careful at first to keep the animal far enough away so that the strength of the fear tendency did not overbalance the strength of the positive food-taking tendency, she found that eventually the sight of the animal itself was enough to initiate pleasant rather than fearful feelings.

Down through the years this kind of model has often been used in the treatment of particular fears. Meyer (1957), for example, cured a woman of a crippling fear of going out by herself by first establishing in her a strong positive feeling toward her therapist and then conditioning this feeling to the outside world. First she walked with him for a little while in the hospital roof garden. Afterward they extended the range of their walks, first to the hospital grounds, then to back streets, then to main thoroughfares. As the patient came to feel more positively toward these formerly feared situations, she was able to behave normally in them even without the therapist's presence.

Other workers have devoted efforts to devising ways of training patients in habits that would counteract every sort of neurotic manifestation. The most widely known of these endeavors produced the progressive relaxation technique of Jacobson (1938). One behavioral component of the neuroses, including their psychosomatic accompaniments, is undesirable muscular tension. It seemed to Jacobson that if a person could train his perceptions to recognize initial signs of the build-up of excessive muscular tension and then train his muscles to relax voluntarily, he would have in his own hands a powerful tool for combating neurotic difficulties, whatever their sources. The Jacobson relaxation techniques form a system of therapy that can be applied by general medical practitioners and physical therapists as well as by psychiatrists.

Another attempt to build a general habit that will eliminate all kinds of neurotic responses is Salter's method of conditioned-reflex therapy (1949). Salter's basic model is the classical Palvovian conditioning experiment. The only one of Pavlov's specific ideas that he uses extensively, however, is the concept of a conflict between inhibitory and excitatory processes in the brain. The neurotic, whatever his symptoms, is a person too much in the grip of inhibitory processes. The thing he needs most is to have his general level of excitation raised. To accomplish this, Salter trains his patients to express their feelings even when they are hostile or sad, to assert themselves on all occasions, to use the word *I* as much as possible, to act on impulse instead of planning ahead. Through such *re*conditioning he tries to overcome the *mal*conditioning of the past.

Salter, along with various other workers who think of therapy as habit change, uses hypnosis or waking suggestion as an accessory technique. The most difficult part of this kind of habit-molding is often to create a situation in which the new response will actually occur. Posthypnotic suggestion may accomplish this. For example, if a singer is crippled by stage fright, some way must be found of making her sing with confidence in front of a crowd, so that confident singing may be reinforced. If she is hypnotizable, appropriate suggestions can be given that she will feel strong and secure when she comes on stage for a certain concert. Once this happens, the applause of the audience will serve to reinforce the kind of habits she is seeking to strengthen and she is started on the road toward the elimination of the stage fright. The procedure will doubtless have to be repeated over a period of time if steady progress is to be made.

During the last 40 years or more, ever since behaviorist psychologists first demonstrated that emotional reactions could be modified by learning, this approach to therapy has been available, but it has never really "caught on." Jacobson and Salter have had their followers, but their methods have never been widely adopted. There is sporadic use of hypnosis for this purpose, but it is not considered standard treatment for habit malfunctions, nor the primary use of hypnosis. This lack of enthusiasm is due partly to the fact that those methods sound better in theory than they actually work out in practice. Some patients change their habits, others do not. The complexities of human life are so great that the isolation of any particular stimulus-response pattern may present insuperable difficulties. Nevertheless, these therapeutic methods have survived as alternatives to the more influential systems. For the individual case and for the theorist or researcher who wishes to strike out in a different direction, there is ready at hand a body of knowledge and experience with these methods on which to draw. It should also be added that this habit-change approach, though drawing on learning theory, is based on a pretty elementary kind of learning theory. Other therapeutic methods utilizing more complex ideas about learning have been developed; these will be mentioned later on. The further application of learning principles to clinical work would seem to be a very important line for psychologists to pursue.

WOLPE'S PSYCHOTHERAPY BY RECIPROCAL INHIBITION

The fullest and most systematic account of habit-change therapy, and therefore the most satisfactory one, has been published by the South African psychiatrist, Wolpe (1958). His theory as to the nature of neurosis underlies the specific techniques he has developed for its treatment. This theory is based primarily on laboratory work in which experimental neuroses in animals were produced and treated. Wolpe's own experiments in this field figure most prominently, but the theory accounts for the findings of other investigators as well.

Let us look first at his theory of neurosis. The basic definition is admirably simple: "Neurotic behavior is any persistent habit of unadaptive behavior acquired by learning in a physiologically normal organism" (Wolpe, 1958, p. 32). Almost every word in this definition is important—*persistent, unadaptive, learning, physiologically normal*—and each can be pinned down to a fairly precise meaning. The central idea is that neurotic behavior has been *learned* and thus can be *unlearned* or replaced by more adaptive kinds of behavior if the right stimulating situation can be set up.

Anxiety, an important concept in almost all theories of neurosis, is important here too. But as Wolpe uses the word, it is synonymous with fear. It may be more pervasive and occur as a response to many more kinds of stimuli, but it is, like any fear, a response to a stimulus. All of its well-known physiological concomitants, such as rapid pulse rate, raised blood pressure, sweating, are part of the total fear response.

How does Wolpe think human neurotic behavior is acquired? First of all, there are predisposing conditions in the make-up of some persons, based either on hereditary physiological idiosyncrasies or on the previous development of anxiety through learning. Second, the person is exposed to a stress situation, which may be one of several types. It may be very intense, painful stimulation such as the prisoner in a concentration camp might undergo. It may be a severe threat or conflict from within the personality. It may be a summation of a number of experiences, no one of them intense enough by itself to produce a neurotic response. Third, there are two kinds of responses, either one or both of which can be conditioned to all stimuli present in the stress situation. The first kind are high-intensity anxiety responses; the second kind are derived responses such as hysterical responses and some kinds of obsessional behavior. Lastly, secondary anxiety-relieving activities may be learned. These include physical avoidance of stimuli, displacement of attention, drug-taking, and anxiety-relieving obsessions.

This formulation of the origin of neuroses suggests the kinds of therapeutic intervention Wolpe thinks are *most likely to succeed* in overcoming them. To *extinguish* or abolish the unadaptive habits would appear to be almost impossible because of the pervasiveness of anxiety responses and their attachment to innumerable stimuli. Furthermore, the person's unwillingness to encounter situations that increase his anxiety make it extremely unlikely that he will ever undergo enough unreinforced trials to produce extinction. What seems a more promising approach is to design a situation in such a way that a response incompatible with the neurotic responses will occur. When this happens the strength of the neurotic response decreases through "reciprocal inhibition." Tersely stated, the principle is as follows: *If a response antagonistic to anxiety can be made to occur in the presence of anxiety-evoking stimuli so that it is accompanied by a complete or partial suppression of the anxiety responses, the bond between these stimuli and the anxiety responses will be weakened* (Wolpe, 1958, p. 71).

The last half of Wolpe's book explains in detail the procedures he uses to put these principles into effect. The first step is to arrange one or more interviews designed to obtain as clear a picture as possible of the nature of the patient's anxiety reactions—what they are like and under what circumstances they occur. A life history is taken, but the emphasis is on the present rather than the past. During this phase, the therapist maintains an objective, nonjudgmental attitude. As part of this diagnostic interviewing he administers a brief personality inventory to assess the amount of neurotic anxiety that is present.

The second step is to explain the model and the plan of attack to the patient. The therapist makes a brief statement in which he shows with down-to-earth examples how a neurosis gets started. He then points out what the pattern seems to have been in the patient's particular case and explains that the task is one of weakening the neurotic habits by strengthening some responses antagonistic to them.

The kinds of responses Wolpe has identified that may be expected to have such inhibitory effects on anxiety are: (1) assertive responses; (2) sexual responses, (3) relaxation responses, (4) respiratory responses; (5) "anxiety-relief" responses, (6) competitively conditioned motor responses, (7) pleasant responses in the life situation (with drug enhancement), and (8a) interview-induced emotional responses and (b) abreaction (Wolpe, 1958, p. 113). The last two kinds may occur spontaneously; the first six must be planned by the therapist so that they occur in some strength in situations where the cues for anxiety are present. Which kind of response he decides to use depends to a considerable extent on what the patient is anxious about.

In some cases the patient is trained to produce the positive response in life situations. A shy, timid person, for example, may be schooled in giving assertive responses. Role-playing may be used as a part of such training. A man suffering from impotence may be shown how, with the cooperation of his sexual partner, he can set up a situation in which the positive sexual response will become strong enough to inhibit his anxiety. Relaxation is used a great deal in connection with those strategies. As Jacobson has shown, a person who knows how to produce relaxation responses in himself can gain control of various situations that would otherwise cripple him.

Perhaps the most interesting special technique that Wolpe describes is what he calls "systematic desensitization based on relaxation." Before putting this into effect, the therapist has drawn up a list of anxiety-producing situations, arranged in order of severity, based on what he has learned from his patient during his interviews. Such a hierarchy will range from situations the patient finds almost intolerable, through those he finds moderately disturbing, down to those that bother him only slightly. He then trains the patient in the Jacobson relaxation techniques. At the first of the special desensitization sessions he hypnotizes him and tells him to relax deeply. At this point he asks him to imagine a certain scene very vividly, raising his hand if he feels disturbed. The therapist uses first a scene from the low end of the patient's list of anxiety-producing situations. Usually this produces no disturbance because it is too weak to counteract the general relaxation. After about two or three seconds of this he moves up to the next situation in the list, asking the patient to imagine it as vividly as possible. If he signals any disturbance the procedure is discontinued, and in any event it is stopped for the day after several such scenes have been reacted upon. The patient is then roused from the hypnotic state and questions about how he felt while it was going on.

Over a series of sessions, therapist and patient gradually work themselves up to the top of the anxiety hierarchy. As the anxiety response
becomes weaker, the person can tolerate a more intense stimulus. If all
goes well, he finds after a number of such sessions that things that used
to throw him into a panic no longer trouble him at all.

The following example illustrates this procedure:

The conduct of desensitization sessions

An account will be given of the exact details of procedure at one patient's
desensitization sessions—her first session and two ~~two~~ successive sessions when
therapy was well under way. This patient had the following anxiety hierarchies
(the most disturbing items being on top, as always):

Hierarchies

A. Fear of hostility
    1. Devaluating remarks by husband
    2. Devaluating remarks by friends
    3. Sarcasm from husband or friends
    4. Nagging
    5. Addressing a group
    6. Being at social gathering of more than four people (the more the
       worse)
    7. Applying for a job
    8. Being excluded from a group activity
    9. Anybody with a patronizing attitude

B. Fear of death and its accoutrements
    1. First husband in his coffin
    2. At a burial
    3. Seeing a burial assemblage from afar
    4. Obituary notice of young person dying of heart attack
    5. Driving past a cemetery
    6. Seeing a funeral (the nearer the worse)
    7. Passing a funeral home
    8. Obituary notice of old person (worse if died of heart disease)
    9. Inside a hospital
    10. Seeing a hospital
    11. Seeing an ambulance

C. Fear of symptoms (despite *knowing* them to be nonsignificant)
    1. Extrasystoles
    2. Shooting pains in chest and abdomen
    3. Pains in left shoulder and back
    4. Pain on top of head
    5. Buzzing in ears
    6. Tremor of hands
    7. Numbness or pain in fingertips
    8. Dyspnea after exertion (shortness of breath)
    9. Pain in left hand (old injury)

First desensitization session (12th interview)[1]

Before this interview the patient had learned to relax most of the muscles in her body. At our last meeting hypnosis had been discussed, and as she was afraid of it, I had tried to reassure her.

After some discussion about other matters, I told her that we would now try to have a hypnotic session. As she was comfortably seated, I said, "Rest a hand on each thigh. In response to suggestions that I shall give you, you will notice various things happen to your hands. However, if at any time you feel anxious at what is happening, you will be able to interrupt the proceedings immediately. You will at no stage lose consciousness."

Her hands having settled comfortably on her lap, I went on, "Look at your hands and keep on looking at them. At the same time I want you to give your fullest attention to the sensations in your hands, whatever they may be. At this moment you may be aware of the texture of your skirt, of the warmth between your fingers and in your thighs, of tingling sensations, perhaps an awareness of your pulse, or the movement of air over your fingers. There may even be other sensations. Concentrate on your sensations, give them your complete attention, no matter what they are, and continue to do so. As you go on watching you will notice small movements appearing in your fingers. It will be interesting to see what finger moves first—maybe the thumb or little finger or index finger or the middle finger or even the fourth finger. (Right index finger moves.) There, your right index finger moved, and now, as you go on watching, you will notice other fingers move, and the general effect of these movements will be to spread the fingers farther and farther apart. (Movements appear in other fingers of the right hand.) Now you begin to notice that as the fingers spread apart, a feeling of lightness appears among the other sensations in your hand, and soon you will observe that your right hand begins to rise. Your right hand will become lighter and lighter and it will begin to lift. There, we can already see some slight arching of the right hand. Your hand goes up higher and higher. (Hand rises.) As it rises you will notice that the palm begins to turn slowly inward, because it is going to rise to your face. When your hand touches your face, you will be aware of a profoundly pleasant, heavy feeling throughout your body. Then, or even before then, your eyes will close. (Her hand slowly rises to her face and her eyes close.) Now you feel so pleasantly heavy and drowsy, you become heavier and heavier.

"Now let all the muscles of your body relax. Let relaxation grow deeper and deeper. We shall concentrate on the various zones of your body in turn. Relax the muscles of your forehead and those of the rest of your face. (Pause.) Relax all the muscles of your jaws and of your tongue. (Pause.) Relax the muscles of your eyeballs. (Pause.) Now relax your neck. (Pause.) Let the muscles of your shoulders and your arms relax. (Pause.) Relax the muscles of your back and your abdomen. (Pause.) Relax the muscles of your thighs and your legs. (Pause.) Let go more and still more. You become so calm, you feel so comfortable, nothing matters except to enjoy this pleasant, calm, relaxed state. (Pause.)

"Now I am going to give you some scenes to imagine and you will imagine them very clearly and calmly. If, however, by any chance anything that you imagine disturbs you, you will at once indicate this to me by raising your hand two or three inches. First I am going to give you a very commonplace

[1] The hypnotic induction procedure follows Wolberg (1948).

scene. Imagine that you are sitting alone in an armchair in the living room of your house. It is a very pleasant sunny day and you are sitting in this chair perfectly at ease. (Pause of about 5 seconds.) Next I want you to imagine the printed word *dentist*. (Pause of about 3 seconds.) Stop imagining this word and concentrate on relaxing your muscles. (Pause.) Now imagine that you are reading the newspaper and that your eye falls upon the headline, 'Prominent citizen dies at 86.' (Pause of about 3 seconds.) Stop imagining those words, and again concentrate on your muscles. Let them go completely. Enjoy this calm state."

After a minute or two, I said to the patient, "In a few moments, I'll count five and then you will wake up feeling very calm and refreshed. (Pause.) One, two, three, four, five."

She now opened her eyes and to my "How are you?" She said that she felt quite calm. Replying to further questions, she said that all three of the scenes had been clear and the only one that had disturbed her was the third one and the disturbance had even in this case been very slight. It may be noted that the first scene had nothing to do with the items on the hierarchy list. It was inserted as a kind of control, and a street scene or a flower or almost anything else which has no obvious relevance to the hierarchy items could equally well have been used. The word *dentist* was used as a kind of sensitivity test because of its vague associations with hospitals and illness.

Seventeenth desensitization session (32nd interview)

Since desensitization to the fear of hostility (sublist A) had progressed much more rapidly than the others, at the last few sessions this sublist had been set aside and our attention concentrated on the death fear and fear of symptoms. Six sessions before, we had begun to deal with funerals (B-6) on the hierarchy list. On the first occasion, the word *funeral* had alone been presented, and thereafter actual funerals had been presented, starting from two blocks away and then at decreasing distances as her reaction declined. At the previous session she had been made to imagine a funeral passing in the street in front of her and this had caused slight disturbance. Imagining a pain in her left shoulder had been just perceptibly disturbing. A scene of a woman in a film weeping had also been introduced because of its association with the idea of death and she had reacted very slightly to it.

At this session she was hypnotized in the same way as in the first session, but as would be expected, the procedure took much less time. When she was deeply relaxed, I spoke as follows:

"I am going to present a number of scenes to your imagination which you will imagine very clearly. It goes without saying that, if by any chance any scene should disturb you, you will indicate it by raising your left hand. First I want you to imagine that you are standing at a street corner and a funeral procession passes you. You may have some feeling of sadness, but apart from this you are absolutely calm. (Brief pause.) Stop the scene. (Pause of about 4 seconds.) Now I want you to imagine the same scene of the funeral passing in the street before you. (Pause of 6 or 7 seconds.) Now just relax. Think of nothing but your muscles. (Pause of about 15 seconds.) Now I want you to imagine the same scene of the funeral again. (Pause of about 8 seconds.) Stop imagining that scene and just relax. If the last presentation of that scene disturbed you even to the slightest degree I want you now to raise your left hand. (Hand does not rise.) Good. Now let yourself go still further. (Pause of about 15 seconds.) Now I want you to imagine last time's scene of the woman in the film weeping bitterly. (Pause of about 4 seconds.) Now stop imagining this scene and just relax. (Pause of about 15 seconds.) Now I want you again to imagine the scene of the weeping woman. (Pause of about 8 seconds.) Stop that scene and again think of nothing but relaxing. If the last presentation of that scene disturbed you in the slightest, please raise your left hand. (Hand does not rise.) Good. Relax. (Pause of about 15 seconds.) Now I want you to imagine that you have a pain in your left shoulder. (Pause of about 10 seconds.) Now stop that pain and think only of relaxing. (Pause of about 15 seconds.) Now again imagine you have a pain in your left shoulder. (Pause of about 10 seconds.) Stop that pain and think of your muscles only. Soon I'll count five and you will wake. (Pause.) One, two, three, four, five."

The patient was not asked during the trance to indicate if she had been disturbed by the shoulder pain, because I assumed—wrongly, as it turned out—that there would be no disturbance. (As stated earlier, patients usually do not spontaneously signal mild disturbances.) On waking, she stated that there had been a very slight disturbance to the first presentation of the funeral scene, less to the second, and none to the third. The weeping woman had not disturbed her at all, but each presentation of the pain in the shoulder had been very slightly disturbing.

Eighteenth desensitization session (33rd interview)

The hypnotic session was, as usual, preceded by a discussion of the patient's experiences of the past few days.

At this session the funeral scene and the one of the woman weeping were abandoned because it had been possible to present them without any disturbance whatever at the previous session. They were replaced by two new scenes, slightly higher on the hierarchy. The pain in the left shoulder was again presented because its presentation had not been completely free from disturbance last time. Having hypnotized the patient and made her relax, I spoke as follows:

"First we are going to have something already well familiar to you at these sessions—a pain in your left shoulder. You will imagine this pain very clearly and you will be not at all disturbed. (Pause of about 4 seconds.) Stop imagining this pain and again concentrate on your relaxing. (Pause of about 15 seconds.) Now again imagine that you have this pain in your left shoulder. (Pause of about 10 seconds.) Stop imagining the pain and again relax. (Pause of about 15 seconds.) Now I'd like you to imagine the pain in your left shoulder a third time, very clearly and calmly. (Pause of about 10 seconds.) Now stop this pain and focus your attention on your body, on the pleasant relaxed feeling that you have. If you felt in the least disturbed by the third presentation of this scene, I want you to indicate it by raising your left hand. (The hand does not rise.) Go on relaxing. (Pause of about 15 seconds.) Next I want you to visualize the following. You are in your car being driven by your husband along a pleasant road in hilly country. On a distant hillside you can clearly see the gray stones of a cemetery. (Pause of 2 or 3 seconds.) Now stop imagining this scene and think only of relaxing. Let yourself go completely. (Pause of about 15 seconds.) I want you again to imagine the same scene of the distant hillside cemetery. (Pause or 4 or 5 seconds.) Now stop imagining the scene and again think of your muscles and of letting them go still more. (Pause of about 15 seconds.) I want you to imagine that while you are standing in a queue at a drugstore you begin talking to the woman next to you and she tells you that her husband has been very short of breath since he had his heart attack. (Pause of 2 or 3 seconds.) Now cut that scene short and relax. (Pause of about 15 seconds.) Now I want you to imagine the same scene again very clearly and calmly. (Pause of about 4 seconds.) Stop imagining this scene and relax."

On waking, the patient reported that the first presentation of the pain in her left shoulder had been very slightly disturbing, but by the third presentation it had not disturbed her at all. The first presentation of a distant cemetery had been fairly disturbing but the second much less so. The woman in the drugstore whose husband had had a heart attack had disturbed her considerably the first time and somewhat less the second time.

Two remarks must be made here. First, it was not imperative to present the two new scenes only twice each, but experience with this patient had shown that new scenes did not entirely lose their power to disturb at the first session at which they were given, so that to force the pace would have taken up time and gained nothing.

Second, it will have been noticed that although the scenes presented follow the general idea of the hierarchy list, they do not conform to it absolutely, and the therapist may introduce variations according to his discretion and his knowledge of the case (Wolpe, 1958, Ch. 9).

This example shows with admirable clarity just how Wolpe proceeds. (The reader may also wish to examine a similar case report by Rachman, 1959). Let us turn now to a discussion of some of the questions it raises.

USE OF ASSESSMENT IN HABIT-CHANGE THERAPY

The therapist who chooses to work according to the procedures we have been discussing finds little use for the customary assessment procedures, with the exception of interviewing. He does not ordinarily think in terms that are used by psychological diagnosticians. The distinctions he needs to make between the major psychiatric groups—for example, hysteria vs. obsessional neurosis—are clear from the discussion of symptoms. So is the answer to the principal question upon which treatment rests: With what situations are this patient's anxiety responses connected?

The one purpose for which Wolpe uses a test is to determine how severe the neurotic reactions are. Just why he chose the 25-item Willoughby Personality Schedule for this purpose he does not say. It is, perhaps, as good as most of the inventories that purport to measure general neuroticism. One major defect is that its form—25 items, each to be rated on a five-point scale—leaves it open to influence from any special kind of response set that may be operating in the patient.

Wolpe indeed has little to say about just how he uses this or any other assessment device in making decisions as to which of the various techniques he outlines—role-playing, real-life practice, hypnosis—should be used in an individual case. This decision would seem to rest on the thorough study of the symptom pattern that occurs in early interviews. The decision as to which patients are not amenable to such therapeutic procedures at all is made on the basis of trial sessions.

If conditioned-response techniques are to become standard treatment procedures for neurosis it would seem desirable to coordinate them with a much more thorough study of the personalities of patients who are treated than has been made so far. Are patients who benefit from this sort of treatment similar to those who benefit from client-centered therapy or psychoanalysis? Does it produce the same kinds of personality change by different means, or does it constitute an entirely different kind of influence?

CRITICAL EVALUATION

In the previous chapter it has been explained that research on any variety of therapeutic procedure can be classified either as *outcome research* or *process research*. Client-centered therapists have done both, but their greatest interest is in process research. The opposite is true for the therapists whose work is explicitly grounded in conditioned response, a process presumed to be well known. Simple outcome research thus seems most important to them. The question that interests them is: Do these methods really benefit patients?

It is to Wolpe's credit that he gives us detailed answers to this question. His criteria for effectiveness of treatment are those formulated by Knight (1941): symptomatic improvement, increased productiveness, improved adjustment and pleasure in sex, improved interpersonal relationships, and ability to handle ordinary psychological and reality stresses. Not all of these criteria are applicable to every patient, and the major emphasis falls on improvement of symptoms. Patients are classified into five groups: (1) apparently cured, (2) much improved, (3) moderately improved, (4) slightly improved, and (5) unimproved.

Of the 210 cases Wolpe has treated by reciprocal inhibition methods, 39 per cent are classified as apparently cured, 50.5 per cent much improved, 7.2 per cent slightly or moderately improved, and 3.3 per cent unimproved. This is an impressive record. As mentioned in the preceding chapter, the proportion of patients cured or much improved usually does not run higher than 60 to 70 per cent.

It is made more impressive by the fact that follow-up information on 45 of the patients in the two top groups showed that only one had relapsed. Forty-four of them had held their own or gained ground over a period of not less than two years.

There is, however, one kind of doubt that arises with regard to these reported results. It is the ever-present possibility of special selective factors in the group of patients on which they are based. Wolpe recognized two points at which selective influences might enter: One is the point at which patients are accepted for treatment in the first place. On this score perhaps we can agree there are no complications. He reports that he undertook to treat anyone whose diagnosis was *neurosis*. The other is the selection of cases to be included in the series on which the report is based. Here he set up what seems at first to be a reasonable criterion— that the patient should have undergone an adequate *amount* of therapy.

However, the judgment as to whether a patient has remained under treatment long enough to give the techniques a fair trial opens up a good deal of uncertainty, and more research on the question would seem to be badly needed. How many persons are not able to accept this kind of therapy? Do they differ in personality characteristics from those who react to it favorably? Are they similar to those who drop out of client-centered or psychoanalytic therapy without really giving it a fair trial? How about the influence of social class, or ego strength, or intelligence?

We shall return to the general problem of attrition in groups of patients who start therapy in Chapter 19. Suffice it to say at this point that here is a major challenge to therapists of all schools and that some progress has been made in the research attack on it.

Wolpe's book is the most systematic account of a program of psychotherapy based on conditioned-response principles. But outcome research has been carried on in a few other specific areas where somewhat similar methods have been applied to the treatment of abnormalities of behavior. One such problem is nocturnal enuresis. Since the 1930's, equipment has been available that is designed to associate bladder distention with waking up. The child lies on a pad constructed in such a way that as soon as any moisture touches its metal parts, an electrical circuit is closed and a bell rings. The bell is, of course, a natural stimulus for awakening. Conditioned-response principles would lead us to predict that the sensations from bladder distention immediately preceding the sound of the bell would soon be sufficient in themselves to wake the patient up. Several outcome studies have reported about 70 per cent success in curing enuresis by these methods. In one of the most complete, that of Baller and Schalock (1956), out of 55 patients treated, 90 per cent showed marked improvement immediately following a few weeks of treatment, and a two-year follow-up indicated that in 65 to 70 per cent of the cases, results were still good. An interesting sidelight is that 24 of the 25 cases interviewed to secure more than the minimum information about the effects of the treatment reported favorable personality changes in addition to the elemination of the enuresis. Both social relationships and general "disposition" were said to have improved.

Another special area in which treatment methods based on conditioned responses have been quite extensively used is alcoholism. The procedure here is to combine an alcoholic drink as a conditioned stimulus with an emetic drug. The vomiting, or at least the nausea, produced by the drug becomes associated with the taste of the alcoholic beverage so that the patient is no longer able to drink it. Voegtlin and Lemere (1950), reporting on 4096 cases they had treated over a 13-year period, indicated that 60 per cent had abstained from drinking for one year or longer, 51 per cent for two years or longer, 38 per cent for five years or longer, and 23 per cent for ten years or longer. Reports from other institutions using these techniques vary. Some show a high percentage of cures, others low.

Fortunately, there has been a careful study of this method and three others carried out by the Menninger Clinic (Wallerstein, 1957). Alcoholic patients were assigned at random to the four kinds of treatment that were to be compared: (1) antabuse (a drug therapy), (2) conditioned-reflex, (3) group hypnotherapy, and (4) milieu therapy (environmental control). The conditioned-reflex technique turned out to be the least successful of the four, with only 24 per cent of the total number of patients assigned to it classified as improved. By comparison, the other physiological treatment with the drug antabuse produced a 53 per cent improvement rate. For the two psychological treatments the proportion of "cures" was 36 per cent for group hypnotherapy and 26 per cent for milieu therapy. An interesting aspect of this study is its analysis of the kinds of personality responding best to each of the treatments. Since the conditioned-response treatment is a highly threatening, unpleasant experience, the aggressive rebel against it and try to defeat its purpose, but those who feel guilty and depressed about their addiction tend to welcome it as a needed punishment.

All in all, research on treating neurosis by eradicating or forming specific habits indicates that the approach holds some promise. What seems to be needed now is a research in which personality assessment would play a larger part. We need to know what kinds of patients react to it most favorably and for what kinds it is likely to fail. If it turns out that these methods work for some persons who are not able to carry out the complex exploration of inner experience that is required for client-centered or analytic therapy, we will have added a considerable resource to the practicing clinician. If, on the other hand, results indicate that this variety of therapy is failing with the same kinds of individuals as the others are, the challenge of developing new ways to help such people must be met. The Wallerstein study cited above is an admirable example of the kind of evaluative research needed in many areas other than alcoholism.

INFLUENCE OF LEARNING RESEARCH ON THEORIES OF THERAPEUTIC CHANGE

In spite of the tremendous prestige and influence of laboratory research on learning, methods of therapy deliberately modeled on such experimental situations have never really become popular in psychology or psychiatry. But what has become a movement of considerable importance in clinical psychology is the attempt to build a theory of what happens in *all* the more common kinds of therapy interviews that will be congruent with learning theory models developed in the laboratory. Dollard and Miller (1950) have brought together the central concepts of Hullian learning theory and Freudian psychoanalysis. Shoben (1949, 1953) shows how the circumstances of the therapeutic interview operate to produce in the patient a new "comfort reaction," replacing the anxiety or fear reaction that has generated the rest of his difficulties. Among others who have applied learning theory to psychotherapy and counseling are Mowrer's (1953), Pepinsky & Pepinsky (1954), and Rotter (1954). Most of these systematic applications have come from the stimulus-response branch of learning theory, rather than the perceptual-cognitive side.

During the 1950's several ingenious attempts to demonstrate the applicability of the learning principles formulated by Skinner (1953, 1957) have been made. The one most discussed has been the Greenspoon experiment (1955) showing that if an interviewer said "Uh huh" every time an interviewee used a plural noun, the frequency of plurals could be significantly increased without the client's awareness of any change. A considerable number of subsequent experiments have shown that the client's *verbal* behavior can indeed be changed by means of selective reinforcement consisting of nothing but unobtrusive indicators of approval on the part of the therapist.

This finding, and the many repetitions of it by others, has raised interesting questions for those who wish to carry on therapy and to understand how it works. What has come to be called the "Greenspoon effect" does not occur under all conditions, though Krasner (1958a), in reviewing 31 studies, reported a majority of positive results. Changes of this sort in verbal behavior may or may not be accompanied by changes in relationships to other persons and increased general competence in the business of living. How safe is it to judge the success of therapy by what the patient is *saying* when he completes it? Other questions can be raised about the practicality and complexity in applying such procedures to clinical populations. Patterson, Helper, and Wilcott (1960), for instance, have shown with disturbed children that there is a negative relation between conditionability and anxiety—the reverse of what is found in normal samples.

Interest in learning theory and interest in psychotherapy have been central concerns of American psychology for many years. Whether they work in laboratory or clinic, most psychologists agree that therapy is in some sense a learning process. However, as was said earlier, the majority of them are not impressed with the techniques Jacobson, Salter, or Wolpe have worked out in an attempt to model therapy on the methods and principles of the experimental laboratory. Experienced psychotherapists are so much aware of the complexity of human personality that systems and methods like Wolpe's inevitably impress them as oversimplifications. What they are interested in, however, is building a personality theory that will synthesize the results of laboratory experiments and the experience gained in therapy. To be sure, nobody has quite "pulled this off" yet, but the challenge remains.

SUMMARY

The task of therapy can be seen as an attempt to change certain habits of the patient. Over the years since the discovery of conditioning by Pavlov and the demonstration of the learning of fear response by Watson, there have been scattered attempts to apply learning principles to psychotherapy. These attempts are based on more than concern with a single habit such as handwashing, and become really complex when therapists attempt to deal with the learning of anxiety or the generalization of responses to new stimuli. Jacobson has attempted to teach muscular relaxation to persons troubled with anxiety. Salter attempted to strengthen excitatory responses and weaken inhibitory responses. Wolpe has tried out a wide variety of techniques aimed at the central principle of eliciting a response which is antagonistic to anxiety in the presence of the anxiety-evoking stimuli. Wolpe reports impressive data on the successes achieved by his method of treatment, but there is a need for others to duplicate and otherwise study the same procedures. Conditioning methods have been used by other researchers with considerable success in cases of eneuresis and mixed success in cases of alcoholism. Since learning is assumed to underlie or influence most maladjustment and mental illness, learning principles would seem to have great potential value for ultimately clarifying the nature of the psychotherapeutic process.

SUGGESTED READINGS

DOLLARD, J., and MILLER, N. E. *Personality and psychotherapy.* New York: McGraw, 1950.

These authors apply the learning theory of Hull to the fields of personality and psychotherapy. Their basic concepts are drives (both primary and learned), cues (stimuli for responses), responses, and reinforcement. Symptoms are learned by virtue of their reinforcing effects, particularly through the reduction of the learned drive of fear. In the use of habits (learned cue-response connections), conflicts often arise. The task of psychotherapy is to strengthen tendencies to approach desired goals and lessen avoidance tendencies.

EYSENCK, H. J. A rational system of diagnosis and therapy in mental illness. In L. E. Abt & B. F. Riess (Eds.), *Progress in clinical psychology,* Vol. IV. New York: Grune & Stratton, 1960. Pp. 46-64.

Eysenck, whose work derives both from Pavlov and the British factor analysts, here describes his so-called "behavior therapy," based on the simple thesis that neurotic symptoms are but learned patterns of unadaptive behavior. As he put it: "There is no neurosis underlying the symptom, but merely the symptom itself. Eliminate the symptoms and you have eliminated the neurosis (p. 60)." His therapy, unlike psychoanalysis, which he calls mentalistic, is concentrated almost entirely on the patient's behavior. Eysenck puts no faith in the notion that removal of one set of symptoms leads to anxiety or alternative symptoms, but asserts that removal of one symptom facilitates the removal of others. Underlying his system of therapy is a system of diagnosis along the major dimensions of neuroticism and introversion-extraversion, with some associated hypotheses about the conditionability of persons falling at different places on these continua.

MEDNICK, S. A. A learning theory approach to research in schizophrenia. *Psychol, Bull.,* 1958, 55, 316-327.
Mednick proposes the idea that schizophrenia is characterized by repeated occurrence of remote associative responses in the context of anxiety-provoking thoughts. The remote associations reduce anxiety, since they remove from awareness other thoughts that arouse anxiety. The author postulates a mechanism to explain the introduction of remote associative responses—that increased drive leads to increased generalization of learned responses.

WILLIAMS, C. D. The elimination of tantrum behavior by extinction procedures. *J. abnorm. soc. Psychol.,* 1959, 59, 269.
This is a one-page report on the handling of a problem which frequently confronts inexperienced parents—a child's screaming and demanding behavior when he is put to bed. Applying the learning principle that non-reinforced responses extinguish themselves, the parents decided to put their twenty-one-month-old boy to bed in a leisurely fashion and then shut the door and let him scream. The length of crying each night was recorded and plotted on a curve. The extinction curve was similar to that obtained in subhuman learning studies. There apparently were no unfortunate side effects.

KLINE, M. V. Hypnosis and clinical psychology. In L. E. Abt & B. F. Riess (Eds.), *Progress in clinical psychology.* Vol. IV. New York: Grune & Stratton, 1960. Pp. 65-84.
Kline's review of theories of hypnosis and research about it indicates that hypnosis is being used more and more in a variety of studies—medical, dental, psychiatric, and psychological. Hypnosis is useful in the management of behavioral problems in obstetrics, surgery, and dentistry as well as for psychotherapy. At the present time hypnosis is not considered to be in itself a form of psychotherapy. It is used by therapists to make more meaningful and penetrating many of the same kinds of interactions that occur in therapeutic interviews where hypnosis is not used.

RESEARCH EXAMPLES

SALZINGER, K., and PISONI, STEPHANIE. Reinforcement of affect responses of schizophrenics during the clinical interview. *J. abnorm. soc. Psychol.,* 1958, 57, 84-90.
This is an early investigation of verbal conditoning using schizophrenics as subjects. The authors interviewed 36 hospitalized schizophrenics, 16 of whom were controls and given no special conditioning period. The 20 in the experimental group were interviewed by two different interviewers.

After a standard introductory period, there were three periods: (1) First came a ten-minute (operant level) period during which the interviewer kept the conversation going to establish a base line of spontaneous "affect" responses. (2) During the second ten-minute (conditioning) period, the experimenter reinforced every self-referent "affect" response with verbal agreement, "I see," "mmm-hmm," or "Yeah." Affect responses were defined as any expression beginning with *I* or *we* and followed by an expression of affect: "I liked her," "I am upset," "We enjoyed it," or "I feel—." (3) In the third ten-minute (extinction) period, the experimenter withheld all reinforcement but continued asking questions.

The interviews were recorded and coded independently by the two interviewers. Intercoder reliability was high. There were also no significant differences between interviewers when they interviewed the same patients, demonstrating that affective verbal responses can be reliably counted. There was no significant difference between the base line of the experimental group and the control group.

Significantly more self-referent affective responses were emitted during the conditioning period. The number of reinforcements was directly related to the resistance to extinction. Though the conditioning effects were significant for the total experimental group, there were wide individual differences within the group and some patients gave no evidence of changing in response to the conditioning procedure.

The authors conclude from the lawfulness of their findings that the clinical interview is subject to investigation by experimental techniques. The experiment demonstrates the applicability of the findings of Greenspoon and others and suggests that Skinner's theoretical concepts can be applied to clinical populations.

There have been a few demonstrations of the applicability of the concepts of verbal conditioning in actual therapy interviews (e.g., Richard et al., 1960). For an excellent review of the literature and a persuasive argument for considering the therapist as a social reinforcement machine, see Krasner's paper for the APA's Second Conference on Research in Psychotherapy.

KING, G. F., ARMITAGE, S. G., and TILTON, J. R. A therapeutic approach to schizophrenics of extreme pathology: an operant-interpersonal method. *J. abnorm. soc. Psychol.,* 1960, 61, 276-286.

This is a very interesting example of the work growing out of Skinner's theories on operant conditioning. Described as a nonverbal method of bringing very regressed chronic schizophrenics into progressively greater interaction with reality. The authors describe and illustrate their Multiple Operant Problem-Solving Apparatus which was built into an eight-by-eight-foot panel in the alcove of a room in a psychiatric hospital. The subject must operate levers in response to certain stimuli. The rewards for correct performance were chocolate candies or cigarettes. The operator of the apparatus used very little verbal communication, at least in the initial stages. Some of the patients were so withdrawn at first that their hands had to be placed on the levers and moved, and the operator had to pick up the candy reward and put it in the patient's mouth. During the different phases of the conditioning process, only a simple mechanical response to a flashing light was required. Later in the series of problems complex cooperative efforts with another patient were necessary if reinforcement was to occur.

For the purposes of this study 48 chronic schizophrenic male patients were transferred to a special ward. They were divided into four groups of 12, matched on age, length of hospitalization, and a specially constructed measure of severity of illness (the Extreme Mental Illness Schedule). The 12 patients undergoing operant-interpersonal therapy were seen three times a week for 15 weeks in therapeutic sessions lasting 20 to 30 minutes. There were three control groups: A verbal therapy group with whom the same amount of time was devoted to individual (and later group) psychotherapy; a recreational therapy group given three to five hours a week of special activities; and a no-therapy group who were given no special attention beyond the usual ward activities.

The results of each of the programs was assessed by several ratings of improvement at the end of the experimental period. In the operant-interpersonal therapy group, 5 of the 12 subjects were rated as showing considerable improvement (one patient even being transferred to an open ward) and three showed minor improvement. The next best results were from recreational therapy, with two being considerably improved and the two showing minor improvement. At the time of a follow-up six months later, the operant group still showed significantly less pathology. Other comparisons favoring the operant method were level of verbalization, motivation to leave the ward, less resistance to therapy, more interest in occupational therapy, and decreased eneuresis, although the amount of many of these changes was not striking. The patients undergoing verbal therapy actually became somewhat more withdrawn verbally.

In interpreting the results the authors speculate about what might be gained by additional and more complex operant interpersonal therapy. They believe that in such extreme cases it is necessary that the therapy be nonverbal, at least at the beginning. They seem to contemplate a development of therapeutic learning machines comparable to the teaching machines now being developed. The authors state their belief, however, that there are probably organic or constitutional factors in schizophrenia which set limits on what may be expected from this kind of treatment.

ORNE, M. T. The nature of hypnosis: artifact and essence. *J. abnorm. soc. Psychol.*, 1959, 58, 277-299.

(NOTE: Hypnosis is such an important psychological phenomenon that it deserves more attention than is being given it in this book, or, for that matter, in scientific psychology in general. As mentioned elsewhere, the primary use of hypnosis is not to change specific habits. It is much more commonly combined with other approaches to therapy, such as psychoanalysis, and employed as a method for accomplishing insight or catharsis more quickly and effectively. There is as yet no adequate body of theory or research to explain hypnotic phenomenon. It might be fruitful to consider hypnosis along with suggestion, attitude change, effects of propaganda, brainwashing, and faith healing in the general area of communication of influence. The Stanford Hypnotic Susceptibility Scale (Weitzenhoffer & Hilgard, 1959), should be an aid to assessment and research. The present article is an important new departure, turning the attention of research workers toward hypnosis as a special aspect of interpersonal relationships and role-playing.)

Orne in these studies sets out to test aspects of the three leading theories of hypnosis: hypnosis as a desire on the part of the subject to play a role, hypnosis as heightened suggestibility, and hypnosis as an altered state of consciousness. A very important innovation which Orne made was to provide for "blind" controls over the hypnotist's knowledge about the past experience of the subject he hypnotizes. This is important because of the many possibilities that the hypnotist will give subtle directions to his subjects.

In the first experiment, the hypothesis was supported that the subject's "knowledge" about hypnosis influences his own hypnotic behavior. In two college classes, students were given lectures and demonstrations of hypnotic behavior. In one class it was emphasized that in induced hand catalepsy, it is the dominant hand that is affected. In the other class this was not mentioned. Volunteers from both classes were then sent to the experimenter without his knowing which class they came from. The result was a significant difference in catalepsy of the dominant hand in the group which had prior "knowledge" about the matter.

The second experiment was a repetition of an earlier study originally done by someone else. It involved having hypnotized subjects "forget" their own past history and assume the history of someone, either a rich person or a poor person. Judgments made under the influence of these two histories were different. In Orne's work a control group was introduced. This group, which was instructed to fake the whole procedure, was mixed in with the group of "real" subjects. The hypnotist did not know to which group any individual belonged. The result was that the behavior of the simulating group in making judgments was indistinguishable from that of the "real" group. Some doubt is thus cast on the validity of hypnotic amnesia, and the idea that hypnotic subjects mainly do what they are asked to do in the experimental situation gains some support.

In the third experiment, nine subjects in a deep trance were asked to hold a kilogram weight at arm's length as long as they possibly could. Later, in a waking state, the same subjects were asked to hold the weight again and were "motivated" by rewards of money and by appeals to their pride. The result was that all but one subject in the waking state were able to surpass their performances during hypnosis. This finding casts strong doubt on the idea that physical capacity can be enhanced under hypnosis.

More informally, Orne investigated differences between "real" and "fake" subjects. He found that fakers flinched less and tolerated more pain from an electric shock than the real subjects. He did find differences, however, in the way the two groups handled hallucinations that the hypnotist suggested. The "real" group tolerated more logical inconsistencies, spontaneously saying such things as, "This is very peculiar. I can see Joe sitting in the chair, and I can see the chair through him."

All these studies point the way to more research on this very important aspect of human behavior. Other investigations on differences between "fake" and "real" should be undertaken. Such studies as we have make it pretty clear that hypnosis is in no sense a mysterious force, but is related to other more common forms of behavior.

15 Psychotherapy as Change in Concepts and Values

Though a considerable number of psychologists would agree that what goes on in a client during therapy is essentially a learning process, they would insist that the basic change that occurs is not so much in particular habits of behavior as it is in general outlook on life. Psychotherapy can be looked upon as the process of helping a person reorganize his ways of conceptualizing himself, his values, and his relations with others. As we have already seen, the theories Rogers has formulated use perceptual and cognitive concepts; however, in practice his therapy aims to elicit feelings rather than directly to produce rational changes in thoughts. In this chapter we shall review several theories which, however much they differ in detail, center around the attempt to change the patient's concepts.

THE VIEWS OF ADLER AND SEVERAL RECENT COGNITIVE CHANGE THEORISTS

Alfred Adler was probably the first among major psychotherapists to design a technique of therapy around the need to change the patient's general conception of his life, or, as he put it, his *style of life*. Each of us, early in childhood, develops his own individual style for solving the special problems of living. This unique pattern of interpreting and responding to experiences continues throughout life and is discernable by the astute therapist underneath all the patient's actions. Interwoven in this life pattern are likely to be mistaken premises which lead to neurotic difficulties. The task of the therapist is to discover what these erroneous assumptions are and to bring them to the understanding of the patient, thus modifying the person's life style to make it fit the facts of life better. Adler, first of Freud's students to break away, did so in protest against the mechanistic and biological conception of man which Freud held. He described his view, in contrast, as holistic, purposive, and social. Adler called his system *"individual psychology,"* intending to imply by this term that he was concerned with the total individual and not his parts. It is a somewhat misleading term in the light of present-day tendencies to contrast individual with social approaches. Actually, Adler's views were highly social. (Adler could very well find a place in our later chapter on interpersonal approaches to psychotherapy if it were not for his overriding insistence that the basic element in understanding a person is the discovery of his implicit concept of life—his life style.) Adler arrived at his emphasis on the social goals of individuals by a rather strange route. While still close to Freud, he saw the relation between a patient's symptoms and whatever bodily organs the patient felt were inadequate or inferior—the idea of *organ inferiority.* His defection from Freud began when he noticed the importance of inferiority feelings in life and how people attempted to *compensate* for these inferiorities. These ideas led him to recognize the significance of the individual's struggle for *power* and superiority over his surrounding social world. The basic pattern of this struggle originated early in life in interaction with the social pressures that arose from his particular *family constellation.* Finally Adler came to the conclusion that the solution to the problem of perennial competition was to develop an attitude of *social interest,* or social feeling (*Gemeinschaftsgefühl*), through which a person would cease to enter into power struggles with others and would associate himself cooperatively, though not submissively, in work for the common good. Thus Adler consciously incorporated a humanitarian value orientation into his conceptions of man's nature and of psychotherapy.

In beginning psychotherapy, the Adlerian therapist starts out with an extensive interview designed to elicit the life style and the patient's basic mistaken assumptions about life. The initial interview covers the patient's present complaints, his objective situation, an extensive review of his family constellation, his earliest recollections, and questions designed to get at the neurotic purposes of his symptoms, which might be, for example, to avoid unpleasantness of life or to gain more attention for himself. This interview results in a "diagnosis" of the patient's basic mistakes, which the therapist may immediately put before him quite frankly. Subsequently, he analyzes further revelations of the patient, pointing to his erroneous assumptions and his selfish social goals. Adlerians, though emphasizing the rational approach to difficulties of adjustment, are particularly alert to what they call the "social *movements*" of the person in the real world, since verbalizations are often used to cover up real underlying purposes. The therapy is usually of a very active kind, with the therapist using many different techniques, some quite dramatic, to get across his analysis of the patient's life style.

The Adlerians, both because their theory requires that they be concerned with the early family constellation and through their general social and humanistic values, have set up many child guidance centers. In these, the theory leads to directive counseling with the whole family. The counselor frequently interviews young children and their parents in front of an audience of other parents, teachers, and professional workers. In a very frank and open way, the counselor analyzes the family interaction which surrounds the development of behavior disorders. The Adlerian system stresses more than most approaches the importance of siblings and the manner in which a child struggles to find an advantageous place in interaction with his brothers and sisters. The usual practice of having an audience is thought to heighten the social influences on parents and children in changing their behaviors; at the same time, this procedure also provides an excellent opportunity for training many people in the Adlerian approach.

All manner of psychological disorders are seen as arising in the family context. For example, if a child's parents gratify his every whim, he quite naturally assumes that the world revolves around him and that the way to get what he wants is through the services of other people. Unless he is disabused of these ideas when he enters school and finds out what the complex world of other children is like, he will constantly be running up against neurosis-generating frustrations. The "mistakes" his style of life is built on must be corrected before he can deal in an effective manner with all of the circumstances he encounters. He is *not* the center of the universe and he will never be certain of persuading people outside his family to treat him this way. He must learn that the major satisfactions of life are *not* things that are handed to us by other people, but are things that we achieve or obtain by our own efforts.

These are only parts of Adlerian personality theory, but they are the parts upon which Adlerian therapy most clearly rests. Dreikurs and others who take this position today (see Ansbacher & Ansbacher, 1958; Dreikurs, Corsini, Lowe, & Sonstegard, 1959) have worked out techniques for helping parents to correct misconceptions in their children by changing their methods of dealing with them; also technicians that help the adult neurotic patient and his therapist identify and outline his life style, see where it is faulty, and modify it accordingly. Many people prefer Adlerian practices because they seem like an appealing common-sense attack upon neurosis and its therapy. It seems reasonable that man should be able to bring his capacity for rational problem-solving thinking to bear even on emotional difficulties.

It is an interesting fact that while Adlerian psychology has always occupied a minority position, apparently not very influential in personality theory as a whole, its essential ideas crop up again and again in the writings of other psychologists, often persons who begin with a Freudian psychoanalytic orientation. Some of these psychologists apparently have had no contact with Adler's work or writings and are unaware that their ideas resemble his. It is as though other persons, when they reach a certain stage in their own development, feel a need to break with Freud on essentially the same grounds that Adler originally did.

Ellis, as one example, recognized when it was brought to his attention that the ideas underlying his method of *rational psychotherapy* are similar in many respects to those of Adler (Ellis, 1957). Ellis has compiled an interesting list of the mistaken ideas he has found most commonly involved in neurosis. They are as follows:

1. That it is necessary to be loved and approved by everyone.
2. That one should be thoroughly competent and adequate.
3. That certain people are bad and should be punished.
4. That it is horrible or catastrophic when things are not as one would like them to be.
5. That unhappiness is externally caused.
6. That if a thing is dangerous, one must be terribly concerned about it.
7. That it is easier to avoid than to face life's responsibilities.
8. That one should be dependent and rely on someone stronger.
9. That the past is all-important.
10. That one should get upset over others' problems.
11. That it is exceptionally difficult to find the solution to human problems and catastrophic if one does not.
12. That human happiness can be achieved by inertia and inaction.

The methods Ellis uses for correcting such misconceptions involve both what he calls "counterpropaganda" and attempts to stimulate the client to take action of various kinds that will convince him that his assumptions are wrong. In another paper Ellis (1958) explains that the aim of this type of therapy is to attack the assertions or self-talk that *sustain* the neurotic process rather than the experience that originated it.

The effective therapist should continually keep unmasking his client's past and, especially, his present illogical thinking or self-defeating verbalizations by (a) bringing them to his attention or consciousness; (b) showing the client how they are causing and maintaining his disturbance and unhappiness; (c) demonstrating exactly what the illogical links in his internalized sentences are; and (d) teaching him how to rethink and reverbalize these (and other similar) sentences in a more logical, self-helping way. (Ellis, 1958, p. 39.)

There have been many other writers who have formulated similar aims and methods. The very influential "psychobiological" approach of Adolph

Meyer (1958; also see Muncie's synopsis, 1959), with its emphasis on common sense and objective practices, on treatment as negotiation, and on "reeducation," points in the same direction. Thorne (1950) finds a place for suggestion, persuasion, advice, and even pressure and coercion in his system of eclectic personality counseling. The most sophisticated and thorough statement of a theoretical system of this kind is Kelly's *Psychology of Personal Constructs* (1955). Kelly has developed a theory based on the idea that a person's psychological processes and behavior follow channels determined by the way he construes events in anticipation. The important thing in therapy is to understand first the personal constructs of the client, for which Kelly has developed an ingenious test. His system proposes that the client be unbound from his particular construct system so that he can try other alternatives. Kelly's therapeutic techniques include helping the client try out a different picture of himself through acting out in his daily life for a specified period of time a planned role. Kelly calls this "fixed role" therapy.

HOW THERAPY INTERVIEWS ARE CONDUCTED— THE PHILLIPS SYSTEM

We shall use as examples of the way therapy of this kind is handled, certain recommendations of Phillips (1956). In this book Phillips elaborates in some detail both the theoretical reasoning and the actual methods of dealing with clients that are involved in what he calls "assertion-structured" therapy. He sets forth first a four-point model in terms of which the client's difficulties are analyzed and plans for therapy formulated. The four key words are: *assertion, disconfirmation, tension, redundancy*. A person's behavior, including the symptoms that motivate him to seek therapy, represents some kind of assertion he is making about himself and his relationship to the world. For example, Mrs. Green, a neurotic woman, may be asserting by the way she acts in all her relationships with other people: "I am weak and helpless. You must take care of me." The *disconfirmation* comes from the fact that others do not make the responses that Mrs. Green shows by her actions she needs to have them make. Mr. Green, as an example, may counter his wife's declaration of helplessness with indifference, or by exhorting her to stand on her own feet, or even by asserting that it is he who needs care! This constant failure to obtain what she needs and thinks she has a right to expect leads to more tension and discomfort. The more tense she gets, the harder she tries to get what she is after. Since the only assertions she knows how to make about life are those she is already making, she reiterates them with more insistence than ever. This produces the *redundancy*, or circular effect, so often noted in describing neurotic behavior, its tendency to get worse rather than better. Mrs. Green may progress from timidity and tears to complete invalidism in her insistence that her husband must take care of her.

Phillips insists that when it comes to formulating a theory that will "rationalize" a form of therapy, "depth" concepts like "the unconscious," "repression," and the like—so widely used since Freud brought them to our attention—are not necessary. The neurotic pattern is visible as an aspect of the person's behavior. The assertions he is making can be inferred directly from that behavior. We need not search for the origin of symptoms in infancy or early childhood or for hidden unconscoius motivational forces. Phillips draws considerably upon the thinking about approach-avoidance conflicts that originated in experimental laboratory studies of the phenomenon. The difficulty a neurotic experiences in changing anything about his pattern of assertions is that he is caught between his positive and negative attitudes toward the same situations. One of the therapist's aims should be to reduce the person's negative feeling enough so that he can move in any positive direction he sees open to him.

In our example, it may be that Mrs. Green can see that if she would learn to drive the family car she would be less dependent on her husband and could manage her household affairs more efficiently. But her fear of driving, growing out of her general lack of confidence in her own capacities, is so strong that, although on several occasions she made arrangements with a driving school for lessons, the feeling grew to panic proportions as the hour set for the lesson approached and she canceled the appointment, afterwards feeling more worthless and unable to cope with life than ever. If the therapist can reduce her fear enough so that she is able to take a first driving lesson, the pattern of her life will have begun to change. All systems of therapy place great emphasis on a warm, secure, dependable relationship between client and therapist. In this system it is all-important because it is the means through which the negative motivation involved in approach-avoidance conflicts is reduced.

The active "teaching" manner in which a therapist attempts to help a patient understand the assertions he is making at the same time that he works for a reduction in the avoidance motives tied up in his particular approach-avoidance conflicts, is illustrated in this excerpt from a recording of the eighth therapy hour with a college student:

Patient. I had a hard time getting to school this morning.
Therapist. Oh, you did?
Pt. Couldn't get out of bed.
Th. This is pretty early for you, eh?
Pt. It is bad on Saturdays but on school days it is just misery. Ah . . . Saturdays and Sundays. The main thing I want to talk about today is responsibility.
Th. Yeah.
Pt. You've been saying it is a matter of my thinking something else is more important——

Th. Momentarily——

Pt. Well, even momentarily . . . well, the only thing I can say is . . . well, the . . . I just can't see this.

Th. OK, what's your notion about it?

Pt. The only thing I can see is . . . ah . . . and it seems very obvious to me . . . Well, this one course, B——, is giving me trouble and I'm afraid of it. I'm afraid because I know there are a lot of other smart people who are going to get A's and I don't think I can get A's.

Th. Shying away from competition?

Pt. Yeah . . . because I don't want the superiority notions I have disconfirmed.

Th. Yeah.

Pt. But . . . ah . . . it certainly is a compulsion . . . it certainly is . . . I mean . . if I were doing something like watching TV, that would be fine . . but I'm sitting there thinking *I gotta get to the work, I gotta get to the work,* but I can't, but I can't . . . then . . . I mean, doing nothing certainly isn't more important than doing something like studying—

Th. But you are doing something, you aren't ever doing nothing, are you?

Pt. Well, I mean——

Th. You're delaying, or you're saying "I can postpone it," or momentarily you're saying it isn't quite *that* important although the long-range is important—the grades at the end of the semester or your preparation as a prelaw student. But isn't your momentary behavior one that says, "This can be delayed," "This can be pushed back," "This can be handled some way other than studying it right now"?

Pt. Well, the behavior, I guess, would indicate that . . . but, as far as what I've done, what I see myself it's a definite compulsion. Here I have so much homework, I'm so far behind, how am I going to do it?

Th. Uh huh.

Pt. How am I going to start? I have so much to do I don't know where to start.

Th. You have so much to do?

Pt. Yeah, then maybe I could get up and walk around . . . and think about it and get my wits together.

Th. Well, now do you say something like that when you have a long distance to go? Travelling? You don't say, "Oh, it's so far I can't get started—I'll never get there.". . . because before you could get there you'd have to take three steps, I'll have to take two, and you can pose the problem of Zeno's arrow here and never get going. That's the problem that says that before you can shoot an arrow a given distance, it has to travel half that distance; before it can travel the remaining distance, it has to travel half *that* distance, and so on and on, and the arrow can never reach its destination because it always has half the remaining distance to go.

Pt. Uh huh.

Th. Maybe you kinda look at your B—— course that way?

Pt. Uh huh. But I should look at it different . . . I should get going.

Th. But you don't look at travelling . . . going some place that is important to you that has no conflict connected with it, no alternatives . . . you don't look at those tasks that way . . . figure out how far you have to go before you get there and let that discourage you——

Pt. You mean thinking beforehand how much there is to do?

Th. Um huh. "It's so overwhelming I can't do it—I'll do something else," you are saying—"It's just so much, I can't compete with these people,

I'm behind already, so why knock myself out, it's all settled, it's a lost battle."

Pt. Of course, if I were going to Florida . . . ah . . . and my parents wouldn't let me have the car, I'd see it was too far for me and therefore I wouldn't go.

Th. That's right, the alternative in the conflict of not going would be so overwhelming you wouldn't pursue the goal. The alternative to going would be so important . . . and that's what we're saying here with respect to your study of B——: the alternatives are more important, however momentary they are, however weak they seem to be as you think of your ultimate goals like grades at the end of the semester. (Pause.) You see my point?

Pt. Uh huh. Course I don't see how to get rid of these.

Th. Well, let's talk about it from that vantage point now. What you're saying is it's not important for you to knock yourself out in a situation where you're behind. If in a race you fall behind, your tendency is to give up if you cannot gain enough ground to win. Or to let it slack so much that there's no conflict any more, no contest—you're out of it. There are too many people competing with you in B—— that are doing better than you, so you're saying: "OK, I'm so far behind I can't compete with you people, so I'll just call it no contest." But that's a choice, isn't it? That's an assertion . . . that's the choice that says that's more important than staying in there and battling it out and doing whatever I can, or retrieving my losses, or whatever. (Pause.) Does that get over to you at all?

Pt. Why yes, sure. Actually, though . . . ah . . . ah . . . though I may think that calling it no contest, it actually isn't any contest——

Th. But there is.

Pt. Yes there is——

Th. There is in reality as far as your matriculation in the course is concerned, and it is in terms of your own reality as the course and the semester move on. But *at the time* you're supposed to get down to study, you find something else to do because these other "something elses" are more attractive, more compatible, stronger at the moment, they have less conflict connected with them, and so on. (Pause.) That's part of the business of your responsibility and self-discipline, isn't it?

Pt. It's all the same thing.

Th. Yeah. All part and parcel. (Pause.) You're saying, "I'll get in the contest when I can win, or when I can achieve the high-level performance I deem my prerogative . . . but . . . I won't . . . if there's anything against me . . . I mean really formidably against me. (E. Lakin Phillips, *Psychotherapy: a modern theory and practice*, Englewood Cliffs, N. J.: Prentice-Hall, Inc., 1956, p. 279.)

One of the advantages of the type of therapy Phillips is recommending is that it is applicable to children and adults in individual or group situations. In cases where a child is the patient, the same therapist would work with all members of the family who need to be brought in, so that the nature of the interacting assertions they are making may become apparent to him. Phillips holds (along with the Adlerians mentioned earlier) that the practice usually followed in child guidance clinics, that of having different therapists for mother and child, has nothing to recommend it. At best it makes treatment take longer; at worst it creates a stalemate of mutual frustration when changes that occur in mother and child are not complementary. The excerpts Phillips includes in his book (1956) to illustrate the conduct of group therapy for mothers are similar in many respects to the individual interview passage given above.

THE USE OF ASSESSMENT IN COGNITIVE CHANGE THERAPY

Because the success of this kind of therapy depends to a considerable extent on the skill of the therapist in identifying the patient's fundamental concepts and values, one would expect assessment to play a larger part in the procedure than it does in Rogerian or conditioned-response therapy. In most of these systems, however, the common psychological tests, such as the Wechsler, the Rorschach, or the TAT, do not contribute so much to the assessment process as do interview and observation. Thorne recommends that tests be given as part of the diagnosis but he does not emphasize them. The Adlerians pay special attention to the patient's description of the family constellation in his childhood home and his report of his earliest recollections. George Kelly has worked out some ingenious new ways of diagnosing an individual's personal constructs. The Role Construct Repertory Test requires him to think first of persons who stand in certain relationships to him and then to classify them, telling how any two of them are alike and a third different. The reasons a person gives for such sortings show what constructs operate in his evaluations of people.

Phillips does not consider the question of assessment at all. He does state that some means of diagnosing conflicts rather than symptoms would be useful, but makes no suggestions about what such a method might be.

In general, we can conclude that there are many questions about the ways in which personality assessment might contribute to therapies that aim at cognitive change—questions that have not as yet been squarely faced, let alone answered. Perhaps because the psychologists representing this point of view tend to be persons who have broken away from a theoretical school in which they had received some indoctrination, they have not yet had time to consider what a thorough-going shift to this position would mean in those areas of clinical psychology that lie outside of therapy.

RESEARCH ON COGNITIVE CHANGE THERAPIES

Because their practitioners see cognitive change theories as radically different from the dominant theories of therapy, there has been some research evaluating outcomes of cases treated in this way. Phillips (1956, pp. 43-50) obtained follow-up information about children treated by a child guidance clinic over a five-year period. Both the therapist who had handled the case and the child's parent were asked to rate the amount of progress each child had made on a seven-point scale ranging from "symptoms much worse" through "no change" to "great change for the better." The 30 cases treated by the assertion-structured method required an average of only 7.37 interviews, as compared with the average of 17.60 interviews for the "depth-oriented" cases, and the average degree of improvement was somewhat higher for the assertion-structured cases.

In another study of 249 cases, Phillips compares both the *efficiency* and the *effectiveness* of the two methods. As a measure of *efficiency* he takes the proportion of cases actually treated by the clinic after there has been some opportunity for a therapist to judge that it is a treatable case. As a measure of *effectiveness* he uses the therapist's or parent's judgment as to whether or not the patient benefited from the treatment he received. Differences in favor of the assertion-structured method are striking. About 90 per cent of the assertion-structured patients completed three or more interviews, and more than 86 per cent of them benefited from the treatment. The comparison figures given for the psychoanalytic depth-oriented therapy are about 24 per cent treated for at least three interviews, and 17 per cent benefiting (according to therapists' ratings—the patients' ratings show an even smaller figure).

This kind of comparison can be made only in a fairly large clinic where several therapists are working in different ways. There are many things we would need to know about this whole situation before we could be sure what the reported results mean. Information is not given in the preliminary report Phillips presents with regard to the nature of the clinic, how many therapists participated and what their qualifications were, how much variety there was in the types of cases encountered, and how individual cases were assigned to particular therapists. But as they stand, the figures certainly support his claims for assertion-centered therapy.

A different kind of evaluation has been reported by Ellis (1957). He tells us that in the years since he began practicing, he has gone through three distinct periods. During the first of these he used orthodox psychoanalysis, during the second a psychoanalytically oriented method, and during the third the rational psychotherapy he now recommends. The kinds of patients he encountered during the three periods, he reports, were quite similar. His judgments of improvement in percentages follow:

	Orthodox Psychoanalysis N = 16 per cent	Psychoanalytic Orientation N = 78 per cent	Rational Psychotherapy N = 78 per cent
Little or no improvement	50	37	26
Distinct improvement	37	45	44
Considerable improvement	13	18	30

The figures speak for themselves. They show quite clearly that Ellis is better satisfied with the results he obtains from the new technique than with those from a fully or partially psychoanalytic approach. But here again the meaning such figures can have for others involves a good deal of uncertainty. How do we know, for example, that increasing experience is not making Ellis a better therapist as the years pass, so that we could expect him to get better results regardless of the method he used? The need for other controls, such as having the judgments of degree of improvement made by someone other than the therapist himself, is obvious. But figures of this kind are at least suggestive.

What we have been considering in this chapter is, of course, a minority position in present-day psychotherapy. It is militantly anti-Freudian in choosing to work on present behavior rather than experiences long past and in placing emphasis on the conscious rather than the unconscious aspects of personality. It differs from Rogers' methods in allowing the therapist to intervene actively in attempts to induce a client to change some unsound premise or assumption. It differs from the viewpoint of those who hope to change habits by conditioned-response methods in stressing cognitive rather than behavioral change.

The psychologists we have classified in this group do not see themselves as linked together in any sort of school or movement. Each of them has independently made his protest against the dominant schools of psychotherapy. But it is in the ideas they hold in common that some of the most challenging questions lie for psychologists interested in the processes of therapy. There is room for more and better research upon these than has heretofore been carried out. It is hoped that as more workers are attracted to this position such research will be forthcoming. There is a great deal of experimental work in perception and concept formation that might ultimately be combined with this therapeutic approach. Leeper and Madison (1959) have taken a step in that direction. They see intensive psychotherapy as producing basic shifts in the perception of the self comparable to the shifts that occur in perceiving the Necker cube, when certain parts of the box appear now as close, and later as distant. In addition, they do not view emotions, feelings, and motives as excluded from cognitive operations or learning, but consider all of these to be embraced by basic perceptual processes.

THERAPY EMPHASIZING MORAL RESPONSIBILITY

There are two approaches to psychotherapy which have much in common with the cognitive change approaches that have been discussed, but which differ from them in one important way. These are the existentialist approach and the approach formulated by O. H. Mowrer. Whereas Ellis and Phillips tend to assume that a change in an unworkable idea, concept, or world view is what brings about a change for the better in a person's behavior, the existentialists and Mowrer hold that it is necessary for the person himself to make a decision or to choose a course of action. That man is free to decide upon his own future course of action is a basic assumption in these formulations, and the emphasis is on this active *volitional* determinant of behavior.

It is obvious that this point of view is much closer to theology than are any of the others we have considered. This is explicitly recognized by many of those who advocate it. Such a rapprochement with religion is in a sense justified by historical tradition. It is only recently that personality difficulties have been classified exclusively as mental *illness*. More dominant than the medical viewpoint throughout most of the centuries of man's recorded history has been the concern of priest, rabbi, and minister with these problems.

The existentialist philosophies and systems of therapy flourished for some time in Europe before they became generally known in this country, but several expositions of them in English are now available (May et al, 1958; Pervin, 1960). The various writers belonging to this school disagree somewhat in details but are in accord on core ideas. One of the simplest and clearest discussions of existentialist principles as applied to therapy can be found in Frankl's little book, *The Doctor and the Soul* (1955).

The central human characteristic Frankl postulates is a *will-to-meaning*. This is a matter of values, and is a highly individual matter. The values that give one life its meaning are not identical with those to be found in another. Each person must find the one unique value pattern capable of giving his life a meaning. It is the task of the therapist to help him in this search.

Frankl distinguishes between creative values, experiential values, and attitudinal values. Creative values are those that inhere in the achievement of tasks. Experiential values are those that inhere in experiencing the Good, the True, and the Beautiful, or in knowing and loving another human being. Attitudinal values inhere in facing destined suffering without flinching. Because these kinds of values are embodied in circumstances of different degrees of rigor and constriction, it follows that if a person can find it, there is always *some* value to be realized, no matter how hopeless his objective situation may appear. Frankl gives an example to illustrate this (Frankl, 1955, pp. xii-xiii):

A nurse in my department suffered from a tumor which proved to be inoperable. In her despair the nurse asked me to visit her. Our conversation revealed that the cause of her despair was not so much her illness in itself as her incapacity to work. She had loved her profession above all else, and now she could no longer follow it. What should I say? Her situation was really hopeless; nevertheless, I tried to explain to her that to work eight or ten hours per day is no great thing—many people can do that. But to be as eager to work as she was, and so incapable of work, and yet not to despair—that would be an achievement few could attain. And then I asked her: "Are you not being unfair to all those thousands of sick people to whom you have dedicated your life; are you not being unfair to act now as if the life of an incurable invalid were without meaning? If you behave as if the meaning of our life consisted in being able to work so many hours a day, you take away from all sick people the right to live and the justification for their existence."

The most salient characteristic of existentialist therapy is apparent in the foregoing example. What Frankl calls *logotherapy*, or "psychotherapy in terms of the mind," seeks to develop in each patient an understanding that life is an *obligation*, a responsibility. The important consideration is not what a person hopes to get from it, but what he has in him to contribute. In deciding what one's contribution is to be, one must understand his own world view, as it has been shaped by all the experiences of his life. It is characteristic of this approach not to discount the world view of a patient because it grows out of his neurotic or psychotic condition. Its validity is independent of its origin. Original works of art, meaningful systems of philosophy have been produced by deviant personalities.

There is nowhere in Frankl's book or in any of the other discussions of existential therapy any complete account of techniques used in working with an individual. The therapists practicing according to this system would probably say that techniques should *not* be standardized. One gets the impression from the brief examples given that the therapist reasons with the patient, asks him questions to stimulate his thinking, or gives instructions which he is to attempt to carry out. With neurotic clients the therapist attempts first to produce a change of attitude toward the neurosis, and then proceeds to analyze the world view the patient expresses. Vivid, concrete language is used, as in the following example:

The patient was instructed to ignore as far as possible her depressive mood, since such brooding understandably but unjustifiably would tend to give her a bleak view of her prospects. It was suggested that she let the depression pass by her as a cloud passes over the sun, hiding the sun from our eyes. She must remember that the sun continues to exist, even if we do not see it for the moment (Frankl, 1955, pp. 103-104).

Many of the ideas Mowrer has been presenting are similar to those found in the existentialist writers, although they were arrived at independently (Mowrer, 1960a, 1960b). There is the same emphasis on decision-making and responsibility, the same conviction that the knowledge an individual gains through neurotic or psychotic experience is valid in spite of its origin. But Mowrer emphasizes moral or ethical considerations even more strongly. The core of all psychiatric difficulties is *guilt*, and in order to cope with them, the patient must in some way come to terms with the *sin* from which the guilt arises. Instead of considering the guilt feelings irrational and trying to diminish their severity, as psychoanalytically oriented therapists typically do, the therapist should accept them as valid indicators of something wrong in the patient's life that must be set right.

The trouble with most kinds of psychotherapy, as Mowrer sees it, is that the patient when in the therapist's office may confess his wrongdoing, but does nothing to atone for it or expiate it. Mowrer puts it this way in one of his statements (Mowrer, 1960*b*):

For the only way to resolve the paradox of self-hatred and self-punishment is to assume, not that it represents merely an "introjection" of the attitudes of others, but that self-hatred is realistically justified and will persist until the individual, by radically altered attitude *and action,* honestly and realistically comes to feel that he now deserves something better. As long as one remains, in the old-fashioned religious phraseology, hard-of-heart and unrepentant, just so long will one's conscience hold him in the vise-like grip of "neurotic" rigidity and suffering. But if, at length, an individual confesses his past stupidities and errors and makes what poor attempts he can at restitution, then the superego (like the parents of an earlier day—and society in general) for-gives and relaxes its stern hold; and the individual once again is free, "well."

Like the existentialist writers, Mowrer has as yet presented no clear account of the techniques or procedures a therapist might use to help a patient. He has referred to Alcoholics Anonymous as a kind of prototype of what is needed in other areas, therapeutic programs that, "whether under religious or secular auspices, will, like Alcoholics Anonymous, take guilt, confession, and expiation seriously and will involve programs of *action* rather than mere groping for 'insight.' "

As yet there have been no attempts to try out various assessment pro-cedures or to evaluate the effectiveness of either existentialist therapy or the kind of treatment Mowrer recommends. It seems likely, however, that the next few years may produce a good deal of such research. As an out-standing experimentalist and learning theorist Mowrer is equipped with the ideas and skills that would be needed to investigate the complex behavior changes involved in such therapy. His earlier volume (1953) is one of the most thorough attempts that has been made to date to bring together theoretical ideas and research techniques, by means of which the therapeutic process may be studied. New and, in some ways, startling as it is, this approach to therapy must be taken seriously. It constitutes a challenge to many of our generally accepted ideas and could produce a major or minor revolution in therapeutic practice if sub-stantiated.

SUMMARY

Some clinicians see the goal of psychotherapy as changed concepts and values. They attempt to help the patient alter his outlook on life. Adler, Phillips, and other cognitive change therapists view the neurotic person as one who has developed erroneous ideas about himself, mistakes which

the therapist helps him to see and rectify. These basic mistakes or assertions have been opposed by the outside world, but since the patient knows
no other way to respond, he asserts his own personal approach even more
strongly, building up a vicious circle of tension. The therapist intervenes
directly to point out his mistakes and convince him of them and to encourage him to try other alternatives. Assessment techniques are only in
an early stage of development, though it would seem that cognitive change
therapy could make much use of assessment. The results of the few research studies available on the outcome of this kind of therapy have been
very favorable to it, but they need to be repeated and extended by other
investigators. Akin to cognitive therapy are recent developments in which
emphasis is put upon change in values and the assumption of moral
responsibility. Frankl attempts to help the patient find his unique value
pattern, one that will give his life meaning, particularly through revealing
to him his obligations in life. Mowrer resurrects the word *sin* to explain
neurotic suffering and asserts that rather than seeking to diminish guilt
feelings, the therapist should help the patient accept them as indicators
of something wrong which he must make right again.

SUGGESTED READINGS

ANSBACHER, H. L., & ANSBACHER, Rowena R. (Eds.) *The individual psychology of Alfred Adler*. New York: Basic Books, 1956.

This is a systematic presentation of Adler's thought through selections from
his writings, with occasional editorial comments. It shows the early development of Adler's thought from his first publications in 1907 on through his
break with Freud in 1911 and then presents Adler's later views on various
topics. Adler's greatest divergence from Freud was over social adaptation. To
Freud this was a result of a restrictive modification of human nature; to Adler
it was a natural disposition obscured by distortions in early relationships and
psychological disorders.

KELLY, G. A. *The psychology of personal constructs*. Vol. I. *A theory of personality*. Vol. II. *Clinical diagnosis and therapy*. New York: Norton, 1955.

Kelly's theory is a revolutionary one in many ways. He does away with
many of the traditional concepts of psychology, like motivation. Instead, he
sees each individual as engaged in construing his world and testing his
hypotheses about it. The most important thing in clinical work is to identify
and influence these dimensions along which a person thinks—his personal
constructs. The sections most relevant to the content of this chapter are the
early introductions to theory and the chapter on "fixed-role therapy." The
reader may be interested in reading the illuminating reviews of these volumes
by Bruner and Rogers in the 1956 volume of *Contemporary Psychology*.

RESEARCH EXAMPLES

FERGUSON, Eva D. The effect of sibling competition and alliance on level of
aspiration, expectation, and performance. *J. abnorm. soc. Psychol.*, 1958, 56,
213-222.

This research project, a Ph.D. dissertation, is one of the few studies stemming directly from Adlerian theory. According to this theory, sibling relationships are very important since personality patterns are a reflection of goals the person establishes in early years within the family constellation. For any child a sibling can be seen as an ally or a competitor in gaining his place in the family. Allies become alike in personality; competitors become different. Two hypotheses were singled out for investigation: (1) In a competitive relationship, a child's performance and aspirations rise when he is informed that his sibling has done more poorly than himself and drop when told the sibling has done better. (2) In an alliance relationship, the reverse is true— the child's performance and expectations change in the same direction as the report of the sibling's performance.

For this study 20 sibling pairs were drawn from child guidance centers to which at least one sibling had been brought as a behavior problem. Another group of 20 sibling pairs was obtained through churches in the community. In each group there were ten pairs of allies and ten pairs of competitors, these being identified on the basis of a preliminary interview with the mother. All subjects came from families of three or more children. The children were between four and one-half and ten years of age.

Each subject was tested individually on two aspiration tasks and one learning task. The aspiration tasks involved putting lines between dots and inserting pegs in a pegboard as fast as possible. The other task was the serial learning of pictures of common objects. In a balanced design each subject was given predetermined statements telling how the sibling compared with him in performance and was then given additional trials.

The results were analyzed for the three different tasks and the different subject groups. The main hypotheses were not upheld, but there were some rather complex differences between allies and competitors. These findings suggested reformulations of the original hypotheses with ego-involvement and status effects brought into the picture.

Any attempt to investigate sibling interactions is important but difficult because there are so many variations among family groups. Such a study as this needs repetition with a larger sample of subjects and modified procedures.

MARTINSON, W. D. Utilization of the Role Construct Repertory Test in the counseling process. *Dissert. Abs.*, 1955, 15, 2102-2103.

The Role Construct Repertory Test (the Rep Test) asks for a list of persons who have played certain important roles in the person's life. The subject then is asked to compare and differentiate among these various persons. In this manner one obtains a person's ways of describing these roles and presumably the important dimensions on which he classifies people. This test is the basic technique used by George Kelly in his theory of assessment and therapy. The reader should consult Kelly's book (1955) for a more complete account of the technique and other illustrations of its application.

This study, reported briefly as an abstract of a doctoral research project, is one of the few applying this very interesting test to a clinical population. Martinson's design involved a test and retest of experimental and control groups of 15 clients each. Both groups took the Rep Test after a routine intake interview. The control group took it again after a voluntary waiting period without counseling, while the experimental group took it again after four counseling interviews.

Predictions as to area of probable interpersonal difficulty were made by the counselor after the initial interview and by the test administrator from the test record. At the end of the four counseling interviews, the counselor rated the success of the counseling outcome. Clients were divided into high- and low-ability students on the basis of college entrance tests. The Rep Test responses were evaluated according to how "positive" they were in contributing to good interpersonal relations.

The analyses of the results produced the following findings and conclusions: (1) Counseled subjects showed a significant increase in the use of positive dimensions on the Rep Test. (2) The clients rated as most successful showed a greater increase of positive evaluations than those rated as least successful. (3) The Rep Test provided a more accurate diagnosis of areas of interpersonal difficulty than did the initial counseling interview. (4) The areas rated as being probable areas of difficulty showed a significantly greater increase in positive evaluation. (5) The number of positive dimensions used was not related to scholastic ability.

There are many further questions one might raise about such a study. The present abstract unfortunately does not provide sufficient detail to enable us to judge the adequacy of many aspects of the research, e.g., the kind of criterion for judging the area of greatest difficulty. There is room for much more research along the lines of detecting role perceptions and cognitive organizations.

OSGOOD, C. F., & LURIA, ZELLA. A blind analysis of a case of multiple personality using the Semantic Differential. *J. abnorm. soc. Psychol.*, 1954, 49, 579-591.

There is a general assumption that mental illness involves a disordering of meanings or ways of perceiving. Osgood and his colleagues have developed a technique for measuring meaning. In the famous case of multiple personality described in *The Three Faces of Eve*, by Thigpen and Cleckley (1957), the Semantic Differential was administered to the patient in each of her three personalities: Eve White, Eve Black, and Jane. The Semantic Differential involves ratings of concepts such as "My father" on a series of bipolar opposites such as good-bad, fair-unfair, and hard-soft. Two concepts can then be compared by statistically computing the differences between them. The distances between a set of concepts could be used in drawing a "semantic structure" for each of the three personalities at the two different times each was tested. The measurements and the drawings are shown in detail in the original article.

Without knowing anything about the case except that it was a case of triple personality and a few items of external information, Osgood and Luria studied the results and interpreted them. With all of the personalities and over the two months between the two test administrations, there was a positive evaluation of the concept "My Doctor." In general, Eve White perceived the world in an essentially normal fashion, being well socialized. However, she saw "Me" as weak and "Sex" and "My spouse" as meaningless. "Love" and "Sex" were widely separated. Eve Black, on the other hand, had achieved a violent kind of adjustment in which she perceived herself as perfect, but became completely disoriented from the norm. She accepted "Fraud" and "Hatred" as positive values. She rejected "Child," "My spouse," "My job," "Love," and "Sex" as bad and passive. Jane displayed the most healthy meanings of the three.

The authors interpreted these findings in terms of identification with the father (the closeness of "Father" and "Me" concepts) and of disturbances in sex relations, among other things. They made some interpretations of the nature of the therapy at different stages. The increasing simplification of the semantic structure during therapy suggested to the authors some dangers in therapy—that the patient was paying for supposedly better adjustment with loss of initiative, creativeness, and differentiation.

This case study is a very interesting one from the methodological standpoint. The validity of the interpretations is not checked in any systematic fashion. The reader may also wish to consult the therapists' own description of the case (Thigpen & Cleckley, 1954).

16 Psychotherapy as Insight and Emotional Reorganization: Psychoanalytic Approach

Most discussions of psychotherapy begin with psychoanalysis. There are excellent reasons for this. Although attempts had been made to treat mental illnesses and maladjustment by verbal methods before Freud's time, they had been sporadic and did not have much influence. It can almost be said that the whole structure of psychotherapeutic practice is Freud's creation. Although it is true that some of those who practice along lines that can be traced back to Freud have now become definitely anti-Freudian in their ideas, even their deviations constitute a kind of recognition. Any person who wishes to work in this area will find that he must orient himself in some way, positive or negative, to the dominant Freudian position.

THE FREUDIAN SYSTEM

It is important always to remember that Freud is the founder of a system both of theory and of practice, and that the two are not inevitably united in any unalterable union. One can adhere to general psychoanalytic theory even though in his therapeutic work he may introduce many techniques derived from other sources. And one can use techniques that have been developed in psychoanalytic settings while remaining skeptical or rejecting the system as a whole.

This is not the place to enter into a discussion of Freudian psychology as a theoretical system. We shall mention only a few of its features that tend to determine the pattern for therapeutic work. The most basic of these ideas is that of the _unconscious_. Figuratively speaking, it is a sort of reservoir of wishes and impulses that have been _repressed_. The concepts of the unconscious and of repression have been discussed briefly in Chapter 2. Fundamental to therapy is the idea that because of the anxiety they generate, some wishes, thoughts, and feelings have been "pushed down" into the unconscious and are thus not available to the patient unless some means can be found to weaken the repressing influence. What he experiences as neurotic symptoms are indirect effects of the conflict between impulses struggling for expression and the repressing forces. Personality difficulties appear baffling and incomprehensible when we do not see their source in this struggle. From the beginning of Freud's work to the present, a major aim of psychoanalytic therapy has been to open up some of the areas of the unconscious to conscious scrutiny.

Another basic Freudian idea is that the roots of a person's behavior go back to the earliest years of his life. Every symptom, every behavior pattern, every feeling, is in theory determined to some extent by the person's experience, and the basic patterns for this experience were set early in his life. This explains the emphasis on "tracing back" in Freudian therapy, an emphasis quite different from some of the other systems we have discussed. It also leads the analyst to expect that the patient will reenact in the therapeutic situation itself the same kind of emotional relationship to his parents that played such a decisive part in shaping his personalty. This aspect of psychoanalytic therapy is what is called _transference_. We will consider transference at greater length in the following section.

Other intricacies of Freudian theory and their elaborations at successive stages of Freud's development have left their effects on the sort of interpretations therapists make as well as on the insights patients acquire, but they do not determine the foundations of the therapist's thinking as do the two cardinal ideas we have discussed, the unconscious and the genetic development of personality. There has been much controversy and many modifications in psychoanalytic theory with regard to such matters as the nature of the instincts and the functions respectively of id, ego, and superego. But the procedures in therapy remain much the same regardless of where one stands on these theoretical issues. For that reason we shall not consider them here. It is expected that every clinical psychologist will become really knowledgeable about psychoanalytic theory before he finishes his training.

In terms of the classification set up in Chapter 11, where we took up the question of how much and what kinds of *change* the different varieties of therapy aim to produce, psychoanalysis occupies the extreme position. Its goal is not the amelioration of symptoms or the replacement of some bad habits by good ones, but rather a basic *reconstruction* of the emotional aspects of the whole personality. We shall later look into such evidence as is available on the degree of profundity of the changes that actually occur and the question as to whether the briefer psychoanalytically oriented variety of therapy can expect to bring about the same kind of personality change as does the extremely time-consuming orthodox form of Freudian analysis. It is enough to say here that perhaps the greatest appeal of this system, for therapist and patient alike, is this hope it holds out that "deep" emotional reorganization may occur rather than limited change of some sort.

SALIENT FEATURES OF ORTHODOX FREUDIAN PSYCHOANALYSIS

An introductory book on clinical psychology is not the place to discuss the details of orthodox psychoanalytic treatment. We can be certain that young clinicians will not be trying out this technique during their graduate years or in the early years of their professional careers, since it requires prolonged and specialized training. Furthermore, in the United States at least, it is difficult if not impossible for a person without a medical degree to obtain full training and accreditation as a practicing psychoanalyst. This situation is a result of the decision made by the first analysts in this country to limit membership in the American Psychoanalytic Association to persons with the M.D. degree, a decision which was strongly condemned by Freud (1950). We shall confine ourselves in this section, therefore, to those basic features of psychoanalytic therapy that one must understand if he is to use the briefer techniques that have been developed as an outgrowth of psychoanalysis.

The physical features of standard psychoanalytic treatment have become familiar to us through hundreds of novels, movies, and television programs, to say nothing of quips and cartoons. The patient lies on a couch with the analyst sitting behind him taking notes, occasionally commenting on what he says. In a typical analysis, both participants work at this task for an hour each day of a five-day week for two or more years. The tools they use are primarily free association and the analysis of dreams. During the period that it lasts, the analysis becomes the center of the patient's life. It is an intense, profoundly moving experience.

When we analyze the process that occurs and try to explain why it does constitute so vital an experience, several aspects of it are apparent. In the first place, the release through free association of emotions that have been held down for a long time constitutes *catharsis*, a purging of the system of feelings that have been poisoning it. In some variations of analytic treatment, such as the narcotherapy so extensively used for treatment of war neuroses, this emotional release seems to constitute the "cure" itself. More typically, however, it is not sufficient to free the patient from his difficulties. Most psychoanalysts themselves do not consider it to be a major therapeutic influence.

The second feature of analytic treatment consists of *interpretation* by the therapist, contributing to *insight* in the patient. If the patient is really able to obey the basic rule and put into words every thought that occurs to him, even if it seems silly or shocking, parts of the total picture that have not before been accessible to conscious awareness begin to emerge. The analyst helps him to put these together and make what could be called "psychoanalytic sense" of them. In this he must always proceed cautiously and tentatively, trying never to confront the patient with anything he will need to repudiate entirely.

But no matter how cautious the interpretations are, *resistance* always develops in the patient. It shows itself in many ways—by long periods of silence, by hostile remarks, by unpunctuality or failure to keep the analytic appointments altogether. This resistance itself becomes something to be interpreted and diminished. The ability to handle this resistance to the task is an important part of the analyst's skill. Resistance is the form repression takes in the psychoanalytic situation. Thus the analyst's principal task is to weaken it. The interpretations he offers of what the patient says and does are designed to do this. Their purpose is not simply to clarify some psychological point suggested by what the patient has said or to lead him to a purely intellectual understanding of his experience. Thus the timing of the interpretive statements the analyst makes and the verbal form they take may be as important as their soundness. They must assist the patient in his task of expressing what is struggling for expression.

Another phenomenon fundamental to psychoanalytic work is *transference*. Freud discovered that a patient whose analysis proceeds to a successful outcome always developed for a time an intense personal attachment to the therapist. Because of the way the whole situation is structured, the patient cannot, of course, know him in any of the ways in which we know our friends in ordinary social life. As he lies on the couch he does not ever see the therapist. Between analytic hours he has no social or professional contact with him. With such an unstructured and socially blank screen on which to picture, or seem to himself to be picturing, his therapist, it is natural that the patient reacts during therapy in the way he has reacted to the most significant persons in his past life. He may *transfer* to him his whole relationship, perhaps, to his father, reenacting even painful early struggles of which he has no clear memory. According to Freudians, it is in this experience that there lies the possibility for profound personality reorganization. It is as though the patient in a sense *relives* the developmental periods in which the basic personality patterns were laid down, and modifies these patterns through this new emotional experience. This experience is what analysts mean by the *transference neurosis*. The resolution of this neurotic attachment to the therapist is of major importance in the patient's recovery.

The transference must of course be understood at all times by the analyst so that he can make sure that it constitutes for the patient this kind of corrective emotional experience. Of late years there has been increasing attention directed to *countertransference*, or the emotional relationship of the analyst to the patient. The analyst must understand his own reactions if these powerful forces are to be channeled wisely.

Along with these processes, there is another that becomes increasingly prominent as the analysis proceeds toward its close. This is called *working through*. The new insights achieved do not automatically transfer to every area of life. Emotional relationships to wife, to son, to colleague, may all need to be reshaped as basic attitudes change. There is much to discuss even after most of the significant unconscious material has been brought to light. And it takes a considerable time to resolve a deep transference—to free the patient from dependence on the analyst. Thus a complete psychoanalysis is very time-consuming, and as a consequence, very expensive. It is likely to require several years and to cost several thousand dollars.

ANALYTICALLY ORIENTED PSYCHOTHERAPY

It is the briefer forms of therapy derived from psychoanalysis that are important for the clinical psychologist to understand. In the general practice of psychotherapists they occupy a much larger place than full-scale psychoanalysis does. The experience the student clinician obtains in a practicum setting is likely to include therapy of this sort.

While the concepts on which psychoanalytically oriented psychotherapy rests come from Freudian theory, the techniques themselves cannot be considered simply as poor substitutes for a complete psychoanalysis. They have advantages of their own. Many analysts prefer to treat the majority of their patients by these briefer methods because they are convinced that results are often more successful than they are after orthodox Freudian analysis (Alexander & French, 1946).

Outwardly this kind of therapy may seem similar to most of the kinds we have described in previous chapters. The patient sits in a chair where he can look at the therapist instead of reclining on a couch. He is told to talk openly about whatever comes into his mind, but such "free" associations as occur are likely to be determined to some extent by factors that pass for what we ordinarily mean by "reality." The intervals between sessions are longer than in psychoanalysis. Once a week is perhaps the most common schedule, and there are seldom more than three sessions a week.

So far as the psychological processes that occur are concerned, they differ from those in standard psychoanalysis mainly because there is much less emphasis on transference and much more on interpretations by the therapist, interpretations that are intended to lead to insight in the patient. The very deep forms of attachment characteristic of psychoanalysis—the so-called transference neurosis—cannot occur in the course of the briefer varieties of therapy. In fact, part of the therapist's task is to head off such a development. When he senses that the patient is beginning to react to him in an irrational, overly dependent manner, he makes it plain that he will not become involved in playing the role of the patient's domineering father. By consistently treating the patient as an adult, he makes it necessary for the patient to modify the childish role he was finding it natural to take. The patient may develop intense feelings toward the therapist in this as in many other kinds of therapy, but they do not have the regressive and "neurotic" quality that they have in orthodox psychoanalysis.

Interpretation is thought to be the most essential skill. The therapist must grasp the hidden meaning of what the patient says and does and communicate his understanding to him. The word *interpretation*, however, is surrounded by a cloud of ambiguity. It covers many sorts of comments a therapist may make, from simply calling the patient's attention to an unrecognized slip of the tongue, to an involved explanation of behavior in terms of psychoanalytic concepts. A common mistake made by inexperienced therapists is to interpret too soon, too much, and in a crudely psychological way. Almost any patient is going to be disturbed if he is told in the first interview that his symptoms are an expression of Oedipal anxiety or anal-aggressive tendencies!

Though the theories on which they are based differ widely, the principal procedural difference between client-centered therapy, as discussed in Chapter 13, and the psychoanalytic variety, is that the Rogerians almost sternly hold back interpretations of what the client says. However, the boundary between the "reflection of feeling" that characterizes the client-centered worker and the cautious, limited interpretation that the psychoanalytically oriented therapist is likely to attempt is not a very clear one. Some research has made it seem probable that if the therapist's remarks go just a little beyond what the patient has actually said (Dittmann, 1952; Speisman, 1959), they produce more therapeutic movement than if they simply reflect what he has expressed. The therapist must expect some resistance from the patient if he interprets at all—and resistances themselves are of course material for interpretation—but if he arouses too much resistance, the patient's defenses against submitting to the whole process of therapy may become impregnable. As Wolberg puts it, "It is important to interpret to the patient only material of which he has at least preconscious awareness" (1954, p. 179). The best procedure is to point out things that will help the patient to make his own interpretation rather than to make it oneself.

Brief psychoanalytic therapy, like the standard variety, requires the stage of "working through," or applying insights that have been gained to all areas of life. At this stage the therapist is pretty certain to let himself become more active than is the orthodox analyst, asking questions, perhaps suggesting things the patient might try to accomplish between interviews. He may interview members of the patient's family in an attempt to bring more favorable influences to bear on him. (This is done, of course, with the patient's knowledge and permission.) There comes a time when the person seems able to carry out his tasks and handle his emotional relationships to others without undue anxiety—a simple way of stating what may involve a great number of changes in habits and outlook. When this happens, it is time for therapy to end.

An Example

Wolberg (1954, p. 461) presents an excerpt from an interview with a man who had, after three months of treatment, gone back to his wife and three children, whom he had left in order to live with a prostitute. The therapist's comments on the case, in brackets, show how he was attempting to use interpretation to help this man come closer to understanding his own emotional reactions.

Pt. I know I shouldn't want Marie [the prostitute] as bad as she is. The whole thing is silly, the kind of person she is, I mean.

Th. But you do seem to want her in spite of her faults. [Reflecting underlying attitudes.]

Pt. I know she is bad for me; Rita [his wife] is so much more of a real person. But I can't get Marie off my mind. I don't want to go back to her, though, because the same mess will happen all over again. I would like to think about Rita all the time, to be thrilled by her. But I can work better now and would like to help Rita get the art training she wants. (Long pause.)

Th. I see. (Pause.) What are you thinking about?

Pt. A flash came to me, a fantasy of my standing on a subway platform. A person in front of me. As the subway approaches, I imagined myself pushing this man off.

Th. What kind of a person is this?

Pt. Unidentified. I couldn't identify the man. I seem to see him with a blue suit. He seems sinister for some reason. Sometimes when I stand on the platform of a subway, I have a fear I may jump off, or that someone may push me off.

Th. But in your fantasy you push this man off. You're angry with him?

Pt. Oh no, I don't feel . . . I didn't feel anything. Just felt like pushing him off. (Yawns.) I'm kind of tired today. I had a hard day at the office, all kinds of pressures. I thought of cancelling my appointment today, because my secretary had forgotten to make it and I forgot it, and I was supposed to talk to one of the out-of-town advertising people. [This sounds like resistance.]

Th. How do you feel about coming here? Do you feel it's an inconvenience to you? [Handling his mention of wanting to cancel his appointment.]

Pt. (Laughs.) It is. I come because I think it's necessary, not because I want it. There isn't anything enjoyable in it.

Th. So maybe you resent coming here. [A tentative interpretation.]

Pt. No, I don't think I resent it, because I know I *should* come. [He rejects the interpretation.]

Th. Mm hmm mm.

Pt. But it is a lot of work to get here; it does take time. It isn't anything I would do for fun. And then I feel that I have the responsibility to my family to get this thing straightened out.

Th. But how do you feel about doing it for yourself?

Pt. Frankly I'm doing it for my family. Indirectly, I suppose, I benefit from it.

Th. You know, I get the feeling that you really resent coming here. [An authoritative interpretation.] Let's take that fantasy. Here in fantasy you do an aggressive thing to someone in a blue suit.

Pt. Yes.

Th. What kind of a suit do I have on?

Pt. (Startled.) Why *your* suit is blue! [The patient seems astonished.]

Th. Maybe I'm the man in the fantasy and you want to get *me* out of the way. If so, you do seem to resent me. [Tentative interpretation.]

Pt. Oh, I almost forgot. [Reaches in his pocket and pulls out a check.] I've been carrying this around for two weeks and always forget to give it to you when I'm here.

Th. There must be a reason for that.

Pt. You mean I might not have wanted to pay you?

Th. That's possible. (Pause.)

Pt. But I did have the intention to pay you. I just forgot.

Th. People forget for definite reasons very often. Could you possibly not have given me the check because you felt critical of me? [A tentative interpretation.] If that's the case, then your giving me the check now is making up with me for being critical.

Pt. (Laughs.) Well, I'll tell you, I have been annoyed having to come here. I've even resented your good intentions. Not that you've ever told me to stay away from Marie, but I've been ashamed to go on the way I did. I've even wanted you to tell me Rita was better than Marie for me. But, damn it, the pull is there, the excitement. I can't go back, but I can't seem to push myself forward either.

Th. You see, there is a contradiction in some of your strivings. Your present stalemate is a result of being wedged in between your desire for Marie and your guilt and sense of responsibility to the family. You want me to make the choice for you and you are angry if I don't. [Authoritative interpretations.]

Pt. Yes, I can see that, and I know that, attractive as Marie is, life with her would be poison for me. I don't need you to build up Rita because she's a person with quality.

Th. Now, were I to make the choice for you, you'd have trouble. For instance, if I told you to give up Marie, I'd become the repressing authority you've been fighting all your life. As a matter of fact, you may find Marie attractive and want to kick over the traces to defy this authority and to do as you please. Then our relationship would get bad, because you'd probably want to defy me. On the other hand, if I encouraged you to give up Rita and to yield to your desires, you would be contemptuous of me. And if you went back to Marie, you'd blame me for exposing you to something from which you got pleasure, but which was very destructive to you. [More interpretations.] (L. R. Wolberg, *The technique of psychotherapy*, 2nd ed., New York: Grune & Stratton, 1954, p. 461.)

RELATED METHODS

The psychoanalytic orientation has extended to many kinds of specialized therapeutic techniques in addition to the more usual interview methods. One of these is interpretive play therapy for children. Little children, of course, cannot verbalize their free associations. Their skill in using words is not well enough developed to enable them to put into words the complex and subtle feelings that trouble them. But they can often act out these feelings or express them through manipulating toys and play materials so that they appear with startling clarity. When three-year-old Jimmy picks up the baby doll, stuffs its head into the toy toilet, and looks around at the therapist with some satisfaction, one need not use much imagination to conclude that he has some negative feeling toward his baby sister.

Not all varieties of play therapy make use of psychoanalytic thinking. What distinguishes this from other kinds is the attempt to use *interpretations* based on Freudian theory to communicate to the child the meaning of his behavior. The difference between the methods used by Anna Freud (1946), Melanie Klein (1949), or Lippman (1956), on the one hand, and those used by Axline (1947), a Rogerian, on the other, parallels the difference between "interpretation" and "reflection of feeling" in interviews with adults. However, within the broad confines of the psychoanalytic approach there is room for much variation and disagreement, as will become apparent to anyone who reads the three child analysts mentioned.

Even more than in the case of play therapy, a wide variety of group therapy techniques have evolved. *Analytic groups* are only one variety, and not the most numerous. They are distinguished from other kinds by the emphasis put on interpretation. The group situation furnishes a wealth of material to be interpreted—what individuals say, how they act toward one another, their behavior toward the therapist, and the like. In analytic groups the aim is to stimulate *individual* insight rather than to produce group solidarity. In many other orientations, the emphasis tends to be more on helping people learn to get along with one another than it is on the individual's understanding of his own reactions. A later chapter will discuss group therapy at greater length.

Another offshoot of psychoanalytic therapy has been the use of artistic expression for facilitating both catharsis and insight. Hospital patients who are unable to communicate verbally with a therapist may be able to express their feelings of terror, their conflicts, or their confusion with the help of paints or crayons. Similarly, nursery school children may express in their finger paintings some of their deep-lying emotional experiences. Other arts, such as the dance, have been used in this same way. To the extent that catharsis or expression itself is helpful, the act of self-expression itself seems to have a therapeutic effect. To the extent that the therapist can understand what the patient's art is expressing, his interpretations of motives and conflicts may constitute first steps toward the patient's self-insight or may lead to the planning of environmental moves to reduce the patient's tension and anxiety. This kind of therapeutic activity is clouded with uncertainty, however. It is usually far more difficult to comprehend the emotional significance of a painting than to grasp the meaning of what is communicated in words, however haltingly. Tangible evidence of favorable outcomes from this kind of therapeutic effort is even harder to discover than evidence for the value of therapy in general. However, it can at least be said that the attempt to use the arts for therapeutic purposes is a venture well worth trying, because in the long run it is likely to increase our knowledge both of therapy and of the motivations at work beneath the surface of artistic creation.

Still another group of workers has been interested in attempting to combine psychoanalytically oriented therapy with the use of hypnosis or drugs. As explained in the discussion of the Orne research study at the end of Chapter 14, hypnosis is a technique that can be used to facilitate different types of therapy. When it is used simply to reduce anxiety or to remove symptoms through suggestion, it has nothing to do with psychoanalysis. But it can be used to enable the patient to bypass resistances and open up deeper and deeper areas of the unconscious to inspection. This process is what is meant by *hypnoanalysis*. *Narcoanalysis*, using a drug such as sodium pentothal, has a similar purpose. In the altered state of consciousness produced by these methods the process of free association is tremendously speeded up, and unconscious feelings of fear or anger come to life again in all their vivid intensity. The difficulty is that the patient, when he returns to his normal conscious state, may not be able to remember these thoughts and feelings or translate them into actions. If the therapist, however, on the basis of such understanding as he has obtained during the hypnotic or drugged period, can bring the patient's repressed thoughts to his awareness and can help him accept and assimilate them, the therapeutic process may be advanced. This is not easily done, but it is a technique at which some therapists have acquired considerable skill. Drug therapy as such is naturally outside a psychologist's field of competence, though as a member of a clinical team the psychologist may share in handling a case, along with a psychiatrist.

THE ANALYTICAL PSYCHOLOGY OF CARL JUNG

Jung was for a time a member of Freud's inner circle. When he left the psychoanalytic group and set up his own center of practice and research in Zurich, he continued to make use of the techniques of therapy that Freudian analysts employ, but developed a theoretical structure very unlike Freud's. Jungian therapists listen to patients' free associations, analyze dreams, deal with transference, and make interpretive remarks. But because of the difference in Jungian theory, the interpretations take a different form from those made by Freudian therapists.

Like the existentialists discussed in the preceding chapter, Jung has emphasized the search for *meaning*. He thinks it can often be found in the accumulated wisdom of the human race, as crystallized in universal symbols and myths, what he calls *archetypes*. These are in some way represented at the unconscious levels of each individual personality. For Jung, then, the purpose of bringing unconscious material to the surface is not to expose traumatic material, but rather to release creative potentialities. Thus Jungian analysts encourage patients to pay attention to their dreams and fantasies and teach them to understand what the symbols they encounter in them may mean. For the analyst himself, the study of mythology and primitive thinking is essential if he is to recognize archetypes in the fantasies of his patients.

While there is in Jungian theory this emphasis on universal symbols, there is in practice an even greater emphasis on individual uniqueness. The therapist's task is to help a person develop and express his unique self. Painting and other kinds of artistic expression are commonly used in Jungian therapy to develop creativity and an active rather than a passive attitude toward one's own experience.

THE USE OF ASSESSMENT IN PSYCHOANALYTICALLY ORIENTED THERAPIES

Some form of personality assessment plays a larger part in the therapies based on psychoanalysis than in any of the other main types we have discussed in previous chapters. The emphasis on interpretation makes it seem desirable for the therapist to understand right from the beginning the most general features of the personality with whom he is working, so that he will be able to react in an appropriate manner, and to anticipate and perhaps forestall difficulties that are likely to arise.

The analyst using the "long method," or standard Freudian procedure, does not ordinarily make much use of tests as a means for understanding a patient. His methods call instead for a number of trial interviews, during which he hopes to size up the major outlines of the patient's personality structure and gauge how suitable for him the analytic procedure is likely to prove. When a form of treatment that will require several years for completion is contemplated, a period of several weeks spent in evaluation of the person's strengths and weaknesses will not seem excessive.

The shorter forms of therapy are more likely to include an assessment made at least partly on the basis of psychological tests. The projective techniques—the Rorschach, the TAT, the Draw-a-Person, and many others—have been widely used for this purpose, along with such standard measuring instruments as the Wechsler intelligence tests and, to some extent, inventories like the MMPI. Often a psychologist's principal task is to make these assessments and then prepare psychological reports on patients for whom some sort of therapy is contemplated.

Such psychological studies serve two main purposes. One is to determine the person's suitability for insight-oriented therapy. Here the elusive concept of "ego-strength" is an important variable. The aim of analytic therapy is to bring unconscious forms of motivation arising from id or superego under conscious ego control. The therapist hopes that the patient's ego will be gradually strengthened in the course of therapy, recognizing that there is a possibility that if it is too weak to start with, the kind of "uncovering" method we have been describing may overwhelm it and thus lead to a state worse than the original one.

A psychological study often provides the therapist with some clues as to how a given patient will respond to various aspects of the therapy—how readily he will form a transference relationship, for example, or how strong resistance is likely to be. Such a study often includes material that will aid in getting interpretations over to the patient, such as letting him see what his reactions to authority or his relationships to his parents have been.

It must be admitted that the evidence for the validity of any of the kinds of statements typically made in psychological reports is limited. There is always a possibility that some inference based on a test score or response may be entirely wrong, and thus may lead the therapist astray rather than help him understand the patient. In particular, assessments based on projective tests tend to overestimate pathology and to underestimate the person's ability to control such tendencies (Soskin, 1959). However, when one considers the amount of uncertainty in this whole field, he cannot be too much deterred by the risk of being wrong. Any kind of therapy involves risks, sometimes, perhaps, great risks. If a careful psychological assessment can add ever so little to the soundness of the decisions a therapist must make, it is justified.

CRITICAL EVALUATION

A comprehensive theory and a well-established method of treatment like psychoanalysis raises hundreds of what we would like to believe are researchable questions. Only a few of them have been attacked, and the answers even when we have them are none too clear. We shall turn in a later chapter to an examination of the many difficulties and complications that arise in doing research on this or any of the other varieties of therapy.

The first and rather common-sense question we raised in connection with each of the previous therapeutic approaches concerns outcomes. How much good does it do? In general, the answers research has given us to this question have not been very favorable. Eysenck (1952), you will recall, collected all the reports he could find in psychiatric and psychological publications where therapists or clinical services had supplied figures showing what per cent of their patients were improved and what per cent unimproved after treatment. For the four reports summarizing the outcomes of psychoanalysis the average percentage of patients rated "improved" was 44. For the other and shorter therapies, the average percentage of patients rated "improved" was 64. How such figures should be interpreted is a tough question. Therapists of different schools use different criteria for judging improvement. Because they have aimed at the thorough reorganization of a personality, psychoanalysts cannot usually be satisfied with the kinds of evidence other therapists typically adduce—disappearance of symptoms, feelings of well-being, and improved social relationships. As stated previously, Eysenck's figures challenge all therapists to find out why such a large proportion of those who seek their help apparently do not benefit from it. Many segments of the educated public, including many psychologists themselves, tend to assume that if it were possible for all unhappy, ineffective people to receive therapy, their difficulties would disappear. Many of them believe that if their resources were sufficient to make full-scale psychoanalytic therapy possible, the results would be better than under shorter forms of therapy. We should not forget that such outcome statistics as we have do not support these conclusions.

During recent years few outcome studies of analytically oriented therapy have been reported. The many complications connected with such studies make investigators more and more reluctant to undertake them. Differences in patients, differences in therapists, differences in circumstances, and many other sorts of complicating factors combine to mask any general effect that can be isolated. Unless one arranges for an adequate control group of untreated patients in whom any changes that occur can be compared with the changes in a group that received therapy, it is impossible to conclude that therapy produced such and such changes. And to find a large enough control group, comparable with the experimental group in all respects *relevant to therapy*, is—well, very nearly impossible. Because these obstacles seem so insuperable, there has lately been a shift of interest toward *process* research, as distinguished from research on outcomes. Its goal is understanding of the processes of human interaction as they occur in therapeutic interviews. Through knowing about these we may come closer to understanding how a personality may be changed.

A large-scale research program is being understaken at the Menninger Clinic (Robbins & Wallerstein, 1959). It may eventually answer many questions with regard to both outcome and process variables. The plan involves using case materials of the kind normally available at the Menninger Clinic, rather than selecting only certain patients as research subjects. Neither therapists nor patients are to know which cases are to constitute the research group. The total sample for the first phase of the study consists of 42 cases, about half of them treated by standard psychoanalysis and half by analytically oriented interview therapy. The data will include information obtained at three points in time: at the beginning of treatment, at its termination, and at a follow-up two years later. (The average length of treatment is three years.) Forms have been developed on which experienced clinicians will abstract from the full case material, the information with regard to three classes of variables: data concerning the patient, the process of treatment, and the patient's life situation. Detailed outlines of the variables included under each of these headings have been made. Some of them will be assessed quantitatively using a paired-comparison procedure. Others will enter into specific predictions concerning the patient's behavior during and after treatment and concerning the kinds of change that will occur. These predictions will be confirmed or disconfirmed by what is found during the assessments at the time of termination and follow-up, thus supporting or failing to support the kinds of thinking ("analytic," "dynamic," or whatever) on which they were based. At the later periods, notes from interviews and other ways of sizing up the process of therapy will be used to throw light on the question of where some predictions went wrong. This should enable the researchers to sharpen their hypotheses and improve their research methods with subsequent series of cases.

Today we find that the influence of Freud's ideas and the psychoanalytic movement he founded has spread into every domain of human living. The number of psychoanalytic papers and books published is so enormous that Grinstein's *Index of Psychoanalytic Writings* (1956-1960) requires five volumes. Psychoanalytic theory has generated more research than any other personality theory (Hall & Lindzey, 1957). Because it has spread so widely, it has tended to penetrate more and more into social sciences in general, especially as the recent developments in ego psychology have made it possible to integrate perception, intelligence, and thought into a psychoanalytic framework. Psychoanalysis is also the dominant theory that underlies practice in many related areas of psychological service, such as social work.

Despite this widespread acclaim, and perhaps partly because of it, the critics of psychoanalysis are numerous. One of them, LaPiere (1959), for instance, has examined the values implied in Freudianism and denounced them as socially irresponsible. He goes so far as to say that they might ultimately destroy the values Western civilization prizes most. The semantic looseness that characterizes psychoanalytic theory and the difficulty of proving or disproving it are objects of criticism by philosophers of science, as illustrated in a recent symposium (Hook, 1959). For all of the research on psychoanalysis, it can be said of it (as also of other personality theories) that its "empirical validity remains largely undemonstrated" (Hall & Lindzey, 1957, p. 557). Psychoanalysis, nevertheless, is still uncrystallized and still growing. Many of its adherents are vigorously attempting to improve its scientific conceptualization, as demonstrated by the report of a recent conference (Bellak, 1959). Madison's intensive analysis (1961) of the foundation stone of Freudian theory, repression, including his concrete suggestions for research, is a major contribution. Meanwhile, Hilgard's Janus-faced summary of the status of psychoanalysis is a good one to remember: "Anyone who tried to give an honest appraisal of psychoanalysis as a science must be ready to admit that as it is stated it is mostly very bad science, that the bulk of the articles in its journals cannot be defended as research publications at all. Having said this, I am prepared to reassert that there is much to be learned from these writings" (1952, p. 44).

SUMMARY

Psychoanalytic ways of thinking are undoubtedly the leading influence in psychotherapy today. Freud based much of his thinking on the concept of the unconscious, a reservoir of impulses and repressed wishes. Psychoanalytic therapy of the orthodox sort is a prolonged and intense process. Its major techniques include free association, catharsis, and interpretation. Change and reconstruction of personality is supposed to come through the release of repression and the resolution of the transference neurosis. Analytically oriented psychotherapists attempt a briefer treatment through a flexible application of a variety of techniques. Psychoanalytic principles have been widely applied and its methods adapted for play therapy, group therapy, hypnoanalysis, and similar types of therapy. Psychoanalytically oriented therapists believe a careful study of their patients is desirable. Projective methods of assessment are frequently used to uncover unconscious as well as preconscious material and difficulties of interpersonal adjustment. Since psychoanalysis is so widespread and influential, it has permeated a great deal of contemporary thinking about personality and psychotherapy. Research on psychoanalytic approaches overlaps very much with research in psychotherapy in general. Vehement criticism of psychoanalysis has matched in intensity some of the fervor of its protagonists. What we need most is a soundly conceived program for testing psychoanalysis, as well as other approaches, using rigorous methods and controls.

SUGGESTED READINGS

FREUD, S. *Collected papers.* Vol. III. *Case histories.* London: Hogarth, 1925.
This volume, one of several in the *Collected Papers,* includes nearly all his cases which Freud described at length. It opens with the "Fragment of an Analysis of a Case of Hysteria," the famous case of Dora, which had much to do with Freud's early theoretical development. There is also the case of Little Hans, the first application of analysis to a child; also the case of Schreber, in which Freud's ideas on paranoia and the mechanism of projection are outlined. Obsessional neurosis and infantile neurosis are taken up in the light of specific cases. Familiarity with Freud's more general works, such as those found in *The Basic Writings of Sigmund Freud* (1938), is assumed.

GILL, M. The present state of psychoanalytic theory. *J. abnorm. soc. Psychol.,* 1959, 58, 1-8.
See this article for an abbreviated but remarkably clear exposition of recent changes in psychoanalytic theory. Gill discusses motivation, drives, maturation, thought processes, and the structural point of view. He indicates that recent changes involve paying more attention to the effects of environment, to the surface features of behavior, to ego functions, and to cognitive and adaptive behaviors. For a much more detailed attempt at systematizing contemporary psychoanalytic theory, see D. Rapaport (1959).

FENICHEL, O. *The Collected Papers of Otto Fenichel.* (First series.) New York: Norton, 1953. See Ch. 28, "Psychoanalytic Method."
This paper on psychoanalytic method, written in 1935, is one of the clearest brief statements of the theory underlying technique. The emphasis is on the use of interpretation to overcome resistance.

MENNINGER, K. *Theory of psychoanalytic technique.* New York: Basic Books, 1958.
This small book, written by one of the world's leading psychoanalysts, is another of the few publications on the conceptual framework of analytic technique. Menninger sees the analytic situation as a contract between therapist and patient. He gives considerable attention to the frustrating nature of this situation for the patient. A critical review of the book by Symonds, himself a writer of books on therapy, may be found in *Contemporary Psychology,* 1959, 4.

DOLLARD, J., AULD, F. Jr., & WHITE, Alice M. *Steps in psychotherapy.* New York: Macmillan, 1953.

This is a very interesting book in the way it presents a case of psycho-analytically oriented therapy. The verbatim transcript is given and commented on by the supervisor of the therapist.

RESEARCH EXAMPLES

SHEVRIN, H., & LUBORSKY, L. The measurement of preconscious perception in dreams and images: an investigation of the Poetzl phenomenon. *J. abnorm. soc. Psychol.*, 1958, 56, 285-294.

This experimental study, carried out at the Menninger Foundation, is one of many investigations into psychoanalytically slanted hypotheses about personality processes. Some of the most basic assumptions upon which Freud founded his system concern the nature of the unconscious as a dynamic motivating part of personality. Freud called dreams "the royal road to the unconscious." Shevrin and Luborsky in this study have brought together the Freudian theory of dreams and the findings and ideas of Poetzl. Poetzl discovered in 1917, quite independently of Freud, that subjects sometimes dreamed about originally unreported parts of a picture they had previously been shown.

The procedure of Shevrin and Luborsky, which was an extension and improvement on earlier work, was as follows: After a complicated picture was flashed for one-fiftieth of a second in a tachistoscope in front of the subject, he was asked to describe it as fully as possible and make a drawing of it. Later, before he left the session, he was asked to remember and write down any dreams he might have the following night and to come back the next day. On the next day, he was asked to describe his dreams and draw anything pictured in them. If he did not report a dream, he was interrogated about his thoughts before falling asleep. He was then asked to close his eyes and let a picture come to mind, which he drew. Later he was shown the original picture and asked if he could see any connections between it and his dreams or images. All of the interview was recorded on tape. The resulting drawings and verbal reports were scored for the number of elements in the dream or image having a conceptual similarity with elements in the picture. High interjudge reliability (.84) was achieved for the measure of "preconscious recall," the number of new picture items appearing in the dreams and images. The dreams and images and reports of recall were also rated independently by judges on their unpleasantness. Twenty-seven persons served as subjects.

In general, these experimenters obtained results which they see as confirming the hypothesis of Poetzl that dream imagery "excludes" conscious perception in favor of preconscious perception, and also confirming Freud's hypothesis that the preconscious perceptions serve as a "cover" for unconscious and threatening ideas which would not otherwise escape the censor. As evidence of this latter point, a .57 correlation was obtained between preconscious recall and unpleasantness.

Such a study as this contains weak links here and there. There is dependence on subjective judgments in many places, and a number of questionable assumptions are made. It is an important line of investigation that needs to be followed up by a number of research workers before we can put much faith in its claimed findings. Readers who consult the article may find it interesting to examine the article following it, a study by Meissner (1958) investigating another side of psychoanalysis—the affective value of symbols.

SPEISMAN, J. C. Depth of interpretation and verbal resistance in psychotherapy. *J. consult. Psychol.*, 1959, 23, 93-99.

This study, done as a doctoral thesis, deals with two important aspects of psychotherapy: the therapist's depth of interpretation and the patient's resistance to interpretations. Speisman's study was stimulated by the disagreement he had noticed between psychoanalytic and nondirective procedures. Fenichel, a renowned analytic theorist, advises therapists to interpret what appears to be just beyond the preconscious, while Rogers suggests that therapists should clarify what the client has already stated. Both are opposed to deep interpretations.

The principal instruments used in the research were two rating scales. One was a seven-point Depth of Interpretation Scale developed earlier. At the one end, a rating of "1" would be given if the therapist's statement was judged to be a mere repetition of material of which the patient is fully aware. At the deep interpretation end, a rating of "7" would indicate that the therapist dealt with inferences about material completely outside the patient's awareness. Moderate levels of interpretation would be rated if the therapist connected two aspects of content mentioned previously or commented on the patient's bodily and facial expressions as manifestations of his feelings. The rating scale for resistance was developed by Speisman to cover three positive categories (the patient's exploration, self-scrutiny, and self-orientation), and three negative categories (the patient's statement of opposition, superficial remarks, and blocking). The reliability of the depth of Interpretation Scale was satisfactory. The Resistance Scale was not as satisfactory in part, and the results are reported only for the ratings for exploration and opposition. The ratings were applied to transcripts from interviews with 22 neurotic patients by a wide variety of therapists. Twelve judges familiar with psychotherapy did the ratings for depth of interpretation. Three different judges rated for resistance, using the patient's transcribed responses only.

The results supported the formulation that deep interpretations lead to the most resistance, moderate interpretations to the least resistance, and superficial interpretations fall between the other two levels. All of the results were in the predicted direction and most were statistically significant. However, the degree of association (as indicated by Kendall's tau) was not high. The author, following Fenichel, concludes that "moderate interpretations encourage free expression by producing a new frame of reference or by making new connections for materials which are close to consciousness" (p. 99). However, deep interpretations touch repressed materials that have no direct connection with consciousness, and superficial interpretations function only with what is already conscious and provide no encouragement for further exploration.

These findings, confirming opinions of experienced therapists, also suggest that more research must be done defining the nature of interpretation and discovering what the optimum amount of interpretation in interviews is. Some of the early work of Rogers and his group on therapist-response classes is relevant. Snyder (1945), for instance, showed by analyzing transcripts that clarification of feeling comprised about half of the counselor's activity and simple acceptance about 30 per cent. There was also a small amount of structuring, approval, and encouragement. Seeman (1949) suggested later that client-centered interviewing had changed; by then, 63 per cent of the therapist's activity was then clarification of feeling. Speisman's study does not, of course, prove that Fenichel was right and Rogers wrong. Actually, Rogerian reflection of feeling would be classified on Speisman's scale somewhere in the moderate range for depth of interpretation. This study does not claim, of course, to report on longer range effects of different therapists' procedures.

17 Psychotherapy as Interpersonal Relations and Communications

Man is a social creature. He is born into a world where he must immediately start depending on others for his very life. The long childhood of man as compared with all other animals has made it possible and, indeed, necessary, for each older generation to·exert powerful influences upon the generation that succeeds it. The prodigious variety of cultures that have arisen and the great changes that have occurred during the history of man on this earth testify to the overriding important of this malleability of man at the hands of man. Many theorists are convinced that undesirable forms of interpersonal relationships must lie at the roots of those disturbed ways of living we call maladjustment, neurosis, or even psychosis.

HISTORY AND VIEWPOINT

On the whole there has been a surprising failure to recognize the full extent of the influence of society upon human behavior. As Gardner Murphy (1959) has said, early writers developed theories of man almost without reference to society and they developed theories of society almost without reference to man. Perhaps the reason for this in the West has been our preoccupation with the individual soul, conceived as an

entity created independently of man's group life. Even in the late nineteenth century, when Freud began to formulate his revolutionary ideas,
social psychology had hardly begun. Freud reacted against the strictness
of Victorian demands for control of impulses. His basic formulations
were individualistic and biologic, with society pictured in the role of
suppressor of individual drives, especially the sexual and aggressive
impulses. However, interpersonal ideas, such as his concepts of the
Oedipal relation and transference, lie close to the center of his system,
and later developments in psychoanalysis have seized upon and expanded his admission of the importance of social influences.

Shortly before World War I, Adler broke with Freud because Freud
would not admit the importance of inferiority feelings and the will to
power in explaining psychological disorders. Adler sought a basically
social interpretation of human motivation, in opposition to Freud's interpretation of motives as instinctual. Traces of Adler's concepts of power
struggle, social interest, life style, and the significance of early recollections and family constellation, concepts discussed in more detail in
Chapter 15, may be found in many recent developments in psychotherapy. In fact it has more than once been suggested that the contemporary "Neo-Freudians" could just as well be designated "Neo-Adlerians."
During the early part of this century social philosophy has developed
greatly and it, together with cultural anthropology, has strongly influenced the rise of several varieties of socially oriented psychotherapy.
Adolf Meyer's approach to psychiatry gave a prominent place to the
social influences as well as biological. Karen Horney, Erik Homburger
Erikson, and Erich Fromm adhere to forms of psychoanalysis modified
by the introduction of social concepts.

The man whose name is most closely connected with the interpersonal
emphasis in psychoanalysis and psychotherapy is Harry Stack Sullivan.
Sullivan's thinking developed out of the ideas of Freud, of psychiatrists
like Adolph Meyer and William Alanson White, on one hand, and social
psychologists, social philosophers, sociologists, and cultural anthropologists, on the other. He defined psychiatry as the study of interpersonal
relations. His ideas are mainly set down in his *Conceptions of Modern
Psychiatry* (1947) and in several volumes of his notes (Sullivan, 1953,
1954, 1956), published by his colleagues and students after his untimely
death in 1949.

Some psychoanalysts, aware that at many points Sullivan deviated
from orthodox psychoanalytic theory, have debated whether Sullivan's
approach should be called psychoanalysis or not. To this discussion
Clara Thompson has contributed the following statement: "If by psychoanalysis one means recognition of unconscious motivation, the influence of repression and resistance on the personality, and the existence
of transference, then Sullivan's thinking fulfills all requirements for being

considered psychoanalysis. He himself was not concerned with this point and preferred to call his therapeutic approach, intensive psychotherapy" (1952, p. 107).

At the focus of Sullivan's theory was his concern with the *anxiety-arousing aspects of interpersonal relations during early development*. As soon as the human being is born he must start depending on interpersonal interactions for satisfaction of his needs. Crying and other acts are ways of getting what he needs from the environment. The nurturant action, or tenderness, of the one who mothers a baby, is vital for its life. If the mother is distraught, insecure, and anxious, the infant becomes anxious also. Anxiety, Sullivan believed, is transmitted by a vaguely defined process called *empathy*. Long before he develops speech, the child can sense feelings; thus the "significant others," especially the parents, have an immense influence in laying the basic foundations for the development of his personality.

The infant begins incorporating a *self-system* consisting of learned ways of avoiding anxiety primarily by *selective inattention* and *dissociation*. Through his perceptions of how he is being appraised and valued by others he begins implicitly labelling some tendencies in himself as the "*bad-me,*" and other tendencies as the "*good-me.*" When such tendencies to judge himself are accompanied by overwhelming anxiety, certain areas of personality may become the "*not-me,*" thus laying the groundwork for later experiences of uncanny emotions, depersonalization, and even schizophrenic episodes and trends.

Sullivan took up the later periods of life and analyzed the interpersonal problems typical of them and the meaning of these problems in terms of self-system development and its dynamisms. Whereas Freud saw the Oedipus complex as deriving from innate predisposition, Sullivan held that a similar outcome might well result from the interpersonal dynamics of the parent-child relationship, if the patient had a harsh authoritarian father and an excessively tender mother. In further development of his theory, Sullivan paid considerable attention to preadolescence and adolescence. During these periods, in addition to the continued need for security, there develops a need to be intimate with others outside the home, especially one's peers. In adolescence and adulthood there is a potential conflict between needs for security and intimacy and needs for sexual satisfaction. Thus the human being develops through a series of changing interpersonal needs. Mental illness results from an over-reliance on one form of operation or dynamism of the self-system, such as obsessionalism, selective inattention, or emotionality.

One other cardinal concept of interpersonal theory should be mentioned. The connecting linkage between persons is *communication*. Sullivan stressed the importance of all sorts of clues by which people interpret the actions of others. He delineated the different modes of communication, and was especially alert to nonverbal communication. The simple, crude empathic feeling the infant experiences before his sensory organization is complete is called communication in the *pro-totaxic mode*. The *parataxic mode* develops a little later as the child experiences reward and punishment in his emotional life. By this term Sullivan meant communication by gesture and symbols not precise enough to serve as labels for a fully differentiated experience. *Parataxic distortion* is a more common-place occurrence than most people realize. It happens when we react to people with unrealistic feelings of fear, mistrust, love, or awe. It happens in professional interviews when the patient reacts toward the clinician as if he were his father. Psycho-analytic transference is, then, an instance of parataxic distortion. Mature and direct communication coordinated with "reality" is termed experi-ence in the *syntaxic mode*. Such communications are open to *consensual validation,* confirmation, or negation in interaction with others. Others following in Sullivan's general framework have further amplified the nature of communication (Ruesch & Bateson, 1951; Ruesch, 1959). One particular development has been the *double-bind hypothesis* (Bateson et al, 1956), in which it is hypothesized that schizophrenia can develop from a situation in which a covertly hostile parent gives the child one message on one level of communication but denies or countermands it on another level; thus the child is caught between the two messages, being, as it were, damned if he does react and damned if he does not.

SULLIVAN'S INTERPERSONAL THERAPY

Sullivan was bent upon developing the concrete implications for therapy of his interpersonal theory. In his professional work, he dealt mainly with schizophrenics and obsessional neurotics. Up to his time, there had been but few attempts to apply psychoanalysis to schizophrenia, and his contribution to this difficult problem was especially important.

Sullivan's therapeutic strategy involved an intensive analysis of char-acter, exposing the patient's way of living and especially his unique methods of dealing with other persons. In the concluding pages of his very readable book on interviewing (1954), he asks what there is in therapy that brings about a favorable change in the person. First he points out that when a person cannot learn from new experience and is prevented from moving forward, it is because sometime in his past it has become dangerous to inquire into certain experiences. The patient has been taught to shy away from an area of life where he feels threatened. Here is how Sullivan puts it:

When a person comes to an interviewer with a problem, the assumption is that this person has been *restrained from using the totality of his abilities*. The problem of the psychiatrist in treatment is to discover what the *handicaps* to

the use of his abilities are. . . . The *real* problem which I hope finally to uncover, to my patient's satisfaction and with his clear insight, is *what stands in
the way* of his making the conventional, and therefore the comparatively simple
adjustment, which is regarded as normal (1954, p. 237).

Again he says (p. 238), "what counts is what you discover about the
person—what particular terrors, menaces, and risks other people hold
for him." The goal is to uncover the person's recurrent interpersonal
mistakes.

Sullivan did not have a ready-made pattern of the "good life" to which
he tried to make patients conform. He saw the person as somehow
hindered, held back from a straightforward adjustment, and his task was
to disentangle him from these hindrances. He stated:

. . . In well over twenty-five years—I have never found myself called upon
to "cure" anybody. The patients took care of that, once I had done the
necessary brush-clearing, and so on. It is almost uncanny how things fade
out of the picture when their *raison d'etre* is revealed. The brute fact is that
man is so extraordinarily adaptive, that, given any chance of making a reasonably adequate analysis of the situation, he is quite likely to stumble into a
series of experiments which will gradually approximate more successful living
(1954, p. 238).

The tactics with which Sullivan works toward the achievement of his
strategy from the inception and early stages of the interview till the
termination are taken up in detail in *The Psychiatric Interview* (1954).
Tying together a wide variety of his ideas, he defined the psychiatric
interview as "a situation of primarily *vocal* communication in a *two-
group* more-or-less *voluntarily integrated,* on a progressively unfolding
expert-client basis for the purpose of elucidating *characteristic patterns
of living* of the subject person, the patient or client, which patterns he
experiences as particularly troublesome and especially valuable, and in
the revealing of which he expects to derive benefit" (p. 4). Sullivan's
terminology tells much about his sociopsychological standpoint. The
thought in this book is clear and it contains many illustrative instances,
but unfortunately we have been unable to find here or elsewhere any
transcriptions of therapeutic sessions as he conducted them.

It is apparent that Sullivan must have possessed extreme sensitivity
for the verbal and nonverbal communications of his patient. As a therapist he considered himself to be a participant observer highly involved
in the process, and therefore hard at work. In trying to unravel the
meanings of the patient's communications the clinician listens to each
statement with critical interest, asking himself if it could mean something other than what first comes to mind. The clinician attempts to
clarify communication and to help the patient face reality as honestly
as possible. Sullivan frequently exemplifies this tactful but critical attitude in the interview. For instance, Sullivan says:

. . . A patient may say, "Well, he's my dearest friend! He hasn't a hostile impulse toward me!" I then assume that this is to explain in some curious fashion that this other person has done him an extreme disservice. . . . And I say, "Is that so? It sounds amazing." Now when I say a thing sounds amazing, the patient feels very much on the spot . . . and tells me more about how wonderful his friend's motivation is. Having heard still more, I am able to say, "Well, is it possible that you can think of nothing he ever did that was at least unfortunate in its effect?" . . . And thus we gradually come to discover why it is necessary for him to consider this other person to be such a perfect friend— quite often a very illuminating field to explore. God knows, it may be the nearest approach to a good friend this man has ever had, and he feels exceedingly the need of a friend (1954, p. 20).

Thus the clinician plays a very active role in questioning in order to clarify communications. "Almost every time one asks, 'Well, do you mean so and so?' the patient is a little clearer on what he does mean" (p. 21). Sullivan believed in very extensive history-taking at the start of therapy. The history-taking often required many interviews and proceeded in a frank and direct manner through clarification of the reasons for seeking therapy, a complete social history, and detailed inquiry about many aspects of personality. Free association to uncover blind spots was used. The patient's relationship with the therapist himself often came in for attention and clarification. The therapist was always on the alert to discover which periods in life or which topics of discussion aroused anxiety in the patient and were associated with his "security operations."

IMPLICATIONS FOR ASSESSMENT

History-taking is a cardinal procedure for anyone who holds views like Sullivan's. He did not see the extensive exploration of life history as a separate assessment device, but rather as the beginning of therapy. In his writings Sullivan paid scarcely any attention to psychological testing, and there has been little emphasis on special assessment devices or tests among his psychiatric followers. A psychologist cannot, however, see why certain psychological tests might not lend themselves to the kind of investigation of interpersonal attitudes, behavior, and communication with which adherents of Sullivan's views are so deeply concerned.

An excellent example of how psychological assessment can be applied to the interpersonal aspects of clinical problems is provided by Timothy Leary (1957), who was indirectly influenced by Sullivan. Leary's system of interpersonal diagnosis, described in Chapter 7, consists of several levels of communication between the person and his inner and outer environment, primarily the levels of overt public communication, conscious self-descriptions, and private symbolization. These levels are mainly assessed by the MMPI, an adjective checklist, and the TAT. It also will be recalled that Leary has developed a scheme for classifying the directions of interpersonal behavior. There are 16 directions or 8 octants, the two fundamental axes being dominance-submission and hostility-affiliation. The circular diagram on which the levels and directions are plotted provides a representation of the patient's interpersonal approach to life. This diagram can be used in planning therapy, and the patient can be studied at different periods to observe shifts in his interpersonal behavior.

Also, as briefly mentioned in Chapter 7, Schutz (1958) has developed tests in connection with a system of his own devising entitled a Fundamental Interpersonal Relations Orientation. He postulates that there are three basic interpersonal needs: inclusion (to be a part of a group), control, and affection. (It will be noted that Schutz's dimensions of control and affection are similar to Leary's dimensions of dominance-submission and hostility-affiliation.) Somewhat like Leary, Schutz also deals with different levels of behavior, differentiating between behavior that is "expressed" or merely "wanted." Schutz's system, like Leary's, is expressed in a set of principles or postulates which he believes will make interpersonal theory more amenable to scientific testing. The major testing instrument, called FIRO-B, is a rational set of scales composed of statements about both expressed and wanted needs for inclusion, control, and affection. Schutz has used his tests in social psychological research and in studying group dynamics. However, there has been but little use of this system in clinical situations as yet.

Several other nascent possibilities for interpersonal assessment may be noted. Ruesch (1957) has detailed very carefully a method of interviewing designed to detect and diagnose disturbed communication. His proposals might be used for developing assessment devices. Assessment methods for the clinic could be developed from techniques used in research in social psychology, where sociometric evaluations and standardized observations are common procedures. One psychologist, Luchins (1959), has proposed a system of training clinical students by requiring them first to make an observational "assessment" of a hospital ward or of a community situation rather than to begin by using standard psychological tests. A thorough-going application of such a radical proposal would seem to require the creative development of many new assessment approaches.

CRITICAL EVALUATION

The interpersonal approach to psychotherapy constitutes an excellent counterbalance to the earlier too individualistic and instinctual formulations of psychoanalysis. Sullivan has been successful in showing us all the importance of social and cultural factors in mental illness. Particularly in his profound concern with schizophrenics and in developing therapeutic methods for use with this form of psychosis, he has made a notable contribution. It has been said that Freud brought understanding and therapy to the neuroses; Wilhelm Reich to the character disorders; and Sullivan to schizophrenia. Any tendency there may have been to found a distinct school around the ideas and methods of Sullivan seems to be fading, but his legacy of the interpersonal and social approach to psychotherapy remains one of the dominant forces in American psychiatry and psychology. In time, his contribution, together with those of Horney and Adler, will very likely merge into the tide of still newer contributions to the sociopsychological and cultural understanding of behavioral disorders.

In evaluating each of the forms of psychotherapy considered in these chapters, we have summarized such research studies of outcome and process as we could locate. Like their more orthodox psychoanalytic confreres, Sullivan and his associates have paid little attention to the formal kind of research psychologists have generally felt should be carried out. Some projects are being started by "neo-Sullivanians" (e.g., by Dittmann in Washington and Jackson and his group in Palo Alto), but as yet there is little to report. If we should widen the scope of relevant research to include all work on interpersonal processes, we would open up a large part of the vast field of social psychology, a field, though ultimately of great import for therapy, now too far removed to serve for our necessarily restricted purposes. The general research on psychotherapy into which this approach merges will be discussed in Chapter 19.

However, we cannot agree with Hall and Lindzey (1957) in what we feel is their unduly hasty criticism of the socially oriented theories of Sullivan, Horney, Fromm, and Adler for not being research-oriented and stimulating to research. To us this criticism seems premature, at least in Sullivan's case. Some significant research has developed out of Sullivan's emphasis on interpersonal relations, of which Leary's interpersonal diagnostic system is one example. The investigations of hospital milieu by Stanton and Schwartz (1957) also grew directly out of Sullivan's interpersonal approach. These investigators, one a psychiatrist and one a sociologist, studied intensively and for several years what was being done in a private sanatarium near Washington. They observed and kept records of the behavior of psychotic patients in a ward and sought to discover how this behavior was related to the ongoing activities of the staff and to interpersonal interactions that occurred between themselves and the patients. They were able to show a connection between periods of heightened disturbance in the patients and disagreements and poor communication among staff members. In general they demonstrated the importance of taking human relationships into account for the understanding of what happens to individual patients. This study has sparked other case studies of hospitals and even of whole communities.

The socially oriented therapists have done their part in the rapidly accelerating development of the behavioral sciences and have done much to heighten and direct this movement. They have also contributed to the group and community therapeutic work that will be mentioned in the next chapter. In their concern with the whole social environment they have sought ways of achieving a "sane society" (especially Fromm, 1955). Sullivan at the time of his death was actively engaged in trying to organize international efforts to promote better social health.

SUMMARY

Partly as a rebellion against the individualistic and biological emphasis of Freudian thinking, Adler, Horney, Fromm, and Sullivan have developed new kinds of social approaches to psychotherapy. In Sullivan's interpersonal system the key to disorder was sought in anxiety-arousing interpersonal relations in early development. The growing child's self-perceptions develop through other persons' appraisals of himself. He begins labelling some parts of himself as good and others as bad. If the accompanying anxiety is great enough to overwhelm him, he may reject portions of his own personality, thus laying the groundwork for later psychotic or near-psychotic experiences. Unsuccessful or unfortunate communication with others lies at the center of psychological disorders, mature and direct communication being coordinated with reality and, in the normal instances, being open to consensual validation. During the therapeutic process, Sullivan spent a great deal of time trying to understand how the patient had been trying to cope with what was happening between himself and other persons and helping him become aware of these relations. He analyzed nonverbal as well as verbal communications. He also emphasized the social milieu of the patient and encouraged the study of hospital wards and communities. Sullivan and the other socially oriented psychiatrists have made rather little use of psychological tests. However, some psychologists, notably Leary, introduced promising innovations in the development of methods of interpersonal assessment. Critical research upon the efficacy of this approach to therapy is scanty and is not always easy to distinguish from research on therapy in general.

SUGGESTED READINGS

SULLIVAN, H. S. *The psychiatric interview.* New York: Norton, 1954.
  This very readable book based on notes from Sullivan's lectures gives us his thinking about the structure of the therapeutic interview and goes into details on therapist-patient interactions. There are many illustrations of interpersonal communications, both verbal and nonverbal. A suggested outline for taking case histories is included.

HORNEY, Karen. *Neurosis and human growth.* New York: Norton, 1950.

This book, Horney's last, is a summary of much of her thought. Her basic assumption is that human beings given a chance will grow toward self-realization, because the real self operates dynamically to guide the person's constructive efforts. However, since the child is also driven by whatever basic anxiety he has acquired from his early experiences, he may have developed conflicts and these can lead to neuroses. The culture has within it conflicts that stimulate neurotic developments.

SPIEGEL, J. P. The resolution of role conflict within the family. *Psychiatry,* 1957, 20, 1-16.

Role theory is an important development that has only recently begun to claim the place it deserves in clinical assessment and therapy. In this article, a psychiatrist, Spiegel, analyzes the family in terms of its members' roles. The family is a small-scale social system, in which many processes are oriented toward the development and maintainance of an equilibrium. Usually family roles complement each other easily, and problems requiring decisions are few, since most of the business of the family runs along fairly automatically. However, strains arising from role conflicts throw the family into disequilibrium. In such cases the family seeks to reestablish equilibrium by manipulation (role induction) or by mutual insight (role modification). Spiegel bases his analysis on work with families where there are disturbed children. For those interested in exploring role theory further, the work of Mangus (1957) in marriage counseling and the theoretical analysis by Sarbin (1954) are important. Kelly (1955) should also be remembered here as one who used "fixed role" therapy.

RESEARCH EXAMPLES

RAUSH, H. L., DITTMANN, A. T., & TAYLOR, T. J. The interpersonal behavior of children in residential treatment. *J. abnorm. soc. Psychol.,* 1959, 58, 9-26.

A very important study for its application of observational methods to the description of individuals and settings in everyday life. Its methods were developed out of earlier work by Barker and Wright as well as certain concepts and techniques of Freedman, Leary, Coffey, and others. The research took place at the National Institute of Mental Health where Redl and his coworkers had been intensively studying hyperaggressive boys for several years. This study covered the period when the six boys in the group were from eight to about ten years of age.

The children were observed twice in each of six settings at 18-month intervals. Each set of observations was made during a brief period of time, after which the observer immediately dictated detailed notes without interpretation. The six settings in which the boys were observed were: breakfast, snacks before bedtime, other mealtimes, structured game activities, unstructured group activities, and an arts-and-crafts period.

The records of the observations were analyzed by a coding scheme. The coder took the attitude of the "generalized other," attempting to answer by his categorization, "What is this person doing to the other? What kind of relationship is he attempting to establish?" The categories coded were based on two polar coordinates: one running from love to hate and the other from domination to submission. Thus four categories of interpersonal behavior were obtained: hostile-dominant action, friendly-dominant action, hostile-passive action, and friendly-passive action. In addition, the authors coded for the intensity of involvement in the action.

The results, presented in considerable detail, were as follows: Over the 18 months the interpersonal behavior of the children shifted considerably, with more change in the way they behaved toward adults than in the way they behaved toward other children. Hostile-dominant behavior decreased and friendly-passive behavior increased. The appropriateness of the behavior toward both children and adults increased. To what extent the changes were due to the natural development of children over the 18-month period and to what extent they were due to individual therapy (each boy received four hours per week) and to the institutional milieu is not clear from this study. The changes were in the direction aimed at by the treatment and it seems reasonable to suppose that they were in part a function of the treatment program.

In general, changes in behavior of the boys toward others were accompanied by reciprocal changes in the behavior of others toward them, both adults and children. In their relations with their peers, each child was likely to receive about as much aggression as he gave out, but from adults they received less than they gave. The authors of this study pointed to the fact that Barker and Wright, working with different subjects in a different setting and using different methods, found many patterns of behavior used by adults in dealing with children that were the same as those observed in this special situation.

It seems very important that there be more research of this kind. The direct study of behavior in everyday living situations would provide a base line that cannot be obtained by the usual clinical and laboratory methods. The interested reader should examine another article by Raush, Dittmann, and Taylor (1959*b*). In the same situation they analyzed with a new mathematical technique the interaction between persons and settings as they influence behavior.

FARINA, A. Patterns of role dominance and conflict in parents of schizophrenic patients. *J. abnorm. soc. Psychol.*, 1960, 61, 31-38.

In this significant study, Farina used an ingenious situational test to examine some hypotheses derived from clinical observations. A number of clinicians have reported that one of the parents of schizophrenic patients dominates over the other to an unusual degree and that there is heightened conflict and hostility between the two. It has also been claimed that schizophrenic patients from father-dominated homes tend to be married, have more friends, and have a generally better premorbid adjustment than patients from mother-dominated homes. The major purpose of this study was to investigate these reported associations between the adequacy of premorbid adjustment and the sex of the dominant parent and amount of conflict between the parents.

The subjects, 36 pairs of white parents, were divided into three groups of 12 each. Parents of the control group had sons who had been hospitalized for pulmonary tuberculosis. Parents of the "Good Premorbid" group had sons hospitalized for schizophrenia about the same length of time as the control group. Parents of the "Poor Premorbid" group had sons who were poorly adjusted before hospitalization for schizophrenia. Good and poor premorbid adjustment were separated on the basis of a scale developed by Phillips (1953). The sons of all three groups were similar in age (average 29 years) and education, and they came from lower-middle-class backgrounds.

The procedure for determining dominance and conflict between the parents was as follows: While one parent was out of the room taking a test, an interviewer asked the other parent to describe how he would handle 12 hypothetical problem situations in child-rearing. Then the activities of the parents were reversed. Finally both of them were brought together before the interviewer. They were presented with the 12 problem situations again and asked to come to a common agreement on how they would handle them. All of the interviews were recorded. The indices of dominance and conflict were derived from the recordings. Indices of dominance included which parent spoke first or last, the total time speaking, and the amount that one parent yielded to the other (discovered from comparisons of the content of the individual interviews with the content of the group interviews with each pair). Indices of conflict were number of interruptions, disagreements, and failures to agree. The three groups were statistically compared on each of these indices.

The results were quite clear. Father-dominance was found to be associated with good premorbid adjustment of the schizophrenic son, and mother-dominance characterized sons with poor premorbid adjustment. The author interprets this result as indicating that it has been easier for the good premorbid group to acquire the expected behavior of an adult male and to achieve a somewhat higher level of maturity. With regard to dominance, the control group was generally in the middle, being significantly less father-dominated than the good premorbid group and significantly less mother-dominated than the poor premorbid group. In regard to conflict present in the parental interaction, the parents of both schizophrenic groups displayed more conflict than the control parents. Conflict was particularly marked in the cases of parents of the poor premorbid group.

This highly important study needs to be repeated and extended. One wonders what kinds of family interaction characterize the homes from which other types of mental patients come. More study of what constitutes normal family interaction is needed. A similar study of parents of schizophrenic daughters should be undertaken. Without further evidence we cannot assume direct causation from this study, but the hypothesis would seem reasonable that if a longitudinal study were carried out, some of these same factors might turn up in the early lives of persons who later become disturbed.

18 Group Therapy and Other Social Approaches

So far we have mostly concerned ourselves with psychotherapy as a form of influence upon individuals. However, the disturbances of individuals are in a sense not confined to the individual alone. Both in their origins and in their effects, psychological ailments and disturbances can be said to reach outward so that other people are involved—the person's family, his working partners, and his friends. Also in our society, individuals, far more than they realize, are embedded in a matrix of social habits and institutions that determine the very texture of their lives and the roles they are permitted to play.

There are many differences between working in any relationship with an individual by himself and working with a group of people. It is true that in individual therapy, which has been the main occupation of therapists, there is already a kind of group—a two-person group or *dyad*. Because this is so, some people have thought that the principles of individual therapy could simply be extended to cover any additional individuals who might happen to be brought together to work with a therapist. However, as the old saying puts it, "three's a crowd," and there is a decided difference between even a two-person and a three-person situation. As the number of persons interacting in a group increases, new possibilities and complications arise. For one thing, since time is limited, the more people there are in a group, the less opportunity

405

each individual will have to talk. As the number in a group increases, the possibilities for the formation of relationships between subgroups of different sizes rapidly expands. In a three-person group, three pairings are possible, but in a six-person group 15 different pairs can be formed. In addition, there are all the varieties of roles in a group that people can be moved to play. When we pass from small groups to sizeable organizations and great institutions, possibilities of a quite different order of magnitude appear. Suffice it to say that an individual functioning in a group may be exposed to vastly different influences than when he is by himself with a single therapist.

GROUP THERAPIES

Because the pressures for therapeutic services have increased greatly during and since World War II, the search for new forms of therapy and new solutions to problems has been intensified. The origins of group therapy, however, go back to a considerably earlier period. Emphasis on group methods was already prominent in the 1920's in the work of Moreno (Dreikurs, 1959). Many would date the beginnings of group therapy with Pratt, an internist who in 1905 organized groups of tuberculosis patients for discussion of their emotional problems (Hadden, 1955). Prior even to this effort there had been, of course, the many kinds of group educational and inspirational approaches, some going back a century or more. In recent years, psychologists, social workers, and psychiatrists have adapted and improved on many of the older group approaches, making use of educational methods and group activities such as acting and role-playing, as well as applying the most prominent theories of therapy to group interaction. This diversity of origins and the diversity of thought among investigators active in it has made group therapy a very broad and lively area of clinical effort, one in which no particular theory or method has achieved a dominant position.

From the many forms which group approaches may take, Frank and Powdermaker (1959) have singled out five common kinds: (1) *didactic groups*, large educationally oriented groups where a group leader presents material and encourages discussion of it; (2) *therapeutic social clubs*, organized for the purpose of increasing mental patients' skills in social participation; (3) *inspirational groups*, which stress group identification and positive group emotions, such as Alcoholics Anonymous; (4) *psychodrama*, in which problems are acted out on a stage; and (5) *free-interaction groups*, which are the usual group therapy situations where an effort is made to induce expression of feelings and ideas in small group meetings. All group approaches provide social stimulation and support for patients and encourage them to test out and develop relationships with other people. Since many mental patients lack social skills, the development of a person in interaction with a group takes on added importance.

A small interaction group most frequently consists of five to ten patients. The seating arrangement is often circular so that each person can see and talk readily with any other. The therapist's responsibility is to encourage discussion and to structure it so that the flow of interaction will be therapeutic rather than damaging, but the main responsibility for the content and manner of interaction usually remains with the patients themselves. One of the things a new group therapist finds difficult is to focus his attention on the group interaction rather than on the problems and dynamics of individuals, as these become evident. He must accustom himself to thinking in terms of such things as kinds of interaction and roles patients take within the group instead of allowing himself to be diverted by individual feelings and reactions. The selection of patients for group therapy can become a rather complicated undertaking. In order that the group may go actively to work on problems it is advisable not to have its members too similar, but there must be enough common ground between them so that it is possible for them to pull together for a good part of the time. The effectiveness of group therapy arises not only from what happens during the group meetings but also from the relationships that develop among its members when the group is not meeting.

Some illustrations of how group therapy may work follow. They are selections from an introductory book by Hinckley and Hermann (1951). Their practice, a modified psychoanalytic one, is fairly common, although it is but one among a wide variety of possible ones. Hinckley and Hermann see the group therapy experience as primarily emotional, though with some rational elements in it. The therapist is expected to assume a kindly parental role in the group, remaining relatively quiet and permissive, but directing the group function in a broad general way. The first excerpt from a transcript of a group meeting, together with comments by the authors, demonstrates the effects of a minimum amount of activity by the therapist in the opening session.

Therapist (enters after men assemble). Hello men. (Members respond with various greetings.) Let's introduce ourselves first of all, and then perhaps talk a bit about ourselves. Jack, would you like to begin?

Jack. We introduced ourselves, Doc, before you got here. So I guess that's taken care of. (Pause.) Well—my problem is asthma. I've had it since I was four and no one knows what it's all about. It left me once when I was given some shots, and I thought that was it. But when I was in the Army I really began to have attacks. I got in school here and finally wound up in the Clinic. There are emotional factors, I guess. One damned thing, though, I'm far from being an emotionally adjusted person!

Albert. What do you mean—who is well adjusted? And how do you know he is?

Jack. Well—you fellows all look well adjusted, and it seems kind of foolish to shoot the bull this way! (At this point regarding the therapist with evident resentment.)

Oliver. You guys call me Oliver in here. My name is Jack, but the other Jack spoke first. (To Jack) I'd really like to correct you. I don't think this is shooting the bull or that being able to talk even is well adjusted. I think that's my problem—that I talk too easily and too much. I think it's worse than your problem. With me it's an attention-getting device, and I do it because I'm anxious.

Jack. (*To Albert*) What do you think about this?

Albert. I don't think either of you is right. Why is Oliver so easy and free, and why are you at the opposite end of the chain? What is normal?

Oliver. I'm not happy unless I'm getting attention. You sounded kind of disgusted there, Al. Well, I dream of suicide every night and of an obituary, and I have no intention of doing it. It's just attention-getting.

Jack. I still say this is just bull!

Therapist. A few moments ago when you said that, you seemed resentful toward me.

Jack (laughingly). Yeah—I guess maybe I was. I don't know why, though.

(Although up to this point the therapist has been mostly silent, one does not feel he maintains this quiet arbitrarily or punitively. After the introductory remarks, the patients pursue their own patterns. They mention some of their symptoms, disagree with each other, and one dares to show some hostility by glancing at the therapist resentfully. Yet, when this display first happens, the therapist accepts it without comment. Later, rather casually, he suggests the possibility of resentment. When Jack's tension is released a little by laughter, the therapist again lapses into silence. Nor does he suggest a cause for Jack's angry feeling or offer any explanation at all. Jack, as a matter of fact, arrives at interpretation indirectly somewhat later during the same session.)

Joel. You can call me Red—everyone does. Say, are all you guys maladjusted? One thing worries me—you fellows are all so darned normal!

Oliver. Another thing that is really my problem is that I'm accident-prone. I get into accidents about once a year—really serious ones.

Jack. You're farther along the scale, maybe, than I am, but in the Army I used to have problems too, very much like that.

Mark. I guess I'm afraid of people. My object is never to be the big wheel. I suppose they found out I had high blood pressure, and that's why they sent me up here to the Clinic. I don't know just why I have it, though. In the Navy I was in the Personnel Bureau. I was a conference reporter in one of the "red rooms."

Jack (laughingly). We're in the wrong room, boys. Let's move.

(The patients compare notes and see their resemblances and their differences. This spontaneous contrast and clarification results in group identity, a feeling one for the other in the permissive presence of the therapist. A less mature therapist easily could seize upon Oliver's admission of being accident-prone for interpretation, could point it up as a possible indication of a need to be self-punishing; or he could use Mark's comments in regard to his war assignment to show need for status. Instead, although undoubtedly aware of the inferential possibilities, the therapist permits the patients to explore further their self-directiveness.) (Hinckley & Hermann, 1951, pp. 22-24.)

There is often a beginning period in which patients work through their discomforts, establish trust in the group and the therapist, and develop a readiness to accept help and participate in the group. As group feeling grows in the early sessions, Hinckley and Hermann see the therapist as encouraging catharsis of feelings and greater freedom of association while at the same time supporting the equilibrium of any patient who appears to be under stress and keeping the group reminded of reality, of problems they have in common. The patients also support each other and are active contributors to the therapy of each other. Transference, or strong emotional feelings toward each other, develops in the group, but not as intensely as in individual therapy. Groups also show resistance to therapy through such behavior as talkativeness, denying certain implications of their symptoms, hostile attempts to break up the group, "flight into health," displacement, and other defenses. The therapist's interpretations may take the form of reflections of feelings, questions, suggestions, or explanations of motives. The following excerpt from an advanced session with another group shows not only the therapist's way of approaching interpretation, but also the interpretations which other patients may give in helping each other:

Therapist. Will you review for us what happened last time, Alice?

Alice. I was scared. I didn't like getting together with people I hardly knew. Telling things about myself was awful.

June. Well, I felt just the opposite. I loved it. I suppose the lesson of the session was that by listening to others and helping them, we learn about ourselves.

Ellen. I'm having a bad day. Someone bumped my car, and I've been fuming. I'm not sure I can contribute much today at all.

June. Now that I think about it, I don't know where to start in regard to my problems. I'm too fat. I know it's from eating too much, but there must be some reason behind it, I know. Why do I pick at food all the time?

Therapist. Tell us something more about your background, if you will.

June. Well, everybody in our family have beautiful figures. They all disapprove of my overeating.

Sara. You mean you have to fight it? You don't look overweight to me.

June (in great surprise). Won't you all come home with me?

Alice. Are you hungry all the time? Are you hungry when you're happy and satisfied?

June. No, I guess not. I was with a fellow over the weekend and had a wonderful time, and I wasn't hungry at all.

Therapist. Sounds psychological. Perhaps you know something of the psychology of overeating.

Alice. My little niece has the same sort of trouble.

June. Well, I suppose when you keep on eating all the time and never really get satisfied, it can't be food you want at all. (Silence) Maybe—maybe—the eating is a substitute for something else that is lacking.

Therapist. You feel something else is lacking?

Alice. She is right. Something else probably is lacking. She wants something, but it's not food. She feels OK—at least not hungry—when she is with her boy friend. (Laughing) Maybe it's love she is looking for.

June (surprised). Why, yes, that could be, couldn't it? How reasonable that seems! But why should I need to look for love?

Alice. Guess I can't help there. I don't know.

June. There must be something wrong in the family—something lacking. Can it be love there, too? Oh, I'm getting confused.

Sara. No, I think you are on the right track. I've got trouble along that line, too, but I don't try to solve mine by eating. I do it in other ways.

Karen. Well, what is this trouble at home? I've got troubles with my boy friend, and I never can get along at home. My mother nags if I don't jump when she wants me to. My boy friend used to take my part, but since my father died, he sides with my mother when he knows about our arguments. My mother ends up crying all the time. Something is wrong.

Therapist. Conflict with parents sometimes does cause painful behavior symptoms. (Hinkley & Hermann, 1951, pp. 83-84.)

PSYCHODRAMA AND ROLE-PLAYING

J. L. Moreno, who has been especially prominent in the development of social approaches to treatment, started his work as a young physician in 1921 by founding the *Stegreiftheater*[1] (the Theater of Spontaneity) in Vienna. Moreno's strong motivation and originality came in part from his reaction against the Freudian psychoanalytic movement which had become dominant in Vienna at that time. Moreno became convinced of the therapeutic importance of acting out personality problems on the stage when he observed changes in people as a result of their spontaneous performances. Over the years he has contributed a number of ideas that have greatly influenced social psychology and sociology, as well as psychiatry and clinical psychology. The beginnings of sociometric approaches can be credited to him. Though he was a pioneer in the development of group psychotherapy, he is best known for his work with psychodrama.

Psychodrama takes place upon a stage, often a specially designed one, in front of an audience. The chief participants are the protagonist (the patient), the director (the chief therapist), the auxiliary egos (assistant therapists or other patients), and the group making up the audience. The therapist-director gets the psychodrama going by asking the patient to act out a scene spontaneously. Auxiliary egos take parts that will support the action and help bring out the problems and conflicts of the patient. The techniques for developing the production are many and varied (Moreno, 1959). The director encourages the patient to achieve catharsis in order to liberate himself from his problems. The goal is to produce a spontaneous, creative person. One of the interesting byproducts of the psychodrama is its importance to the patient-audience. In one mental hospital a patient about to be discharged was asked what had helped him most in the hospital. He replied that the psychologist's psychodrama

[1] The word *Stegreif* itself is interesting. It means "stirrup." To speak "from the stirrup" is to speak extemporaneously.

sessions had given him the most help. This was a patient who had never actively participated in the psychodrama, but as a member of the audience he believed he had profited greatly, presumably by working through the problems vicariously.

On a level less elaborate than psychodrama, many therapists use *role-playing*. It can become the primary technique in therapy or remain an auxiliary method resorted to occasionally. Some situation that has arisen quite naturally in a group therapy may be taken as a starting point. A patient tells of his mother's harsh treatment when he started having dates in high school. The therapist asks the patient to describe a particular time when he came home from a date. Members of the group are assigned to play the mother and the other significant persons involved. Roles may be switched around and much discussion results. Another occasion for the use of role-playing is in preparing patients for job interviews or future stressful situations. Ossorio and Fine (1960), aiming to benefit chronic patients, have used role-playing and psychodrama as techniques for changing the social atmosphere in hospital wards and especially for increasing communication. There are many other possibilities.

FAMILY THERAPY

In looking at the social influences upon the development of persons, we are not likely to find any that have a greater impact than the family. So it is natural that we should look to the family in treating patients. In the course of out-patient work, marital partners are often brought into therapy. The extensive mental health survey mentioned in an earlier chapter (Gurin et al, 1960), found that marital problems were the most commonly reported reasons for seeking psychological help. The close relatives of hospitalized adults whose cases are being diagnosed are usually interviewed and contacts with them are continued later into the counseling the patient is given to help him return to his former situation. The family is even more important in therapeutic work with children. The usual tactics of the child guidance clinic include observing the child in play therapy while the mother is interviewed in a separate therapeutic session at the same time. Traditions in this field are being modified in recent years and different arrangements for family therapy are being tried out.

In his *Psychodynamics of Family Life,* Nathan Ackerman (1958) shows over and over again the interdependence of the individual, his family, and the society of which he is a part. No patient can be adequately understood in isolation from his family. Ackerman says that the first member of the family to consult the clinic, "the primary patient," is "an emissary in disguise of an emotionally warped family group" (p.

104). This primary patient may or may not be very disturbed. Ackerman makes a family diagnosis on the basis of interviews and home visits in order to discover something about family relationships and the sort of equilibrium maintained in the home. On the basis of such a diagnosis he will attempt to arrange a flexible program of therapy involving members of the family. They may be treated all together, or some may be treated individually; he may mix the group and individual approaches over the period during which therapy is continued.

A number of other psychiatrists and psychologists have been exploring what have been called "family group therapy" (Bell, 1961), "family unit therapy" (Bowen, 1960), "family counseling" (Dreikurs et al, 1959), or in general *conjoint therapy,* in which several members of a family meet together with a therapist and try to work out their problems by direct interaction. This kind of therapy with groups that are living together presents challenges and opportunities that do not occur in groups organized specially for the therapy sessions. Arguments that start in the consultation room tend to carry over into the home. Understandings developed in therapy would seem to transfer better, too.

The Clay family provides an example of conjoint family therapy in a child guidance clinic. It consists of mother, father (a well-to-do business man), a 13-year-old boy (Dick), and a 10-year-old girl (Janet). The original complaint in the mother's application to the clinic was her fear that Dick's rebellious ways at home and school were indications that he was becoming delinquent. Mrs. Clay and Dick were having such quarrels that she was in favor of sending him away to a military school. After a diagnostic study, the clinic staff decided to offer therapy to the family. Following the general guidelines recommended by Bell, the therapist met the father and mother and outlined the plan of treatment to them to see if they would accept it. He explained to the parents that Dick's disturbance was part and parcel of the whole family situation, encouraging them to let him see how each of them was concerned and upset. He proposed that the family meet as a group for one and one-half hours each week with the therapist. The purpose of the sessions would be to help each member of the family express his feelings about his problems better, to develop closer understanding of each other, and to find improved solutions of their common problems. In order to do this, the therapist explained, it would be very important in early sessions that the parents should not dominate the conversation. Instead the children were to be encouraged to tell all of their problems and "gripes," with the parents merely indicating that they would do everything reasonable to improve the situation. As another part of the plan, the therapist agreed that in the future he would not see or talk with any member of the family individually. If one of them should telephone or write him, he would tell what was said to the rest of the group. The reason for such a rule is that the family must at all times be treated as a unit and not broken down into factions each of which might have a different relation with the therapist. This plan was acceptable to Mr. and Mrs. Clay and therapy was begun.

The following transcript is from the beginning of the fourth family group session, when the family is still wrestling with the children's complaints, but by this time the therapist is allowing the parents gradually to become more active. In this session some of the family dynamics are apparent. Note the power struggle going on in the family between Mrs. Clay and Dick. The father in other sessions seems to be subtly encouraging the boy's rebellion. In this session, he seems to be showing an excessive interest in the details of the boy's school misdemeanors. However, the minute Dick criticizes his mother, his father quickly jumps over to her side. Both parents use moralizing in their attempts to alter the boy's behavior. The mother shows her need to maintain rigid controls clothed in religious terms. Many of these ways of trying to hold him down are threatened by the boy's clearly developing adolescent independence. She seems to have very little empathy for what her children need, but feels a great responsibility for getting them to lead the "right" kind of life. The therapist encourages Dick to express some of his feelings. Dick exhibits strong strivings both for attention and independence, almost equally strong, along with feelings of rejection. The importance of another interactive system, the school, is brought out in this transcript. In this session the therapist's activity is oriented toward encouraging family interaction. Several of the therapist's introjections serve to orient the group to feelings of individuals. There is somewhat less emphasis on understanding group interaction than would be common in other sessions. In this session Janet is relatively quiet, perhaps because the therapist fails to encourage her more to let herself go in the beginning interchange.

Therapist. I think last time one thing that was mentioned was that we need a lot more understanding, and that's our task here—to try to understand each other. The purpose of this kind of meeting is to help the family to talk together and to see how each other feels about things.

Mrs. Clay. I felt that something was brought out last time that was really helpful to me and that is that I spend too much time moralizing and talking. I think I have overdone that.

Therapist (to Dick and Janet). How did the rest of you feel about that? Do you agree with Mom on that? (Janet laughs.) On the moralizing and talking? Both of you?

Janet. Well, I think that she talks a little bit too much, but not too much. I mean she talks a little too much at times, but it isn't too bad.

Mrs. Clay. Janet felt this week that I dug into her about eating too much and gaining weight. (Laughs.)

Therapist. Oh, is that right? Would you tell us about that?

Janet. Oh, it was yesterday at the party. I had some cookies and I started to eat them. She'd say, "Now, Janet, don't you eat any of those."

Mrs. Clay. I said, "Now don't eat all of them." (Laughs.) She had a whole pile of them. (Laughs again.)

Therapist. And this is something that you would just as soon not be reminded of.

Janet. Oh, I might be reminded but not every single second.
(Pause.)

Therapist. How about you, Dick. How have you been?

Dick. Oh, I wasn't home hardly any of the time. When she (the mother) was home, I wasn't and when I was home, she wasn't, so I didn't have hardly any trouble.

Mr. Clay. I think that it has been a little easier week this time. I don't know how Dick is coming out on his school problems, but I think that it has been a little better, partly because he has had his own way.

Dick. The teachers sent me five times to the office this week. That's an improvement.

Mr. Clay. Improvement? Do you mean that you've gone to the office more times? How many times? Once a day?

Dick. No, I went three times in one day. Twice. One time in two different days.

Mr. Clay. The average has been worse than that?

Dick. It's usually been about two times every day.

Mr. Clay. Do they come from the same or different teachers?

Dick. Oh, it's usually the same one. I have my ideas and I'm not going to back down. If you do back down you are a lost soul. You've got to have your own head.

Mr. Clay. You have a point there. But sooner or later you back up against something you can't control and then what are you going to do?

Dick. I'm going to just push right forward.

Mr. Clay. You can't sometimes.

Dick. Hmmm.

Mr. Clay. I wonder what the answer is. It seems to me that everyone is going to have to knuckle down some place sometime. It's just a matter of when and how quick.

Mrs. Clay. It has been awful easy for me to have a high standard in life. I have it for myself as well as others, but I think that I am coming to realize that I can't influence others—that if I keep my standard for myself that then I'll have to let others choose their standards. I think I have been getting a little more peace in my mind and realizing that I am responsible to God for myself and to train others, but the results are not my——

Dick (interrupts). Mother, this isn't church. Good night!

Mr. Clay. Well, those things have to be said.

Dick. She can do it in church—not here. A bunch of preaching!

Mr. Clay. Most people have to learn the hard way, but they'd like you to learn some other way than the hard way, but I kind of think that you are going to have to learn the hard way, however hard it is. If you're going to fall, you'll just have to fall.

Mrs. Clay. Well, I've just wanted to prevent that, but I don't think that can be done.

Therapist. Is it that you feel irritated with Dick or that you feel that the children need to learn on their own?

Mr. Clay. I kind of feel, maybe I'm sounding off here against Dick, but that's not necessarily the case, that not the last couple of years but previous to that he didn't get all that was coming to him, not only him but the rest of us in this room. Their discipline wasn't as tough as it might have been. And now that it is starting to tighten up again, they are kind of behind the eightball and they don't know what to do about it. They don't want to give in—they have had their own way for a while—and now the fun begins.

Therapist. How do you feel about this, Dick?

Dick. I'm not backing down.

Therapist. That seems to be your theme, doesn't it?

Dick. Boy, there's going to be something that's really going to come up. Someone is going to have to work hard. I'm not going to back down.

Therapist. It's important for you to keep your own head all the way.

Dick. Yeah.

Mr. Clay. I think Dick has said exactly what his major trouble is, if you call that a trouble—Dick doesn't think so—he thinks it's a good point. Well, nobody can be boss all the time—there isn't any question. That is the reason I say that everybody is going to have to lower their head and get it bloody sometime in order to learn that they can't run the whole show. The sooner we realize it, the better off we are. I don't mean that they should cow-tow to everybody, but at the same time sooner or later they are going to run up against somebody that's not going to fool with that kind of stuff. If it's on the job, they may get canned, and if it's other places there are other results.

Therapist. I wonder what Dick could tell us to help us to feel how it feels to have to fight to keep from being pushed around.

Dick. When I was in school did I tell you how I got to the office?

Therapist. How?

Dick. Well, we were—yeah, I'll tell about yesterday. There was a party at school. A friend and I, we were passing out the punch and I was doing okay. One of the other guys started talking to me and he was talking and we got to laughing about something. The teacher got mad and after the party was all over he said, "Would you mind going to the office?" So we went to the office and he said, "I don't want you guys to make a fool of us anymore." I said, "Well, if I knew I was making a fool of you I'd of made a big one." And then at the time I said that he came over to me and said, "If you are going to say any more I'll bend you over." So I went back and sat down. As soon as we got out I said, "The next time I go to the office I'll bend *him* over," and I think he heard me—I'm pretty sure he did.

THE THERAPEUTIC USE OF ENVIRONMENTAL CONDITIONS

It is commonly recognized that a person's environment has a great deal to do with how well he feels and how much satisfaction he takes in life. The advice of a friend or a physician to go on a vacation when you are under tension or "worn out" is often good advice, even if it is not a cure-all. Sometimes a change of jobs will revitalize a person. Social workers know the importance of the proper kind of foster home for a neglected or disturbed child. The sheltered workshop, the day hospital and the night hospital for mental patients, and the rest home for the aged are examples of environment especially developed to provide the necessary support for persons who are only marginally adequate to the demands of life. The psychologist's techniques of assessment and therapy need to be extended so that they cover the adjustment of patients and environments to each other. Here is a great challenge, indeed.

Sometimes interpersonal therapeutic techniques can be applied in the natural environment itself. Redl (1959) has proposed what he calls the *life space interview,* an on-the-spot handling of emotional problems. Suppose, for instance, in a residential treatment home, most of the boys suddenly turn on one of their number, tease him unmercifully, and reduce him to angry tears and wild fighting. When the melee is over, the psychologist who was on the scene may be able to use this immediate moment as an opportunity to give "emotional first aid" to the boy. Perhaps he might even be able to conduct a brief and informal therapy session, skillfully helping the boy to see the situation more realistically and to detect what it is about his own behavior that may have helped elicit the teasing. Such impromptu therapy may have greater possibilities for effectiveness than if the boy has to wait until the next therapy hour to discuss a matter that is already cold or perhaps repressed, pushed out of mind. In a similar manner in recent years "aggressive" social workers have been working directly with delinquent gangs on the streets. One is reminded of the finding in the Korean conflict that psychiatric breakdowns had a better chance of recovery if they could be treated close to the front lines. It must be admitted that this kind of "therapy *in situ*" raises serious problems concerning the selection and training of personnel.

Institutions such as mental hospitals, schools for mental defectives, and prisons are slowly beginning to understand the rehabilitative effects that the right kinds of environmental conditions and institutional personnel can have. Mental hospitals are trying to become more therapeutic and less custodial, and there is a movement to leave patients in their own community as much as possible. As long as it was thought that mental illness was a dangerous "disease" that must be treated by isolating and imposing special restraints on the patient, everything that was done to or for him was dehumanized, and little attention was paid to the possibly ameliorating effects that might be produced by the right social influences. Occasionally reformers would plead for more humane treatment. The newly awakened interest in the therapeutic effects of the environment is reminiscent of the "moral treatment" that emerged at the end of the eighteenth century with Pinel's breaking of the mental patient's chains (Carlson & Dain, 1960). Later in the nineteenth century the harsh and cruel treatment of patients returned in full force. One exception has been the long history of the town of Gheel, Belgium, where chronically ill mental patients have led nearly normal and useful lives in foster homes in the community. Gheel now has a population of 24,700, and because of this foster-home plan, over 10 per cent are patients. Only a few of them require conventional hospitalization, even though most of them have been classed as incurable and have failed to respond to treatment in public institutions (Amrine, 1960). Thus we see that the treatment of mental illness and deviant behavior in general is related to public and professional attitudes.

In the mental hospitals themselves there has been a new look at the impact of their surroundings on the lives of its inmates. A number of studies of institutions (Belknap, 1956; Caudill, 1958; Greenblatt et al, 1957; Stanton & Schwartz, 1954) have shown the importance of staff attitudes and of the social and emotional climate on the patients themselves. Ideas of the therapeutic use of environment, such as *milieu therapy*, have developed. Maxwell Jones (1953, 1961) and others like him (Rapoport, 1960) have given a boost to this kind of thinking by calling the institution a *therapeutic community* or metaphorically viewing the community itself as the "doctor." Improvement of the environment is not intended just to make the institution more pleasant, though this may also happen, but to encourage everybody to take a developmental view of patients, teaching them a more effective and satisfying way of living. This particular view affects even the architecture of hospitals. The psychiatrist Linn (1959) has recommended that hospitals should be small, certainly with less than 1,000 patients, and located near population centers. Instead of the isolated cell, on the one hand, or the huge dormitory, on the other, patients are placed in small living groups. They have daily meetings where the staff is careful to communicate plans and problems that arise in the living situation and where patients can express themselves. A certain amount of government in the hands of the patients themselves may involve them in significant decision-making about immediate problems. Recreational and occupational therapy is used extensively so that patients may have some fun, all the while developing social and manual skills.

ASSESSMENT PROCEDURES

The desire to be able to evaluate small groups and institutions has produced demands for many new assessment techniques. As the chapters on assessment pointed out, most psychological tests are oriented toward the description of individuals, not situations. Some conventional tests, like the TAT, and some sentence completion forms may be useful in revealing an individual's attitudes and feelings toward interpersonal matters. Also, the different individuals who make up a group can be tested with instruments like the Rorschach or MMPI and the results compared for similarities and differences. However, one study (Sohler et al, 1957) has shown that the Rorschach and other projective techniques are better at showing individual characteristics than the relations between members of a family. The diagnostic procedures of Leary (1957), described in the last chapter, provide an interpersonal framework with which to evaluate individuals. Groups can be studied by sociometry, but except on the fairly simple level of plotting diagrams of choice patterns, the measurement of groups for assessment purposes is in an elementary stage. Assessment procedures therefore rely mostly on the old standbys of interviewing and observation. In the process of adapting these to group and institutional situations, new methods of observing and rating group behavior and role-playing as it occurs in groups are gradually being evolved.

A major assessment problem in group therapy is selection of those patients who are likely to benefit from it. There have been studies in which patients were classified into different diagnostic categories, but because of the diversity of techniques and therapeutic situations, it is very difficult to draw useful generalizations. It would seem, however, as Coffey (1954) has pointed out, that extreme ranges of ability within a group make communication difficult. He urges that in selecting patients for group therapy one should avoid wide differences in education, intelligence, or cultural background. Groups, it appears, function best when the group members represent a variety of roles. Coffey concludes that the intake worker's impressions of whether or not persons will do well in a group are often better than the clinical psychologist's diagnostic techniques. Ullman (1957), in a study of patients selected for therapy groups in a VA hospital, used Finney's Palo Alto Group Therapy Scale, a new social perceptions test, and the TAT. He found the latter two predicted both how patients would behave and whether or not they would still be in the hospital six months later significantly better than chance. He also found that test behavior was a better indicator of whether the person would remain in the hospital than of how he would behave in the group.

In psychodrama, Moreno (1959) recommends that a sociometric test should be given each member of the group after it has become established. Each member is asked to express his preferred choices and rejections of other members, and from these data a sociogram is constructed. Moreno may ask individual members to reveal in advance their own impressions of what the sociogram will show in order to compare what they predict with what is actually obtained. For many group problems there are few specific assessment procedures. With training and experience the clinician begins to be perceptive of significant shifts going on in the group, of just what roles are taken by its members, and occasionally of the need of certain patients to receive special individual therapy.

We now turn to some assessment procedures developed for married couples and family groups. Since these are persons who live closely together, and since therapy is often directed at increasing understanding of the other person with whom one lives, it is often helpful to have a way of checking discrepancies between the reactions of various members of the same family. For instance, a mother may be asked to answer a set of test questions the way she thinks her son would answer them. Then her "predictions" can be compared with her son's actual answers. Data like these can be used for initiating discussions in therapy. There have been some beginning attempts at developing techniques specifically designed for *family assessment*. Titchener and Emerson (1958) have developed a Family Relations Inventory consisting of 250 statements which provide each member of the family with a way of indicating what he thinks are his relations with the others. Anthony and Bene (1957) have devised an "objective" technique for exploring a child's emotional relations to his family. The PALS test by Williams (1958) is another device for getting children to evaluate both their parents. All of these family tests are still in an early stage of development, but they open up promising avenues of research. There are also many marital adjustment tests, and tests for studying how parents believe children should be brought up. Romano (1960) advocates the use of Leary's interpersonal system in counseling married couples to disclose any difficulties in communication that may exist as well as differences in their interpersonal and general social reaction patterns.

If we are trying to understand what is going on in some natural living group, of whatever kind, direct observation of the situation is bound to be essential. It often comes as a surprise to the less experienced clinician to see how different the behavior of a person in an individual interview is from his behavior when he is among his colleagues or with his family. Home visits are emphasized in the family assessment methods of Ackerman (1958). Ward observations are customarily done by professionals who specialize in studying hospitals. Any method of assessing natural living groups and organizations is bound to require a great deal of exploratory endeavor and many innovations, and they must be inspired by a thorough knowledge of both clinical and social psychology (see Luchins, 1959).

In connection with our stress upon the therapeutic importance of the environment, one or two practical points about the psychological practices prevalent in hospitals should be made. For one thing, the effort to obtain a good deal of knowledge about each patient puts a burden on a small department. Usually it is impossible to give a lengthy test to everyone. Some hospitals therefore have resorted to using short screening batteries as a basis for planning therapeutic efforts. Similarly, to assist in the proper selection of personnel, there are devices for screening employees to detect sadistic or sociopathic or other damaging tendencies.

Examples of such tests are the psychiatric attitudes battery of Reznikoff and associates (1959) and the Custodial Mental Illness Scale of Green-blatt and others (1957). Still another feature of the hospital environment that is important is the provision of vocational planning and of the services of a counseling psychologist, who assesses the abilities and strengths which the patient retains despite his psychopathology and then finds ways of relating these to what is available in the form of work within the hospital and later in the community.

CRITICAL EVALUATION

Of the several kinds of therapy which utilize social relations the most attention has been devoted to group therapy (cf., reviews such as Kadis & Markowitz, 1948; Gundlach, 1960, Corsini et al, 1960). No large propor-tion of this voluminous literature is systematic research. Most of it is given over to clinical observation and general reflections on the subject. There is very little in the way of synthesis of basic sociopsychological research using small groups and group therapy. Good reasons can be cited for this, because many obstacles lie in the path of significant re-search upon group therapy—the problem is complex, a sound conceptual framework is lacking, and the subject tends to run into emotional and interpersonal resistances (Bennis, 1960).

As often happens with a new idea, people try it on new groups and in new ways, and the publications that result boil down to little more than this: "We tried group therapy with wayward girls and we liked it." As part of an attempt to survey the applications of group therapy, Corsini (1957) sent a questionnaire to two hundred institutions. Re-spondents indicated that they considered the following kinds of patients suitable for group therapy in the order listed, beginning with the most suitable: psychoneurotics, nonpsychotics, passive individuals, and psy-chosomatics. The following were considered poor prospects, beginning with the least suitable: psychopaths, organics, persons with character disorders, persons with active delusions, and persons who are grossly bizarre, hostile, hyperactive, or senile. The listing is not greatly different from the usual prognosis for any kind of psychotherapy.

There has been much discussion of the relative merits of group and individual psychotherapy. The two have been compared in a number of research studies. In general there is agreement that the two approaches are indeed different and that each has its own special advantages and disadvantages. Frequently patients participate in both kinds of therapy at the same time. The decision when to use one and when to use the other is made mainly on the particular local "run" of clinical experience and on the availability of therapists. One early argument for group therapy was that it saved time and personnel, since one therapist could see many patients simultaneously. This argument is now considered to be misleading, since individual and group approaches produce different effects. For certain kinds of patients and problems group therapy should be chosen because in such cases prognosis is better, not because it is thought to be economical.

The largest study of the outcomes of group therapy was made by Powdermaker and Frank (1953). Their cases were 124 men in a VA hospital, half of whom received group therapy and half of whom did not. The outcome, according to the criterion of physicians' judgments, showed that 61 per cent of those who had both individual and group treatment improved, and 52 per cent of those who had only individual therapy improved. In general, group therapy had a stimulating effect upon purposeful activities and verbal communication. The experimental group developed more expressiveness in reacting to stress than the control group. This study has been criticized by some for the inadequacy of the criteria, because the group therapists had not had much training in the method and because it was beset with administrative difficulties. In another outcome study, Sacks and Berger (1954) found that schizophrenic patients who had experienced an active kind of group therapy did not achieve a higher rate of discharge than a control group of nontreated patients; however, more patients participating in the therapy were able to move to a ward for improved cases.

There have also been a few studies of the effects of different kinds of group therapy. Coons (1957) found that group therapy emphasizing interaction proved more beneficial than therapy emphasizing insight. Haskell (1958) and Mann and Mann (1958) found that role-playing in groups improved interpersonal adjustments more than group meetings limited to discussion. We can say, in conclusion, that the problem of how valuable group therapy is certainly is not settled. Some of what we shall say in the next chapter will be appropriate to group therapy since the problem of what to take as the criterion of improvement continues to plague all appraisals of the effectiveness of psychotherapy.

Because studies of the process of group psychotherapy are complex, relatively few have been attempted. Many of the techniques in laboratory studies of small groups might possibly be adapted for use in this field. Bale's Interaction Process Analysis, for instance, can be used with therapeutic groups (Psathas, 1960), though probably categories would be needed that more adequately reflect the emotionality prevailing in group meetings. Gundlach (1960) has briefly described an interesting research project in which recorded interchanges were analyzed for "inappropriate responses." His hypotheses were that the defensive misperceptions of patients are central to their difficulties, and that the essence of therapy is to call these misperceptions to the patient's attention. During the course of group therapy, he found, a marked decrease in the inappropriate behavior occurred. In another interesting line of research, Winder and Hersko (1958) analyzed patients' remarks in group sessions. They report that several members in the group tended to share a common concern, which they call a theme. Frequently a single theme would dominate a session and certain themes tended to recur. The nine themes which tended to occur frequently are as follows, in order of highest to lowest frequency: (1) hostility to authority figures, (2) hostility to peers, (3) warmth for authority figures, (4) warmth for peers, (5) expression of need for help, (6) fear of losing self-control, (7) responsibility for self and others, (8) jealousy, (9) recognition of dependency. Talland and Clark (1954) had patients rank topics of discussion in psychoanalytically oriented group therapy; they found a positive correlation between rankings for helpfulness and rankings for disturbing effect. They concluded that just the topics that could only be discussed in intimate groups, such as sex, anxieties, childhood memories, shame and guilt, were the ones the group benefited most from talking about. Studies such as these will give the reader an idea of the variety of possible ways of studying processes of group therapy.

Therapy taking a family as the group is so new that little has been done to evaluate it. Some significant attempts have been made by several clinicians to conceptualize processes in disturbed families and their treatment (Ackerman, 1948; Bateson et al, 1956; Jackson, 1960; Spiegel, 1957; Wynne et al, 1958), but research procedures are yet to be developed.

One extensive and well-designed study applies both to group therapy and to mileu therapy. Fairweather and others (1960) studied the effectiveness of four different therapeutic programs in a Veteran's hospital. These four programs included (a) a control group to whose members an individual work assignment had been given but no therapy; (b) a group whose members were given individual therapy and individual work assignments; (c) a group that had both group therapy and individual work assignment; and (d) a group that lived together, participating in group therapy and group-oriented activities. The total number of patients systematically assigned in an analysis of variance design was 96, including nonpsychotics and acute and chronic psychotics. A variety of criteria of improvement were employed including several kinds of tests, ward observations and Q sorts. The short-term psychotics made the best posthospital adjustment, the nonpsychotics the next best, and the chronic psychotics the poorest. In general, all three kinds of therapy produced more change than was found in the control group. The group-living approach and the individual approaches produced the greatest changes, but the two treatments affected the criteria of improvement in different ways. This complex design, revealing interactions among several variables, could very well serve as a model for further research studies. It is presented more extensively at the end of this chapter.

Many of the newer approaches to institutional treatment have not been tried very long. The British have used concepts about the therapeutic community for about ten years longer than the Americans. Jones (1953) mentions a follow-up study of such a setup that showed very favorable results. Patients in this country as well as Britain seem to be remaining in institutions for shorter periods of time since the newer staff attitudes and also the new drug therapies have become effective. A concomitant increase in readmission is also evident, so that institutions are now said to have "revolving doors" instead of doors that just open and shut. What the ultimate effect on mental illness will be is not clear, but there is no doubt that the greater diversity in methods of treatment will result in more disturbed people having closer contact with the community, which means that certain social readjustments and innovations are going to be required.

SUMMARY

Therapy applied simultaneously to groups of individuals differs in its problems and effects from individual therapy. There is a wide variety in the kinds of group therapy, including educational groups, social clubs, inspirational groups, groups participating in psychodrama, and free interaction groups. Most commonly a group consists of five to ten patients. The goals of the interaction can be adapted to fit different theories; for example, its purposes might be insight, emotional expression, or knowledge of interpersonal interaction. Psychodrama, developed by Moreno, is a way of acting out conflicts both verbally and nonverbally. Through the director's suggestions and with the help of auxiliary actors, the patient is helped to gain insight into his own behavior and to try out different roles of behavior himself. Role-playing provides a flexible technique for therapy and training. In the treatment of families, different methods are tried, such as family unit therapy (a recent development), in which the whole family meets with the therapist in a direct effort to improve understanding and interaction. Therapy can sometimes be extended into the natural living situations of patients—so-called "life-space interviewing." In recent years more of an attempt has been made to deal with social influences in institutions in the form of milieu therapy and a therapeutic community. Assessment devices for group and institutional work are still in an early stage of development. Studies of the outcome of group therapy are rather few; and it cannot be claimed that they indicate much difference in effectiveness between group and individual therapies. Study of the process of group therapy is still in its early stages, but there have been analyses of interactions, themes of sessions, and other kinds of study. Research in group therapy is still in its infancy, and research on family therapy and institutional treatments has barely started.

SUGGESTED READINGS

CORSINI, R. J. *Methods of group psychotherapy.* New York: McGraw, 1957.

Corsini, a psychologist widely experienced in group therapy, here describes a variety of techniques usable with groups. He finds potential values in all the theories of group therapy and holds that their differences consist mainly in where the emphasis is placed. An attempt is made to classify the mechanisms that operate in group therapy. Techniques may be distinguished on three continua: directive-nondirective, verbal-actional, and superficial-deep. The last section of the book is composed of excerpts from verbatim transcripts of group sessions. Another introductory text is Bach (1954).

ACKERMAN, N. W. *The psychodynamics of family life.* New York: Basic, 1958.

Over a period of many years, the psychiatrist Ackerman has been developing his ideas of family dynamics and of therapeutic techniques by which they can be improved. He starts out from a psychoanalytic base, but incorporates a good many innovations, indicating his acceptance of the role of social and cultural influences. The primary concepts he stresses are the psychological identity of the person, the stability of behavior, and its adaptibility. The book contains a description of how he approaches family diagnosis and of his varied methods of treating a whole family. He also discusses mental health and social values. Pauline Sears (1960) in reviewing this book warns that there is danger in inferring social values solely from experience with pathological cases, especially in the absence of research on normal families.

BINDMAN, A. J. Mental health consultation: theory and practice. *J. consult. Psychol.,* 1959, 23, 473-482.

Bindman discusses the functions of a psychologist (or other professional person concerned with health) in his relations with the community. He contrasts these functions with those of education and therapy, making several points such as that the person who comes in for consultation about his problems has done so on his own initiative, that the consultant usually enters the consultee's social system, that the consultee is usually of a different professional background, that the consultant gives his advice but does not himself initiate plans, and that the consultant does not have any administrative control over the consultee. Bindman illustrates his description of this relationship with a report on a consultation with a teacher over a crisis with a problem child. It seems clear that consultations of this sort with persons in the community are becoming a larger and more important part of clinical work.

ROSE, A. M. (Ed.) *Mental health and mental disorder, a sociological approach.* New York: Norton, 1955.

This book is a series of important writings on sociological theories of mental illness and research upon it. The sections on ecological research, research in the mental hospital, group psychotherapy, and mental hygiene in relation to class structure are those most pertinent to the present chapter. The reader may also wish to refer to the subject of mental health in other cultures in the book by Opler (1959).

RESEARCH EXAMPLES

ENDS, E. J., & PAGE, C. W. Group psychotherapy and concomitant psychological change. *Psychol. Monogr.,* 1959, 73, No. 10, 1-31 (Whole No. 480).

This report covers only a part of a large research program in a state hospital. The purpose of this portion of the program was to assess the usefulness of group psychotherapy with alcoholic patients. The patients were usually kept in the hospital for 60 days, and many of them were not self-motivated to participate in therapy. The two questions initially raised were the following: Does the addition of Rogerian group-centered therapy to a general hospital program for alcoholics make a detectable difference in outcomes? Does the therapeutic movement differ when it is continued for 30 sessions instead of 15?

From male alcoholic admissions to the hospital all those meeting certain requirements of age, intelligence, lack of organic pathology, and absence of psychosis were randomly assigned either to the group given therapy or to a control group, with a total of 28 persons in each. Those given group therapy were divided for treatment into six separate subgroups. All subjects in both therapy and control groups had taken pre- and post-MMPI's and self and ideal-self Q sorts preceding and following the six-week period of the study. Q technique was used to analyze the Q sorts. Patients' Q sorts were also compared with a criterion-sort by five psychologists for what they considered the healthiest answers. The authors report their several indexes and the findings in some detail.

When the changes occurring in therapy and control groups were compared, there were a large number of significant differences. Five of eight Q-sort changes were significant. For instance, those given therapy changed significantly in self-acceptance and movement toward the pretreatment ideal-sort. Also there was greater improvement on a large number of the MMPI scales for the group given therapy. Doubling the number of group therapy sessions from 15 to 30 without increasing total elapsed time resulted in significantly greater therapeutic improvement. The authors concluded that at the end of 15 sessions the average group patient was just on the threshold of his greatest therapeutic progress.

This study suggests the value of Rogerian group therapy with alcoholics. Its main limitation is that the question remains unanswered whether the changes carry over into behavior after discharge from the hospital.

PSATHAS, G. Interaction process analysis of two psychotherapy groups. *Internat. J. Group Psychotherapy*, 1960, 10, 430-445.

This research project is more interesting for its methodology than for its findings, though its findings are also valuable. It is one of a very few applications of small-group research procedures to groups undergoing therapy. Psathas applied Bales' Interaction Process Analysis to two therapy groups of four members each and compared the results with results obtained with those from a laboratory problem-solving group.

The methodology was as follows: Three group therapy sessions during each of three different periods (which were respectively early, middle, and late in the whole series) were recorded and observed through a screen permitting only one-way vision. Thus there were 9 recorded sessions for each of the two groups receiving therapy. The observations of the interactions and the tape-recordings were analyzed by Bales' method, which requires scoring each remark of each person in one of 12 categories. The categories in the social-emotional area include some that are positive, such as showing solidarity, showing release of tension, and agreeing; and some that are negative, such as disagreeing, showing tension, and showing antagonism. Other categories are task-oriented and apply to remarks where answers are attempted such as giving suggestions, advancing opinions, and supplying orientation. Still other categories are task-oriented but involve asking questions, such as asking for orientation, asking for opinions, asking for suggestions. After all the interactions had been classified in categories, the mean profile of each individual was drawn, the changes over successive sessions were studied, and comparisons were made with norms from previous laboratory group studies.

The results of the study showed the existence of significant differences between the groups given therapy and the laboratory groups engaged in problem-solving. The differences reflected the different emphases of the groups, one emphasizing discussion and the other decision-making. For instance, the therapy group gave suggestions and disagreed less often. Over the entire series of sessions, the individual members of the therapy group were more variable. This study is limited by the small sample of therapy groups, but the same methods might well be applied more widely in studies of different kinds of groups.

FAIRWEATHER, G. W., SIMON, R., GEBHARD, M. E., WEINGARTEN, E., HOLLAND, J. L., SANDERS, R., STONE, G. B., & REAHL, J. E. Relative effectiveness of psychotherapeutic programs: a multicriteria comparison of four programs for three different patient groups. *Psychol. Monogr.*, 1960, 74, No. 5, 1-26 (Whole No. 492).

This is a complicated and well-designed study carried out in a section of the VA neuropsychiatric hospital at Perry Point, Maryland. The amount of effort going into it is suggested by the long list of participating researchers. The subjects, 96 male patients, were randomly assigned on admission to the various procedures.

The plan of the research required placing 8 patients in each of the 12 cells of a three by four analysis of variance design. The three classifications by *diagnosis* were (a) nonpsychotics, that is patients classified as neurotics or as having character disorders; (b) short-term psychotics, that is patients with a psychotic diagnosis but with less than one year of previous hospitalization; (c) long-term psychotics, that is patients with more than one year of previous hospitalization. All patients were given routine work assignments and post-hospital planning. The four classifications by *treatment* were (a) a control group, which was given nothing special in addition to the routine procedures; (b) an individual psychotherapy group; (c) a group psychotherapy group; and (d) a group-living group, which lived in a single-ward dormitory, worked together on the hospital newspaper and also received group therapy. Each group given treatment consisted of eight patients randomly assigned from each of the three diagnostic classifications.

The *criteria* of improvement were multiple. Each patient was tested and rated at admission and upon discharge with a battery of assessment devices. The tests included the MMPI, the TAT, the Holland Vocational Preference Inventory, and a special Q sort. Changes on the test scores provided some of the criteria. The patients were rated on a special ward behavior scale, a hospital job behavior scale, and if in group therapy, on the Finney (1954) Group Therapy Scale. They were also evaluated six months after discharge or at the termination of the study by reports and ratings of success in adjustment. One important finding of the study was the low correlation among many of these commonly used criteria of therapeutic success. There were two relatively independent clusters: the subjective self-evaluation as revealed by tests, and the objective interpersonal evaluation as revealed by follow-up items and the group therapy rating. The only measure taken while the patients were in the hospital that correlated with follow-up success was the psychologists' ratings of behavior during group therapy; this finding suggests that such a group situation duplicates most closely the more-or-less intense interpersonal situation in which patients will find themselves when they leave the hospital.

As might be expected of such a complex study, the *findings* were numerous and somewhat complicated. In some cases the diagnostic classifications showed significant differences; sometimes the treatment approaches were significantly different; at other times the interaction between diagnosis and treatment was significant. As an example of the latter, though it was found that neither treatment groups nor diagnostic groups showed significant differences on Q-sort changes in self-descriptions, the *interaction* between diagnosis and treatment was significant. The reason was that nonpsychotics and short-term psychotics showed large changes only when they *had* had any kind of therapy, but not if they had *not* had therapy. The rest of the results were such that the totals cancelled out any general findings for diagnoses or treatments. Such a finding demonstrates the need to design studies so that interactions can be tested for significance.

Some of the leading findings were as follows: (*a*) When it came to length (number of days) of treatment, there were differences within both diagnostic classifications and treatment groups. Individual therapy took the longest time and group living the next longest. Short-term psychotics and nonpsychotics required the least treatment, with duration almost equal. However, length of time in treatment had little relation to post-hospital adjustment. (*b*) On measures of change within the hospital there were generally significant differences. The three therapy groups usually showed changes and the control group did not. Among the four treatments, either group living or individual therapy usually showed the greatest difference. (*c*) On the several follow-up measures, only one showed significant differences between treatments, but this was an important one, namely getting employment. The percentage of patients from the various treatments who became employed full-time was as follows: group living, 42 per cent; group therapy, 33 per cent; individual therapy, 42 per cent; and control, 8 per cent. With regard to diagnostic classification, many of the follow-up measures were significant. Short-term psychotics made the most adequate post-hospital adjustment, nonpsychotics next, and long-term psychotics the poorest. Statistical interactions in this case were not significant.

More studies like this need to be made, varying the methods, the kinds of patients and the criteria. The intracacies of the problem of therapy would seem to require studies at least as complicated and carefully planned as this one. For an interesting study of milieu therapy and the social organization of patients, see Murray and Cohen (1959). They found that as the degree of mental illness increases, there is a decrease in social organization and in relationships involving positive or negative feelings. Milieu therapy seems effective in reversing this trend.

19 Research

on Psychotherapy

Though psychologists may argue about the value of psychotherapy either in general or in some specific form, they would all agree that research in psychotherapy must go on. It is obvious that if we are ever to attain more certainty about its methods, their possibilities and their limitations, research will be the means through which it has to come. It is less obvious but even more important that therapy affords us one of the best opportunities we have for the study of personality. Probably most, if not all psychoanalysts feel that Freud's greatest contribution to humanity was not the "curing" of a limited number of neurotic patients, but his opening up of a vast new territory to the scrutiny of scientists and others who hope to understand human behavior better—physicians, counselors, social workers, writers, clergymen, and artists. To come down to a specific instance, many client-centered counselors would point to the research studies through which Rogers' theoretical formulations have been tested and constantly modified as perhaps the major result of more than twenty years of endeavor in the field of therapy.

PSYCHOLOGISTS MUST DO RESEARCH ON THERAPY

Because of the way in which he has been trained, the psychologist plays a leading role in research on therapy. Its fusion of research and practice is one of the unique features of clinical psychology as a professional field. Research techniques are not stressed to this extent in the training of any other member of the therapeutic team. Psychiatrists sometimes become

428

research workers, but their professional reputations do not ordinarily depend upon their doing so. Nearly all social workers are trained for service, not research. Generally speaking, it is the psychologist who must accept major responsibility for the research task if it is to be done.

It has been the experience of many psychologists who are practicing therapists that a research orientation contributes to their own stability in the face of the inevitable uncertainties and disappointments that therapy relationships bring. The fact that a patient over whom one has worked hard and with whose welfare one is keenly identified does not improve can have a corroding effect on a therapist's self-confidence. When a patient manifests resistance or negative transference, it is natural that the therapist should feel anxiety or hostility. Then there is the ever-present danger that he may do or say something in the supercharged atmosphere of the course of therapy that will have damaging effects on the patient's life. These emotional hazards are difficult to describe to the student who has not yet had the experience of being a therapist, but they are very real. Various means for dealing with them are available—perhaps a personal analysis, which may help the therapist to become aware of his own vulnerable spots, perhaps a sufficiently secure grasp on an overall theory to bolster the therapist's confidence that he is doing the right thing. The fact that the psychologist is at other times engrossed in carrying on research helps in two ways. It lessens any guilt feelings which grow out of the mistakes he realizes he has made and that he can identify by their consequences, after they have occurred, since the researcher in him realizes that he cannot be expected to act on principles that no one has as yet discovered. He can say to himself, "I could not have been sure, on the basis of evidence now available, what I should have said or done at this juncture. Therefore I need not blame myself." Furthermore, the research attitude has a way of making every case meaningful and impor- tant, regardless of its outcome. In the overall research enterprise, where the getting of hunches that can build up to formal research hypotheses is as important as the organized effort to test these hypotheses, each case pays dividends if something has been learned from it.

Research in psychotherapy, as we have said before, can be divided into two large classes: investigation into its _outcomes_ and into its _processes_. Outcome research answers such questions as: Was the treatment suc- cessful? Which of several approaches or techniques works best with a certain type of case? How lasting are its effects? What characteristics in patients encourage us to predict a favorable outcome? What character- istics in therapists tend also to make a favorable outcome more probable?

Process research is concerned with what is happening as therapy pro- ceeds. It is directed to such questions as: In what way do the things the patient says change from interview to interview? How frequently does he make remarks indicating anxiety, inferiority feelings, hostile attitudes toward others? What proportion of his remarks in each successive interview have to do with himself? with members of his family? with the therapist? How are the patient's remarks during any one therapy hour related to the therapist's remarks that preceded them? What kinds of remarks are accompanied by physiological indicators of emotion, such as changes in respiratory activity, heart rate, or blood pressure?

Generally speaking, the outcome studies are designed to produce evidence on the basis of which the effectiveness of psychotherapy can be increased. The process studies are designed to uncover information that will throw light on personality manifestations wherever they occur. Both types are complex and difficult, but enough work has been done to make research workers confident that the problems are not insoluble.

OUTCOME RESEARCH

We have referred several times to Eysenck's formidable challenge to psychotherapists (1952). His summing-up of the reports that had been published on the outcomes of psychotherapy indicated that on the average only two-thirds of the patients showed improvement. Even more disturbing were the comparisons between different kinds of treatment that suggested that the more intensive and prolonged therapies were producing poorer results than the briefer forms. The highest proportions of improved cases were found among groups of patients who had received minimal treatment from ordinary physicians or custodial care in mental hospitals.

A great many kinds of criticisms can be directed at the Eysenck paper for such things as lack of comparability among the populations from which the various samples were drawn, lack of uniformity in the meaning different authorities would attach to "Greatly improved" or "Slightly improved," and the absence of information as to just what kind of therapy was given in each case. However, the conclusions which Eysenck believes he has found evidence for are very similar to the findings of Levitt (1957), who investigated therapy with children, and to the failure to demonstrate differences in improvement rates for different psychiatric therapies (Appel et al, 1953). Even if one discounts the statistics and refuses to accept the conclusion, a challenge certainly remains. In a sizable proportion of cases, psychotherapy fails in its purpose. Why?

The more psychologists attempt to design outcome research investigations, the more they become convinced that the question: Does psychotherapy do any good? is not the right question to ask. The processes of psychotherapy, they come to realize, are too complex and vary too much from place to place, from therapist to therapist, and from patient to patient, to permit evaluation of them as a whole, in one lump. Progress, it now appears, has come as the large question has been broken down into smaller questions that are less complicated and more precise. We shall examine some of these more limited research strategies and consider examples of the ways they have been used. But first let us turn to some of the difficulties that beset the investigator of psychotherapy, whatever the specific question he sets out to answer may be.

One of these difficulties has to do with the *criteria* to be used in evaluating the success of treatment. In the treatment of many physical illnesses we can rely mainly on the patient's own statements to tell us whether the treatment has been effective. If he says his pain is gone and he feels well and happy, the physician is satisfied to let him go. This would not be the decisive factor in cases where the patient is known to have cancer, tuberculosis, or other disease identifiable as being pathology of a known type. In such cases, the person is not considered "cured" as long as the condition persists, no matter how well he feels.

Psychotherapists tend to distrust *patients' reports* on how they are feeling as indicators of how successful therapy has been, or at least they try to supplement these with other kinds of evidence. There are many sources for a person's statements about his aches and pains, his feelings of discouragement and contentment, so that such statements may not indicate that the therapy, or any other causal condition, has brought about basic or lasting changes. Hathaway (1948) has called attention, as we have mentioned before, to the "Hello-Goodbye" effect that may be operating. When the patient comes in for his first interview, he often tries, consciously or unconsciously, to prove that he is ill enough to need help. When he has decided to end treatment, he shows by his report on his feelings—perhaps out of common politeness or a desire to meet social expectations—that he appreciates the help he has received.

Some other kinds of evidence of improvement may also be suspect. One common practice is the use of therapists' *ratings* of the progress made in each case. It is obvious that bias can operate here. The therapist needs to believe that he is doing a good job and may, quite innocently, tend to magnify the changes. The danger of this can be removed to some extent now that simple methods of recording interviews are available, by having another therapist who has had no contact with the case do the judging, first listening to interviews taken from different stages and then evaluating the degree of improvement. But this method is time-consuming and still subject to the kinds of biases that may slant any subjective judgments.

Another way of measuring improvement is to give *personality tests* of some sort before and after therapy. This constitutes a useful check on more subjective methods, but it is open to question on the grounds that therapy would not be expected to affect the traits that many of these tests measure. Furthermore, the validity of many personality tests has not been established. As a consequence we can never be sure in the case of failure to get significant changes whether therapy was ineffective or whether the test failed to get at the quality we were trying to assess. The MMPI, the TAT, and the Rorschach have been used most frequently in such studies, but a variety of other tests have also been used as evidence of change.

One other kind of evaluation rests on objective records or ratings of the patient's *behavior and life adjustment* before and after therapy. Such ratings are subject to the errors that beset all rating methods and there are often practical difficulties in obtaining them. Objective events and even partially objectifiable ones, including discharge from a hospital, avoidance of trouble with the law, percentage of time employed, estimated number of friends, and production of creative works, would seem to be excellent indexes of therapeutic success. In some studies it is possible to use these, but oftentimes the bewildering variety of individual situations in which patients live make it very difficult to develop any scales adequately comparing one patient and another. Even with single indexes, such as job success, there is difficulty. With one person therapeutic success might be achieved if he were able to maintain his job, but with another patient success would be indicated by his leaving this job and moving to another. Luchins, Aumack, and Dickman (1960) have pointed out that improvement ultimately depends on a change in appraisals of others. This view leads to a study of the social field in which the patient is operating now or might operate in the future. The therapeutic problem is to decrease negative appraisals and increase positive ones. Change is then seen as an interaction between the individual and his environment. The difficulties of such an approach, attractive as it is, reside in specifying criteria of improvement which would not be subject to the same problems as all of the others mentioned above. Also in studies involving going into the community and conducting a follow-up of the patient, there are many practical problems of finding adequate informants to report on the patient's behavior and in keeping in touch with patients in a highly mobile society.

In explaining what the difficulties are in assessing the outcomes of therapy, we would not wish to give the impression that the problem is insoluble. Each of the methods outlined can be refined and improved by devoting some consideration to its deficiencies, and a combination of several of them constitutes a fairer indicator than any one taken separately. The self-report, for example, has been made more precise and accurate by the use of Q-sort methods, in which the patient assigns descriptive statements to categories based on his judgment of how strongly they apply to him. The rating by therapists can be made more reliable and free from personal distortions by using several judges instead of one. Tests can be made more useful by fitting them into a careful theoretical analysis that produces at the beginning of the study hypotheses as to what kinds of change are to be expected.

In the few careful outcome studies in which there has been an attempt to use several of these criterion measurements on the same cases, it has become clear that they do not all give the same results. In the University of Chicago study of client-centered therapy (Rogers & Dymond, 1954), for example, ratings by friends of the clients on changes in emotional maturity were similar to ratings made by the counselor but were not related at all to the clients' own reports. Kelman and Parloff (1957) studied changes in fifteen neurotic patients in group therapy, using some special techniques they had devised to measure comfort, effectiveness, and self-awareness. Out of 21 correlations between separate measures of change, only one was high enough to be significant at the .05 level. In the VA study by Fairweather and his associates (1960), mentioned in the last chapter, an intercorrelation of 13 therapeutic criteria produced two rather independent clusters: one having to do with effectiveness of social behavior (follow-up items and final group therapy ratings) and the other with patients' self-reports on tests. It may well be that different patients change in different ways, so that any composite measurement of overall rating of improvement masks individual changes that are real and important. This question is open to further investigation.

The second major problem that presents itself in connection with outcome studies on psychotherapy is the problem of *controls*. Even if significant change along some measurable dimension can be shown to occur, how do we know that this results from the therapy and not from some other influence upon the person's life? The standard scientific method for dealing with such a question is to set up a control group, similar in all other respects to the group receiving the special experimental treatment, but receiving no special treatment at all during the time the investigation lasts. This classical method is difficult to apply to research on outcomes of therapy. If we select a control group similar to the therapy group in age, sex, social status, intelligence, and a dozen other characteristics, including even measured neuroticism, it will still differ from the experimental group in the one characteristic most relevant to therapy, namely motivation for change. The only way to equate the control group to the therapy group in this characteristic is to make it, too, up of persons who have actually applied for therapy, but who are not given it. There are obvious ethical and practical objections to doing this. Some compromise solutions of this problem are possible. In the Rogers and Dymond (1954) study to which reference has been made, one control group was made up of persons who were asked to wait 60 days to begin therapy after they had applied for it. It was then possible to compare changes in this group during the 60-day no-therapy period with changes in the therapy group during the same period of time. However, even here there is evidence that the equating has not been altogether accomplished, since the wait period introduces special motivational problems of its own. Frank (1959) reports using the random assignment of out-patients to individual therapy, group therapy, and minimal contact, the latter group being used as a control. By the time patients had been followed for two years, however, quite a change had occurred in the characteristics of the different groups because of the difficulties in keeping in touch with patients and various circumstances that kept some in treatment and eliminated others.

Besides the problems in equating experimental and control groups of subjects, there are the no less serious problems of equating therapists and therapeutic techniques. If the research worker is attempting to compare the effects of one technique with the effects of another, it is important that he rule out the possibility that any difference he finds actually arises from the fact that one therapist is more skillful than the other. If, to control this factor, he designs his study so that all therapists at some time make use of all techniques before the study is complete, he still faces the possibility that any given therapist gets better results with the particular technique he finds most natural or congenial. Fortunately, statistical techniques based on analysis of variance now make it possible to sort out what, for short, we may term *therapist effects, treatment effects, patient effects,* and *interaction effects* of different kinds from the total outcome *variance,* even though it is not possible to rule out any one of them experimentally.

There is another control problem more troublesome in some ways than any of the others. It arises from the *placebo effect,* mentioned in an earlier discussion of research design. An injection of distilled water will often produce in patients the same effects that are being claimed for a new drug. Such placebo effects are not confined to subjective descriptions of feelings. Actual physiological changes often occur. It is evident that any kind of psychotherapy may also have a placebo effect (Rosenthal & Frank, 1956). In fact, this is the most plausible explanation for the often-noted fact that almost all techniques, even though they are diametrically opposed to one another, chalk up therapeutic successes.[1]

Really to demonstrate that a certain kind of therapy is efficacious, it is logically necessary to demonstrate that its effects are greater than these placebo effects. Thus it is probably a sounder policy to provide a control group with some kind of minimal therapy than to leave it completely untreated. This idea is being followed in the Psychotherapy Research Project of the Phipps Psychiatric Clinic at Johns Hopkins University (Frank, 1959). Interestingly enough, this is ethically and practically a far more feasible policy also.

A number of other specific problems are encountered in designing re-

---

[1] Borgatta (1959) amusingly incorporates this idea into an article proposing "placebo therapy." The clinic keeps delaying treatment until the patient stops requesting it. The case is then considered a success. Readers will also enjoy the humor of Borgatta's earlier article (1954) on the concept of deumbilification, in which he spoofs clinical theories like psychoanalysis.

search on the outcomes of psychotherapy, all of them arising from the *complexity* of the process to be studied. Since therapy often goes on for a long time, the changes that occur during one stage may be different from those occurring earlier or later. Patients differ. So do therapists. Communication is far from perfect, and either a patient's perception of what a therapist means to convey or a therapist's grasp of a patient's meaning, or both, may be far from accurate. The general question Eysenck raised, Does psychotherapy do any good? is probably unanswerable. But many narrower questions bearing on outcomes are open to investigation through skillfully planned research—and good luck! Many moves can be made toward obtaining sound, dependable information about what kinds of therapeutic techniques, what kinds of therapists, and what kinds of treatment conditions have the most beneficial effects on specific kinds of patients.

Various research strategies have been tried for dealing with these more limited questions. One of these is to contrast cases judged to be success- ful with those judged to be therapeutic failures within the framework of the theory on which the therapy is based. The first step is to set up one or more hypotheses with regard to the difference between the cases that appear to have been successes and those that resulted in failure—hypotheses that may concern characteristics either of the patient, or the therapist, or of the interaction between them. The second is to develop some way of assessing the hypothesized characteristics and then to compare a group of successes with a group of failures, applying statistical significance tests. It is, of course, possible to compare cases of success and failure on any characteristics that happen to have been recorded for them, starting with no particular initial hypotheses. If this purely empirical procedure is used, the results should be cross-validated before they are accepted.

One example of this research technique is the study of client-centered therapy by Tougas (reported in Rogers & Dymond, 1954, Ch. 12). The theory underlying this approach to therapy considers changes in perception of the self as the most essential thing that occurs during the therapy experience. Research on the authoritarian personality (Adorno et al, 1950) suggests that persons high in ethnocentrism would find this kind of change particularly difficult. Thus one might hypothesize that there would be less therapeutic movement in such cases. As a measure of ethnocentrism, Tougas employed an inventory called the Self-Other Attitude Scale even before therapy was begun. He compared the scores made by the 21 clients their therapists had rated "improved" with those of the 6 clients they had rated "unimproved." As hypothesized, there turned out to be a significant difference in the score for ethnocentrism. The result was particularly interesting in that it corresponded with results Barron (1953) had obtained on a group of patients in a California clinic, where treatment had been based on a different theory of personality.

Another interesting example of "success versus failure" research is the study reported by Betz and Whitehorn (1956). Here we have no prior theoretical formulation, simply an empirical search for characteristics that would distinguish between a group of psychiatrists who achieved high success rates in treating schizophrenics and a group whose success rates were low. Two kinds of differences emerged. One, identified from the case records, seemed to be a difference in general manner of approaching the patient. The successful physicians were more likely to formulate diagnoses in terms of the personal meaning and motivation of the patient's behavior than in terms of psychopathology, to select personally-oriented rather than psychopathologically oriented goals for therapy, and to show active personal participation during the therapy sessions. The second kind of difference showed up on the Strong Vocational Interest Blank, not in the scores for their own occupation, but in eight other occupations without apparent relation to the psychiatric profession. The differences were tested in another group of cases and survived cross-validation.

Another research problem that has generated a considerable number of studies is the question why some patients break off therapy before they get really into it, while others continue. Continuing in therapy does not, of course, guarantee that desirable personality changes will occur, but early termination practically guarantees that they will *not*. A considerable amount of time therapists spend in out-patient clinics is thus wasted on persons who come in for an interview or two and then do not return. The study by Lorr, Katz, and Rubinstein (1958) is one of a series that have been carried out in VA clinics to develop techniques of identifying those patients who are likely to terminate therapy prematurely. Thirteen VA centers cooperated in this study, permitting the assembling of 291 usable cases. Only those cases were used that could be classified into one of two groups, the *terminators*, those who had come for six weeks or less, and the *remainers*, those who had continued for 26 weeks or more. Personality characteristics that seemed to be relevant in previous studies were measured. The combinations of these measurements that differentiated most sharply in half the group of subjects was cross-validated on the other half. Anxiety was the best single predictor. Patients whose level of anxiety is too low seem not to have the motivation to keep up treatment. As a result of the study some rather simple combinations of measured characteristics were perfected for use in predicting perseverance in therapy in this kind of clinic. Frank and associates (1957) from an extensive study with 91 out-patients concluded that patients who remain in treatment are of higher socio-economic class; have more social integrity, general perseverance, and manifest anxiety; are influenceable and ready to talk about what distresses them and also about their liabilities. This list certainly sounds like a job description for the patient in psychotherapy! Frank and his associates remind us that the factors determining improvement may be different from those for remaining in treatment. Lindemann and others (1959) showed that evidences of the following characteristics at time of entry were predictive of a long stay in a VA psychiatric hospital; being unmarried, diagnosed psychotic, rated severely incapacitated, legally incompetent, and not alcoholic (alcoholism was much more common among the nonpsychotic). Such studies as these show that it is possible to make prognoses with respect to matters like length of stay in a psychiatric hospital or continuing in therapy, but that the different factors which enter into the prediction are dependent on the nature of the clinical population and the kind of clinical service.

In another study Hiler (1958) has investigated *differences between therapists* that seem related to remaining in therapy and terminating it. Professional affiliation—whether the therapist was a psychiatrist, a psychologist, or social worker—was not a significant differentiator. Sex was. Female therapists were less likely to lose their "unproductive" patients than were males. (Productiveness, previously shown to be related to terminating therapy, was assessed by simply counting the number of Rorschach responses the patient had given.) Therapists rated high for "warmth" held a larger fraction of their unproductive patients than others did. Therapists rated below average for the group on "competence" lost more of their *productive* patients than did the more competent therapists.

Another research strategy in investigating outcomes of therapy is to compare two or more *different techniques of therapy.* A major study of this sort has been carried out at the Phipps Psychiatric Clinic of Johns Hopkins University (Frank, 1959). The subjects were 54 out-patients. There were three therapists, each of whom at different times used three methods—group therapy, averaging 15.8 sessions, individual therapy, averaging 17.7 sessions, and what was called minimal therapy, which consisted of occasional brief contacts, averaging 9.3 per patient. Each therapist treated six patients by each of the three methods. The outcomes evaluated were decreases in discomfort (from an inventory of 41 symptoms and feelings filled out by the patient) and ineffectiveness (from ratings by interviewers of 15 types of social behavior). Evaluations were made after six months of therapy (or earlier if therapy was terminated before six months were up), again six months later, and at yearly intervals from then on. As mentioned earlier, after two years the attrition was so great that the follow-up studies could be considered of only limited value. At the time this report was published its results were not available for inclusion. They will be awaited with great interest, since the question of the relative value of group and individual therapy for neurotic patients is exceedingly important from a practical standpoint, if from no other.

Many other examples could be given of research approaches to limited questions concerning the outcomes of therapy. But those we have cited should suffice to indicate that in spite of difficulties that at first glance appear almost insuperable, it is possible to formulate hypotheses to be investigated and to work out good research designs. We turn now to the other major area of research on therapy—to investigation of the *process*.

PROCESS STUDIES

The aim of process research is to understand as fully as possible the complex changes in personality that occur during the course of therapy. Such understanding could be important not just to therapists and their patients but to all students of personality. We may look upon therapy as a kind of special laboratory in which psychological phenomena not ordinarily visible present themselves for examination. In a broad sense, all of Freud's observations on which the theoretical structure of psychoanalysis is based can be considered process research. Most psychologists, however, thinking like scientists, would prefer to narrow the scope of the term somewhat and require that the observations be made, analyzed, and interpreted on the basis of some preformulated plan.

The raw material for process research is usually the therapeutic interview itself. Technological advances during the last quarter century such as one-way-vision screens and mirrors permit observation while the interview is actually in progress, and sound recording and sound films make possible detailed and repeated scrutiny of almost everything that occurs.

There is one seemingly grave obstacle to such research that arises from the doubts many therapists have felt about the ethics of such an invasion of privacy. Then there is the possibility that the presence of recording equipment or cameras in the room may distort the interview and give it a shape differing at least somewhat from that it would have taken were two persons talking alone under normal circumstances. As time has passed, however, these problems have come to appear less serious than they did at first. Patients are usually willing to give their permission for their interviews to be observed or recorded because they have confidence in the therapist's integrity and believe he is speaking the truth in promising that only professional uses will be made of the data. In most cases they quickly become accustomed to the research equipment and seem after a few minutes not to pay any further attention to it, although admittedly there are individual differences in this respect and a few persons do not find it easy to disregard (Shakow, 1959). Thus it is now generally accepted among research-minded psychiatrists and psychologists that full recordings of interviews, with the knowledge of the client, are both feasible and ethically permissible.

Another group of problems encountered in planning and carrying out process research arises from the enormous complexity of the data. The general question, What is going on during this therapeutic session? is just as difficult to answer, in fact just as unanswerable, as the general question, Does therapy do any good? What we have to be content to do is to select out of the interview protocols certain kinds of data that can be used to answer certain specific questions. There are many ways in which this can be done.

There is another way of decreasing the complexity of the data to be analyzed. Some hypotheses with regard to what goes on during therapy can be tested by setting up experimental interviews with subjects who are not patients. If the process under consideration is a result or concomitant of a certain kind of behavior on the part of the therapist, it should show up in these experimental interviews designed to produce it. The Greenspoon (1955) experiment in verbal conditioning to be discussed in detail later in this chapter is an example of the use of experimentally set-up interview situations to study a kind of process that may be important in therapy. Also, one of the writers (Sundberg, 1952) has used "pseudopsychotherapeutic sessions" in which interviewers using whatever native skills they possess attempt to "help" an actor who is playing the part of a neurotic. It was found that observers of varying sophistication in therapy differ with respect to their preferred interviewing style. College sophomores tended to perceive directive advice-giving as good therapy, but clinical psychologists and the actor himself preferred less active, permissive approaches. Fiedler and associates (1959) have studied groups for quasi-therapeutic effects. These methods have much to recommend them. Their major weakness is the fact that the experimenter can never be sure that the other aspects of actual therapy situations, such as the motives of the client, would not have important influences.

After these preliminary remarks on the general problem, we now turn to an account of some research strategies that have been used. Probably the most frequent is some sort of *content analysis* of interview protocols. The first step is to break the interview typescript up into units of some sort. These units can then be categorized in accordance with some predetermined system. Often the unit used is each separate verbalization —everything a patient says before he pauses or is interrupted by the therapist and everything the therapist says in reply. Each time there is a shift in who is speaking, a new unit is distinguishable. Larger units covering whole topics of discussion, or smaller, sentence-by-sentence units have also occasionally been distinguished. The units can be analyzed in several ways. One possibility is to compare the frequencies of certain types of verbalization at different stages of therapy, another is to observe sequences. We seek to discover what kinds of verbalizations in patients follow certain kinds of remarks made by the therapist. Another way of going at the analysis is to make a prediction based upon the assumption that some principle (or hypothesis) of a personality theory is correct and then use frequency tabulations as a way of confirming or disconfirming the theoretical principle on which the prediction was based. A number of studies using these various methods have already been mentioned in previous chapters, but we will refer to them again here.

A good example of a research program in which both theoretical reasoning and empirical observation of interview sequences are used as a basis for the formulation and testing of hypotheses is the work being done by Bordin and his colleagues and students at the University of Michigan (Bordin, 1959). They have singled out several variables derived from psychoanalytic theories of therapy, among them "depth of interpretation." As indicated in the previous chapter, interpretation plays an important part in all psychoanalytically oriented therapy. Bordin defines it as "any behavior on the part of the therapist that is an expression of his view of the patient's emotions and motivations. . . . The greater the disparity between the view expressed by the therapist and the patient's own awareness of these emotions and motivations, the deeper the interpretation." Studies from this Michigan group reported by Raush and others (1956) show that the ratings judges make of therapist responses for depth of interpretation are not undimensional, but involve three kinds of distinction. Another study in this series by Speisman (1959) investigated the relationship between depth of interpretation and patient resistance rated from transcripts of interviews. As stated in the review at the end of Chapter 16, he found that interpretations at a moderate level of depth met with the least resistance. This fits in with the finding in an earlier study by Dittmann (1952) that when the therapist's responses are somewhat "deeper" than pure reflection of feeling, they are most likely to be followed by patient responses showing therapeutic movement in a forward direction. Client-centered therapists have tested many of their hypotheses by content analysis methods (Cartwright, 1957). Psychoanalytic hypotheses are increasingly being studied in this same manner.

A second strategy in process research is *to compare the actual behavior during interviews of therapists representing different theories or schools*. Fiedler (1950a, 1950b, 1951) initiated this kind of research by asking both expert and inexperienced therapists of three different schools —Freudian, Adlerian, and Rogerian—first to express by Q-sort methods their concepts of an ideal therapeutic relationship and later to supply him with some of their recorded interviews which could be judged by both trained and untrained judges as to how closely they approximated the ideal therapeutic relationship. The results have been widely quoted. There turned out to be very little difference in the concept of what an ideal therapeutic relationship should be, in the opinion of experts of the three schools. The inexperienced workers differed more from one another.

In general, experts differed more from nonexperts of their own school than they did from experts of other schools.

More recently Strupp (1955, 1958, 1960) has been comparing Rogerian and Freudian therapists with respect to variables more closely related to interview behavior, using first statements by the patient, and later a sound film of an interview, as ways of delivering a standard stimulus to each of his therapist subjects. The principal differences between Rogerians and Freudians have to do with the "reflection of feeling." Client-centered workers use it much more frequently than do the therapists with a psychoanalytic orientation. Aside from this, the differences are not pronounced.

A third research strategy is *to concentrate on the structural aspects of the interview interaction,* ignoring its content for the time being. Much exploratory work in this area has been done by Saslow and Matarazzo (1959), using a piece of equipment called an *interaction chronograph* in a standardized interview situation. As the earlier chapter on the interview in assessment indicated, a number of variables are measured by this method—things like the number of times the patient speaks, the average duration of his remarks, the average duration of his silences, the number of times the patient interrupts the interviewer, and the like. Corresponding measurements can be made for the interviewer. Research so far has indicated that these variables can be judged with a high degree of reliability and that they have a fair amount of stability from one time to another and from situation to situation. Thus they may constitute a kind of standard measuring instrument by means of which changes occurring during therapy can be identified.

Still a fourth research strategy has been the *analysis of physiological changes* occurring during therapy interviews (Lacey, 1959). Any physiological measure that reflects functioning of the automatic nervous system can be used in this way. Data have been accumulated on changes in psychogalvanic response (PGR), muscle tension, respiration rate, heart rate, and a number of other variables. These indicators turn out not to be, however, as clear a method for evaluating the emotional changes that are involved in therapy as had been hoped. There are individual differences in spontaneous activity that occur regardless of the stimulating situation. There are individual differences in the pattern of reactivity to the same stimulating situation, and still further individual differences in how stereotyped this pattern is. What these mean is that if any one indicator—PGR, for example—is being used as an indicator of emotional processes occurring during therapy interviews, one patient may register striking fluctuations from period to period without feeling anything in particular, whereas another may show very few of these responses even though his emotional experience is profound. It is, of course, possible to use a number of indicators simultaneously, but in this case the problem of equating the measurements on different scales becomes troublesome. Furthermore, there is some evidence that these physiological manifestations may adapt out or become extinguished if the subject is repeatedly exposed to the same stimulating situation. His PGR measurement can fall to zero even though his reported anxiety persists.

In spite of these difficulties and complications, physiological measurements do constitute a resource in research on psychotherapy. One example of an ingenious study demonstrating an important fact is the report by Coleman, Greenblatt, and Solomon (1956). They measured changes in heart rate during 44 interviews and correlated these measurements for different periods with judgments made by an independent observer of the affective states that characterized the therapeutic interactions during these periods. Heart rate measures proved to be a very sensitive indicator of affective reactions. It was highest during periods labeled "anxiety," lowest during periods labeled "depression," and intermediate in periods labeled "hostility." But what was more surprising than these results was the finding that the *therapist's* heart rate fluctuated in almost the same way as did the patient's. This suggests the possibility of a physiological indicator of the elusive variable "empathy."

Another research strategy that attracted immediate attention when first presented and has already led to a considerable number of research investigations is illustrated by a study which has come up in discussing other topics in this book. Greenspoon (1955) showed that by saying "mmm-hmm" every time a subject used the plural form of a noun he could produce an increasing number of plural responses without any awareness on the part of the subject as to what was going on. What he was doing was *applying to an interview situation the principles underlying the shaping and control of behavior through reinforcement* that have been formulated by B. F. Skinner. Since approval from another person is one of the most effective reinforcing agents, any kind of interviewer behavior indicating approval might be expected to have such a reinforcing effect. In subsequent studies using a variety of situations and of verbal responses to be conditioned, similar results have been obtained by interviewers who say "good," or smile, or lean forward, or simply nod their heads (Krasner, 1958).

While there have been only a few attempts to apply this technique to therapeutic interviews, most of them using hospitalized schizophrenics, the possible significance of this relationship between the interviewer's manifestations of approval and the interviewee's changing verbal behavior as a general explanation of how the process of therapy works has generated a great deal of interest. Much more must be known before firm conclusions can be drawn. What is especially important to discover is whether the verbal or motor changes occurring in response to reinforcement during the therapy interview are paralleled by other changes in the patient's behavior and experience. It would be of little value to increase the frequency of optimistic, self-confident responses in the patient's verbal interview behavior if he continued to feel as anxious and inferior as ever in his life outside the small world of the therapy room.

GENERAL CONSIDERATIONS

While research on psychotherapy is one of the most challenging and even exciting activities in which a clinical psychologist can engage, it is an activity rather difficult to pursue except as part of an organized research program. There are many areas in psychology where small-scale experiments by single individuals are possible, but this is not one of them. It takes a long time to accumulate a usable series of research cases, still longer if they are to be followed-up for a period of several years. Controls that permit checking on particular therapist and patient effects can hardly be set up unless more than one therapist participates in the study. Thus the future of research on psychotherapy depends to a large extent on how successfully research programs can be set up and maintained in clinical settings. Almost all of the studies we have cited as examples in the previous section were parts of such programs. The APA conference report *Research in Psychotherapy* (Rubinstein & Parloff, 1959) gives an account of several of these projects now in operation.

There should definitely be in the training of every young clinician, whether in the university or in a practicum setting, some opportunity to prepare himself for participating in large-scale research programs and some knowledge about how they are initially organized. The skills required are not identical with those needed for the independent personal research project that often forms the basis for the Ph.D. dissertation. Many Ph.D. dissertations, of course, are reports of research done as parts of a large, organized research program.

The other general consideration important in the area of research on therapy is the need for imaginative, original approaches to the problem. Too great a reliance on existing theories of personality or on methods used in previous studies is to be avoided. Because of the complexity of therapy, new ways of conceptualizing it, new and original kinds of evaluation, and special statistical techniques may be of great value. There are still large areas of behavioral change relevant to psychotherapy that have scarcely been noticed. We need to study the changes that occur under natural living conditions, as well as to relate psychotherapy to laboratory findings on learning and the effects of drugs on behavior. There can be no advance prescription for originality, and no satisfactory way of selecting persons likely to manifest this characteristic. But to the extent that theoretical and methodological stereotypes can be avoided, it seems valuable for us to try to avoid them here.

As was stated at the beginning, research on psychotherapy is an undertaking that may well pay enormous dividends in human happiness if we can use it to help us understand better not just the process of treatment itself, but many other interpersonal relationships and personality changes as well. The well-trained clinical psychologist can make one of his most useful contributions here.

SUMMARY

The major share of responsibility for the systematic study of psychotherapy falls upon psychologists. Most studies of psychotherapy may be classified as either outcome or process studies. The study of therapeutic outcomes is made difficult by problems such as what criteria should be used to measure success, the selection of control groups, and the general complexity of changes in human behavior. The criteria of change most often used are patient's reports, therapists' ratings, changed scores on personality tests, and objectively determinable changes in the way the patient adjusts to life. Outcome studies are concerned with how improvement is related to the characteristics of patients, to the characteristics of therapists or their techniques, or to the environment of the patient. One study of physicians who were successful in treating schizophrenics, as compared with those who were not, showed that they were more likely to formulate diagnoses in terms of personal meaning and motivation rather than in terms of psychopathology. The characteristics of patients who break-off therapy compared with those who continue it is another subject for study. Those who continue seem to be characterized by possessing more anxiety and having a higher socioeconomic status, as well as other characteristics.

Process studies are concerned with what happens during a single therapeutic session and with changes occurring during a series of sessions. One approach to controlling and limiting the complexity of the situation is to set up experimental situations that simulate therapy with normal subjects. It is a question how much this approach actually simulates therapy, but eventually there should be a synthesis of experimental findings with clinical findings. Process studies often analyze the content of transcribed interviews for such variables as the special interpretative techniques of the therapist and indicators of distress in the patient. From some studies like this it appears that interpretations that are moderately close to the patient's own perceptions are best, as opposed to very deep or very superficial interpretations. Several comparisons of the interview behavior of therapists from different schools have been made. One series of studies suggests that experience is more important than the particular theories of the therapists. Highly controlled interviews are sometimes used as a method of studying patients' ways of interacting in therapy. Physiological changes occurring in the patient would seem likely to shed interesting light on the processes of therapy, but there is so much individual variability in response patterns that progress in this field has not fulfilled original expectations. In short, research on psychotherapy has undeniably produced some very interesting results, but the impression remains that so far we are only able to see a little way into the darkness. It is a field that will challenge the originality and reward the persistence of clinical psychologists who have been adequately trained to undertake research.

SUGGESTED READINGS

RUBINSTEIN, E. A., & PARLOFF, M. B. (Eds.), *Research in psychotherapy*. Washington, D. C.: Amer. Psychol. Assn., 1959.
   This book contains the papers, and the discussions that followed them, at the first conference on research in psychotherapy, sponsored by the American Psychological Association and the National Institute of Mental Health. Unlike a good many publications of conference proceedings, this one is really full of ideas and sound thinking by leading research workers. A wide variety of research problems are taken up, including such topics as the use of controls, the assessment of change, and therapist-patient relationships. The gist of some of the papers has been included in the present chapter, but it would be desirable for most readers to become more closely acquainted with them. A second conference on research in psychotherapy was held in May, 1961.

MOWRER, O. H. (Ed.) *Psychotherapy: theory and research*. New York: Ronald, 1953.
   A series of contributions by Mowrer and 21 other experts. The first third of the book is devoted to theory, concepts and applications, including chapters on the general philosophy of psychotherapy, the relation of learning to therapy, and the implications of therapy for public health. The other two-thirds of the book is given over to a wide variety of other topics such as research on client-centered therapy, a method of measuring tension in written documents (the distress-relief quotient), therapists' feelings toward their patients, studies of changes in tension and verbal behavior during therapy, as well as several chapters on ways of measuring interpersonal and intrapersonal differences by a variety of statistical techniques.

Reviews of research on psychotherapy and counseling

Almost every year there is a review on this subject in the *Annual Review of Psychology*. Although not as research-oriented,, the articles in the series *Progress in Psychotherapy* are valuable. Zax and Klein (1960) have reviewed procedures for measuring changes following psychotherapy. Staudt and Zubin (1957) reviewed the work on evaluation of somatic therapies. The Public Health Service (Greenhill et al, 1955) has published a review of the problem of evaluating mental health activities, including almost 984 annotated references to studies published before May, 1954.

RESEARCH EXAMPLES

NICHOLS, R. C., & BECK, K. W. Factors in psychotherapy change. *J. consult. Psychol.*, 1960, 24, 388-399.

The subjects for this study were 75 undergraduates who came to a college clinic for at least five psychotherapeutic interviews. The mean number of interviews was 15. They had completed the CPI and they took a sentence completion test before and after therapy. The results of therapy were rated both by the client and by the therapist. From the assessment instruments 30 changes in scores were available, including the score changes on the 18 scales of the CPI.

A factor analysis of the change scores produced six factors, of which the following four showed significant improvement: a cluster of CPI scales partially representing the tendency to present oneself in a good light; a cluster of CPI scales measuring poise, ascendency, and self-assurance; a therapist rating factor; and a client rating factor. The fact that these different factors showed little interrelationship is consistent with earlier studies showing that such changes occurring in psychotherapy depend on the kind of instrument and the vantage point from which one observes.

As an additional part of the study, Nichols and Beck obtained data from control subjects enrolled in an introductory psychology class, of whom 42 were matched with 42 clients from the therapy group on age, sex, and initial scores on the CPI. A post-test was given the controls after the same amount of time as had elapsed for the experimental group. An attempt was also made to produce in them a somewhat similar set toward taking the test by telling the controls at the time of the post-test that the effects of the course were being evaluated. They were also given a modified form of the client rating scale at the same time.

The results were that the control group also changed on the two CPI factors and the client rating factor. However, the therapy group showed significantly greater improvement on the CPI factor on poise and interpersonal effectiveness and on the self-rating factor.

One obvious doubt about the significance of this study is connected with the comparability of the control group. The reported findings will have to be checked in other kinds of clinical settings and with other clinical populations. It does seem clear that there is a certain lack of relationship between the criteria of improvement commonly used, which needs to be considered in any therapy study.

GRAYSON, H. M., & OLINGER, L. B. Simulation of "normalcy" by psychatric patients on the MMPI. *J. consult. Psychol.*, 1957, 21, 73-77.

Grayson and Olinger asked 45 male patients consecutively admitted to a VA hospital to take the MMPI on admission. A day later they were asked to take it again but this time to answer "the way a typical well-adjusted person would." To check on the differences between the two, the authors independently and blindly sorted the original and simulated profiles. A patient was considered to have simulated improvement if both investigators correctly sorted his two profiles and if the second one showed a reduction in height of scores. On this basis, 73 per cent of the patients were considered to have simulated improvement. Most of the patients did not produce a "normal" profile, but such changes as they made tended to be in the direction of reduced severity of their symptom pattern.

Later a comparison was made between those of the original group of patients who were discharged from the hospital and those who had to remain hospitalized. Neither in total score on the original performance nor the simulated performance were the two groups different. Only in respect to the change from the first MMPI to the second, i.e., the amount of simulated improvement, was there a significant difference. Of the group able to make a change, those who had original MMPI's closer to their simulated MMPI's were most often discharged; in other words, at entrance they were closer to their perception of what was normal.

Other studies should carry the implications of this one further. What is the nature of the patient's perception of normal behavior? This perception would seem to be related to the knowledge component of role-taking ability. Why are some patients unable to simulate normality? Are there certain aspects of behavior and experience which are easy to simulate even by very disturbed patients?

BANDURA, A., LIPSHER, D. H., & MILLER, PAULA E. Psychotherapists' approach-avoidance reactions to patients' expressions of hostility. *J. consult. Psychol.*, 1960, 24, 1-8.

The purpose of this study was to determine the ways in which a therapist's anxieties over the patient's expressed hostilities influence therapy. The therapists studied were 12 advanced students of clinical psychology. Staff members and supervisors rated these therapists on several scales, notably with respect to any evidence of hostile attitudes.

The recorded interviews of 17 parents undergoing psychotherapy with these therapists in a child clinic were analyzed. The patient's responses in an interaction were coded for degree of hostility and the object of hostility. The therapist's responses were coded for "approach" reactions which encouraged the patient's expression of hostility, and "avoidance" reactions, which disapproved of, ignored, or otherwise avoided the patient's expression of hostility. Of the 4734 interaction sequences that were coded, there were 34 per cent in which the patient expressed hostility. The therapists' reactions to these expressions of hostility were about equally divided between approach and avoidance.

The results showed that therapists who were rated as tending to express their own hostility directly and therapists who were rated as having low need for approval were more likely to permit and encourage their patients to express hostility. Therapists were more inclined to use avoidance techniques when hostility was directed toward themselves than when it was directed toward others. Patients were more likely to drop a hostile attitude or topic after an avoidance response by the therapist than following an approach response.

This carefully planned study gets at a very important aspect of therapy. It would be interesting to relate the therapists' general style of approach and avoidance to longer range effects. Through a series of several interviews, in what direction does the patient move in his expression of hostility? Which approach is more effective with a given kind of patient? Some theories of therapy assume that the expression of hostility is desirable and therapeutic. Is this true? It would be interesting to compare results of a student-therapist group like this with a group of expert therapists, since experience should be —in fact has been shown to be—a very important variable in therapy.

Four

THE DEVELOPMENT
OF CLINICAL PSYCHOLOGY

20 Personal Development of Clinicians

The book would be incomplete without a look at the most important part of clinical psychology—the persons who have made it what it is and who seek to perfect it both as a science and as an art or practice. We shall examine some personal histories of clinicians and the assessment research on psychologists and make some suggestions about the kinds of experiences which seem to be valuable for clinical work.

CASE REPORTS OF SOME PSYCHOLOGISTS

As we think about the different clinical psychologists we have known, we are impressed with the wide variety of personalities, interests, and backgrounds among them. The profession of clinical psychology has proved broad enough to make use of many talents. The brief autobiographical sketches that follow illustrate a few of the backgrounds and events that have shaped the lives and the services of clinical psychologists.

Dr. K., a clinician in a large government hospital

In the following paragraphs, Dr. K. describes in his own words his present work and how he came to choose clinical psychology for a career. At the present time he is in his mid-thirties, married, and the father of two children. He received his Ph.D. about seven years ago after completing the VA clinical psychology training program.

My professional life at present is busy and varied. Besides working full-time for a government hospital, I teach at a medical school and have a private practice. The working hours in a week often total sixty, but I do not consider myself overworked—in fact, I consider myself fortunate to lead an interesting and stimulating life. What do I do at the hospital? As a supervisory psychologist, I work with psychology trainees in their testing and treatment activities. The ward I am assigned to has been experimenting with a night-hospital program for those patients still hospitalized but who work in the community during the day, and I have been made administrator of that program. Our ward has over 100 patients in a group therapy program—I am responsible for assigning patients to groups and arranging for supervisory conferences with hospital consultants on problems which arise in group handling. I am occasionally called on to lecture on the nature of mental illness to groups of hospital workers who are either regularly employed or are receiving training. My position with the government offers opportunities in testing, treatment, administration, training, lecturing, and carrying on research.

My duties in the medical school at present consist of lecturing to junior students once a week on the forms of mental illness and on personality theory. These duties have varied from time to time. I have worked in the out-patient psychiatric clinic and have assisted in departmental research projects. I find time for these activities during the day because my night-hospital duties require me to work at the hospital one evening a week.

The remainder of my working hours I devote to private practice of individual and group therapy. My patients come to me by referral from physicians and psychiatrists or from finding my name in the classified pages of the telephone book. Those whose condition is too serious for me to work with I refer to psychiatrists in the neighborhood. My approach is analytically oriented and I attempt to set therapeutic goals which can be reached in one or two years.

Whence came my interest in psychology—and, specifically, clinical psychology? This is a difficult question to answer. I have always felt curiosity about people. At one time, in high school and while an undergraduate, this expressed itself as an interest in literature (I suppose for its portrayal of human experience in behavior and feeling) and this led me to consider seriously the career of teaching in English or the Humanities. However, during my sophomore and junior years, courses in psychology awakened my interest in the *origins* of human behavior, which has continued unabated ever since.

One of the reasons I find clinical psychology exciting is the fact that the final answers are not in. There are many basic questions in the areas of intelligence, perception, personality development, group dynamics, etc., etc. Thus I feel that I am part of an expeditionary force on the outer frontier of human knowledge, and that I may be fortunate to be on the scene to share the thrill of discovery of what exists in the inner world of the mind. Clinical psychology is probably too unobstructed for those who feel secure only when they deal with closed systems—so I recommend it only to those who are challenged, not confused, by uncertainty.

Dr. R., a psychologist in a child guidance clinic

Dr. R. is one of the most highly respected clinical psychologists in his community. He is very effective both in clinical work and in professional relationships. He has been elected to high office in several professional organizations. In contrast with his present social status, it is interesting to see in the following account some of the underlying personal feelings which he believes got him into psychology. At the time of writing he is in his mid-forties, having received his Ph.D. about ten years previously.

One of the easiest things in the world is to look back and "misperceive" one's own motives. That is precisely what most persons probably do when asked how they "got into" the occupational field in which they find themselves in adult life. Nevertheless, I shall try.

Since I came from a minority group background with a feeling for the oppressed and from a childhood which constantly emphasized in discussion and practice the importance of people, it would not be unexpected that my interest should turn to medicine. But, fortunately or unfortunately, I was destined for bitter disillusionment when as a premed junior in college I was called into the office of one of my science professors to be told that in his opinion, and in spite of the fact that I had "satisfactory" grades, I was not the "type" to become a physician and I ought to change majors immediately. Without this man's recommendation my chances for medical school were minimal. Another of my professors suggested that I try the business department, but here I was told that it was too late to start the program and that no one could take any business courses without the prerequisite full year introductory course in that field. As a possible help to me in my dilemma it was suggested that I take a battery of psychological tests. I shall never forget my interview giving me the "results" of these tests (and my confused, forced indecision certainly made me a ripe target for psychological instruments) and the summary statement of the person in charge of the testing, "Frankly, R., I don't see how you can succeed at anything."

This "advice" did several things: first, it made me angry; secondly, it increased my need for personal and academic support and for acceptance by someone; thirdly, it raised a big question in my mind regarding the efficacy of psychological tests. The anger made me work harder for grades and recognition than I ever had before; the need for support and confidence in myself and a statement by the speech professor suggesting confidence in me led me to take further courses in public speaking; the doubts about psychological tests remained as a gnawing problem to emerge at a later date.

Successful completion of college took me on to graduate school majoring in speech and with a growing interest in speech correction, in which I obtained a master's degree. Meanwhile interest in psychology was increasing, both in its application to speech correction and to other kinds of personal problems, especially those which involved communication and the understanding or acceptance of people's feelings. When World War II came, I was assigned to clinical work in an army hospital on the basis of my graduate courses in psychology. After the war, the GI Bill gave me a financial opportunity I had never had before to continue studying for a Ph.D.

My advanced work was not altogether the usual clinical training, being modified in the direction of its application to children's problems. This was largely a result of the support, interest, and thinking of another professor who stressed the importance of giving every child a "good start." In addition, it had been suggested, and accepted by me, that *child* clinical psychology was almost an open door for activity where it was unnecessary to cross swords with any other profession. When children are concerned, there is much less tendency to become jealous over professional proprieties.

Seldom have I regretted emerging, occupationally, as whatever I am. The work has not always been "satisfying" but the learning is continual. My interest in teaching has remained. Nearly every term I teach an evening course at a nearby state college. Undoubtedly, my choice of what I should teach—psychological diagnosis and psychological testing—has been influenced by my own unfortunate experience with psychological tests. The diagnostic interest remains and finds its outlet both in my regular work as a psychologist in a child clinic and also in private diagnostic work. My interest in the welfare of people finds its major satisfaction in therapeutic endeavor—in collaboration with other disciplines and the resources of the community—with children and their parents.

Thus, I now find myself leading the "full life" of diagnostic and therapeutic work in a child clinic, carrying on diagnostic work with both children and adults in private practice, teaching university extension courses in psychological diagnosis and testing, and having a growing interest in community interaction and cooperation in the field of mental health.

Dr. T., an investigator of human abilities

The following is a summary from the autobiography of a distinguished psychologist, written when he was in his mid-fifties. At the time of writing, he was the chairman of a leading department of psychology. Though not a member of the clinical division of the APA, his contributions to clinical psychology were of such importance that it seems appropriate to include him among clinicians.

Dr. T. grew up on a Midwestern farm. His ancestors were Scotch-Irish, Welsh, German, and French, most of them farmers and none of them with a college education. He was the 12th of 14 children. His father was a quiet man who read a great deal and was extraordinarily fond of children. His mother was less calm and less understanding of the children. The only thing he remembers of his early childhood that might be related to his later interest in psychology is the keen eye of his brothers and sisters for the peculiarities of others whom they mimicked and made jokes over. He also remembers being impressed when a touring phrenologist "read his bumps" when he was nine or ten years old and predicted great things for him. He attended a one-room grade school which had no library. He learned things easily and completed school early. Throughout his life he read a great deal. He was, however, poor in sports, which added to his feelings of inferiority and his tendencies toward introversion. Dr. T.'s higher education was sporadic. He planned on going into education and actually taught for a few years in a small high school. In the small college he attended he was excited by two teachers whose views on psychology and philosophy clashed. His interest in developmental psychology was augmented when he married at age 22 and became a father. He borrowed money and returned to a state university where he completed his B.A. at age 25 and his master's degree a year later. He read psychology widely, but was most impressed by what he read on the characteristics of mental defectives, geniuses, and criminals. His choice of leadership in children as the topic for his master's thesis was influenced by recently published reports on suggestibility in groups. His master's thesis was published, and though later he considered it scientifically worthless, he felt it had been of great value in his personal development.

Being much in debt, it was difficult for him to continue graduate work, but with the encouragement of his wife and by further borrowing, he was able to go to one of the leading universities of the East. His three years in this university, noted for its brilliant staff and its atmosphere of stimulation and academic freedom, brought to fruition his research skills and knowledge. What Dr. T. mentions as being the most stimulating experience there was a weekly seminar attended by all of the graduate students in the home of a great psychologist. Each week a student presented a paper which was avidly discussed and debated by the others. In his autobiography he mentioned the importance of his interactions with brilliant fellow students for his own development. He wrote that everything he had done in later life was foreshadowed by his interests at that time. "The small progress one makes after the age of 25 or 30 toward higher levels or new fields of achievement is a hard blow to one's pride. . . . One is reminded of a remark that Samuel Johnson made when he reached the age of 57: 'It is a sad reflection, but a true one, that I knew almost as much at eighteen as I do now.'"

Chance factors entered into the course of Dr. T.'s life on several occasions —the timing of job offers, the occurrence of serious illness. After getting his Ph.D. he spent several years as principal of a high school and later as an instructor in a college of education. He described these years as "fallow," but the stimulation of colleagues and the experience of teaching in these years was useful. At age 33 he was invited to one of the great universities on the West Coast where he remained for the rest of his career. At this university, given a light teaching schedule and freedom to do what he wished, Dr. T. began the experimental studies of children's intelligence which were to be a large part of his life work. Six years later he published his first book on the subject—a book which gained worldwide attention and usage. The other main lines of interest were giftedness in children and sex differences, in which he made notable contributions. His extensive reading of American and foreign literature pertinent to his field continued. He reports that his favorite among all psychologists was Binet, not because of his test, but because of his originality, open-mindedness, and rare charm.

Dr. T. is now dead, but his contribution to psychology both directly and through his many students has earned him a place among the most outstanding men in the history of the field. The original autobiography of Dr. Lewis Terman can be read in Murchison's *History of Psychology in Autobiography*, Vol. II (Terman, 1932).

THE LIFE HISTORIES OF CLINICAL PSYCHOLOGISTS

In the autobiographies of Drs. K., R., and T., we see divergent backgrounds and influences. There are also some similarities. All of them are very much interested in people. They all wind up teaching, at least part-time. They all had to possess the capabilities and motivation necessary to take a student through college and graduate work. But these case reports number but three out of thousands. What commonalities hold for most clinicians' lives? In the long process of moving from childhood to adulthood and old age, a small number of people out of the population of a country become psychologists, and of these only some practice clinical psychology throughout their professional lives. Can we detect any special characteristics of this particular kind of life history? Where are the special decision points? What kind of a selection process goes on to winnow out a mature and effective clinician from the myriad possibilities?

Early background and characteristics of psychologists

One question psychologists frequently ask themselves is, "How did I get into this profession?" Some say they are miscarried ministers, writers or physicians; some say they came into psychology to try to solve their own personal problems; some say they have always been curious about people—like the little boy in the *Peanuts* cartoon who says he wants to study people when he grows up because he's "just plain nosey." The exact reasons why any given person chose psychology are undoubtedly complex and multiply caused. Some light is thrown on the question from the survey of psychologists by the American Psychological Association (Clark, 1957). A large sample of psychologists who got their doctors' degrees in the 1930's and 1940's answered questionnaires about their backgrounds, training, and present situation. Concerning the family background of psychologists it is clear that education has been a vehicle of upward social mobility. Only about a third of the fathers of psychologists were professional men; another third were in managerial and office work, and the remaining third were in clerical work, sales, or working-class occupations. About a third of the psychologists' fathers and mothers had only a grammar school education. Roe has studied prominent research scientists in various scientific disciplines. In her study of psychologists (1952, 1953), she frequently found a family concern with social status, family patterns involving overprotection and firm control, and present resentment and difficulty with the parents. In their religious backgrounds Clark reports psychologists are very varied, but in comparison with the general population it is likely that psychology, like some other sciences, draws a higher proportion of persons with liberal Protestant and Jewish backgrounds and a smaller number of Catholics than would be expected from the proportion of such persons in the general population. A majority of the psychologists in the APA survey made their decision to go into psychology while in college years. In undergraduate work the large majority were able to achieve high grades. They reported being influenced in their decision to enter psychology by a great variety of things. Prominent among them were good teachers and interesting courses, a scientific interest in human behavior, and a personal interest in knowing more about human beings. Roe's studies of psychologists (1952, 1953) led her to conclude that psychologists "are from childhood very much more concerned with other persons than are those who go into such fields as physics and biology. That personal relations loom so large in their lives may well have affected the theories of personality development now current" (1956, p. 171). The last comment seems a very important one for psychologists to keep in mind in judging the development of their field. In Gough's research with the California Psychological Inventory (1957), psychology graduate students show a characteristic profile. On the average, in comparison with the general population, they can be described as independent, more given to achieving by independence than conformance, intellectually superior, perceptive, ambitious, forceful, resourceful, quick, clever, spontaneous, insightful, flexible, adventurous, and showing social presence. Many of these characteristics would be true of graduate students in other fields as well.

Characteristics of clinical psychologists

So far we have been concerned with all kinds of psychologists. Among people going into psychology, there is the question of who would go into clinical work. Entering graduate students in clinical work are very similar to other graduate students in psychology in possessing a high level of intelligence and professional and scientific interests (Kelly & Fiske, 1951.) Kriedt (1949) has been able to distinguish between the interests of several specialties which psychologists enter and has developed special scales for the Strong Vocational Interest Blank. Kriedt describes clinical psychologists as being differentiated from other psychologists by having stronger artistic, literary, teaching, verbal, and social service interests. It was found by Kelly and Fiske (1951) that clinical psychologists are quite similar in interests to psychiatrists.

Kelly and Goldberg (1959) in a follow-up of the 248 VA clinical psychologists who were studied at the time of their entrance into graduate work in 1947 and 1948 were also able to note some of their special characteristics. They found differences between those who subsequently engaged primarily in academic or research work and those who occupied administrative positions. They also tried to find the distinguishing characteristics of those who took up the practice of psychotherapy. The academic clinical psychologists were characterized as being bright, theoretically oriented, widely read but not socially active; their reported childhood backgrounds were characterized by considerable intrapsychic disturbance, lack of athletic ability and leadership, relative isolation and solitude, curiosity, and good school marks. Administrative clinical psychologists were characterized by extroversion, coming from a harmonious and religious family background, early participation in athletics, class leadership, somewhat less curiosity, good grades but somewhat lower measured intelligence. The overlap between academicians and administrators was quite low, but the therapists were not distinguished as a separate homogeneous group, contrary to the expectations of the experimenters. Like the academician, the therapist also had experienced family frictions and a sense of inferiority as a child; by the time he entered graduate school he already had pronounced interests in clinical work, and applied psychological work in general. Thus we see a process of decision and differentiation among individuals going into clinical psychology.

Though it is possible to find differences among psychologists who go into different specialities, one major point of the clinical psychology assessment program should not be missed: It is very difficult to predict future success in clinical work from any of the traditional tests or from complex procedures aimed at the clinical evaluation of entering graduate students. The extensive assessment of VA trainees, reviewed at the end of Chapter 10, showed little relationship with criteria of later success (Kelly & Fiske, 1951). The most generally useful measures were two objective tests, the Miller Analogies (widely used as a test of ability to do graduate work) and the Strong Vocational Interest Blank. The best predictions were to intellectual aspects of success in graduate work with correlations running from .35 to .60 even in the restricted range being studied. The monographs by Kelly and Fiske (1951) and Kelly and Goldberg (1959) clearly show that there is great diversity among the individuals who are later judged successful in psychodiagnosis, psychotherapy, and academic work in clinical psychology. It is also true that there was great diversity among the judges who served to establish criteria—that is, different universities and training centers adopt different criteria for judging candidates.

TRAINING EXPERIENCES IN CLINICAL PSYCHOLOGY

Graduate school training is the essential formative experience for professional work. On the average, clinical psychologists take five years of graduate work to obtain the Ph.D. (Kelly & Goldberg, 1959), though the time varies greatly, with some individuals, who may hold part-time jobs, taking much longer. In their graduate years students develop their professional identity. They learn the principles, concepts, and skills of their vocation which they will carry into future work. It is a period of intensive indoctrination to which they will react positively or negatively, in varying proportions, for the rest of their lives. During these years, they must clear many selective hurdles—course work, seminar papers, supervised clinical work, "preliminary" doctoral examinations, original research—all of which are used to appraise them as persons and as scholars and future practitioners. The cost in money, effort, and time is great. Many graduate students are married, putting extra burdens on wives and children. What is the effect of all these pressures, this selection? It is hard to give a clear answer, but certainly the program demands great motivation, persistence, ability, and general effectiveness of personality.

The early period of graduate school usually emphasizes general psychology, followed by a gradual turn to more and more specialized courses through the ensuing years. Preparation for clinical work often starts with observation, interviewing, and testing of normal people. Later, in the practicum, the student is supervised in diagnosing actual patients and in taking a few cases in psychotherapy. The introductory knowledge and skills learned in courses are put into practice under the supervision of psychologists in clinics and hospitals. The detailed description of courses and practicum work in clinical psychology will not be undertaken here. Such descriptions have been published from time to time in the *American Psychologist* and more information is readily available by writing to any psychology department that offers graduate training in clinical psychology.

Along with the formal learning there is much to be learned informally. Many graduate schools have a unique traditional atmosphere and emphasis, which the new student quickly feels and usually identifies with. Prominent research psychologists emphasize the importance of learning from apprenticeship relationships with older research workers. Research assistantships and seminars with ongoing research projects provide valuable experience. Clinical practicum training often is a kind of apprenticeship under master diagnosticians or therapists. A summer job as a psychiatric attendant may reassure the student that he is headed in the right direction before he reaches formal clinical training. Perhaps there is as much to be learned from associating closely with other graduate students facing similar problems as from any other source.

At the same time that contacts are being made with the many positive aspects of clinical training and experience, its negative aspects will become apparent. Training of this specialized kind increases the distance between the clinician and the "common man" with whom he will work. It requires a kind of compulsive delay of reward and an attention to books and abstract ideas that is sometimes almost neurosis-producing. Someone has said that the price of specialization is narrowness. Clinical psychologists are likely to overemphasize some things and overlook others. As an example, it has been shown in several studies mentioned in an earlier chapter that clinicians given normal protocols to judge tend to accentuate the abnormal and pathological in them unrealistically. Clinicians trained as they are today often fail to see the most obvious everyday influences on behavior and prefer to find or invent deep unconscious motives as explanations. In therapy, there are grounds for questioning seriously the effectiveness of clinicians from highly educated middle-class backgrounds in treating disturbed people with lower-class backgrounds. There seems to be too wide a disparity in values and understanding of each other's behavior. Also, many manual laborers and poorly educated people do not communicate well verbally and do not care for "talking therapy." Perhaps this is the reason Hollingshead and Redlich (1958) found that lower-class patients were more often given drug and shock treatments than middle-class patients. Also in work with delinquent boys, some investigators have found that a counselor or social worker is more effective if he comes from a similar background, perhaps even to the extent of having had a police record himself when a youngster. The studies of clinical prediction, as we have previously seen, show that the people who can predict best are close to the norms of the group they are predicting.

These examples, and perhaps many others the reader can think of, point to the highly selective character and the trained narrowness of clinicians. So it becomes obvious that we need to become aware of our strengths and weaknesses—a difficult assignment. The fact that many highly educated clinicians cannot at present accomplish much with delinquents and lower class patients does not end the problem. One solution may be to have these clinicians work through other people selected for their ability to undertake special methods and forms of contact. Another solution would be to improve training methods by some radical innovations.

THE CLINICAL PSYCHOLOGIST AT WORK

During graduate school days and the years shortly thereafter, the identity of the clinical psychologist has usually become pretty firmly crystallized. Formative experiences in academic work and clinical training have oriented him to follow lines of effort in pursuit of certain values. He may have become a devout adherent of S-R learning theory or Gestalt psychology, of psychoanalysis or psychometrics. He discovers that certain kinds of research or service suit his interests and temperament. He has found his profoundly admired "heroes." His professional identity automatically insures that he has a basis both for his positive choices and for his defenses against the onslaughts of people who adhere to other views. He tests out this identity against his experiences after graduate school.

In these early postdoctoral years, there are many choice-points at which the "switches become set" for later professional development. What kind of psychological work do I want to do? Where should I go? What lines of research interest me? What kinds of clinical problems should I work with? There is still considerable flexibility about changing lines and places of work. It is said that on the average a psychologist makes three moves before he settles down. One reason for the geographical mobility of psychologists is that their reference community is not limited to the city or region of residence. Professional literature, meetings, and correspondence keep them in touch with psychologists all over the country or even the world. The job market is thus a very wide one. When a psychologist goes into private practice, there is perhaps more need to remain in a given community, since building up an active practice depends on one's reputation and liaison with referral sources. Only a small percentage of psychologists are in full-time private practice, however; the vast majority are connected primarily with academic or clinical institutions.

These early years constitute the most likely ones for creative contributions to psychology (Lehman, 1960; Pressey, 1960). Yet this period is also a difficult one because of many demands upon the time of the new clinician. Creativity can take many forms—innovations in clinical procedures as well as in research. However, if we select publications as the index of creativity, the creative productivity of clinical psychologists is not highly impressive. In the Kelly and Goldberg follow-up of VA trainees (1959) only 30 per cent of them had more than one publication to their credit during the first five years after the Ph.D. Whether non-VA clinicians would be different, and how much is published during these years in other fields of psychology are unanswered questions. There are many possible reasons (rationalizations?) for this state of affairs: poor research training, deficient motivation, heavy demands for service in clinical settings, and heavy academic teaching loads. Another possibility is that our expectations that clinical psychologists should publish are too high. It is true that much emphasis in psychological training is placed on research; yet many psychologists are primarily motivated for service and make their contribution through using psychological procedures to help people. Perhaps the conflict between research and service and the difficulty of achieving much along both lines is part of the reason that a large number of clinicians are dissatisfied. In the Kelly and Goldberg study (1959) 40 per cent of the respondents stated that if they had their lives to live over again they would choose either another field of psychology or some other profession, such as medicine or law. Again, without comparisons with other professional groups it is difficult to interpret such a figure. In a survey of 158 psychologists in the state of Oregon, very few, only 8 per cent, stated they would definitely go into another occupation if they were starting over again (Wiens, Brody, Matarazzo, & Warnath, 1961).

As the years go by, of course, there tend to be shifts in the work that a particular clinician does. For one thing there seems to be a tendency to change from direct work with patients to other activities. In Clark's APA survey (1957), clinicians who had been out of graduate school ten to twenty years reported that only a fourth of their time was devoted to straight clinical service, while those out of graduate school for four years reported a third of their time went into clinical work. The older clinicians reported more administrative work and teaching. Experienced clinicians also have more responsibility for supervising and training students. In their careers in psychotherapy, that most intimate and often threatening activity, psychologists, like the psychoanalysts described by Wheelis (1958, Chapter 7), undoubtedly face crises of belief and skepticism as they grow older, resulting in some of them leaving the field and others shifting their theoretical alliances.

How stable the present roles of the clinical psychologist will be cannot be foreseen. Perhaps totally new kinds of activity will emerge. The increasingly large bulk of literature now published and the broadening of the work of psychologists into community consultation, applications to many fields, new research, and so on make the field a dynamic, changing one. These changes make the training of new recruits difficult. Pressey (1960) recently has pointed out the impossibility of training adequately for future developments in any scientific field. Postdoctoral work and refresher courses are becoming increasingly necessary.

THE PERSONAL CHARACTERISTICS OF CLINICIANS

Assuming a clinician has the necessary abilities and training, and recognizing that there is a great variety of situations in which a clinician may work, what special personal characteristics does he need beyond those of reputable persons in general? The following qualities seem important: understanding and respect for other people, for himself, and for the communities in which he works. Let us look further at what is meant by these qualities and how they might be developed.

Understanding and respect for others

Man must have been concerned to some degree with *understanding* and *respect* in human relationships probably as long as he has existed. In their broad connotations they are among the ideals upheld by all great ethical and religious systems. There are, however, some pertinent aspects of them that have received special research attention and systematization from psychologists.

Understanding others has been studied under terms like "ability to judge others," "knowledge of others," "empathy," and "interpersonal perception." (For major reviews and discussions see Taft, 1955, and Taguiri & Petrullo, 1958.) One finding that emerges in many studies is the greater ability of judges to predict the responses of other individuals if the judge himself comes from a background similar to that of the person being judged. In part, this is a kind of statistical artifact (usually called *assumed similarity*), since a person who happens to have average characteristics can predict the average reactions of the group simply by stating his own reactions. Furthermore, the clinician cannot be sure his training gives him any special powers in judging others. As we have noted in a number of studies mentioned earlier, naive students, secretaries, and others proved equally able to predict the responses of others. Often, as we have also seen, prediction is very good if the predictor knows only such simple facts as the age, sex, and occupation of a person.

Prediction may even worsen if the person knows more about the other person. This ability to predict from simple background facts, called *stereotype accuracy*, is also sometimes thought to be an artifact. But this is a finding on which one might capitalize. Any knowledge of people can be useful if the knowledge is correct. The implication for the training and personal development of the clinician is that he might intentionally try to develop his knowledge of different categories of people—not just individuals—obtaining norms of important groups with whom he is later to work by living with them and by survey research. He would discover their common problems, their feelings, what they know, what their world is like. He should become especially familiar with age differences (what the usual problems of a 65-year-old man or of the 16-year-old boy are; what sort of experiences such classes of individuals are likely to have), how the sexes differ (in the case of the typical suburban housewife and her husband, what their common interests are, their rivalries), such expectable occupational differences as those between the abilities or the problems of a steelworker and a garbage man, or office worker, or the differences between persons on different educational levels. Perhaps there are other differences that are important: regional, ethnic, religious, physical differences. People are constantly reminded of many of these characteristics and traits and are pressured to react in accordance with them. They enter into the shaping of their behavior and experiences. We might hypothesize that there is utility in the proper development of these normative impressions for various social and personal characteristics. But the utility needs to be demonstrated by research. Furthermore, the psychologist knows very well that his stereotypes may be wrong in many individual cases, and that he should use them only for initial hypotheses. Rare cases, people who do not fit even enlightened normative notions, do exist, and they often show up at clinics. In fact, as we have emphasized throughout this book, the clinician's job is to go beyond the stereotype and the norm—to the understanding of individuality itself.

After reviewing the literature, Taft (1955) concluded that the main components of the ability to judge others seem to be three: possession of appropriate judgmental norms, judging ability (in great part a combination of general intelligence and social intelligence), and motivation (including a desire to be accurate and free from prejudice which prevents objectivity). Just what kind of training will most enhance ability to judge others is not now at all clear. Since there is some suggestion that aesthetic and dramatic interests are related to this ability, specific training in "taking the role of the other," through psychodrama or other role-playing techniques, might be helpful. Familiarity with great literary portrayals of emotional problems may help give one insight into others. Whether the present kinds of training that psychologists get is helpful is a question. There are even some shreds of evidence that physical scientists may do better than psychologists in predicting behavior (Taft, 1955). Perhaps clinicians are selected for emotional involvement with people (as against stand-offish objectivity), or maybe they are overly concerned with certain aspects of personality, such as the inner dynamics of a person, and this prevents them from making a balanced judgment of persons.

It could be argued that ability to judge others is not very important for some kinds of clinical work. Perhaps in therapy such things as personal interest, a respect for the person, and emotional warmth and acceptance are more important. In fact, the judgmental attitude itself (which may be correlated with ability to judge others) may threaten the effectiveness of therapy rather than increase it. Rogers (1957) is one psychologist who argues that "unconditional positive regard" is primary, though he would not deny the need for an empathetic understanding of the client. If this is the case, then psychologists, or at least those who are going into therapy, should be selected and trained for interpersonal warmth and interest in others. As yet little has been done in the way of research to define these qualities, though they would seem to be very important ones. Also the question whether there is any correlation between ability to judge others and therapeutic skill is still unsettled. Until we know more about these things, it would seem important that a psychologist have both the ability to judge people soundly and objectively and the ability to establish warm therapeutic relationships. Every clinical psychologist might be able to do a great deal to enhance his understanding of other persons by consciously striving to hold himself more open to experiences with others and seeking in every way he can think of to widen his knowledge of human experience and behavior.

Understanding and respect for self

Another quality of the good clinician that is frequently cited as important is his own self-knowledge. Since the clinician is a kind of interpersonal instrument himself, his blind spots and biases enter into his clinical work, and he needs to understand as fully as he can just how he is reacting to others. Patients, like people in general, can be unpleasant; they may be irritating, dependent, hostile, demanding, or manipulating. As every professional person knows, even one's colleagues may become difficult. The threats of clinical work can make the clinician anxious and lead to defensiveness, submissiveness, or many another unadaptive reaction. Also, undue involvement with the patient or countertransference may lead to unwise and untherapeutic behavior. External pressures in the clinician's life—a quarrel with his wife, a near accident on the way to work—can upset the clinician as much. Kerr and his associates (1949), studying worry patterns of psychologists, found them subject to anxiety about economic problems, health, and failures at various points in life just as other people are. Clincians cannot be expected to be entirely free from the effects of their own feelings. In fact, these feelings are very important aspects of therapy itself. However, if a psychologist can be alert to mounting anxieties in himself and can deal with them sensibly and keep them under control, it is more likely that he can be of help to the client. Brammer and Shostrom (1960, p. 225) list many signs that should make the psychologist alert to his own feelings toward patients: finding oneself tightening up, feeling no emotional response when the patient becomes upset, being argumentative or competitive with the patient, feeling that this patient is the best or the worst client one has ever had, noticing that one is habitually late for the interview with a certain client or runs over the hour, or feeling the urge to do something overly active in helping the client.

What can the clinician do to increase understanding of himself? The first step is to become aware of one's feelings and impulses to action. Just being aware of oneself is already a large part of the battle. Some people attempt a kind of self-analysis. Freud, the pioneer, had to analyze his own dreams. However, it is generally easier to see oneself when another person is cooperating in doing the looking. Through supervision of psychotherapy and other clinical work, this other person can help the student get a better understanding of his behavior. Some mode of supervision can be continued in a less formal and intense way into independent clinical work. Most clinicians feel that it is a great help to continue consultations about cases as long as they do clinical work. Talking a therapy case over with a colleague or a consultant helps in securing perspective. In private practice—just where consultation may be more difficult to arrange—it becomes especially important as a way of insuring that the clinician will not become too isolated from others doing similar work.

Not only in therapy but also in psychodiagnosis a device to insure self-calibration is needed. Perhaps clinicians, like the astronomers, might develop ways of computing the *personal equation* of individual observers. In some training places, students learn to interpret tests by sorting Q decks or checking adjective lists to record their impressions of a patient. Then they can note how they differ from other students or the instructor and can discuss these differences.

There has been much discussion as to whether it is necessary that every clinical psychologist should have had personal psychotherapy.

Traditional psychoanalytic training requires a "didactic analysis." There is now general agreement that this analysis is not just training received from a master, but is a thorough therapeutic analysis (Ekstein, 1960). Many psychologists believe that a personal experience of some kind of psychotherapy is essential for doing psychotherapy itself. In a survey of 70 clinical psychologists, Seeman (1950) found a high agreement in favor of making personal therapy at least available to the trainee. However there was substantial agreement that real evidence is still lacking on whether the most effective therapists are the better adjusted ones, or the ones who have undergone some form of therapeutic experience. In the APA study of private practice in Los Angeles (Clark, 1957), 77 of 100 respondents had received some personal psychotherapy or counseling, and the majority considered the experience as the most important thing in their training. It would seem probable that this figure might be lower in a less populous area and where there is less emphasis on psychoanalysis. Strupp (1955a) found that analyzed psychotherapists showed differences in responses in therapy from unanalyzed ones; the analyzed ones tended to be more active and handled transference phenomena more consistently. But it is certainly clear that having had a personal psychoanalysis, even from the best training institutes, does not automatically release a person from difficulties or make him free to learn and behave ideally in interpersonal relations. Such a conclusion is suggested by the studies of staff relations in good mental hospitals (Caudill, 1958; Stanton & Schwartz, 1954).

The decision to participate in personal therapy must be an individual matter. Undoubtedly many prospective psychologists would benefit from such an experience. The precise effects of psychotherapy are still a serious subject for research, as we have seen, but the chances are that a good therapist will be able to help a person develop his self-insight considerably. In making a decision for or against personal therapy the psychologist or student has to weigh the advantages against costs in time and money. Since a very close relationship with the therapist is likely to develop, it is most important to select a therapist whose personality and viewpoint are compatible with one's own. In coming to such a decision himself the student or psychologist can gain more understanding of the problems of patients who come to therapy.

Understanding and respect for the community

In the course of clinical work, the psychologist will have many occasions for interaction with his community. In referring patients he must be aware of the needs and perhaps the biases of social agencies and private practitioners in the community. If he is in private practice himself he will in large measure be dependent on the goodwill of referral sources. As a minimum every clinical psychologist should have available at his finger-tips such knowledge about the community as the names and functions of the major social agencies, the services available for delinquents and retarded children, names of the leading medical men concerned with mental health, and the steps to be taken in referring a psychotic patient. Beyond his personal contacts with the community in handling cases, he will find himself being invited to address many groups—the PTA, nursery school mothers, meetings on mental health. He may be a con-sultant at VA hospitals and a member of committees in the fields of mental health, retardation in children, gifted child programs, recreation, delinquency, or alcoholism. Thus be becomes immersed in community affairs.

Another quality of a good clinician is the ability to exert an influence through his ideas and skills on the community in which he works. In such an interaction he works cooperatively but not submissively with others. He sees how his own role can contribute not only to his clinic or hospital but to the community around him. In many communities, psychologists as experts in human problems will have a hand in evaluating the deficiencies in mental health services, of training and educational facilities, and in determining the directions the community should take. This kind of understanding requires a basic motivation for understanding social structures that is sometimes lacking in clinical psychologists—and is not always strengthened by their training, since there is often a single-minded emphasis on the behavior of isolated individuals. In order to understand other persons (and himself, too), he must be aware of people's roles in groups and of group pressures and dynamics. Organizations with bureaucratic structures are likely to require conforming behavior, making the introduction of changes a delicate matter (Argyris, 1957). In order to raise the general level of mental health in the community the clinical psychologist needs to be very much aware of what is going on.

How is such knowledge of the community to be obtained? Much can be learned from the easily accessible sources—local newspapers, radio, and TV programs. They will provide initial information on local issues and problems, especially those related to mental health. The psychologist may attend meetings of community groups concerned with psychological and social matters. With his eyes open, but not saying much at the start, he will soon learn to identify the major community problems and local power groups. Sometimes as part of their clinical training, students can observe and participate in community mental health affairs, as Mills (1955) has demonstrated. With proper support and encouragement from the community, research by psychologists and sociologists can help un-cover the more exact kinds of information about the community which are the best basis for action.

Not all psychologists can be community experts, but there ought to be some psychologists specializing in community affairs. In reviewing the training needs for psychologists in state and local mental health programs, Carter (1957) especially stressed four areas beyond the psychologist's traditional contribution through diagnosis and treatment of individual patients: (1) *consultation* to referring agencies about cases, to agency staffs on psychological principles and resources, and to public interest groups on psychological aspects of community problems; (2) *education and training* for community mental health in a wide variety of ways; (3) *research and evaluation,* using the psychologist's special scientific training, for such matters as assessing the mental health needs of the community, evaluating the effects of rehabilitation programs; and (4) *administration and supervision* in state and community mental health committees and programs. The psychologist's potential contribution is as a "scientist-professional," who believes in the efficacy of scientific methods and constantly searches for evidence, while serving and advising his community.

CREATIVITY IN CLINICAL PSYCHOLOGY

Clinical psychology is a broad field wide open to those who wish to discover and invent. After all his centuries of struggle, man knows far too little about himself that is systematized and tested. Psychology as a science is less than a century old, and clinical psychology has arrived at a prominent position only in the last few decades; yet we promise much— sometimes too much. So-called human nature and its potentialities are great mysteries, the understanding of which seems now more important than ever before because of the perils attending the rapid development of physical science. Also in biological and psychological science the pace of development is becoming enormously fast—new drugs influencing the mind, a human embryo in a test tube, computer simulation of human problem-solving. The range of possibilities for mass good and mass evil seems to have increased enormously. By comparison our socioclinical progress is very slow indeed.

Creativity can be called innovating problem-solving. It is not just the production of something new or original, though certainly originality is involved. To be effectively creative, one must also be adaptive; the new device, method, or theory must contribute to the solution of a tangible and tough problem. There are many opportunities for real problem-solving in clinical work itself. The development of a clear diagnostic picture of a person or the communication of an insightful and helpful interpretation to a patient in therapy is a creative act. There are problems to be solved creatively with clinical organization, administration, and leadership. There are problems in clinical research. All of these await a creative touch. Many creative solutions may be purely local phenomena known only to the clinical team and the patients involved, but they are still important. Some of these creative developments become systematized and communicated to others. Some of these creative contributions become so widely known and used that they influence the whole world. The prime example is the work of Sigmund Freud. His insights into motives have changed man's view of himself so much that the world is not the same since he lived. There are other psychologists whose inventions of theories and procedures have had great influence—James, Jung, Galton, Watson, Binet, Lewin, to mention only a few. Some psychologists living today will have as much influence.

There is little research directly dealing with creativity as it attacks clinical problems, though there has been a great deal of interest and research on creativity in recent years (for summaries of a large number of studies see Stein & Heinze, 1960). Concerning the accomplishments of psychologists in general, the studies of Roe (1952, 1953) have been mentioned and also some of Clark's findings (1957). Clark's study for the APA compared a general sample of psychologists with "significant contributors" to psychology nominated from a list of psychologists who have a high number of publications. These eminent psychologists tended to show an earlier preference for psychology, to have been trained at certain renowned universities, to be at present on university staffs, to be more active in the APA, to read more psychological literature, to have stronger interests in research and scholarly activities than in helping people, and to be working on long-term planned research programs. The APA study points to the conflict that we have suggested earlier—namely, the conflict between the research and service interests of clinical psychologists. Each psychologist has to decide how his time is to be spent. Some prefer to work with the immediately pressing problems of clinical work, for which they seldom get credit through publication, though their work may be both valuable and creative. Others prefer to do research on clinical problems that are of more general and long-range significance. Clinical psychology needs both kinds of people.

Creativity also seems to be related to a stage in development. As mentioned before, the major creative contributions tend to come fairly early in the life of the scientist. Terman, the great student of giftedness, wrote; "In nearly all fields of science, the best work is done between ages 25 and 35, and rarely later than 40. The peak productivity for works of lesser merit is usually reached 5 to 10 years later; . . . The lesson for us . . . is that the youth of high achievement potential should be well trained for his life work before too many of his most creative years have passed" (1954, p. 226). Lehman's research on creativity in scientists (1960) confirms this conclusion. However, it must be remembered that there are variations in the age at which people are maximally creative. Freud was about 40 before he turned to the study of mental disturbances and wrote his most important books. Anderson and Goodenough (1935) found a sex difference in number of publications of psychologists, with women reaching their peaks later than men. Psychologists do tend to keep up the quantitative output of publications even into their 60's and 70's. In a general survey of research on the older years, Anderson concluded that "aging results in efficiency or economy of effort at the cost of variability or versatility" (1959, p. 793). Whether the remaining energies of the elderly are turned to being less trifling or less brilliant is still an individual matter.

The conditions under which creativity in students will be best encouraged, and even trained, demand study. Pressey (1960) has urged that psychologists encourage gifted students to get into college earlier and give them early experience in research. The importance of scholarships and research fellowships is stressed by Clark (1957), though in later, postdoctoral years, financial support does not seem as important for researchers as in the graduate years. As mentioned elsewhere, a number of eminent research psychologists (APA Education and Training Board Ad Hoc Committee, 1959) believe that the *art of research* must not be overlooked. They asserted a student may learn best through apprenticeship in an ongoing research program where he gets to see both the early groping efforts to formulate a problem along with intermediate steps and the completed products of research. They also wish to have variety in training for research encouraged rather than a highly standardized curriculum.

One of the most extensive studies of the personal characteristics of creative individuals has been conducted by the Institute of Personality Assessment and Research, in Berkeley, California, under the general direction of MacKinnon. A wide variety of artists and scientists have been studied. A number of the studies are still unpublished, but already some general impressions can be stated. Creative persons seem to have the following traits (Crutchfield, 1961): cognitive flexibility, ideational fluency, originality of perceptions and thought, openness to experience both from the inner self and the outer world, tendencies to adopt an intuitive rather than a sense-dependent approach, strong theoretical and aesthetic interests, preference for complexity, freedom from excessive impulse control, interest in independent rather than conforming achievements, individualistic orientation, and a strong and sustained motivation for one's chosen field of work. The process of creating does not occur in a single dramatic flash. It requires a trained mind and persistence in seeking answers. Those who have chosen to face human problems are confronting the greatest challenges. Since new findings and insights often upset old beliefs, and since the great anxieties of human life often work to suppress honest search for answers, the creative clinical psychologist must possess much personal courage.

SUMMARY

The clinician and his development are important aspects of clinical psychology, since he himself is so very much part of what he does. Clinicians come from a variety of backgrounds and spread out to work in a wide variety of tasks. There is some evidence that later preferences for academic or administrative work are forecast by the characteristics students possess when they enter graduate school. Among those who specialize in the various fields of psychology, several studies have been able to detect differences of attitudes and interests. Clinicians are characterized more by an interest in helping people than are laboratory experimentalists. Despite an extensive assessment study it has proved difficult to predict success in the nonacademic aspects of clinical work. Nevertheless, it would seem that personal characteristics and training are very important for the development of the clinican. Among general personal characteristics which clinical psychologists should possess are understanding and respect for others, for themselves, and for community welfare. It seems very probable that the high degree of selection and specialization of the clinician has not only advantages but disadvantages—especially, among the latter, the distance that separates him from the poorly educated lower socioeconomic patients he works with. Consequently he needs to broaden his experience and become aware of the limitations imposed by his training. The professional identity of the clinician seems to be particularly molded by his work in graduate school and by the experience of his early postdoctoral years. Creative contributions such as research publications usually come early in one's career. For this reason it seems important that a student be encouraged to finish training as soon as possible. Clinical work can supply the rich experiences and stimulate the kind of thinking (especially the formulation of fruitful hypotheses) that are needed to stimulate significant research work. Yet in clinical work there is often a conflict between research and practice—a conflict which might be resolved when the clinician establishes his identity both as a scientist and as a professional worker.

SUGGESTED READINGS

HATHAWAY, S. R. A study of human behavior: the clinical psychologist. *Amer. Psychologist*, 1958, 13, 257-265. (Reprinted in Braun, 1961.)

In a frank look at the development of clinical psychology, Hathaway points out the conflicts, frustrations, and struggles over prestige that have beset the science and the profession. He shows how clinical psychologists have tried to achieve a place as respected "doctors" while still avoiding the discomforts of being "on call" and having direct responsibility for patients; how psychologists have turned to research for security, although often the most satisfying rewards and the largest measure of personal recognition comes from clinical service that is frequently quite unscientific; how much of the training of psychologists is unneeded in practical clinical work; how many of the trappings of the psychologist, such as projective methods and personality "dynamics," have little if any scientific validity; how diagnostic testing is said to be important but the teaching faculty often does very little of it; how psychotherapy, thought prestigeful, is frequently dull and uninteresting; and how clinicians blur their specialty by trying to include all manner of human problems in their purview instead of concentrating on truly clinical problems. Hathaway concludes that clinical psychologists need to channel their energies into work with mental patients under a disciplined and recognizable training program, to explore the possible use of ancillary technicians for some psychological procedures, not to let themselves become overly involved in academic pursuits, to revive the respectability of testing, diagnosis, and the evaluation of psychopathology, and to attempt vigorously to meet the service needs in the expectation of which the public supports their profession. This article is reprinted in the book by Braun (1961), where the reader might find several other pertinent articles.

LUCHINS, A. S. *A functional approach to training in clinical psychology: via study of a mental hospital.* Springfield, Ill.: Thomas, 1959.

Luchins views a hospital or clinic as a place where students learn about the functioning of the installation itself—its administrative and social organization, its network of formal and informal communication channels, the roles and role conflicts. The primary task of the student is to become acquainted with the facility by observing on wards, interviewing personnel, participating in activities with patients, and by organized discussion and study. Luchins describes how principles and research in social-experimental psychology might be integrated with applied clinical practice.

JONES, E. *The life and work of Sigmund Freud,* Vol. I *1856-1900, the formative years and the great discoveries.* New York: Basic Books, 1953.

This first book of a trilogy by a close friend and student of Freud is a particularly interesting account of his early years, ending with his first publications in psychoanalysis, including his magnum opus, *The Interpretation of Dreams.* Jones attempts to find some of the personal reasons for Freud's interests and creative insights. The reader will probably also wish to read the two later volumes which complete the biography.

WHEELIS, A. *The Quest for Identity.* New York: Norton, 1958. See Ch. 7, Vocational hazards of psychoanalysis. Pp. 206-246.

Wheelis frankly discusses the conflicts and disillusionments of a career in psychoanalysis. He shows the adolescent problems of identity, the loneliness and inadequacy which underly the choice of this career. He reports how training analyses do not live up to expectations and how deep and honest doubts about his effectiveness lead the practicing analyst into dogmatism or some other form of adjustment. He presents the feelings of the analyst in response to the hostility and love of the patient. This literary, and perhaps autobiographical, account by a psychoanalyst gives the reader an understanding of how many of psychotherapists feel.

SYMPOSIUM: Psychoanalysis as seen by analyzed psychologists. *J. abnorm. soc. Psychol.,* 1940, 35, 3-323.

In this symposium a number of prominent psychologists comment on their experiences in psychoanalysis. They include Boring, Landis, J. F. Brown, Symonds, Murray, Shakow, and Frenkl-Brunswik. Hans Sachs and Franz Alexander comment on the reports. Several see their experiences as unsuccessful but the majority are favorable.

BARRON, F. The psychology of imagination. *Sci. Amer.*, 1958, 199, 151-166.

This article by a member of the Institute of Personality Assessment and Research at the University of California is an easily readable introduction to some psychological research and findings on unusually creative people. Illustrations of a number of assessment techniques are provided. The entire September issue of 1958 is devoted to creativity in science and several of the other articles are likely to interest the reader.

21 Professional Development of Clinical Psychologists

Becoming a professional psychologist, or becoming a member of any profession, carries with it certain implications of responsibility, a willingness to uphold standards of training and conduct, relationships with colleagues and professional societies—in general, both privileges and duties. In addition to such matters, there are the important personal concerns of one's prestige, economic status, and sense of professional identity. In this chapter we shall explore a number of these topics.

THE ORGANIZING OF A PROFESSION

Clinical psychology, though a newly developed and still not crystallized specialty, clearly bears the marks of a profession—high standards of training, grave responsibilities for the welfare of clients, considerable independence in regard to policy-making for itself, self-policing on ethical matters, and freedom to pursue creatively the problems that fall in its domain. The decade following World War II was certainly the most significantly formative period of the growing profession, one in which clinical psychology developed much of the character it has today and will doubtless keep for some time. During this period clinical psychologists shaped their professional organizations, adopted their first certification procedures, hammered out an official code of ethics, and set up the machinery for insuring standards of training. The manifestations of clinical psychologists' concern for their professional development are chronicled in the official journal of the American Psychological Association, the *American Psychologist*.

In order to institute and maintain vigorous professional activities, a large organization is needed. At the present time the largest and most active of national groups of psychologists is the American Psychological Association. Much of the growth of the APA is a result of the great increase in the use of applied psychology, and this is reflected in the present membership of the APA, the large majority of whom function primarily in applied fields. The largest of these fields is clinical psychology, with which about 37 per cent of the membership consider themselves to be primarily affiliated (Clark, 1957).

The APA has been very active in promoting professional development. Its journals contain reports of research, articles on theory and methods, critical reviews, and discussion of all sorts of professional topics and issues, and the organization holds an annual meeting attended by thousands of psychologists. The Division of Clinical Psychology, one of the 22 divisions of the APA, puts out a *Newsletter* which reports on professional problems and developments and conducts its alloted portions of the program at the annual APA meetings. Clinical psychologists are often members of other divisions of the APA as well—especially the divisions of counseling psychology, rehabilitation, school psychology, personality and social psychology, and experimental psychology. All of these, as well as other national organizations, such as the American Orthopsychiatric Association and the American Association for the Advancement of Science, provide useful and stimulating opportunities for clinical psychologists to join in the development of their specialty.

State organizations and local organizations act on special professional problems. The improvement of mental health resources in a particular state or region, the legal problems of psychology as they are affected by state laws, and civil service standards and rates of compensation have a vital bearing on psychologists' activity and welfare. Representatives of such organizations often work with the members of state legislatures in framing legislation bearing on the professional activities of psychologists and do what they can to facilitate the enactment of the laws they favor. This kind of political activity, though long familiar to other professions, has been a new experience for psychologists, who until recently were mostly content to remain in their academic "ivory towers."

CERTIFICATION OF PSYCHOLOGISTS

In order to maintain high professional standards, there must be methods for screening persons who believe themselves qualified to practice and making clear to the public which persons have met these standards.

Otherwise, the lay person who seeks psychological help can have no way of knowing whether a self-styled "psychologist" is adequately trained and competent, and not a quack. Since the demand for help with personal problems is great, many unqualified people have been able to pose as psychologists and even to make a good living out of doing so. A few years ago the yellow-page section of the Los Angeles telephone directory contained several pages of advertising and a long list of self-styled psychologists, psychoanalysts, marriage counselors, and hypnotists. Several of them advertised, "We can lift your burdens with one visit," and asserted that they could cure all manner of problems, including impotence and enuresis. Since any advertising beyond a simple listing of name, degree, and field of specialization is condemned by professional organizations, we can be pretty certain that such high-sounding claims are made by quacks.

On the national level, the APA has taken steps to set standards for psychologists in clinical, counseling, and industrial psychology and to award certification to qualified practitioners. The requirements for certification by the American Board of Professional Examiners are as follows: the Ph.D. degree from an APA-approved university training program, five years of qualifying experience, recommendations from experts, and satisfactory performance on written and oral examinations. The written examination for clinical candidates covers knowledge of research, diagnosis, and therapy. Those passing the written tests take oral examinations involving an observation of diagnostic work with an actual patient or client and a discussion of methods of treatment, research, and the professional problems that arise in their specialty.

At the state level, it is becoming increasingly common to impose some form of regulation over the standards of practicing psychologists. A direct and simple way of doing this is for a state psychological association to develop *self-certification,* or nonstatutory certification. As the name implies, the state organization itself voluntarily reviews the qualifications of its members who apply for certification and sees that proper standards are maintained. Many states now have self-certification procedures, and the public is informed of certification by directories and appropriate public notices. These procedures are helpful, but unless the words *psychologist* or *psychological* are legally defined and protected, anyone can use them.

Statutory certification requires the enactment of laws by the state legislature. Sometimes such a law involves issuing licenses to practice, thus insuring more control than simple certification, since it spells out what the members of the licensed profession can and cannot do. A major difficulty arises when the attempt is made to define the services of a psychologist, especially those engaged in psychotherapy and counseling, in a way that will not restrict or infringe on the prerogatives of other professions such as psychiatry and the ministry. Straight certification avoids this difficulty by limiting the use of the professional label only. Typically a certification law states that a person cannot call himself a "psychologist" or offer services designated as "psychological" to the public for remuneration unless he has met certain standards. These standards of experience (excluding early "grandfather" provisions to authorize practice by experienced persons who may not have met the formal educational requirements) usually require the Ph.D. from a recognized university plus two years of experience. In a few states there is certification at the level of the master's degree. Well over half of the states in the United States now have either statutory or self-certification.

There has been some criticism of the certification development within psychology itself (Deutsch, 1958), but most of the opposition has come from outside. The medical profession, especially psychiatry, has sometimes seen the recognition of psychology as an independent profession as a threat. In many states, however, psychiatrists have come to see the advantage of certification as a protection for the public and as valuable for promoting general professional development. There has been scattered opposition from other groups here and there, so that getting a bill through a legislature requires careful preparation and tactical skill.

ETHICAL STANDARDS OF PSYCHOLOGISTS

One of the accomplishments of the American Psychological Association of which psychologists can be justly proud is that over the years an official statement of ethical standards has been developed. An interesting aspect of this undertaking was its adoption of a semi-inductive approach. A committee of psychologists went realistically to work on the project, drawing on their understanding of operational and experimental methods. They called upon their colleagues for descriptions of specific instances of psychologists at work where ethical issues had arisen. The following are examples of the "critical incidents" of good, poor, or undetermined ethical conduct which the committee gathered, all of them taken from the booklet entitled *Ethical Standards of Psychologists* (APA, 1953a):

A nonpsychologist colleague recently requested an endorsement for an article which he had written for a lay publication. The article dealt with the self-evaluation of parents and contained a "test," complete with item weights, which the reader could take and determine whether he or she was an "excellent, good, average, or poor" parent. The publisher requested an endorsement from a psychologist to the effect that this article was in accordance with psychological principles. The psychologist refused on the grounds that the article gave the impression of scientific validity, when none was there (p. 34).

At a social gathering composed mostly of nonpsychologists, a therapist in the group, when asked about his work, proceeded to discuss for apparent purposes of entertainment the details of several life histories of clients with whom he was working (p. 53).

A school examiner had used the Rorschach almost exclusively for estimating mental ability. Recommendations for grade placement and instructional treatment are based directly on these findings, without corroboration from other standardized instruments (p. 40).

A child is brought to a clinic because of difficulties in learning to read. It is found that his difficulties are due largely to low intelligence. Without unethical intent, but from a desire not to hurt the parent, a vague report is given which disguises the facts somewhat (p. 64).

A psychologist working for a clinic for veterans on a salary basis does personal counseling. On several occasions, veterans have offered money as an expression of their appreciation of the work of the psychologist. He refused to accept the gift with an explanation that the service is free and that acceptance of a gift would violate the fundamental basis on which the service is offered (p. 71).

A psychologist obtained results which he had reason to fear would discourage a form of democratic behavior in which he believed. He was unable to conduct further research on the problem. He withheld publication of his results while he tried to get other psychologists to repeat his work. Failing in this effort, he published his own study after two years (p. 119).

Some hundreds of situations were classified and studied by the committee. On the basis of these the APA published a monograph of principles (APA, 1953b). Later another committee reviewed these principles and simplified and reformulated them on the basis of further experience. The APA code of ethics in effect at present (APA, 1959) will be reviewed again after an additional trial period.

The preamble of this ethical code sets the tone for the whole document:

The psychologist is committed to a belief in the dignity and worth of the individual human being. While demanding for himself the rights of freedom of inquiry and freedom of communication, he accepts the responsibilities that these freedoms imply. He maintains integrity with respect to the facts of his science and in his relationships with other psychologists and with the public. He does not use his psychological knowledge or insights to secure personal advantage, nor does he knowingly permit his services to be used by others for purposes inconsistent with his own ethical standards (APA, 1959, p. 279).

The eighteen principles of the code specify general standards of responsibility, competence, representations to the public, relationships with clients and with other professional people, the use of psychological tests, and credit for publications. For clinicians, the heart of the ethical code resides in statements about responsibility to the client. Two of the most important sections are reprinted below in their entirety:

Principle 6. *Confidentiality*. Safeguarding information about an individual that has been obtained by the psychologist in the course of his practice or investigation is a primary obligation of the psychologist. Such information is not communicated to others unless certain important conditions are met.

a. Information received in confidence is revealed only after most careful deliberation and when there is clear and imminent danger to an individual or to society, and then only to appropriate professional workers or public authorities.

b. Information obtained in clinical or consulting relationships, or evaluative data concerning children, students, employees, and others are discussed only for professional purposes and only with persons clearly concerned with the case.

c. Clinical and other case materials are used in classroom teaching and writing only when the identity of the persons involved is completely disguised.

d. The confidentiality of professional communications about individuals is maintained. Only when the originator and other persons involved give their express permission is a confidential professional communication shown to the individual concerned. The psychologist is responsible for informing the client of the limits of the confidentiality.

e. Only after explicit permission has been granted is the identity of research subjects published. When data have been published without permission for identification, the psychologist assumes responsibility for adequately disguising their sources.

Principle 7. *Client Welfare.* The psychologist respects the integrity and protects the welfare of the person or group with whom he is working.

a. The psychologist in industry, education, and other situations in which conflicts of interest may arise among varied parties, as between management and labor, defines for himself the nature and direction of his loyalties and responsibilities and keeps these parties informed of these commitments.

b. When there is a conflict among professional workers, the psychologist is concerned primarily with the welfare of any client involved and only secondarily with the interest of his own professional group.

c. The psychologist attempts to terminate a clinical or consulting relationship when it is reasonably clear to the psychologist that the client is not benefiting from it.

d. The psychologist who asks that an individual reveal personal information in the course of interviewing, testing, or evaluation, or who allows such information to be divulged to him, does so only after making certain that the person is aware of the purpose of the interview, testing, or evaluation and of the ways in which the information may be used.

e. In cases involving referral, the responsibility of the psychologist for the welfare of the client continues until this responsibility is assumed by the professional person to whom the client is referred or until the relationship with the psychologist making the referral has been terminated by mutual agreement. In situations where referral, consultation, or other changes in the conditions of the treatment are indicated and the client refuses referral, the psychologist carefully weighs the possible harm to the client, to himself, and to his profession that might ensue from continuing the relationship.

f. The psychologist who requires the taking of psychological tests for didactic, classification, or research purposes protects the examinees by insuring that the tests and test results are used in a professional manner.

g. When potentially disturbing subject matter is presented to students, it is discussed objectively, and efforts are made to handle constructively any difficulties that arise.

h. Care must be taken to insure an appropriate setting for clinical work to protect both client and psychologist from actual or imputed harm and the profession from censure (APA, 1959, p. 280).

The consideration of ethics does not stop with a statement of principles. The profession must enforce its ethical code. To this end, the APA reviews complaints about the professional conduct of its members and makes decisions. It is the responsibility of a profession to supervise and guard the public against unethical behavior by its members.

RELATIONS WITH OTHER PROFESSIONS

Human behavior—complex and interrelated as it is with all sorts of phenomena—is naturally the object of study and practice by many disciplines and professions. No one of these possesses an exclusive and proprietary right to the whole field of human life. Thus the psychologist will find that he will often cooperate closely with many other professional persons in working with patients and clients. This interdependence is perhaps most obvious in the case of children. For one thing, the life of the child is intimately tied in not only with his home but also with what happens in school. Teachers and principals are deeply concerned with the behavior problems of children. They are often the first to notice a child's disturbance. What is happening to the child in school must be understood in order to carry out many forms of treatment. In addition to the teachers, the pediatrician is concerned with the health of the child. When youngsters become delinquent, the juvenile court authorities are likely to enter the picture. If the child is in a foster home, or seriously deprived, the welfare department is likely to work with his case. Frequently the church connections of the family bring a clergyman into relationship with the clinic. In a hospital situation professions such as nursing, occupational therapy, and social work are involved. In such cases the psychologist sees that he needs to develop a number of different relationships that may be helpful to the patient or client and promote his mental health.

There are easy referrings back and forth among the professions in a community with good professional relationships. Very frequently psychologists receive referrals from schools, physicians, and ministers. In return the psychologist will consult with other professionals and make referrals when the case enters an area of their competence. The clinical psychologist should be aware of the limitations of his own skills and knowledge as well as the competence of others in his community to accomplish what he cannot alone. He will make sure that a case has been adequately studied medically. In most private clinical work he will insist on a physical examination to determine the role, if any, of organic factors before he embarks on psychotherapy (Blau, 1959). He will not work with a psychotic person unless in close liaison with a psychiatrist.

In some situations, as in vocational and educational counseling, it will not normally be necessary to have medical coverage, since this work is clearly labelled to the public as being restricted to problems such as occupational adjustment. Of course, if the psychologist does not have expert knowledge of occupations, and the client or patient needs special vocational guidance, the psychologist must then consult with or refer his client to an appropriate person in the community. The same is true of speech correction, reading disabilities, or legal and religious problems.

The extent of referral is, of course, limited by the community facilities. In a small town without special facilities, a psychologist may have to stretch a point and take on cases in which he has limited skill. But he should always know his community and the region well enough to know where to get the best available help for his client. He will have directories of professional services in his office so that he can make distant referrals when necessary. In the directories of the American Psychological Association and the American Psychiatric Association, he can readily check the names of psychotherapists. There are usually city or state directories of social welfare services. National directories are published by some national organizations.

The three largest kinds of institutional systems with which psychologists affiliate are education, industry, and medicine. In organizational units of each of these systems the psychologist is seldom the administrative head, for his is a staff or consultant relationship. He consults, advises, or treats individuals and groups. He may have considerable influence, but the main job of the organization is usually something else—teaching children, supplying medical treatment, manufacturing, or carrying on a business. The psychologist needs to understand his position and role in relation to others. Each of these situations presents certain ethical and professional problems. All of them demand good human relationships. On the whole, the psychologist is welcomed in these situations.

The only professional groups with which psychologists have had any considerable amount of conflict have been with some representatives of medicine and psychiatry. The nub of the conflict is over the entrance of clinical psychologists into independent practice of psychotherapy, a function in which the professions overlap in their offerings to the public. There is practically no friction from the psychiatrist's side over the psychologist's private work in testing, doing research, or consulting with organizations. Furthermore, the psychologists do not question in the slightest the prerogatives of the medical profession where it is a matter of physical or organic disorders or where nonpsychological means of treatment, such as drugs or electroconvulsive therapy, are being used. These matters are legally under the physician's control. In fact, an APA publication on relationships with other professions specifies: "The profession of psychology approves the practice of psychotherapy by psychologists only if it meets conditions of genuine collaboration with physicians most qualified to deal with the borderline problems which occur (e.g., differential diagnosis, intercurrent organic disease, psychosomatic problems)" (APA, 1954, p. 13).

It is important to gain perspective on this conflict. Both as professionals and as students of human behavior, we should see both sides. A book edited by Krout (1956) and entitled *Psychology, Psychiatry, and the Public Interest* presents the viewpoints of both professions. The argument of the psychiatric profession runs as follows: The treatment of human illness of all kinds traditionally and legally has been the responsibility of medical practitioners for centuries. Only the physician can be responsible for the diagnosis and treatment of mental illness. Physicians are experts on the functioning of the whole man, and it is always very difficult to disentangle the "mental" from the "physical." The medical profession welcomes the appropriate utilization of the psychological skills of other professional groups as long as they are under the supervision of physicians. Furthermore, among physicians it is the psychiatrist who is particularly competent by training and experience to deal with mental illness.

The psychologist's argument runs as follows: Psychologists by training and experience are qualified to deal with psychological problems, that is, problems that involve such processes as learning, motivation, personal development, and interpersonal relations. Granting psychiatric and medical responsibility for cases of organic disorder and psychosis, there remains over and above these a tremendous public need for counseling and psychotherapy where an individual's problems are psychological. When psychologists have good training and experience, it is unnecessary for them to be supervised by physicians regarding psychological matters. Moreover, many psychologists resent being excluded from the major American psychoanalytic associations, which through control by medical men in the early days restricted membership to those having the M.D. degree. This was done in spite of Freud's denial that medical training was important in psychoanalysis (Freud, 1950) and his defense of nonmedical colleagues. This restriction has been maintained in spite of the great contributions to psychoanalysis of distinguished nonmedical persons such as Anna Freud, Theodor Reik, Otto Rank, Erich Fromm, and Erik Homberger Erikson.

Underlying the dispute between the two professions are some other motives. The emergence of clinical psychology as an independent service to the public presents an *economic* challenge to medical interests. Aside from their repugnance at being restricted from selfish motives, most professional people are convinced that the demand for psychotherapeutic services is so great that there is room for many more people to render these than are now doing so.

Another conflict is over *power* in an emerging area. Many of those exercising control naturally do not like to be faced with a demand that they share the authority over an important sector of human endeavor. However, psychologists feel that their background and training entitle them to a more independent position than that of supervisees of medicine. Some political control of services in a large area of human relationships is involved. Again it would seem that both humanitarian needs and the vast number of human beings with psychological problems would argue for contributions from all who are capable.

Bolgar (Krout, 1956) feels that the conflict arises out of feelings of professional *insecurity* in both groups. Psychiatrists have long been considered marginal in comparison with the basic science of medicine; clinical psychologists may similarly be looked down upon as marginal by experimental psychologists. The professional egos of clinicians are weak, and they feel threatened by the other group. That there is some basis for this evaluation is suggested by Thorne (1961). He found much evidence for defensiveness in his survey of clinical shortcomings. He concluded that this indicated there was "a general state of immaturity and demoralization" in the field, and that "clinical psychology and clinical psychiatry are young fields in which social pressures have placed far greater demands for solutions of pressing problems than there are valid answers for" (1961, p. 162). Hathaway also analyzed the clinical psychologist's insecurity and envy in discussing the development of the profession:

But, like many other humans, these psychologists had striven to feel significant in the world and to gain cultural and financial security, and the physician was the most obvious and desirable example for imitation. . . . The intellectual path to power and achievement was clearly established for use. From the culture, the physician not only carried the prestigeful power of life and death but also was reputed to have great psychological wisdom in what used to be called the philosophy of living. People sought the physician for information about sex; and, if anyone was troubled in ways that appeared not obviously criminal or that appeared a bit deviant from ordinary behavior, then the physician (actually any physician, not just the psychiatrist) was the accepted advisor. He had to keep things in confidence, and he had studied and dissected human bodies; he was the only person, except family, before whom the opposite sex could appear undressed with propriety and to whom one would bring psychological and physical excreta. Naturally, our clinical progenitors were attracted by the applied psychological aspects of so secure a position (Hathaway, 1958, p. 259).

The psychologist's sense of professional identity might be strengthened if he could accept himself as a scientist-professional who must honestly face the areas of his ignorance, meanwhile constantly searching for better solutions and making practical decisions on the basis of what he knows now, which is the best he has to offer. However, there are conflicts between research and service which are not easy to resolve. In any case, as Bolgar has put it, a strong feeling of identity, a secure knowledge of oneself as playing a consistent role that has permanent values, results in the strength to cope with one's own inner expectations and with the pressures that impinge on one from without.

Part of the conflict arises from *the definition of what human problems and disorders are*. It seems to be largely a historical accident that the so-called "mental illnesses" fell into the domain of medicine instead of education or theology. There have been a few spectacular associations between mental disturbances and organic causation, notably when syphilis was discovered to be the cause of general paresis. However, when official psychiatric diagnostic nomenclature includes such titles as "personality trait disturbances," "adjustment problems," and "transient situational disorders," it has moved a long way from organic causation. These problems arise in such areas as learning, personal development, and conscience. They are problems for behavioral scientists and specialists in learning and social psychology. They are also the concern of educators and clergymen. Lindner has pointed out that the labels, *sickness, illness,* and *disease,* we have fallen into the habit of using have "made us prey to all the ancient traditions, superstitions, and phantasies underlying and sustaining the image of the 'medicine man,' the 'healer,' and the 'magician'" (1956, p. 155). He calls "sheer gibberish" such statements as "Alcoholics are sick people" or "Crime is an illness." As mentioned earlier, some psychiatrists, notably Szasz (1960) have pinpointed the fallacies and dangers in "the myth of mental illness." (For a rebuttal see Ausubel, 1961). This conflict may be resolved in part when the boundaries of the domain of behavior have been more clearly defined and when the extent of the behavior specialist's possible contribution is realized.

Meantime the conflicts with psychiatry and the medical profession are a continuing problem for psychology, but they should not blind us to the real cooperation that is going on between psychologists and psychiatrists on a personal level right now. Also on the national level, both organizations have committees trying to work out better relations. (See a joint report on relations, APA, 1960.) The ever-present fact of great public need suggests that it would be better if each profession would turn more of its energies toward solving human problems and become less eager to point out what is wrong with the other.

THE DANGERS OF PROFESSIONALISM

The achievement of maturity by a profession requires self-knowledge. As we have suggested before, such knowledge should include a keen scrutiny of the groups with which it affiliates or identifies. Psychologists, as well as other professionals, need to be aware of the negative as well as the positive aspects of the development of the profession. In an excellent analysis of professionalism, Bisno (1960) recalls Tolstoy's admonition that any man can find good reasons to justify the way in which he makes his living.

Bisno first points out the great importance of professions in American life. When strangers meet, one of the first questions is, "What do you do?" Status, prestige, power, economic reward are tied in with professional affiliation. Although the stated goal of every profession is social good and the welfare of the client, Bisno finds striking evidence that this aim is often neglected in actual professional activity. Economic enhancement and maintenance of status take precedence over public needs when it comes to admitting candidates for training, setting up qualifications for professional membership, catering to wealthy and prestigeful clients, and emphasizing individual therapy as against preventive measures on a large scale.

Bisno, in a spirit of pseudoprofundity proposes two "laws." The Law of Professional Velocity asserts the following:

The internal dynamics of the process of professionalization result in an upward and onward motion of the profession which is expressed in a continuous pressure toward extending the educational requirements for desired professional statuses irrespective of the absence of public clamor for such professional velocity (1960, p. 10).

Bisno's second law, the Law of Professional Dissociation is as follows:

As the process of professionalization goes on the professionals proceed to disassociate themselves from the uninitiated, respectfully referred to as subprofessionals, technicians, aides, the untrained, and laymen (1960, p. 10).

By increasingly higher standards and the achievement of social distance for the elect, professionalism acts ultimately to restrict the situation and make it so rigid that public needs are no longer well served. The profession becomes more and more commercialized. The professional person is seen less and less as a dedicated humanitarian and more and more as a man with marketable skills. Vested interests begin to discourage social change. It is no secret that the American Medical Association takes strong political stands and spends large sums of money on propaganda and in engaging lobbyists who work against the expansion of measures promoting public health. Some professional groups, no less than labor unions and corporations, have developed tremendous political power. Looking at themselves, some psychologists have become aware of the dangers in increasing professionalism and its concomitant shift to taking a political and social stance, which could be one outcome of the increase in private practice by clinical psychologists. We also have the conflict over whether to grant certification to master's level people or to restrict it to the Ph.D. The needs of the public and the kind of service required would suggest that the master's degree is sufficient for much psychological work.

THE GOOD PROFESSION

Facing up to the problems of professionalism, the APA has approved a statement originally prepared by Fillmore Sanford (1951) on the aspirations of the "good profession" of psychology. The following points are intended to suggest how the profession should develop:

1. A good profession guides its practices and policies by a sense of social responsibility.
2. A good profession will devote relatively little of its energy to "guild" functions, to the building of its own in-group strength, and relatively much of its energy to serving of its social functions.
3. A good profession will not represent itself as able to render services outside its demonstrable competence.
4. A good profession has a code of ethics designed primarily to protect the client and only secondarily to protect the members of the profession.
5. A good profession will find its unique pattern of competences and focus its efforts on carrying out those functions for which it is best equipped.
6. A good profession will engage in rational and cooperative relations with other professions having related or overlapping competences and common purposes.
7. A good profession will be characterized by an adaptive balance among efforts devoted to research, to teaching, and to application.
8. A good profession will maintain good channels of communication among the "discoverers," the teachers, and the appliers of knowledge.
9. A good profession is free of nonfunctional entrance requirements.
10. A good profession is one in which preparatory training is validly related to the ultimate function of the members of the profession.
11. A good profession will guard against adopting any technique or theory as the final solution to its problems.
12. A good profession is one whose members are socially and financially accessible to the public.
13. A good profession is a free profession (APA, 1954, pp. 4-8).

Psychologists are in a peculiar position in regard to the nature of a profession and its values. On the one hand, they are interested in the ethical conduct of their affairs as psychologists. On the other hand, they are interested in ethical conduct and values as objects of scientific study. In the latter role, psychologists can help to clarify and guide the development of the right values among people in general. Their psychological knowledge may contribute to the development of ways of behaving that flow from the possession of high values. Hobbs has made the following points:

Psychological knowledge should result in more ethical behaviors: (*a*) by clarifying the process of decision-making; (*b*) by divesting repressed responses already in the individual's repertory of their anxiety-producing potential, thus making them useful in problem-solving; and (c) by adding to the response repertory of the individual a number of alternative ways of behaving (Hobbs, 1959, p. 224).

Because psychology has an enormous potential for good or evil as it develops into a more verified science of human behavior, the development of a good psychological profession is particularly important. Like the physicists with the atomic bomb, psychologists have already begun to develop techniques which have enormous power. Consider for example some of the implications of brainwashing, mass communication, stimulation of the "pleasure center," hypnosis, sensory deprivation, and conditioning. Aldous Huxley in *Brave New World* foresaw the early conditioning of children to fit them harmoniously into chosen kinds of roles in society. Orwell's *1984* showed how a totalitarian regime could impose nearly complete surveillance over individual behavior. These are forecasts of future potentialities which are awesome to consider. Faced with the possibility that they may decide to employ such powerful psychological methods, psychologists not only need to be loyal to the highest ethical standards, but they must also plan how they should relate themselves to the political forces which will decide just how psychology is to be utilized. In a democratic society, psychologists should be as committed to the development of independent thinking as the physician is to the preservation of life. All signs point to grave responsibilities for psychologists and their fellow behavioral scientists in the future.

SUMMARY

The development of a clinical psychologist involves his participation in professional organizations on national, state, and local levels. The American Psychological Association has a very active history of supporting and shaping standards of competence and training in clinical work. Through a number of years and a series of revisions the APA has provided statements of ethical standards to which clinical psychologists adhere. The primary and final interest of the clinician is the welfare of the client and of society. A growing number of states legally certify psychologists, thus preventing quacks and untrained persons from calling themselves psychologists. Another approach followed by many state organizations is self-certification of their qualified members. In the many situations in which psychologists work they cooperate with the members of several other professions. Good relations with others are important for the welfare of clients and patients. There has been considerable conflict, sometimes becoming bitter, with medical organizations and especially psychiatry, centering around the practice of psychotherapy by clinicians. If the growth of the profession of clinical psychology is to be sound, the dangers of a rampant professionalism which loses sight of the public good must be guarded against. Since techniques for influencing human behavior may be misused, psychologists are likely to be faced with serious issues in the future, issues which will require them to become very clear about which values they should put first.

SUGGESTED READINGS

American Psychological Association. Ethical standards of psychologists. *Amer. Psychologist*, 1959, 14, 279-282.

This version of an ethical code has been approved by the Board of Directors of the APA and is the official statement used by most groups certifying psychologists. Its 18 principles cover in brief form most situations where ethical problems might arise in professional experiences of psychologists. For interesting illustrations of incidents of good and poor ethical conduct, see the earlier version of the standards (APA, 1953a).

American Psychological Association. *Psychology and its relations with other professions*. Washington, D.C.: Amer. Psychol. Assn., 1954.

Here is the cooperative product of extended and conscientious work by many of the APA members who set out to state in brief form the nature of psychology as a profession, the aspirations of the profession, and the basic principles which should guide the relations between psychology and other professions. Genuine collaboration with other professions is called for and the responsibilities and privileges of psychologists in independent private practice, in clinics, in counseling, and in industrial psychology are explicitly recognized.

ZANDER, A., COHEN, A. R., & STOTLAND, E. *Role relations in the mental health professions*. Ann Arbor: Research Center for Group Dynamics, Institute for Social Research, Univer. of Michigan, 1957.

The place of the interprofessional team in the field of mental health is commonly accepted, and cooperation among team members is held to be important and necessary for the functioning of clinics and hospitals. This book reports an interview study of how 165 clinical psychologists, 156 psychiatrists, and 159 social workers who were members of clinical teams conceive their roles and their interpersonal relations. Findings included such important points as the social workers' great need for acceptance and the psychiatrists' rating of psychologists as their equals. It also revealed some problems of status and the need for better cooperation. The study is limited by having relied solely on verbal reports, without observation of actual interactions.

BLAU, T. H. *Private practice in clinical psychology*. New York: Appleton-Century-Crofts, 1959.

This book provides a very practical, down-to-earth introduction to the procedures of setting up and maintaining a private practice. Based on his experiences in private practice, Blau discusses relationships with other professional people in the community, referral sources, ethical standards, clinical functions, fees, and legal considerations. He illustrates with recommended forms and reports.

DANIEL, R. S., & LOUTTIT, C. M. *Professional problems in psychology*. New York: Prentice-Hall, 1953.

This book is an excellent introduction and survey covering a broad array of the activities of psychologists. It is not limited to clinical or applied psychology. It is intended to meet many needs of graduate students, and is also of value as a reference book for professional psychologists at all levels. Daniel and Louttit review the historical development of psychology, present a survey of psychological literature and bibliographies, discuss ways of reporting psychological research, and cover many organizational, vocational, and legal problems of professional life. There are appendixes presenting abbreviations, references to apparatus and techniques, lists of journals in the field, and an annotated list of reference books. Louttit, who was editor of *Psychological Abstracts* for many years, and his colleague here present a comprehensive survey of useful information for psychologists.

ROGERS, C. R., & SKINNER, B. F. Some issues concerning the control of human
    behavior: a symposium. *Science*, 1956, 124, 1057-1066.
    In this symposium two of the leading figures in contemporary psychology confront each other. Skinner comes from a tough-minded experimentalist background. Aware of social problems, he wrote *Walden Two* describing an ideal society where persons could be conditioned for better behavior. Skinner argues in this symposium that fear of control has falsely led people to a blind rejection of intelligent planning. Rogers, coming from a tender-minded background which emphasizes the sanctity of the individual and his experience, argues that Skinner underestimates the place of values in his optimistic reliance on scientific method as the instrument for shaping human lives.

Joint Commission on Mental Illness and Health. *Action for mental health.* New
    York: Basic Books, 1961.
    This is the final report of an extensive survey of the resources and conditions of mental health in the United States, initiated by an act of Congress in 1955. The recommendations of this study are summarized in twenty pages at the beginning of the book. These recommendations place a very strong accent on governmental support for research. Other recommendations set standards and goals for training of personnel and the care of mental patients. For example, the report asserts that there should be a full-time mental health clinic available for each 50,000 of population and that no further state hospitals of more than 1,000 beds should be built. This is a stirring and clear call to do something about mental illness. It should be read, at least in summary, by everyone contemplating work in the field of mental health.

22 Where Is Clinical Psychology Going?

Where is clinical psychology going? We undertake the hazardous enterprise of discussing this question because it seems useful to look ahead. It may help in formulating our understanding of the clinical field if we outline some of its different values and directions even though we cannot make confident predictions. It may be of personal help to some students entering this field to try to see what shape their lives may be taking ten or fifteen years hence. If they do not like any of the pictures, they can still shift to some other profession. If they strongly prefer one of the alternatives sketched, they can prepare themselves to enter it and to throw their influence on that side.

It is less difficult to analyze several alternative trends than to predict which of them will prevail. The roots of the kinds of growth to which we shall be referring seem to be already established. What is impossible is to attach to each trend the appropriate degree of probability that it will prevail, to the exclusion of others. Furthermore, other trends may be shaping up and may be at such an early stage of development that we are not able yet to see them at all; they may turn out to be the ones that dominate the future. After this cautious introduction, the reader's scepticism should be properly aroused, and we may safely look at the directions in which clinical psychology may move in the years ahead.

490

FIRST POSSIBLE DIRECTON:

Clinical Psychologists as Specialists in Medical Psychology

From the beginning there has been an association between clinical psychology and medicine. During the time when psychologists were seen primarily as technicians, psychiatrists thought of them as "ancillary" workers comparable to laboratory technicians and physical therapists. As clinical psychology grew in knowledge and influence, the relationship between psychiatrist and psychologist has become in many places more of a partnership in all the aspects of diagnosis and treatment of mental illness and maladjustment. Furthermore, as awareness of the psychosomatic nature of many kinds of illness has grown, psychologists have increasingly found places in general hospitals and clinics. Along with these developments has come an emphasis on psychology in the training of medical students. Thus considerable numbers of psychologists are now teaching and doing research in medical schools.

A clinical psychology defined essentially as medical psychology would be focused on *illness*, physical as well as mental. An individual psychologist would need to use assessment procedures suitable for a wide variety of patients, not just for those who are hospitalized for a mental disease or who seek psychotherapy. He would need skill in consulting and collaborating in many kinds of medical treatment as well as in providing psychotherapy. His research might be concerned with psychological aspects of any illness or any kind of treatment—the personality patterns of diabetics, ways of preparing patients psychologically for surgery, the effects of a new drug on learning, a comparison of hypnosis as an anesthetic with a chemical anesthetic, when both are used in the same kind of situation. Not just psychopathology but the psychological *side* of pathology in general would be his province.

SECOND POSSIBLE DIRECTION:

Clinical Psychologists as Specialists Who Provide Psychological Treatment

Along with the growth of clinical psychology has come an increasing emphasis on psychotherapy, a tendency to see this as the core activity of the profession. Perhaps most high school and college students who become attracted to this career are aware of the therapy possibility first. There is an element of drama and excitement in this kind of venture— here seems to be a chance to really know people and have some influence on them—as well as an appeal to the desire to help suffering human beings. While it is often said that a psychologist is *merely* a mental tester or *merely* a vocational counselor, seldom, if ever, is it said that a person is *merely* a therapist.

The growth of private practice illustrates this trend. Especially in the larger cities, considerable numbers of clinical psychologists are going into practice as psychotherapists on a full- or part-time basis. Assessment is only an incidental part of their activity. Their research, if they manage to find time for it at all, is often on the subjects related to therapy itself.

It is largely because of this tendency for clinical psychologists to concentrate on therapy that so much attention has been devoted during the decade of the 50's to certification, licensing, and other legal considerations. Ways of distinguishing between competent and incompetent practitioners are essential if the public interest is to be served. Though as we have noted already, several actions have been taken, both by legislatures and by professional organizations, many problems in this area remain unsolved. Much attention will need to be given them in the years ahead if this trend toward psychotherapy becomes the dominant one in clinical psychology.

Perhaps the most urgent of these problems has to do with the nature of the training program that would best prepare psychologists for practice. As was mentioned in the first chapter of this book, there is considerable sentiment, though at present shared only by a small minority, in favor of training programs where the emphasis will be put on therapeutic skill rather than on scientific knowledge.

Another outgrowth of this trend in the development of the profession has been the establishment of postdoctoral training facilities. Present Ph.D. programs do not provide enough training in psychotherapy to insure that a graduate comes out a skilled practitioner. Experience under competent supervision is an important means of obtaining such skill. In many clinical centers, postdoctoral training programs have been set up. Fellowships may be available that permit young Ph. D.'s to participate in them. Also institutes, workshops, and other short-term educational ventures are being extensively utilized.

There is even a possibility that this trend may influence the training of psychiatrists as well as psychologists. It is possible that future training programs in psychotherapy will not make the distinction, now insisted upon, between the trainee with a medical degree and the one with a degree in clinical psychology, but will combine the resources of medicine and psychology, as they are applicable to this particular task.

Desirable as this trend toward concentration on therapy seems to be in many ways, the authors of this book, like many other psychologists, are not altogether in sympathy with it. The main reason is that we believe our *knowledge* of psychotherapy, as indicated in Part III, is still too shaky to constitute a foundation for such a professional edifice. Psychological treatment is still far less certain in its effects than it is thought to be both by many who practice it and many who seek it. A great deal more research is needed, and there is no guarantee that research concentrated on therapy itself will give us the answers we seek. Crucial answers may come instead from research in the special areas of perception, learning, development, personality—in fact, in any of the areas where general psychological research is being done.

THIRD POSSIBLE DIRECTION:

Clinical Psychologists as Specialists in Human Relations

Even more recently there has come a challenge which clinical psychologists are attempting to meet in areas not previously thought of in connection with mental illness and maladjustment. Our concern is rapidly being broadened to include interest in the whole life span of almost any person. The demand has arisen that psychologists be able to help the aging, as well as children and young adults. There is increasing concern with problems arising in such areas of life as work and marriage as these are encountered by healthy persons as well as by neurotics, by the stable as well as the unstable. Psychologists are getting opportunities to demonstrate what role they can play in institutions like industrial plants and schools and to show how successful they can be in easing tensions and promoting constructive human relationships.

Within such an institution as the mental hospital, where clinical psychologists are typically expected to serve, this same emphasis on human relations has been growing. Studies of hospitals as social institutions and the roles that physicians, nurses, aides, and patients themselves play in such social structures have been made. Programs of treatment aimed at setting up "therapeutic communities" are being tried out. The mental health movement, with its emphasis on prevention rather than cure of emotional difficulties has been a force in this same direction. Psychologists are participating in many aspects of this movement.

This social emphasis has permeated the work clinical psychologists are doing in each branch of what have been their conventional fields—assessment, therapy, and research. Clinical assessment techniques are being applied to the task of choosing high-level executives in large business organizations as well as to the task of screening out unstable workers not suitable for repetitive work. Aides and nurses as well as patients, teachers as well as students, are being tested. Where something in the nature of treatment is called for, sometimes total group situations are being studied and attempts made to modify their structure. Research on relationships rather than individuals is being carried out.

It is obvious that this trend, like the others we have considered, has implications for the planning of training programs. If it becomes dominant, clinical psychology graduates may need to know considerably more about social psychology and social organization than they are customarily exposed to now. If the problems of essentially normal persons of all ages in the areas of education, work, marriage, and leisure are included in the province of clinical psychology, the overlap between clinical psychology and some other areas, such as counseling and industrial psychology, becomes marked. It may be that there will be a common core of "generic" applied psychology (perhaps called clinical psychology) which will serve as the foundation for all specializations.

CONFLICTS AND PROBLEMS IN PROFESSIONAL DEVELOPMENT

It is apparent when one examines these trends carefully that there is some incompatibility among them. A planning commission, given the task of setting a course for all clinical psychology for the next ten years, could not make a decision to do all of these things simultaneously. For example, to move in the direction of medical psychology requires the forging of stronger bonds than have existed heretofore between psychology and medicine, while to move in the direction of specialization in psychotherapy involves increasing independence from medicine. Psychotherapists who spend the largest portion of their time in face-to-face interviews with troubled individuals require somewhat different kinds of theoretical knowledge and quite different skills from psychologists engaged in preventive mental health work in the community. Medical psychologists need thorough preparation in physiology. Human relations specialists must know social psychology just as thoroughly.

The thing that actually makes such conflicts less urgent than they would otherwise be is the diversity within the profession, from place to place, and from person to person. University departments differ widely on what they emphasize; students differ widely in what they seek. With the present lack of consensus about what psychological services our society needs most, it is fortunate that such diversity exists. However, it confronts the student with the task of discovering, if he can, which department has the point of view he will find congenial. There is no easy way to do this, since policies and goals of a training program are often not explicitly stated and may change as time passes. But the attempt to set up and maintain communication between faculties and students, actual and prospective, about the objectives of the graduate program should be made.

There are other kinds of conflicts, inconsistencies, and professional problems that have not been resolved. There are, for example, large areas of overlap among the different professional specialties. We have referred earlier to the conflict between medicine and psychology as to who should be allowed to engage in psychotherapy. Psychiatric social workers have also carried on therapeutic work under medical supervision, and there is no clear distinction between their activities and those of clinical psychologists engaged in treatment. Other groups of psychologists, represented by separate divisions of the American Psychological Association—the divisions of Counseling Psychology, School Psychology, and Rehabilitation—overlap both in membership and in definition of duties with the group represented by Division 12, the division of Clinical Psychology. As the goals of clinical psychology change, these areas of overlap change. There seems to be no way at present of stating clearly and explicitly *who* should be doing *what* in supplying psychological services and training those competent to render these services.

In addition to these conflicts among possible lines of development and among professional groups, there are the conflicts that arise for each individual psychologist with regard to the use of his time. The sharpest of these is the everpresent struggle between *research and practice*. It seems likely that this conflict will continue regardless of which trends in the development of the profession become dominant. Whatever a clinical psychologist is doing in a practical way—assessment, treatment, or consultation—he is constantly reminded that our present knowledge is inadequate for the tasks at hand. Psychology has taken on the major responsibility of obtaining the needed knowledge, and each individual psychologist has an obligation to participate in the total research endeavor.

There is no universal solution to this problem. To some extent it is a matter of arbitrarily reserving a portion of one's time for research activities, even when knowing in advance that some other important tasks will remain undone, some patients remain unserved. To some extent, it is a matter of thinking about the unique characteristics of particular situations and identifying special kinds of research that can best be done where one is. To some extent it is a matter of reshaping administrative policies to provide for research activity as an integral part of a total program. To some extent, it is a matter of developing channels of communication so that the hunches and hypotheses one gets as a clinician from intensive interaction with individuals can be tested by other specialists in large-scale research programs.

The whole problem is complicated by considerations of prestige. Research ranks higher than practice in the prestige hierarchy accepted by most psychologists. Thus a person who might prefer to spend most of his time in actual work with patients may, if he is strongly achievement-oriented, give up a position in a service agency in order to accept a pure research position, even though he finds it less congenial. Another person may feel vaguely guilty because he is making no research contribution, even though the ideas he is passing on to others, ideas generated by his practice, constitute a considerable contribution to the meaningfulness of the research these others are doing.

The broad definition of science we have tried to set up throughout this book should make individual solutions of the practice versus research problem possible. The generating of ideas and theories to be tested is as important a part of scientific activity as is the testing of hypotheses. It is the psychological profession as a whole that is responsible for the increase in psychological knowledge. There is room for much diversity of individual talents in the conduct of the large enterprise. What we need to work out are various kinds of arrangements by means of which all practitioners can participate in one way or another.

CONFLICTING TRENDS AND TRAINING DECISIONS

In this somewhat confusing picture of what clinical psychology is and where it is going, certain features stand out clearly enough that they can be used as a basis for the decisions that must be made by individuals and professional groups. Such decisions, in turn, will help to clarify the picture.

One fact to be recognized is that the shape of a profession like clinical psychology depends to a considerable extent on what is happening in society at large. World War I led to an enormous amount of research and practice in intelligence testing and the measurement of other more specialized abilities. World War II focused attention on personality deviations and stimulated the use of psychologists in assessment and treating such conditions. Clinical psychology emerged from these war years radically changed in its goals, and vastly increased in size and influence. Immediately after the war the support given on its own initiative by the Veterans Administration to the training of clinical psychologists further increased the numbers of graduate students choosing this professional specialty and helped to establish the policy that a Ph.D. rather than an M.A. degree should be considered the appropriate minimum level of training. In the years since World War II, funds granted by the Public Health Service have aided directly or indirectly in building up many more graduate training programs than were in existence during earlier periods, have subsidized the training of promising graduate students, and have encouraged research activity by student and graduate psychologists.

There is every reason to believe that clinical psychology will react to changing social needs and opportunities in the future as it has in the past. These reactions to circumstances do not occur automatically, however. What will probably be needed are periodic conferences, such as the Boulder, Stanford, and Miami conferences mentioned in Chapter 1—

conferences in which changing circumstances can be analyzed and general policies formulated. The activities of committees and boards, at local, state, and national levels of professional association, also play a large part in keeping the profession in step with the times.

The training policy that seems to be best suited to present circumstances and foreseeable future trends is one that combines breadth with specialization. The basic graduate program for all students should concentrate on breadth. The new Ph.D. should have an adequate store of knowledge in most if not all of the major areas of psychology as well as sound training in research. He must have the opportunity to develop a high degree of specialized knowledge and skill later, through experience, in-service training programs, and postdoctoral fellowships. If this policy is followed, young psychologists emerging from graduate training programs should be able henceforth to act in step with changing trends and with their own developing research interests.

PROSPECTS FOR CONTINUED GROWTH

Even though we cannot predict with certainty just what clinical psychologists will be doing in 1975 or 1980, we can be certain that large numbers of them will be doing *something*. Increasing awareness of a number of different social needs is producing an ever-increasing demand for trained workers. For example, there is widespread concern today about mental hospital patients. Few educated men and women of our time are content with the old "asylum" concept of patient care. They see hospital patients not as inmates in custody, but as human beings in need of care and treatment. To carry out the programs of treatment that enlightened public opinion is ready to support would require far more workers in all of the mental health fields than are now available.

Social trends of various sorts are stimulating the desire, if not the need, for psychotherapy. Although some writers hold that the uncertainty, mobility, and rapid cultural change that have characterized the last half century are producing more neurotic and psychotic reactions in proportion to the size of our population than in the preceding fifty years, there is no real evidence of this. The difference between our own and previous periods is rather that more and more persons are learning that help is possible—that crippling psychological handicaps should not be accepted as inevitable or permanent. In the modern world, there seems to be a *revolution of rising expectations*, not only about the material goods of life but also about the psychological manner of living. Thus the demand for treatment, both by private practitioners and by social agencies, becomes ever more insistent.

New needs for psychological services constantly emerge. The national effort to help the physically handicapped to live productive, independent lives creates opportunities for psychologists both in dealing with complex individual attitudes and feelings in disabled clients and in helping to train other rehabilitation workers. The national effort to identify and develop the talents of all gifted individuals creates new opportunities for practicing school psychologists and for psychologists who share in the training of teachers and counselors. Interest in mental retardation and funds for research have increased greatly in recent years. The National Institute of Health at Bethesda, Maryland, has grown as a result of increasing Congressional appropriations into a huge organization for stimulating research both intramurally and all over the country. Psychologists also look to the National Science Foundation for support. The need for research has been accented by the trend-setting report of the Joint Commission on Mental Illness and Health (1961). It is likely that federal funds will be provided in even greater amounts.

It is common knowledge that psychology is one of the fastest growing professions of our time. At the time of the founding of the American Psychological Association in 1892, it had a membership of 31. In 1960 there were 18,000. Members are being added at the rate of more than 1,000 per year, and of this number a considerable proportion, probably at least one-half, consist of persons engaged in clinical psychology and the other applied areas. Boring once jokingly reported that if the growth curves for world population as a whole and for American Psychological Association membership continue unchanged, the number of APA members will in 2100 just equal the world's population of 10,700 million persons! (Clark, 1957, p. 13).

Putting joking aside, and also the possibility that a nuclear war may break out, the demand for psychological services of many kinds practically insures that positions will be available for at least 1,000 new Ph.D.'s each year. This number is a conservative estimate of the rate at which psychologists will be coming out of established graduate training programs in 1965 (APA, 1959, p. 34). Albee (1959) conducted a survey of American manpower needs in the field of mental health for the Joint Commission on Mental Illness and Health. He found a severe shortage of professional personnel. Even among positions in state and county hospitals which were already provided for in the budgets, there was a 25 per cent shortage. If one takes into account expert opinion of the personnel needs for adequately dealing with mental health problems, the shortage is very serious. Albee points to the root of the problem —the lack of support for intellectual achievement in the society as a whole. While private waste and spending for frivolous and even injurious things (cosmetics, tobacco, alcohol, gambling, the annual expenditures for which far outweigh that spent on the schools) is seldom questioned, there is a great hue and cry over Federal aid to education, and local schools have difficulty in passing bond issues. The reason that this basic weakness in support for education creates professional personnel shortages is that the persons selected for advanced work must come from the pool of college graduates, which in turn must come from the pool of high school graduates. When many capable people are not motivated enough to go on to graduate from college, and when the school instruction is weakened because teaching does not attract top quality people, the pool is diminished. The situation is further complicated by the fact that all the professions and high-level occupations must dip from this common pool. With the increased emphasis on physics, engineering, and mathematics in the post-Sputnik era, other professions are naturally affected. Albee ends on a gloomy note:

We must conclude this survey with the prediction that our country will continue to be faced with serious personnel shortages in all fields related to mental illness and mental health for many years to come. Barring the possibility of a massive national effort in all areas of education, with all the social changes such an effort would imply, or the possibility of a sharp breakthrough in mental health research, the prospects are pessimistic for significant improvements in the quantity or quality of professional services in these fields (1959, p. 259).

It is of the greatest importance that the quality of clinical psychologists be high. Quality depends upon selection as well as training. Intellectually, psychology graduate students have always constituted a high-level group. For example, on the Miller Analogies Test, extensively used in the selection of graduate students, psychology students have been one of the top groups. With increasing enrollments in undergraduate colleges and more governmental support for education, perhaps it will be possible to maintain this level of ability and still increase the total number of graduate students admitted to training programs. Other personal qualities, while harder to assess, must also be taken into consideration.

The future demands much of us. We must be alert to changing circumstances and social trends as they affect the constantly changing pattern of our profession. Psychologists will think, choose, decide, and share in planning their own destiny. In this young science and profession, the doors are open for creative development. In the minds of men we serve and study lie the potentialities for the shape of the future. The challenge is great and the rewards and satisfactions are promising.

SUMMARY

Though the future is unpredictable, it is helpful to try to analyze the ways clinical psychology might go. At least three directions are discernable—toward specialization in medical psychology, toward specialization in psychotherapy, and toward a broad specialization in human relations. It seems likely that clinical psychology will move most rapidly in the third direction, broadening its applications to normal and near-normal people, engaging in community consultation and preventive work, and making closer its association with social psychological research. However, clinical psychology has become so large that there is room for specialization in many different areas. The conflict between research and practice is a real conflict for many psychologists, especially the younger ones. Clinical psychology has chosen to be both scientific and professional. Clinicians resolve this conflict in various ways—by combining research with their service work or by specializing in either practice or research. In any case, the future development of knowledge and contribution to human welfare depends on a vigorous interaction between research and practice. All the signs point to the growth of clinical psychology as an increasingly important profession in a society disposed to benefit by and reward its services and acclaim its achievements.

APPENDIX A: Fifty Tests of Importance in Clinical Psychology

In developing the following list, the authors have asked themselves: What are the 50 tests and techniques which would be of most value for clinical psychologists to know? Thinking of the wide panorama of more-or-less standardized procedures, we wanted to select a good beginning sample for the student-clinician to have available cognitively for his understanding of publications and for entry into clinical work. As our first step in answering the question, we have tried to set up some objective criteria for selection. We have reasoned that clinicians and student-clinicians should know tests that are in very common usage, are frequently mentioned by experts, and have a high number of publications. Such widely acclaimed tests, even though some may not be of greatest value to the clinician, are at least part of the testing heritage against which other tests are compared and evaluated. We have thus arrived at three criteria: (1) Usage by at least half of the 185 clinical services responding to a survey of testing practices (Sundberg, 1961); (2) mention in the subject-matter index by at least five of ten leading clinical textbooks (Garfield, 1957; Hadley, 1958; Louttit, 1957; Pennington & Berg, 1954; Rotter, 1954; Rubinstein & Lorr, 1954; Shaffer & Lazarus, 1952; Thorne, 1955; Wallen, 1954; and Watson, 1951); and (3) rank in the upper 10 per cent of number of publications among tests listed in the two latest *Mental Measurements Yearbooks* (Buros, 1953, 1959) under the sections on individual intelligence and personality testing[1] (80 or more publications in the 1959 edition, or 55 or more publications in the 1953 edition).

[1] These two sections were selected as being most closely aligned with clinical work in contrast to many of the other sections covering educational achievement, etc. This restriction does, however, prevent us from indicating frequency of publications

501

All tests meeting one or more of these three criteria are listed—a total of 30. Their status is indicated by symbols to the left of the title of the test as follows:

     * tests used by one-half of the clinical services.

     † tests mentioned by one-half of the textbooks.

     ‡ tests in the upper 10 per cent of publications.

For the remaining 20 tests of the total of 50, the authors have made selections to round out the testing picture and bring it up to date. The list has largely been chosen with clinical diagnostic problems in mind, but a number of research techniques have been added at the end. Unless otherwise indicated, tests usually are administered individually. Evaluation of norms, reliability, and validity is not attempted here, the list being intended to provide a background for reading and an introduction to the field. The student is urged to become acquainted with the tests and evaluate them as suggested in Chapter 6.

INTELLIGENCE OR GENERAL ABILITY

    † *Arthur Point Scale of Performance Tests.* A collection of performance tests including formboards, mazes, block designs, etc., all standardized on the same sample and yielding an IQ. Ages 4½ to adult.

    * *Draw-A-Man* (Goodenough). An old and simple procedure for obtaining a rough estimate of intelligence by scoring a child's drawing for details, proportion, etc. Ages 5 to 15. See Harris' revision (in press), the Harris-Goodenough Test of Psychological Maturity.

    Full-Range Picture Vocabulary Test. A rapid measure for vocabulary "in use," the subject being asked merely to point at which of four pictures illustrates the word spoken by the examiner. Useful for patients who verbalize poorly. Ages 2 to adult. For another test developed along the same lines, see the Peabody Picture Vocabulary Test (Dunn, 1959).

    Kent Series of Emergency Scales (Kent E-G-Y). A short series of questions useful as a quick screening device and providing a rough index of intelligence. Different forms for ages 5 to 14, but can be used for adults with suspected mental deficiency.

    ‡ *Porteus Maze Test.* A series of printed labyrinths on which the subject draws his way from the starting place to the exit. Described as a measure of foresight and planning. A useful clinical tool found to be affected in cases of brain damage and delinquency. Age 3 to adult. See Porteus (1959).

    Progressive Matrices. A series of designs each with a missing part, for which the subject is to choose among several alternatives. Very simple oral directions. Can be used as group test. Developed and used widely in Great Britain. Norms for ages 8 to 65 years. See Burke's review of research (1958).

    †‡ Stanford-Binet Intelligence Scale. The old "work-horse" of psychological examiners, brought up to date in 1960. Arranged by mental-age levels. Now provides IQ's as standard scores. Ages 2 to adult, but not standardized for older adults.

---

for ability, achievement, and interest tests in the list. These three criteria make the list rather dated, reflecting the popularity of research on the early personality inventories and the enthusiasm with projective techniques of the 1950's. Still, one can argue that these highly popular tests, though often of dubious validity, do serve to illustrate important attempts in the field.

* *Wechsler Adult Intelligence Scale* (WAIS). Six verbal subtests (information, comprehension, arithmetic, similarities, digit span, and vocabulary) and five performance subtests (digit symbol, block design, picture completion, picture arrangement, and object assembly) provide a Verbal IQ, Performance IQ, and Full-Scale IQ. Ages 16 and over, with normative information up to 60 years of age and over.

*†‡ *Wechsler-Bellevue Intelligence Scale.* An earlier form of the WAIS covering ages 10-70.

*‡ *Wechsler Intelligence Scale for Children* (WISC). The children's form of the Wechsler test, with norms for ages 5 to 15.

INTELLECTUAL DEFICIT AND THINKING DISORDERS

† *Concept Formation Test* (Hanfmann-Kasanin or Vigotsky test). A technique requiring subjects to sort blocks of various shapes and colors. Not challenging enough for subjects of higher intellectual levels. Still largely experimental but used in a clinical sense for studying disturbances of thought in cases of schizophrenia and brain damage.

*† *Goldstein-Scheerer Tests of Abstract and Concrete Thinking.* A series of clinical techniques for testing a patient's ability to conceptualize, including sorting of objects and copying of designs. The Weigl color-form sorting task is sometimes used alone as a simple concept formation task. No rigorous standardization, but offering good opportunities for clinical observation.

† *Shipley-Institute of Living Scale for Measuring Intellectual Impairment.* A paper-and-pencil test that can be administered in a group as a quick screening device. Provides separate scores on vocabulary and abstractions sections. The conceptual quotient is based on the assumption that an unusually low abstraction score in comparison with vocabulary suggests intellectual deficit due to brain damage or some functional disorder.

Wechsler Memory Scale. A rapid and practical way to examine a patient's memory in a standard fashion. Parts briefly sample the patient's information, orientation to time and place, immediate recall, memory span, etc. Limited adult norms are provided.

* † ‡ *Visual-Motor Gestalt Test* (Bender-Gestalt). The subject's task on this test is simply to copy nine designs as they are presented one at a time. The brief and nonthreatening task is used to reveal perceptual distortions suggesting brain damage, developmental retardation, and personality characteristics. Most common use, for differential diagnosis of organicity (Schulberg & Tolor, 1961). Scoring has been standardized (Pascal & Suttell, 1951) and certain signs for detecting organicity are showing validity (Quast, 1961). Also see manual by Hutt and Briskin (1960).

SPECIAL ABILITIES, APTITUDES, AND ACHIEVEMENT

Test of Mechanical Comprehension (Bennett). A series of questions about pictures illustrating mechanical principles. Widely used. Can be given to groups. Has shown to have validity in predicting success in mechanical trades, engineering, and flight training. Grades 9 and over.

APPENDIX

Durrell Analysis of Reading Difficulty. A standard procedure for diagnosing reading difficulties in children, including rate and comprehension of oral and silent reading, listening comprehension, word recognition, and word analysis. Valuable checklist for identifying reading errors, providing rich clinical information. Grades 1 to 6.

General Aptitude Test Battery (GATB). Developed for use by employment counselors. Includes 12 tests that use either simple apparatus or paper-and-pencil forms. Scores on 9 factors (intelligence, verbal aptitude, numerical aptitude, spatial aptitude, form perception, clerical perception, motor coordination, finger dexterity, and manual dexterity). Occupational Ability Patterns showing critical scores for many occupations have been developed.

Minnesota Clerical Test. Measures subject's speed and accuracy in comparing name pairs and number pairs. Can be given to groups. Studies show moderate validity using ratings of office supervisors and commercial teachers as well as on-the-job performance. Grades 8 to 12 and adult.

Sequential Tests of Educational Progress (STEP). Group tests covering achievement in reading, writing, mathematics, science, social studies and listening. Also an essay part. Items related to many of the intellectual skills outlined in the *Taxonomy of Educational Objectives* (Bloom, 1956). Grades 4-6, 7-9, 10-12, and 13-14. (The STEP tests have been chosen rather arbitrarily as an example of achievement tests for schools. There are many other possibilities, the Metropolitan Achievement Tests and the Iowa Tests of Education Development.)

INTERESTS, VALUES, AND ATTITUDES

† Kuder Preference Record—Vocational. Widely used and researched. A forced-choice technique providing scores on interests in the following kinds of activities: mechanical, computational, scientific, persuasive, artistic, literary, musical, social service, clerical, and outdoor activities. Group test. Grades 9-16 and adults.

† *Strong Vocational Interest Blank for Men.* An extensively investigated interest inventory. Compares the subjects responses with those of successful men in a large number of occupations. Can be used with groups. Ages 17 and over.

‡ *Study of Values* (Allport-Vernon-Lindzey). An inventory requiring the subject to state preferences among several activities representing different values. The values, derived from Spranger, are theoretical, economic, aesthetic, social, political and religious. Group test. Grades 13 and over.

PERSONALITY INVENTORIES

‡ *Adjustment Inventory* (Bell). Has a large number of publications since its first appearance in the 1930's. Developed by internal consistency methods to cover adjustment in four areas: home, health, social, and emotional. Can be used for groups. Grades 9-16 and adults.

California Psychological Inventory. Largely empirically developed. Provides 18 scales covering "positive" social characteristics, such as responsibility, social presence, socialization, tolerance, and achievement by independence, and including three scales for detecting unusual test-taking attitudes. (Gough, 1957). Can be given to groups. Ages 13 and over.

‡ *California Test of Personality.* Since its publication in 1939, has accumulated a large number of publications. Some improvements in the 1953 revision. One of the very few tests of personality for elementary grades. Provides 15 scores on such topics as self-reliance, feeling of belonging, and family relations. Group test. Grades kindergarten to 3, 4-8, 7-10, 9-16, and adults.

Cornell Index. A civilian adaptation of a quick military screening questionnaire, requiring the person to check whether he has a wide variety of psychiatric symptoms. Provides only one score. May be used as a survey from which to start an interview. (In a counseling situation the Mooney Problem Check List would serve a similar purpose more appropriately.) For adults and groups.

Edwards Personal Preference Schedule (EPPS). Developed in forced-choice format to control for social desirability. Provides 15 scores of the subject's reports on his "needs" such as achievement, intraception, dominance, abasement, and aggression. Can be given in groups. College age and adults.

*†‡ *Minnesota Multiphasic Personality Inventory* (MMPI). Most widely used and researched personality inventory. Originally provided for scores on 4 "validity" scales covering test-taking attitude and 9 "clinical" scales such as depression, hysteria, and schizophrenia. Now has many other scales developed from its item pool. Refer to Hathaway and Meehl (1951), Welsh and Dahlstrom (1956), and Dahlstrom and Welsh (1960). Both individual and group forms. Ages 15 and over.

†‡ *Personality Inventory* (Bernreuter). An older test, which like the Bell Adjustment Inventory has been largely superseded by the MMPI, but still has an extensive list of publications. Provides 6 scores: neurotic tendency, self-sufficiency, introversion-extroversion, dominance-submission, confidence, and sociability. Can be used as group test. Grades 9-16 and adults.

Sixteen Personality Factor Questionnaire (16PF, Cattell). Based on a comprehensive factor analysis. Scores provided on intelligence plus 15 personality factors, including such dimensions as dominance, stability, and radicalism. Group. Ages 16 and over.

PERSONALITY-PROJECTIVE TECHNIQUES

† *The Blacky Pictures.* A series of 12 cartoon drawings designed to elicit material related to psychosexual development as hypothesized by psychoanalytic theory. Provides both for structured questioning and free story-telling. Ages 5 and over.

† *Children's Apperception Test* (CAT). A set of 10 drawings about animals to which the subject must tell stories. Ages 3-10.

* *Draw-A-Person Test* (Machover). A general technique in which the person is simply asked to draw a person and then to draw a person of the opposite sex from the first one. Goodenough's Draw-A-Man test was an earlier predecessor. Personality interpretations of questionable validity (Swenson, 1957) but widely used for a quick, interesting approach. Children and adults.

*‡ *House-Tree-Person Projective Technique* (H-T-P). After drawing a house, a tree, and a person, the subject is asked a series of guided questions. The manual provides quantitative scoring. Ages 5 and over.

† *Make A Picture Story* (MAPS). A series of 22 backgrounds against which a variety of cardboard figures can be placed, about which the subject tells a story. Ages 6 and over.

*†‡ *Rorschach*. The most widely used and published clinical assessment procedure. The subject tells what he sees in 10 inkblots during the "free association" stage, following which the examiner inquires regarding the location of the percept and which blot characteristics (form, color, etc.) suggested the percept. According to a survey by Lesser (1961), the most widely used scoring and interpretative system is that of Klopfer (Klopfer, Ainsworth, Klopfer, & Holt, 1954), with Beck's system (1950, 1960) second most common. Many innovations and modifications on the Rorschach including Holtzman's more structured and quantified inkblot technique (Holtzman, Thorpe, Swartz, & Herron 1961). Children and adults.

†‡ *Rosenzweig Picture-Frustration Study* (P-F). A set of cartoons presenting frustrating situations in response to which the subject must write what the frustrated character would say. Based on Rosenzweig's theory. Scored for the direction of aggression and type of reaction. A wide amount of research. Can be used as a group test. Children's form. Adults.

† *Sentence completion tests*. This is a general category rather than a specific test, in which there are many forms, including widely used tests by Rhode (1957), Forer (1957), and Rotter and Rafferty (1950). The subject's task is to construct the remainder of a sentence after a few initial words. Some scoring systems have been developed but interpretation is largely impressionistic. Can be given in groups. Older children and adults.

†‡ *Szondi Test*. Six sets of eight pictures each, from which the subject must choose the two most liked and the two most disliked. It is recommended that the test be repeated six times. The pictures are of mental patients, and Szondi's questionable theory is that the subject's choices reflect his reactions to the genetic characteristics of the patient. Little demonstrated validity. The use of choices and profiles for the results and the repetition of the test are interesting innovations in projective testing. Ages 4 and over.

*†‡ *Thematic Apperception Test* (TAT). A series of 20 pictures (from which a smaller number is often used for clinical work) to which the subject makes up stories. Scoring systems including ones based on the original Murray need-press theory are available, but interpretation is usually impressionistic. Many research publications. Note the particularly well-designed validity study by Henry and Farley (1959). Contributions to interpretation and texts by Tomkins (1947), Shneidman (1951), Henry (1956), Lindzey (1952), and others. Many adaptations of this basic technique including the Blacky and CAT methods mentioned above and an objective group test, the Picture Arrangement Test (Tomkins & Miner, 1957). Children and adults.

† *Word association tests*. Like the sentence completions this is a general technique, for which the clinician might want to make up his own form. The procedure is simply to instruct the subject to say the first word that comes to his mind when the examiner pronounces the stimulus word. The reaction time and emotionality of the subject are noted as well as the content. The

best-known list of words is the Kent-Rosanoff, for which Jenkins and Russell (1960) present norms and norm changes between 1910 and 1952. Children and adults.

MISCELLANEOUS AND RESEARCH TECHNIQUES

Adjective checklist. This simple technique consists of a list of terms which the subject checks as a self-description or a judge uses to describe others. The results, mainly valuable for training and research purposes, can be analyzed in a variety of ways described by Gough (1960a).

Gesell Developmental Schedules. A series of observational procedures using specified objects for evaluating infant development in 4 areas: motor, adaptive, language, and personal-social behavior. Not a standardized test. (If a more rigorous measurement procedure for infants is needed, see the Cattell Infant Intelligence scale.) 4 weeks to 6 years.

Hospital Adjustment Scale (HAS). A set of 90 statements descriptive of the behavior of hospitalized psychiatric patients designed to be completed by a psychiatric aide or nurse or other person familiar with the patient's day-to-day activities. Scores are provided on adjustment in communications and interpersonal relations, self and social responsibility and work and recreation, and there is a keying for "expanding" and "contracting" personality traits.

Q sort. The subject sorts a large set of statements on cards into piles ranging from least characteristic to most characteristic of himself. Oftentimes the piles of cards must have a limited number so that the distribution approximates the normal curve distribution. Mainly used for research purposes as a standardized method of personality description amenable to useful statistical procedures—such as Q technique. (For an excellent introduction see Nunnally, 1959, pp. 377-383). One Q-sort deck on which there has been considerable research is the California Q deck (Block, 1961).

Role Construct Repertory Test (Rep Test). After identifying significant persons in his life, the subject indicates their similarities and differences by comparing them. Analysis provides clues to the subject's personal constructs or ways of thinking about others. See Kelly (1955). Group and individual forms.

Semantic Differential. Originally developed by Osgood and his associates (1957) for research on the psychology of connotative meanings. Requires the subject to rate a given object or concept, such as "mother" or "sex" on many rating scales. These different concepts can then be compared for their connotative closeness or distance. Three major rating factors have emerged: evaluation, potency, and activity. Interesting application to the case of "The Three Faces of Eve" (Osgood & Luria, 1954).

Sociometry. A general technique, discussed in somewhat more detail in Chapter 7. A procedure to determine the relationships of individuals in a group from their statements of preferences. See Gardner and Thompson (1959) for a standardized approach with school children.

‡ ‡ *Vineland Social Maturity Scale.* Uses the reports of an informant being interviewed by the clinician regarding the observed behavior of the patient or client in the areas of locomotion, communication, socialization and occupation. Results are scored on social competence by age levels. Particularly useful in evaluating mental deficiency. Birth to adult.

APPENDIX B: Guide for a History-Taking Interview

The following outline is a suggested guide for interviewing an adult patient regarding his own description of himself and of his life history (his anamnesis, or self-report). With some modification it would be an appropriate outline for interviewing adolescents and for obtaining information from the patient's relatives. For other case-history outlines and discussions, see Berg (1954), Hadley (1958), Menninger (1952), and Thorne (1955). Wells and Ruesch (1945) present a check sheet (reprinted in Berg, 1954) for recording important events or descriptive terms which come up in the course of the interview. It is to be understood, of course, that the following list is a guide only, that oftentimes there will not be time or necessity for such an extensive case study, and that any actual interview is flexible in following an outline. Nevertheless this guide will serve to call to mind important material to be covered in understanding the patient.

A. *Identifying data* (The details of this are usually dictated by routine procedures of the hospital or clinic. There will frequently be a "face sheet" on the patient's chart with this information on it. However, if these data are not available it is important for the clinician to ascertain them. Included in such data would be the patient's name, sex, address, date and place of birth, marital status, educational status, occupation, income, religion, names of close relatives, etc.)

B. *Reason for coming*
   1. Present problem or complaint.
   2. History of complaint; ideas about how it started.
   3. Nature of referral or how patient learned about coming here.

    4. Previous experience with clinics or hospitals about this problem.

    5. Expectations about how clinic might help.

C. *Present situations*
1. Description of an ordinary day in the patient's life, from rising in the morning to going to bed; any major variations on weekends, etc.
2. Descriptions of each member of present family, and other significant people.
3. Changes currently planned in situations—work or school, recreation, family.

D. *Family constellation* (family of orientation)
1. Description of mother and father (age now and at time of their marriage, general description of personality, and relationship with patient).
2. Description of each brother and sister (number of years older or younger than patient, general description of personality, and relationship with patient).
3. Patient's role in the family (the "good little sister," "the black sheep," etc.).
4. Alliances and frictions in the family. Changes in family constellation such as divorce, death.

E. *Early recollections*
1. Descriptions of earliest events clearly recalled (noting age, people involved, and patient's feelings about incident).

F. *Birth and development*
1. Term and conditions of birth.
2. Ages of walking and talking.
3. Problems of infancy and childhood (feeding difficulties, nailbiting, thumb sucking, fears, night terrors).
4. Social relations in childhood (outgoing or seclusive tendencies, lying, stealing, cruelty, truancy).
5. Patient's view of own childhood (pleasant, unhappy).

G. *Health*
1. What childhood diseases and when.
2. Other illnesses, injuries, operations, handicaps.
3. Patient's estimate of habitual degree of health and bodily weaknesses and strengths.

H. *Education and training*
1. Schools attended, dates of attendance, class standing.
2. Subjects of special interest, of strength and weakness.
3. Patient's evaluation of adequacy of past training and present learning needs.

I. *Work record*
1. Descriptions of jobs in chronological sequence.
2. Reasons for changing jobs.
3. Attitudes toward work, responsibility, saving, indebtedness.

J. *Recreation, interests*
1. Nonpaid work (work around the home, volunteer work).
2. Interests, what patient reads, what kinds of physical activities he pursues, membership in groups, religious activity, creative pursuits.
3. Patient's evaluation of adequacy of self-expression.

K. *Sexual development*
  1. First awareness (how learned about sex, attitude, and reactions).
  2. Evolution of sex interest, sex pace, fantasies, dreams.
  3. Kinds of sexual expression (masturbation, homosexual, and hetero-sexual).
  4. Patient's evaluation of adequacy of his sexual expressions.

L. *Marital and family data*
  1. Date(s) and circumstances surrounding marriage(s) (where met, length of engagement, honeymoon).
  2. Pregnancies and children (ages, preferences).
  3. Major events in course of marriage, changes.
  4. Present family interaction (how decisions made about buying major items, going on trips, etc.; amount and kind of communication; roles played by each member of family).
  5. Comparison between present family and family of orientation.
  6. Patient's evaluation of present family strengths and problems.

M. *Self-description*
  1. Patient's description of self as if writing a story about a person, or describing his role in a play.
  2. Outstanding characteristics—assets and limitations.
  3. Sources of worry, doubt, anxiety, remorse.
  4. Concrete difficulties would like to overcome in next few months or years; what adjustments have been tried.
  5. Patient's description of what he would do if he were suddenly free of his symptoms, complaints, or problems.
  6. Patient's description of two persons most like him and most unlike him.
  7. Patient's ideal (the person he would like to be like).

N. *Choices and turning points in life.*
  1. The most important turning points of life.
  2. How patient went about making decisions at these turning points.
  3. A concrete illustration of a success and of a failure.
  4. Main resources of help and encouragement in times of crises, decisions, or uncertainty.

O. *Any additional points patient sees as omitted in above history.*

References

ABT, L. E. The development of clinical psychology: a transactional approach. In D. Brower & L. E. Abt (Eds.), *Progress in Clinical Psychology.* Vol. II. New York: Grune & Stratton, 1956. Pp. 1-13.

ACKERMAN, N. W. *The psychodynamics of family life.* New York: Basic Books, 1958.

ADORNO, T. W., FRENKEL-BRUNSWIK, Else, LEVINSON, D. J., & SANFORD, R. N. *The authoritarian personality.* New York: Harper, 1950.

AKUTAGOWA, R. *Rashomon and other stories.* New York: Bantam Books, 1952.

ALBEE, G. W. *Mental health manpower trends.* New York: Basic Books, 1959.

ALEXANDER, F., & FRENCH, T. M. *Psychoanalytic therapy: principles and application.* New York: Ronald, 1946.

ALLEN, F. H. *Psychotherapy with children.* New York: Norton, 1942.

ALLEN, R. M. *Personality assessment procedures.* New York: Harper, 1958.

ALLPORT, G. W. *Personality: a psychological interpretation.* New York: Holt, 1937.

ALLPORT, G. W. What units shall we employ? In G. Lindzey (Ed.), *Assessment of human motives.* New York: Rinehart, 1958. Pp. 239-258.

ALLPORT, G. W. *Pattern and growth in personality.* New York: Holt, Rinehart, & Winston, 1961.

ALPERT, R. Personal communication. 1961.

American Psychiatric Association, Mental Hospital Service. *Diagnostic and statistical manual of mental disorders.* Washington: Amer. Psychiat. Ass., 1952.

American Psychological Association. *Ethical standards of psychologists.* Washington: Amer. Psychol. Ass., 1953. (*a*)

American Psychological Association. *Ethical standards of psychologists, a summary of ethical principles.* Washington: Amer. Psychol. Ass., 1953. (*b*)

American Psychological Association. *Psychology and its relations with other professions.* Washington: Amer. Psychol. Ass., 1954.

American Psychological Association. Ethical standards of psychologists. *Amer. Psychologist,* 1959, 14, 279-282.

American Psychological Association & American Psychiatric Association. Joint report on relations between psychology and psychiatry. *Amer. Psychologist,* 1960, 15, 198-200.

American Psychological Association, Board of Scientific Affairs. Technical communication in psychology: a statement of the problem. *Amer. Psychologist,* 1959, 14, 267-271.

American Psychological Association, Committee on Psychological Tests. *Technical recommendations for psychological tests and diagnostic techniques.* Washington: Amer. Psychol. Ass., 1954. (Reprinted from *Psychol. Bull., Suppl.,* 1954, 51, 201-238.)

American Psychological Association, Committee on Training in Clinical Psychology. Recommended graduate training program in clinical psychology. *Amer. Psychologist,* 1947, 2, 539-558.

American Psychological Association, Education and Training Board Ad Hoc Committee. Education for research in psychology. *Amer. Psychologist,* 1959, 14, 167-179.

AMRINE, M. Psychology in the news. *Amer. Psychologist,* 1960, 15, 630-631.

ANASTASI, Anne. *Psychological Testing.* (2nd ed.) New York: Macmillan, 1961.

ANDERSON, H. A., & ANDERSON, Gladys L. (Eds.) *An introduction to projective techniques.* New York: Prentice-Hall, 1951.

ANDERSON, J. E. The use of time and energy. In J. E. Birren (Ed.), *Handbook of aging and the individual.* Chicago: Univer. of Chicago Press, 1959. Pp. 769-796.

ANDERSON, J. E., & GOODENOUGH, Florence L. Age and sex differences in productivity of American psychologists. *Psychol. Bull.,* 1935, 32, 675-676.

ANSBACHER, H. L., & ANSBACHER, Rowena R. (Eds.) *The individual psychology of Alfred Adler.* New York: Basic Books, 1956.

ANTHONY, E. J., & BENE, Eva. A technique for the objective assessment of the child's family relationships. *J. ment. Sci.,* 1957, 103, 541-555.

APPEL, K. E., LHAMON, W. T., MYERS, J. M., & HARVEY, W. A. Long-term psychotherapy. In *Psychiatric treatment: Proc. Ass. Res. nerv. ment. Dis., N. Y.* Baltimore: Williams & Wilkins, 1951.

APPEL, K. E., LHAMON, W. T. MYERS, J. M., & HARVEY, W. A. Long-term psychotherapy. In *Psychiatric treatment: Proc. Ass. Res. nerv. ment. Dis., N. Y.* Baltimore: Williams & Wilkins, 1953. Pp. 21-34.

ARGYRIS, C. *Personality and organization, the conflict between system and the individual.* New York: Harper, 1957.

ARIETI, S. (Ed.) *American handbook of psychiatry.* Vols. I & II. New York: Basic Books, 1959.

ASCH, S. E. Forming impressions of personality. *J. abnorm. soc. Psychol.,* 1946, 41, 258-290.

ASH, P. The reliability of psychiatric diagnoses. *J. abnorm. soc. Psychol.,* 1949, 44, 272-276.

ASHBY, J. D., FORD, D. H., GUERNEY, B. G., Jr., & GUERNEY, Louise F. The effects on clients of therapists administering a reflective and a leading type of psychotherapy. *Psychol. Monogr.,* 1957, 71, No. 453.

AUSUBEL, D. P. Personality disorder *is* disease. *Amer. Psychologist,* 1961, 16, 69-74.

AXLINE, Virginia M. *Play therapy.* Boston: Houghton, 1947.

BACH, G. R. *Intensive group psychotherapy.* New York: Ronald, 1954.

BALES, R. F. Small-group theory and research. In R. K. Merton, L. Broom, & L. S. Cottrell Jr. (Eds.), *Sociology today.* New York: Basic Books, 1959. Pp. 293-305.

BALLER, W., & SCHALOCK, H. D. Conditioned-response treatment of eneuresis. *Except. Child.,* 1956, 22, 233-236.

BANDURA, A., LIPSHER, D. H., & MILLER, Paula E. Psychotherapists' approach-avoidance reactions to patients' expressions of hostility. *J. consult. Psychol.,* 1960, 24, 1-8.

BARKER, R. G., SCHOGGEN, Maxine F., & BARKER, Louise S. Hemerography of Mary Ennis. In A. Burton & R. E. Harris (Eds.), *Clinical studies of personality.* New York: Harper, 1955. Pp. 768-808.

BARKER, R. G., & WRIGHT, H. F. *One boy's day.* New York: Harper, 1951.

BARKER, R. G., & WRIGHT, H. F. *Midwest and its children, the psychological ecology of an American town.* Evanston, Ill.: Row, Peterson, 1955.

BARRON, F. Some test correlates of response to psychotherapy. *J. consult. Psychol.,* 1953, 27, 235-241.

BARRON, F. *Personal soundness in university graduate students, an experimental study of young men in the sciences and professions.* Berkeley: Univer. of California Press, 1954.

BARRON, F. The psychology of imagination. *Scient. Amer.,* 1958, 199, 151-166.

BARTLETT, F. C. Fifty years of psychology. *Occup. Psychol.,* 1955, 29, 203-216.

BASS, B. M. The leaderless group discussion. *Psychol. Bull.,* 1954, 51, 465-492.

BASS, B. M., & BERG, I. A. (Eds.) *Objective approaches to personality assessment.* Princeton, N. J.: Van Nostrand, 1959.

BATESON, G., JACKSON, D. D., HALEY, J., & WEAKLAND, J. H. Toward a theory of schizophrenia. *Behav. Sci.,* 1956, 1, 251-264.

BAUGHMAN, E. E. A new method of Rorschach inquiry. *J. proj. Tech.,* 1958, 22, 381-389. (*a*)

BAUGHMAN, E. E. The role of the stimulus in Rorschach responses. *Psychol. Bull.,* 1958, 55, 121-147. (*b*)

BAUGHMAN, E. E. The effect of inquiry method on Rorschach color and shading scores. *J. proj. Tech.,* 1959, 23, 3-7. (*a*)

BAUGHMAN, E. E. An experimental analysis of the relationship between stimulus structure and behavior on the Rorschach. *J. proj. Tech.,* 1959, 23, 134-183. (*b*)

BECHTOLDT, H. P. Construct validity: a critique. *Amer. Psychologist,* 1959, 14, 619-629.

BECK, S. J. *Rorschach's test.* (2nd ed.) Vol. I. New York: Grune & Stratton, 1950.

BECK, S. J. *The Rorschach experiment: ventures in blind diagnosis.* New York: Grune & Stratton, 1960.

BECK, S. J., & MOLISH, H. B. (Eds.) *Reflexes to intelligence: a reader in clinical psychology.* Glencoe, Ill.: Free Press, 1959.

BECKER, J. Achievement related characteristics of manic-depressives. *J. abnorm. soc. Psychol.,* 1960, 60, 334-339.

BELKNAP, I. *Human problems of a state mental hospital.* New York: McGraw, 1956.

BELL, J. E. *Family group therapy.* (Public Health Monograph No. 64) Washington: U. S. Govt Printing Office, 1961.

BELLAK, L. (Ed.) *Conceptual and methodological problems in psychoanalysis.* (Annals of the New York Academy of Sciences, Vol. 76, Art. 4) New York: New York Academy of Sciences, 1959. Pp. 971-1134.

BENNIS, W. G. A critique of group therapy research. *Int. J. Group Psychother.,* 1960, 10, 63-77.

BERDIE, R. F. A program of counseling interview research. *Ed. psych. Measmt,* 1958, 18, 255-274.

BERENSON, B. G., BIERSDORF, Kathryn C., MAGOON, T. M., MAXWELL, Martha J., PUMROY, D. K., & RICHEY, Marjorie H. A checklist for recording test-taking behavior. *J. counsel. Psychol.,* 1960, 7, 116-119.

BERG, I. A. The clinical interview and the case record. In L. A. Pennington & I. A. Berg (Eds.), *An introduction to clinical psychology.* (2nd ed.) New York: Ronald, 1954. Pp. 91-127.

BERG, I. A. Response bias and personality: the Deviation Hypothesis. *J. counsel. Psychol.*, 1958, 5, 130-135.

BERG, I. A. The unimportance of test item content. In B. M. Bass and I. A. Berg (Eds.), *Objective approaches to personality assessment*. Princeton, N. J.: Van Nostrand, 1959. Pp. 83-99.

BETTELHEIM, B. *Truants from life*. Glencoe, Ill.: Free Press, 1955.

BETZ, B. J., & WHITEHORN, J. C. The relationship of the therapist to the outcome of therapy in schizophrenia. In N. S. Kline (Ed.), *Psychiatric Research Reports* No. 5. Washington: Amer. Psychiat. Assn., 1956. Pp. 89-105.

BIBER, Barbara, MURPHY, Lois B., WOODCOCK, Louise P. & BLACK, Irma S. *Life and ways of the seven-to-eight year old*. New York: Basic Books, 1952.

BIJOU, S. W. Therapeutic techniques with children. In L. A. Pennington & I. A. Berg (Eds.), *An introduction to clinical psychology*. (2nd ed.) New York: Ronald, 1954. Pp. 608-631.

BINDMAN, A. J. Mental health consultation: theory and practice. *J. consult. Psychol.*, 1959, 23, 473-482.

BINGHAM, W. V. D., MOORE, B. V., & GUSTAD, J. W. *How to interview*. (4th ed.) New York: Harper, 1959.

BIRREN, J. E. (Ed.) *Handbook of aging and the individual*. Chicago: Univer. of Chicago Press, 1959.

BISNO, H. Professional status and professional policies: a heterodox analysis. *Counseling News and Views*, 1960, 12, 4-11.

BLAU, T. H. *Private practice in clinical psychology*. New York: Appleton-Century-Crofts, 1959.

BLOCK, J. A comparison between ipsative and normative ratings of personality. *J. abnorm. soc. Psychol.*, 1957, 54, 50-54.

BLOCK, J. *The Q-sort method in personality assessment and psychiatric research*. Springfield, Ill.: Thomas, 1961.

BLOOM, B. S. (Ed.) *Taxonomy of educational objectives, handbook I: cognitive domain*. New York: Longmans, 1956.

BORDIN, E. S. *Psychological counseling*. New York: Appleton-Century-Crofts, 1955.

BORDIN, E. S. Inside the therapeutic hour. In E. A. Rubinstein & M. B. Parloff (Eds.), *Research in psychotherapy*. Washington: Amer. Psychol. Ass., 1959. Pp. 235-246.

BORGATTA, E. F. Sidesteps toward a nonspecial theory. *Psychol. Rev.*, 1954, 61, 343-352.

BORGATTA, E. F. The new principle of psychotherapy. *J. clin. Psychol.*, 1959, 15, 330-334.

BORING, E. G. When is human behavior predetermined? *Sci. Monthly*, 1957, 84, 189-196.

BOULDING, K. E. *The image*. Ann Arbor: Univer. of Michigan Press, 1956.

BOWEN, M. A family concept of schizophrenia. In D. D. Jackson (Ed.), *The etiology of schizophrenia*. New York: Basic Books, 1960. Pp. 346-372.

BRAMMER, L. M., & SHOSTROM, E. L. *Therapeutic psychology*. Englewood Cliffs, N. J.: Prentice-Hall, 1960.

BRAUN, J. R. (Ed.) *Clinical psychology in transition*. Cleveland: Howard Allen, 1961.

BRIGGS, P. G. Eight item clusters for use with the M-B History Record. *J. clin. Psychol.*, 1959, 15, 22-28.

BRONOWSKI, J. *Science and human values*. New York: Messner, 1958.

BRONOWSKI, J. The creative process. *Scient. Amer.*, 1958, 199, 59-65.

BROWER, D., & ABT, L. E. (Eds.) *Progress in clinical psychology.* Vol. III. New York: Grune & Stratton, 1958.

BRUNER, J. S. & TAGIURI, R. The perception of people. In G. Lindzey (Ed.), *Handbook of social psychology.* Vol. II. *Special fields and applications.* Reading, Mass.: Addison-Wesley, 1954. Pp. 634-654.

BUGENTAL, J. F. T. Explicit analysis: a design for the study and improvement of psychological interviewing. *Educ. psychol. Measmt,* 1954, 14, 552-565.

BURDOCK, E. I., Sutton, S., & ZUBIN, J. Personality and psychopathology. *J. abnorm. soc. Psychol.,* 1958, 56, 18-30.

BURKE, H. R. Raven's Progressive Matrices: a review and critical evaluation. *J. genet. Psychol.,* 1958, 93, 199-228.

BUROS, O. K. (Ed.) *The 1940 mental measurements yearbook.* Highland Park, N. J.: Ment. Measmts Yearb., 1941.

BUROS, O. K. (Ed.) *The third mental measurements yearbook.* New Brunswick, N. J.: Rutgers Univer. Press, 1949.

BUROS, O. K. (Ed.) *The fourth mental measurements yearbook.* Highland Park, N. J.: Gryphon, 1953.

BUROS, O. K. (Ed.) *The fifth mental measurements yearbook.* Highland Park, N. J.: Gryphon, 1959.

BURTON, A. (Ed.) *Case studies in counseling and psychotherapy.* Englewood Cliffs, N. J.: Prentice-Hall, 1959.

BURTON, A., & HARRIS, R. E. (Eds.) *Clinical studies of personality.* New York: Harper, 1955.

BUTLER, J. M. Client-centered counseling and psychotherapy. In D. Brower & L. E. Abt (Eds.), *Progress in clinical psychology.* Vol. III. New York: Grune & Stratton, 1958. Pp. 93-106.

BYRD, E. A study of validity and constancy of choice in a sociometric test. *Sociometry,* 1951, 14, 175-181.

CALLIS, R., ENGRAM, W. C., & McGOWAN, J. F., Coding the Kuder Preference Record—Vocational. *J. appl. Psychol.,* 1954, 38, 359-363.

CAMPBELL, J. D., & CARON, H. S. Data processing by optical coincidence. *Science,* 1961, 133, 1333-1338.

CARLSON, E. T., & DAIN, N. The psychotherapy that was moral treatment. *Amer. J. Psychiat.,* 1960, 117, 519-524.

CARLSON, J. S., & FULLMER, D. W. *College norms.* Eugene: Counseling Center, Univer. of Oregon, 1959.

CARTER, J. W. The training needs of psychologists in community mental health programs at state and local levels. In C. R. Strother (Ed.), *Psychology and mental health.* Washington: Amer. Psychol. Ass., 1956.

CARTWRIGHT, D. From cells to societies. (A review of R. R. Grinker (Ed.), *Toward a unified theory of human behavior.* New York: Basic Books, 1956.) *Contemp. Psychol.,* 1957, 2, 121-123.

CARTWRIGHT, D. S. Annotated bibliography of research and theory construction in client-centered therapy. *J. counsel. Psychol.,* 1957, 4, 82-100.

CASEY, R. S., PERRY, J. W., BERRY, MADELINE, & KENT, A. (Eds.) *Punched cards, their applications to science and industry.* (2nd ed.) New York: Reinhold, 1958.

CATTELL, R. B. *Description and measurement of personality.* Yonkers-on-Hudson, N. Y.: World, 1946.

CATTELL, R. B. *Personality and motivation structure and measurement.* Yonkers-on-Hudson, N. Y.: World, 1957.

CAUDILL, W. *The psychiatric hospital as a small society.* Cambridge, Mass.: Harvard Univer. Press, 1958.

CHARMS, R. D., LEVY, J., & WERTHEIMER, M. A note on attempted evaluation of psychotherapy. *J. clin. Psychol.*, 1954, 10, 233-235.

CHASSAN, J. B. Statistical inference and the single case in clinical design. *Psychiat.*, 1960, 23, 173-184.

CHODORKOFF, B. Self-perception, perceptual defense, and adjustment. *J. abnorm. soc. Psychol.*, 1954, 49, 508-512.

CHOWDRY, KALMA, & NEWCOMB, T. M. The relative ability of leaders and non-leaders to estimate opinions of their own group. *J. abnorm. soc. Psychol.*, 1952, 47, 51-57.

CLARK, K. E. *America's psychologists, a survey of a growing profession.* Washington: Amer. Psychol. Ass., 1957.

CLARK, K. E. The mountain's mouse. (A review of D. W. MacKinnon et al., *An assessment study of Air Force officers,* Parts I-V, and *The use of trait ratings in an assessment of 100 Air Force captains.* Lackland Air Force Base, Texas: Personnel Laboratory, Wright Air Development Center, Air Research and Development Command, U. S. Air Force, 1958). *Contemp. Psychol.*, 1960, 5, 72-73.

COBB, S. Technique of interviewing a patient with psychosomatic disorder. In A. Weider (Ed.), *Contributions toward medical psychology.* Vol. I. New York: Ronald, 1953. Pp. 225-233.

COFFEY, H. S. Group psychotherapy. In L. A. Pennington & I. A. Berg (Eds.), *An introduction to clinical psychology.* (2nd ed.) New York: Ronald, 1954. Pp. 586-607.

COLBY, K. M. *A primer for psychotherapists.* New York: Ronald, 1951.

COLBY, K. M. *Energy and structure in psychoanalysis.* New York: Ronald, 1955.

COLBY, K. M. *A skeptical psychoanalyst.* New York: Ronald, 1958.

COLEMAN, R., GREENBLATT, M., & SOLOMON, H. C. Physiological evidence of rapport during psychotherapeutic interviews. *Dis. Nerv. Sys.*, 1956, 17, 71-77.

COONS, W. H. Interaction and insight in group psychotherapy. *Canad. J. Psychol.*, 1957, 11, 1-8.

CORSINI, R. J. *Methods of group psychotherapy.* New York: McGraw, 1957.

CORSINI, R. J., DANIELS, R., & MCFARLAND, R. Group psychotherapy. In E. A. Speigel (Ed.), *Progress in neurology and psychiatry.* Vol. XV. New York: Grune & Stratton, 1960. Pp. 526-534.

COUCH, A., & KENISTON, K. Yeasayers and naysayers: agreeing response set as a personality variable. *J. abnorm. soc. Psychol.*, 1960, 60, 151-174.

COUTU, W. *Emergent human nature.* New York: Knopf, 1949.

CRITES, J. O. A coding system for total profile analysis of the Strong Vocational Interest Blank. *J. appl. Psychol.*, 1959, 43, 176-179.

CRONBACH, L. J. Report on a psychometric mission to Clinicia. *Psychometrika*, 1954, 19, 263-270.

CRONBACH, L. J. Assessment of individual differences. In P. R. Farnsworth (Ed.), *Annual review of psychology.* Vol. VII. Stanford, Calif.: Annual Reviews, 1956. Pp. 173-196.

CRONBACH, L. J. The two disciplines of scientific psychology. *Amer. Psychologist*, 1957, 12, 671-684.

CRONBACH, L. J. *Essentials of psychological testing.* (2nd ed.) New York: Harper, 1960.

CRONBACH, L. J., & GLESER, GOLDINE, C. Assessing similarity between profiles. *Psychol. Bull.*, 1953, 50, 456-473.

CRONBACH, L. J., & GLESER, GOLDINE, C. *Psychological tests and personnel decisions.* Urbana: Univer. of Illinois Press, 1957.

CRONBACH, L. J., & MEEHL, P. E. Construct validity in psychological tests. *Psychol. Bull.*, 1955, 52, 281-302.

CROW, W. J. The effect of training upon accuracy and variability in interpersonal perception. *J. abnorm. soc. Psychol.*, 1957, 55, 355-359.

CROW, W. J., & HAMMOND, K. R. The generality of accuracy and response sets in interpersonal perception. *J. abnorm. soc. Psychol.*, 1957, 54, 384-390.

CRUTCHFIELD, R. S. Conformity and character. *Amer. Psychologist*, 1955, 10, 191-198.

CRUTCHFIELD, R. S. The creative process. In *The creative person: proceedings of a conference presented at the Tahoe Alumni Center, October, 13-17, 1961.* Berkeley, Calif.: Institute of Personality Assessment and Research, 1961. Pp. VI. 1-VI. 16.

CUADRA, C. A., & ALBAUGH, W. P. Sources of ambiguity in psychological reports. *J. clin. Psychol.*, 1956, 12, 109-115.

DAHLSTROM, W., & WELSH, G. S. *An MMPI handbook.* Minneapolis: Univer. of Minnesota Press, 1960.

DAILEY, C. A. The practical utility of the clinical report. *J. consult. Psychol.*, 1953, 17, 297-302.

DALLENBACH, K. M. Phrenology vs. psychoanalysis. *Amer. J. Psychol.*, 1955, 68, 511-525.

DANIEL, R. S., & LOUTTIT, C. M. *Professional problems in psychology.* New York: Prentice-Hall, 1953.

DATEL, W. E., & GENGERELLI, J. A. Reliability of Rorschach interpretations. *J. proj. Tech.*, 1956, 19, 372-381.

DAVIDSON, H. A. The commitment procedures and their legal implications. In S. Arieti (Ed.), *American handbook of psychiatry.* Vol. II. New York: Basic Books, 1959. Pp. 1902-1922.

DEMMING, J. A., & PRESSEY, S. L. Tests "indigenous" to the adult and older years. *J. counsel. Psychol.*, 1957, 4, 144-148.

DEUTSCH, Cynthia P. After legislation—what price psychology? *Amer. Psychologist*, 1958, 13, 645-651.

DEUTSCH, F., & MURPHY, W. F. *The clinical interview.* Vol. I. *Diagnosis.* New York: International Universities, 1955.

DEUTSCH, M. Field theory in social psychology. In G. Lindzey (Ed.), *Handbook of social psychology.* Vol. I. *Theory and method.* Reading, Mass.: Addison-Wesley, 1954. Pp. 181-222.

DITTMANN, A. T. The interpersonal process in psychotherapy: development of a research method. *J. abnorm. soc. Psychol.*, 1952, 47, 236-244.

DITTMANN, A. T. Systematic psychoanalysis as research. (Review of D. M. Bullard (Ed.), *Psychoanalysis and psychotherapy: selected papers of Frieda Fromm-Reichmann.* Chicago: Univer. of Chicago Press, 1959.) *Contemp. Psychol.*, 1960, 5, 366-367.

DITTMANN, A. T., & WYNNE, L. C. Linguistic techniques and the analysis of emotionality in interviews. *J. abnorm. soc. Psychol.*, 1961, 63, 201-204.

DOLLARD, J., AULD, F., JR., & WHITE, Alice M. *Steps in psychotherapy.* New York: Macmillan, 1953.

DOLLARD, J., & MILLER, N. E. Personality and psychotherapy. New York: McGraw, 1950.

DREIKURS, R. Early experiments with group psychotherapy. *Am. J. Psychother.*, 1959, 13, 882-891.

DREIKURS, R., CORSINI, R., LOWE, R., & SONSTEGARD, M. (Eds.), *Adlerian family counseling, a manual for counseling centers.* Eugene: Univer. of Oregon Press, 1959.

DRYER, B. V. *The image makers.* New York: Harper, 1958.

DUNCKER, K. On problem-solving. *Psychol. Monogr.,* 1945, 58, No. 5.

DUNN, L. M. *Peabody Picture Vocabulary Test manual.* Minneapolis: Amer. Guidance Serv., 1959.

DUVALL, Evelyn M. *Family development.* Chicago: Lippincott, 1957.

EDWARDS, A. L. *The social desirability variable in personality research.* New York: Dryden, 1957.

EDWARDS, A. L. Social desirability and personality test construction. In B. M. Bass & I. A. Berg (Eds.), *Objective approaches to personality assessment.* Princeton, N. J.: Van Nostrand, 1959. Pp. 100-118.

EISENSTEIN, V. W. (Ed.) *Neurotic interaction in marriage.* New York: Basic Books, 1956.

EKSTEIN, R. A historical survey on the teaching of psychoanalytic technique. *J. Amer. Psychoanal. Ass.,* 1960, 8, 500-516.

ELLIS, A. Rational psychotherapy and individual psychology. *J. indiv. Psychol.,* 1957, 13, 38-44.

ELLIS, A. Rational psychotherapy. *J. gen. Psychol.,* 1958, 59, 35-49.

ENDS, E. J., & PAGE, C. W. Group psychotherapy and concomitant psychological change. *Psychol. Monogr.,* 1959, 73, No. 10 (Whole No. 480).

ENGLISH, H. B., & ENGLISH, Ava C. *A comprehensive dictionary of psychological and psychoanalytical terms.* New York: Longmans, 1958.

ERIKSON, E. H. *Childhood and society.* New York: Norton, 1950.

ERIKSON, E. H. Identity and the life cycle. *Psychol. Issues,* 1959, 1, No. 1 (Whole No. 1).

EYSENCK, H. J. The effects of psychotherapy: an evaluation. *J. consult. Psychol.,* 1952, 16, 319-324.

EYSENCK, H. J. A reply to Luborsky's note. *Brit. J. Psychol.,* 1954, 65, 132-133.

EYSENCK, H. J. The effects of psychotherapy: a reply. *J. abnorm. soc. Psychol.,* 1955, 50, 147-148.

EYSENCK, H. J. A rational system of diagnosis and therapy in mental illness. In L. E. Abt & B. F. Riess (Eds.), *Progress in clinical psychology.* Vol. IV, New York: Grune & Stratton, 1960. Pp. 46-64.

EYSENCK, H. J. (Ed.) *Handbook of abnormal psychology.* New York: Basic Books, 1961.

FAIRWEATHER, G. W., SIMON, R., GEBHARD, M. E., WEINGARTEN, E., HOLLAND, J. L., SANDERS, R., STONE, G. B., & REAHL, J. E. Relative effectiveness of psychotherapeutic programs: a multicriteria comparison of four programs for three different patient groups. *Psychol. Monogr.,* 1960, 74, No. 5 (Whole No. 492).

FARBEROW, N. L. Validity and methodology in projective tests. *J. proj. Tech.,* 1959, 23, 282-286.

FARINA, A. Patterns of role dominance and conflict in parents of schizophrenic patients. *J. abnorm. soc. Psychol.,* 1960, 61, 31-38.

FEIGL, H. Philosophical embarrassments of psychology. *Amer. Psychologist,* 1959, 14, 115-128.

FELIX, R. H. New directions in patterns of patient care. Paper presented at the Fourth Annual Meeting of the Western Mental Health Council of the Western Interstate Commission for Higher Education, Salt Lake City, Utah, June 22, 1961. *Ment. Hlth. Train. and Res. Highlights,* 1961 (November), 3-5.

FENICHEL, O. *The collected papers of Otto Fenichel.* (First series.) New York: Norton, 1953.

FENICHEL, O. *The psychoanalytic theory of neurosis.* New York: Norton, 1945.

FERGUSON, Eva D. The effect of sibling competition and alliance on level of aspiration, expectation, and performance. *J. abnorm. soc. Psychol.*, 1958, 56, 213-222.

FIEDLER, F. E. A comparison of therapeutic relationships in psychoanalytic, nondirective, and Adlerian therapy. *J. consult. Psychol.*, 1950, 14, 436-445. (*a*)

FIEDLER, F. E. The concept of an ideal therapeutic relationship. *J. consult. Psychol.*, 1950, 14, 239-245. (*b*).

FIEDLER, F. E. Factor analyses of psychoanalytic, nondirective, and Adlerian therapeutic relationships. *J. consult. Psychol.*, 1951, 15, 32-38.

FIEDLER, F. E., HUTCHINS, E. B., & DODGE, Joan S. Quasi-therapeutic relations in small college and military groups. *Psychol. Monogr.* 1959, 73 (Whole No. 473).

FINNEY, B. C. A scale to measure interpersonal relationships in group psychotherapy. *Group Psychother.*, 1954, 7, 52-66.

FISHER, G. M. Differences in WAIS Verbal and Performance IQ's in various diagnostic groups of mental retardates. *Amer. J. ment. Defic.*, 1960, 65, 256-260.

FITZHUGH, Kathleen B., FITZHUGH, L. C., & REITAN, R. M. Psychological deficits in relation to acuteness of brain dysfunction. *J. consult. Psychol.*, 1961, 25, 61-66.

FJELD, S. P., ATKINSON, HARRIETTE S., LUCERO, R. J., MEYER, B. T., & RECHTSCHAFFEN, A. A behavorial census of a state hospital population. *Psychol. Monogr.*, 1957, 71, No. 12 (Whole No. 441).

FLANAGAN, J. C. The critical incidents technique. *Psychol. Bull.*, 1954, 51, 327-358.

FLANAGAN, J. C., & SCHMID, F. W. The critical incident approach to the study of psychopathology. *J. clin. Psychol.*, 1959, 15, 136-139.

FOA, U. G. Convergences in the analysis of the structure of interpersonal behavior. *Psychol. Rev.*, 1961, 68, 341-353.

FORER, B. R. The fallacy of personal validations: a classroom demonstration of gullibility. *J. abnorm. soc. Psychol.*, 1949, 44, 118-123.

FORER, B. R. The Forer Structured Sentence Completion Test. Los Angeles: Western Psychological Services, 1957.

FOSTER, A. Writing psychological reports. *J. clin. Psychol.*, 1951, 7, 195.

FRANK, J. D. Problems of controls in psychotherapy as exemplified by the psychotherapy research project of the Phipps Psychiatric Clinic. In E. A. Rubinstein & M. B. Parloff (Eds.), *Research in psychotherapy.* Washington: Amer. Psychol. Assn., 1959. Pp. 10-26.

FRANK, J. D., GLIEDMAN, L. H., IMBER, S. D., NASH, E. H., JR., & STONE, A. R. Why patients leave psychotherapy. *Arch. neurol. Psychiat.*, 1957, 77, 283-299.

FRANK, J. D., GLIEDMAN, L. H., IMBER, S. D., STONE, A. R., & NASH, E. H. Patients' expectancies and relearning as factors determining improvement in psychotherapy. *Amer. J. Psychiat.*, 1959, 115, 961-968.

FRANK, J. D., & POWDERMAKER, FLORENCE B. Group psychotherapy. In S. Arieti (Ed.), *American handbook of psychiatry.* Vol. II. New York: Basic Books, 1959. Pp. 1362-1374.

FRANKL, V. E. *The doctor and the soul.* New York: Knopf, 1955.

FREUD, Anna. *Psychoanalytic treatment of children.* London: Imago, 1946.

FREUD, S. *The interpretation of dreams.* New York: Macmillan, 1913.

FREUD, S. *On the psychopathology of everyday life.* New York: Macmillan, 1914.

FREUD, S. *Collected papers.* Vol. III. *Case histories.* London: Hogarth, 1949. (Originally published in 1925.)

FREUD, S. *New introductory lectures on psychoanalysis.* New York: Norton, 1933.

FREUD, S. *The basic writings of Sigmund Freud.* A. A. Brill (Ed.), New York: Modern Library, 1938.

FREUD, S. *Outline of psychoanalysis.* New York: Norton, 1949.

FREUD, S. Postscript to a discussion on lay analysis. In *Collected papers.* Vol. V. London: Hogarth, 1950. Pp. 205-222. (Originally published in 1927.)

FROMM, E. *The sane society.* New York: Rinehart, 1955.

GAGE, N. L. Judging interests from expressive behavior. *Psychol. Monogr.,* 1952, 66 (Whole No. 350).

GARDNER, E. F., & THOMPSON, G. G. Syracuse Scales of Social Relations. Tarrytown-on-Hudson, N. Y.: World, 1959.

GARFIELD, S. L. *Introductory clinical psychology.* New York: Macmillan, 1957.

GARFIELD, S. L., HEINE, R. W., & LEVENTHAL, M. An evaluation of psychological reports in a clinical setting. *J. consult. Psychol.,* 1954, 18, 281-286.

GARRETT, H. E. *Statistics in psychology and education.* (5th ed.) New York: Longmans, 1958.

GHISELLI, E. E. The measurement of occupational aptitude. *Univer. Calif. publ. Psychol.,* 1955, 8, 100-216.

GIEDT, F. H. Comparison of visual, content and auditory cues in interviewing. *J. consult. Psychol.,* 1955, 19, 407-416.

GILL, M. The present state of psychoanalytic theory. *J. abnorm. soc. Psychol.,* 1959, 58, 1-8.

GLANZER, M., & GLAZER, R. Techniques for the study of group structure and behavior: I. Analysis of structure. *Psychol. Bull.,* 1959, 56, 317-332.

GOLDBERG, L. R. The effectiveness of clinicians' judgments: the diagnosis of organic brain damage from the Bender-Gestalt test. *J. consult. Psychol.,* 1959, 23, 25-33.

GOLDMAN, L. *Using tests in counseling.* New York: Appleton-Century-Crofts, 1961.

GOODMAN, L. A. The use and validity of a prediction instrument. I. A reformulation of the use of a prediction instrument. II. The validation of prediction. *Amer. J. Sociol.,* 1953, 58, 503-513.

GOUGH, H. G. The Home Index. (a 24-item objective home status index: suitable for use with children ages 10-18), 1949.

GOUGH, H. G. Predicting social participation. *J. soc. Psychol.,* 1952, 35, 227-233.

GOUGH, H. G. Potential uses of personality scales in schools and colleges. *Proc. fifth annual western regional conference on testing problems,* April 13, 1956. Los Angeles: Educational Testing Service, 1956. Pp. 3-20.

GOUGH, H. G. *California Psychological Inventory manual.* Palo Alto, Calif.: Consulting Psychologists Press, 1957.

GOUGH, H. G. The adjective checklist as a personality assessment research technique. *Psychol. Rep.,* 1960, 6, 107-122. (Monogr. Suppl. No. 2.) (*a*)

GOUGH, H. G. Cross-cultural studies of the socialization continuum. *Amer. Psychologist,* 1960, 15, 410. (Abstract) (*b*)

GOUGH, H. G. Theory and measurement of socialization. *J. consult. Psychol.,* 1960, 24, 23-30. (*c*)

GRAYSON, H. M., & OLINGER, L. B. Simulation of normalcy by psychotic patients on the MMPI. *J. consult. Psychol.*, 1957, 21, 73-77.

GRAYSON, H. M., & TOLMAN, R. S. A semantic study of concepts of clinical psychologists and psychiatrists. *J. abnorm. soc. Psychol.*, 1950, 45, 216-231.

GREENBLATT, M., LEVINSON, D. J., & WILLIAMS, R. H. (Eds.) *The patient and the mental hospital.* Glencoe, Ill.: Free Press, 1957.

GREENHILL, M. H., FORD, L. S., OLSON, W. C., RYAN, W. C., WHITMAN, S., & SKEELS, H. M. *Evaluation in mental health.* Washington: U. S. Department of Health, Education, and Welfare, 1955.

GREENSPOON, J. The reinforcing effect of two spoken sounds on the frequency of two responses. *Amer. J. Psychol.*, 1955, 68, 409-416.

GRINKER, R. R. (Ed.) *Toward a unified theory of human behavior.* New York: Basic Books, 1956.

GRINSTEIN, A. *The index of psychoanalytic writings.* New York: International Universities Press, 1956-1960. 5 vols.

GRONLUND, N. E. *Sociometry in the classroom.* New York: Harper, 1959.

GUMP, P., SCHOGGEN, P., & REDL, F. The camp milieu and its immediate effects. *J. soc. Issues*, 1957, 13, 40-46.

GUMP, P., & SUTTON-SMITH, B. The "It" role in children's games. *The Group*, 1955, 17, No. 3, 3-8.

GUNDLACH, R. H. Group psychotherapy: new clinical and experimental approaches. In L. E. Abt & B. F. Riess (Eds.), *Progress in clinical psychology,* Vol. IV. New York: Grune & Stratton, 1960. Pp. 149-168.

GURIN, G., VEROFF, J., & FELD, Sheila. *Americans view their mental health.* New York: Basic Books, 1960.

HABBE, S. Some characteristics of clients who seek guidance. *Amer. J. Orthopsychiat.*, 1939, 9, 802-806.

HADDEN, S. B. Historic background of group psychotherapy. *Int. J. group Psychother.*, 1955, 5, 162-168.

HADLEY, J. M. *Clinical and counseling psychology.* New York: Knopf, 1958.

HALBOWER, C. C. A comparison of actuarial versus clinical prediction to classes discriminated by MMPI. Unpublished doctoral dissertation, Univer. of Minnesota, 1955.

HALES, W. M. Profile patterning and coding of the Rorschach Test: a preliminary report of research methods and materials. *J. consult. Psychol.*, 1952, 16, 37-42.

HALL, C. S., & LINDZEY, G. *Theories of personality.* New York: Wiley, 1957.

HAMMOND, K. R., & ALLEN, J. M. *Writing clinical reports.* New York: Prentice-Hall, 1953.

HANNA, J. V. Estimating intelligence by interview. *Educ. Psychol. Measmt.*, 1950, 10, 420-430.

HANVIK, L. J. Some psychological dimensions of low back pain. Unpublished doctoral dissertation, Univer. of Minnesota, 1949.

HARRIS, D. B. *Children's drawings as measures of the psychological maturity of children: a revision and extension of the Goodenough Draw-A-Man Test.* New York: Harcourt, Brace, & World, in press.

HASKELL, M. The drug addict, role playing and group psychotherapy: the need for a new approach. *Group Psychother.*, 1958, 11, 197-202.

HATHAWAY, S. R. Some considerations relative to nondirective counseling as therapy. *J. clin. Psychol.*, 1948, 4, 226-231.

HATHAWAY, S. R. A case with low back pain. In A. Burton & R. E. Harris (Eds.), *Clinical studies of personality.* New York: Harper, 1955. Pp. 70-85.

HATHAWAY, S. R. A study of human behavior: the clinical psychologist. *Amer. Psychologist*, 1958, 13, 257-265.

HATHAWAY, S. R. Increasing clinical efficiency. In B. M. Bass & I. A. Berg (Eds.), *Objective approaches to personality assessment.* New York: Van Nostrand, 1959. Pp. 192-203.

HATHAWAY, S. R., & MEEHL, P. E. *An atlas for the clinical use of the MMPI.* Minneapolis: Univer. of Minnesota Press, 1951.

HATHAWAY, S. R., & MONACHESI, E. D. (Eds.) *Analyzing and predicting juvenile delinquency with the MMPI.* Minneapolis: Univer. of Minnesota Press, 1953.

HEARN, G. *Theory building in social work.* Toronto: Univer. of Toronto Press, 1958.

HEBB, D. O. The American revolution. *Amer. Psychologist,* 1960, 12, 735-745.

HENRY, W. E. *The analysis of fantasy.* New York: Wiley, 1956.

HENRY, W. E., & FARLEY, JANE. The validity of the Thematic Apperception Test in the study of adolescent personality. *Psychol. Monogr.,* 1959, 73, No. 17 (Whole No. 487).

HERBST, P. G. The measurement of family relationships. *Hum. Relat.,* 1952, 5, 3-36.

HERBST, P. G. Family living—patterns of interaction. In O. A. Oeser & S. B. Hammond (Eds.), *Social structure and personality in a city.* London: Kegan Paul, 1954.

HERBST, P. G. Situation dynamics and the theory of behavior systems. *Behav. Sci.,* 1957, 2, 13-29.

HILER, E. W. An analysis of patient-therapist compatibility. *J. consult. Psychol.,* 1958, 22, 341-347.

HILGARD, E. R. Experimental approaches to psychoanalysis. In E. Pumpian-Mindlin (Ed.), *Psychoanalysis as science.* Stanford: Stanford Univer. Press, 1952. Pp. 3-45.

HIMMELWEIT, H. T., & SUMMERFIELD, A. Student selection—an experimental investigation. II. *Brit. J. Sociol.,* 1951, 2, 59-75.

HINCKLEY, R. G., & HERMANN, Lydia. *Group treatment in psychotherapy.* Minneapolis: Univer. of Minnesota Press, 1951.

HINSIE, L. E., & CAMPBELL, R. J. *Psychiatric dictionary.* (3rd ed.) New York: Oxford Univer. Press, 1960.

HOBBS, N. Science and ethical behavior. *Amer. Psychologist,* 1959, 14, 217-225.

HOFFMAN, B. The tyranny of multiple-choice tests. *Harpers,* 1961, 222, 37-44.

HOFFMAN, M. L. An interview method for obtaining descriptions of parent-child interaction. *Merrill-Palmer Quart.,* 1957, 4, 76-83.

HOFFMAN, P. J. The paramorphic representation of clinical judgment. *Psychol. Bull.,* 1960, 57, 116-131.

HOLLINGSHEAD, A. B., & REDLICH, F. C. *Social class and mental illness: a community study.* New York: Wiley, 1958.

HOLMEN, M. G., KATTER, R. V., JONES, Ann M., & RICHARDSON, I. F. An assessment program for OCS applicants. *HumRRO Tech. Rep.,* 26, 1956.

HOLT, R. R. Clinical and statistical prediction: a reformulation and some new data. *J. abnorm. soc. Psychol.,* 1958, 56, 1-12.

HOLT, R. R., & LUBORSKY, L. *Personality patterns of psychiatrists* (Menninger Clinic Monograph Series, No. 13). Vol. I: *A study of methods for selecting residents.* New York: Basic Books, 1958. Vol. II: *Supplementary and supporting data.* Topeka, Kan.: Menninger Foundation, 1958.

HOLTZMAN, W. H. Can the computer supplant the clinician? *J. clin. Psychol.,* 1960, 16, 119-122.

HOLTZMAN, W. H., THORPE, J. S., SWARTZ, J. D., & HERRON, E. W. *Inkblot perception and personality.* Austin: Univer. of Texas Press, 1961.

HOOK, S. (Ed.) *Psychoanalysis, scientific method, and philosophy.* New York: New York Univer. Press, 1959.

HORNEY, Karen. *Neurosis and human growth.* New York: Norton, 1950.

HORROCKS, J. E., & NAGY, G. The relationship between the ability to make a diagnosis and to select appropriate remedial procedures. *J. gen. Psychol.,* 1948, 38, 139-145.

HOVEY, H. B. The questionable validity of some assumed antecedents of mental illness. *J. clin. Psychol.,* 1959, 15, 270-272.

HOVEY, H. B. *Self-interview inventory.* Chicago: Psychometric Affiliates, 1958.

HOVLAND, C. I. (Ed.) *The order of presentation in persuasion.* New Haven: Yale Univer. Press, 1957.

HOVLAND, C. I. Computer simulation of thinking. *Amer. Psychologist,* 1960, 15, 687-693.

HUBBARD, Ruth M. What constitutes a psychological examination? In R. I. Watson (Ed.), *Readings in the clinical method in psychology.* New York: Harper, 1949. Pp. 334-348.

HUBER, J. T. *Report writing in psychology and psychiatry.* New York: Harper, 1961.

HUTT, M., & BRISKIN, G. *The clinical use of the Revised Bender Gestalt Test.* New York: Grune & Stratton, 1960.

INGLIS, J. Psychological investigations of cognitive deficit in elderly psychiatric patients. *Psychol. Bull.,* 1958, 55, 197-214.

JACKSON, D. D. (Ed.) *The etiology of schizophrenia.* New York: Basic Books, 1960.

JACKSON, D. N., & BLOOMBERG, R. Anxiety, unitas or multiplex? *J. consult. Psychol.,* 1958, 22, 225-227.

JACOBSON, E. *Progressive relaxation.* Chicago: Univer. of Chicago Press, 1929.

JAHODA, Marie. *Current concepts of positive mental health.* New York: Basic Books, 1958.

JENKINS, J. J., & RUSSELL, W. A. Systematic changes in word association norms: 1910-1952. *J. abnorm. soc. Psychol.,* 1960, 60, 293-304.

Joint Commission on Mental Illness and Health. *Action for mental health.* New York: Basic Books, 1961.

JONES, E. *The life and work of Sigmund Freud.* Vol. 1. *1856-1900, The formative years and the great discoveries.* New York: Basic Books, 1953.

JONES, M. *The therapeutic community.* New York: Basic Books, 1953.

JONES, M. Intra and extramural community psychiatry. *Amer. J. Psychiat.,* 1961, 117, 784-787.

JONES, Mary C. A study of the emotions of preschool children. *Sch. Soc.,* 1925, 21, 755-758.

JOURARD, S. M. Self-disclosure and other-cathexis. *J. abnorm. soc. Psychol.,* 1959, 59, 428-431.

KADIS, Asya L., & MARKOWITZ, M. Group psychotherapy. In D. Brower & L. E. Abt (Eds.), *Progress in clinical psychology.* Vol. III. New York: Grune & Stratton, 1958. Pp. 154-183.

KAHN, R. L., & CANNELL, C. F. *The dynamics of interviewing: theory, technique and cases.* New York: Wiley, 1957.

KELLER, J. E., ROSENBLUM, S., & EBLING, G. The Keysort card system as a research and administrative aid in a residential school for retarded children. *Amer. J. ment. Defic.,* 1956, 60, 706-713.

KELLY, E. L. Clinical psychology—1960; a report of survey findings. *News-*

letter, Division of Clinical Psychology of the APA, 1961, 14, (Winter issue), 1-11.

KELLY, E. L., & FISKE, D. W. *The prediction of performance in clinical psychology.* Ann Arbor: Univer. of Michigan Press, 1951.

KELLY, E. L., & GOLDBERG, L. R. Correlates of later performance and specialization in psychology, a follow-up study of the trainees assessed in the VA Selection Research Project. *Psychol. Monogr.,* 1959, Vol. 73, No. 12 (Whole No. 482).

KELLY, G. A. *The psychology of personal constructs.* Vol. I. *A theory of personality.* Vol. II. *Clinical diagnosis and therapy.* New York: Norton, 1955.

KELMAN, H. C., & PARLOFF, M. B. Interrelations among three criteria of improvement in group therapy: comfort, effectiveness, and self-awareness. *J. abnorm. soc. Psychol.,* 1957, 54, 281-288.

KENT, A. V. A machine that does research. *Harpers,* 1959, 218, 67-71.

KERR, W. A., NEWMAN, H. L., & SADEWIC, A. P. Lifetime worry patterns of American psychologists. *J. consult. Psychol.,* 1949, 13, 377-380.

KING, G. F., ARMITAGE, S. G., & TILTON, J. R. A therapeutic approach to schizophrenics of extreme pathology: an operant-interpersonal method. *J. abnorm. soc. Psychol.,* 1960, 61, 276-286.

KIRK, Barbara A. Classifying the literature in counseling psychology. *J. counsel. Psychol.,* 1958, 5, 89-97.

KIRK, Barbara A., & HEADLEY, R. R. Factors related to voluntary discontinuance of contact during counseling. *J. consult. Psychol.,* 1950, 14, 386-392.

KIR-STIMON, W. A follow-up study of counseling with anxiety neurotics. *Personnel guid. J.,* 1956, 34, 474-480.

KLEIN, Melanie. *The psychoanalysis of children.* London: Hogarth, 1949.

KLINE, M. V. Hypnosis and clinical psychology. In L. E. Abt & B. F. Riess (Eds.), *Progress in clinical psychology.* Vol. IV. New York: Grune & Stratton, 1960. Pp. 65-84.

KLOPFER, B., AINSWORTH, Mary D., KLOPFER, W. G., & HOLT, R. R. *Developments in the Rorschach technique.* Vol. I. *Technique and theory.* Yonkers-on-Hudson, N. Y.: World, 1954.

KLOPFER, B., KIRKNER, F. J., WISHAM, W., & BAKER, Gertrude. Rorschach Prognostic Rating Scale. *J. proj. Tech.,* 1951, 15, 425-428.

KLOPFER, W. G. *The psychological report.* New York: Grune & Stratton, 1960.

KLUCKHOHN, C., & MURRAY, H. A. Personality formation: the determinants. In C. Kluckhohn, H. A. Murray, & D. M. Schneider (Eds.), *Personality in nature, society and culture.* (2nd ed.) New York: Knopf, 1955. Pp. 53-67.

KNIGHT, R. P. Evaluation of the results of psychoanalytic therapy. *Amer. J. Psychiat.,* 1941, 98, 434.

KOESTER, G. A. A study of the diagnostic process. *Educ. psychol. Measmt,* 1954, 14, 473-486.

KOGAN, L. S. Statistical methods. In D. Brower & L. E. Abt (Eds.), *Progress in clinical psychology.* Vol. I. Sec. 2. New York: Grune & Stratton, 1952. Pp. 519-535.

KOGAN, L. S. Research in clinical psychology. In L. A. Pennington & I. A. Berg (Eds.), *An introduction to clinical psychology.* (2nd ed.) New York: Ronald, 1954. Pp. 661-680.

KOGAN, L. S. Statistics in clinical research. In D. Brower and L. E. Abt (Eds.), *Progress in clinical psychology.* Vol. II. New York: Grune & Stratton, 1956. Pp. 326-339.

KOSTLAN, A. A method for the empirical study of psychodiagnosis. *J. consult. Psychol.,* 1954, 18, 83-88.

KRASNER, L. Studies of the conditioning of verbal behavior. *Psychol. Bull.*, 1958, 55, 148-170. (*a*)

KRASNER, L. A technique for investigating the relationship between the behavior cues of the examiner and the verbal behavior of the patient. *J. consult. Psychol.*, 1958, 22, 364-366. (*b*)

Kremers, J. *Scientific psychology and naïve psychology.* Groningen, Netherlands: Nordhoff, 1960.

KRIEDT, P. H. Vocational interests of psychologists. *J. appl. Psychol.*, 1949, 33, 482-488.

KROUT, M. H. (Ed.) *Psychology, psychiatry and the public interest.* Minneapolis: Univer. of Minnesota Press, 1956.

LACEY, J. I. Psychophysiological approaches to the evaluation of psychotherapeutic process and outcome. In E. A. Rubinstein & M. B. Parloff (Eds.), *Research in psychotherapy.* Washington: Amer. Psychol. Ass., 1959. Pp. 160-208.

LAPIERE, R. *The Freudian ethic: an analysis of the subversion of American character.* New York: Duell, Sloan & Pearce, 1959.

LAZARUS, R. S. Personal communication, 1962.

LEARY, T. *Interpersonal diagnosis of personality.* New York: Ronald, 1957.

LECKY, P. *Self-consistency: a theory of personality.* New York: Island Press, 1945.

LEDLEY, R. S., & LUSTED, L. B. Reasoning foundations of medical diagnosis. *Science,* 1959, 130, 9-21.

LEEPER, R. W. *Lewin's topological and vector psychology: a digest and a critique.* Eugene: Univer. of Oregon Press, 1943.

LEEPER, R. W., & MADISON, P. *Toward understanding human personalities.* New York: Appleton-Century-Crofts, 1959.

LEHMAN, H. C. The age decrement in outstanding scientific creativity. *Amer. Psychologist,* 1960, 15, 128-134.

LEIGHTON, A. H., CLAUSEN, J. A., & WILSON, R. N. (Eds.) *Explorations in social psychiatry.* New York: Basic Books, 1957.

LESSER, E. Popularity of Rorschach training in the United States. *J. proj. Tech.,* 1961, 25, 179-183.

LEVITT, E. E. The results of psychotherapy with children: an evaluation. *J. consult. Psychol.,* 1957, 21, 189-196.

LEVY, L. H., & ORR, T. B. The social psychology of Rorschach validity research. *J. abnorm. soc. Psychol.,* 1959, 58, 79-83.

LEWIN, K. Forces behind food habits and methods of change. *Bull. Nat. Res. Council,* 1943, 108, 35-65. (Reprinted in K. Lewin, *Field theory in social science.* New York: Harper, 1951.)

LEWIS, N. D. C. American psychiatry from its beginnings to World War II. In S. Arieti (Ed.), *American handbook of psychiatry.* New York: Basic Books, 1959. Pp. 3-17.

LINDEMANN, J. E., FAIRWEATHER, G. W., STONE, G. B., & SMITH, R. S. The use of demographic characteristics in predicting length of neuropsychiatric hospital stay. *J. consult. Psychol.,* 1959, 23, 85-89.

LINDNER, R. M. *The fifty-minute hour: a collection of true psychoanalytic tales.* New York: Rinehart, 1954.

LINDNER, R. M. Who shall practice psychotherapy? In M. H. Krout (Ed.), *Psychology, psychiatry and the public interest.* Minneapolis: Univer. of Minnesota Press, 1956. Pp. 148-160.

LINDZEY, G. Thematic Apperception Test: interpretive assumptions and related empirical evidence. *Psychol. Bull.,* 1952, 49, 1-25.

LINDZEY, G., & BORGATTA, E. G. Sociometric measurement. In G. Lindzey (Ed.), *Handbook of social psychology.* Vol. I. *Theory and method.* Reading, Mass.: Addison-Wesley, 1954. Pp. 405-448.

LINDZEY, G. (Ed.) *Assessment of human motives.* New York: Rinehart, 1958.

LINN, L. Hospital psychiatry. In S. Arieti (Ed.), *American handbook of psychiatry.* New York: Basic Books, 1959. Pp. 1829-1839.

LIPPITT, R., WATSON, Jeanne, & WESTLEY, B. *The dynamics of planned change.* New York: Harcourt, Brace, 1958.

LIPPMAN, H. S. *Treatment of the child in emotional conflict.* New York: Mc-Graw, 1956.

LITTLE, K. B. Problems in the validation of projective techniques. *J. proj. Tech.,* 1959, 23, 287-290.

LITTLE, K. B., & SHNEIDMAN, E. S. Congruencies among interpretations of psychological test and anamnestic data. *Psychol. Monogr.,* 1959, 73, No. 6 (Whole No. 476).

LOEVINGER, Jane. Objective tests as instruments of psychological theory. *Psychol. Rep.,* 1957, 6, 635-694.

LOEVINGER, Jane, & OSSORIO, A. Evaluation of therapy by self-report: a paradox. *J. abnorm. soc. Psychol.,* 1959, 58, 392-394.

LOFQUIST, L. H. *Vocational counseling with the physically handicapped.* Appleton-Century-Crofts, 1957.

LORR, M. Rating scales and checklists for the evaluation of psychopathology. *Psychol. Bull.,* 1954, 51, 119-127.

LORR, M., KATZ, M. M., & RUBINSTEIN, E. A. The prediction of length of stay in psychotherapy. *J. consult. Psychol.,* 1958, 22, 321-327.

LOUTTIT, C. M. *Clinical psychology of exceptional children* (3rd ed.) New York: Harper, 1957. (a)

LOUTTIT, C. M. Publication trends in psychology: 1894-1954. *Amer. Psychologist,* 1957, 12, 14-21. (b)

LOUTTIT, C. M., & BROWNE, C. G. Psychometric instruments in psychological clinics. *J. consult. Psychol.,* 1947, 11, 49-54.

LUBORSKY, L. Intraindividual repetitive measurements (*P* technique) in understanding psychotherapeutic change. In O. H. Mowrer (Ed.), *Psychotherapy, theory and research.* New York: Ronald, 1953. Pp. 376-389.

LUBORSKY, L. A note on Eysenck's article "The effects of psychotherapy: an evaluation." *Brit. J. Psychol.,* 1954, 65, 129-131.

LUCHINS, A. S., AUMACK, L., & DICKMAN, H. R. *Manual of group therapy.* Roseburg, Ore.: Veterans Administration Hospital, 1960.

LUCHINS, A. S. *A functional approach to training in clinical psychology: via study of a mental hospital.* Springfield, Ill.: Thomas, 1959.

LYKKEN, D. T. A study of anxiety in the sociopathic personality. *J. abnorm. soc. Psychol.,* 1957, 55, 6-10.

MACCOBY, Eleanor E., & MACCOBY, N. The interview: a tool of social science. In G. Lindzey (Ed.), *Handbook of social psychology.* Vol. I. *Theory and method.* Reading, Mass.: Addison-Wesley, 1954. Pp. 449-487.

MACCORQUODALE, K., & MEEHL, P. E. On a distinction between hypothetical constructs and intervening variables. *Psychol. Rev.,* 1948, 55, 95-107.

MACFARLANE, Jean W., ALLEN, Lucille, & HONZIK, Marjorie P. *A developmental study of the behavior problems of normal children between 21 months and 14 years.* Berkeley: Univer. of California Press, 1954.

MACKINNON, D. W., et al. *An assessment study of Air Force officers.* Parts I-V. Lackland Air Force Base, Texas: Personnel Laboratory, Wright Air Development Center, Air Research and Development Command, U. S. Air Force, 1958.

MADISON, P. *Freud's concept of repression and defense, its theoretical and observational language.* Minneapolis: Univer. of Minnesota Press, 1961.

MANDLER, G., & KESSEN, W. *The language of psychology.* New York: Wiley, 1959.

MANGUS, A. R. Role theory and marriage counseling. *Soc. Forces,* 1957, 35, 200-209.

MANN, J. H., & MANN, Carola H. The effect of role-playing experience on self-ratings of interpersonal adjustment. *Group Psychother.,* 1958, 11, 27-32.

MANNHEIM, K. *Ideology and utopia: an introduction to the sociology of knowledge.* New York: Harcourt, Brace, 1936.

MARKS, P. A. An assessment of the diagnostic process in a child guidance setting. *Psychol. Monogr.,* 1961, 75, No. 3 (Whole No. 507).

MARTINSON, W. D. Utilization of the Role Construct Repertory Test in the counseling process. *Dissertation Abstr.,* 1955, 14, 2102-2103.

MASLING, J. The effects of warm and cold interaction on the administration and scoring of an intelligence test. *J. consult. Psychol.,* 1957, 23, 336-341.

MASLING, J. The influence of situational and interpersonal variables in projective testing. *Psychol. Bull.,* 1960, 57, 65-85.

MAY, R., ANGEL, E., & ELLENBERGER, H. F. (Eds.) *Existence.* New York: Basic Books, 1958.

MAYR, E. Cause and effect in biology. *Science,* 1961, 134, 1501-1506.

McARTHUR, C. Analyzing the clinical process. *J. counsel. Psychol.,* 1954, 1, 203-208.

McCLELLAND, W. *Selection for secondary education.* London: Univer. of London Press, 1942.

McNEMAR, Q. Review of E. L. Kelly & D. W. Fiske, *The prediction of performance in clinical psychology.* Ann Arbor: Univer. of Michigan Press, 1951. *J. abnorm. soc. Psychol.,* 1952, 47, 857-860.

McQUITTY, L. L. Differential validity in some pattern analytic methods. In B. M. Bass & I. A. Berg (Eds.), *Objective approaches to personality assessment.* Princeton, N. J.: Van Nostrand, 1959. Pp. 66-82.

McREYNOLDS, P. Perception of Rorschach concepts as related to personality deviations. *J. abnorm. soc. Psychol.,* 1951, 46, 131-141.

McREYNOLDS, P. The Rorschach concept evaluation technique. *J. proj. Tech.,* 1954, 18, 60-72.

McREYNOLDS, P., & COLLINS, Beverly. Concept-forming behavior in schizophrenic and non-schizophrenic subjects. *J. Psychol.,* 1961, 52, 369-378.

MEDNICK, S. A. A learning theory approach to research in schizophrenia. *Psychol. Bull.,* 1958, 55, 316-327.

MEEHL, P. E. An investigation of a general normality or control factor in personality testing. *Psychol. Monogr.,* 1945, 59, No. 4.

MEEHL, P. E. Configural scoring. *J. consult. Psychol.,* 1950, 14, 165-171.

MEEHL, P. E. *Clinical versus statistical prediction.* Minneapolis: Univer. of Minnesota Press, 1954.

MEEHL, P. E. Wanted—a good cookbook. *Amer. Psychologist,* 1956, 11, 263-272. (*a*)

MEEHL, P. E. When shall we use our heads instead of the formula? Paper read at the Amer. Psychol. Assn., 1956. (*b*)

MEEHL, P. E. A comparison of clinicians with five statistical methods of identifying psychotic MMPI profiles. *J. counsel. Psychol.,* 1959, 6, 102-109. (*a*)

MEEHL, P. E. Some ruminations on the validation of clinical procedures. *Canad. J. Psychol.,* 1959, 13, 102-128. (*b*)

MEEHL, P. E. The cognitive activity of the clinician. *Amer. Psychologist,* 1960, 15, 19-27.

MEEHL, P. E. Logic for the clinician. (Review of T. R. Sarbin, R. Taft, & D. E. Bailey, *Clinical inference and cognitive theory*. New York: Holt, Rinehart, & Winston, 1960.) *Contemp. Psychol.*, 1961, 6, 389-391.

MEEHL, P. E., & DAHLSTROM, W. G. Objective configural rules for discriminating psychotic from neurotic MMPI profiles. *J. consult. Psychol.*, 1960, 24, 375-387.

MEEHL, P. E., & ROSEN, A. Antecedent probability and the efficiency of psychometric signs, patterns, or cutting scores. *Psychol. Bull.*, 1955, 52, 194-216.

MEISSNER, W. W. Affective response to psychoanalytic death symbols. *J. abnorm. soc. Psychol.*, 1958, 56, 295-299.

MENNINGER, K. A. *A manual for psychiatric case study.* New York: Grune & Stratton, 1952.

MENNINGER, K. A. *Theory of psychoanalytic technique.* New York: Basic Books, 1958.

MEYER, A. *Psychobiology: a science of man.* Trans. and comp. by E. E. Winters & A. M. Bowers. Springfield, Ill.: Thomas, 1958.

MEYER, Priscilla R. Counseling and adjustment after long mental illness. *J. counsel. Psychol.*, 1960, 7, 275-277.

MEYER, V. The treatment of phobic patients on the basis of learning principles. *J. abnorm. soc. Psychol.*, 1957, 55, 261-266.

MICHAEL, W. B. Development of statistical methods especially useful in test construction and evaluation. *Rev. educ. Res.*, 1959, 29, 106-129.

MILLER, G. A., GALANTER, E., & PRIBRAM, K. H. *Plans and the structure of behavior.* New York: Holt, 1960.

MILLER, J. G. Toward a general theory for the behavioral sciences. *Amer. Psychologist*, 1955, 10, 513-531.

MILLS, E. S. Broadening student experience in mental hygiene and abnormal psychology. *Amer. Psychologist*, 1955, 10, 74-78.

MORENO, J. L. Psychodrama. In S. Arieti (Ed.), *American handbook of psychiatry.* Vol. II. New York: Basic Books, 1959. Pp. 1375-1396.

MORRIS, C., EIDUSON, Bernice T., & O'DONOVAN, D. Values of psychiatric patients. *Behav. Sci.*, 1960, 5, 297-312.

MOSAK, H. M. Early recollections as a projection technique. *J. proj. Tech.*, 1958, 22, 302-311.

MOUSTAKAS, C. E. *Children in play therapy.* New York: McGraw, 1953.

MOWRER, O. H. (Ed.) *Psychotherapy: theory and research.* New York: Ronald, 1953.

MOWRER, O. H. What is normal behavior? In L. A. Pennington & I. A. Berg (Eds.), *An introduction to clinical psychology.* (2nd ed.) New York: Ronald, 1954. Pp. 58-88.

MOWRER, O. H. The role of the concept of sin in psychotherapy. *J. counsel. Psychol.*, 1960, 7, 185-188. (a)

MOWRER, O. H. "Sin," the lesser of two evils. *Amer. Psychologist*, 1960, 15, 301-304. (b)

MUDD, Emily H., & KRICH, A. (Eds.) *Man and wife: a sourcebook of family attitudes, sexual behavior, and marriage counseling.* New York: Norton, 1957.

MUNCIE, W. The psychobiological approach. In S. Arieti (Ed.), *American handbook of psychiatry.* Vol. II. New York: Basic Books, 1959. Pp. 1317-1332.

MURPHY, G. Social psychology. In S. Arieti, (Ed.) *American handbook of psychiatry.* Vol. II. New York: Basic Books, 1959. Pp. 1733-1742.

MURRAY, E. J., & COHEN, M. Mental illness, milieu therapy, and social organization in ward groups. *J. abnorm. soc. Psychol.*, 1959, 58, 48-54.

MURRAY, H. A. *Explorations in personality.* New York: Oxford, 1938.

MURSTEIN, B. I. A conceptual model of projective techniques applied to stimulus variations with thematic techniques. *J. consult. Psychol.*, 1959, 23, 3-14.

MURSTEIN, B. I., & PRYER, R. S. The concept of projection: a review. *Psychol. Bull.*, 1959, 56, 353-374.

MURSTEIN, B. I., & WHEELER, J. I. The projection of hostility on the Rorschach and Thematic Stories Test. *J. clin. Psychol.*, 1959, 15, 316-319.

MUSCIO, B. The influence of the form of the question. *Brit. J. Psychol.*, 1916, 8, 351-389.

NEWMAN, S. H., BOBBITT, J. M., & CAMERON, D. C. The reliability of the interview method in an officer candidate evaluation program. *Amer. Psychologist*, 1946, 1, 103-109.

NICHOLS, R. C., & BECK, K. W. Factors in psychotherapy change. *J. consult. Psychol.*, 1960, 24, 388-399.

NUNNALLY, J. C., Jr. *Tests and measurements.* New York: McGraw, 1959.

NUNNALLY, J. C., Jr. *Popular conceptions of mental health.* New York: Holt, Rinehart, & Winston, 1961.

ODUM, C. L. A study of time required to do a Rorschach examination. *J. proj. Tech.*, 1950, 14, 464-468.

Office of Strategic Services Staff. *Assessment of men.* New York: Rinehart, 1948.

OLDFIELD, R. C. *The psychology of the interview.* (3rd ed.) London: Methuen, 1947.

Opler, M. K. (Ed.) *Culture and mental health, cross-cultural studies.* New York: Macmillan, 1959.

ORNE, M. T. The nature of hypnosis: artifact and essence. *J. abnorm. soc. Psychol.*, 1959, 58, 277-299.

OSGOOD, C. E., & LURIA, Zella. A blind analysis of a case of multiple personality using the Semantic Differential. *J. abnorm. soc. Psychol.*, 1954, 49, 579-591.

OSGOOD, C. E., & SUCI, G. J. A measure of relation determined by both mean difference and profile information. *Psychol. Bull.*, 1952, 49, 251-262.

OSGOOD, C. E., SUCI, G. J., & TANNENBAUM, P. H. *The measurement of meaning.* Urbana: Univer. of Illinois Press, 1957.

OSSORIO, A. G., & FINE, L. Psychodrama as a catalyst for social change in a mental hospital. In J. H. Masserman & J. L. Moreno (Eds.), *Progress in psychotherapy.* Vol. V. *Review and integrations.* New York: Grune & Stratton, 1960.

PARKER, C. A. As a clinician thinks . . . *J. counsel. Psychol.*, 1958, 5, 253-261.

PARSONS, F. *Choosing a vocation.* New York: Houghton, 1906.

PASCAL, G. R. Psychological deficit as a function of stress and constitution. *J. Pers.*, 1951, 20, 175-187.

PASCAL, G. R., & SUTTELL, Barbara J. *The Bender-Gestalt Test: quantification and validity for adults.* New York: Grune & Stratton, 1951.

PATTERSON, G. R., HELPER, M. E., & WILCOTT, R. C. Anxiety and verbal conditioning in children. *Child Develpm.*, 1960, 31, 101-108.

PEAK, Helen. Problems of objective observation. In L. Festinger & D. Katz (Eds.), *Research methods in the behavioral sciences.* New York: Dryden, 1953.

PENNINGTON, L. A., & BERG, I. A. (Eds.) *An introduction to clinical psychology.* (2nd ed.) New York: Ronald, 1954.

PEPINSKY, H. B., & PEPINSKY, Pauline N. *Counseling: theory and practice.* New York: Ronald, 1954.

PERVIN, L. A. Existentialism, psychology, and psychotherapy. *Amer. Psychologist,* 1960, 15, 305-309.

PETRULLO, L., & BASS, B. M. (Eds.) *Leadership and interpersonal behavior.* New York: Holt, Rinehart, & Winston, 1961.

PHILLIPS, E. L. *Psychotherapy, a modern theory and practice.* Englewood Cliffs, N. J.: Prentice-Hall, 1956.

PHILLIPS, L. Case-history data and prognosis in schizophrenia. *J. nerv. ment. Dis.,* 1953, 117, 515-525.

PHILLIPS, L., & RABINOVITCH, M. S. Social role and patterns of symptomatic behaviors. *J. abnorm. soc. Psychol.,* 1958, 57, 181-186.

PHILLIPS, Jeanne S., MATARAZZO, Ruth G., MATARAZZO, J. D., SASLOW, G., & KANFER, F. H. Relationships between descriptive content and interaction behavior in interviews. *J. consult. Psychol.,* 1961, 25, 260-266.

POLANSKY, N., & KOUNIN, J. Clients' reactions to initial interviews: a field study. *Hum. Relat.,* 1956, 9, 237-265.

PORTEUS, S. D. *The Maze Test and clinical psychology.* Palo Alto, Calif.: Pacific Books, 1959.

POWDERMAKER, Florence B., & Frank, J. D. *Group psychotherapy.* Cambridge, Mass.: Harvard Univer. Press, 1953.

PRESSEY, S. L. Toward earlier creativity in psychology. *Amer. Psychologist,* 1960, 15, 124-127.

PSATHAS, G. Interaction process analysis of two psychotherapy groups. *Int. J. Group. Psychother.,* 1960, 10, 430-445.

QUAST, W. The Bender Gestalt: a clinical study of children's records. *J. consult. Psychol.,* 1961, 25, 405-408.

RACHMAN, S. The treatment of anxiety and phobic reactions by systematic desensitization psychotherapy. *J. abnorm. soc. Psychol.,* 1959, 58, 259-263.

RAIMY, V. C. Self-reference in counseling interviews. *J. consult. Psychol.,* 1948, 12, 153-163.

RAIMY, V. C. (Ed.) *Training in clinical psychology.* Englewood Cliffs, N. J.: Prentice-Hall, 1950.

RAPAPORT, D. The structure of psychoanalytic theory: a systematizing attempt. In S. Koch (Ed.), *Psychology: a study of a science.* Study I. *Conceptual and systematic.* Vol. 3. *Formulations of the person and the social context.* New York: McGraw, 1959. Pp. 55-183.

RAPOPORT, R. N. *Community as doctor.* Springfield, Ill.: Thomas, 1960.

RAUSH, H. L., DITTMANN, A T., & TAYLOR, T. J. The interpersonal behavior of children in residential treatment. *J. abnorm. soc. Psychol.,* 1959, 58, 9-26. (*a*)

RAUSH, H. L., DITTMANN, A. T., & TAYLOR, T. J. Person, setting, and change in social interaction. *Hum. Relat.,* 1959, 12, 361-378. (*b*)

RAUSH, H. L., SPERBER, Z., RIGLER, D., WILLIAMS, J., HARWAY, N. I., BORDIN, E. S., DITTMANN, A. T., & HAYS, W. L. A dimensional analysis of depth of interpretation. *J. consult. Psychol.,* 1956, 20, 43-48.

REDL, F. Strategy and techniques of the life-space interview. *Amer. J. Orthopsychiat.,* 1959, 29, 1-18.

REICHENBACH, H. *Experience and prediction, an analysis of the foundations and the structure of knowledge.* Chicago: Univer. of Chicago Press, 1938.

REITAN, R. M. Validity of the Trail Making Test as an indicator of organic brain damage. *Percept. mot. Skills,* 1958, 8, 271-276.

REMPEL, P. R. The use of multivariate statistical analysis of MMPI scores in classification of delinquent and nondelinquent high school boys. *J. consult. Psychol.*, 1958, 22, 17-23.

REZNIKOFF, M., BRADY, J. P., & ZELLER, W. W. The psychiatric attitudes battery: a procedure for assessing attitudes toward psychiatric treatment and hospitals. *J. clin. Psychol.*, 1959, 15, 260-265.

RICE, S. A. Contagious bias in the interview. *Amer. J. Sociol.*, 1929, 35, 420-423.

RICHARD, H. C., DIGNAM, P. J., & HORNER, R. F. Verbal manipulation in a psychotherapeutic relationship. *J. clin. Psychol.*, 1960, 16, 364-367.

RICHARDS, T. W. *Modern clinical psychology.* New York: McGraw, 1946.

ROBBINS, L. L., & WALLERSTEIN, R. S. The research strategy and tactics of the psychotherapy research project of the Menninger Foundation and the problem of controls. In E. A. Rubinstein & M. B. Parloff (Eds.), *Research in psychotherapy.* Washington: Amer. Psychol. Ass., 1959. Pp. 27-43.

ROBINSON, J. T., & COHEN, L. D. Individual bias in psychological reports. *J. clin. Psychol.*, 1954, 10, 333-336.

ROE, Anne. Analysis of group Rorschachs of psychologists and anthropologists. *J. proj. Tech.*, 1952, 16, 212-224.

ROE, Anne. A psychological study of eminent psychologists and anthropologists and a comparison with biological and physical scientists. *Psychol. Monogr.*, 1953, 67, No. 2.

ROE, Anne, GUSTAD, J. W., MOORE, B. V., ROSS, S., & SKODAK, Marie. (Eds.) *Graduate education in psychology.* (Report of the Conference on Graduate Education in Psychology of the Amer. Psychol. Assn., Miami Beach, Florida, Nov. 29-Dec. 7, 1958.) Washington: Amer. Psychol. Ass., 1959.

ROGERS, C. R. *Counseling and psychotherapy.* Boston: Houghton, 1942.

ROGERS, C. R. *Client-centered therapy.* Boston: Houghton, 1951.

ROGERS, C. R. The necessary and sufficient conditions of therapeutic personality change. *J. consult. Psychol.*, 1957, 21, 95-103.

ROGERS, C. R. Persons or science? a philosophical question. *Amer. Psychologist,* 1958, 13, 142-149.

ROGERS, C. R. A tentative scale for the measurement of process in psychotherapy. In E. A. Rubinstein and M. B. Parloff (Eds.), *Research in psychotherapy.* Washington: Amer. Psychol. Ass., 1959. Pp. 96-107. (a)

ROGERS, C. R. A theory of therapy, personality, and interpersonal relationships, as developed in the client-centered framework. In S. Koch (Ed.), *Psychology: a study of a science.* Study I. *Conceptual and systematic.* Vol. III. *Formulations of the person and the social context.* New York: McGraw, 1959. Pp. 184-256. (b)

ROGERS, C. R. Significant trends in the client-centered orientation. In L. E. Abt & B. F. Riess (Eds.), *Progress in clinical psychology.* Vol. IV. New York: Grune & Stratton, 1960. Pp. 85-99.

ROGERS, C. R. *On becoming a person.* Boston: Houghton, 1961.

ROGERS, C. R., & DYMOND, Rosalind F. *Psychotherapy and personality change.* Chicago: Univer. of Chicago Press, 1954.

ROGERS, C. R., & SKINNER, B. F. Some issues concerning the control of human behavior: a symposium. *Science,* 1956, 124, 1057-1066.

ROHDE, Amanda R. *The sentence completion method.* New York: Ronald, 1957.

ROKEACH, M. *The open and closed mind.* New York: Basic Books, 1960.

ROMANO, R. L. The use of the interpersonal system of diagnosis in marital counseling. *J. counsel. Psychol.*, 1960, 7, 10-19.

ROSE, A. M. (Ed.) *Mental health and mental disorder, a sociological approach.* New York: Norton, 1955.

ROSE, D. W. The study of behavior settings as an aid in mental hospital analysis: a methodological exploration. Unpublished master's thesis, Univer. of Oregon, 1959.

ROSENTHAL, D., & FRANK, J. D. Psychotherapy and the placebo effect. *Psychol. Bull.*, 1956, 53, 294-302.

ROSENZWEIG, S. Idiodynamics in personality theory with special reference to projective methods. *Psychol. Rev.*, 1951, 58, 213-233.

ROSENZWEIG, S. A transvaluation of psychotherapy—a reply to Hans Eysenck. *J. abnorm. soc. Psychol.*, 1954, 49, 298-304.

ROTTER, J. B. *Social learning and clinical psychology.* New York: Prentice-Hall, 1954.

ROTTER, J. B. Some implications of a social learning theory for the prediction of goal-directed behavior from testing procedures. *Psychol. Rev.*, 1960, 67, 301-316.

ROTTER, J. B., & RAFFERTY, J. E. The Rotter Incomplete Sentences Test. New York: Psychological Corp., 1950.

RUBIN, M., & SHONTZ, F. C. Diagnostic prototypes and diagnostic processes of clinical psychologists. *J. consult. Psychol.*, 1960, 24, 234-239.

RUBINSTEIN, E. A., & LORR, M. (Eds.) *Survey of clinical practice in psychology.* New York: International Universities Press, 1954.

RUBINSTEIN, E. A., & PARLOFF, M. B. (Eds.) *Research in psychotherapy.* Washington: Amer. Psychol. Ass., 1959.

RUESCH, J. *Disturbed communication, the clinical assessment of normal and pathological communicative behavior.* New York: Norton, 1957.

RUESCH, J. General theory of communication in psychiatry. In S. Arieti (Ed.), *American handbook of psychiatry.* Vol. I. New York: Basic Books, 1959. Pp. 895-908.

RUESCH, J., & BATESON, G. *Communication, the social matrix of psychiatry.* New York: Norton, 1951.

RUESCH, J., & KEES, W. *Nonverbal communication.* Berkeley: Univer. of California Press, 1956.

SACKS, J. M., & BERGER, S. Group therapy techniques with hospitalized chronic schizophrenic patients. *J. consult. Psychol.*, 1954, 18, 297-302.

SAHLINS, M. D. The origin of society. *Scient. Amer.*, 1960, 203, 76-87.

SALTER, A. *Conditioned-reflex therapy.* New York: Creative Age, 1949.

SALZINGER, K., & PISONI, Stephanie. Reinforcement of affect responses of schizophrenics during the clinical interview. *J. abnorm. soc. Psychol.*, 1958, 57, 84-90.

SANFORD, F. H. Annual report of the executive secretary. *Amer. Psychologist*, 1951, 6, 664-670.

SARBIN, T. R. A contribution to the study of actuarial and individual methods of prediction. *Amer. J. Soc.*, 1943, 48, 593-602.

SARBIN, T. R. Role theory. In G. Lindzey (Ed.), *Handbook of social psychology.* Vol I. *Theory and method.* Reading, Mass.: Addison-Wesley, 1954. Pp. 223-258.

SARBIN, T. R., TAFT, R., & BAILEY, D. E. *Clinical inference and cognitive theory.* New York: Holt, Rinehart, & Winston, 1960.

SASLOW, G., & MATARAZZO, J. D. A technique for studying changes in interview behavior. In E. A. Rubinstein & M. B. Parloff (Eds.), *Research in psychotherapy.* Washington: Amer. Psychol. Ass., 1959. Pp. 125-159.

SASLOW, G., MATARAZZO, J. D., & GUZE, S. B. The stability of interaction chronograph patterns in psychiatric interviews. *J. consult. Psychol.*, 1955, 19, 417-430.

SCHAFER, R. *Psychoanalytic interpretation in Rorschach testing*. New York: Grune & Stratton, 1954.

SCHMIDT, H. O., & FONDA, C. P. Reliability of psychiatric diagnosis: a new look. *J. abnorm. soc. Psychol.*, 1956, 52, 262-267.

SCHOFIELD, W., & BALIAN, Lucy. A comparative study of the personal histories of schizophrenic and nonpsychiatric patients. *J. abnorm. soc. Psychol.*, 1959, 59, 216-225.

SCHULBERG, H. C., & TOLOR, A. The use of the Bender-Gestalt in clinical practice. *J. proj. Tech.*, 1961, 25, 347-351.

SCHUTZ, W. C. *FIRO, a three-dimensional theory of interpersonal behavior*. New York: Rinehart, 1958.

SCHWAB, J. J. What do scientists do? *Behav. Sci.*, 1960, 5, 1-27.

SCRIVEN, M. Explanation and prediction in evolutionary theory. *Science*, 1959, 130, 477-482.

SEARS, Pauline S. Treat all, not each. (A review of N. W. Ackerman, *The psychodynamics of family life*. New York: Basic Books, 1958.) *Contemp. Psychol.*, 1960, 5, 18-20.

SEARS, R. R. *Survey of objective studies of psychoanalytic concepts*. New York: Soc. Sci. Res. Council, 1943.

SEEMAN, J. A study of the process of nondirective therapy. *J. consult. Psychol.*, 1949, 13, 157-168.

SEEMAN, J., & RASKIN, N. J. Research perspectives in client-centered therapy. In O. H. Mowrer (Ed.), *Psychotherapy: theory and research*. New York: Ronald, 1953. Pp. 205-234.

SEEMAN, W. Clinical opinion on the role of therapist adjustment in psychotherapy. *J. consult. Psychol.*, 1950, 14, 49-52.

SEIDEL, Claudene. The relationship between Klopfer's Rorschach Prognostic Rating Scale and Phillips' case-history prognostic rating scale. *J. consult. Psychol.*, 1960, 24, 46-53.

SELYE, H. *The stress of life*. New York: McGraw, 1956.

SHAFFER, G. W., & LAZARUS, R. S. *Fundamental concepts in clinical psychology*. New York: McGraw, 1952.

SHAKOW, D. Discussion of papers by Leary and Gill, and Rogers. In E. A. Rubinstein & M. B. Parloff (Eds.), *Research in psychotherapy*. Washington: Amer. Psychol. Ass., 1959. Pp. 108-115.

SHAPIRO, A. K. A contribution to a history of the placebo effect. *Behav. Sci.*, 1960, 5, 109-135.

SHEVRIN, H., & LUBORSKY, L. The measurement of preconscious perception in dreams and images: an investigation of the Poetzl phenomenon. *J. abnorm. soc. Psychol.*, 1958, 56, 285-294.

SHOBEN, E. J., Jr. Psychotherapy as a problem in learning theory. *Psychol. Bull.*, 1949, 46, 366-392.

SHOBEN, E. J., Jr. Some observations on psychotherapy and the learning process. In O. H. Mowrer (Ed.), *Psychotherapy: theory and research*. New York: Ronald, 1953. Pp. 120-139.

SHNEIDMAN, E. S. *Thematic test analysis*. New York: Grune & Stratton, 1951.

SILVERMAN, L. H. A Q-sort study of the validity of evaluations made from projective techniques. *Psychol. Monogr.*, 1959, 73, No. 7.

SINES, L. K. The relative contribution of four kinds of data to accuracy in personality assessment. *J. consult. Psychol.*, 1959, 23, 483-492.

SKINNER, B. F. *Science and human behavior*. New York: Macmillan, 1953.

SKINNER, B. F. *Verbal behavior*. New York: Appleton-Century-Crofts, 1957.

SMITH, E. E. Defensiveness, insight, and the K scale. J. consult. Psychol., 1959, 23, 275.

SMITH, M. B. Research strategies toward a conception of positive mental health. Amer. Psychologist, 1959, 14, 673-681.

SNEDDEN, D. Measuring general intelligence by interview. Psychol. Clinic, 1930, 19, 131-134.

SNYDER, W. U. An investigation of the nature of nondirective psychotherapy. J. gen. Psychol., 1945, 33, 193-224.

SNYDER, W. U. Client-centered therapy. In L. A. Pennington & I. A. Berg (Eds.), An introduction to clinical psychology. (2nd ed.) New York: Ronald, 1954. Pp. 529-556.

SNYDER, W. U. Some investigations of relationship in psychotherapy. In E. A. Rubinstein & M. B. Parloff (Eds.), Research in psychotherapy. Washington: Amer. Psychol. Ass., 1959. Pp. 247-259.

SNYDER, W. U. The psychotherapy relationship. New York: Macmillan, 1961.

SOHLER, Dorothy T., HOLZBERG, J. D., FLECK, S., CORNELISON, Alice R., KAY, Eleanor, & LIDZ, T. The prediction of family interaction from a battery of projective techniques. J. proj. Tech., 1957, 21, 199-208.

SOMMER, R. Studies in personal space. Sociometry, 1959, 22, 247-260.

SOSKIN, W. F. Bias in postdiction from projective tests. J. abnorm. soc. Psychol., 1954, 49, 69-74.

SOSKIN, W. F. Influence of four types of data on diagnostic conceptualization in psychological testing. J. abnorm. soc. Psychol., 1959, 58, 69-78.

SPEISMAN, J. C. Depth of interpretation and verbal resistance in psychotherapy. J. consult. Psychol., 1959, 23, 93-99.

SPIEGEL, J. P. The resolution of role conflict within the family. Psychiatry, 1957, 20, 1-16.

STAINBROOK, E. The community of the psychiatric patient. In S. Arieti (Ed.), American handbook of psychiatry. New York: Basic Books, 1959. Pp. 150-160.

STANTON, A. H., & SCHWARTZ, M. S. The mental hospital. New York: Basic Books, 1954.

STARK, W. The sociology of knowledge: an essay in aid of a deeper understanding of the history of ideas. Glencoe, Ill.: Free Press, 1958.

STARKWEATHER, J. A. Content-free speech as a source of information about the speaker. J. abnorm. soc. Psychol., 1956, 52, 394-402.

STAUDT, Virginia M., & ZUBIN, J. A biometric evaluation of the somatotherapies in schizophrenia. Psychol. Bull., 1957, 54, 171-196.

STEIN, M. I., & HEINZE, Shirley J. Creativity and the individual. Glencoe, Ill.: Free Press, 1960.

STEPHENSON, W. The study of behavior. Chicago: Univer. of Chicago Press, 1953.

STERN, G. G., STEIN, M. I., & BLOOM, B. S. Methods in personality assessment. Glencoe, Ill.: Free Press, 1956.

STOTSKY, B. A. How important is psychotherapy to the hospitalized patient? J. clin. Psychol., 1956, 12, 32-36.

STOTSKY, B. A., DASTON, D. G., & VARDACK, N. An evaluation of the counseling of chronic schizophrenics. J. counsel. Psychol., 1955, 2, 248-255.

STRONG, E. K., Jr. Vocational interests of men and women. Stanford, Calif.: Stanford Univer. Press, 1943.

STROTHER, C. R. (Ed.) Psychology and mental health. Washington: Amer. Psychol. Ass., 1956.

STRUPP, H. H. The effect of the psychotherapist's personal analysis upon his techniques. J. consult. Psychol., 1955, 19, 197-204. (a)

STRUPP, H. H. An objective comparison of Rogerian and psychoanalytic techniques. *J. consult. Psychol.*, 1955, 19, 1-7. (*b*)

STRUPP, H. H. The performance of psychoanalytic and client-centered therapists in an initial interview. *J. consult. Psychol.*, 1958, 22, 265-274.

STRUPP, H. H. *Psychotherapists in action.* New York: Grune & Stratton, 1960.

STUBBLEFIELD, R. L., & CAMP, Bonnie W. Use of the Keysort System in maintaining clinic records for research. *Amer. J. Orthopsychiat.*, 1959, 29, 827-828.

SULLIVAN, H. S. *Conceptions of modern psychiatry.* Washington: Wm. A. White Foundation, 1947.

SULLIVAN, H. S. *The interpersonal theory of psychiatry.* New York: Norton, 1953.

SULLIVAN, H. S. *The psychiatric interview.* New York: Norton, 1954.

SULLIVAN, H. S. *Clinical studies in psychiatry.* New York: Norton, 1956.

SUNDBERG, N. D. The relationship of psychotherapeutic skill and experience to knowledge of other people. Unpublished doctoral dissertation. Univer. of Minnesota, 1952.

SUNDBERG, N. D. The acceptability of "fake" versus "bona fide" personality test interpretations. *J. abnorm. soc. Psychol.*, 1955, 50, 145-147.

SUNDBERG, N. D. A note concerning the history of testing. *Amer. Psychologist*, 1954, 9, 150-151.

SUNDBERG, N. D. The practice of psychological testing in clinical services in the United States. *Amer. Psychologist*, 1961, 16, 79-83.

SUPER, D. E. The preliminary appraisal in vocational counseling. *Personnel guid. J.*, 1957, 36, 154-161. (*a*)

SUPER, D. E. *The psychology of careers.* New York: Harper, 1957. (*b*)

SUTTON-SMITH, B. A formal analysis of game meaning. *Western Folklore*, 1959, 18, 13-24.

SWENSEN, C. H., Jr. Empirical evaluations of human figure drawings. *Psychol. Bull.*, 1957, 54, 431-466.

Symposium: Automation technics in personality assessment. *Proc. Mayo Clinic*, 1962, 37, 61-82.

Symposium: The impact of computers on psychological research. *Behav. Sci.*, 1960, 5, 170-187.

Symposium: Psychoanalysis as seen by analyzed psychologists. *J. abnorm. soc. Psychol.*, 1940, 35, 3-323.

Symposium: Research design in clinical psychology. *J. clin. Psychol.*, 1952, 8, 3-64.

Symposium: Statistics for the clinician. *J. clin. Psychol.*, 1950, 6, 1-76.

SZASZ, T. S. The myth of mental illness. *Amer. Psychologist*, 1960, 15, 113-118.

TAFT, R. The ability to judge people. *Psychol. Bull.*, 1955, 51, 1-23.

TAFT, R. Multiple methods of personality assessment. *Psychol. Bull.*, 1959, 56, 333-352.

TAGIURI, R., & PETRULLO, L. (Eds.) *Person perception and interpersonal behavior.* Stanford, Calif.: Stanford Univer. Press, 1958.

TALLAND, G. A., & CLARK, D. H. Evaluation of topics in therapy group discussion. *J. clin. Psychol.*, 1954, 10, 131-137.

TALLENT, N. On individualizing the psychologists' clinical evaluation. *J. clin. Psychol.*, 1958, 14, 243-245.

TALLENT, N. Psychological consultation in psychiatry. *Dis. nerv. System*, 1960, 21, 1-7.

TALLENT, N., & REISS, W. J. Multidisciplinary views on the preparation of written clinical psychological reports: III. The trouble with psychological reports. *J. clin. Psychol.*, 1959, 15, 444-446.

TAYLOR, J. L., & TEICHER, A. A clinical approach to reporting psychological test data. *J. clin. Psychol.*, 1946, 2, 323-332. (Reprinted in R. I. Watson (Ed.), *Readings in the clinical method in psychology.* New York: Harper, 1949. Pp. 244-258.)

TERMAN, L. M. Trails to psychology. In C. Murchison (Ed.), *A history of psychology in autobiography.* Vol. II. Worcester, Mass.: Clark Univer. Press, 1932. Pp. 297-331.

TERMAN, L. M. The discovery and encouragement of exceptional talent. *Amer. Psychologist*, 1954, 9, 221-230.

THIGPEN, C. H., & CLECKLEY, H. M. A case of multiple personality. *J. abnorm. soc. Psychol.*, 1954, 49, 135-151.

THIGPEN, C. H., & CLECKLEY, H. M. *The three faces of Eve.* New York: McGraw, 1957.

THOMAE, H. Problems of character change. In H. P. David & H. von Bracken (Eds.), *Perspectives in personality theory.* New York: Basic Books, 1961. Pp. 242-255.

THOMPSON, Clara. Sullivan and psychoanalysis. In P. Mullahy (Ed.), *The contributions of Harry Stack Sullivan.* New York: Hermitage House, 1952. Pp. 101-115.

THORNDIKE, R. L. Predicting psychiatrists' psyches. (A review of R. R. Holt & L. Luborsky, *Personality patterns of psychiatrists.* Vol. I. New York: Basic Books, 1958; Vol. II. Topeka Kan.: Menninger Foundation, 1958.) *Contemp. Psychol.*, 1960, 5, 116-118.

THORNE, F. C. *Principles of personality counseling.* Brandon, Vt.: J. clin. Psychol., 1950.

THORNE, F. C. *Principles of psychological examining.* Brandon, Vt.: J. clin. Psychol., 1955.

THORNE, F. C. *Clinical judgment, a study of clinical errors.* Brandon, Vt.: J. clin. Psychol., 1961.

TIEDEMAN, D. V. A model for the profile problem. *Proc. 1953 Invitational Conf. on Testing Problems*, Educational Testing Service, 1954. Pp. 54-75.

TITCHENER, J., & EMERSON, R. Some methods for the study of family interaction in personality development. In B. Pasamanick & P. H. Knapp (Eds.), *Social aspects of psychiatry.* Amer. Psychiat. Ass.: Psychiatric Research reports, No. 10, 1958.

TOMKINS, S. S. *The Thematic Apperception Test: the theory and technique of interpretation.* New York: Grune & Stratton, 1947.

TOMKINS, S. S., & MINER, J. B. The Tomkins-Horn Picture Arrangement Test. New York: Springer, 1957.

TORRANCE, E. P. A theory of leadership and interpersonal behavior under stress. In L. Petrullo and B. M. Bass (Eds.), *Leadership and interpersonal behavior.* New York: Holt, Rinehart, & Winston, 1961. Pp. 100-117.

TRANKELL, A. The psychologist as an instrument of prediction. *J. appl. Psychol.*, 1959, 43, 170-175.

TYLER, Leona E. Towards a workable psychology of individuality. *Amer. Psychologist*, 1959, 14, 75-81.

TYLER, Leona E. Research explorations in the realm of choice. *J. counsel. Psychol.*, 1961, 8, 195-201. (*a*)

TYLER, Leona E. *The work of the counselor.* (2nd ed.) New York: Appleton-Century-Crofts, 1961. (*b*)

ULLMANN, L. P. Selection of neuropsychiatric patients for group psychotherapy. *J. consult. Psychol.*, 1957, 21, 277-280.

ULLMANN, L. P., BERKMAN, V. C., & HAMISTER, R. C. Psychological reports

related to behavior and benefit of placement in home care. *J. clin. Psychol.*, 1958, 14, 254-259.

VANDENBERG, S. G. Medical diagnosis by computer: recent attempts and outlook for the future. *Behav. Sci.*, 1960, 5, 170-174.

VEITH, Ilza. Psychiatric nosology: from Hippocrates to Kraepelin. *Amer. J. Psychiat.*, 1957, 114, 385-391.

VERNON, P. E. *Personality tests and assessments.* New York: Holt, 1953.

VINCENT, C. E. (Ed.) *Readings in marriage counseling.* New York: Crowell, 1957.

VOEGTLIN, W. L., & LEMERE, F. An evaluation of the aversion treatment of alcoholism. *Quart. J. Stud. Alcohol,* 1950, 11, 199-204.

WALLEN, R. W. *Clinical psychology, the study of persons.* New York: McGraw, 1956.

WALLERSTEIN, R. S. (Ed.) *Hospital treatment of alcoholism.* New York: Basic Books, 1957.

WASHBURN, S. L. & DEVORE, I. The social life of baboons. *Scient. Amer.,* 1961, 204, 62-71.

WATKINS, J. G. Psychotherapy: an overview. In L. A. Pennington & I. A. Berg (Eds.), *An introduction to clinical psychology.* (2nd ed.) New York: Ronald, 1954. Pp. 483-501.

WATKINS, J. G. *General psychotherapy, an outline and study guide.* Springfield, Ill.: Thomas, 1960.

WATSON, R. I. *The clinical method in psychology.* New York: Harper, 1951.

WATSON, R. I. A brief history of clinical psychology. *Psychol. Bull.,* 1953, 50, 321-346.

WEIDER, A. (Ed.) *Contributions toward medical psychology.* Vols. I & II. New York: Ronald, 1953.

WEITZENHOFFER, A. M., & HILGARD, E. R. *Stanford Hypnotic Susceptibility Scale.* Palo Alto: Consulting Psychologists Press, 1959.

WELLS, F. L., & RUESCH, J. *Mental examiners' handbook.* (2nd ed.) New York: Psychological Corp., 1945.

WELSH, G. S., & DAHLSTROM, W. G. *Basic readings on the MMPI in psychology and medicine.* Minneapolis: Univer. of Minnesota Press, 1956.

WHEELIS, A. *The quest for identity.* New York: Norton, 1958.

WHYTE, W. H., Jr. *The organization man.* New York: Simon & Schuster, 1956.

WIENER, D. N. Subtle and obvious keys for the MMPI. *J. consult. Psychol.,* 1948, 12, 164-170.

WIENER, D. N., & RATHS, O. N. Contributions of the mental hygiene clinic team to clinic decisions. *Amer. J. Orthopsychiat.,* 1959, 29, 350-356.

WIENS, A. N., BRODY, D. S., MATARAZZO, J. D., & WARNATH, C. F. The habits and practices of professional psychologists in Oregon. Report of the Oregon Psychol. Ass. Board of Examiners, 1961.

WILLIAMS, C. D. The elimination of tantrum behavior by extinction procedures. *J. abnorm. soc. Psychol.,* 1959, 59, 269.

WILLIAMS, W. C. The PALS tests: a technique for children to evaluate both parents. *J. consult. Psychol.,* 1958, 22, 487-495.

WILLIAMSON, E. G., & BORDIN, E. S. Evaluating counseling by means of a control group experiment. *Sch. Soc.,* 1940, 52, 434-440.

WILLIAMSON, E. G., & BORDIN, E. S. An analytical description of student counseling. *Educ. psychol. Measmt.,* 1941, 1, 341-354.

WILSON, D. P. *My six convicts.* New York: Rinehart, 1951.

WINCH, R. F., & MORE, D. M. Does TAT add information to interviews? Statistical analysis of the increment. *J. clin. Psychol.,* 1956, 12, 316-321.

WINDER, A. E., & HERSKO, M. A thematic analysis of an outpatient psycho-therapy group. *Int. J. group Psychother.*, 1958, 8, 293-300.

WIRT, R. D., & BRIGGS, P. F. Personality and environmental factors in the development of delinquency. *Psychol. Monogr.*, 1959, 73, No. 15 (Whole No. 485).

WITTENBORN, J. R., & HOLZBERG, J. D. The generality of psychiatric syndromes. *J. consult. Psychol.*, 1951, 15, 372-380.

WITTENBORN, J. R., HOLZBERG, J. D., & SIMON, B. Symptom correlates for descriptive diagnosis. *Genet. Psychol. Monogr.*, 1953, 47, 237-301.

WITTSON, C. L., & HUNT, W. A. The predictive value of the brief psychiatric interview. *Amer. J. Psychiat.*, 1951, 107, 582-585.

WOLBERG, L. R. *Medical hypnosis.* Vol. I. New York: Grune & Stratton, 1948.

WOLBERG, L. R. *The technique of psychotherapy.* New York: Grune & Stratton, 1954.

WOLFE, D. M. Power and authority in the family. In D. Cartwright (Ed.), *Studies in social power.* Ann Arbor: Univer. of Michigan, 1959. Pp. 99-117.

WOLPE, J. *Psychotherapy by reciprocal inhibition.* Stanford, Calif.: Stanford Univer. Press, 1958.

WYATT, D., & CAMPBELL, D. A study of interviewer bias as related to interviewer's expectations and own opinions. *Int. J. Opin. Attit. Res.*, 1950, 4, 77-83.

WYNNE, L. C., RYCKOFF, I. M., DAY, Juliana, & HIRSCH, S. I. Pseudomutuality in the family relations of schizophrenics. *Psychiatry*, 1958, 21, 205-220.

YANDELL, R. J. An investigation of the configural use of true-false personality test items in predicting a job performance criterion. Unpublished doctoral dissertation, Univer. of California, Berkeley, 1955.

YARROW, L. J. Maternal deprivation: toward an empirical and conceptual re-evaluation. *Psychol. Bull.*, 1961, 58, 459-490.

YATES, A. J. The validity of some psychological tests of brain damage. *Psychol. Bull.*, 1954, 51, 359-379.

ZANDER, A., COHEN, A. R., & STOTLAND, E. *Role relations in the mental health professions.* Ann Arbor: Univer. of Michigan, 1957.

ZAX, M., & KLEIN, A. Measurement of personality and behavior changes following psychotherapy. *Psychol. Bull.*, 1960. 57, 435-448.

ZIGLER, E., & PHILLIPS, L. Social effectiveness and symptomatic behaviors. *J. abnorm. soc. Psychol.*, 1960, 61, 231-238.

ZIGLER, E., & PHILLIPS, L. Case-history data and psychiatric diagnosis. *J. consult. Psychol.*, 1961, 25, 458.

Index of Research Examples

Index of Cases and Illustrations from Cases

Index of Names

Abt, L. E., 55, 152
Ackerman, N. W., 166, 411-412, 419, 422, 424
Adler, A., 42, 290, 357-360, 394
Adorno, T. W., 62, 435
Ainsworth, Mary D., 161, 506
Akutagowa, R., 177
Albaugh, W. P., 249
Albee, G. W., 498-499
Alexander, F., 379
Allen, F. H., 296
Allen, J. M., 233, 251
Allen, Lucile, 91
Allen, R. M., 159
Allport, G. W., 65, 68, 189
Alpert, R., 274
American Psychiatric Association, 11, 13, 481
American Psychological Association, 19-21, 23, 30, 67, 72, 136, 139, 147, 149, 256, 274, 456, 461, 466, 469, 470, 475, 477-482, 484, 486, 487, 488, 498
Amrine, M., 417
Anastasi, Anne, 142, 158
Anderson, Gladys L., 159
Anderson, H. A., 159
Anderson, J. E., 470
Ansbacher, H. L., 359, 371
Ansbacher, Rowena R., 359, 371
Anthony, E. J., 419
Appel, K. E., 301, 430
Argyris, C., 467
Arieti, S., 13, 31
Armitage, S. G., 354
Asch, S. E., 264, 266
Ash, P., 126
Ashby, J. D., 330
Auld, F., Jr., 390
Aumack, L., 432
Ausubel, D. P., 32, 484
Axline, V., 325, 383

Bach, G. R., 424

Bailey, D. E., 85, 198, 211-214, 219, 221, 262
Baker, Gertrude, 161
Bales, R. F., 275
Balian, Lucy, 188, 192, 195
Baller, W., 349
Bandura, A., 447
Barker, Louise S., 169
Barker, R. G., 45, 61-62, 169-170
Barron, F., 188, 268, 435, 473
Bartlett, F. C., 29, 85
Bass, B. M., 179, 181, 278
Bateson, G., 112, 396, 422
Baughman, E. E., 161
Bechtoldt, H. P., 150
Beck, K. W., 446
Beck, S. J., 32, 506
Becker, J., 281
Belknap, I., 417
Bell, J. E., 412
Bellak, L., 389
Bene, Eva, 419
Bennis, W. G., 420
Berdie, R. F., 312-313
Berenson, B. G., 154
Berg, I. A., 95, 140, 149, 238, 278, 501, 508
Berger, S., 421
Berkman, V. C., 249
Bettelheim, B., 31
Betz, B. J., 436
Biber, Barbara, 158
Bijou, S. W., 300
Bindman, A. J., 424
Binet, A., 18, 136, 303
Bingham, W. V. D., 128
Birren, J. E., 161
Bisno, H., 485
Black, Irma S., 158
Blau, T. H., 15, 89, 90, 93-94, 238, 248, 480, 488
Block, J., 69, 222, 507
Bloom, B. S., 178, 268, 504
Bloomberg, R., 150
Bobbitt, J. M., 126

548

Subject Index

Abnormality, 9
  as habit, 337-340
  social view of, 43
  See also Mental illness, Psychosis, Psychoneurosis
Achievement, in manic-depressives, 281-282
Acquiescence set, 140
Adjective checklist, 264, 507
Adjustment Inventory (Bell), 504
Adlerian therapy, 301-302
Administration: clinical psychologists in, 461-462, 468
  problems in research, 67
Admission to clinical service, 17-18
Affect, *see* Emotion
Aggression, 402-403
Aging, 160-161, 470
Alcoholism, group treatment, 370, 424-425
Alternatives: clarification, in treatment, 183
  identification, in assessment, 258
American Board of Examiners in Professional Psychology (ABEPP), 476
American Psychiatric Association: diagnostic system, 11
  relations with psychology, 484
American Psychological Association: Division 12 (clinical psychology), 24, 475, 495
  ethical standards, 477-480
  growth, 19, 475, 498
  planning for clinical training, 19-21
  survey of psychologists, 456, 461, 469
Analytical psychology, 385
Anamnesis, 117, 251-252, 508-510
Anomie, 43
Anxiety: defenses against, 41, 395
  hierarchy, 343
  interpersonal theory, 395
  patients coming to clinic, 17
  psychotherapy, 293, 340-341, 351, 442
  relation to conditioning, 342, 351
  study in sociopathic personalities, 280

Anxiety (*Continued*)
  underlying neurotic habits, 338
Approach-avoidance conflict, 362, 447
Archetypes, 385
Art: clinical psychology as, 28, 29
  therapy, 384
Arthur Point Scale of Performance Tests, 502
Assertion, in therapy, 342, 361
Assessment: analysis chart, 230-232
  case history, value in, 223-224, 261
  choice patterns, 171, 184
  clinical and programmatic, 82
  communication and report-writing, 225-252
  compared with psychodiagnosis, 81
  course or process, 86-88
  decision-making, 83-84, 256-258
  definition of, 80-83
  effectiveness, 256-263
  of families, 154, 193-194, 403-404, 419
  future, 277-278
  inevitability, 82-83, 256-257
  information as sample, correlate, and sign, 198-199
  of interpersonal systems, 172-176
  life history, 183-188, 398
  observation, 153-154
  place of interview in, 127
  place of tests in, 132-135, 154-157
  programmatic, 267-273
  psychotherapy, planning, 134, 256
  referral influences on, 88-91
  research in, 253-283
  situations, 164-196
  social implications of, 97-98
  stages, 86-88, 271-272
  training, 261-262, 270
  use in therapy, 326-327, 347-348, 365, 385-387, 398-399, 417-420
  uses of computers in, 273-278
  working image, 85-86
Assumed similarity, 462
Aunt Fanny reports, 235
Authoritarianism, 62, 281-282, 435